A YEAR OF PROPHECY

Saint Germain Stumps America

ELIZABETH CLARE PROPHET

PEARLS OF WISDOM
TEACHINGS OF THE ASCENDED MASTERS
Mark L. Prophet • Elizabeth Clare Prophet
VOLUME THIRTY • 1987

SUMMIT UNIVERSITY PRESS®

A Year of Prophecy
Saint Germain Stumps America

Elizabeth Clare Prophet

Pearls of Wisdom 1987
Volume Thirty

Published by
The Summit Lighthouse®
for Church Universal and Triumphant®

For information, write or call Summit University Press, Box A, Livingston, MT 59047-1390. Telephone: (406) 222-8300.

LIBRARY OF CONGRESS CATALOG CARD NUMBER: 89-61581

INTERNATIONAL STANDARD BOOK NUMBER: 0-916766-96-9

Printed in the United States of America

Summit University Press®
First Printing

The Ascended Master Saint Germain

Harry Langdon

The Messenger Elizabeth Clare Prophet

Contents

Christ's Ascension in You

May 28 – 31, 1987
Kansas City, Kansas

Freedom 1987

July 1 – 5, 1987
Heart of the Inner Retreat, Royal Teton Ranch, Montana

The Summit Lighthouse - Twenty-Ninth Anniversary

The Consolation of the Divine Mother
On the Occasion of the Feast of the Assumption of the Blessed Virgin

Part I

Part II

Part III

Saint Germain Stumps New York

Saint Germain Stumps America

Vol. 30 No. 1 | Beloved Gautama Buddha | January 4, 1987

The Golden Sphere of Light

The Saving of That Which Can Be Saved

New Year's Eve Address 1986

Beloved of the Golden Sun of the Infinite One,

How art thou now transported into another golden sphere[1]—a sphere of memory that does become a reality only in the Eternal Now. For the mortal cannot capture the infinitude of a presence of a once-manifest golden age so long past, now forgot.

Come, then, for I would speak to you in this golden sphere, once thy habitat, once the kingdom of joy. And this joy, beloved, is the true bliss of the Divine Union, a joy of a paradise that seemed as though it would never end.

This golden sphere, beloved, where I am taking you is in fact the causal body and the point of origin of a planet closest to the sun, identified to you by beloved Lanello as "Hedron." What you know of Hedron is its descent into a cult of pleasure, but I bring you to the golden sphere of a paradise that was beyond all necessity of human pleasure.

For here I would that you might experience for an hour with me this night what it is to be in the warmth of the golden sunshine of love and to know the fullness of all joy in all chakras of being, oneness with the twin flame and with God. So, beloved, it is a reprieve from a planet called "Earth" where you sojourn and have entered to tarry with the Lord and to toil for the hour of his appearing.

In this my address to you and all devotees of Buddha, whether known by any other name (for the devotee of God is always the devotee of Buddha, though he shun the connection)—all, then, are taken by me, for all need surcease from the burden and strain of contemplation of that which may be coming upon

Earth, that which has been abuilding for centuries, that karma which is due which the Lightbearers alone know how to stay.

Thus, hearts of Light, it is a giant sphere that takes us there for contemplation upon a perfection so light, so beautiful, so immediately the transfer of the temple of Helios and Vesta—truly the first point of qualification of this 'sun-light' [by a planetary body] followed by the calling and the office of other planetary bodies of the seven spheres.

Beloved ones, to enter here now you may see the beauty, the verdure, the fragrance, the harmony of an existence that each and every one of you knows exists somewhere in the vast somewhere. It is a memory like this, beloved, that endows all human existence with hope, with certainty of faith and conviction born of experience that Earth is not as God intended it to be and that there is an Eternal Now waiting for the soul.

I give you a moment to explore—with eye and swiftness of Mercurian feet, winged-sandaled—meadows, forests, streams, vast bodies of water, sky and lightness, elemental life, visible angels—not overpopulated nor under, for on a small orb such as this many can evolve when harmony is as natural as the grace of birds and flowers in springtime.

Sit back, as it were, beloved, and relax in this atmosphere. Absorb from this great causal body of golden light and pink glow-ray a peace, a recharging, a sense of divine purpose and ultimate goals, and know that all that separates you from this experience is time, space, and karma—*kal-desh.*

These things are not impenetrable obstacles. Time can be transcended when it is mastered. Space can be penetrated when it is absorbed. Karma can be dealt with, for all that is required is to deal with the day's allotment. Cast it into the sacred fire early that thy work might be a gain in self-mastery for the next karmic assignment and spiritual lesson.

Now then, this golden sphere does not leave one passive, without activity and challenge, [it affords] new vistas, almost a sense of urgency to unfold cosmic splendor and science. Here Ascended Masters, unascended ones see the immediacy of becoming God and more of God. Earth's playground—or playpen—is a very limited challenge. From this level the whole of the Spirit/Matter Cosmos beckons. Any one of you can consider those things that would take your heart and mind and diligence if you but had the hours, if you had taken from you the struggle and the dire challenges of earthly existence. Know, then, that there is no plateau in infinity, no end of opportunity, discovery, happiness, creativity.

In the wonder of this beauty where many [of the inhabitants of Hedron] could see to the very heart of the Sun itself, the presence of Helios and Vesta, there eventually came about on the part of some, absent of true gratitude and appreciation for these opportunities unlimited, a desiring for other discoveries in lesser spheres, in lower vibrations.

Why, then, would they desire less than all of this? Because in the lower domain, you see, they would achieve notoriety and a human kind of a godhood not subject to a hierarchical chain of command; they would achieve independence and the fulfillment of a desire for a pleasure that would slowly begin with a titillation of the outer senses instead of the stimulus of the inner sensitivities of the soul.

Gradations of vibration are subtle, beloved, and the one least aware of his own fluctuation is the individual himself. Only a single blind spot, and one (thinking he is yet in the corona of the Sun) may have strayed many miles from the highest vibrations of Maitreya. Many have not understood what is known as the fall of angels, but I tell you, beloved, the descent is always by imperceptible degrees.

Now, if you but think of this eventuality on Earth, you are very much aware, for instance, that those who are ignorant know not that they are ignorant, even as in the animal kingdom the animal that is clumsy knows not that he is clumsy. You have all seen insensitivity of conscience, of awareness of Christ Self allow individuals to rationalize heinous crimes against humanity, all manner of perverse relationships and actions against one another justified for some so-called righteous cause, even as you have seen individuals locked into pockets of self-deception believing they are God-fearing and of the highest path or, on the other hand, aware they have chosen the left and yet so very certain it is correct.

Thus, if you will attempt to understand the mysteries of life from examples and equations of Earth, you may come to some very practical as well as sobering conclusions to the questions you ask—primarily: Why would one leave the very center of the throne of grace in the heart of God in the Great Central Sun to descend for experimental purposes or other reasons?

I show you gradations of Light and Darkness and how these have resulted, in fallen angels, as a direct opposition to the Most High. This is easier to understand than the apathy of the sons and daughters of God who stray just a little and all of whose actions seem to be Godlike and for righteousness. These pedal in one place. They know not what place they are in; they have no sense of co-measurement—neither betwixt Earth and the lower astral plane nor Earth and the Golden City of Light or the Golden Planet of Light in this sphere where we are.

Blessed ones, the shadows creep and fall across the unsuspecting soul. No matter what plane of occupation, whether the etheric or in dense Earth, once one has entered the decision to be in relativity, a relative good and evil based on a position and a defense of one's right—"my right"—from thenceforth, beloved, one can calculate neither the plummeting nor the ascent. Something apart from oneself must report the goings and the comings—the rise and fall of the soul.

That something and that someone is the Mediator. But then, who can approach the level of the Mediator? Therefore, we have sent World Teachers into that zone betwixt the golden sphere and the planes of evil and foul spirits—World Teachers and the living Guru, one, someone, to embody the standard of the Law of the I AM and that one also to descend to the plane of the Christ Self.

Beloved El Morya has this night given a sobering picture to his children.[2] I come desiring to give a larger view and a release from Earth. Earth is heavy in this hour, beloved, as you well know, but remember you are with me in the golden sphere of Life, nestled near to Helios and Vesta.

Just as you have sensed in the leaving of the cities at sea level and in the coming to the mountain of God that all that is below is, as it were, an illusion, so from the perspective of the golden sphere you once called Home, you may see how the dilemma of the human mind and the fallen angels traps millions to an unreality that is so real—as real, then, as Death and Hell when it devours a soul.

Blessed ones, I give to you a peace—a peace beyond all telling, even beyond understanding.[3] It is a peace you need for all the years ahead. It is the inner peace of Light, of a sense of Destiny, of arriving at such a golden sphere when the work at hand is concluded. For, you see, the golden sphere swings and may touch the lowest dimensions of Matter, as when a child takes a ball attached to a string and turns it in circles it does reach the height and the depths.

There is a causal body for each planet of the system and there are spheres of light that contain the record of all good in that collective causal body. The causal body of each planetary home contains the entire momentum of the [members of the] Great White Brotherhood and unascended souls [who have evolved upon it] and may be called upon to "swing round." And in that swing it becomes congruent to those earthbound, as you say, and can transmit in an instant a light and a power that can also consume on an instant.

This consuming, to the inhabitants of such a sphere so touched by the sphere of the causal body, can seem as utter destruction, desolation, or annihilation, as though someone flashed a light and a goodly portion of the known world were to be changed. This is a method of drawing a world abruptly back into an alignment with the inner blueprint. It is not the preferred method, beloved, but it does avert ultimate chaos and destruction of souls.

What occurs in this method is a reducing of the identity of all. For to take from the individual his karma or his human creation before he has gained a mastery of the light in the opposite dimension—that is, in the dimension of the I AM Presence—is therefore to reduce his identity. For one's karma and one's human creation is one's self until one has transmuted it and ascended to a higher level of self-awareness.

Thus, if you can imagine a flash of light as a nuclear explosion coming upon the planet only for a split second, in that moment God would have the power to reduce all equally, let us say, by ten percent, by fifteen percent, depending on what reduction would be necessary in order to avert an utter calamity or cataclysm. This has been done in the past. Entire evolutions have been "dwarfed," you might say—reduced in life span, reduced in stature. Thus, as the Evil was cut back, so the potential for greater Good was also cut back until that evolution should come unto a love for and an obedience to the Higher Law and LORD.

The drawback to this solution to a planetary equation that was once the dilemma of Hedron or Maldek and is fast becoming the dilemma of Earth is that there is no lesson learned. There is the same potential for Evil as [that which] created the greater danger in the first place. Without the intercession of World Teachers, those so reduced will simply continue on in their old ways and the Darkness will mount again as new Nimrods come forth to build new towers greater than before.

So you see, beloved ones, there is a certain futility to this solution; for the planets that have received it have not merited further World Teachers, having been given many, even as many have been sent to Earth. Thus, without an Intercessor, a Maitreya, they have simply built again, just as the grass grows and the weeds return once the fields have been cut or the lawn mowed.

Thus, the advantage is a certain gaining of time. And this time was gained in Earth through the flood of Noah, the sinking of continents, and the reduction of the life span [of the evolutions] on Terra. And even withal, teachers were sent again and again. Yet, the joy of it all is that there has been a harvest of souls who have ascended for the gaining of that time, for the setting back of the potential of Evil on Earth. Thus, there is in the annals of Earth, as we read them this night from the golden sphere, some salutary word that souls have been won for the ascension and have attained a Godhood which otherwise might have been lost.

The question is, then: How many souls have ascended from planet Earth apart from those who came with Sanat Kumara or who were emissaries of Venus or who were of angelic realms apart from his coming? We look to measure, then, the condition of Earth by a numbering of those souls who have responded to the ministrations of many. We understand that the ministering servants themselves have ascended. The question is: Have any from among humanity?

Beloved ones, I cannot say that the Lords of Karma have determined to release these statistics to you in this hour. I can only tell you that the harvest is disappointing and the level of disappointment may be measured by yourselves by your own observations of the activities of humanity in this hour.

As you have heard the dictation of Saint Germain, you understand what is at hand.[4] Some of you have wondered, would we say more? Would we draw back the veil?

Our presence here is by the grace of the Lightbearers and we address the Lightbearers this evening that you might understand with comfort and enlightenment from the higher abode of your spirit that each and every one of you is tenderly cared for and shall always be. As you did not always make your home in this physical octave or body temple, so I can assure you that for the Lightbearer the adjustment to higher octaves and etheric life is a welcomed reprieve between embodiments and this transition is only a Hell and a Darkness to those who have so created it.

One of the dilemmas which face the Cosmic Council and the Lords of Karma at this juncture of the history of this system of worlds is that some among the Lightbearers descended too far, lost the way, identified with fallen angels through only a splinter of pride which grew and festered and began to dominate their existence. These Lightbearers, then, lost the momentum, lost the wind in their sails.

It is about these Lightbearers that we are most concerned, that the Darjeeling Council and the Messengers are concerned—that they, having a memory of higher spheres, not sensing the gradations of consciousness over which they have crossed, do not have a sense of the danger, do not have a sense of the jeopardy in which their souls are placed when such forces of Darkness [as are being witnessed today] are coming nearer and nearer a confrontation on the planet.

This planet where they should be but pilgrims, sojourners in the way, easily able to take their leave of it, has now become to many of these children of the Sun a prison house from which they cannot escape. They have lost the key to open the prison doors and unless some make the call, no angel will come to open those doors. This is a far greater dilemma to Sanat Kumara than the plight of a mankind that has ever walked the easy, downward way.

We seek to save that which has lost the First Estate, those who were once in the kingdom of joy. It is our hope that in saving these there might be an engrafting of the Word[5] unto those who have it not. Unless, then, the firstfruits be saved from psychicism and all manner of false prophecy, how, then, can there be another opportunity for humanity at large?

You are alive in a day when the sophistication on planet Earth of the Serpent and his seed—the proud talkers, philosophers, from the professors to the economists to those who lead labor unions to those who manage the governments of Soviet and Communistic states—is such that, blessed ones, the subtlety and the weight of the lie is a smothering blanket and it does take, oh, such a steel, as the steel sword of Serapis, to be unbending toward the sympathy of these fallen angels who have such vast "social" programs whereby they expect to raise and equalize the race of humanity and the nations.

Our concern, then, is not for the Lightbearers who shall clean escape the moment they depart this octave. Our concern, as Morya stated, is for the ones who are totally convinced they have found the right path and the right teacher; though they are surrounded by false chelas and false gurus in these other movements, yet they follow suit, for their memory is dull. These, then, we must rescue by an all-out effort if by the hour of Wesak we are to come to a place for a larger dispensation for Earth as a whole.

We are, then, gratified as we rejoice and sing together in this golden sphere of joy's kingdom to know that many books are gone forth, that hearts have pledged to publish *The Coming Revolution,* that many hearts have pledged and are actively stumping their areas and the nations, that many are spreading the Word, and also that many have increased the light and the candlepower of their threefold flame so as to have placed themselves out of harm's way in the previous twelve months since I have addressed you at the New Year's conclave of the Royal Teton.

Understand, then, that our gratitude for the good, the effort, and the accomplishment is why we are here this very night. We have something to stand on of worth, and it is the development of the heart of those who have understood how to develop the heart. Thus, there is an increase of Light* on Earth almost, but not quite, commensurate with the increase of Darkness.† Those who have it must let it shine and teach and transfer it. Those who do not must be thankful and humble enough to realize it when they are confronted by the Messenger.

Blessed ones, to know that one has erred or failed is the most important news one can receive when in a situation where opportunity is yet available. The news of victory is no news to the victor. For he has known all along that he has prepared himself well, that he has qualified himself, and that he deserves the victory. And he is certain that in God he shall achieve it—and so he does. But, beloved ones, failures are more unexpected because they follow folly, miscalculation, an ambition that is blind, a pride that is blind, a rebellion that is blind and that is not seen until the shell of illusion is broken by a failure: "What went wrong?"—and then the soul-searching begins.

With these words you can understand why at times the Cosmic Council has decreed not merely to set back an evolution but to bring total destruction and to begin anew. It is not our desire, nor is it the desire of any of the hosts of heaven, to see such utter pain and destruction come upon Earth as has been contemplated. But I must ask you to ponder the question we ponder at the level of the Darjeeling, Indian, and Royal Teton councils, at the level of the Buddhas, at the level of the Lords of Karma. The question is, beloved: What else will awaken the souls of Earth if not cataclysm or nuclear war? They *must* be awakened. The death of souls must be stopped. What will stop it, if not utter catastrophe?

Again, look to the profile of lives you have known. Have you not seen that catastrophe in a household or family has brought them closer to God if they are of God and of the seed of Christ, and that in others such eventualities have brought a hardening of the heart toward God, an anger toward God, a closing of the petals of the chakras, and then a defiance which ensues of any coming representative of God?

Thus, according to their point of origin, souls react one way or another. But the desired reaction of the Law is always that the Lightbearer might return to his First Love and First Estate.

*Christ consciousness †the weight of planetary karma produced by the collective consciousness of Antichrist

I ask you, then, to look at the questions that you ask and to know that these have been the topic of our discussions in our council chambers. And as we, too, have gone to the heart of God and even into the Great Silence, our answer is that we would desire that the Teachings of the Ascended Masters would bring about this awakening, this return, this conversion that could avert planetary chaos erupting. This is our desire.

Blessed ones, in some areas you are more familiar with the ways of the world and the thoughts and feelings of the people than we are in our highest consciousness. When we descend to Earth we descend often through the chela's mind, knowing that there there is a certain screening by the Christ and a certain greater awareness that goes beyond outer appearances.

And so, beloved, it is to those in physical embodiment that the answer to this question belongs: Can, will the Teachings of the Ascended Masters prevent mankind's karma from descending?

This I will tell you, beloved—that there are dispensations available and forthcoming to those who in all practicality and balance and self-mastery can be our spokesmen running with our message. Saint Germain himself will speak to you on the morrow and what he may unveil or reveal I leave to his discretion.

My message, then, to you is to calculate with practicality and honesty the part you can play in postponing the day of karmic reckoning, or the descent of Damocles' sword. The vigils held by the Mother in this place, reinforced by yourselves, will avail much. The scattering of the books as the seed of the sower will avail much.

Prayer for the Lightbearer must be fastidious. A transfer of the Word can be imparted only by those who have the Word. Thus, beloved, seek that divine experience outlined by El Morya, not for yourself alone but for the having of the Light that it might be transmitted. The equation remains: How the Light increases in each individual Keeper of the Flame may determine much.

We have not lost hope for the children of the Sun nor for the sons and daughters of God. But our hope in the practical sense is meager for the masses who have turned their backs again and again upon our light, teaching, and representatives for tens of thousands of years. They reproduce after their kind, beloved, almost as cattle. And one cannot find the point of opening where there is a desire to receive the divine spark which we may transfer to them through our own. Thus, we must concentrate on the saving of that which can be saved, understanding that their salvation can yet gain time even for those who have absolutely no interest in the things of the Spirit or of God, even if they are instructed day and night by the most precious angel.

Can and should, then, a civilization be saved that is self-perpetuating in this attitude of mankind? Or should the matrix of this civilization and this kind of man be shattered that the new golden-age man and golden-age woman of the seventh root race might appear and that the Christed ones might fulfill their responsibilities and gain a dimension of Cosmos?

If you can answer these questions, beloved, and I think that you can if you ponder them against the backdrop of cosmic law, then you will come to a realization of certain key factors and solutions in your own life (these have been mentioned before but they are easy to see from this golden sphere of light)—that those who value eternal Life and understand that it must be lived here and now must truly come apart from mortality and the herds of mortals fulfilling Death from the moment they are born. These must surely understand that their children need, require, and deserve a better example, a better way of life, that they must be pushed and pulled back up the mountain of God whence they once descended in response to the music of Hell that lured them down.[6]

The equation of physical survival was touched upon by Saint Germain. It should be foremost in your mind. Why do you need to survive, beloved? Because you need to be in physical embodiment until you have balanced sufficient karma to warrant that you should no longer return to a place of such a low vibration as Earth. To cut off that opportunity before it is fulfilled has too many dire consequences to the individual.

When you place the goal first of the balancing of karma, it does not mean that you abandon families, jobs, calling, responsibility, but rather that you enter into all of these with greater vigor, spirituality and accelerated pace in order that you might not be caught in any of the pitfalls associated with human relationships or the karma-balancing process.

This place requires great preparation to be a place prepared for survival. Let us see that the day that has begun be one where you set priorities for the year, the foremost of which should be the determination of how and where you can best physically survive no matter what may come upon the planet. In a position of survival, you may then once again return to the task of enlightenment. The enlightenment of self is key—and of other Lightbearers. This is a certainty.

I will tell you, then, beloved, that the golden sphere of light where you now abide is about to be transferred over the Inner Retreat and the Royal Teton Ranch. As all Lightbearers have entered it, now the golden sphere itself does begin to move toward planet Earth. When it is fully accomplished ere six hours have passed from the conclusion of my address, you will know that there is a very large golden sphere of light that literally touches the Earth in its lower portion.

It is like a tree house into which you climbed as a child. This place, beloved, forms the figure-eight flow with the "Place Prepared" below. It provides you with a haven of paradise even as you work the works of God at hand. It provides you with an inner blueprint and a power source that you have not known.

This sphere, beloved, is positioned with its center being the throne which I occupy as Lord of the World. Thus, I was called to other octaves by the Cosmic Council and Sanat Kumara many weeks ago, and to me they presented this proposal. For Hedron has long gone beyond the pale of restoration and has become, as you know, an asteroid belt.

Therefore, the Cosmic Council decreed: Why not deliver this sphere to those Lightbearers of Earth who have demonstrated the responsibility and the ability to produce what is necessary? Why not give to them access to so great a reservoir of light and kingdom of joy that those who have been called by Serapis to ascend and stand with him as the stalwarts of Thermopylae[7] might have almost unlimited wealth, abundance, opportunity, wisdom—and at the same time an escape hatch if the various courses of action should come to pass which have to do with the return of mankind's karma?

Thus, beloved ones, this golden sphere of light becomes the citadel of the Western Shamballa. Now that Western Shamballa, truly centered over the Heart, gains an auric field and a causal body built by Lightbearers long ago. And, precious ones, those somewhat burdened by the frankness of Morya, which is our own as well, may now take some heart and measure of hope. For you, beloved, were a part of the building of this kingdom of joy and this causal body; and therefore, because you are here—having volunteered to redeem the karma not only of Earth but of Hedron (for many of its fallen evolutions have reembodied here)—you, then, by your presence have also allowed this event to take place.

Thus, in truth, many upon Earth who did not go the way of the pleasure cult completely but regained their senses and stood fast have, to your credit, substance in this causal body. Thus, you have a point of polarity with it and now, for the first time in thousands of years, access to this cumulative momentum of world good.

This sphere has been sealed until this hour, beloved. Now it is come, accessible solely to the true Son of God, the true Chela, the true Lightbearer. You may, then, begin this day, January 1, 1987, understanding the meaning of the initiation of a cycle.

Beloved ones, I must tell you sadly that correspondingly there is also delivered to this planet a dark sphere of the karma of mankind. It is like the lower sphere of the Silex coffee maker, except in this instance it is not in a figure-eight flow with the golden sphere. For you stand—and all Lightbearers collectively stand—in that [figure-eight] relationship to the golden sphere. And thus, the dark sphere is below. It is also below in altitude, beloved. It is below [vibrationally, hence] in the astral plane.

It is given to you through my heart, my love, and my presence here to return to identification with the golden sphere of the kingdom of joy at any time or hour throughout this life unto the finishing of your course. And from the perspective of that sphere you may observe pain, suffering, and calamity among mankind, not as from an ivory tower but as from the lotus throne of the Western Shamballa where you may surround me, seated on your own lotus throne as a bodhisattva of grace. And from that point of equanimity you may direct almost, as it were, a straw into the darkness of the lower sphere and pull up by the magnet of your heart, by the sacred fire breath, Lightbearers caught and tumbling in that karma that is delivered.

Thus, the right hand of the Mighty Angel of the Judgment is raised. From high in the upper atmosphere of Earth the angel does stand and the right hand of the angel, beloved, does descend. And with this descent, mankind must deal with a greater portion of their karma for their failure to accept the Light and even for their persecution of the Light and the Messenger of the Light.

So let those who have touched the hem of our garment, who have seen and known the Truth and gone aside from it, hear me. For you are caught, unable to enter the golden sphere of light and therefore subject to the depravity and the depredations coming upon the Earth.

Seek God while there is time. All who have doubted or maligned the Messengers have had abundant proof of their office and mantle—even the evildoer. Repent, then, from your ways, all ye who have abandoned this path; and let the good, the Lightbearer entering in, value his acceleration and increase it. If you but raise, then, the size of the threefold flame, if you but enter into a oneness with the golden sphere to a point of several degrees as we would measure it, know, then, that you have access to other millions who will be touched by your heart.

Those who are accelerating have every reason to accelerate more, for these have the highest momentum and may swiftly gain a higher. Those who have slacked off and entered laggard ways may instantaneously leave these and enter in to this hope and promise.

Let there be no regrets. The year '86 is past. And it is too late. But a new year has begun. For some it is a clean, white page. For I, Gautama, out of my heart extend myself to you who know enough to have remorse, who know enough to receive instruction, to be tutored, and to regain a lost spirituality. For you, I will do all that the Great Law allows me—and the Law of Love *does* allow me. For some whose density has carried them downstream have awakened to the call of Morya, and they shall return and they may become the swift and the strong with renewed zeal. May it be so. For, beloved, I do tell you that the years of opportunity are few and small. Make the most of them.

Now then, to comfort ye all, a messenger of Sirius walks down the aisle of this room to hand to me here in this place (where I AM also even as I AM in the golden sphere approaching) the scroll containing the thoughtform for the year 1987.

Beloved ones, it is "A Proclamation from the God Star Sirius to the People of Earth." I shall read it to you:

> O people of Earth, the Four and Twenty Elders speak to you in this hour, and in our speaking we send light rays to activate and quicken consciousness.
>
> People of Earth, the LORD God has sent to you his Son Saint Germain in this hour of trouble. Hear him. Heed him. Know him.
>
> To that end, we impress upon the ethers the image, the word, the vibration of Saint Germain and the blueprint of Aquarius—Aquarius, then, as a sign and as a sphere, as a grid of light, of lines connected by Maltese crosses. This geometric form, in the shape of planet Earth, is represented in white lines on a field of dark blue. This thoughtform, O people of Earth, is the matrix that you may determine and decide to fill in in order that you might make the change to Aquarius.
>
> People of Earth, we show you, then, the handwriting on the wall. We show you that surely there shall come upon you the full karma and karmic accountability delivered by the Four Horsemen and in the seven last plagues delivered by the Archangels. None will stay the hand of this descent

unless you turn from your ways at once and embrace the Master and his gift of the violet flame.

People of Earth, the time has run out. Your destructive ways have gone too far and the Great Law cannot allow it to continue. Therefore, from the Great Central Sun come messengers of Light, legions of angels in the service of the God Surya. These angels are sent to the side of every man, woman, and child of Earth to transmit to your senses the oncoming tide that at a certain point cannot be turned back.

These angels will lead you at inner levels to the Royal Teton Retreat and on the outer to the teachings of Saint Germain. Heed him and heed these teachings and you will discover the gift of miracles and the gift of prophecy. You will learn the science of changing the future by transmuting the past. You may become alchemists in the twinkling of an eye if you so choose. You may discover God within your heart and live forever.

Seek and find Saint Germain! He is the Master who once again pledges his life to the deliverance of Earth.

People of Earth, it is the last time. This Master of Light therefore comes in a final intercession in a final hour. May the children of the Sun run to greet him with Portia standing in the Seventh Ray waiting to take you each one by the hand.

People of Earth, this is our message. It is brief and to the point. The Teaching is set forth. The Opportunity is given. Take it and be free.

Beloved, this proclamation is signed by the hand of the God Surya and each one of the names of the Four and Twenty Elders is written in gold as signature. These names have never before been released and they shall not be pronounced to you, but they are written in the proclamation and therefore may be known by you at inner levels.

Thus, this is an answer—a beginning and, you might say, a partial answer. The equation must be filled in by those who now at will may drink the nectar of the golden sphere of light. When I say "at will," beloved, this will involves your alignment with your blueprint, the blueprint of Aquarius, and the will of God—your embodying of the Cosmic Christ.

Through your own Christ Self, the Mediator, you now have access to unlimited light for the solution to the problem. You, then, must now devise those solutions, work them, fulfill them. So be engaged in self-mastery. So feel the urgency of self-mastery as never before. For above all, it is the wayward Lightbearers who stand to lose the most and be lost.

To the rescue, then, I say! Look to the New Day. Those who have earned it may enter it each night. Those who have not may yet pay their dues and fulfill the requirements.

My profound blessing and love to each and every one who knows me as I AM and loves me as I love you. My blessing to those entering in. My legions attend those who yet struggle and must be cut free.

Part the Red Sea. The command is given not to angels and Cosmic Beings but *to you,* beloved. So do it. So be it. So know, in the oneness of God all things are possible.

"The Summit Lighthouse Sheds Its Radiance O'er All the World to Manifest as Pearls of Wisdom."

This dictation by Gautama Buddha was **delivered** through the Messenger of the Great White Brotherhood Elizabeth Clare Prophet on **New Year's Eve, December 31, 1986,** at the Royal Teton Ranch, Montana. (**1**) In his Christmas Day address 1986, Jesus announced that the God and Goddess Meru had come from Lake Titicaca to "establish a corridor of light from the etheric retreat over the Royal Teton Ranch to the etheric retreat of the Feminine Ray at Lake Titicaca," opening a highway whereby our calls might "reach South America in time." The Master announced that the God and Goddess Meru had placed themselves within golden white spheres to be sustained above the Ranch as their presence with us and that "their great momentum of victory over witchcraft, Death, Hell, and black magic is brought to bear in this hour on the threat of suicide worldwide. . . . They are ready to turn back and bind the entire momentum of this force in answer to your call." See "The Coming of the Divine Teacher," 1986 *Pearls of Wisdom,* vol. 29, no. 78. (**2**) See El Morya, December 31, 1986, "Purity of Heart," 1986 *Pearls of Wisdom,* vol. 29, no. 80. (**3**) Phil. 4:7. (**4**) See Saint Germain, November 27, 1986, "A Prophecy of Karma of the United States of America," in *Saint Germain On Prophecy,* Summit University Press, pp. 206–22, Book Four, $5.95 (add $.50 for postage), or 1986 *Pearls of Wisdom,* vol. 29, no. 75. (**5**) James 1:21. (**6**) As recorded in *The Forgotten Books of Eden,* the children of Jared (descendants of Seth) were lured down the Holy Mountain of God by the children of Cain, who committed all manner of abominations and enticed them with sensual music from the valley below. See Elizabeth Clare Prophet, "Prologue on the Sons of Jared Taken from the Second Book of Adam and Eve," *Forbidden Mysteries of Enoch: The Untold Story of Men and Angels,* containing all the Enoch texts, including the Book of Enoch and the Book of the Secrets of Enoch, Summit University Press, pp. 353–63, $12.95 (add $1.00 for postage). (**7**) **Stalwarts of Thermopylae.** See Mark L. Prophet and Elizabeth Clare Prophet, *Lords of the Seven Rays,* Summit University Press, pp. 150–52, Book One, $5.95 (add $.50 for postage); and Serapis Bey, December 28, 1985, "The Descent of the Mighty Blue Sphere," 1986 *Pearls of Wisdom,* vol. 29, no. 15, pp. 127–29 and 130, n. 2, "Leonidas."

Vol. 30 No. 2 *Beloved Saint Germain* *January 11, 1987*

The Vow

A New Day and a New Covenant

Hail, Keepers of the Flame!

My beloved sons and daughters, I salute you in the heart of America's Rocky Mountains. [27-sec. standing ovation]

My dearest friends and compatriots—compatriots of universal freedom whose loyalties are to Life, Light, Love, Peace and Enlightenment that transcend all boundaries—I say to you, a year ago I looked at the year through the mind of the Divine Mother and I looked upon each one of you. And my very first act upon receiving my freedom, beloved, was to go to the heart of the Central Sun. There I did kneel and implore in your behalf an ascendancy, a focalization, a coming to grips with personal, organizational, and planetary karma—not the least of which, initiations and testings of the soul.

Now I gaze upon your faces ripened by adversity, your souls fired in the trial that has been upon our Mother and our Church and all of you. Each step of the way, including every soul's surrender of Camelot and Los Angeles and all for which it stood, I have been present, beloved, trusting, hoping, praying and interceding where the Great Law would allow, that you would arrive at that point of Spirit where I might address you as I so have desired to address you.

Not all have reached the mark, as Morya has so stated. But the quorum and the balance of at least 51 percent of those who call themselves Keepers of the Flame have provided me a sound chalice and a heart of love that I may therefore this moment pour my love to you and the meditations of my heart.

Beloved, I bless and love all and come to rekindle a fire that in some has waxed low. But, blessed ones, it is a new year. Those who see in the dawn of a new day, ushered in by Archangel Uriel this morn, the error and the folly of their indulgences of the past year may once again return to the point of Reality by the grace of my Guru, the Great Divine Director. He has stepped forth to sponsor those who have erred in this movement. For he has said, "Saint Germain, let not your dispensation be troubled by standing once again for those who know the Path [but do not follow it]. I shall offer my own heart as you may deliver your address and your vow."

Thus, beloved, those who would make up for lost time may appeal fervently to the Great Divine Director and the Lords of Karma that they may rise up over base selfishness, self-indulgence and fantasies contributing to the blockages in the various chakras. Therefore, beloved, let all come in his mantle.

Hear me now, for I would speak finally of that dispensation which I propose. I would speak to you, then, of the principle of the vow and why holy vows have been taken through the ages. A vow, beloved, is the victory of the oneness of the Word. A vow is more than a promise. It is more than a human word or a human contract. A vow is the pledging of one's life and being and soul to a mission or to a cause.

Understand, then, that many of you have taken steps of commitment. In many cases, though not understood by yourselves, these commitments have been partial, where consciously or unconsciously the individual has said, "I will keep a little part to myself." Or the individual has said, "I will commit an hour a week or three hours a week to this or that community cause."

And many have kept exactly the commitments they have made. Others have rushed forward in the emotion of the moment and the fervor of others' deeper spirituality to commit all and even to vow. Yet they have fallen by the wayside with the blowing of the strong cold wind or the enticements of the warmer winds of the south.

Thus, beloved, I allow you to understand my heart and my life. According to the dispensation given to me, I am able to do the following—and it is to vow my life, my causal body, and my service to planet earth so long as there are those in embodiment who are capable of making the identical vow. I will not tell you in numbers how many, for in some cases one heart so infilled by the Buddha Gautama, one heart such a vessel of Maitreya, may count for many. But I will say that it is a tally of a geometry of a weight of sacred fire, an Omega balance in the earth that will allow my presence to fully and finally intercede in all these things projected upon the screen of mankind's returning karma.

Thus, beloved, we come to understand what is the principle of a holy vow. It is a commitment to serve in a holy order as a brother or a sister, to espouse certain virtues such as poverty, chastity, obedience. A vow is an entering into God, and it is God entering in to oneself. A vow is a promise that one does not break, for one understands one has made this vow directly to his heart and in so doing has evoked from the heart of God a commensurate measure of support, even privilege, even rank in the spiritual hierarchy of the planet. In order to make a vow, one must have had the maturity of thinking through a lifetime and the meaning thereof—and whether or not one is willing to give an entire lifetime to such a cause.

Today the breaking of vows by priests or the religious has become commonplace. They have felt justified, for they have found the established Church wanting. In the case where vows are made to human institutions or human beings, one can easily have a change of heart. But if the vow be made to the Universal God, one can change institutions [as a means of its implementation] without breaking that vow. One can take a vow to sponsor the education of the heart on a planetary scale and one can espouse that vow through every available avenue.

Thus, you understand it is not good to make vows to the untrusty human consciousness but rather to look into the face of God or one of his ascended representatives and to know that one has the will, the disposition, and the character to enter in to such a vow.

In the Old Testament the vow was called a covenant. It was always made by God unto his people. The essence of the covenants, broken again and again by man and not God, was his promises to love, to protect, to illumine, and to care for his own so long as they would love him by obedience, by refusing to go after other idols, including the idols of self and the fallen angels and the gods of Baal and materialism and Death itself.

One would think that a commitment to God, in order to receive the promises, should not so often have been broken. But all covenants have been broken, beloved. Thus the plight of the world and the seed of Israel and Judah today.

Realize, then, that Christ came to give a new covenant.[1] And that covenant was a transfer by his Body and his Blood of the renewal of the divine spark—a regeneration. And that new covenant, beloved, does come into full manifestation by the descent of the Holy Christ Self and the fullness of Christhood in you. In other words, the covenant, which is the [contract between the parties to the] vow, is not fully enjoyed by both parties to that vow until it is claimed by both sides.

Therefore, understand that as I come in the lineage of the prophets and as your Messengers come in the lineage of the prophets, so we bear the good tidings of the new covenant of Sanat Kumara, who gave to you for the closing months of the year the opportunity [whereby] he declared, beloved, that he would hold the balance of your karma while you performed the necessary services that required Herculean strength, tenacity of will, and truly the love of a purpose and a vision that must be held in view in order to keep on keeping on through the hours of the day and the night and in order to summon the strength from on high.[2]

This many have done, while others have slunk away and said, "It is too hard. I must have this and that in my ordered life. I am not here to work through the day and the night, to neglect my family or my this or my that." Beloved hearts, I have stood by and literally wrung my hands as I have seen cowards reborn, called "wimps"—who *are* wimps, for they are spineless—fail to understand a period of sacrifice or even to comprehend that there must be a means of separating the "humans" from the Sons of God, the goats from the sheep.

Do you not remember how those were chosen to fight the battle, those who carried sword and armour? Blessed ones, they were told to drink of the waters of the river. And those who laid down their swords while they drank were cast aside, and those who kept their swords were chosen.[3]

As Morya said, we have a right to test and know the mettle of our chelas apart from the glory and the drama of an exclusive property in Malibu and a famous leader—or infamous, as they have attempted to make her and myself. We have a right to know who will survive a nuclear war among you and who will be the crybabies—and I tell you, we have discovered it!

And there is no other word but *failure* for those who cannot rise to the occasion of sacrifice when the very angels of Sanat Kumara stand by with their flame in hand ready to transfer it to a heart if that heart would only cry out and say, "O God, give me the strength to fulfill this task for Saint Germain!"

Thus you understand my silence during which many have asked: What is Saint Germain doing with his new dispensation? When will he speak of it? Thus, beloved, I speak of it when I know that I have hearts who can be trusted and who are not here for the merry-go-round or the titillation of senses.

Let it be known that there were outcasts in Israel and there are outcasts today. Let it be known that there are those who may still go down in ignominy preferring their satin beds and creature comforts, and there are those who will stand and still stand as my minutemen and -women of the hour.

Thus, first of all, let the criticism of the Messenger and of the strictness of our order cease. Let it be understood that we have drawn the line in the entire Community, including in Montessori International. Let chelas come to our school. Let nonchelas be not pampered by their parents or by themselves.

Blessed hearts, whether you are parent or Community member, do not point the finger at our decision, our discrimination, and our discernment. The battle at hand is frightful. We draw a circle of light and we demand that those who choose to be in it *cease* their bellyaching, *cease* their fantasies concerning members of the opposite sex, *cease* their human consciousness and recognize that in the time it took to play this piece, the "Rakoczy March,"* blessed hearts, in that short a time, *you* could cease to exist through a nuclear first strike.

Now, if you desire to dally in your demanding of rights for creature comforts another round, I suggest you contemplate just how much dalliance there will be in the world that is left. And I shall not speak of it again! The discipline of Maitreya be upon you and your own woes as well! For I, Saint Germain, am not permitted to engage my vow with God with you when you have proven or prove yourselves faithless—faithless to our covenant or rule of order in this Community.

This year has seen leaders of local study groups becoming involved in affairs with new students, both leaving the Path, thus using the energy of the altar either for psychic channeling and delivering private messages from the Masters to their little groups or for the arousing of the untransmuted baser energies. It is well-known that the Holy Ghost and the power of the Brotherhood that does go forth will indeed activate all momentums of Darkness as well as of Light. This is why we have Keepers of the Flame Lessons. This is why we have studies and disciplines. It is necessary to remember them. It is necessary to guard oneself.

How can so great a Light as Sanat Kumara come into your midst when the very presence of the Light causes you to criticize your neighbor or to lust after another man's wife or to neglect your own family? Keepers of the Flame, be on guard!

This is my final opportunity and I guard it well. Therefore, you also should understand that you keep the flame of Maitreya and you ought to be concerned when you observe violations of the

*The "Rakoczy March" from Hungarian Rhapsody no. 15 by Franz Liszt, 4 min., 36 sec., was played as the meditation music before the dictation.

flame and recognize that your silence on human compromise, seeking popularity, places in jeopardy the entire Community. There are none so fooled and so damned (which means judged by the Law) as those who allow human rationalization to compromise the most basic principles of our Path.

Beloved ones, there is more than one reason for our silence during these recent months—and the inconvenience of the move has not been the entire matter. It has been because for all that has been given and gone forth there is a desire on the part of our students to appropriate the light to their private uses and to mold a new image and a new way of life for the Community that is apart from the path of chelaship which Morya has established. And not the example of the Messenger or the qualified staff has in any way deterred those who have said, "We will do it our way. We will prove that we can take the Teachings and do it our way. We will show that these rules and principles are no longer prevailing."

Beloved ones, thus does begin the compromise of the founding principles of every religion. Beware of it. We know of the psychics and other religious leaders who take our teachings, our books, and our decrees and blend them with their version of an anti-Guru, anti-Christ path. So they have said, in Germany and elsewhere, "Why can we not take the decrees and the songs and leave the rest? We do not need the Messenger. We have our own messengers and our own seers." Thus, beloved, no graver mistake has ever been made than by those who stand neath the boot of the Soviet, only miles from the border.

If you speak of apathy and indifference, speak, then, of somnambulance! Speak of those who sleep in their pride of intellect and of the false theologians who have come out of that nation,[4] always destroying the spirit and confounding the innocent with their misuse of the letter.

Blessed hearts, it is a shame to turn aside my mouthpiece. It is a shame to look at human idiosyncrasies or the pressures upon this instrument and to judge by some imagined divine standard that the Messenger does not measure up. Beloved hearts, early in her training—very early, in an hour when the burden of the bearing of world karma was too great for Mark Prophet to bear—this Messenger, by the age of twenty-three, was bearing the burden of half of the weight of planetary karma with Mark.

We do not condemn for situations that may have occurred of burden to our Messengers in the attempt to bear this cross for you. Truly, what freedom of youth had been hers was gone in that moment when passing through Georgetown, driven by Mark, the first 10-percent weight came upon her body and she cried out and said to him, "Mark, what has come upon me?" And so he did tell her, "A percentage of the planetary weight."

Beloved hearts, when this does come upon an individual all other interests of life are surrendered—no more time for playing the piano, for painting paintings of art, for doing those things of a social nature. And even the simple joys of family must be set aside for the keeping of the flame upon the altar of humanity.

It was with the passing of Mark that the full weight came upon the Messenger of that planetary karma as well as the initiation of the descent into Death and Hell and specifically the assignment to deal with those individuals who had plagued the house of Rakoczy and the entire Great White Brotherhood for centuries—personal enemies of mine and of yourselves who must be dealt with.

Thus, you have heard of those seven years of the Dark Night of the Spirit that ended in 1980 with the betrayal of the one to whom it was given to stand at her side that he might ultimately choose the Light and not the Darkness—choose Life and not Death.[5] For to him was given the vow in ancient times, by Mark himself in a prior incarnation, that if he should obey the Truth and come into the covenants of God he should be given the opportunity of bearing the seed of the Christed One.

Thus, beloved, such an ancient vow of thousands of years ago must needs be fulfilled yet by the Messengers. And so it came to pass. The gift was offered, the cup was extended and it was dashed in pieces not once but again and again by this one who could not enter in to the heart of the Divine Mother and receive thereby the initiations for salvation.

Blessed ones, if the Messengers ascended and unascended had not agreed to all of this, that judgment and that trial (whereby some of the most vicious of individuals who have ever attacked the Great White Brotherhood were brought to judgment—not only those involved in the case, beloved, but many unseen supporters and those who betrayed Justice herself in that courtroom) would not have come to pass. Many were judged through this trial, beloved, and those of a like vibration to all players who played their parts of infamy.

Thus, not one but entire classes of fallen ones have gone before the Court of the Sacred Fire. And though they may still have tenure in physical form, I tell you they are as dead as charred wood and absent, devoid of the Spirit. Thus, they have a decay rate. Let us move on.

Blessed ones, in the hour of the ascension of Mark, the Keepers of the Flame who made their inner vows did determine to share in the bearing of the burden of this weight of world karma borne by the embodied Messenger. Thus, by the grace of the true chelas of Morya and Saint Germain who endured through the trials and temptations of the Messenger, she has endured and remained in embodiment to serve our cause. And you have remained! And a bond of hearts fused as one has come out of all of this.

And you have understood the profound lessons of the history of your Messengers and your part therewith over hundreds of thousands of years of the going forth of the Mother in the attempt to rescue the fallen ones. As you have been told, their opportunity is up. Now the Mother and you may devote yourselves entirely to the Lightbearers. And you must do so swiftly, for they are caught in psychic snarls beyond belief.

If you consider how so easily you are drawn apart by the machinations of your own mind to stray from my heart though you love me still, let me tell you, beloved, those who have a little more karma, a little less light are swept away by false-hierarchy impostors of myself who cleverly, *cleverly* disguise themselves as teachers of righteousness. The personality cult and the hypnosis practiced by the leader is all-enveloping. It must have your forthright decree work.

Thus I come today. It is indeed a New Day and a New Covenant. For it is to this end that two thousand years of your own trek and that of your Messengers has brought you here—brought you here to this Inner Retreat. It is the sign of hope, beloved, of what promise and hope can be like—a crystal image in the heart, even unknown to the outer mind, whereby a soul will trudge through karma and circumstance and burden for the crystal image placed there by the living Christ.

Beloved hearts, the image of the giant jet of water coming out of the earth* that Jesus placed in the heart of Martha allowed her to endure and survive two thousand years of attempting to hold the balance of the nations. Promises sealed in your own hearts have brought *you* to this place, beloved, when you have passed through adversity and all temptations that beset your generation.

Blessed hearts, hope—hope is a most valuable quality. And therefore I desire to see you not disperse this year before having heard the message of the blessed Archeia Hope, consort of Gabriel.

And so, beloved, having passed through a most difficult and arduous childhood, dealing not alone with karma but those false

*Old Faithful Geyser, Yellowstone National Park

initiations given by those who have left the throne of grace, at a certain point I quickened the mind of the Messenger at the age of seventeen to go to Europe, to go to Switzerland and to study French. I had seen the long languishing of the soul and how this soul pursued God in the face of unseen odds—not the mere sometime abuses of parents but the entire forces of Hell behind this plot upon her lifestream.

Thus understand that by that age, through prayer and communion she had earned a dispensation from my heart. I sponsored her, then, for six months in Switzerland—and there, for the first time in her life to know the breath of freedom and the joy to be oneself without the burdens that had been upon that household.

But I will tell you of a few vignettes that I yet cherish. It was when she came upon the Lake of Geneva where in a past life she had been assassinated and there saw a man-made giant jet of water, rejoiced and thrilled to see this jet of water rising into the sky from the lake itself. This was the inner quickening of the image placed there by Jesus when she was Martha. Mind you, at this hour of her life she knew nothing of me or my name or this path but only the inner walk with Christ.

And so, beloved, with only that gleaned from early religious training, with no Catholicism whatsoever but inspired by myself, she took a ten-day layover in Paris much to the consternation of her parents, went there and what do you suppose?—went to the altar of many cathedrals in a pilgrimage to pray for the Hungarians who in that year of 1956 were crushed by the Soviets, to pray and to commune, and unknown to herself to physically anchor my flame for the staying of the hand of the impending karma of that continent. It was at Christmastime with the misty rains of Paris that she made her way by map cathedral to cathedral, I at her side in a city where she had been guillotined at the hands of mob violence.

Blessed hearts, I wish to tell you that at every point of the path of this Messenger unto the very present she could have made the wrong choice or given up and all that we have looked toward to fulfill should have been lost. I tell you this, beloved, so that you may know that you may do likewise and gain your victory; for the attainment won and expressed is a mantle of a living Guru that you may claim in the physical octave.

How sad it is that those who have [recently] passed from the screen of life did not call upon her for help when they needed it most. Thus, we say to you, beloved, understand the burdens and the joys of an office and how an office is won. And realize that at any moment failure could have resulted in the end of this mission.

You are as important as the Messenger and perhaps more so. For without the supporting body, the Word could not be implanted or delivered. Now, if you are as important, beloved, do you not also deserve as important bestowals and initiations and testings? Do you not also deserve so great a Light as the reward for dealing with so great a Darkness?

We are grateful that our Messengers have bared themselves to you that you might know that there is a human side to all who take embodiment. And whether there be weaknesses or stresses or gaps that you might identify in the human, this is only that you might realize for yourself, as for the Messengers, that our mission does not rest upon human mistakes or foibles. Our mission rests upon the divine afflatus, the descent of the Holy Ghost, the power of God present that overrides all of these, smoothens the rough places, and is able to deliver the violet flame for the exaltation of every son and daughter of God!

I speak, then, to those who weary themselves, their families, and us in the prolongation of their psychological problems and their physical ailments. Blessed ones, if you will remember sins committed against you by another, I can only say, God pity you, for you contain the seeds of your old age and your demise. I say, God pity you who have not known me or the violet flame!

And I have cried out to many a disturbed person who has come, disturbed by the very fact of desiring to manipulate others and thereby attracting to himself demons, possessing and otherwise, and I have said, "Is there not a violet flame? Have you not called to the violet flame? Do you not believe in the violet flame? Have you no mercy upon your God, your family, the angels who tend you? Where is the violet flame? Where is mercy?" And this is what the Law will not allow—the unmerciful servant,[6] the unmerciful heart, the one who says he forgives but never forgets and thus has not transmuted the wrongs of a true brother of Light.

Blessed ones, we all, I included, have passed through many periods in the human consciousness in many embodiments for which we have no pride. And when we look at these moments, we are grateful for the Holy Spirit, the violet flame, and those who have sponsored us. Thus, if there were to be held against me or you all of the foibles and mistakes of all past lives, there would be no salvation.

Now, the Christian viewpoint would have it, beloved, that inasmuch as the grace of God is greater than all of these it is possible to achieve salvation by confessing the name of the Lord Jesus Christ as one's Saviour. Thus salvation has become much like the drugs that are taken today—take a little pill and the pain goes away and you are saved from the crucifixion.

I speak, then, beloved, of a false theology built on half-truths, a false political system built on half-truths. And those who think they are wise, prating about—they go here and there and they draw false conclusions from false premises and they lead all astray.

Blessed ones, I will tell you of the final initiation of the Messenger in Los Angeles. It was to deal with a confrontation of Death and Hell. It comes to all, beloved. It is well that you know of the Messenger's initiation, for you must have a keen vision.

You must know that the last time she left here in late fall to return to Los Angeles, descending into the city and into the airport she saw [through the eye of an Archangel and said to herself], "This is a city of death and all whom I see are the living dead." And it was so, as far as those who happened to be in the airport at that time. For I did portray vividly a panorama of the dead/wounded dying, that she might know, by stark contrast to the Inner Retreat and the spiritual life, the challenge that remained. And so she saw clearly through my heart that this "death" and the "city of death"* would seek to devour her ere she should leave. And so, praying earnestly, she went about the business of concluding my book and others.

Blessed ones, you should know of the projections of Death that were played upon her by masterminds of the false hierarchy twenty-four hours a day, waking and sleeping. These projections were vivid as movies, as though on film, portraying a blow-by-blow account of what her demise should be in the coming weeks. Having scarce the time to separate herself from the writing of the books, there grew in her an inner resolve of resistance to Death and a transmittal to the decree tags† of the understanding of this force and its modus operandi that I gave to her.

And this is the key, beloved—whether it is the death wish of the various sects of religion on earth wishing and willing the death of the Messenger, whether it is Russian psychics or KGB agents who have masterminded the ability to probe the human mind and penetrate it, whether it is from Mars or Pluto or the moon or Hell itself, those embodied or disembodied, Death yet exists in the astral plane and it will come knocking at your door one of these days as surely as Death knocked clearly and loudly at

*the astral overlay of the lower astral plane shrouding the "City of the Angels" with the vibrations and the consciousness of the denizens of death

†groups of chelas who keep the flame of God 24 hours a day making the rounds of the hours to keep the vigil of Life in community and for the planet

the bedroom door of your Messenger in Los Angeles.

And this occurred at the hour of 4:00 a.m. And at that hour the loud rap came twice—a physical sound bringing her to the awakened state and then the instantaneous knowledge that though the sound were physical, the presence was astral.

After moments and minutes of silence assessing this knock, which came only days before her departure, and assessing the astral vibration and all of the compounding of these projections of Death, there began to be heard in the farthest star, where angels waited breathless for the response, the cry and the call that went forth: "Archangel Uriel, enter this house and bind Death and Hell!" These calls of the Messenger continued unabated beyond an hour until the Peace of the Archangel had devoured and bound the enemy.

Blessed hearts, within twenty-four to thirty-six hours of that event, the Messenger with her daughters seated here experienced a carefree return to youth, of joy and laughter and fun and jokes. Beloved, it was the victory over Death, whose victory is always the LORD's if only the one assailed will make the Call.

The tragedy of this year, beloved, is the passing of certain individuals who succumbed to Death and the suicide entity, all of whose families are in this movement and who watched their loved ones slip into compromise after compromise. And I tell you, these compromises with the suicide entity began decades and lifetimes ago. And these individuals had the opportunity to see the example of the Messengers, to follow in their gait, to know that the preparation for the meeting of this test is intense.

One must know that it does come. One must know that though death be predestined by your karma and your stars and may surround and grip you, *predestination is not the law of Cosmos.* Nay, the free will of the individual to overcome a predestination of karma and to rise again—this is the law of the Great White Brotherhood whereby we have defeated Death time and again.

Let the record be clear. As one has stood in your midst to defy the enemy, so when your hour does come, the full mantle of this experience may be upon you multiplying your Christhood. And you, one in the embrace of our physical mouthpiece, may conquer.

I say to you, begin now and cast out Death and Hell from your consciousness and see this as more important than the latest human attraction. And let there be less animal magnetism in this Community. Let God act in your life and do not so easily succumb to Death entities who come in the guise of sympathetic attractions, involvements, the tying up of one's energy, et cetera, et cetera.

Beloved hearts, you cannot have kept from you the testings of Death and Hell. You must be ready. And it is toward this end that the Masters who have preceded me have spoken to you. I say all of this so that you may understand the point of the vow. The vow to serve Saint Germain and my cause has never been more needed, more critical, more serious. So I precede it, then, with an explanation of the Path itself.

Those not upon this Path, those not willing to aim for the balancing of 100 percent of their karma, those who would take their own way, blessed ones, though they be sincere, though they would make the vow, are not able to keep it. Better, then, to not make the karma. This, too, is a concept that has been twisted by those who say, "Well, as long as I am making bad karma, I might as well slink away in the night. It would be better for all." And this, too, is the lie of the suicide entity. And it is cowardice!

O beloved, if you think that the eye of Morya is stern toward the coward who is on the Path, let me tell you, be ready for the eye of Saint Germain! For I have stood and seen the crimes against humanity.

What percentage of those in these rooms gathered do you think were among those murdered by World Communism? As the Messenger listened intently to the delivery of her son,[7] I showed her your faces in other lives with those Russian or Ukrainian or Eastern European characteristics. And one by one she saw the record of the martyrdom of those whom I singled out to her vision, beginning with Mark and herself and one of her children. You may also know that it was the blood of Christ in their lifestreams that became the foundation of the Bolshevik revolution when they were murdered in the House of Special Purpose.

Blessed hearts, know, then, that our mission in this hour is well planned. It is as follows: I will give myself to those who have taken the vow and who have renewed heart to be disciplined as chelas under our Messenger. Those who have received the discipline and have had enough, even as we have had enough, will not be disciplined again unless they request it. We will work through those, then, who can keep a vow, worldwide.

Certain members of this immediate family and staff have taken a vow to publish *The Coming Revolution*. And you have heard that vow of Sean at the conclusion of his delivery.* Blessed ones, that commitment will be multiplied by our dispensation. It is a life that is vowed, not merely a vow for a particular project. When we have this we will see what we can do to do exactly what has

*". . . The Masters have great hope for us and faith in us. I can say this, speaking as the voice of my father, Mark Prophet, and I pledge myself to the Coming Revolution in Higher Consciousness and the Battle of Armageddon. My fellow Community members, will you join me?"

been called for—the reeducation first of America and the Lightbearers and then of the larger population.

The outlining by the God and Goddess Meru, Lanello, Mother Mary, and Jesus[8] may be studied following dinner by those of you who have not heard these dictations. And you may take notes during the listening and thereby understand what is set before you.

The consideration is the following, beloved, and it has been well thought through by the Messenger and her son. If we, then, move full force to expose the Soviets and their plan for a first strike against the United States, we will then make of ourselves targets, even the targets of the first strike. What, then, is the choice? To lay low and compromise like all of the rest or to take our stand and shout our message from the housetops and send it forth in our magazine and in our lectures and conferences.

What, then, would be the results of these choices? To lay low and ipso facto already begin to carry the party line would be to face the eventuality that is certain—that is, the nuclear attack and war on this soil, which could be followed by a complete takeover and life under a Soviet dictatorship.

It was well put by Sean. We would not want to live in such a situation. We have no fear of Death or dying. We have no fear of War. But we will not live or give our lifeblood to a Soviet dictatorship!

Thus you see, beloved, the choice may seem to be either death by a Soviet nuclear first strike or death by submission to a Soviet society that would result from not engaging in the battle that has already begun.

It is very clear that one thus becomes a member of Serapis Bey's chosen ones. And the battle at Thermopylae ought to be studied.[9] The standing for a principle, beloved, is more important than life itself. But those who have not faced and defeated the last enemy who is Death,[10] those who know that they are playing games, deceiving themselves and attempting to deceive the Messenger—these cling to life and would avoid this choice or this vow. They would rather live a little while longer in their compromise and their way than to become enfired with a fervor of freedom and to take the ultimate stand.

It is for want of taking the ultimate stand on the part of the leadership of the free nations, the religious people, and the good people that there be few with whom I can work directly in the giving of myself. Who takes an ultimate and a complete life-and-death stand on anything these days, beloved? But this is a requirement of my dispensation and vow.

Thus, I do not even ask you to enter into it this day, for it shall require of you soul-searching, perhaps a period of self-purging and submission to more severe disciplines than those to which you are accustomed that you might see how you fare, [in order] to be certain. Then, of course, I must make the choice of those who step forward—those whom I can work through and with and sponsor, those whom I cannot. For it is I who pay the ultimate price in this hour and in this situation.

I would like you to recall that when the Messenger gave her first Stump messages, even as early as during her trip to Ghana and Liberia and then later in the seventies, she was preaching a message of anti-Communism based on the Fátima message and on facts such as those given today. Blessed ones, she was met with boos and hisses, with large percentages of the audiences leaving when at the conclusion of her spiritual teaching she would sound the warning and expose the Soviets and the Marxists.

Therefore, in deliberation with my heart and our reasoning together we concluded that the hour was to give a spiritual teaching and let children become grounded in the milk of the Word, in the violet flame, in the decrees, and in the buoyancy of the Light, and then let them be introduced to the International Capitalist/Communist Conspiracy once they should arrive at Summit University. This, then, remained our plan. And it was pursued and many came into the Teaching without arousing the serpent mind before they had the preparation to receive the strong meat of the Word.[11]

Now, beloved, you have heard Sean call for those who will go forth not only with the spiritual message but with my message, which is indeed interpreted as a political one although it sets aside all barriers of politics. I say to you, let us abandon the right wing. Let us abandon the left wing. And as Morya said, let us not be caught in the middle of the road.

Blessed ones, "right" means a perspective to the right of Truth, and "left" means a perspective to the left. Now, if you would be centered in Truth and have Truth centered in you, you must be above this politicking. You must understand that the right-wing individuals who should have espoused my cause long ago, who have known me and known my name in their midst, thanks to these Messengers and the previous ones—they in their pride have refused to be associated with me. Therefore, those who have denied me before men, them do I deny before the Father this day![12]

Therefore, as a cardinal principle, I say to you, let not my message be tainted with the jargon of the right wing or the left wing. See to it that you therefore present a platform upon which every candidate to office may stand as an independent Lightbearer—not as a libertarian or an anarchist in the ultimate sense of independence, but as one who is independent beneath his I AM Presence and Holy Christ Self, who does stand beneath the Tree of Life, who champions Truth wherever it is found, who may also recognize that certain points in the entire spectrum of world thought are worthy of championing.

Therefore, listen to the enemy as well as the friend and seek in God what I have called the "Awareness/Action." It is not enough to present the plight, the problem, the dilemma, or to read the handwriting on the wall. Those who see and know all of this and who have access to us must present to the people of America *an awareness which is a foundation for action.* Today's actions supporting the Sandinistas, the lethargy in America, and so forth are based upon nonawareness or a psychic awareness.

First, let there be awareness of cosmic principles of freedom and destiny on earth. Based upon the awareness of the exact geopolitical configuration of the hour, let hearts one with me, then, present my platform of action, subject by subject—from education to drugs to Communism to pornography and so on.

Blessed ones, it is not enough to prophesy a doomsday, as many extremists on the right have done with such emotion and fanaticism as to utterly turn off those who should be listening to dire forebodings of world karma. And these have been turned off by the very ones who should have engaged my flame. And I tell you, their fanaticism comes, beloved, from the fact that they love freedom. And the force does entangle them and cause them grave consequences of misuse of the Light—even the Light [as portion of my attainment] that I once gave to them.

The message of the spiritual teaching is fundamental. The books that have been published this fall [1986][13] must be devoured and underlined, for it is a platform of teaching.

Beloved ones, it is an easy course set before you. You have, practically, only to take a book in hand and read it to new classes of students, even before you have studied it yourself. You can learn it with them. The teaching is plain. It needs no ad-libbing. It can be fed direct. You can gather with a circle of students and simply allow each in his turn to read from these books and then at the conclusion give decrees and have discussion or questions and answers.

Thus, delay not. For with the coming into your hands, no later than by Lincoln's birthday, of my book *Saint Germain On Prophecy* you will desire to deliver a stronger message and a more fierce confrontation with the forces of Darkness lodged in the planet. You will get the picture of the urgency and the circle of prophecy that we have been sending forth since the early part of this decade.

With the studying of this release, beloved, you will come into an hour of realization and of quickening, if you have not already done so, that will impel you to desire to deliver our message into the very political arena as you strive to avert the election to the office of the president of one who will lead this nation to war.

Thus, I warn you in advance: If you yourself are not cleared of fanaticism, you will immediately be cast in the role of a Lyndon LaRouche or a right-wing fanatic. And then the world will cease to listen to you or me or the Messenger.

Therefore study well how the message has been presented. And, of course, you cannot be illiterate politically. You must read certain periodicals regularly and know their bias, right or left, so that you may understand what is happening. Although the Messenger has set the pace for awareness of political events, not all have followed suit.

And those who are our ministers, beloved, are those who must lead this activity in bringing the awareness of what is happening always in the International Capitalist/Communist Conspiracy, always with the eye on the Soviets and their Western supporters. For there is where all decrees must be directed, not merely on Saturday night but at every session. Not long invocations but very specific and incisive ones will give us the authority to act. If you do not know the danger, you cannot defeat it.

Take care, then, I say, when you deliver this message into a field saturated with the disinformation of the Soviet Union that you do not fall prey to the character assassination and the deathblows of a public and a media who are quick to denounce and ridicule those who stand for the cause of freedom. The deliberation of your hearts is necessary, so seek to do so in an organized manner and neglect not our call. Neglect not our call that has gone forth before and that we give again.

The vow that I have taken is to serve with this earth until the true Lightbearers are free. The vow I propose to take, having accomplished this, is to stand with all others who have accepted the transfer of the flame of freedom from our best servants. The specifics of the vow must be, then, to defeat World Communism before it defeats the West and to defeat in

the West those betrayers of the Word before the very foundations of Western civilization crumble for their presence in that foundation. To this end I will answer your calls, and that is where the revolution begins.

If you feed to the Messenger the facts and the information of what is happening on the earth and if she does make the call, I promise you that the causal bodies of all who take this vow will combine with the entire Spirit of the Great White Brotherhood and mine to defeat the Adversary (wherever and through whomever he appears) and to turn the tide.

In the meantime, all must act as though already engaged in a war that began at the conclusion of World War II. You are in a war this day. Let every penny that comes to your hands be used to prepare for personal physical survival for yourselves and your children. And let the organization as a whole plan, then, to have a sufficiency of food and protection to endure any type of attack. When this is accomplished, I tell you, you will be fearless and have a new freedom.

In the meantime, the doubt and the fear somehow lurks—what will we do if this happens on the morrow? Beloved, if you move swiftly and defeat the forces that oppose this Community, you will have your base and you will survive. But remember, the hour is very short.

The significance of this day of January 1, 1987, is the coming of the golden sphere of light—of which it was not known if it would be possible until a certain proving, then, of yourselves in your initiations—and the very certain coming of the dark sphere of planetary karma.

The significance of the hour is that the Four Horsemen move on and intensify in their delivery of karma and that many will suffer. The significance of the hour is that the base must be prepared and continue to be prepared and that all of you who have responsibilities around the world must know that unless this place be prepared for and by yourselves it will be too late to get ready when the time comes.

Let this, then, be your first priority. It is not necessary to move here but it is necessary to contribute financially. For, beloved ones, bomb shelters and food-storage barns that are necessary are very costly. Therefore, recognize that this is the greatest insurance policy you could take. There is no other guarantee but God and God in you who prepare.

Therefore, beloved, I rejoice that in this hour my son and yours, America's son, has presented himself to me and to the

Messengers that he might become an ordained minister of this Church. Thus, he did deliver to you this day his first sermon, and I call him now that I might in truth ordain him.

[Sean Christopher Prophet approaches the altar.]

LORD God Almighty, thou who didst send me forth to anoint thy son David, even the soul of Jesus Christ, receive now unto thy heart this son of David that he might fulfill his inner vow made long ago for the building of the temple.

LORD God, he does kneel to receive the very first steps, yet thou knowest his Inner Light. Receive him as revered. Let thy mantle drop upon him now as holy angels now anoint this head with oil.

Sean Christopher Prophet, I, Saint Germain, who have held thee in my arms from the beginning, do now clothe you with my own mantle, for you have demonstrated again and again no desire for popularity or reputation but to speak my Truth both to the ignorant and the cunning. In guilelessness you have preached many sermons in full hope for a response, only to be spurned and ridiculed. Thus, let it be known by this company that you have been my minister, my ambassador "plenipotentiary" for some hours of this life and many hours of previous lives.

Therefore I take in this moment this point of consecration. It is the bishop's ring worn by your father, Mark, which you may aspire also one day to wear. You may gaze upon the power of the hand of Mark when you see the ring size of the index finger, as [on which] he wore it—truly an ancient emissary of the Lord Christ. With this ring, then, I thee wed in the Guru/Chela relationship.

It is thy vow that I accept as the firstfruits of my new calling to the earth. By the flame of Zadkiel, who also blessed me, receive now the initiations of the priesthood of the Order of Melchizedek, the sign of the Seventh Ray ministering servant, and a cloak of the original priesthood of the Israelites.

So there is emblazoned upon the brow HOLINESS TO THE LORD.[14] Thou art sealed, then, in the protection and mantle of thy office, both thou and thy seed and thy family. May this protection and ordination extend to all Keepers of the Flame who keep the harmony with thy mission, as it is mine.

I bring to you, then, the congratulations and the rejoicing of the first Mother of the Flame, Clara Louise.

This ring she wore then is now pressed into the crown chakra as a blessing of her fiery lifestream, one with Serapis, Amen Bey, and the seraphim. This one who held thee in her arms following thy birth does now stand as thy sponsor with your own beloved Jesus, once thy father, and Mark, thy father. Therefore, rise to receive the Communion cup of the new wine.

Beloved, on this occasion, I, Saint Germain, serve the golden wine of the golden grape, not the red wine, signifying by this Communion the opportunity of the son of God for that transmutation and translation whereby the Blood of Christ does become that golden light of the crown of wisdom. As thou once asked the LORD for an understanding heart, so I have asked the Maha Chohan to bless this bread and wine that thou might drink in the true wisdom of leadership, of the understanding of my heart, and the step-by-step Awareness/Action, Alpha/Omega, Blood and Body of Christ that is to be taken.

So now receive the Body of the Divine Mother as thou dost break the bread of Life with her. Receive now this Communion and drink ye all of it.

[Sean Christopher Prophet receives Holy Communion taken with the Mother of the Flame.]

Now in memory of Melchizedek, who did break bread and serve wine to Abraham,[15] know that it is in the tradition of this priesthood that thou mightest rise to bear the flame of freedom by the message of my heart, thy heart—one.

Son of God, rise to claim thy mantle. In the name of the Father and of the Son and of the Holy Spirit, in the name of the Divine Mother, the Spirit of the Great White Brotherhood saluteth thee.

I, Saint Germain, choose, then, in this hour to shake thy hand as a brother of Light.

May you also know me in my son. And those who would sing "I can say that I shook Lanello's hand"[16] may in this hour shake the hand of the one who has shaken my hand and pledge for a beginning that friendship with Sean. For I tell you truly, no truer friend there is to any man than this Sean Christopher Prophet.

I seal you, one and all, in the flame of hope unto your own ordination to your divine destiny. As the door is opened by one, it can be opened by the few and the many.

I, Saint Germain, salute you and seal you in this hour unto God Victory. [52-sec. standing ovation]

"The Summit Lighthouse Sheds Its Radiance O'er All the World to Manifest as Pearls of Wisdom."
This dictation by Saint Germain was **delivered** through the Messenger of the Great White Brotherhood Elizabeth Clare Prophet on **New Year's Day, January 1, 1987,** at the Royal Teton Ranch, Montana. (**1**) **The new covenant**. Jer. 31:31–34; Matt. 26:28; I Cor. 11:25; II Cor. 3:6, 14; Heb. 8:6–13; 9:15; 10:16, 17; 12:24. See also Jesus Christ, December 25, 1985, "'Rise, Peter: Kill and Eat!' The Engrafting of the Threefold Flame," 1986 *Pearls of Wisdom,* vol. 29, no. 14, pp. 107–20. (**2**) See Sanat Kumara, July 27, 1986, "The Empowerment of Christhood," 1986 *Pearls of Wisdom,* vol. 29, no. 71, p. 622. (**3**) Judges 7:4–7 gives the account of Gideon's 300 who lapped the water "as a dog lappeth," chosen apart from those who knelt upon their knees to drink. This may or may not be the scene Saint Germain is referring to. (**4**) In addition to Karl Marx, chief theorist of modern Communism, and Friedrich Nietzsche, who proclaimed "God is dead," other **theologians and philosophers** have emerged from Germany distorting Christ's message, including: David Friedrich Strauss, Ferdinand Christian Baur, Rudolf Bultmann, Martin Dibelius, Hermann Samuel Reimarus, William Wrede, Johannes Weiss. For more on these, see Mark L. Prophet and Elizabeth Clare Prophet, *The Lost Teachings of Jesus I,* Summit University Press, p. 332, n. 9, and pp. 340–43, n. 44. (**5**) Deut. 30:19. (**6**) Matt. 18:23–35. (**7**) Prior to the dictation, Sean Christopher Prophet delivered the New Year's Day sermon on **"Apathy in America."** Presenting facts, figures, and case histories, the Messengers' 22-year-old son challenged America's entrenched pacifism, apathy and indifference in the face of continued Soviet atrocities. He set forth the thesis that "apathy is the state of consciousness that breeds and allows Communism to exist" and that "will bring World Communism into this country and/or an annihilating Soviet first strike" unless the people are reeducated on a planetary scale. His address included readings from Aleksandr Solzhenitsyn and *Saint Germain On Prophecy.* (**8**) See Mother Mary, December 24, 1986, "The Clay Vessels Must Be Broken"; Lanello, December 25, 1986, "Endowing Time with Eternity"; Jesus Christ, December 25, 1986, "The Coming of the Divine Teacher"; God Meru, December 28, 1986, "To Win a World for Cosmos," 1986 *Pearls of Wisdom,* vol. 29, nos. 76–79. (**9**) See Mark L. Prophet and Elizabeth Clare Prophet, *Lords of the Seven Rays,* Summit University Press, pp. 150–52, Book One. (**10**) I Cor. 15:26. (**11**) Heb. 5:12–14; I Cor. 3:2. (**12**) Matt. 10:33; Luke 12:9. (**13**) **New publications, Fall 1986**: *The Lost Teachings of Jesus,* I and II, *Lords of the Seven Rays,* and *Corona Class Lessons.* (**14**) Exod. 28:36–38. (**15**) Gen. 14:18, 19. (**16**) See "I Shook Lanello's Hand," song 517 in *The Summit Lighthouse Book of Songs.*

Decree for Freedom's Holy Light*
by Saint Germain

Mighty Cosmic Light!
My own I AM Presence bright,
  Proclaim Freedom everywhere—
In Order and by God Control
I AM making all things whole!

Mighty Cosmic Light!
Stop the lawless hordes of night,
  Proclaim Freedom everywhere—
In Justice and in Service true
I AM coming, God, to you!

Mighty Cosmic Light!
I AM Law's prevailing might,
  Proclaim Freedom everywhere—
In magnifying all goodwill
I AM Freedom living still!

Mighty Cosmic Light!
Now make all things right,
  Proclaim Freedom everywhere—
In Love's Victory all shall go,
I AM the Wisdom all shall know!

I AM Freedom's holy Light
  Nevermore despairing!
I AM Freedom's holy Light
  Evermore I'm sharing!
Freedom, Freedom, Freedom!
  Expand, expand, expand!
  I AM, I AM, I AM
Forevermore I AM Freedom!

*Give this decree nine times three times a day for personal and planetary freedom. Do this for thirty-three days and see how your life and divine plan accelerate into Higher Consciousness!

Pearls of Wisdom®

published by The Summit Lighthouse

Vol. 30 No. 3 *Sean C. Prophet* *January 18, 1987*

"On the Defense of Freedom"

I
Apathy in America

Elizabeth Clare Prophet:

This New Year's Day, January 1, 1987, our message will be delivered by our son, Sean Christopher Prophet.

Good afternoon and happy New Year.

["Happy New Year, Sean!"]

Our subject today is "Apathy in America."

Apathy is tantamount to suicide. And we've heard from beloved Jesus that "Communism is organized suicide."[1] So we can conclude that apathy is the state of consciousness that breeds and allows Communism to exist.

Apathy in America today and into the 1990s is by nature a willing espousal of the values of the beast of socialism. The American people are willfully apathetic and do not want to be told the truth. They will resist that truth when it is given to them in any form because that truth would force them to change their outlook and their attitudes in such a way that they would rather die than change.

The false prophets in the established churches and in the media are responsible in large part for this entrenched apathy. This state of consciousness will bring World Communism into this country and/or an annihilating Soviet first strike, as Saint Germain has said.[2]

In any event, it will mean an end to freedom and opportunity for spiritual and technological evolution. We've heard from many of the Ascended Masters on this subject, and they have given us hope. However, the only thing that can change the world situation and reverse or abate this prophecy is the complete and total reeducation of the people on a planetwide scale and the giving of the violet flame and "Archangel Michael's Rosary for Armageddon" by Americans and the people of the earth.

I'd like to examine now the construction of the word *apathy* and several synonyms. *Apathy,* as defined by Webster's dictionary, is a "lack of feeling or emotion," or "impassiveness." The second definition is a "lack of interest or concern," or "indifference."

The construction of the word is *a-* + *pathos—a,* of course, meaning "without"; and *pathos* is from the Greek, "suffering, experience," or "emotion." It means "an element in experience or in artistic representation evoking pity or compassion," also "an emotion of sympathetic pity."

And so we observe that the people of America are without the capacity to feel compassion—except in a very superficial way—for those around the world who are suffering; and they are not prepared to challenge the cause of that suffering in any direct way that is effective to end that suffering. That is the real meaning of the word *apathy.* It's when people do not have the capacity to confront the cause of suffering and to defeat it.

From "apathy" to "indifference" we zero in on the state of being "apathetic" or "indifferent":

Indifferent is defined as "neither good nor bad."

Definition 1: "marked by impartiality," or "unbiased."

2: "that does not matter one way or the other; that has nothing that calls for sanction or condemnation in either observance or neglect: of no importance or value one way or the other."

3: "marked by no special liking for or dislike of something; marked by a lack of interest in or concern about something," and again "apathetic."

4: "being neither excessive nor defective."

5: "being neither good nor bad: mediocre" and "being neither right nor wrong."

6: "characterized by lack of active quality: neutral."

7: "capable of development in more than one direction; especially: not yet embryologically determined."

We also have the synonym *impassive:*

1: "unsusceptible to pain; unsusceptible to physical feeling: insensible; unsusceptible to or destitute of emotion: apathetic."

2: "giving no sign of feeling or emotion: expressionless."

3: "not moving in any way: motionless."

And we are given again some synonyms for the word *impassive*—one being *apathetic,* with this defined as "a puzzling or deplorable indifference or inertness"; and "stolid," which "implies an habitual absence of interest, responsiveness, or curiosity concerning anything outside of an accustomed routine."

So we've come full circle and that's the end of our definitions. I will now go through on a point-by-point basis and talk about each one.

First we have *indifferent*—**"neither good nor bad."** We've seen the popularization in society today, even by the established churches, of the notion that "good" and "evil" are relative terms and the espousing of situation ethics. It's also been in the schools—the teaching of secular humanism. And that has evolved as a philosophy and a way of life for many people in this country. It is an extremely dangerous ideology.

Aleksandr Solzhenitsyn has had considerable contact with the ideology of Communism, which is not really any different from secular humanism. He spent a good deal of his life in the Soviet Union. He was born there. He won the Nobel Peace Prize in 1970 while still in the Soviet Union, and for his writings and works he was exiled therefrom. Prior to his exile, he spent eight years in labor camps where he garnered many of the experiences that have made him such a dynamic speaker and such a freedom fighter.

From this he wrote *The Gulag Archipelago* in three volumes and *One Day in the Life of Ivan Denisovich.* I believe he had a job as a teacher. He was living in a small home and he was constantly bothered by the Soviet secret police, so he hid his writings. The entire book of *One Day in the Life of Ivan Denisovich* was written on six sheets of paper! This is the extent to which individuals in the Soviet Union are forced to go to get their message to the West.

I'll read to you now from one of Solzhenitsyn's speeches—one he made before the AFL-CIO in 1975, published in *The Voice of Freedom.* He has written other things since then, but I believe this to be extremely important.

> Communism has never concealed the fact that it rejects all absolute concepts of morality. It scoffs at any consideration of "good" and "evil" as indisputable categories. Communism considers morality to be relative, to be a class matter. Depending upon circumstances and the political situation, any act, including murder, even the killing of thousands, could be good or could be bad.
>
> It all depends upon class ideology. And who defines class ideology? The whole class cannot get together to pass judgment. A handful of people determine what is good and what is bad. But I must say that in this very respect Communism has been most successful. It has infected the whole world with the belief in the relativity of good and evil.
>
> Many people besides the Communists are carried away by this idea today. Among enlightened people it is considered rather awkward to use seriously such words as "good" and "evil." Communism has managed to instill in all of us that these concepts are old-fashioned concepts and laughable. But if we are to be deprived of the concepts of good and evil, what will be left? Nothing but the manipulation of one another. We will decline to the status of animals.[3]

Many parts of the world are well on their way.

President Reagan gave a speech in 1983 in which he called the Soviet Union an "evil empire."[4] He was reviled for this and many in the media gave an outcry, saying that he was hindering the cause of world peace and that he was a warmonger. What else should he have called it when the facts are so clear? When is a spade not a spade?

We come to **Definition 1** of *indifferent*—and that is **"marked by impartiality,"** or **"unbiased."** I'd like to talk about the media in this case and their treatment of President Reagan and the entire American way of life.

The media prides itself on being unbiased. And for a free and independent media to be unbiased when the facts about Communism are as clear-cut as they are is at least hypocritical if not an act of treason. For journalists to be "unbiased" about two political systems, it stands to reason that both systems should meet the standards of human dignity.

One cannot be unbiased when faced with the animalistic nature of the Soviet system. To treat the Soviet Union as an equal to the United

States of America is, in fact, bias of the worst kind. Any decent human being would be biased against Adolf Hitler, so why not against the perpetrators of a far more serious and long-term holocaust?

By neglecting to provide the American viewer with the full scope of Soviet activities—while scrutinizing every domestic issue—the media, which has been given a direct line into American living rooms, imparts a negative bias towards our government and a distrust of our leaders. The excuse which has sometimes been given about the lack of coverage of the Soviet Union and Communist-backed insurgencies is that they control physical access to a given country, usually banning the media.

Now, Americans have an extreme distaste for those who withhold information or hide the truth. Witness what is going on right now in Washington. We have two former members of the government—John Poindexter and Oliver North—who have, within their constitutional rights, taken the Fifth Amendment and refused to testify. They are being reviled. And many in the media are calling this an act of treason.

So why do we not apply the same standards to the Soviet dictators?

The Soviets withheld information about Chernobyl for three days. This is a matter of global consequence. It will cost thousands of lives in Western Europe because people were not evacuated due to the fact that they did not have the information.

A few months after Chernobyl there was a conference of the International Atomic Energy Agency and many scientists went to get the Soviet view of what happened at Chernobyl. It seems that most scientists came away satisfied and were even praising the Soviets for their new openness. Basically, the West has already forgiven them for their three-day silence, and Chernobyl is a part of history.

We should interview the Soviets and let them speak about their environmental pollution and their "wars of national liberation" and let the American people decide. We have the right to have investigative reporters bringing us continual updates on Soviet activities worldwide, much as we are given updates on our own government's doings.

Soviet state spokesmen like Vladimir Posner and Georgi Arbatov, who speak regularly on American television posing as "objective" spokesmen or scholars, have no objective viewpoint and nothing new to say. They are representatives of the Politburo and the Soviet Communist Party Central Committee and are simply spouting that line.

We need to interview the members of the Communist Party Central Committee, the real decision makers, and put them on the spot. If they have nothing to hide, let them withstand the direct scrutiny of Ted Koppel or other probing reporters. And let them be asked *real* questions and be confronted with the evidence and be called to accounting by *informed* reporters who can challenge their lies with facts! [14-sec. applause]

If they will not grant interviews, let us show it, "60 Minutes" style, with the door slamming in the camera lens. If they threaten our networks or our network correspondents or throw the networks out of the country, let us say so on the evening news so that the American people may see the manipulation and blackmail that occurs behind the scenes.

Finally, let us insist on free access to the Soviet people by the press, without the threat of imprisonment or loss of status in society for granting frank interviews with Western reporters. Let us have watchdog groups that constantly report to the American people and track Soviet citizens who are brave enough to be interviewed. If they are harassed by their government, let there be a worldwide outcry against this barbaric society that does not allow its citizens the freedom to speak their minds!

We must get over the idea that *bias* is a dirty word. Webster defines *bias* as simply "an inclination of temperament or outlook." As representatives of the American people, the journalists are our eyes and ears and thus have a duty to be biased in favor of our interests and the protection of our way of life.

These journalists are not elected but they can influence policy in a very real way. Therefore, their views should reflect a cross section of the views of the electorate. However, they are also in the position before the fact of shaping those views. Thus, by the abuse of the power of the press in presenting a one-sided view, *their view,* a vicious cycle has developed.

Word choice has become a way that the media has imparted bias without changing the empirical content of a story. The very word *anti-Communist* has been poisoned by the media. Accusations of McCarthyism have surfaced whenever anyone mentions Communism—to the point where no journalist dare use the term in its true sense for fear that he will end his career.

I will read again from Solzhenitsyn:

> Whoever says "anti-Communism" is saying, in effect, anti-anti-humanity. A poor construction. So we should say: that which is against Communism is for humanity. Not to accept, to reject this inhuman Communist ideology is simply to be a human being. It isn't being a member of a party. It's a protest of our souls against those who tell us to forget the concepts of good and evil.[5]

Many times in frank discussion about the Soviet system, when you confront people with a heinous act or crime that the Soviet government has perpetrated they will say, "Sure, there's not a Russian behind every tree." But there might be! We might, in fact, be putting ourselves in mortal danger by not thinking that there's a Russian behind every tree.

I've also been called a "knee-jerk anti-Communist." Well, what does that mean?

Many times the media will substitute the word *Marxist* or *leftist* for the term *Communist,* such as with the government of Nicaragua or other Soviet client states. They will not call them Communists. They also use the term *Russian* interchangeably with the word *Soviet.* As Solzhenitsyn has said, this is a dangerous practice.

This reading is from a book by Solzhenitsyn, *The Mortal Danger: How Misconceptions about Russia Imperil America.* This section is titled "Russia and the U.S.S.R.":

> To begin with, there is the careless and inaccurate use of the words "Russia" and "Russian" in place of "U.S.S.R." and "Soviet." (There is even a persistent emotional bias against the former: "Russian tanks have entered Prague," "Russian imperialism," "Never trust the Russians," as against "Soviet achievements in space" and "the triumphs of the Soviet ballet.") Yet it ought to be clear that these concepts are not only opposites, but are *inimical.* "Russia" is to the Soviet Union as a man is to the disease afflicting

> him. We do not, after all, confuse a man with his illness; we do not refer to him by the name of that illness or curse him for it.
>
> After 1917, the state as a functioning whole—the country with its government, policies, and armed forces—can no longer be referred to as Russia. It is inappropriate to apply the word "Russian" to the present authorities in the U.S.S.R., to its army, or to its future military successes and regimes of occupation throughout the world, even though the official language in each case might be Russian. (This is equally true of both China and Vietnam, only in their case no equivalent of the word "Soviet" is available.)
>
> A certain American diplomat recently exclaimed: "Let Brezhnev's Russian heart be run by an American pacemaker!" Quite wrong! He should have said "Soviet heart." Nationality is determined not by one's origins alone, but also by the direction of one's loyalties and affections. A Brezhnev who has connived at the ruin of his own people in the interests of foreign adventures has no Russian heart. All that his ilk have done—to destroy the national way of life and to pollute nature, to desecrate national shrines and monuments, and to keep the people in hunger and poverty for the last sixty years—shows that the Communist leaders are alien to the people and indifferent to its suffering.
>
> (This is equally true of the ferocious Khmer Rouge, the Polish functionary who may have been reared by a Catholic mother, the young Communist activist, taskmaster over a group of starving coolies, or the stolid Georges Marchais with his Kremlin-like exterior; each has turned his back on his own nationality and has embraced inhumanity.)
>
> For present-day purposes the word "Russia" can serve only to designate an oppressed people which is denied the possibility of acting as one entity, or to denote its suppressed national consciousness, religion, and culture. Or else it can point to a future nation liberated from Communism.
>
> There was no such confusion in the 1920s when progressive Western opinion exulted over Bolshevism: the object of its enthusiasm was then named "Soviet" outright. During the tragic years of the Second World War, the concepts "Russian" and "Soviet" seem to have merged in the eyes of the world (a cruel error, which is discussed below). And with the coming of the cold war, the animosities generated were then directed principally toward the word "Russian." The effects are being felt to this day; in fact, new and bitter accusations have in recent years been leveled against all things "Russian."[6]

This is a real tragedy for the Russian people—that they should be associated with this Soviet Communist dictatorship which keeps them in bondage and gives them a bad name.

Definition 2 of *indifferent:* **"that does not matter one way or the other; that has nothing that calls for sanction or condemnation in either observance or neglect: of no importance or value one way or the other."**

How many times have we heard that the Soviet Union and the United States are both corrupt, both are likely to cheat on arms control, and both abuse human rights equally in the Third World? It's a very common liberal argument.

This is the perfect outpicturing of **Definition 2a** of *indifferent:* **"that does not matter one way or the other."** In fact, the indifference has tipped the scales in favor of the Soviets. Our press and media are harder on our own government than they are on the Soviets, fostering the illusion of equality.

We'll take the example of Amnesty International, a human rights group that is dedicated to the exposure and condemnation of human rights violations wherever they occur (according to them). Amnesty International is likely to report approximately the same volume on Eastern and Western human rights abuses in a given time period. Though it would seem that this is fair, it is not, because the two sides are not equal in human rights abuses by any stretch of the imagination. This dulls the sensitivity of the West to reports of Soviet human rights abuses. "We do the same thing," they say.

Indifference is then established. Equality is established. The concept of a "good nation" versus the "evil empire" seems ludicrous. Thus Amnesty International, while posing as a human rights group, serves the cause of Communism. It would be better that they said nothing.

If you ever need evidence of Sino-Soviet crimes, you need look no farther than the *Guinness Book of World Records*. Under the section of crime, World Communism is center stage.

The mass murder of the Chinese people on their own soil which took place in Communist China under Mao Tse-tung is the worst crime in history, with estimates varying between 32.25 to 61.7 million from 1949 to 1971.[7]

Second in line in *Guinness* is the Soviet Union with its great purge of 1936–38 under Stalin, listing 8–10 million victims. The Ukrainian famine and purges (also under Stalin) claimed an additional 10–15 million.

These estimates are on the low side. When you include all Communist murders, including the more recent genocides in Cambodia and Afghanistan, you see that the Soviets and other Communists have murdered 190 million people since 1917.[8] 190 million! This is more than the entire pre-World War II population of the United States of America! These executions have been mostly for political crimes and some for no crime at all, as in the Ukrainian famine caused by Stalin.

What sort of a system is this, to do such a thing? We'll ask Solzhenitsyn.

> The system was installed by armed uprising.
> It dispersed the Constituent Assembly.
> It capitulated to Germany—the common enemy.
> It introduced execution without trial.
> It crushed workers' strikes.
> It plundered the villagers to such an unbelievable extent that the peasants revolted, and when this happened it crushed the peasants in the bloodiest possible way.
> It shattered the Church.
> It reduced twenty provinces of our country to a condition of famine. . . .

> A system that, in the twentieth century, was the first to introduce the use of hostages, that is to say, not to seize the person whom they were seeking, but rather a member of his family or someone at random, and shoot that person.
>
> This system of hostages and persecution of the family exists to this day. It is still the most powerful weapon of persecution, because the bravest person, who is not afraid for himself, still shivers at the threat to his family.
>
> It is a system which was the first—long before Hitler—to employ false registration, that is, to say: "Such and such people have to come in to register." People would comply and then they were taken away to be annihilated.
>
> We didn't have gas chambers in those days. We used barges. A hundred or a thousand persons were put into a barge and then it was sunk.
>
> It was a system which deceived the workers in all of its decrees—the decree on land, the decree on peace, the decree on factories, the decree on freedom of the press.
>
> It was a system which exterminated all additional parties, and let me make it clear to you that it not only disbanded the party itself, but destroyed its members. All members of every other party were exterminated. It was a system which carried out genocide of the peasantry; 15 million peasants were sent off to extermination.
>
> It was a system which introduced serfdom, the so-called "passport system."
>
> It was a system which, in time of peace, artificially created a famine, causing 6 million persons to die in the Ukraine in 1932 and 1933. They died on the very edge of Europe. And Europe didn't even notice it. The world didn't even notice it—6 million persons![9]

If any of you should run into someone who compares Communism to other authoritarian regimes in other parts of history that have been supposedly "just as bad," here's the evidence. It is documented that in Russia during the eighty years prior to the Bolshevik Revolution of 1917, during which time there was sedition, assassination attempts and the actual assassination of a tsar (when the country was in a state of turmoil due to political, social, and economic changes), an average of seventeen persons per year were executed. During the Spanish Inquisition at the height of its terror, perhaps ten persons per month were executed.

Immediately following the Bolshevik Revolution, the Cheka, which was the predecessor to the modern KGB, was murdering a thousand a month without trial. Stalin, not to be outdone, killed forty thousand per month, not counting the artificial famines. Forty thousand per month executed without trial or hope!

Now, according to *Guinness,* the great Nazi holocaust which we hear so much about comes in a distant third with "only" 5.8 million victims. But just because the dead of Hitler's war machine scored third is no reason we should ignore them; nevertheless, to spotlight these atrocities while avoiding the record of World Communism is to invite this hellish nightmare to repeat itself. Our fixation with the holocaust sends the message to the Communists that *their* murders, continuing to the present, must be acceptable because we do not speak of them.

Witness: the people of Tibet have lost 1.2 million lives, one-sixth of their population—from starvation, execution, torture, prison and forced labor conditions, battles and uprisings, and suicide—under Chinese rule since 1950. Now even unborn Tibetans are being exterminated by way of aggressively pursued forced sterilization and forced abortion, including full-term babies murdered at birth.[10]

Yet the holocaust is to this hour held up as the pinnacle of Evil, with endless television specials, books and documentaries. We even have Elie Wiesel, who has just won the Nobel Peace Prize for his work on the holocaust and on world peace. He doesn't mention a thing about the Communist holocausts—only about nuclear disarmament. While horrible beyond description and painful to the present, the Nazi holocaust killed only 3 percent of the number killed by World Communism.

Where are the television shows on World Communism? Who will speak out against this terror? It is easy to decry Hitler. He is dead, he is no threat. The Soviets are alive and marching in every corner of the globe and no voice speaks out against them, save the few. Only when Evil is denounced as Evil will it come to an end. Failure to denounce Evil is indifference in its most pernicious form.

In Definition 2b of *indifferent,* Webster states that indifference finds **"nothing that calls for sanction or condemnation in either observance or neglect":** the state of indifference finds **"no importance or value one way or the other."**

Is there nothing in the Soviet regime that calls for sanction or condemnation?

What about South Africa, whose crackdown on dissent has resulted in worldwide sanctions and condemnation, even though the crackdown is as a result of a ruthless, "necklacing," Soviet-backed Communist insurgency? South Africa was an ally of ours. They have many strategic minerals which are vital to us in our war against the Communists. Yet we sanction them and we continue to trade and give money to the Soviets.

What is going on?

Did you know that the "evil" South Africans feed and give medical care to sixty-three thousand black Mozambican refugees who have fled their black-ruled Communist "paradise"? Why does Mozambique, a Soviet client, have to put land mines on its borders to keep its population from escaping to "tyranny" in South Africa?

But how many people in America even know where Mozambique is? When my sister told her USC roommate she was writing a letter to the editor about Mozambique, her roommate said, "Who is she?"

Our failure to address international injustice across the board is national indifference on a grand scale—*by the only nation that has the power to do something about it.*

Definition 3: "marked by no special liking for or dislike of something; marked by a lack of interest in or concern about something: apathetic."

A poll recently taken by *Newsweek* magazine revealed that when asked to rate one's feelings toward a particular country on a scale of one to ten, Americans rated the Soviet Union a two. This would seem to signify that our nation dislikes the Soviets. However, they are unwilling to back up their inherent dislike for the Soviets with any action. What most Americans want is peace, disarmament, and a nuclear freeze.

Americans are so afraid of war—that war might break their little bubble—that their fear neutralizes their sense of loyalty and duty. But war is far less dangerous than totalitarianism. All the wars in this century have taken perhaps 60 million people, whereas the Communists have killed 190 million people. Which would you rather have: war or totalitarianism? At least with war you have a fighting chance to survive as a free people!

It is clear that most Americans do not like the Soviets but from their actions it would appear that they do not dislike them either. This is indifference—"marked by no special liking for or dislike of something." America continues to supply the Soviets with grain, credit, and technology. This is nothing new. We have built the Soviet Union since its prerevolutionary days and continue to do so. And we have built ourselves a formidable enemy.

World Communism is not the crime of the century: the crime of the century is the apathy of the Americans! We are the ones who could have prevented and can still prevent World Communist genocide perpetrated by an evil ideology and an evil system which fulfills Jesus' prophecy for our time: "The brother shall betray the brother to death, and the father the son; and children shall rise up against their parents, and shall cause them to be put to death."[Mark 13:12]

I will read again from Solzhenitsyn, *The Voice of Freedom:*

> We are slaves there from birth. We are born slaves. I'm not young anymore, and I myself was born a slave; this is even more true for those who are younger. We are slaves, but we are striving for freedom. You, however, were born free. If so, then why do you help our slave owners?
>
> In my last address I only requested one thing and I make the same request now: when they bury us in the ground alive— . . . as you know, this is a very unpleasant sensation: your mouth gets filled with earth while you're still alive—please do not send them shovels. Please do not send them the most modern earth-moving equipment.
>
> By a peculiar coincidence the very day when I was giving my address in Washington, Mikhail Suslov was talking with your senators in the Kremlin. And he said, "In fact, the significance of our trade is more political than economic. We can get along without your trade."
>
> That's a lie. The whole existence of our slave owners from beginning to end relies on Western economic assistance. As I said the last time, beginning with the first spare parts used to reconstruct our factories in the 1920s, from the construction in Magnitostroy, Dneprostroy, the automobile and tractor factories built during the first five-year plans, on into the postwar years and to this day, what they need from you is economically absolutely indispensable—not politically, but economically indispensable—to the Soviet system.

The Soviet economy has an extremely low level of efficiency. What is done here by a few people, by a few machines, in our country takes tremendous crowds of workers and enormous masses of materials. Therefore the Soviet economy cannot deal with every problem at once: war, space (which is part of the war effort), heavy industry, light industry, and at the same time the necessity to feed and clothe its own population.

The forces of the entire Soviet economy are concentrated on war, where you won't be helping them. But everything which is lacking, everything which is needed to fill the gaps, everything which is necessary to feed the people, or for other types of industry, they get from you. So indirectly you are helping them to rearm. You're helping the Soviet police state.

To get an idea how clumsy the Soviet economy is, I'll give you the following example: What kind of country is it, what kind of great power, which has tremendous military potential, which conquers outer space, but has nothing to sell? All heavy equipment, all complex and delicate technology, is purchased abroad. Then it must be an agricultural country? Not at all; it also has to buy grain.

What then can we sell? What kind of economy is it? Can we sell anything which has been created by socialism? No! Only that which God put in the Russian ground at the very beginning, that's what we squander and that's what we sell. What we got from God in the first place. And when all this will come to an end, there won't be anything left to sell.

The president of the AFL-CIO, George Meany, has quite rightly said that it is not loans which the United States gives to the Soviet Union, it is economic assistance. It's foreign aid It's given at a level of interest that is lower than what American workers can get for their home mortgages. That is direct aid.

But this is not all. I said in my last address and would like to repeat it again, that we have to look at every event from the other point of view—from the point of view of the Soviet Union. Our country is taking your assistance, but in the schools they're teaching and in the newspapers they are writing and in lectures they are saying, "Look at the Western world, it's beginning to rot. Look at the economy of the Western world, it's coming to an end. The great predictions of Marx, Engels and Lenin are coming true. Capitalism is breathing its last. It's already dead. And our socialist economy is flourishing. It has demonstrated once and for all the triumph of Communism."

I think, gentlemen, and I particularly address those of you who have a socialist outlook, that we should at last permit this socialist economy to prove its superiority. Let's allow it to show that it is advanced, that it is omnipotent, that it has defeated you, that it has overtaken you. Let us not interfere with it. Let us stop selling to it and giving it loans. If it's all that powerful, then let it stand on its own. . . for ten or fifteen years. Then we will see what it looks like.

I can tell you what it will look like. I am being quite serious now. When the Soviet economy will no longer be able to deal with everything, it will have to reduce its military preparations. It will have to abandon the useless space effort and it will have to feed and clothe its own people. And the system will be forced to relax.[11]

Americans do not care that they are picking up the tab on the world's largest concentration camp! They lack interest in this issue. They're simply indifferent. It just doesn't seem to matter to them that their money and technology are going to support slavery. No politician has ever put this on his agenda in a serious way. When the citizenry is impassive their leaders reflect it, which is to say we have no leaders.

With our voter turnout for the last congressional election as low as 37 percent of those eligible, our apathy is complete. This 37 percent represents about 17 percent of the overall population. Our future is being decided by 17 percent of the population! What's more, there is a 20-percent illiteracy rate among adult Americans and an even higher level of low literacy—such as being able to read road signs but not text.

How many of our voters are educated on the issues? If they get their information exclusively from television, not many. We can assume that maybe one in ten takes the time to independently research each issue on the ballot. The rest base their vote on the information they receive from the media. It is certain that they will not hear much about the evils of World Communism from their television sets and more than likely that they will hear a lot about peace and disarmament.

Thirty-seven percent voter turnout, educated or not, means that the majority of the public is not interested in the destiny of our nation. This is **Definition 3b—"marked by a lack of interest in or concern about something."**

Apathy is a reaction to a reality that is too terrible to accept, particularly when individuals feel powerless to act against that reality. This has come out in a variety of ways. People who fear nuclear war will live "for the moment" because they feel they might not be alive tomorrow. If they are not going to be alive tomorrow, why should they vote or care about the issues? This is a step toward spiritual suicide.

Americans also have a fear of the Soviet war mentality on a subconscious level which begets a fear that they might anger the Russians and bring on their wrath if they do not learn to live with them. Apathy and pacifism then become acts of desperation on the part of an anxious people—which the German *angst* best conveys. This state of mind is only one step removed from actual physical suicide.

We come to **Definition 4—"being neither excessive nor defective."** America has been subject to many changes in national outlook. One of the most profound was that which took place with the coming of age of the early baby-boom generation in the 1960s. Born into an era of prosperity, many lacked direction and purpose and turned their youthful energies toward protest. Patriotism went out of style and was replaced by internationalism and the lack of support for things American, including the Vietnam War.

This movement was led by the poets and minstrels of the era—the rock stars. John Lennon and his contemporaries provided the "leadership" and "ideals" that somehow our government was no longer capable of providing. Unfortunately, the rock stars led the nation down a primrose path. Peace and love are great but they mean nothing to the Communists except to prove to them that the West is growing weak and spineless.

What manifested in the protests and flag-burning was not apathy. It was activism at its worst. But this activism served to redirect and break down our national will and in fact increased the mounting wave of national apathy that was a major factor in our loss in Vietnam and the subsequent Cambodian genocide. Following the American pullout from Vietnam, seventy-five thousand Vietnamese were executed for political reasons by the Communist government between 1975 and 1983. And worse, four million innocent Cambodians were killed from 1975 to 1979 by their Communist countrymen, the Khmer Rouge. And their blood is on the hands of the American people!

As we entered the 1980s and the Reagan era, flag-waving was back. This time it was superficial, though, and served only to convince ourselves that we were in such great shape that we need do nothing further. Thus, Americans will not be excessive in defense of freedom; but neither do they feel they are defective. And most Americans are smug about it.

We come to **Definition 5: "being neither good nor bad,"** or **"mediocre; being neither right nor wrong."** This is a very curious state of affairs—how someone can think that they can be in the middle, "neither good nor bad."

Many of you may have heard of Ian Anderson, the lead singer of the group Jethro Tull. He is known to be extremely cynical. This is a sample of his lyrics: "Here's the everlasting rub— / Neither am I good nor bad. / I'd give up my halo for a horn / And the horn for a hat I once had." This is the ultimate rebellion. He's placing himself above God and the Devil and answering to no one. That is what the American people are doing. They want to answer to no one—"neither good nor bad."

The Bible is very clear on this issue, saying in Revelation 3:15, 16: "I know thy works, thou art neither cold nor hot: I would thou wert cold or hot. So then because thou art lukewarm, and neither cold nor hot, I will spue thee out of my mouth."

We must take a unified national stand in order to survive. If we refuse to think in terms of Absolute Good and Absolute Evil, we will be swallowed up by the Evil. God cannot and will not (according to his own Law) protect us if we will not see Evil. We will be as the lukewarm ones whom he spews out of his mouth. God will allow the Soviet Union to destroy our nation as our judgment, much as he allowed the Assyrians to dominate and destroy the Israelites. History is repeating itself. And "those who cannot remember the past are condemned to repeat it,"[12] to quote Santayana one more time.

You cannot be "neither good nor bad." You cannot be "neither right nor wrong." If you choose not to decide, you still have made a choice. If you do not stand for Absolute Good, you have already chosen Absolute Evil. The conclusion of C. S. Lewis in his *Screwtape Letters* is: once a soul has chosen mediocrity, the Devil has already won.

This brings us to **Definition 6** of *indifferent*—**"characterized by lack of active quality: neutral."**

Neutralism and pacifism are diabolical and seductive concepts. I have developed these concepts further in "The Psychology of Pacifism and the Strategy of Nuclear War," published in *Heart* magazine, Winter 1985. You may want to reread that. I recently reread that article and there were things in it that I had forgotten, even though I wrote them.

Suffice it to say that Americans and the rest of the population of the NATO alliance flirt dangerously with these concepts.

Solzhenitsyn has spoken out on neutralism:

> This is very dangerous for one's view of the world when this feeling comes on: "Go ahead, give it up." We already hear voices in your country and in the West—"Give up Korea and we will live quietly. Give up Portugal, of course; give up Japan, give up Israel, give up Taiwan, the Philippines, Malaysia, Thailand, give up ten more African countries. Just let us live in peace and quiet. Just let us drive our big cars on our splendid highways; just let us play tennis and golf, in peace and quiet; just let us mix our cocktails in peace and quiet as we are accustomed to doing; just let us see the beautiful toothy smile with a glass in hand on every advertisement page of our magazines."[13]

It's a sad state of affairs. Just before I left my last job in the television industry to return to my studies at Northwestern, I had a friend who I'd been talking politics with say to me, "Well, Sean, what's your prophecy? What do you say is going to happen in the next five or ten years?"

"Well," I said, "if things go as they are, we're going to have the Soviets here in our government or we will have already been the victim of a first strike."

He looked at me for a while, looked away and then said, "Boy!... Well, ten years is a long time."

Nuclear war is unique. When the Allies were attacked in the first half of the twentieth century, it was our ability to crank up weapons production quickly and outproduce the enemy that was crucial to our victory in the two world wars—along with the sacrifice of those who gave their lives for their country.

In a nuclear war, what you have is what you use to fight the war—period. There is no time for production. Hence, you must always act as if you are at war. The British ought to know this. Prior to World War II, when they were faced with the choice of building either an offensive bomber force or a strategic defense, they opted for strategic defense. As a result, they won the Battle of Britain and saved their nation from a Nazi invasion. Yet one of the liberal opposition parties in England today—the Labor Party—has already pledged, if elected, to remove all nuclear weapons from their territory.

There is a similar situation in Canada. The extremely liberal New Democratic Party (NDP) has pledged it will withdraw Canada from NATO if it comes to power. Due to parliamentary politics, the NDP might conceivably force a Liberal Party government to do the same—and the Liberals are currently in first place in the polls. The consequences of a Canadian withdrawal from NATO could potentially be catastrophic if they forced the United States to remove its radars and optical tracking systems that are part of our warning system against ballistic missiles, cruise missiles and aircraft.

Lately, when taking their positions on defense, the American people have counted on the balance of nuclear forces, which they have been told exists between the superpowers, to prevent war. They think that we don't need any more weapons because we already have enough to kill each other ten times over.

This is a fallacy. There is no overkill. Overkill is a simplistic argument which adds up the number of megatons on both sides, figures out how many Hiroshima-sized bombs that makes, multiplies that by the number of people killed at Hiroshima, and claims we don't need any more weapons.

Mount St. Helens released about five hundred times the force of the bomb dropped on Hiroshima, yet it killed only seventy-two people. Bombs only kill people if there are people under them to be killed. And we know from Soviet military doctrine that they do not target people. They would just as soon disarm us and take our country whole.

The Soviets target military installations, such as missile silos. And you need two or three weapons for each missile silo to be sure you have destroyed it. They can destroy our land-based missiles in a first strike because our missiles are not mobile and they know exactly where they are. Thus, we *do* need more missiles. *We need mobile, land-based missiles. And we need them now!*

The American people are unsophisticated in their belief of overkill. It is a gross oversimplification. They do not understand the issues which face them. And they must understand those issues soon or we will face the ultimate destruction.

We must always act as if we are at war. The war is going on in many other countries in the world. Just because it's not here, just because it doesn't touch us, just because, as Solzhenitsyn said, we can drive our cars and—probably not many people here play golf, but you get the picture—doesn't mean we're not a part of it and it's not a part of us.

There is no balance between the superpowers. The Soviets have, and have had since the mid-seventies, military superiority. Our nation cannot act neutral and survive. The will of the people must back a consensus for action—now. Nuclear deterrence is not defense. Defense takes the will of the people—to sustain and back their armed forces to protect their interests. Will is the most important aspect of defense.

We have the second most powerful military in the world. And yet we will not even come to the necessary and sufficient defense of the freedom fighters in Afghanistan or Nicaragua. This is a lack of will. We could invade Nicaragua and Cuba and drive those Communists out in probably two months, if we so chose. And we should! [17-sec. applause]

We Americans are soft. No American alive today has ever seen war on our soil. Every American alive today will see war on our soil if we do not stand strong during this time of relative peace.

In the Soviet Union those who love freedom understand that a price must be paid. They are willing to be locked up and tortured for what they believe in, for they have nothing else. They have very few consumer goods in the Soviet Union—nothing to distract them from the cause of freedom.

Irina Ratushinskaya is a Russian who loves freedom. I will read you her story now. This is from the *Chicago Tribune*. The headline is "Soviets Let Dissident Poet, Who Wrote in Soap, Leave."

> KIEV, U.S.S.R.—Dissident poet Irina Ratushinskaya, considered by many Western critics and Soviet emigre writers to be among the most talented Soviet literary figures, received permission Saturday to leave the country.
>
> During an interview in her Kiev apartment, Ratushinskaya said she would depart the Soviet Union with more than 250 new poems secretly composed on a bar of soap during her 3½ years in a labor camp.
>
> The poems were committed to memory and the soap scrubbed to obliterate any evidence of the underground verses that could result in additional months tacked to her 12-year sentence for "anti-Soviet agitation and propaganda."

This is how they treat their writers.

> Ratushinskaya, 32, was unexpectedly released from prison Oct. 9 in what was deemed a goodwill gesture prior to the Reykjavik summit. She and her husband, Igor Gerashchenko, 33, hope to leave for London next week on a medical visa granted Saturday.
>
> The poet said she also is planning to visit the Chicago area, where she has been invited to read her poems at Northwestern University and the University of Illinois at Chicago.
>
> Soviet authorities had blocked numerous official invitations mailed from the West in the two months since she was freed.
>
> But Ratushinskaya received a number of invitations through protected diplomatic channels from Great Britain and the United States, among them a letter from Northwestern University Medical Center promising treatment for the respiratory ailments, heart problems and kidney disorders she contracted in prison.
>
> Ratushinskaya and her husband said they do not plan to renounce their Soviet citizenship, and both pledged to return in order to work for democratic reforms.
>
> But as Ratushinskaya's conversation was interrupted numerous times by painful spasms of a raw, hacking cough, it became clear that medical treatment is, for now, the first priority.
>
> "I went into prison a healthy woman. They took care of that right away," she said of the strict labor camp in central Russia.
>
> After her conviction in April, 1983, for circulating her unofficial verses, Ratushinskaya lost 44 pounds on a prison diet of bread and water one day, soup the next.

April 1983. Tell this to anyone who doesn't think this is going on now. I am sure everyone in this room can remember where they were in April of '83. And I am equally sure that this torture is going on today.

> Because of her frequent protests over prison conditions, she spent a total of 120 days in a solitary confinement cell kept at a temperature just above freezing.
>
> In 1985, prison authorities told her she would be held for life, and she said she staged a hunger strike for better treatment that "brought me near death." She was refused any medical attention.
>
> Writing poetry was banned in the camp and could result in an extended sentence. Paper and pen were given to inmates only for writing two letters a month, which had to pass through censors.

But Ratushinskaya said she unfettered her creative muse by composing verses on a bar of soap, using a burnt and sharpened match-head as a quill to scratch in the letters and words.

"When I finished a poem, I would wash my hands and it would be gone," she said in her first personal interview with a Western reporter since returning from the labor camp.

Ratushinskaya composed 250 poems during her captivity, and had to memorize each one to avoid detection. As a ritual to help maintain her sanity, she would spend an hour every day cataloguing the verses in her head.

A correspondent, testing her ability to know a huge volume of poetry by heart, selected titles at random from her portfolio and asked her to repeat them in full.

In a husky voice free from the falsetto that is a cultural affectation of so many Russian-speaking women, Ratushinskaya began reciting verses shaped by Christian imagery, regional nationalism and stark memories of dark prison nights.

She also managed to smuggle many poems out of prison, but declined to describe the method because it is still being used as an underground channel of communication by gulag inmates.

This brings up an issue which has come up many times. Every time someone escapes or every time they catch someone smuggling Bibles into the Soviet Union, the Western media publishes the method! This is wrong. Here we have these freedom fighters and they grant interviews and they tell how they escaped and the Western media publishes it! And the Soviet Union, in turn, seals that method of escape.

We visited a museum at the Berlin wall which shows all the ways by which people have escaped. I am sure it is frequented by all the Soviet authorities. This is an important issue. We should protect the possibilities for freedom at every hand. Our loyalties as world citizens ought to be to the freeing of every body and soul from the bondage of totalitarian systems.

Since her release, Ratushinskaya has written nine new poems, but has not begun a major planned work of prose for fear it would be confiscated when she leaves the country. *She also has not been allowed to own a typewriter.*

Tell this to the professors in the political-science departments of the universities of America—who sit at their word processors in their air-conditioned offices pontificating on the need for 'peace' while Russian literary genius languishes for want of paper or typewriter!

Her most recent poem, completed Oct. 24, is written to a "country of thoughtful train stations and eternally poor women," and says in part:

With doubt, you have punished all your children
Be they strong or weak.
Your questions, until dawn.
Your reprimands, until gray hair.
And how shall we live, you and me?
You are looking, but covering your eyes with your hands.
To forget? To curse? To make the sign of the cross?

> Sitting in her apartment in Kiev's academic neighborhood, Ratushinskaya looked the part of a Beat Generation poet with her raven-black hair cut to pageboy length and dark turtleneck. Her bookshelves included Russian translations of Twain and Cervantes.
>
> She speculated little on the cause of her early release from prison and the other events of the last months, except to say that they may reflect discussions in the Kremlin over reforms in the Soviet system and a strategy to improve its image abroad.
>
> "I believe there are talks at high levels about democratization, and that has brought about the release of some political prisoners," she said.[14]

Now, the only reason there would be any talks about democratization would be as an image tool for the Western media and to keep the American people asleep. Those at the top of the Soviet system will never democratize because if they did it would mean that they would have to loosen the reins of power and in so doing their leadership would be overtaken. They will never do this. Entertain no illusions.

This article was from the point of view of her being inside the Soviet Union. A later article which shows a picture of her in London speaking with Prime Minister Margaret Thatcher following her exit from the Soviet Union expresses her freedom of conscience voiced as free speech to a free press:

> Meanwhile, dissident Soviet poet Irina Ratushinskaya, allowed to leave the Soviet Union last week, met with British Prime Minister Margaret Thatcher in London Monday. . . . Her husband said *she intended to remain in the West.*[15]

In her previous article she said that she was going to stay in the Soviet Union. This is because she was afraid to speak her mind for fear that she would not be allowed to leave. So now she's here, now she can speak her mind.

We need to be willing to pay the price, as Americans have always paid the price, spiritually, economically and militarily to keep the West free—that the flame of hope be not extinguished in the hearts of the oppressed.

But the American people do not realize that this is their calling. For them not to face up to the reality that the Russian people are kept in constant psychic domination and fear is very, very naive. We look at their society as a mirror image of our own, thinking that every institution in our society has an equivalent in Soviet society, including courts. And it is not the case. You'd be surprised at what people I've talked to mistakenly think about the Soviet Union.

It is clear, then, that our media could save thousands if not millions of lives by keeping the pressure on the Soviets. You can look at those evening news anchormen. The blood is on their hands and on the hands of the forces of control at CBS, NBC and ABC. They have the power to mold and marshal public opinion, hence the absolute power to save these lives.

And since they're not doing it, we must!

There was another story that I recently read of an inmate who died because the Western press ignored him. This is taken up by Jeane Kirkpatrick in a Christmas editorial published by the *Chicago Tribune.* But first let's hear again from *The Voice of Freedom:*

> We, we the dissidents of the U.S.S.R., don't have any tanks, we don't have any weapons, we have no organization. We don't have anything. Our hands are empty. We have only a heart and what we have lived through in the half century of this system. And when we have found the firmness within ourselves to stand up for our rights, we have done so. It's only by firmness of spirit that we have withstood.
>
> And if I am standing here before you, it's not because of the kindness or the good will of Communism, not thanks to detente, but thanks to my own firmness and your firm support. They knew that I would not yield one inch, not one hair. And when they couldn't do more they themselves fell back.
>
> This is not easy. In our conditions this was taught to me by the difficulties of my own life. And if you yourselves—any one of you—were in the same difficult situation, you would have learned the same thing. Take Vladimir Bukovsky, whose name is now almost forgotten.
>
> Now, I don't want to mention a lot of names because however many I might mention there are more still. And when we resolve the question with two or three names it is as if we forget and betray the others. We should rather remember figures. There are tens of thousands of political prisoners in our country and—by the calculation of English specialists—seven thousand persons are now under compulsory psychiatric treatment.
>
> Let's take Vladimir Bukovsky as an example. It was proposed to him, "All right, we'll free you. Go to the West and shut up." And this young man, a youth today on the verge of death said: "No, I won't go this way. I have written about the persons whom you have put in insane asylums. You release them and then I'll go West." This is what I mean by that firmness of spirit to stand up against granite and tanks.[16]

Former United States ambassador to the United Nations, Jeane Kirkpatrick, gives us, then, some thoughts on this same issue. This is entitled, "Keeping a Spotlight on the Oppressed":

> It has become traditional for major newspapers in many American cities to focus in the weeks before Christmas on the most needy people in their area in hopes that the glow of the season will stimulate special sympathy and generosity for those oppressed by poverty, old age, ill health, bad luck and bad management of their own lives.
>
> It is a good tradition that illuminates the social problems of great cities by showing how they affect the lives of concrete persons. Similarly, great political abstractions like freedom, repression and pluralism also are most easily grasped when their impact is seen through the experiences of particular people. Human rights activist and former gulag inmate Anatoly Shcharansky told American audiences last week that focusing public attention on

> particular prisoners can make a life-and-death difference.
>
> The recent death in a Soviet prison of Anatoly Marchenko was caused not just by Soviet abuse, Shcharansky said, but by Western indifference. Recalling his own long imprisonment, Shcharansky told a New York audience: "In my case there were strong campaigns all over the world; protests from the top levels and grassroot levels. In this [Marchenko] case, the public opinion of the West reacted quite differently. The results you see yourself."
>
> Shcharansky's view is shared by other former political prisoners—Huber Matos, Armando Valladores, Jacobo Timerman, among many others—who have credited their release and survival to international public attention. Spokesmen for Iran's Baha'i community credit public attention with the dramatic decline in government executions of Baha'i members [from 100 in 1983 to three in 1986].
>
> In this Christmas season, we should focus on just a few of the world's neediest political prisoners who are being denied their most basic human rights.
>
> Dr. Josef Begun, a 55-year-old Soviet citizen of Jewish descent, has been convicted three times for the crimes of teaching Hebrew, cultivating the study of Jewish culture and history and seeking permission to emigrate to Israel. Dr. Begun, a mathematics graduate of Moscow University, first applied for an exit visa in April, 1971.
>
> During his current imprisonment,* Begun has been subjected to especially harsh treatment. He has spent several periods in a special punishment cell [for giving a lecture on the Holocaust and wearing a yarmulke]. His health has deteriorated seriously, his coronary heart disease exacerbated by the harsh conditions under which he must live.
>
> Begun, recently hospitalized again, was never active in politics. His crimes consisted of giving Hebrew lessons when he was denied all other employment. . . .

This is what the Soviets do to individuals who speak out for political or religious freedom. They deny them employment. And since the government is the only employer, they have nothing. They have nowhere to go, no place to turn to. So they must seek, then, to gain employment from the underground.

> Begun is not alone in paying a heavy price for his religious interests. Richard Schifter, assistant secretary of state for human rights, pointed out recently that during the last 12 months at least 90 other Soviet citizens have been sentenced to long prison terms for religious practices.
>
> Dr. Anatoly Koryagin, 47, is the Ukrainian psychiatrist who in the late 1970s exposed the Soviet practice of confining political dissidents and religious observers to psychiatric hospitals, where they are given pain-inducing, mind-destroying drugs. Now, however, it is Dr. Koryagin who needs help.
>
> For blowing the whistle on these practices, now well documented, Dr. Koryagin was sentenced to seven years in prison and sent to the dreaded Chistopol prison, where he has suffered

*Begun was released from prison February 20, 1987.

repeated beatings, a grossly inadequate diet and seriously deteriorating health. Now that his sentence has been extended,* his wife—who has not been allowed to visit him for more than two years—and his friends are gravely concerned for his life.

But Soviet citizens are not the only ones who risk harsh punishment for exercising human rights. There are other prisoners in other lands.

What can we do for these and thousands of others who have been brutally denied their legal and human rights in Eastern Europe, Africa, Asia, Iran and elsewhere? Anatoly Shcharansky tells us these countries want access to Western technology and credits. Therefore, he says, "linkage can help open the gates."

So can our continuing attention.[17]

Another friend of mine whom I have spoken with at length about politics said to me when Shcharansky was released and spoke in New York, "Sean, what do you think of this Shcharansky character?" I said, "Well, I think he's a great freedom fighter and I am glad that he was released." And he said, "They ought to hang the so-and-so. He'll probably make millions on his book."

Can you believe this callous indifference? These attitudes are fairly widespread, too. People cynically feel that Soviet dissidents have betrayed their country and that all they want to do when they get to the West is exploit their fame and take advantage of capitalism. That's what people believe.

Our attention on these dissidents is activism—the opposite of apathy. And that is what is needed.

Indifferent—**Definition 7: "capable of development in more than one direction; especially: not yet embryologically determined."** This last definition is the key to America's future—**"not yet embryologically determined."**

America is in its infancy and has yet a grand destiny to capture and fulfill. Even the quality of indifference implies the capability for development in new directions.

The Soviet Union fears this development. They fear a united West because they know they could not triumph against it. That is why Western public opinion is so important to them. That is why they devote so much of their time and energy to appeasing the public, such as by releasing dissidents who become favorites of the American media.

They will even put themselves at a disadvantage to score points with the American electorate. For example, they initiated a unilateral nuclear test ban in 1985, calling on America to follow suit. Each time we tested a weapon, they said to the world, "Look, America is the aggressor. They are testing and we are not. Furthermore, we'll extend our test ban to show good faith in hopes of creating world peace and an end to the arms race."

You know, of course, that some of the most important nuclear tests in recent years have been on the Star Wars program. We've been testing the X-ray laser and other nuclear-driven devices. These are vital to our future and it would serve the Soviet cause well if we stopped testing. To do so would not be serving the cause of world peace, however.

*Koryagin was released from prison February 18, 1987.

This is nothing but unabashed rhetoric of the worst kind. Sure, they may not have set off any nuclear bombs in the last year and a half, but what about toy bombs, blowing off children's hands? What about bayoneting pregnant women in Afghanistan? What about 1–2 million Afghans martyred in the most heinous act of genocide since the Ukrainian famine? This really shows the Soviet spirit of peace!

Oddly, many of these brutalities went unreported in the American media. A study commissioned by Sen. Gordon Humphrey reported that in 1985 the three major networks devoted less than one hour total to coverage of Afghanistan.[18] But night after night we hear of South Africa, U.S. "aggression" in Nicaragua, and the Iran/contra affair.

I do not believe that Americans are so apathetic that they would let these things go by if they knew. If the people knew of the 1–2 million Afghan deaths and countless maimings, as well as of the 5 million refugees who have fled, they would demand an end to it.

Thus, the solution lies in the reeducation of the people. Solzhenitsyn should be quoted in every elementary and secondary school, college campus and institution of learning. Every American has the right to know the truth about World Communism *and* its capitalist collaborators. And we should start them young instead of allowing our children to be indoctrinated with socialist philosophies and mentalities.

Our message as presented at the Teaching Centers and Study Groups of Church Universal and Triumphant must go beyond the spiritual message. Saint Germain has spelled it out and he is talking to the American people. We must be his mouthpiece. We must watch the news, even if it is depressing. We have the obligation not only to be up-to-date on the facts but also to decree on them nightly. We must anticipate every move of the Soviets and do all in our power to prevent a Soviet first strike and a complete Communist takeover in Central America as prophesied.

It is our duty as soldiers in Armageddon to be informed. We must interpret world events in light of prophecy and present our findings with the documented research to back them up. The time for preaching a spiritual teaching devoid of politics is over. The Spirit of prophecy abroad in the land bears relevance to every area of our lives, but nowhere more vitally than in the political arena. Politics involves the use and abuse of the power of the people. Therefore, our survival depends on the acceptance by the American people of Saint Germain's message as a political message. That is exactly where the ancient prophets of Israel and Judah stood and that is where my father and mother stand today.

Saint Germain has not minced words about dealing with the Soviets. He has made two statements which Americans should be concerned about: One is that we have every reason to believe, to be concerned, and to be prepared for a Soviet first strike upon these United States;[19] and the other is that if the Nicaraguan contras are not aided and supported, totalitarian encroachment in this hemisphere will not be stopped without bloodshed in these United States.[20]

This should end debate on both issues.

As we know from history, however, Saint Germain has been ignored by people at their peril. Europe has been subject to war on its soil for nearly two centuries because Saint Germain has been ignored. Let us pray and act in time that it does not happen here.

Now, Mother has been working this fall on an extremely important book which she announced at Thanksgiving—that is *Saint Germain On Prophecy.* I've read the advance text of this book and I assure you that it is the most important book that Mother has ever written. It will change the world—if people are ready for change.

It will not only be sold through our national bookstore accounts but it will be sold in grocery stores and drug stores, where the common people can have access to the teachings. [21-sec. applause]

I am sure all of you are familiar with Saint Germain's messages of the past year. These messages are included in this book, *Saint Germain On Prophecy,* along with a special section on Saint Germain's embodiments and his work as the Wonderman of Europe and the sponsor of America. There is also a section of dictations by the beings of the elements talking about coming earth changes, and the most exciting section of all—Saint Germain's interpretation of the prophecies of Nostradamus. [13-sec. applause]

Nostradamus, who gained a reputation as a learned physician and healer, as well as a prophet in his own country and time, is highly thought of today even beyond the new-age movement. A number of people have written books about Nostradamus and they have interpreted him in a number of ways. But according to Saint Germain, their approach has not always been correct. Saint Germain has given Mother new interpretations whereby we see that certain coming events spoken of in dictations of the Ascended Masters were actually predicted by Nostradamus four centuries ago. These interpretations by the one who originally dictated the quatrains in the "upper room" at Salon have never before been released.

Now for those who need more evidence than the current prophecies of Saint Germain through the Messenger, Nostradamus is very clear. Without going into a lengthy discourse on *Nostradamus* as I am sure all of you will want to read it for yourselves, I can tell you that Nostradamus predicted much of what is coming to pass before our very eyes, and the Master's message for today is contained in part in the prophet's copious works.

Now, I should explain for those who are not familiar with his writings that Nostradamus wrote in a cryptic style due to the religious persecution that was taking place in his time. Not only did he write in code, he sealed his prophecies in four-line verses called quatrains in sets of one hundred called centuries. Originally, the sixteenth-century seer wrote the quatrains in chronological order, but he had to mix them up so that there would not be any clear message for which he could be punished by the ruling authorities.

The prophecies are so obscure that it is difficult to tell when they will come true. Sometimes dates can be fixed through astrological clues or a technology described. Nostradamus' meaning is often unclear until the events he predicts come to pass or are about to come to pass. He was very precise and said that he meant his verses to have only one meaning and application.

The interpretation of Nostradamus is equally important as the interpretation of the Bible—because he spoke of events that may come to pass in our lifetime. A good number of his quatrains bring out the ride of the Four Horsemen. Thus, if he is misinterpreted, we will suffer for want of knowledge in discerning the signs of the times.

Nostradamus even foretold the current Iran/contra crisis in Washington. He said that there would be such sedition through spies and traitors that the "profligate ones," i.e., the U.S. Congress and the American people, would be in despair:

> The device of flying fire
> Will come to trouble the great besieged chief:
> Within there will be such sedition
> That the profligate ones will be in despair.[21]
>
> VI.34

Indeed, there is such sedition in America and by Americans today—through technology transfers to the Soviet Union and traitors like the Walker spy ring (whose espionage has enabled the Soviets to track our submarines)—that both Congress and the people are in despair as to how to counter the Soviet threat which is, in fact, supported by our own technology.

The question is: How far must our nation be torn down, by both the profligate and the seditious ones? How many must lose their lives and how many years must our civilization be set back in the process?

If the Soviet Union were to conduct a first strike against our military targets, we would be virtually helpless to retaliate. They could invade and conquer us. An all-out nuclear war in which they attacked our cities would put us back to an agricultural society or worse and kill four-fifths of all Americans.

If America is physically destroyed or conquered, the blame lies with us. The fallen ones are on their way to being judged. We are the Lightbearers and we are responsible for the future of our nation. "For evil to triumph, all that is required is that good men do nothing"—a very famous quote from Edmund Burke.

World Communism needs the cooperation of the West. Without it, it would itself be destroyed in a very short time. Look at the devil Peshu Alga, who recently went to his final judgment.[22] He needed his consort as the negative polarity to ground his "deified evil." Without that electrode of the feminine (or negative) polarity, Peshu Alga could never have committed the crimes against God that he did. The Soviets are like Peshu Alga and America, the consort. It is up to us. We have to stop being the negative electrode for an anti-God ideology and an anti-God system! Let's start by stopping technology transfers to the betrayers of humanity.

Americans, if they allow this to go on, are in fact worse than the Russians. The Russian people are powerless to do anything. The American people have "all power given unto them in heaven and earth" to do everything about it. This is the supreme testing we now face as a nation.

If we allow this to happen—if we stand by, do nothing, and allow America to remain without a strategic or civil defense against a Soviet first strike, if we allow freedom to be lost in this hemisphere through our failure to support the freedom fighters in Central and South America, if we allow Congress and the powers that be to betray the contras, then heaven help us! For we will be judged more severely than the Russian people. Russian people are not responsible—it is fallen ones who make up the Soviet leadership who are to blame for the murder and mayhem that follow in the wake of Communist world takeover, nation by nation! But Americans *are.* We Americans are responsible.

There is the matter of the aid to the contras—an issue which has divided the nation. One would think that organized religion would support aid to the freedom fighters who oppose Communism. Communism has been the biggest enemy of religion since 1917 and has slaughtered millions of religious devotees worldwide. Don't you remember what Lenin said? "We must combat religion—this is the ABC of all materialism, and consequently Marxism."[23]

Does it surprise you to hear, then, that the *Chicago Tribune* recently reported that a private network of church groups in the United States had given $42 million in aid—not to the contras, but to the Communist Sandinista government of Nicaragua—in 1985?

They have this philosophy they are preaching now called "matching funds." They tell their congregations that President Reagan is a terrorist and that he is foisting war upon the people of Central America and that their congregations have to donate money to help establish and maintain peace in Central America. And that money is shipped to the Sandinistas as aid.

What can we say about the false pastors of our time, except "Let the LORD's judgment be upon their heads!"

I will read to you now from chapter 16 of *Saint Germain On Prophecy.* This section is entitled "The LORD's Prophecy Concerning the False Prophets of Peace":

> Not only is this denouement of the twentieth century to be reckoned with by a people who have forsaken their God (Europeans, who, though they may deny it, in actuality have been heavily saturated by 'fallout', the dark karma, from Chernobyl), but also must it be dealt with by the profane priests and prophets (European as well as some American Catholic, Protestant and Jewish theologians along with the psychic peaceniks):
>
> > So this is what I AM THAT I AM as the Lord of Hosts [Sanat Kumara] says about the prophets:
> >
> > "Now I will give them wormwood for their food, and poisoned water to drink, since from the prophets of Jerusalem godlessness has spread throughout the land." I AM THAT I AM, Lord of Hosts, says this:
> >
> > "Do not listen to what those prophets say: they are deluding you, they retail visions of their own, and not what comes from the mouth of I AM THAT I AM; to those who reject the word of I AM THAT I AM they say, 'Peace will be yours,' and to those who follow the dictates of a hardened heart, 'No misfortune will touch you.'"
> >
> > (But who has been present at the council of I AM THAT I AM? Who has seen it and heard His Word? Who has paid attention to His Word in order to proclaim it?)

> Now a storm of I AM THAT I AM breaks, a tempest whirls, it bursts over the head of the descendants of the Wicked One; the anger of I AM THAT I AM will not turn aside until He has performed, and has carried out, the decision of His heart. You will understand this clearly in the days to come.
>
> "I have not sent those prophets, yet they are running; I have not spoken to them, yet they are prophesying. Have they been present at my council? If so, let them proclaim my words to my people and turn them from their evil way and from the wickedness of their deeds!
>
> "Am I a God when near—it is I AM THAT I AM who speaks—and not one when far away? Can anyone hide in a dark corner without my seeing him?—it is I AM THAT I AM who speaks. Do I not fill heaven and earth?—it is I AM THAT I AM who speaks.
>
> "I have heard what the prophets say who make their lying prophecies in my name. 'I have had a dream,' they say, 'I have had a dream!'" [Jeremiah 23:15–25, Jerusalem Bible]

And again the prophet Jeremiah converses with I AM THAT I AM who appears to him in the Person of the Lord of Hosts:

> "Ah, Lord I AM THAT I AM," I answered, "here are the prophets telling them, 'You will not see the sword, famine will not touch you; I promise you unbroken peace in this place.'"
>
> Then I AM THAT I AM said to me,
>
> "The prophets are prophesying lies in my name; I have not sent them, I gave them no orders, I never spoke to them. Delusive visions, hollow predictions, daydreams of their own, that is what they prophesy to you.
>
> "Therefore, I AM THAT I AM says this:
>
> "The prophets who prophesy in my name when I have not sent them, and tell you there will be no sword or famine in this land, these same prophets are doomed to perish by sword and famine.
>
> "And as for the people to whom they prophesy, they will be tossed into the streets of Jerusalem, victims of famine and the sword, with not a soul to bury them: neither them nor their wives, nor their sons, nor their daughters. I will pour down on them their own wickedness [karma]." [Jeremiah 14:13–16, Jerusalem Bible]

What follows is "The LORD's Chastisement of the House of Joseph."

But to America, Britannia and the English-speaking peoples—the seed of Joseph, of his sons Ephraim and Manasseh—the LORD has declared through the lovable Amos:

> Seek I AM THAT I AM and you shall live, or else He will rush like fire on the House of Joseph and burn it up, with none at Bethel able to put out the flames.

> It is He who made the Pleiades and Orion, who turns the dusk to dawn and day to darkest night. He summons the waters of the sea and pours them over the land. I AM THAT I AM is his name.
>
> He blazes out ruin on the stronghold and brings destruction to the fortress—trouble for those who turn justice into wormwood, throwing integrity to the ground; who hate the man dispensing justice at the city gate and detest those who speak with honesty.
>
> Well then, since you have trampled on the poor man, extorting levies on his wheat—those houses you have built of dressed stone, you will never live in them; and those precious vineyards you have planted, you will never drink their wine.
>
> For I know that your crimes are many, and your sins enormous: persecutors of the virtuous, blackmailers, turning away the needy at the city gate. No wonder the prudent man keeps silent, the times are so evil.
>
> Seek Good and not Evil so that you may live, and that I AM THAT I AM as the Lord of Hosts may really be with you as you claim He is.
>
> Hate Evil, love Good, maintain justice at the city gate, and it may be that I AM THAT I AM as the Lord of Hosts will take pity on the remnant of Joseph. [Amos 5:6–15, Jerusalem Bible][24]

Both Saint Germain and Nostradamus have predicted the ultimate triumph over Evil and World Communism. It is prophesied. We have to make it happen. Even so, we have to change the prophecy of destruction and death in order to fulfill the prophecy of the triumph of Good.

Now I'm going to read to you the final chapter in Book Two of *Saint Germain On Prophecy*—"Nostradamus' Conclusion of the Matter."

> Nostradamus foresaw the end of Soviet Communism. It is an astonishing prediction of an event anticipated by the martyrs of Soviet Communism who have been massacred by the millions, of whom it is written:
>
>> And when he had opened the fifth seal, I saw under the altar the souls of them that were slain for the word of God, and for the testimony which they held:
>>
>> And they cried with a loud voice, saying, How long, O Lord, holy and true, dost thou not judge and avenge our blood on them that dwell on the earth?
>>
>> And white robes were given unto every one of them; and it was said unto them, that they should rest yet for a little season, until their fellowservants also and their brethren, that should be killed as they were, should be fulfilled. [Revelation 6:9–11]

That's from Revelation 6.

> But Nostradamus' prediction is even more remarkable since it places the point of the unraveling of the Big Lie near Kiev at the Dnieper, about 15 miles from the Chernobyl Nuclear Power Plant:

Here's the quatrain and you'll see that it takes much interpretation:

> The law of More will be seen to decline:
> After another much more seductive:
> Dnieper first will come to give way:
> Through gifts and tongue another more attractive.[25]
> III.95

Of this most transparent prophecy Leoni writes, "For the reader in the second half of the twentieth century, this is one of the most interesting of all the prophecies of Nostradamus—one full of portentous meaning for this era. . . . We now have the generic name 'communism' to apply to the utopian ideologies of which Sir Thomas More's *Utopia* is the common ancestor. Undoubtedly this work, published in Latin when Nostradamus was in the midst of his education, was read by him.

"The prophecy implies a widespread success of this ideology prior to its decline, and mentions that the decline will start where the Dnieper is located. This is the principal river of the Ukraine. In Nostradamus' day it was one of the most backward parts of Europe, part of the Polish-Lithuanian state for three hundred years, and hardly an area Nostradamus would choose for the locale involving any contemporary movement of this nature, such as the Anabaptists.

"Accordingly, it is not unreasonable to speculate on a possible twentieth-century fulfillment of this prophecy, involving the Soviet Ukraine and perhaps its chief city (which is on the Dnieper), Kiev. The nature of the more seductive law and the more attractive tongue are subjects for further speculation."[26]

Utopia is many things to many people. Historians have taken *Utopia* as a blueprint for British imperialism, humanists as a manifesto for total reform of the Christian renaissance, and literary critics as a work of a noncommitted intellectual.

In it More describes an ideal society where all property is held in common and food is distributed at public markets and common dining halls. With its sweeping condemnation of all private property, *Utopia* influenced early Socialist thinkers. Karl Kautsky, the German Socialist theoretician, saw *Utopia* "as a vision of the socialist society of the future"[27] and hailed More as the father of the Bolshevik Revolution.

Yet More's Utopian society and Soviet Communism have striking differences. For instance, in *Utopia,* citizenship was dependent upon the belief in a just God who rewards or punishes in an afterlife.

Professor John Anthony Scott says that More's "views on communism and private property have been explained as an expression of the medieval monastic ideal, in which Christian men and women took vows of poverty and chastity, shared all things in common, and devoted themselves through prayer and good works to the service of the poor and the sick."[28]

Now let us examine Nostradamus' prophecy for the decline of World Communism and the far-reaching consequences of the judgment of Wormwood at Chernobyl.

In previous chapters we've learned that *chernobyl* is Ukrainian for "wormwood," the name of a bitter herb that grows in the place that bears its name. (This information was also published in a 1986 Pearl of Wisdom.[29]) The judgment of a fallen angel named Wormwood is prophesied in Revelation 8. The *New York Times* reported that Russians have been pondering this scripture as prophetic of the nuclear accident at Chernobyl.

Quatrain III.95 describes three kinds of society: The first is an idealistic communism embodied in *Utopia* ("the law of More"). After it declines there appears "another"—the second form of communism—which is "much more seductive," World Communism Soviet-style.

Communism, as we know it, is a seductive metaphysical theory that could not be farther from the basic principles of Thomas More in its atheism, aggression, and unvarnished imperialism. It has been seductive since the first alluring promises of "Peace, Land, and Bread" were made by the Bolsheviks in 1917.

In reality Soviet Communism has from the beginning sown the seeds of its own decline. But the day and date of the initiating of the spiral of its decline is calculated at the triggering of events which give way at the Dnieper—the Chernobyl disaster.

That the Soviet Union is due to self-destruct is evident from its karmic history. The only mitigating factor of the due date has been and continues to be the intercession of Western capitalists and the international bankers, spies, fifth-column sympathizers and agents of the United States government—conscious and unconscious.

The Soviet Union was never a duly elected or popularly supported regime. In effect, Lenin and his confederates waged a premeditated war against those whom they ruled. He realized long before the Bolshevik Revolution that that would be the case and cultivated terror as an instrument of revolution and governance. As early as 1905 he was looking forward to the use of terror such as gripped France in 1793 "to settle accounts with Tsarism" following the revolution.[30]

In 1908, Lenin wrote about "real, nationwide terror, which reinvigorates the country and through which the Great French Revolution achieved glory."[31] On the night of July 16, 1918, the Emperor Nicholas II, his wife, four daughters, and the czarevitch were brutally murdered in the basement of the House of Special Purpose by order of Lenin. Their bodies were burned and thrown into an abandoned mine shaft.

Lenin and his confederates also recognized that since they could never rule popularly they would have to institutionalize terror as a means of control. Thus the Cheka, or secret police, was created to be the direct agent of state power. Some years later Lenin's favorite Bolshevik historian, Pokrovsky, said that the secret police "sprang from the very essence of the proletarian revolution."[32] Between 1918 and 1919, the Cheka executed one thousand people a month without trial.

The Soviet Union is ruled by a dictatorship that installed

itself by force and maintains itself by terror. It is compelled to continually increase its power to stay in power, lest it be overthrown. Indeed, it cultivates violence as a form of vital energy.

This is just the feeding of the fallen ones off the lifeblood of the Lightbearers. They need to have this killing in order to survive.

By the time Lenin was no more in 1924, five hundred thousand people had already died in Soviet prisons or camps.[33]

In 1937–38, during the heyday of Stalin's great terror, forty thousand people were shot each month. While the estimates vary, the Soviets have killed somewhere between 35 and 45 million of their own people since 1917.

Because of its obsessive need for power and control, the Soviet state must of necessity stifle economic production. Prior to the Bolshevik Revolution, Russia was a net exporter of wheat. After the Revolution, the Communist leadership succeeded in institutionalizing agricultural shortages.

Likewise, prior to the Revolution "airplanes and automobiles *of indigenous Russian design* were produced in quantity," says Antony Sutton.[34]

But not so after the Revolution. As we have already seen, the Soviet Union was built by the West, simply because it could not build itself. Soviet Communism cannot produce a viable economy. And because of its political and economic weaknesses, it cannot change. Today it is still essentially the same state created by Lenin and Stalin whose traditions are embodied by paranoid leaders clinging tenaciously to power over their subjects.

The current rulers in Moscow manage a far-flung empire of gulags (prison camps), forcibly "treat" dissidents with painful, personality-destroying drugs in special psychiatric hospitals, and still haul people off to be shot.

The KGB (the latest edition of the secret police [and descendant of the Cheka]) still practices terror against the Soviet population. It is joined in this endeavor by an even more sinister, more secretive organization—the GRU, or Soviet Military Intelligence. Once a GRU agent is recruited, he's an agent for life. Those who try to defect are incinerated in a crematorium. "Few people, inside or outside of Russia, have ever heard of the GRU," says Robert Moss. "Yet its budget for foreign intelligence operations is larger than that of the KGB."

I must tell you there's a book which everyone here should read. It's called *Inside the Aquarium* by Viktor Suvorov. It's about the GRU. The GRU is the most diabolical organization on this planet. In their training they have instituted something which I don't think any society has ever done before—and that is the use of so-called puppets. Now, a puppet is a prisoner—most likely a political prisoner—and specifically a prisoner in good physical shape. They use these people for hand-to-hand combat training and they kill them. So you can bet that every GRU or KGB agent has already killed several people before he ever gets to the West. It's nothing new to *them*. But it should give *us* pause:

If they are conditioned to kill their own people to further the ends of the state and World Communism, who won't they kill!

Puppets are also used to clean up accidents like Chernobyl. Somebody had to tunnel underneath that reactor and dig it out. Who do you think they got to do it? Lightbearers, political prisoners—with virtually no protection.

Continuing on page 196 of *Prophecy:*

> Moss says that the GRU has "been responsible for some of the most stunning coups in the annals of Soviet espionage." Among other things, GRU agents "stole the secret of the atomic bomb for Russia."[35] Today they are in the United States like red ants carrying off technology for the Red Army.
>
> Oppression is present everywhere in the Soviet Union. But it is in keeping with the law of karma that the unraveling of the Soviet Empire should begin near Kiev. For it was at Kiev that Stalin waged war against the peasants, and thus came to pass the *darkest* and most diabolical period in Russian history.
>
> According to historian Robert Conquest, during the early part of this century the Russian intelligentsia saw the peasants as "the People incarnate, the soul of the country, suffering, patient, the hope of the future." But they could also be stubborn and resistant to change. And that bothered the Communists. Lenin complained that the peasant, "far from being an instinctive or traditional collectivist, is in fact fiercely and meanly individualistic." Stalin thought the peasants were scum.[36]
>
> The first stage of Stalin's war was directed against the "kulaks"—supposedly rich, greedy, brutal farmers who, according to Soviet propaganda, exploited the labor of others. In reality, the kulaks were highly productive farmers who might typically own between ten and twenty-five acres of land and as many as three cows. They formed the backbone of Soviet agriculture and the foundation of the Russian food chain. Nevertheless, the Bolsheviks quickly moved against them. "The *kulak* was an ideological enemy," says Antony Sutton, but his ability to produce made him "at least up to 1928–29, indispensable."[37]
>
> Starting in the winter of 1929, Stalin had them "dekulakized," i.e., deported to work camps in the Arctic in the dead of winter. Conquest, who chronicled this tragic chapter of history in his recently published *The Harvest of Sorrow,* writes that upon arrival the peasants had to build their own shelter. Three million died in the early stages of this "resettlement" process, mostly children.
>
> Stalin then pressed ahead with the collectivization of agriculture. He succeeded in ruining it and killing tens of thousands of peasants who resisted in the process. Then he began his assault on the Ukraine and surrounding areas.
>
> The Ukrainians, many of them kulaks, had been a problem for the Soviets from the beginning. In the free elections of 1917, they voted overwhelmingly against the Bolsheviks. They had strong nationalistic yearnings, their own flourishing culture, and they resisted collectivization.

> But Stalin had a way to deal with them. In 1932–33 he engineered a genocidal famine. His method was simple. In July of 1932 he requisitioned 6.6 million tons of grain from the peasants of the Ukraine. It was more than they could possibly produce. But Stalin forced them to deliver what they did have and sent "brigades" with crowbars to search the peasants' houses to make sure they were not holding out. If they found grain, they shot the peasant who hoarded it or sent him to a labor camp.
>
> Stalin sealed the border between Russia and the Ukraine and famine set in. Between 1932–33, 7 million people died of hunger, 6 million of them Ukrainians.

We've already referred to this. Solzhenitsyn talked about this forced starvation of a people by their Satanic overlords. It is a well-known fact. It is basically ignored. Now will you believe that the U.S.S.R. is the "evil empire"!

Another process which Solzhenitsyn described is the present-day policy of the removing of the remaining farmers from lands they are permitted to farm on their own. (A few were allowed to return to self-determination after collectivization because the collectives weren't meeting their quotas!) Those farmers who still exercise private control over their plots, "for the glory of the Motherland," use about 2 percent of the nation's farmland. But they produce 30 percent of the nation's milk, eggs, and vegetables and about 60 percent of its potatoes, berries, and fruit. (The collective farms simply can't compete with free enterprise!)

Yet these farmers are being taken from their land, put into concrete industrial buildings, and told what part of the land they can work. Solzhenitsyn said they started in 1975 and should be finished within fifteen years. By 1990 there should be no Soviet farmers left on their own land.

Taking up from page 198,

> The conclusion of the matter is the third type of society described in quatrain III.95: "Through gifts and tongue another more attractive." The key to deciphering this line lies in the words "through gifts" of the Holy Spirit and "tongues" of angels. In other words, this line describes a pristine and primitive form of communism—the Community. . . of the Holy Spirit.
>
> This society supersedes the first two and is a return to Eden. It is built on the ideals of the earliest golden ages and those to come. Its foundation is the God flame of its members who endow every aspect of its life with the light, love and presence of the Trinity.
>
> Here the Universal Christ is the basis of an individualism where members of society are free to declare: "I am my brother's keeper" and to fulfill it voluntarily, creatively in a world climate of spiritual freedom. This spiritual freedom is reflected in an abundant life based on the free sharing of the fruits of one's labor—as Christ said, "Freely ye have received, freely give."
>
> The Spirit of this Community is abroad in the hearts of the people today and it will take hold and flourish after coming earth changes—long after Soviet Communism passes away—as it surely will. For at Chernobyl, Wormwood and his karma fell where he created it.

Yes, Chernobyl—Star of Wormwood, Star of Soviet Destiny,
How art thou, so great a star, fallen from heaven burning, burning like a ball of fire![38]

This is the end of Book Two of *Saint Germain On Prophecy.*
[25-sec. standing ovation]

All of you and the members of this Community worldwide are the Spirit of that Community and the Masters have great hope for us and faith in us. I can say this, speaking as the voice of my father, Mark Prophet: I pledge myself to the Coming Revolution in Higher Consciousness and the battle of Armageddon.

My fellow Community members, will you join me?
["Yes!" 56-sec. standing ovation]

Thank you all for being here so that I could deliver that message.

"The Summit Lighthouse Sheds Its Radiance O'er All the World to Manifest as Pearls of Wisdom." The delivery by the Messengers' son, Sean C. Prophet, of his first sermon on **New Year's Day, January 1, 1987,** at the Royal Teton Ranch, was edited for print as this week's Pearl. (**1**) Jesus Christ, December 25, 1986, "The Coming of the Divine Teacher," 1986 *Pearls of Wisdom,* vol. 29, no. 78, p. 682. (**2**) Saint Germain, November 27, 1986, "A Prophecy of Karma of the United States of America," 1986 *Pearls of Wisdom,* vol. 29, no. 75, p. 648, or *Saint Germain On Prophecy,* Summit University Press, p. 208, Book Four. (**3**) Aleksandr I. Solzhenitsyn, July 9, 1975, "Communism: A Legacy of Terror," in *Solzhenitsyn: The Voice of Freedom* (Washington, D.C.: American Federation of Labor and Congress of Industrial Organizations, n.d.), p. 30. (**4**) George J. Church, "Hardening the Line," *Time,* 21 March 1983, p. 12. (**5**) Solzhenitsyn, "Communism: A Legacy of Terror," in *The Voice of Freedom,* p. 30. (**6**) Aleksandr I. Solzhenitsyn, *The Mortal Danger: How Misconceptions about Russia Imperil America* (New York: Harper & Row, 1980), pp. 3–5. (**7**) However, the Mongol extermination of Chinese peasantry in the fourteenth century was a 35-million-soul genocide. The parallel is chilling when we consider that the hunters and the hunted reincarnated in the twentieth century for a replay of the bloody scene. Here history is repeated by the same slayers of the same victims. (**8**) No precise enumeration of the **number of deaths worldwide caused by Communism since 1917** is possible. This is the result of the loss of (or inability to keep) records due to civil war, state-organized famines, forced relocations, collectivization, terror, political executions, disease, malnutrition, and the general hardship that accompanies the takeover and process of consolidating power by the Communists—and the suppression of such information as a matter of state policy. Nevertheless, eyewitness accounts, demographic information and such historical records that have survived have enabled scholars to make reasonable estimates of the loss of life at the hands of Communism.

The breakdown of 190 million deaths due to Communism, nation by nation, follows. It should be noted, however, that the 190-million figure may significantly underestimate actual losses since it is impossible to factor in all the deaths caused by forced relocation, disease, dangerous work (such as prisoners in the Soviet Union who handle radioactive ores without proper protective gear), malnutrition and people who simply disappear.

Soviet Union, 110 million dead: Alexander Solzhenitsyn, *Warning to the West,* p. 129; **China,** 64 million: *The Human Cost of Communism in China,* p. iv (prepared by the U.S. Congress, Senate Committee on the Judiciary, 1971); **Cambodia,** 4 million killed by Khmer Rouge: *Current Biography,* 1980, s.v. "Pol Pot"; **Afghanistan,** 2 million: Jan Goodwin, *Caught in the Crossfire,* p. 21; **Vietnam,** 1.4 million: Guenter Lewy, *America in Vietnam,* p. 453, and *Los Angeles Times,* 1 May 1985, sec. 2; **Korea,** 4 million: Lewy, p. 450; **Poland,** 1.2 million: *Encyclopaedia Britannica,* 15th ed., s.v. "Poland, History of"; **Ethiopia,** 1.1 million: *New American,* 17 February 1986, p. 18, and *Insight,* 4 August 1986, p. 4; **Mozambique,** 175,000: *New American,* 2 March 1987, p. 21, and internal memorandum of the Office of U.S. Foreign Disaster Assistance, 28 December 1986; **Angola,** 70,000: *Human Events,* 19 August 1978, p. 11; **Hungary,** 32,000: *World Almanac and Book of Facts,* 1987, p. 578; **El Salvador,** 50,000: Interview with Alejandro Bolaños of the Nicaraguan Information Center, 13 June 1987; **Nicaragua,** 30,000: Interview with Alejandro Bolaños; **South Yemen,** 12,000: *Time,* 3 February 1986, p. 43. The total thus far is 188 million deaths. Additional deaths have occurred in the Soviet Union since 1959, in Cambodia (before and after Pol Pot), in China since 1970, in East Germany, Czechoslovakia, Yugoslavia, Romania, the Baltic Republics, Cuba, Zimbabwe, and at the hands of Communist guerrilla movements around the world. "How long, O Lord!" (**9**) Solzhenitsyn, June 30, 1975, "America: You Must Think about the World," in *The Voice of Freedom,* pp. 7–8. (**10**) The Tibet Fund, "Text of U.S. Tibet Committee Appeal to President Reagan and the United States of America on the 28th Commemoration of Tibetan National Day," March 10, 1987. (**11**) Solzhenitsyn, "Communism: A Legacy of Terror," in *The Voice of Freedom,* pp. 45–47. (**12**) George Santayana, *The Life of Reason,* vol. 1, 1905–1906. (**13**) Solzhenitsyn, "America: You Must Think about the World," in *The Voice of Freedom,* p. 12. (**14**) Thom Shanker, "Soviets Let Dissident Poet, Who Wrote in Soap, Leave," *Chicago Tribune,* 14 December 1986. (**15**) "Sakharov Returns, Speaks Out," *Chicago Tribune,* 23 December 1986. (**16**) Solzhenitsyn, "America: You Must Think about the World," in *The Voice of Freedom,* pp. 21–22. (**17**) Jeane Kirkpatrick, "Keeping a Spotlight on the Oppressed," *Chicago Tribune,* 23 December 1986. (**18**) Reported in a Library of Congress Congressional Research Service study commissioned by Sen. Gordon J. Humphrey (R-N.H.), which analyzed 1985 news coverage by ABC, NBC, and CBS. (**19**) See note 2 above. (**20**) Saint Germain, July 4, 1986, "A Prophecy of America's Spiritual Destiny Restored," 1986 *Pearls of Wisdom,* vol. 29, no. 64, p. 558, or "A Prophecy of Karma: Prophets Who Must Prophesy in America," in *Saint Germain On Prophecy,* p. 197, Book Four. (**21**) Edgar Leoni, *Nostradamus and His Prophecies* (New York: Bell Publishing Co., 1961), p. 289. (**22**) See Archangel Michael, December 29, 1984, "The Judgment of Peshu Alga," 1985 *Pearls of Wisdom,* vol. 28, no. 2, pp. 14–15, 19, and 25, n. 2. (**23**) V. I. Lenin, "Religion," 1933. (**24**) *Saint Germain On Prophecy,* pp. 186–89, Book Two. (**25**) Leoni, *Nostradamus,* p. 217. (**26**) Ibid., pp. 617–18. (**27**) John Anthony Scott, Introduction to *Utopia,* trans. Peter K. Marshall (New York: Washington Square Press, 1965), p. xvii. (**28**) Ibid., pp. xvii–xviii. (**29**) 1986 *Pearls of Wisdom,* vol. 29, no. 50, pp. 457–58, n. 4. (**30**) Vladimir Ilyich Lenin, *Collected Works,* 3d Russian ed., 8:62, in U.S. Congress, Senate Committee on the Judiciary, *The Human Cost of Soviet Communism,* 91st Cong., 2d sess., 1970, p. 7. (**31**) Vladimir Ilyich Lenin, *Collected Works,* 4th Russian ed., 13:435, in U.S. Congress, Senate Committee on the Judiciary, *The Human Cost of Soviet Communism,* 91st Cong., 2d sess., 1970, p. 7. (**32**) U.S. Congress, Senate Committee on the Judiciary, *The Human Cost of Soviet Communism,* 91st Cong., 2d sess., 1970, p. 7. (**33**) Ibid., p. 1. (**34**) Antony C. Sutton, *Western Technology and Soviet Economic Development: 1917 to 1930* (Stanford, Calif.: Hoover Institution on War, Revolution and Peace, 1968), p. 344. (**35**) "Inside the G.R.U.," *Parade,* 6 September 1981, p. 6. (**36**) Robert Conquest, *The Harvest of Sorrow: Soviet Collectivization and the Terror-Famine* (New York: Oxford University Press, 1986), pp. 19, 20. (**37**) Sutton, *Western Technology: 1917 to 1930,* p. 113. (**38**) *Saint Germain On Prophecy,* pp. 190–99, Book Two.

Pearls of Wisdom®
published by The Summit Lighthouse

Vol. 30 No. 4 | *Beloved Archeia Hope* | *January 25, 1987*

The Eternal Now Is My Hope

The Cosmic Conception of a Golden Age

Unto all who have hope, hope is given, even as unto those who have shall more be added. Blessed hearts, a grain of hope can magnetize an ocean of hope. But those who are without hope, beloved, defile the honor of God, show their mistrust of him, and deny the trinity of faith, hope, and charity. Thus, the demons of despair, despondency and death come as destroyers of hope.

Beloved, understand, then, why the flame of hope is my charge and destiny. For to keep alive but a flicker of hope in the hearts of the children of the Sun, this, then, is to preserve the opening for the entrée of the Lord Christ or any angel or Cosmic Being into the world of that one.

The flowers and all of Nature, the stars, even the blue of the sky is a promise of present and future hope, beloved. Thus, God has painted the very canopy and backdrop of a universe to inspire hope that whispers in the heart, "All is not lost."

Beloved, faith is the foundation of hope. Faith, then, in the absolute Good of tomorrow, if it is not evident today, allows hope to take the soul soaring to new heights of opportunity and potential.

Blessed hearts, do you understand for how many of earth's evolutions there is no hope in this hour—no hope of a better tomorrow? Hope not only absent in their own hearts but hope absent by the economic systems under which they toil. Where there is famine, then, and poverty, where there is not even the strength of mind or will or heart to think upon a better future, hope is not only absent but hope is not even conceivable. It does not even exist as an option in the mind. To choose to be hopeful or not has long ago ceased to be.

Thus, we come, beloved, in an hour of cynicism, fatalism,

psychic prediction and all manner of prognostication that has declared the finality of death through the Four Horsemen and mankind's returning karma. We come, our angels of Light, Gabriel with me. We come, then, to expand a purity that is like steel. Can you imagine compressed light so fiery as to be stronger than the strongest wall, harder than the hardest hardness known? It is the concentration of light that does make the aura impervious to despair.

Blessed ones, the opening of despair is through the drug culture and the rock music. This opening into the youth of the world is followed by all forms of masquerading suicide entities. Do you realize, beloved, that in the moment of the decision to take one's life, the only hope held is of death itself, which is a perverted self and a perverted hope?

Know this, then, beloved—that the fire of Astrea, that the calls for the continual clearing of the astral plane and the naming of these entities day after day will surely reap the harvest of Lightbearers sought by beloved Saint Germain. Though the human cannot be guaranteed, the Lightbearer who is free from all illusions and entanglements with the fallen ones can almost of a certainty be guaranteed to receive the light.

Now, beloved, there are hurdles to be passed to be sure, but once there is a clearing, and a certain crystal perception of consciousness occurs as though a peep into the infinite—a peep in the cosmic mirror as to what one may be like, how one may look when cleansed by the flaming presence of hope—this is enough.

Beloved, the greatest preachers, evangelists, deliverers of the Word have been those who could deliver my flame of hope. Once the individual seizes hope based on an inner knowing and a belief in the laws of God and [a belief] that these exist to support his endeavor, to support him in moving forward away from past failure, he is seized again with newness of Life.

Blessed ones, when people find hope and joy in the little things of life—when they even devise for themselves certain intricacies of thought that bring them nearer to our bands, whether children or adults—do not in an advanced awareness of the Path dash these precious though perhaps humble cups of hope from them. And even if they at times may hold hope focused in the wrong individual or the wrong system, we have concluded many times that rather than bring disillusionment to the soul, we would allow a little bit of error sprinkled in to preserve a way and a path that, because it embodies not only hope but Truth herself, will eventually lead that one out of the lower levels to the highest realms.

You see, beloved, one reason that individuals follow psychic meanderings and lesser paths is that these vibrate exactly with their subconscious, with their electronic belt. Almost like a chameleon being the same color of a leaf, so these blend in with a false path and a false guru or perhaps one that is half and half.

Our trust in the living flame of God is great. As you give the calls to Astrea for the youth and mankind, there is a lifting of veils of illusion and psychicism. And suddenly, by the power of the legions of Hope and Gabriel, our bands, they [people on paths which do not offer the fullness of Truth] realize in a moment's descent of the Holy Spirit that they have seen all that they can see with this or that teacher or this or that instruction. And as though the Holy Spirit would suddenly carry them to another place, they are brought face to face with the reality of the Archangels and the Sons of God ascended.

So you see, beloved ones, the great miracle of hope as the flame of purity carried by all of us of the Fourth Ray is the wonder itself that so many, by comparison, of the evolutions of earth have indeed grasped the Teachings of the Ascended Masters. Many more than you realize have incorporated into their lives precepts of Truth tucked into our books that have become a leaven of hope.

Hope is indeed a leaven, beloved, and it is expansive. My aura is expansive to include the stars, for I see hope everywhere in Cosmos and whatever I see, there I AM. And so, my angels who travel in my cosmic aura and mantle become also the components of my being of hope.

Thus, I am known as the Divine Mother of Hope. And some who have ascended on this ray of hope, grasping hope above and beyond all else that did assail them, have become living representatives of my aura. They carry the tie to my Presence, beloved, in heaven itself. Thus, these saints and angels are continually ministering unto all lifewaves, intensifying some hope—some hope that will lead to the heart of God.

Sometimes, then, stimulated by our light, individuals who have not cleared the aura may turn the energy of hope into false schemes—gambling, tying themselves to individuals who take them down other paths of illusion. Thus, it is then that we look to Astrea's legions and the full fire of the Holy Spirit to draw them back and point them in the direction of an upward path.

False hope is dangerous, beloved—most dangerous. For when the disillusionment comes, there is very little left. Thus, you see, this is one of the plots of the sinister force—bringing individuals from disillusionment with their leaders, with their parents, with their friends who betray them, to then say, "If this or that one be not true, who can I trust, where can I go?" And many fall into a heap of hopelessness, often because they can find no self-worth.

It is a mighty task, beloved, that is set before us. We seek swiftly to weave a layer of light twixt the individual and the returning karma of the year and the dark sphere. If we can place but a filigree of hope around each lifestream, but a veil, we can perchance prevent the assimilation of so much darkness returning. Thus, our legions are very, very occupied in this hour, beloved, preparing lifestreams, intensifying the full fire of Serapis Bey that those who are of the Light of God, those who are his children, might cling to that hope even though they understand not the law of karma of this age.

Hope, then, enables the individual to weather the storms of life and to know even from Nature that the vilest of storms, and even cataclysm itself, does spend itself and pass and then the calm does return. So in the cycles of Nature and of Life becoming Life and passing on, one knows that the sine wave of hope is infinite.

Now, beloved ones, the mighty purpose of our coming is to above all give hope to you who have been students of the Ascended Masters for many years, who have come, then, as it were, to the puzzle of life, the very conundrum of self—how to shed the snake-skin and yet in the process to retain an identity and to realize Christhood.

This brings us, then, to the reason for the universities of the Spirit. We recommend that you take the book of the *Lords of the Seven Rays* and read Book One and Book Two simultaneously. When you have read the foundation of Morya's life, his past, his performances and his teachings, turn then to Book Two and read his dictations. Then, with the anchoring of the Alpha and the Omega of the Master, pursue the call of the will of God, pursue Morya with the greatest love, and know that it is self-knowledge and the application of the Law itself that enables one to maintain the flame of hope.

And what is hope but the ascension flame itself? What is hope but life itself? Life without hope is not life at all. Every newborn child comes with hope—hope of surmounting the past incarnation, hope for the clean white page that is given and the new opportunity. One can see this hope on the brow of the newborn child. One can see hope in the baby's cry, for the cry signifies that the child still bears hope that the cry will be answered.

Beloved ones, it is when the individual ceases to cry that one ought to be concerned—ceasing to cry out to God, saying instead,

"What's the use? He will never answer anyway." Thus, beloved, neglect not our flame when you pray for those oppressed.

And remember, dearest hearts, that the goal of the ascension is not merely a goal of reunion with God, but the goal of the ascension is to intensify ascending currents in the aura, in the garment, in the sacred fire that rises upon the spinal altar. This blazing, accelerating flame that swirls around one's presence becomes that very garment, first of the transfiguration, then the resurrection, then the ascension.

The goal of the ascension, beloved ones, is to be the living presence of the ascension flame on earth. As you set for yourself this goal, recognize, then, as you have been taught, that it too is a magnet and therefore it must be sustained in a mighty way.

The ascension flame as the flame of the hope of the Divine Mother, beloved, is a communicator and a receiving station of communication with all worlds in the Matter cosmos and worlds above. For this flame is pure light! light! light! light! light! that expands as from the Goddess of Light, the Queen of Light, and the Goddess of Purity. These beings with myself, beloved, and others of the Archeiai and the ladies of heaven have appeared to many a child as a fairy godmother, as a fairy queen with trooping elementals.

And do you know, this is the greatest delight of little children, and they love to hear stories of fairy queens and fairy godmothers and goddesses. It is because we carry this flame of white fire, divine hope, and the child can see the pattern of the ascent.

Thus, if you would wear the garment that heals on contact, beloved, know that this garment must be free from psychicism, which is the antithesis of hope and the ascension flame, free of Death and Hell and astral substance. And psychicism, beloved, is not merely the mark of those who go after the spirits that mutter and peep and other sources of lower entities for their daily guidance. It is much more than this, beloved. It includes the idolatrous cult, the selfish self, the self engaged in too much misuse of the sacred fire and expending of the life-force.

There are many psychics in the world, beloved, who have never gone to see a psychic and would not term themselves psychic and yet they are. Many of these consider themselves in direct contact with the Ascended Masters. For them, wishing has been the belief that the wish has come true. But it takes more than wishing, beloved. It takes attainment and prayer. It takes a divine contact that may begin with hope but must increase through the expansion of this mighty cable to the heart of God, expanding and pushing back the lower vibrations.

The fire of the ascension flame, beloved, as hope, does indeed therefore bring to you the quickening of the gifts of the Holy Spirit, especially all discernment of spirits that is coming through Paul the Venetian and the Holy Spirit. Understand, then, that it is the white flame of purity that enables you to know exactly the vibrations that come upon you or upon the earth. The all-knowing Mind of God is truly present in the flame of purity.

The flame of purity, then, that is the living presence of hope begins in the heart. One must love. It is always the beginning, as Morya has said. It is a path of the heart and the Presence face-to-face. Thus, we say simply, "Blessed are the pure in heart: for they do see God."

Now, there are illusions whereby people entertain the belief that they are pure in heart; but again, beloved, unless one be cleansed by Astrea, unless the Divine Mother is thy love and goal, you shall find, then, there is yet lurking behind the individual's self-image of purity the record of the hatred of the Mother of Purity. See, then, that thou be not fooled.

Take, then, the opportunity as Jesus did at Luxor to follow the very first steps. Would you not desire to go over his footsteps? Would you not desire, beloved, to be absolutely certain that you have left nothing within the heart or aura or mind that the force can catch you on—a point whereby a clever and mischievous demon may cause you grief?

Grief, blessed, is followed by the weeping entity. Grief is an absence of hope as the absence of the loved one. Internalize hope. Internalize the essence, the heart, the attainment of the one departed.

Is it not beautiful that God has sent wondrous presences into mortal form? Some are like beautiful flowers plucked early with the first breath of summer, but not before all who are intended to see and know them have had the experience of placing the fingers of the mind upon that blessed flame, flower of hope. And when they are gone, one retains the vision, one retains the hope, not only of a hereafter but of a here and now where one says:

> I AM THAT I AM! I claim the full mantle of hope and purity and light and ascension's flame of this one who has tarried with me as my friend. And I shall be a friend to that one departed by embodying all hope that that one had for the fulfillment of life here and hereafter.

Thus, to incorporate, to embody other parts of the Mystical Body not seen is the purpose of living and passing through the veils of time and space.

Beloved ones, have you ever noticed that as long as there is an accomplished pianist around, everyone listens to that pianist and does not bother to play himself? But when that one is no longer present someone must fill the vacuum. And as Nature abhors the vacuum, so one is raised up.

When there are those who do things for you, including to carry the Light and hold back the Darkness and be the embodiment of the Great White Brotherhood, it is easy to remain the chela and to have or retain no necessity of hope of being the Master. But when the Master ascends, beloved, Necessity, who is always the Mother of Hope's invention, does come and say, "Unless you be the master of this situation, all these little ones will be scattered, will be gone astray, will have no hope. You *are* our only hope!"

So she says to you. And so you say to yourself—and the one who has self-worth says this in the confidence, the strength, the boldness, and the humility of the God-enfired son: "I AM the hope of this my family, my community. Lo, I AM the hope of the world! I AM the hope of the world, for I AM an Archeia of Hope."

But, beloved, remember the law as Jesus said it. He said, "So long as I AM [the I AM of me is] in the world, I AM the Light [Christ consciousness] of the world." Many have forgotten this qualifying statement.* Therefore, taking into account the eventual absence of his physical incarnation, Jesus did say, "When the I AM of me is ascended, *ye* are the Light [Christ consciousness] of the world. A city that is set on an hill cannot be hid."

This city of light cannot be hid. It is a city of hope. Does not each and every one of you hope for many things regarding this Community? Ye are indeed the hope of a world that may yet know not that you exist. Yet they have contacted the vibration on inner planes and they lean upon that light of hope of your aura as though it were a staff, as though it were a real and physical support.

O let the Body of God be infused with hope in this hour! Let all the earth know that by hope, multiplied by the Cosmic Christ and all God qualities, the full golden age can, does, and shall manifest!

O blessed hearts, do you know one thing that you have absolute and complete control over? It is this—that the golden age *can* manifest in this hour *where you are!* Where the individualization of the God flame is in you, the golden age can already be in session and progress in your aura. Would you not like to entertain angels and children and say, "Come into my house. Here is a circle of a golden sphere which I have lowered into manifestation"? Would you not like those who seek hope to have a hope of a future better world for themselves?

*The qualifying statement of the oft-quoted "I AM the Light of the world" is "So long as I AM in the world," which is to say "So long as the Christ of me is in embodiment," i.e., "So long as I am in physical incarnation."

Blessed ones, the avatars who have ascended, even the saints who have not balanced their karma, have inspired this hope upon all downtrodden—that somewhere there is a golden age happening. You have viewed it as the etheric cities of light. Now, beloved ones, see it as your aura expanding. Be inside a giant globe. Visualize and position the mountains, the streams, the paradise, the beautiful ones, the happiness. Hear the birds of hope singing.

Blessed ones, I said: You have the absolute control of the manifestation of *your* life. And this is a statement of my hope—a hope that is never future. For when I hope, beloved, it is done. I have only to begin to send forth hope and the object of my hope is instantaneously precipitated. For I refuse to acknowledge past, present, or future. The Eternal Now therefore is my hope, and therefore moment by moment my hopes are satisfied.

Blessed ones, it is important to hope in the realm of the possible. For if you continually hope for that which cannot be, for it violates the Law—it is not practical nor probable nor possible according to all calculations—you will soon be lost in daydreams and fantasies where nothing comes to pass. Thus, beloved, the secret of hoping and rejoicing in hope is to hope for those things which you know can, should, must, shall, and are now presently possible for you.

The present, beloved, is the matrix, or womb, of hope. The Eternal Christ descends. You have a hope in your aura. It is the most powerful matrix. In the human sense you may pass through cycles of time and years. Have you not come to a place where something magnificent has suddenly come into your life and then remembered that three years ago or a decade ago you once had a hope, and since that hope you forgot the hope but your life took a course whereby it was indeed fulfilled?

Have you not noticed that there has been in reality no time? Time is collapsed. The moment of the hope and its fulfillment are one. All sorrow is past. You live in the bliss of a hope that is now.

Therefore, beloved, set the greatest, most powerful matrix of hope which I give to you, which is also presently possible. And it is the golden-age happening of your aura! Do you understand this, beloved? It is a happening now!

Imagine, then, with golden robes and golden spheres of light, how hope, then, becomes illumination's flame, which is why the trinity of the threefold flame is called faith, hope, and charity. Illumine the world with golden wisdom's flame of hope, beloved. Understand the white fire core is there.

You need no longer speculate, "Will the golden age come to

earth?" It is here in me. That I know, O God. It is where I am, and more than this I cannot even desire. For I am with Hope filling Cosmos with my golden age.

What is the golden age, beloved? Is it age one or ten or twenty-five or fifty or a hundred? The golden age, beloved, is the age when *you* find consummation in the Mind of Sanat Kumara. He, the Eternal Youth, has inspired upon this earth the eternal hope.

Blessed hearts, I seal you in this mystery of the world and the universe of your microcosm. And I say by the fiat of Almighty God of the Fourth Ray, I draw a circle of hope around you as the base of your ovoid of light. I seal you in white-fire hope protection. And I impress upon you the unit of golden age that is solely, uniquely your individualization of the God flame.

> O Lord Gautama Buddha, thou who art Shamballa, Lord Gautama Buddha, thou who dost ensoul a planet with thy Buddhas incarnate, with thy bodhisattvas, thou who dost here and now embody the golden age of earth, *intensify* the Great Central Sun Magnet of golden-flame illumination's light, white-fire purity and manifest now in thy aura budding golden yellow-white centered lotuses of these thy Keepers of the Flame!
>
> Now, Gautama, let their lotus blossoms expand in the preordained positions they hold in the very heart center and cosmic rings of causal body of golden age of earth!

So, beloved, expand the cosmic conception of the golden age. See, then, Gautama Buddha centered in his own causal body and see how he fills not only the earth but universes beyond. See yourself, then, suspended—each one, individual God flames of hope, individual units of Hierarchy of golden age.

> O God and Goddess Meru, thou who hast set the power and the foundation, I, then, with Gabriel beloved do manifest here with Alpha and Omega our twin flames, twin pillars of white-fire hope, life, ascension!

These pillars, beloved, are sealed as twin pillars of living flame, electrodes of light. They are pillars of the ascension, beloved, and they are in the fastnesses of these wilderness lands. Beloved ones, those who shall take their initiations of Maitreya unto the hour of the complete absorption unto ascension's flame shall be sealed, healed, and assisted mightily by our twin pillars of living fire.

Let those who fear and doubt have these demons of the night *bound* and cast into the lake of sacred fire! Now I say to all of you, if you re-create your fear and doubt, then I shall say, *Woe* to you!

For ere I come again, the Law may descend that requires both thee and thy fears and doubts to be removed from this place.

Therefore, in the name of the Cosmic Council I speak to you, beloved. Legions of Astrea and my bands strip from you in this twenty-four-hour cycle all fear and doubt concerning thy reason for being and all else. Therefore, accept it. Fill the aura with life, light, hope, faith and charity! And know, beloved, that never, never, never again in all eternity, which is now, need you ever accept a needless fear or doubt. So, it is done and sealed by the Great Central Sun Magnet, by the white fire core of being.

I say, in the name of Saint Germain, let this Body of God, universal and triumphant, be *healed* of all schism caused by fear and doubt! I have decreed it, O beloved. Will you accept it? ["Yes!"]

Will you receive me into your heart that I may abide there forever as the living flame of hope? ["Yes!"]

Then will you trust, beloved, that if hope's call is not answered, for karma's adversity must first be passed, that from the beginning unto the ending, after you have crossed the abyss and the wide chasm, there shall be the fulfillment of promise and the rainbow shall declare it? Will you thus have the patience to let Hope have her perfect work in you? ["Yes!"]

Do not weary, my beloved. Attend thy LORD and thy God, who shall perfect thee even as thou dost seek to be perfected in his Word and Work.

I love you with an all-consuming Love, out of which the Father/Mother God taught me in the very beginning to fashion a flame of living hope. Hope, then, is the gift of the Divine Mother's love. Unto Love, then, I return, beloved. May you follow the white petals of the rose of hope to the pink petals of eternal bliss.

In the name of the Cosmic Christ, I seal you forever. And I implore you, in the name of Saint Germain, give my hope to all. Let my name be known. Let *The Healing Power of Angels* be in the hands of those who need it most.

O beloved, there are some who will not last too much longer without that teaching. Bear it to them as a lamp, as the power of a spoken word, a written word sealed. But, above all, beloved, bear them the flame of hope with good cheer, joy, comfort, and illumination that will lock their hearts into a point of the Law that proves to them God will never, never, never forsake the soul who yet has hope.

"The Summit Lighthouse Sheds Its Radiance O'er All the World to Manifest as Pearls of Wisdom."
This dictation by Archeia Hope was **delivered** through the Messenger of the Great White Brotherhood Elizabeth Clare Prophet on **Friday, January 2, 1987,** at the Royal Teton Ranch, Montana.

Pearls of Wisdom®
published by The Summit Lighthouse

Vol. 30 No. 5 *Beloved Mighty Victory* *February 1, 1987*

The Purging of Chicago

Hail, legions of Victory!

I AM Victory! Welcome to my heart of God's Victory!

Keepers of the Flame, rejoice. For I AM come to this city to establish an intensity of my flame that shall be as a mighty pillar of fire inundating and counteracting all forces of anti-Victory and moving out by the power of the LORD's Spirit and his hosts to counteract that defeatism that is abroad in the land today.

[28-sec. applause]

Indeed I AM Mighty Victory. And the LORD hath said to me this day, "O my son whom I have called Victory, no other flame but Victory can defeat the forces of Death in America and the earth. Go, then, to my city of light, ancient focus of a golden age. Go forth to unleash that Word!"

O beloved ladies and gentlemen of the heart of freedom, I say to you, with hearts noble as these and many more let us see how in the twinkling of God's eye the Spirit of Victory may infuse this land! And so I place my flame in the heart of the Goddess of Freedom above the nation's capitol.

And I cry, as the LORD God does cry, as the Archangel Michael has cried, and the Angel of Unity does stand: O beloved, go forth north, south, east, and west and remind them, "O brothers, ye are indeed brethren. Remember ye are brethren in the light!"

Therefore, O brothers of the Holy Spirit worldwide and sisters of the fraternity of the Woman of the Sun, come forth now, I say. For in this land there is a fire of heart ready, then, to burst. And so may it be said of this generation of Lightbearers that they saw the vision of a golden age and they did indeed see the forces of Darkness pitted against it and they did solemnly choose and vow before the LORD God Almighty that the *Darkness shall not be!* [18-sec. applause]

O beloved ones, fail not the Spirit of Victory. Fail me not, for I am thy brother also. And I come in the name of the Lord of the World to lend my Spirit and my legions with those of the Seven Archangels to see what can be done, to see what keepers of this flame of Liberty might do in this hour leading toward that hour of Wesak for the turning of the tide.[1]

O beloved, let your determination match the saints robed in white and those who are under the altar of God[2] for a season waiting, waiting, I say, for ye all to also enter that Life that is Power, that is Wisdom, that is Love.

Blessed hearts, receive, then, by the inverting of the baton of the Great Divine Director. As there is the inversion of this rod of power, then, heaven comes to earth to meet you in this hour, even as earth has a taste of heaven. So, in the presence of the Great Divine Director, I say to you, let your auras absorb the electromagnetic fields of the legions of Victory! And let that Victory be truly the word of the age.

There is a victory of the flesh. There is a victory of the spirit. One enters the other, and the soul who is the bride of Christ does enter the transfiguration of her Lord. I quicken, then, the memory of the soul and reason for being.

Beloved, all have come to this hour of Victory. So many know it not. I regret that more cannot hear this word.

Beloved, the hour of Victory is that for which you have been prepared and for which you have prepared yourselves diligently. And yet you have reached the ceiling of the offerings of Church and State—the politicians, the economists, and the wolves in sheep's clothing everywhere apparent and nonapparent yet most transparent to us, for you see, beloved, they lack the spark of Victory! There is no Victory where the joy of the Holy Ghost in the full fusion of the soul in the living Word is absent.

Thus, mankind have reached a ceiling of human solutions. And few there be who can lead them to the divine solution. In fact, most have become so cynical as to suspect that there could be any mouthpiece of the heavenly host who could deliver any message that could assuage the grief, the fear, the doubt of the people of God in the earth.

Therefore, in the name of the Almighty One I enter the arena and I come, beloved, with the assistance of Cosmic Beings of Light. These are not dead spirits! But we are they who are alive forevermore in God, who have not worn mortal form for tens of thousands and hundreds of thousands of years.

Blessed hearts, have you contemplated that you are also as old as God is, who conceived you "in the beginning" a living soul and sent you forth?

Thus, we are determined that this ceiling of limitation of self-knowledge of the sons and daughters of God shall be driven back by many hosts who have gathered, responding to the determination of fervent hearts in every religion or outside of the religions of earth.

Blessed ones, many see the handwriting on the wall and do read it. Many understand. But I say, it is the response that counts! And when the response of the people is limited by their leaders, I say, of all conditions this is most tragic in the earth.

Thus, I see losses of territory in this century that ought to have been dedicated to freedom by those who were free and could have done something about it. We cannot look back except to learn the lessons of history. And let us learn well that the enemies of the Light in the personages of the fallen angels—they have come, they have played their roles of infamy, and they have gone down in ignominy.

Yet, beloved, by the actions of individuals few in number the course of the downward spiral of history was set. And now you who have come again in your hour of Victory must deal with deeds that others have sown. And the harvest is nigh! And the reapers come and they not only reap the works of these fallen angels, but they seize the tares as well—genetic strains of evil.

Thus, beloved, just at an hour when the LORD's hosts do intercede to bind those dedicated not to Life but Death in the earth, there is that moment when the seas and the lakes would overflow and the mountains would tremble and the earth should shrug. And in that moment a people have arisen—torchbearers of an age.

The question, then: Will they understand the timing of the hour? Will they understand that as in all battles of history those who could endure have saved not only their nations and families but the course of a planet itself?

Will those who have known Saint Germain cease, then, from their toilings and revelries and understand that in a matter of weeks and months the fate of history may be decided? By thinking man,* but him not alone. By spiritual man—by those who work, those who love, those who know that God is nigh to deliver a people who will appeal, who will apply themselves to the urgency and not fail.

*Homo sapiens

Blessed ones, if you will understand how the presence of angels of Victory can press into the earth and yet some (who are of the earth) in the very pressure of our presence can feel more that spirit of anti-Victory in themselves and defeatism, depression and cynicism, you will also understand how they must, then, make a decision by the lever of the mind and the will and the heart to say, "I will not be defeated, in the name of God! I will fulfill my destiny!"

Some have said this, beloved, without a shred of recourse to things beyond the empirical—yes, courageous hearts who have endured the centuries of barrenness of the religious tree of life. Yet the spark has ignited. It has become a flame. And that all-consuming flame is a passion for peace, for freedom, for the art of love, not war.

Blessed ones, others have made the decision to let the embers die. And in them the spark has gone out. And they have become what is known as a castaway:[3] as the Lord said, empty, empty houses full of dead men's bones[4]—that is, possessed by other ghosts of Christmas past who have taken up their lodging in that emptiness. And thus they have no rudder, no compass, no navigator. They are without Father or Son or Holy Spirit, and the love of the Mother has waxed cold.

Blessed ones, at some time in life there comes to every individual the pain of knowing a loved one that one cannot help, for the loved one has stubbornly refused to let go of the force of anti-Victory.

Beloved ones, to the victors belong the spoils of the spiritual tree of light. Understand that anti-Victory as defeatism must be defeated *by you* within yourself, within the mind and the subconscious, by an act of will and a decision that says, "I can do all things through God, who strengthens me." There is no Victory without him. And in him you live and he in thee, beloved.

Surrender to this one idea: those who determine to succeed by the pride of the mind or whatever else and leave out that Holy Spirit, that power of the immortality of the soul in God—they shall not pass in this age. For the darkness has waxed gross in the earth.

Blessed ones, ye are the Light* of the world. The Light† of the heart of every Keeper of the Flame of Liberty is the primordial Light of a planet largely in darkness. Remember the key word of the Son of God. I remind again of it that you will not forget who you are. He said, "So long as I AM in the world, I AM the Light of the world."[5]

*Christ consciousness †Threefold Flame

Beloved, you are in the world, not I. You cannot say that Mighty Victory is the Light of the world. But you can say, "I AM the Spirit of Mighty Victory incarnate! And the I AM THAT I AM of me *is* the Light of Victory in the earth."

When the responsibility for turning the tide of a nuclear age is put upon the heavenly hosts, blessed ones, a grave mistake based on ignorance of the true divine doctrine is made. You must act, knowing that all things depend upon the Spirit of the LORD in you.

This earth was given to those who wear these bodies that you wear, beloved. Remember this. We may intercede by the authority of your decree, but this is not our battle except you enjoin us by your call. The battle is to the Lord and the Lord of you, the Holy Christ Self.

Very few are in the driver's seat. Thus they accept the ceiling of cynicism in life. "Someone else must solve the problem," they say. The government, the Congress, NATO, the UN—always someone else is left to deliver a world.

There is only one God you can know and He is the God whose voice speaks in your heart. Oh, I beg you on behalf of all who have ever lived on earth and ascended and all who are scheduled to ascend in the next thirty years, Respond to that voice! Some of you do not even speak to one another in love, let alone respond to the most loving, the most wise and powerful voice of all—the voice of the hidden man of the heart.[6]

Blessed ones, to the ingenious will the Spirit of Victory come. And by the power of the Cosmic Christ, may God truly deliver this nation and earth through you and so many others who receive the ministrations of my angels in this hour yet are ill-equipped to receive either me or my Messenger or this creed.

Is it not wondrous that we can live and let live and that knowing the power of this form of prayer we can acknowledge that others, too, reach God and that this is a mutually reinforcing system whereby the greatest Lightbearers of all walks of life do supply some need, some support while receiving the same from others?

A fiery vortex of light is abuilding now and has been for some time, preparing for the release of the spoken Word into this city. It is composed of millions of angels, beloved, and of the fire they have brought from the Central Sun for this occasion of our communion of saints as Above, so below.

My eye is upon the corruption of this city, its former political machines and those who have survived in organized crime or racist groups of all sorts or militant groups. Blessed ones, the day has come, and it is the day of reckoning when this city should be, must be, and shall be purged. Let it be purged by Light, beloved, that can absorb the Darkness and leave a people in peace. Let it be so, for the vortex is set. It is in position to the very depths of the earth under the city.

Beloved ones, I tell you the truth. The purging shall come by Light [*Christos*] and violet flame, guarded by your own God-Harmony, else one day, if it is not transmuted, the purging shall come by water and by fire.

Let it be known, then, that the Almighty has set to you this day a task which you and others like you can fulfill. Recognizing the seriousness of the necessity for Light to increase and for Darkness to be bound without a violent reaction or overreaction of the forces of Nature, know, beloved, that responsible sons and daughters of God in the earth who see the course that is set and take their stand create new levels of opportunity for a dispensation to others yet to be awakened to their own Christhood.

Therefore, I, Victory, draw a circle of fire. It has a radius, beloved, of 100 miles. Its center is in a particular place which I show to the Messenger in downtown Chicago. Therefore, you may easily take and draw this circle and see on the map what the areas of concentration are.

Let it be known, then, that a people whose hearts were afire for God one day on the first of February in Aquarius 1987 did receive an impetus from the Central Sun, did receive an awakening, an enlightenment, and did determine to act before it was too late.

May you know the profound meaning of life and the protection of that life when life is ultimately threatened. Beloved, may you know that those things which threaten life on earth are so intense and intensifying in many hearts—from abortion to suicide, from dread disease to drugs to totalitarian movements to brainwashing to encroachment upon the body and the mind by toxins or vile thoughtforms and sounds.

Beloved, it is not difficult to understand the meaning of the Fourth Horseman, to observe life and what it has become. Will you not understand, then, the daily challenge of Death that comes knocking at the door to convince you to surrender some portion of your personhood in God rather than take a stand for life.

O beloved, the demons of Death are of the ultimate subtlety. Can you believe that a planet could be convinced that those things prophesied shall not come upon the earth? Yet this is what the forces of anti-Victory, defeatism, and Death have done. Those who have lived a little while remember when it was not so.

Therefore, act. Rouse yourselves, beloved! For this is, you might say, a final opportunity for this city and area. Let it be for the turning back of all that which was plotted on the graph of karma by the deeds of mortals—some who knew not what they did and some who entered the league of conscious Evil.

In this day, in the Holy Spirit of God, I, Victory, plant my rod in the center of this vortex. May it blossom as Aaron's rod. May it bloom as the rod of Joseph. Thus, Saint Germain and Joseph of Arimathea—let them have, then, the green branch and new life.

In ye all I place a portion of my flame of Victory, and not alone my flame but my heart. All else I have laid upon His altar. Thus, beloved, the vortex is sealed—and ye also if ye will it so.

Call, then, to the angels of Victory. They will comfort, they will enlighten, they will heal! They will rejoice with you day by day. They will strengthen and transfer from the heart of the Father new life.

Here, take, then, my heart and my flame. I am with you in Christ always unto the end of your karma, my beloved.

"The Summit Lighthouse Sheds Its Radiance O'er All the World to Manifest as Pearls of Wisdom." This dictation by Mighty Victory was **delivered** through the Messenger of the Great White Brotherhood Elizabeth Clare Prophet on **Sunday, February 1, 1987,** at the Blackstone Hotel in Chicago, Illinois. (**1**) Wesak, May 13, 1987, marks the conclusion of the ten-year dispensation for **the turning of the tide** announced by Gautama Buddha in his May 3, 1977, Wesak address. See Gautama Buddha, "One Decade for the Turning of the Tide: The Great Central Sun Messengers, the Cosmic Christs, and the Buddhas Come Forth," 1978 *Pearls of Wisdom,* vol. 21, no. 28, pp. 148–50, or "The Radiant Word," 1986 *Pearls of Wisdom,* vol. 29, no. 65, pp. 577–78. (**2**) Rev. 3:4, 5; 6:9–11; 7:9, 13, 14. (**3**) I Cor. 9:27. (**4**) Matt. 23:27. (**5**) **"So long as I AM in the world. . ."** John 9:5. See Archeia Hope, January 2, 1987, "The Eternal Now Is My Hope," 1987 *Pearls of Wisdom,* vol. 30, no. 4, p. 79. (**6**) I Pet. 3:4.

THE RADIANT WORD

Victory I AM!

Excerpt from a Pearl of Wisdom by Mighty Victory, May 8, 1959

. . . Today I bring to each of you who will accept it the substance of my Victory—that golden flame which contains within it my living feeling of victorious accomplishment in all you do. This is a very real and tangible gift!

Whenever you need victorious accomplishment over anything, remember that *I AM* in the universe and that *I AM* no farther away from you than your own heartbeat. You see, the light which beats your very heart is God's life and therefore a very real part of that Victory which I AM.

Therefore, whenever confronted by any set of circumstances which portends less than God-success for you, may I suggest that you make the following call:

> My very own beloved I AM Presence and beloved Mighty Victory, I consciously and determinedly refuse acceptance into my feelings or any other part of my world of anything but God-Victory right here and now!
>
> In reality, that Victory I AM! My very life is that Victory!
>
> Mighty Victory, flood my entire being and world with your feelings thereof which compel victorious accomplishment for me. Help me to fully accept it as being real and true even before it appears for me in outer manifestation.

Try me out and keep on calling until you have given me sufficient opportunity to make you the Victory I AM!

We know full well that, for the unascended, it is so easy for him to yield his world to the pull of the senses and limiting appearances, for that is the way of the world in which he lives. All unascended consciousness is one, even as our Ascended Master consciousness is one in our octave. That is why, especially in these changing days, as the life of the entire universe is spiraling upward in its return to the Godhead from whence it came, we must have at least some of the life from those embodied upon your star consciously claiming Victory in order to be able to anchor and expand that God-virtue *here.*

Victory! Victory! Victory! must be claimed in all they do, until claiming Victory becomes a fixed and unalterable habit with them. Help to this end I am particularly well prepared, ready and most lovingly willing to give at any moment, day or night. . . .

From everlasting to everlasting I AM the Victory of all life everywhere! My power ever increases as the ages roll. Accept me and my help, beloved ones, for I live but to expand God-Victory.

Be my friend, even as I am yours and let me, through your victories, draw to myself more and more friends on earth. Let me make your world a living example of what my power of Victory can do for all.

Come along with me! The best is yet to be. You cannot yet imagine what I can do with Victory!

Pearls of Wisdom®
published by The Summit Lighthouse

Vol. 30 No. 6 | *Beloved Saint Germain* | *February 8, 1987*

The Pillar of Violet Flame

The Healing Power of the Seventh Ray

Hail, O Lightbearers of the Nations!

I descend into this City of the Angels with legions of violet flame angels who are come, then, for the freedom and the liberation of your souls, your minds, and your bodies.

Fear not, for the hour of your liberation is come if you will it so. For our God has willed it, and he has sent me to you this day to deliver not only my prophecy but my light as his own light directly to your heart and heart center.

Children of the Sun, ye are of an ancient memory and one with the forces of Light. Ten thousand years and more you have awaited this hour of your coming and mine for the fervent release of the Seventh Ray to an age beset with the accumulation of the karma not alone of two thousand years but many.

Beloved, the cycles have turned. Aye, they have turned for thee and for me. The cycles, then, confer in time and space a delivery of the Word and a lowering from your own God Self, from your own I AM Presence, that intensity of sacred fire that in the twinkling of the eye of God can indeed transmute that Fourth Horseman's delivery of Death and Hell.[1]

Therefore, people of the Light, do not tarry in the false teachings of a false hierarchy that does not extend to you a vision of what in actuality is coming upon the nations but concerns itself rather with personal entertainment or even the promise of deliverance through UFOs.

I tell you, beloved, the hour has come when the Lightbearer must choose between the path of the Divine Mother and the true ascension or the path of the UFOs, which promise a flesh-and-blood deliverance but, beloved, cannot give you that which you already have, which only you can acquire through the magnificent consummation of your spirit with the living presence of God!

Let God, then, be your Saviour and none else! Let God be your teacher/deliverer, for he is a consuming fire.[2] And those of us who are among the immortals, those who are the Ascended Masters, show you now at inner levels the pathway of your soul that you can win and thereby endow a planet with victory even as you take your own in this life.

Indeed, it is possible for you to transcend all of the cycles of your karma in this age. But whatever the calling or the choosing of your soul, remember it cannot be accomplished without the Holy Spirit's gift to you of the violet flame. And truly it is given in this hour. And there is no mantra more necessary to your deliverance and survival—for the violet flame is a physical flame!

And, beloved, it is the physical atoms of the earth that are burdened with disease and death and toxins and chemical pollutants which burden the body and prevent the mind from being the chalice of the diamond-shining Mind of God, which is your rightful inheritance from the Universal Christ.

Maitreya is his name yet he is an Ascended Master and has not incarnated in this hour. Beloved ones, he is here to overshadow everyone and not any single lifestream. Therefore, claim your union with the hosts of the LORD where you are and go not after the spirits that mutter and peep[3]—fallen Atlanteans who will come and tell you many tales except the one that is needed, which is your deliverance from the returning karma that, I tell you, is being delivered upon all in this hour through the Four Horsemen.

Blessed ones, it is the Cosmic Christ personified in your own Christ Self that does stand between you and the returning karma of an age. January 1, 1987, is the hour I have predicted for the acceleration of darkness. I do not desire to deliver such a prediction but I say it that you might arm yourselves well and protect your children and your communities, your nations and the planetary body.

Fear not, beloved. For the fallen angels who would promise deliverance through a prophecy of peace or psychicism or those aliens from other systems are only there to deter you from the true and living God who has loved you with such a fervor as to place the divine fire in your very breast.

Beloved ones, I have walked among you in recent centuries and long ages past. Many of you have known me. And I say to you that the adoration of the Light and the sacred fire, its expansion in your heart, gives to you the coequality of an equation where you and Christ are one. Behold the Second Coming of Christ—not alone as the sign in the heaven[4] but as the sign of your emergent Godhood!

Moses has delivered unto you the sign of the I AM THAT I AM.[5] I tell you, this nation is the Place Prepared for the return of the twelve tribes amongst Jew, Christian, and all alike who have been raised up from the four corners of the earth.

I tell you truly, the hour is not too late for you to turn around those things descending. I have said it once, but I shall say it again. For as I stand in your presence and you allow it, I may transfer to you that violet flame—that spirit of freedom whereby you may know this Truth that shall set you free.[6]

I say it, beloved, that when you apply the spiritual science and the true path of the balancing of karma to the problems of the economy, to the problems of defense, education, drugs in America, you can make all the difference. For God is no respecter of persons.[7] You need not be a follower of mine or this Messenger or any particular religion but only a devotee of the living flame of God above you and in the Central Sun and in this temple that is vibrant of life, that you call home for this lifetime.

Beloved ones, devotion to the Law of the One and the one Source makes of all one manifestation of Light. Therefore, we see many sons but one God alone. And in that heartfelt union of the Light there is strength, there is deterrence, there is defense, there is eternal Life, there is the conquering of death in your cells and atoms.

Speak to the viral attacks upon you that come as AIDS or cancer and say: "Thus far and no farther! You have no power over me! Now get thee hence out of my temple! For where I AM, there is the flame of God, and I consecrate in his name this temple to be the temple of the LORD's Spirit."

Thus, beloved ones, take up the decree written down long ago by the Messenger Mark Prophet and command, "O atoms, cells, electrons within this form of mine...!" Thus, beloved, command them to "be all Light!" Then visualize the sun in the center of every atom and molecule, especially where there is the report to you of that terminal disease. Command the Light, dispel the Darkness, and take, oh, take, beloved, my gift to you of the violet flame!

Why is it my gift, beloved? For God has given it unto me to give to you—for so many thousands of years ago I espoused the flame of the seventh age and ray—in many incarnations that then ensued.

Beloved, I was a priest and a high priest in the Temple of the

Violet Flame on Atlantis. Yes, I studied with Melchizedek at the retreat of Lord Zadkiel that now is in the etheric octave over the Caribbean. Beloved ones, I was indeed there when the Lord Jesus Christ received his initiation, long before his incarnation final, to be "a priest forever after the Order of Melchizedek."[8] This calling is unto you to study and learn of the Seventh Ray and the Seventh-Ray Masters.

Therefore, I call forth from the Central Sun a pillar of violet flame fire that shall be set in the heart of this city. Unto it, then, beloved, have recourse. Call upon the pillar of violet flame that is an ancient pillar of the Seventh Ray.

It is because the hour is short that I come to you this day and that I deliver my message. Beloved, I love you with the intensity of the Almighty One, with the love of the camaraderie that we have shared in prior centuries. I know thee, who thou art, O thou child of the Most High, thou striving one, devoted yet burdened. I know the thoughts of thy heart and thy prayers. I come, then, as your Saint Joseph to care for you even as I cared for the Christ Child.[9]

Beloved ones, I do understand the burden of your heart. Thus, I have given to you the mantra "I AM the Light of the Heart." Oh, enter into the deepest mysteries of God and recognize that they are all contained in your heart, in the cells and atoms. The laws are written there. A whole cosmos is inside of you!

In fact, once you were beings of a cosmos waiting to be born. Once with twin flame you saw the face of Father/Mother God and rejoiced that Elohim created you to go forth and manifest the divine polarity in universes unborn. You indeed came trailing clouds of glory, beloved.

Yet there was a losing of the way at the influence of the fallen angels who in their pride defied the LORD God in his sons and descended into density, were cast into the earth and made to take on physical bodies such as those you wear. For they were determined to move against the Divine Manchild who is the Christ—the *Christos,* or Light—the Anointed One of every one of you.

Thus, beloved, you have lost the way of the understanding that some minds in this universe set themselves to Absolute Evil, which is to destroy the potential and the realization of that potential of Christhood by each and every one of you.

They have taught the lie of "only one Son of God"—that only Jesus could attain to this. Yet the only begotten Son of God is the Cosmic Christ who is individualized in ye all as that potential whom Jesus incarnated, externalized, and was fully the representative of for the Piscean age.

Beloved hearts, fallen angels in embodiment and aliens with no good purpose, though they also speak about love, have come to this planet for one purpose alone—as pied pipers to lead the sons and daughters of God away from the Divine Source and the reunion with Light.

Because you have been taught by philosophers, psychologists, and even some men of the cloth that there is no evil or evil intent, you therefore have been lulled to sleep concerning that debacle of nuclear war that hangs as a threat—a threat against whom? The Lightbearers, beloved. For it is they who will lose all. And when I say "all," I mean the opportunity at the end of an age to found a golden age and to bring it forth hand in hand with the heavenly hosts, the Archangels, and elemental life.

The hour of Opportunity* is at hand and has never been greater for the victory of a universal enlightenment and an age of peace. Beloved ones, I implore you and I come to ask you this. I ask you to buy fifty years of peace for me and I will show you what the heavenly hosts working through you may do to save this planet utterly from disease and death and war.

Blessed hearts, to implement this you must call upon your representatives and demand the immediate defense of this nation, whether or not you think it logical or reasonable that an Ascended Master such as I should plead to you for physical defense.

Believe me, then, on the common sense of it, that there is a necessity for physical defense to guard physical life. And I tell you, you need the bodies you wear and the minds you have, free and uncontaminated by nuclear holocaust, in order to balance your karma. That balancing of karma does come through service and through the violet flame.

Beloved ones, your life and opportunity are more precious than they have ever been in any past age. Do not underestimate, then, the envy and the revenge of the fallen angels who have worked as the devil works, without any break whatsoever, to stop *you* from realizing the full Sonship of that Cosmic Christ.

It is the dawning of Aquarius and of the age of awareness. And so, you are at this convention. Blessed ones, take the science of the spoken Word—for the spoken Word is a sword of the Spirit—and through it accelerate mightily. Value your life and service. Help one another and determine that this nation which I sponsored in the beginning shall live and survive to fulfill her immortal destiny.

You are here, beloved, because I sponsored you in the hour of your birth. And some of you who have not traveled abroad

*Portia, the twin flame of Saint Germain, is also known as the Goddess of Opportunity.

have not understood how I have borne your karma as I have not borne it for any other nation, that you might set a path of freedom and liberty not alone in government but in fields of health, medicine, science, education, and law.

Blessed hearts, before Almighty God I have vowed my sponsorship of this land of opportunity because it is the best hope whereby mankind might survive in freedom to know the path that you know, which they have not yet touched.

In the name of the Goddess of Liberty, Cosmic Mother whose temple is over the city of New York and whose statue is enshrined there, I bring you in my hand and heart the flame of Liberty. May you understand its portent in the third century of America's destiny. Oh, look up and live, beloved of the Light!

I would deliver to you the healing power of the Seventh Ray. And I shall be, therefore, in the Heart of the Inner Retreat for some days surrounding the celebration of the Declaration of Independence, July 4th. I summon you to this high place and mountainous retreat where the light of the Holy Spirit flows and I may again transfer to you a just portion of the violet flame and your own divinity.

For this day I can give only that which the Law allows for each lifestream—that which you are able to receive. Blessed ones, it is an increment of light that will not hurt you but will help you. And thus, the governing action of the Cosmic Christ allows only that which the body can receive and yet remain in balance to take place.

Therefore, my beloved—those who have known me forever, those who only recently have made my acquaintance—I tell you that I took the name Saint Germain, for it means "holy brother." May you think of me always as your friend and brother on the Path. And may you know that I may not enter your world to intercede for you unless you call my name in the name of God and ask.

Therefore, say it to me any hour of the day or night—"In the name of Almighty God, Saint Germain, help me now!" I promise you that an Electronic Presence of myself shall be at your side with the speed of light.

And if you desire to increase your capacity to receive my assistance, then take up the calls to the violet flame and see how your aura will actually turn a violet color so that friends may see it and feel the impact of the Seventh Ray.

When your aura is so charged, beloved, I may then enter it and repolarize your very physical form to the light of God that never fails, to the inner blueprint and the image of Christ in which ye are made!

From the beginning unto the ending, I AM Saint Germain, one with the Keepers of the Flame worldwide. O beloved, let me help you! Receive me now as your friend forever.

Angels of the Seventh Ray, now surround this my U.S.A., the entire border. Let it be now walls of light, violet flame, blue lightning, and a pillar of fire! So may it be in the LORD's Day and in the descent of the vengeance of our God[10] that is his judgment that the people of Light might know the protection and divine intervention.

So call it forth and reinforce it, for angels of Light do establish it.

In the name Jesus Christ, I serve.

[36-sec. standing ovation]

"The Summit Lighthouse Sheds Its Radiance O'er All the World to Manifest as Pearls of Wisdom."
This dictation by Saint Germain was **delivered** through the Messenger of the Great White Brotherhood Elizabeth Clare Prophet on **Saturday, February 7, 1987,** at the Whole Life Expo, held at the Pasadena Convention Center, Pasadena, California. The Messenger delivered her lecture "Saint Germain On Prophecy: Coming World Changes" prior to the dictation. (**1**) Rev. 6:7, 8. (**2**) Deut. 4:24; 9:3; Heb. 12:29. (**3**) Isa. 8:19. (**4**) Matt. 24:30. (**5**) Exod. 3:13–15. (**6**) John 8:32. (**7**) **God is no respecter of persons.** Deut. 10:17; II Sam. 14:14; Acts 10:34; Rom. 2:11; Eph. 6:9; Col. 3:25; I Pet. 1:17. (**8**) **"A priest forever. . ."** Ps. 110:4; Heb. 5:5–10; 6:20; 7:11–28. (**9**) Saint Germain was embodied as Saint Joseph, father of Jesus. (**10**) **The LORD's Day, the Day of Vengeance of Our God.** Isa. 2:10–22; 13:6, 9, 13; 34:8; 61:2; 63:4–6; Jer. 46:10; Ezek. 30:3; Joel 1:15; 2:1, 2, 31, 32; Zeph. 1:7–10, 14–16; Zech. 14:1; Mal. 4:1–6; I Thess. 5:2; II Pet. 3:10; Rev. 1:10; 19:11–21.

Christ Wholeness

In the name of the beloved mighty victorious Presence of God, I AM in me, my very own beloved Holy Christ Self and beloved Jesus the Christ, I pour forth my love and gratitude to my beloved body elemental for his faithful service always. (Pause to visualize your precious body elemental in an ovoid of the pink flame of divine love.)

I now command my body elemental to arise and take complete dominion over every imperfect condition which may be manifesting within my physical body!

Beloved body elemental, move into action now to mend the flaws under the guidance and direction of my own beloved Holy Christ Self, beloved Jesus the Christ, and the immaculate design of my lifestream released from the heart of my own beloved Mighty I AM Presence—O thou Great Regenerator!

In the name of the mighty Presence of God which I AM and by and through the magnetic power of the sacred fire vested in the threefold flame burning within my heart, I decree:

1. I AM God's Perfection manifest
   In body, mind, and soul—
   I AM God's Direction flowing
   To heal and keep me Whole!

Refrain: O atoms, cells, electrons
   Within this form of mine,
   Let heaven's own Perfection
   Make me now Divine!

The spirals of Christ Wholeness
   Enfold me by his might—
   I AM the Master Presence
   Commanding, "Be all Light!"

2. I AM God's perfect image:
   My form is charged by Love;
   Let shadows now diminish,
   Be blessed by Comfort's Dove!

3. O blessed Jesus, Master dear,
   Send thy Ray of Healing here;
   Fill me with thy Life above,
   Raise me in thine arms of Love!

4. I AM Christ's healing Presence,
   All shining like a mercy sun—
   I AM that pure Perfection,
   My perfect healing won!

5. I charge and charge and charge myself
   With radiant I AM Light—
   I feel the flow of purity
   That now makes all things right!

Pearls of Wisdom®
published by The Summit Lighthouse
Vol. 30 No. 7 *Beloved Archangel Raphael and Mother Mary* *February 15, 1987*

Healing, Karma, and the Violet Flame

The Law and the Fiery Trial

O wise ones and some who are yet wise in your own foolishness, I AM Raphael Archangel which stand in the presence of God! Therefore, beloved, I bring to you, from the Great Central Sun, fires of Immortality and Life, fires of Healing, if ye would be healed.

Therefore I say, choose ye this day whom ye shall serve—Life or Death.[1] For those who would abide in the sweetness of Death have not the real desire for Life. Should Life, then, as infinity and light and everlastingness be bestowed, it would instantly be requalified with the desire of Death.

Therefore, beloved, a house divided against itself cannot be a fount of healing—except, of course, one is content with an exchange of astral or human-consciousness energies. These may be felt, may be passed to one another and may seem to clear, then, life or mind. But, beloved, the only permanent healing, and the healing which is ours to bestow, is a healing unto spiritual as well as physical wholeness.

Our emphasis, then, must be upon those who have indeed the "can-do" spirit and understand that all healing must be self-healing—healing by the Higher Self whom the soul does lovingly embrace as her Lord and as her Self.

In the name Jesus Christ, I serve. In the name Sanat Kumara, Gautama Buddha, Maitreya, I serve.

Let it be understood that God is no respecter of persons,[2] that all sons who have attained to the ultimate consummation of Light, therefore one with God, may be invoked for a transfer of cosmic power of healing.

O beloved, seek that which is real and know that healing

must be a purging—a purging of mind and heart and soul. Let virtue be the sign, then, of the conquering ones of this age who espouse a law and have the courage to embody the virtue of the Law, the light of the Law, and the letter as well as the spirit of the Law.

Blessed ones, you cannot take the mess of pottage, selling your birthright as Christed ones,[3] and then turn about and expect to be renowned healers. Let the individual be selfless before God. Let him be a nameless one! And let God appear. Let the aura be so charged with a magnificence of light that the touching of the garment is sufficient for a transfer of wholeness.[4]

Beloved, this is an age when healing has become difficult for many—and even self-healing. Some are even disillusioned with so many alternatives and diets and pills and another and another selling their wares saying, "Lo, I have the elixir of life!"

Why is it so, beloved? As you have understood, it is karma—karma descending—that exacts a certain fiery trial. And I have noted well with beloved Mary, my consort, that those of the new-age movement who have understood Truth profoundly have yet stepped back and said, "I cannot endure the fiery trial." Thus, they have become the nonaccountable ones in an age of non-accountability.

Realize that every soul must face her God and her karma. Let her learn well, then, the powers of intercession available but let her understand there is a price to be paid.

Think not that the violet flame may be invoked to transmute today some spot or blemish of consciousness and then, when one is free and healed by the violet flame, that one may again indulge in the same pattern and invoke the violet flame again and again.

You see, beloved, this attitude toward the graces and gifts of God lacks holiness, reverence and a sense of being the beloved son, responsible unto the Father.

For every healing that does take place through you or about you, someone *must* pay the price, beloved. For all energy in Cosmos must be in equilibrium. Therefore, if a dark karma is set aside or removed, the light of God or the light of self-proclaimed healer must be the price.

Now, beloved, many do not understand how heavy is the karma of souls who are bearing heavy diseases in their bodies. It is well that you acquaint yourself with the Law of God and realize that if by the Great Law this individual must learn a lesson through this experience and yet you pray for healing and continue to pray, the Law may answer by requiring you to place upon the altar the price—in fact, the quotient of energy misused by that lifestream in a previous life which did result in this disease.

Do you understand, beloved, that there are also forms of healing where, by prayer or hypnosis or mental willing, the disease is pushed back into the astral body or into the etheric body, there to lodge as karma denied? An individual may suddenly be healed of migraine headaches through hypnosis or other practices of so-called metaphysics.

Beloved ones, this may come about rather easily to the practiced one, adept in the uses of these methods. But, beloved, a heavy karma does accrue to such practitioners when the violet flame is not used to consume the record of the cause and core of that karma. And the individual who did assent to the easy way (that is not the way of Life) will see sometime in the future, in this life or a future embodiment, the same problem recurring and coming to the surface to be dealt with as karma that must be transmuted ere the physical symptoms may disappear.

Thus, some bear in their bodies burdens that others dispense with easily, even by the recitation of a mantra without accountability. There are easy paths and easy religions.

But I speak to you from the octaves of light as an Archangel. I have known you for ten thousand times ten thousand years. I have observed your comings and your goings—your fulfillment of the path of Truth as well as your meanderings in the qualifications of error. All that you have ever been of the Light you may call forth from your causal body to enhance your instrumentation of God's healing.

I say to you, beloved, even this Messenger did begin early in life desiring to heal. Saint Germain, then, taught her, with the assistance of Mary, that each one must come to the understanding of the responsibility of karma and that individuals can indeed be healed when they will apply the violet flame and be willing to serve to set life free that they have wronged.

Thus, beloved, understand that healing is a process which is a culmination of many others. Sometimes those who have not perfect sight desire their sight more than they desire to see God. Often, then, poor eyesight or diseases of the eyes or even blindness is an indication of the karma of refusing to see the Truth or to see Almighty God face-to-face.

Thus, examine the motive and the desire for healing and assess this in yourself as well as in others who come to you for prayer and assistance. It is well to help all in the body and in the spirit—to give comfort, compassion and all means of remedies available.

Take care, then, that you understand that the unlawful healing that is given may accrue to your own karmic record. And that unlawful healing, beloved, is the manipulation of the laws of God and of his Spirit to deliver one who must yet experience his own accountability in the wrestling of the soul in that fiery trial of which I speak.

Beloved, how, then, shall the people escape the torment of the last plagues? I tell you, it is possible. But let every man consider his communion with the Holy Spirit and with the sacred fire. Let each one consider how he may burst forth in song and life to lose himself and his self-concerns in the comforting and healing of others.

Let the violet flame be the universal unguent and even the elixir of youth. And let those who seriously desire union with God be prepared, then, to stand, face, and conquer in his name all that assails them.

I AM Raphael of the Fifth Ray of Science. I have inspired many a cure, a method, even an alternative way upon the scientists and the medical profession as well as upon those who have found the better way of life. Blessed ones, these are dispensations that come through the Lords of Karma, and when they are in your hands they are made available to all—and justly so.

My warning concerns, then, those grey areas—whether of psychic healing or healing of any other form where there is an interference with karmic law and where there is danger to the practitioner who unknowingly takes to himself the burdens of karma by various techniques practiced.

In this light of the new age, I pray you perceive that the greatest healer of all is he who first heals himself by the known methods of God-Mastery taught by the Ascended Masters.

When you complete the healing of the electromagnetic field that is effected by the power of transfer of light through the auric emanations of Archangels, when you can stand in a closed circuit of Alpha and Omega, beloved ones, then you will be the instrument of a light not your own, and not your own to direct, that will flash forth and heal, in the immediate environs or across the planet, those whose karma allows the intercession of grace.

Let your light be raised up. Let the Kundalini rise. Let the chakras become blazing suns. And see what you might accomplish for a planet in distress!

I give to you now my own beloved Mary, who would speak to you of your early vow.

Beloved Mother Mary

The Vow to Heal a Planet
Study the Healing Arts at Fátima

O my beloved children of the Sun, I am your Mother, so very near. And I come, mindful of the Fátima message and of prophecies due to descend upon earth.

I ask you, then, to realize that God has given to me in your behalf a presence, a calling, and a dispensation. When you say the word "Hail, Mary, full of grace," you are giving the salutation to the Mother Ray, the Ma-Ray that is in the heart of the Great Central Sun, which it is my ordination to convey to you through my heart.

I am an Archeia, therefore a consort of an Archangel. My beloved Raphael did keep for me a flame of love in heaven as I descended to earth—not in one life alone but in a number of lifetimes preparing, then, to give birth to Jesus in his final incarnation as the Christ.

In this day I surround you with my swaddling garment of light. I hold you in this immaculate embrace that is a healing power to restore the mind and soul and body to the original blueprint that is in your higher etheric body.

I speak, then, of your vow to be on earth in this hour when many would require healing. I ask you, then, in hearing the words of my beloved Raphael to remember to call upon God, ourselves, and many angels to bring healing where healing is possible. And if the Law does not allow it in the flesh, then call, oh, for the healing of the soul and the spirit that it might take flight from the body in the end to enter new planes of glory and edification to prepare for a final round unto the ascension.

It is the healing of the whole man that we are about. And we ask of you not only this but to remember the vow to heal a planet by becoming the instrument of such radiant light of the Central Sun. Pursue, then, all avenues of healing that are open to you lawfully. And, beloved, pursue the healing of souls.

Souls are in torment and require the healing of the Holy Ghost. You may learn of the gifts and graces that you may earn under the tutelage of the Lords of the Seven Rays. You may seek to increase the aura by devotion, decree, and service. And you may call to me and Raphael, for our etheric retreat is above Fátima in Portugal. There you may come at night [your soul in her etheric garment apart from the physical during the sleep state] and study the healing arts. Not far away is the university of the Spirit of Hilarion over the isle of Crete.

Do, then, call to God and your guardian angels to take you at night in your finer bodies where you may study and learn what are the golden-age methods of healing and how, when the planet is delivered of a certain karma and a certain band of fallen angels incarnate who oppose the real cures that could be available today for cancer and other terminal diseases—how through you and others there may come about finally the liberation and the revelation of the true healing arts.

Some who know it not have been inspired by us and have brought forth their methods. They have been persecuted. They have been pursued by those who have taken the law to wrest it to the destruction of those cures that ought to be available to everyone upon earth.

It is not the LORD God who has decreed that mankind must suffer from these dread diseases. But it is, beloved, a certain clique of fallen angels who have crept in unawares with their spiritual wickedness in high places[5] who have prevented the little people—my people—from having those cures and that application of science which could have delivered their bodies that their souls might have pursued the true spiritual calling of their lives in this very life.

The plagues themselves descending were never designed unto Death and Hell. They are a karma, yes, but the LORD has perceived and has sent the intercessor in the person of the Cosmic Christ to inspire all with the means of deliverance.

I say to all who are so inspired, be not bound by the money beast! Freely ye have received, freely give.[6] Therefore, let the world have what God has given you for healing. Minister to the poor in spirit and the broken in body.

Some have promised to give and have been taken aside by their desire for wealth or money. Blessed hearts, millions are dying. Give and give again that you might be emptied—that you might be filled of the Spirit and renewed to give again.

Did it ever occur to you, beloved, that God may have given to you a gift of healing or a knowledge because it is meet, for your karma demands that you serve life even as you may have done disservice to life in the past? Count every blessing, then, and talent and even genius as opportunity to make all things right.

I desire to see you free, even free from the desire to heal. I desire to see you become instruments of whatever light and love

God would deliver through you. Thus, a little bit of nonattachment would liberate you to know the highest calling of your life.

In the purest heart of my Son Jesus, I extend to you the light—truly the light that is the answer to every need and call. Sent by the Father this day, I seal you in the will of God, the wholeness of God, and his never-failing compassion.

As I am one with Raphael, we establish, then, a circle of fire about you if you receive us, that our angels might better minister unto you and through you alway.

So when you are ready, may the Holy Spirit deliver unto you gifts of healing—freely received, freely given in his name.

"The Summit Lighthouse Sheds Its Radiance O'er All the World to Manifest as Pearls of Wisdom." These dictations by Archangel Raphael and Mother Mary were **delivered** through the Messenger of the Great White Brotherhood Elizabeth Clare Prophet on **Sunday, February 8, 1987,** at the Whole Life Expo at the Pasadena Hilton, Pasadena, California. The Messenger conducted a 4-hour "Self-Healing Workshop" prior to the dictations. (**1**) Josh. 24:15. (**2**) **God is no respecter of persons**. Deut. 10:17; II Sam. 14:14; Acts 10:34; Rom. 2:11; Eph. 6:9; Col. 3:25; I Pet. 1:17. (**3**) Gen. 25:27–34; Heb. 12:16, 17. (**4**) **Touching the garment**. Matt. 9:20–22; 14:35, 36; Mark 5:25–34; 6:56; Luke 8:43–48. (**5**) Jude 4; Eph. 6:12. (**6**) Matt. 10:8.

THE RADIANT WORD

"EYES RIGHT"

Excerpt from a Pearl of Wisdom by Beloved Mother Mary, October 23, 1959

. . . You may or may not know that your physical eyes tell a great story about your individualization with its many past experiences. The military expression "eyes right" is one of the few that has always intrigued me when contacting the many soldiers who have called upon me. It is very good taken as a command from the Presence to persist in seeing only right and truth.

Dear ones, everything you have ever beheld tells its story as it was recorded in your eyes, for most of you know that much can be revealed by looking into the eyes of another. Would it not be well, therefore, for us to engage ourselves in a cooperative service for the purification of each chela's own world?

Give me your attention daily and, as you stand before your mirror, call and ask me to purify all your past perceptions of imperfection. Then, after your call, see your eyes as I do—as blessed orbs of luminous beauty, veritable windows of the soul through which God can gaze joyfully upon all his creation and see the perfection that Light has placed there right behind the screen of appearances.

Vest all men with heaven's holy orders, for what you see in others appears more readily in yourselves. And this that you do for them, each one, is done for me.

As the cosmic law permits, I shall call directly to your own beloved I AM Presence which sees in secret. And the Presence, you may be sure, shall reward you openly by the gift of clearer vision—physical, mental, and spiritual.

The transmutation of your threefold vision will so enhance the power thereof that those seeing you will perceive God, the I AM Presence, shining in your eyes. And by this perception the grace of God shall flow to them also (which oft occurred, according to legend, in the lives of many of the saints), thus transforming those on whom you fix your gaze from glory to glory as the power of God expands its grace to flash forth the greater light of the All-Seeing Eye directly from your own I AM Presence.

Another suggested decree for use by our gracious readers—this one from beloved Morya El—follows:

In the name of my own beloved I AM Presence, I decree:

O "I AM Eye" within my soul
  Help me to see like Thee
May I behold the Perfect Plan
  Whose Power sets all free!

No double vision fills my sight
  The way is pure and clear
I AM the viewer of the Light
  The Christ of all appears!

I AM the Eye that God does use
  To see the Plan Divine
Right here on earth His way I choose
  His concept I make mine!

O loving Christ thou living Light
  Help me to keep thy trust
I AM thy concept ever right
  So "see" like Thee I must!

Pearls of Wisdom®
published by The Summit Lighthouse
Vol. 30 No. 8 *The Beloved Goddess of Liberty* *February 22, 1987*

The Tent of the LORD

And so the LORD's servant does come.

And I AM the Goddess of Liberty.

Thus, my face [is] to the Sun and to the Son of God yet beholding the Dark Night of the Spirit descending upon America—once "the beautiful." Blessed hearts, it is difficult for me to dictate to you in this hour. Thus, the difficulty is reflected in a silence requested.

Beloved ones, we the Lords of Karma are engaged in this very moment in the deliberation concerning the karmic weights in the earth. Saint Germain, besides going up and down the land, has been present, pleading before us as always. Our counsels reflect those of the Cosmic Council, of the Four and Twenty Elders who surround the great white throne of grace.

Therefore, with one track upon the moment-by-moment events and eventualities and the other that I extend to you by the LORD's servant, so I must deliver to you, beloved, an understanding of the burden of Saint Germain, though he has received the balancing of that karma made [incurred] by those who have received the gift of his dispensations.

Beloved, there is an intercession that he cannot make. And this I would speak of. It is the weight, as though it would burst, of the fallen ones themselves. Neither the Knight Commander nor the Lords of Karma nor the Lord of the World may mitigate or stand between the fallen ones and their own descending karma.

What does keep, then, this karma from becoming physical? I will tell you. It [what keeps it from becoming physical] is like a giant tent the size of the nation. And the light of the Lightbearers becomes like a mighty fan; and therefore as the light is held by the Lightbearers, this tent is billowed up. And as it is held up, as one would say, by the wind of the Holy Spirit of the embodied saints, so it does press [up] against the Darkness and prevent it from descending.

Beloved, if any of you have observed such a canvas tent or one of synthetic material held aloft by air alone, you can understand that if the fan should cease or lessen, so the tent should descend. Therefore, beloved, has Saint Germain cried out even unto his own as he has cried unto us, "Give to me those fifty years and we will see that we can bring about a golden age of Light!"[1]

But, beloved, it is a cry made almost in desperation, with a tear in the eye not alone of Saint Germain but also of Jesus.

Therefore, beloved, you would say that on a day-to-day basis this commodity of karma does rise and fall almost like the stock market. When Keepers of the Flame and Lightbearers send forth the light, the descending karma of the seed of the wicked is held back for another and another opportunity for souls of Light to find their Presence, to find the angels of the LORD, and to be cut free by legions of Light who would take them aside, then, from those areas of the greatest karma of the seed of the wicked.

Beloved ones, it is not hard to see or to tell that through the misuse of the media in the "new cities" of New York and Los Angeles[2] the greatest karma of the nation is made. For the multiplication of Evil and of Darkness by the media has truly sown seeds of corruption worldwide. Therefore, beloved, it is in these areas where the [karmic] weight [for the misuse of the All-Seeing Eye of God, i.e., the third eye] is heaviest that our concern is great.

During these hours of your prayer, legions of Light have performed a miraculous service in this area [Los Angeles] for the binding of forces of Darkness impending, in answer to your call. Blessed, then, are children of the Light and Christed ones whom the angels would cut free to be not in this place, to tarry not here.

Beloved, it may be a point of wonder or interest for you to know and understand that because of the unpredictability of human free will or even of the continuing mischievous and malicious deeds of the wicked it is not possible even for us to determine absolutely the hour and the day of the descent of the karma of the fallen ones any more than it is possible even for the experts to predict the rise and fall of the markets in the earth.

One thing we would like to be certain of is that Keepers of the Flame pay greater attention to the moments and the hours that they might be filled with invocations, decrees, the Archangel Michael Rosary, and the violet flame. This, then, will put a mighty wind in the tent of the LORD that is above this nation while you yourselves go forth to cut free the Lightbearers.

The dates, then, far from being fixed as those who believe in predestination would consider, are subject to the rise and fall, the waxing and the waning of the devotions of Lightbearers as well as to those hidden and unseen forces that trigger from time to time greater outbursts of darkness through terrorism and through karma descending by cycles of the stars and of the deeds of men from day to day.

This one thing I will tell you, then, of a certainty. As it is written, so it shall not be turned back: Of the seed of the wicked it is decreed they shall not escape their karma.[3] Unless, then, there is the conversion and the turning to the Light, you can expect that the accounts are due of the sowing of Darkness by this group of fallen ones throughout America and the nations.

The day is far spent that neglectful parents and well-meaning citizens should correct the injustice and the travesty upon the children of the earth. Indeed, the day is far spent, beloved. They have had decades to rise and challenge the oppressors of the innocent.

Thus, where the karma of the wicked is certain, where will fall the karma upon those who have turned their backs upon the crying issues of the times? Oh, how he, the Knight Commander, has sent his angels to prod them, to nudge them, to urge them, to push them, even in the face of the most horrendous manifestations of corruption and decay through drugs and darkness in their own children!

Beloved ones, did they cry unto the LORD and take the word of the Messenger or the Archangels? Nay, they entered into discussion groups, mutual comfort groups. And psychology has held the day as the solution to the problems diabolical that have arisen out of the pits of Death and Hell to torment souls of Light.

The day is far spent when the people of this nation could have and should have accepted the powerful intercession of their God and come to their knees in realization of what has been falling through their fingers, slipping away from them—even the grasp of Reality and Life. And they—as those who could have, should have [acted] and knew better—turned their backs and entertained themselves into fantasy upon fantasy in that diabolical misuse of the television and the media.

Blessed ones, the LORD *will* save his own before they are

utterly corrupted in soul and spirit! Thus, be mindful, for the LORD helps those who help themselves.

As to when and how these seed of the wicked shall be judged, it is indeed an edict of the LORD that is shielded from us all but which will be triggered when the weight of karma of the fallen ones is heavier than the rising incense of the devotions of the children of the Light. Ultimately, nothing will withstand this judgment. Therefore, get thee out of the way of a sinful society and know that thou art anointed in this hour to survive by illumination's golden flame and oil.

Blessed ones, those of entrenched Darkness will not allow a golden age. Therefore, they are disallowed in this hour from entering in. Those grey ones who have failed to prevent them will see a certain karma. And those of the Light who have given their lives to a cause will be upheld if they are not so foolish as to remain in harm's way.

Let the angels pluck thee when they will, O beloved. For one is taken and another is left.[4] And take care of the little child who places his hand in thine own.

Thus, beloved, consider the vastness of planetary cycles and the future of the I AM Race. And consider that the LORD GOD* has decreed this day:

> Lo! I have sent mine own Son Jesus the Saviour and living Christ. And they have not received him nor become like him nor assimilated his Body and his Blood. Therefore, they are judged for having not received Me in the Person of my Son.
>
> Woe! to the false pastors and false shepherds who have led the children of Light astray. I, the LORD GOD, declare this day: They are cut free from you by my legions of Light!
>
> I have sent my angels to deliver my children from the grasp of the coward and the betrayer who has failed to accept the Christ-standard in himself and has become worse than a blind leader of the blind—yea, a betrayer of my Son in these little ones.
>
> Thus, may the Lost Teachings of Jesus prevail and be sent forth to save mine own before the hour and the day of My Coming.

Beloved ones, these are the words of the LORD GOD and of the Father.

Remember, then, that Saint Germain has told you of the

*I AM THAT I AM ELOHIM

increase of Darkness January 1, 1987.[5] So it has come to pass. And some who live in that Darkness perforce have not necessarily noticed the degree of the increase. Beloved, it is alarming even to the Lords of Karma.

Conserve energy. Be thrifty. Determine how, where, and when to survive this descent of the LORD's judgment upon the betrayers of his Word. For it shall come swiftly. Thou hast no part with it. Depart, we say.

Let the sacred fire of the I AM Presence now become the visible guide—the pillar of fire by night, the cloud of witness of the Great White Brotherhood going before you by day.[6]

Keepers of the Flame, I AM your Mother of Exiles. I AM your Mother of Liberty. Keep up the LORD's tent until every one of these little ones is secure! Let the LORD's tent be sustained now by thy sacred fire breath.

In the heart of the gods of Nature and of the earth and the sea and the fire and the wind, I AM the Goddess of Liberty. I return with all my forces to the council of the Lords of Karma that we might find some way to deliver the Lightbearers of the earth, one and all.

In the eye of the vortex of God we serve. May his eye be upon you. And may you follow, then, that light—even the light of the causal body and the rainbow of God—to the heart of the I AM THAT I AM.

I touch you in this moment by my hand upon the third eye for a sealing, quickening, and awakening. Be it unto all Keepers of the Flame who hear this release.

"The Summit Lighthouse Sheds Its Radiance O'er All the World to Manifest as Pearls of Wisdom." This dictation by the Goddess of Liberty was **delivered** through the Messenger of the Great White Brotherhood Elizabeth Clare Prophet on **Sunday, February 8, 1987,** at the Los Angeles Airport Hilton, Los Angeles, California. (**1**) Saint Germain, February 7, 1987, "The Pillar of Violet Flame," 1987 *Pearls of Wisdom,* vol. 30, no. 6, p. 95. (**2**) **"New cities."** In quatrain VI.97, Nostradamus predicts what seems to be a nuclear attack upon the "great new city"—interpreted by some to mean New York City. In quatrains I.87 and X.49, he describes earthquakes around the "new city"—possibly New York or Los Angeles. (See *Saint Germain On Prophecy,* pp. 96–100 and 143–51, Book Two.) Here the Goddess of Liberty reveals that in reference to the misuse of the third-eye (New York) and seat-of-the-soul (Los Angeles) chakras of the nation, both cities can be termed the "new city." This, however, does not clarify which of the two (or whether both) cities are indicated by Nostradamus in his several prophecies. (**3**) I Thess. 5:3. (**4**) Matt. 24:40, 41; Luke 17:34–36. (**5**) Saint Germain, "The Pillar of Violet Flame," p. 92. (**6**) Exod. 13:21, 22; Num. 14:14; Neh. 9:12, 19; Ps. 78:14.

THE RADIANT WORD

"God Has Decided to Save the Earth!"

Given in Washington, D.C., July 4, 1976
by the Beloved Goddess of Liberty

. . . When you feel homesick for our bands, when you feel joy, when you hear our footsteps in the way but it seems that you cannot quite reach us, rise up on your tiptoes and reach a little farther. For we really are no farther than your highest aspirations, your innermost dreams, your prayers to God, your hope for the children, your love for America and her people.

We are in your dreams and in your loves. We are in your longing. We are in your decrees. We are very much a part—and so when light as cosmic lightning strikes upon your soul with the blessing of the Comforter and of celestial sons and daughters, feel touched and know that heaven is very near. And heaven by so many manifestations confirms its love for you.

I stand on that island waiting for those who would walk through the open door of my heart. I have sent joy and love and the promise of freedom to generations—so many who have had the dream, the dream of the Great White Brotherhood. All love me, all place their trust in me. And yet the sternness of my face reveals the discipline of grace, of feminine principle and the seriousness of the hour.

I come from the God Star Sirius this night. I come from where the deliberations of the Four and Twenty Elders concerning all manifestations of earth are underway. And, one and all, I hear them say: "God has decided to save the earth." Simple words—words given to a child.

I am that child. I am the child of Liberty. I adore Liberty, I live in Liberty, and I send forth Liberty to all. Before the almighty ones, I am but a child and so these simple words are enough for me. I live in the comfort of the LORD God of Hosts. I am nestled in his Cosmos. I am secure in starlight, in sunshine, in the wind and in the rain. I am secure because God made me and because I know he is in me.

Let these lessons be taught to young and old alike. Let them be spread abroad throughout the land. Let them be repeated as the report from the Lords of Karma. We could tell you of the intricacies of the plan, but then if you would gaze upon the rose and enjoy the rose, you would really rather not know, for the moment, the intricacies of the plan.

Someday and somewhere you will know, but suffice it to be that God has decided to save the earth. And when you ask how and why and where and who, the answer is: "Through you!"

My love to you. My wisdom to you. And all of my power, yours to command. Let us see now what the Lords of Karma can do to draw you into that starry light, that focus of the Son of God. Let us see what the Lords of Karma will do as we see once again what you will do when you go forth in the flame of Victory.

Take the torch from my heart. Will you carry it for me? . . .

And now the curtain is drawn on the bicentennial celebration of the Ascended Masters and their chelas. And now all is sealed within you by our love. Go forth in love. Live in the love of the Mother and the Spirit, the Son and the Father. Be sealed, be healed, be made whole, and through you see how America and the world will also be made whole.

Children of the Sun, Children of the Sun, Children of the Sun, we are indeed one.

Pearls of Wisdom®
published by The Summit Lighthouse

Vol. 30 No. 9 *Beloved Archangel Uriel, Sanat Kumara, Enoch, and Lanello* *March 1, 1987*

The LORD's Descent with Ten Thousand of His Saints!

Joyous Hearts of the Central Sun—
Not Alone Children but Sons and Daughters of the Sun:

I AM Uriel Archangel! I stand in the midst of a holy people, even as I stand in the Presence of God.

Lo! I AM come. And lo, above this city and vortex of light, that from the beginning was pillars of fire of Alpha and Omega, descends the LORD Sanat Kumara with, indeed, ten thousand of his saints.[1] Lo! they descend. And the witness on this august occasion is none other than your own beloved father Enoch.

Therefore, I stand here before this altar, and Enoch to my right. Our heads are raised on high, for we gaze upon this phenomenon of the descent of the LORD with ten thousand of his saints. Beloved, it is appropriate to greet them with shouts of acclamation and "Hail!" Leap, then, to touch the hem of their garments! [24-sec. standing ovation with joyous shouts]

May you, then, be seated as I tell you of the purpose of their coming.

Lo! he does come, and that for judgment. To this end, beloved, the hour has turned and the cycle for a golden age and the sweeping of a planet, ere it descend. Thus, if the judgment come not, the golden age shall not appear.

Blessed hearts, as this very area and these two cities lie on an ancient focus of a fiery coil of light, so I say, these two centers are become now twin pillars—able, if ye will it so, to so contain the descent of the LORD's judgment that in fact, and in no other area could it be so predicted, the Lightbearers of the city may hold the light and contain the judgment that this may take place for the clearing of the city and the area that does indeed represent the white fire core of North America.

Thus, with a fiery vortex the light does descend in anticipation of the release of the fourteen-month cycle of Serapis Bey in seven days. Blessed hearts, understand the geometry, understand the formula of God—that by grace this judgment descends where it need not cause earthquake or cataclysm, whether in the earth, the economy or the psyche of souls, but rather might be the plucking out of the tares from the wheat, the binding of the seed of the wicked and the seizing of astral hordes that would steal the light of sacred fire.

Blessed ones, this day of judgment could not be held back. Yet, by the intercession of Keepers of the Flame and saints above, this judgment is not nationwide or continentwide but rather confined to an area of containment. For should it descend, beloved, upon the nation, many would fall and the Darkness should be far more grave!

Thus, beloved, for the purity that is held, for the fiery coil of light sustaining the ancient record of purity here, it may come to pass that in response to the descent of the judgment begun here, Keepers of the Flame worldwide *shall* pour down a rain of violet flame and calls to Astrea in order that the effect of this judgment might be peaceful change without upheaval.

Mind you, beloved, this is a fire that is intense and even of the wrath of God. It could not be turned back, for the people in a planetary sense have neglected their God and failed to respond to Saint Germain.

Blessed ones, your Knight Commander is most solemn in this hour, as is beloved Jesus the LORD. And he does summon angels to brace, then, the earth and elemental life and to enfold you who have indeed accepted at inner levels the responsibility for holding the balance in this hour.

Therefore, beloved, as this becomes the place of the instigation of the descent of Light for the binding of the Watcher and the Fallen One and even for the chastisement of the righteous, so it is the LORD's intent that the victorious outcome might expand in rings of light as many are wakened through the quickening power of God, as many come to understand that the purpose of this judgment as the Day of Vengeance of our God is as an atonement for a nation whose karma hangs heavy as ripened fruit, some of it now rotting upon the ground.

You have heard, then, the word of the Goddess of Liberty—or shall hear it—that the judgment of the seed of the wicked could not be held back. Well, blessed hearts, because the faithful are in the earth, it has been held back for a nation and reserved for the place of the faithful, who are the true, who will not fail, then, to sustain the Light* in this period of burden.

Blessed ones, would it be so that we might see this occur city by city. It is an experiment. You might consider it a "chance" taken by the Cosmic Council. But, beloved hearts, we do not take chances. But we must be in fact obedient to cosmic law. And therefore, we have taken the course of the lesser of all "evils," hoping against hope that while the Law is satisfied the Lightbearers might make all the difference.

Blessed hearts, there is not an ascended being or cosmic one or angel of God who could stand between this earth and karma.

To whom much is given, much is expected![2] And therefore, I say to *you,* O America, I AM Uriel, Angel of the LORD's Judgment! And I AM in Him and He is in me. Beloved, I AM the Presence of the Cosmic Christ and LORD Jesus. I AM the Presence of the Christ of the entire Spirit of the Great White Brotherhood. I AM the Messenger of your own Christ Self!

Choose you this day whom ye will serve, America and Keepers of the Flame of Liberty! For the judgment will cleave asunder even a man from his false gods and a woman from her idolatry. Therefore, suffer the two-edged sword to descend and be thou made whole!

I command you, O soul! Leap into the arms of Christhood and live forevermore in God, for as the embodiment of that Cosmic Christ Universal my hand is outstretched unto thee. And I shall not let thee go save thou withdraw by vibration or by that tug-of-war with an Archangel that does no longer allow me to enter the patterns of free will.

You have come and you have endured in light. Therefore, this hallowed place I consecrate as a haven of safety, as a place sealed on the very line of property. And therefore, should anything foul or unclean assail thee as, lo, the angels of the LORD come to bind all that is not of the Light in this city, I say, then, come into this Home of Light. For this place and this alone I now guard as a pillar of fire, as a light extended. So let it be known that Keepers of the Flame of this city have a place of refuge.

Blessed hearts, ye are blessed when ye are in the eye of God but more so when the eye of God is in thee. Let it be, then, a complete circle of devotion that fears not to ascend to his throne, as Enoch was so taken even by our bands.[3] And fear not this descent of the LORD this night. For I tell you, the judgment is a liberation of those who love the Law of God. And it is a removal

*the Light as the Divine Decree and as the Christ consciousness

of those who have defiled it from the beginning unto the end. Let America, then, be free because a remnant in this city have stood and still stand.

Remember, beloved, that in the eye of the vortex is peace and safety,[4] and often on the periphery there is turmoil and chaos and old night. Thus, do not envy those of other cities where the darkness hangs so heavy but the judgment will not come until men, so burdened by karma, are pained and cry out for the judgment to descend, almost as they would rather know death than suffer in agony.

Blessed hearts, there is indeed something to be said for the lightning storm and thunder descending at spiritual realms—for the aftermath of the clearing of the air.

Thus, elemental life, go, then, to the four corners of this city! Go, then! And now hold the mighty sheet of the LORD. And at the sign of Sanat Kumara, so begin then to tremble the sheet until the shaking and the quaking of the earth does force the demons to be delivered out of the earth, out of the water, out of the air, out of their tampering with the nuclear fire.

So, the LORD Sanat Kumara does declare! Hear him as he does cry out:

Beloved Sanat Kumara

Let the Glory of the LORD Descend!

O legions of the Central Sun, I, the Ancient of Days, decree it so. Affirming the Word in the Beginning, I affirm it in the Ending: I AM the Ancient of Days come to deliver my own!

So, let the glory of the LORD descend now, O ye hosts! Now let the glory descend! And let this light be for the sealing of my saints and the binding of the untoward ones who are indeed the spoilers in the earth from the beginning.

And there was silence in heaven, as before the coming of the great notable Day of the LORD. And after the silence, so the thunder. And after the thunder, the rain, and in the midst of the rain, the lightning. And God does touch the earth with his rod.

Now you will see in the atmosphere over this place the full-gathered momentum of light of the Retreat of the Resurrection Spiral.[5] It is sealed in a sphere. It shall multiply your own effort. Intercede, then, if ye will, O Lightbearers, on behalf of a City Foursquare, a nation, a continent. Intercede, then, and know the great geometry of thy God, who shall take up all light ever released in decree or dictation, initiation and love by the Messengers and staff and Keepers of the Flame of La Tourelle.

The forcefield of Omega shall not be superimposed over this building. Nor shall its atoms be endowed with this momentum of the Spirit of the Resurrection. But unto thy heart the momentum shall be, in this scintillating sphere of light, the power to effect local and worldwide change, multiplied in every decree and call that you offer.

Thus, offer it in thine own name—the inner name and the white cube. Offer it in the name of thy God for Saint Germain and a people who must, *must* have opportunity to know him.

This I decree for America, for I AM the Ancient of Days. I AM he that sitteth upon the throne, even the great white throne.[6] And I decree, this people must—they *must* have the opportunity in the name of divine justice to know Saint Germain! I, Sanat Kumara, have decreed this! And upon you is a light and a mantle of beloved Portia and Lady Venus. May the Divine Mother upon you clear the way with the Messenger and angels for this nation to know their God of Freedom, to know their God and live!

I will leave no stone unturned to reach for the Lightbearer and the wayfarer and the pilgrim. I, Sanat Kumara, vow to do it through *you* if you will open your hearts and chakras unto me.

So, shall the pity be not a tear in the eye of Saint Germain or Jesus or any angel or elemental that a soul was lost for having not heard the name Saint Germain or of the light of violet fire or of the means to avert world calamity. Let it now be shouted from the housetops. Let it be broadcast. And let there be an opening of hearts.

I come, then, for the initiation of hearts. I spare you, then, the intense fire but allow a gentle process of gradual cleansing for those who have not yet cleansed or cleared or even begun to expand that threefold flame as they should, though they have tarried long in our service.

I have compassion for thee, my beloved. I would that ye could swiftly expand that flame. Understand, beloved, with each microscopic increment of increase of the threefold flame, every cell and atom of the body and the four lower bodies must suffer a period of adjustment. I give you this teaching, beloved, that you might understand that the Divine Mother within you does indeed experience pain and travail.

Condemn not oneself. Fear not to advance. Fear not that the flame must expel from within those cells karma, misqualified substance. If ye would have the light expand to the plane of the Son of God in your heart, O Lightbearers, ye must understand the 'all-chemistry' of God!

Thus, groan not when the adjustments come within the four lower bodies but cry unto God and say, "O LORD, expand my narrow room! Expand my narrow room!" And thus, the room of the cells and the organs will be expanded. Debris comes to the surface. Let it be swept, then, by violet flame.

Understand when you enter this path, beloved, it is indeed climbing Everest and more. You cannot turn back. You cannot decelerate. Even to look down may cause a precipitous fall. This is the way of immortality and the Ruby Ray. *This is the path of the Sacred Heart.*

Because you have feared it and feared this alchemy, you have sealed your hearts from me, beloved! I, Sanat Kumara, speak to my own in the earth! You have not been willing, then, to go through that so-called crucifixion in the flesh to receive the increment of fire that was yours in the beginning, which you have lost by diminishment.

Understand, then, that to give birth to thy Christhood is pain, travail, and the discipline to tend the mind, tend the astral body, tend the repository of memory and the physical body. For these must needs be expanded!

O beloved, growing pains are upon children and greater adjustments for those in the teen years. Can you not see the process of giving birth to thy God and thy Cosmic Self? Oh, how the world has need of thy example!

The angels of Uriel shall not leave thee—with their golden pink glow-ray, with their violet flame that does cushion this transition. Watch and pray.

I have spoken. I trust you have understood a certain measurement and co-measurement of what is called the mighty work of the ages. I said *work! Work* while ye have this Light with you.[7] *Work,* then, fearlessly and be aggressive in the binding of those demons.

Oh, in Jesus' heart know, then, the I AM THAT I AM. Thy brother stands to be indeed thy friend, thy comrade on life's way. His arm strong around the shoulder holding thee tight is an extension of the Electronic Presence and heart.

You can do it because *I know* you can, *God knows* you can—many have done it and *you know* you can. The question, beloved, remains: Will you do it? ["Yes!"]

Remember in the hour when the darkened smoke of personal and planetary karma descends—remember thy First Love.

Beloved Archangel Uriel

A Canopy of Light over the Twin Cities

My Beloved,

I, Uriel, witness to you the ascent, then, of Sanat Kumara instantaneously to heights of thirty-three thousand feet and beyond this place.

A canopy of light is over the Twin Cities covering a fifty-mile radius with an intensity of a spotlight of sacred fire—with an additional fifty as a penumbra.

As thou art held in the hollow of the hand of God, hear then the words of thy father Enoch:

Beloved Enoch

"I Have Chosen to Walk the Earth..."

My Beloved,

I have petitioned the Father that I might speak to you from my heart and on behalf of Saint Germain.

Some of you were with me in my life as Enoch. Some of you saw Atlantis with me. You remember vividly the temptations of the fallen angels which had begun long ago in Lemuria. You know, beloved, that these fallen ones have drawn mankind in this hour to depths of degradation not thought possible.

Surely, then, all that I have written of the judgment of the Watchers must come to pass.[8] Let my knowledgeable ones, well-taught by the Messengers, understand the directing of sacred fire and legions of Astrea into the earth for the uprooting of the roots of wickedness and karma of these fallen ones as they are bound and taken from the screen of life and, following transition, clearly removed from the astral plane and from the planet.

Be not lulled that some men who are evil die, for the good also die. But be alert to the dispensation of the Fourth Ray on Friday eve. For this is the time, beloved, to descend not only with Archangel Michael but also with Astrea for the carving out of the earth of the diseases of these fallen ones—the viruses and plagues spawned in their laboratories of Atlantis, passed into the waters and the groundwaters in the earth to be released for generations.

Blessed ones, I did reveal to the Messenger recently that these fallen ones programmed their offspring genetically to have a certain inherent immunity to the very viruses they created. Not until recent years and dispensation from the Lords of Karma, then, has the returning karma for the creation of plague upon mankind seriously affected the generations of the Watchers.

Blessed hearts, God is not mocked![9] They are reaping what they have sown. But in the midst of this, the call must go forth for the selective and discriminate judgment of the fallen ones and the protection of the Lightbearers as that judgment does descend.

So it can be. As you recognize this place as a haven and surely the place of refuge (as even in the cities of Sodom and Gomorrah, twin cities of the plain, there was the home of Lot where the Ascended Masters might frequent[10]), so we shall come to this Home of Light during the period of darkening woes, which need not affect the Lightbearer if he remain wise, loyal, and constant.

Faithfully, I AM your father. And I have chosen to walk the earth for a time as a prophet and patriarch and to do so through this Messenger that the presence of the prophets of old and the patriarchs might be felt in the land and a people might be quickened to earlier ages, even to Eden and the Mystery School, that their yearning might increase and that the judgment of the Watcher might increase. As Sanat Kumara has placed it in my heart, so I AM able, then, to multiply his action through the call and heart of the Messenger.

Your access to the Messenger's heart as true chelas of Morya enables you to make the call, then, for her mantle restored[11] and my Presence with her to indeed multiply your own call, even as it is multiplied by the sphere of light that is the harvest of seven years of the retreat of La Tourelle.

Now my heart's desire is only to be with you and to be a part of you. You are indeed the hope of all elemental life and their joy. They rejoice as you call in the name of their hierarchs and send them on missions for the overturning of the plots of the wicked. Develop a momentum with the Master Alchemist Saint Germain and you shall see how the adepts were able to use elementals for good, even in the period of world changes.

I come to praise Saint Germain that you might know of his tireless efforts and of the support of Cosmic Beings and the Brotherhood in his intense effort to intercede where no intercession was thought possible.

Blessed ones, you might consider that the Keepers of the

Flame are the x factor in the equation that can tip the scales in favor of Light. Never has heaven tended more tenderly, watched more watchfully the emergent disciple disciplining himself in earth.

Oh, how we would brace you and embrace you! As the Law compels the Call and the Call compels the answer, and as we would answer as never before, O do thou, beloved, call in our behalf for dispensations of the Cosmic Council and the Sun behind the sun that we might help you more and give more help to Saint Germain.

Therefore, as the world waits, as the world waits, beloved, to see each succeeding dawn—some with fear and anxious anticipation and others ignorantly unaware of those things that hang heavy in the skies—so, Uriel, Archangel of the dawn, does greet every heart of Helios and Vesta.

As Saint Germain has said, "I will be in the Heart of the Inner Retreat," so, many of us begin already the preparations and the pilgrimage. May Keepers of the Flame assemble to keep the vigil, the vigil for freedom, even before the beginning of the conference.

Blessed hearts, last Wesak you heard not from the Lord of the World Gautama Buddha. He did decline to speak, for rather than give to you dire predictions, he did forbear, allowing another twelvemonth for you to make the difference. Now then, in approach of Wesak, I, Enoch, take my place beside every decree leader, every chela wherever the decree of the Word is given.

I AM Enoch. My journeying by the power of angels to the seven heavens,[12] beloved, does allow me to summon the Seven Archangels and their heaven worlds into the earth. Lest there be cataclysm as a result of this summoning, let the Keepers of the Flame cushion the layers of the earth with violet fire.

Oh, what a glorious period of transition unto the golden day of the golden age! Many ancients walk up and down America—many, beloved, for love of Saint Germain. They preach, they rebuke. The souls hear them. Thus, they begin to be attuned to this mouthpiece and the prophecies of the Ascended Masters. Our prayer is that the Darkness shall swiftly pass into the sacred-fire vortex you invoke and that the Light shall come.

I give you, then, my heart, my light as I serve you now through the Messenger Holy Communion.

Bring now the bread and the wine.

Our Father in heaven, thou who hast placed upon me the title and mantle "Father," in the name I AM THAT I AM,

Enoch of the Light, bless now this bread and wine as the instrument of my heart, thus reestablishing the tie through my heart unto the Lord of the World and the Ancient of Days and the Cosmic Christ and the Sacred Heart of Jesus to all descendants of this seed that I bore to earth, even the seed of Sanat Kumara.

In this Communion, O blessed, let there peel away a single layer of density. As it does take place in this week, beloved, identify not with it but accelerate this peeling of the layer of density by the power of Alpha and Omega.

Therefore, I affirm in thy Christ: All power in heaven and earth is given unto me![13] Unto thy Christ it is given unto thyself to claim. Let us see, then, the astute ones wash and be washed. And observe, then, how the density will pass out of thy life freely as long as thou dost not hold thy tatters close to thy flesh.

Let go, O beloved! For I come now in the name of the One who has descended with ten thousand of his saints. Receive me, my own, my child, my heart. Drink me while I am drinking thee.

[Holy Communion is served by the Messenger.]

Beloved of the Light, I therefore seal you in the flame of Mighty Victory.

No idle or chance words are these, beloved. For the Noble One and the Mighty Victory secured from the Central Sun in anticipation of this event the opportunity for the sealing of the Keeper of the Flame of Liberty. For so great an approbation, I, your father Enoch, counsel you: Keep the flame of Liberty and therefore have forever the sealing of Victory.

So it is a sealing of a day in timelessness and spacelessness. Thus with its conclusion, beloved, there is the return now not only to time and space but to its karma, that ye might master it, subdue it, and defeat it.

In the name of Christ, I AM forevermore Enoch of the Light. I AM victorious. So are my own. *Ye are my own.*

The Messenger:

Beloved Keepers of the Flame, may the flight of the hummingbird mark your time and space and your comings and your goings in God. Let us meditate on the "Humming Chorus" as we have our love offering in this hour. [The "Humming Chorus" from *Madame Butterfly* by Giacomo Puccini played during love offering.]

Beloved, beloved Lanello is standing at the altar to bless the love offering. He has been speaking to your souls since I have been seated. He faces now the Chart and offers this prayer:

Beloved Lanello

"I Will Not Leave Thee!"

O my Father, I am grateful for thy care to our own. Receive me as thou hast received them. Through my heart do thou bless their love offering, their peace, their right-mindfulness, their compassion, their mercy toward us.

We, then, who have served as their mentors, O father Enoch, desire also to succor each one. May it be that in this hour all who have been touched by our witness forever might have revealed to them, even in their sense of aloneness or injustice, our hearts' purest devotion to their Christhood.

I AM Lanello, placing my ascended, winged sandals and feet in footprints that have nigh covered this altar.[14] So it is comfortable to wear the old shoes and even the old suit by way of a co-measurement with those yet draped with flesh.

Thus, I, Lanello, O Father, by thy leave, breathe of my Spirit into this house, even as it is the Spirit, the Holy Spirit, and thine own I AM THAT I AM.

Keepers of the Flame of the liberty of the white fire core of America, I will not leave thee. My strong arm about thee, I AM here unto the finish when the LORD shall say through his angel, "Truly it is done, it is finished, it is sealed. Enter thou into the joy of thy LORD."

I bless thy faithful body elementals and angels by the Spirit in me. So, it is done.

The Messenger:

Facing the Chart, Lanello releases fohatic keys and intense light. He speaks and chants in tongues of angels. By his sounding of ancient words he is clearing a funnel of light from heaven to earth in the small space between the lectern and the Chart. So it shall serve thee as thou servest it.

He faces the audience, continues the mudras, releases the light, continues chanting in a holy sound. It is a sound against the backdrop of many voices and these are the voices of the priests of Melchizedek, among whom he is counted as a high priest. They chant in the background in many numbers as he continues his intoning of God's word in a language not spoken on earth since the last golden age.

As he continues this very important inner work, may the ushers retire as we sing to the Elohim "Let Their Voice Be Heard!" Please stand for the action of Elohim which Lanello is invoking. The Elohim Seven have surrounded the Twin Cities with their legions to release a balancing action complementing Sanat Kumara's action, which will be anchored physically through you as you sing this song.

[song 345, "Let Their Voice Be Heard!"]

Lanello has concluded his inner work, dissolved his nearly physical body into a vortex like a whirlwind of light and gone up as you would imagine one of the mighty hierarchs of the fire elementals or as Zarathustra to ascend into a flame.

The sound of the priests of Melchizedek is faded and is no more and we do return now gently to time and space and karma.

"The Summit Lighthouse Sheds Its Radiance O'er All the World to Manifest as Pearls of Wisdom."

These dictations by Archangel Uriel, Sanat Kumara, Enoch, and Lanello were **delivered** through the Messenger of the Great White Brotherhood Elizabeth Clare Prophet on **Saturday, February 21, 1987,** upon the dedication of the sanctuary of Minnehaha House, the Church Universal and Triumphant Minneapolis/St. Paul Community Teaching Center, Minneapolis, Minnesota. (**1**) Jude 14; Enoch 2. (**2**) Luke 12:48. (**3**) Gen. 5:24. (**4**) I Thess. 5:3. (**5**) "La Tourelle" in Colorado Springs was the headquarters of Church Universal and Triumphant from January 1966 through the summer of 1976 and a Community Teaching Center from then until the sale of the property, November 1984. Beloved Omega consecrated it as the **Retreat of the Resurrection Spiral** on April 11, 1971. At the time of the passing of the property into other hands, the light of the entire retreat and forcefield was withdrawn and held in the etheric octave until the opening of the vast Retreat of the Divine Mother over the Royal Teton Ranch and adjacent park and wilderness lands. (See Sanat Kumara, December 15, 1985, "The Retreat of the Divine Mother," 1986 *Pearls of Wisdom,* vol. 29, no. 10, p. 72.) During Sanat Kumara's dictation, the sealed sphere of light—the harvest of seven years' momentum of light released at the Retreat of the Resurrection Spiral in decree, dictation, initiation and love by the hierarchy of the Great White Brotherhood through the Messengers and staff and Keepers of the Flame—was transferred from the Retreat of the Divine Mother and positioned in the atmosphere on the etheric octave over **Minnehaha House.** (**6**) Rev. 20:11. (**7**) John 9:4, 5; 12:35, 36. (**8**) **Judgment of the Watchers.** Enoch 1:3–6; 10:15–20; 12:5–7; 14:1–7; 16:1; 92:16. See Elizabeth Clare Prophet, *Forbidden Mysteries of Enoch: The Untold Story of Men and Angels,* containing all the Enoch texts, including the Book of Enoch and the Book of the Secrets of Enoch, Summit University Press, $12.95 (add $1.00 for postage). (**9**) Gal. 6:7. (**10**) Gen. 19:1–3. (**11**) See Sanat Kumara, January 26, 1986, "The Ancient Mantle Is Restored," 1986 *Pearls of Wisdom,* vol. 29, no. 24, pp. 223–25. (**12**) Secrets of Enoch 3–21. (**13**) Matt. 28:18. (**14**) The altar and platform in the newly decorated sanctuary at Minnehaha House were at La Tourelle in Colorado Springs. They were originally designed by Mark and Elizabeth—and built by Elizabeth's father—for their first sanctuary at Beacon's Head, Vienna, Virginia.

Vol. 30 No. 10 *Beloved Saint Germain* *March 8, 1987*

Spiritual Survival

Hail to the Light!

In the invincible flame of freedom, I, Saint Germain, have chosen to place myself in these Twin Cities of light for the drawing of a circle of fire—and that not of a nuclear event but of a flame of freedom that does devour far more efficaciously those momentums of war about to be unleashed upon this planetary home.

We shall not allow it! But, beloved, it is not in our hands but your own. As we have taken our ascension from this earth, having played our roles on the stage of life, we are now here to sponsor your effort for the liberation of continents.

Do you not know how by the Mind of God in the twinkling of an eye[1] the consciousness of a nation may shift upward into the Light? Well, I know it. And I know as well how when false prophets and false pastors cover the land with an equally forceful message they may take down to lower levels of defeatism almost an entire population. So blow the winds of change and human consciousness.

Would to God that Liberty had her spokesmen in all fields and places! For the revolution of Light must truly probe education, beloved, lest the Word itself be lost, lest history fade into the mists and all sense of a continuum of identity be taken, then, from a mighty people—aye, and Lightbearers from distant stars.

Some of you recognize yourselves as pilgrims in a strange land. I have known this experience. But one day long ago I was touched by the one called the Great Divine Director. This being of such stupendous light and of long acceleration in the higher octaves did once shepherd my soul as I would now shepherd yours. He has been the mentor and guru of many an Ascended Master. And I myself, in my love for my Teacher, was determined that the link to higher octaves should not be lost on earth.

Nations rise and crumble. Civilizations are here and then they are not. But the thread of contact with the Great White Brotherhood does endure—and the mystery schools and the Master/disciple relationship. This we nurture. And I am one who does frequent, therefore, the retreats of light in the Himalayas. There I receive students as well as in the Royal Teton Retreat.

Beloved, the Lords of the Seven Rays are fully prepared and already teaching your souls at inner levels. The very reason for your coming this day is to make contact on the outer with those Seven Masters who may direct the course of your individual self-mastery.

See, then, how swiftly in this twinkling of the eye of God you may shed illusion and realize your true being. See how even the violet flame consumes, resolving what you call "psychological hang-ups" that keep you bound to limitation and that desire, somehow not quenched, to have the last word, to get even, to render upon an enemy his due.

O Love, I speak to thy soul! Let go of all of these things and come into the prominence of Divine Reality. Let the Sun of the Presence shine upon you. Let the Sun of Righteousness[2] rise within you! You are not helpless mortals but God-free beings, immortals veiled in flesh who have forgotten for a while those higher octaves. You know they are there, for your soul is taken to realms of light by angel ministrants at night.

Now, beloved, because you are undaunted in your belief that there *is* an answer and there is a solution to the equation of life, I have come to tell you that there is a spiritual survival that you must secure that the identity of the soul be not fragmented at the hour of transition called death.

This you may secure by our spiritual path that has brought the new-age teaching as an advancement not only of Christianity or Judaism but of all world's religions. For Hinduism and Buddhism, Taoism, Confucianism and the path of Zoroaster all do require the infusion of the new dispensation of the new age. And yet their priests and pundits and pastors do yet retain the smugness that refuses to know that there is today a higher truth than they have known or practiced.

Blessed ones, dispensations come through the original founders and then again in two-thousand-year increments. This is the hour, then, that the son of man, your own soul, must rise to enter the new identity of the Son of God.

This is indeed Aquarius. Shall we find, then, the earth a pile of ash and that not white ash[3] but nuclear fallout and destruction?

Shall we find, then, that war shall steal from us all that for which we have yearned, fought for, lived for, come into embodiment for?

Cannot, then, more than two hundred million Americans recognize that they came to these shores for a higher calling than to amass wealth? Will they so easily continue to sell their souls with their technology to those who have never been trusted [by the Hierarchy] with the secrets of the higher science? Blessed ones, it is for each one of you to answer this question and then to let your life take a course consistent with the highest truth you know and will admit.

I will tell you why five thousand have not come to hear me or my Messenger. It is not that they do not fear the oncoming woes prophesied. It is not that they would not like to know the answer or have their lives be saved by divine intercession.

They are not here, beloved, because they resist the change necessary to become a fitting vessel of the Light who is the real Saviour. People want their cake and they want to eat it too, beloved. They want their humanness and they want their divinity. As oil and water do not mix, so these cannot become synthesized in the individual.

Sacrifice—an unpopular word. It used to be known as a prerequisite to the mystics of all ages. If you desire the higher life, then let go of some of the bondage and the baggage here below. What is so deleterious and damnable about the resistance to change is this—that the winds of Aquarius and the violet flame will take from you only that which is excessive, which is dense, which is ignorant, which is self-limiting.

The violet flame does etch in fire and crystal the image of the divine man that ye are! It is not alone for transmutation of karma. The violet flame is that which seals the creation in the glory of God in the seventh day and the Sabbath rest, when all that you have ever brought forth in all aeons is now sifted by the violet flame. And the jewels and the nuggets, the virtues, the inventions, the music of the spheres that you have brought forth—all these are immortalized together with your own soul by the violet transmuting flame. And the rest that is not worth keeping is consumed under the studious ministration of angels of the Seventh Ray.

I call them now to your service if you will have them. Their hierarch is known as Zadkiel. In his retreat, the retreat of the Archangel, there is the training program for the priesthood of the Order of Melchizedek.

Would you not know of the Mystery School, now in etheric octaves of light, where your own Jesus received the initiation whereby the LORD said, "Thou art a priest forever after the Order of Melchizedek"?[4] There is no scriptural record of this occurrence, only the pronouncement.

But I tell you, my beloved brother Jesus did frequent that temple when it was physical on Atlantis, did submit to the path of initiation and training, and therefore was born into this priesthood [in his final incarnation] as an attainment already won.

And thus Melchizedek himself, the ancient one who served wine to Abraham and broke bread of Communion,[5] did come to earth from other worlds to initiate the orders of Seventh Ray ritual, which have to do with the rituals of science, of the atom, and of religious worship itself.

Thus, beloved, he too, as it is written, was "made like unto the Son of God."[6] These mysteries, slipped into scripture and not removed by those who tampered with holy writ, contain keys that unlock your spiritual destiny.

Thus, as you will read in *The Lost Teachings of Jesus*, if Melchizedek also was made like unto the Son of God as Jesus was, is it not a crack in the door to realize that all evolutions were made after the image and likeness of the Son of God,[7] which image ye may enter by free will, by love, by obedience to Brahma, Vishnu, Shiva? Yes, by any other name, the Trinity yet have this identity of the Personality of Father, Son, and Holy Spirit.

Blessed ones, the spiritual survival secured by you through this teaching liberates you to give this life and more for the saving of nations from economic or nuclear holocaust. Do you see, beloved?

When you have reestablished the lines of contact with the highest octaves of light and the hosts of heaven, when you understand that the light of the temple is for the weaving of the Deathless Solar Body and you are dedicating that light of the Divine Mother daily to the reestablishment of your wedding garment—when you know by the fire that burns on the altar of being that you are truly one with God through this Seventh Ray ritual, you can afford to give your life that others might know true Life and conquer Death and Hell.

It does not take lifetimes to accomplish this. You have desired to be a healer. So be it. Let God heal through you. You have desired to be a liberator of men and nations. So be it. Allow him to use your hands and feet and your heart. Allow us to help you.

I have stressed that the time is short. You have the vote, you have the voice, you have the communications media. Let it not be said when thy tenure on earth is fulfilled, "What might have been . . ."

I have shown the Messenger an individual in Washington

today, the one through whom change might have occurred. Yet he kept silent when in a position of military authority to do something about this knotty equation. I say, let not the Gods be defeated by mortals' foibles, inconsistencies, ignominy. Nay! let the sword of an Archangel cut through, then, the knot of human karma and the snarl.

Blessed ones, remember the twinkling of the eye of God. Remember, the eye that is in thee is the All-Seeing Eye of God. Remember that a beacon light may pass through this center for the healing of life, if you will but sacrifice a single life.

You have had many [lives] in pleasure and indulgence. You have drunk of every cup the world has offered. Can you not say no, resist it, and speak of the Holy Grail? Can you not forgo the revelry of this world for the new wine that you shall drink in your Father's kingdom?[8] Would you do it for ten if you knew that your life given should spare them? Or would you say, "It is not worth ten. I would rather have my life"?

What if your sacrifice meant the victory of a hundred? Still preferring thine own? What of ten thousand? What if your voice turned a nation, and a hundred million lived because you feared not reputation or to have the enemy rise up and attack you in the press and in all manner of calumny, ruining your reputation, your name, because you exposed the Lie and delivered a people?

What is the sacrifice worth? We have never thought sacrifice was worth the mere self. We have not sacrificed for our own blessing or attainment. We have sacrificed for worlds.

But to us, one life delivered is worth our all—one child now become an anointed one, fully endued by the Light* from on high. To us, we would lay down our life, do so daily, have done so in the past, that one of you should rise to be a Christed one. For we believe in God and one God. We know that that one saved, taught, loved, tutored—that one, one with God, is worth the whole of a planet and may be the instrument of its deliverance.

I come to you today for your sakes, not mine. For America's love I come—for Freedom's Goddess.

Blessed ones, all have known the Path at some time or another through the ages. This day you may be newly acquainted with my heart, or you may have been my student for twenty years. It is not the length, the endurance; it is in the twinkling of the eye of God. It is when you declare that Death has sounded its trump for you for the last time—when you decide:

"This day am I begotten of the LORD! I will no longer descend to human foibles and thereby desecrate my soul, my

*Christ consciousness

God, my nation, my earth, my best friend, my twin flame, my child. I can reintroduce honor, for I will call forth the light of my God and he shall answer me. I shall invoke the cosmic honor flame that I remain committed to the integrity of my world community, and not go back into the shadows of cowardice and Death."

Death is less of an offense unto the Almighty than cowardice, lukewarmedness, revelry in things unreal.

How many times must the senses be titillated to be weary of the process? Have you felt the tingling of the light in your chakras? Have you felt the burning in your heart as the disciples did in the presence of the Lord?[9] Have you sought the sacred fire and known in your heart that those cloven tongues[10] would descend upon your crown that you might see through the eyes of Buddha? Blessed ones, there is greater joy and bliss in store for thee through one ounce of sacrifice than all the world has offered thee in lifetimes.

I am Saint Germain, an individual in God like yourself. I am one. You are one.

Blessed ones, what you can do to work planetary change is unlimited. I said it is unlimited! The infinite power of God *is* available to you, greater than all nuclear power or weapons. This is not a theory or a metaphysical statement. It is a law that you can make physical by the spiritual fire merging in the chalice of being. May none ever be compelled to look back upon this century and say, "What might have been . . ."

Let a leap be taken into the eye of God, which by its steady gazing will dissolve in you those things that you think you cannot let go of. Know this—God desires your happiness, has ever and shall provide you with true companionship on the Path. When you raise your vibration by raising up the light, you shall draw unto yourself, by Christhood and not spiritism, those of a like wavelength who are worthy companions.

Let the unprofitable chela that shows no fruit depart from us![11] There are others yearning to let the fruit of their Tree of Life be plucked for the healing of nations.[12] The fig tree cursed[13] is indeed the unprofitable disciple who has known the LORD, the Light, and his Law, soaked it in in selfishness, but given nothing to Community.

The Light will not serve those who do not serve it. But I tell you the Light shall serve, in all of the magnitude of the God Star itself, any and all who will bend the knee to that unfailing light of God and give it wide berth in their lives.

Now, then, the hour of the summoning of Zadkiel's angels has come. May you stand to receive this august company.

O Zadkiel of the flame of the Seventh Ray and Age, Angel of the LORD, I, Saint Germain, summon thee! These, then, are the precursors of our age and dispensation.

Archangel Zadkiel, I command thee in the name Jesus Christ, in the name Almighty God I AM THAT I AM, send ten thousand violet flame angels to this city to anchor now the action of the ten thousand saints who come with the LORD![14]

Let the violet flame precede in the earth—in these souls, in their bodies—the LORD's judgment that when the Light come to separate the real from the unreal, that unreal is in any case already excised by the potency of the violet flame.

Thus, a single thimble of violet flame, as an elixir of Life, is given to you to drink by the violet flame angel who does stand before you. Angels of Light of the Seventh Ray form, then, a great coil of light in their formation over this city.

Know, then, that as you have entertained strangers this day—perhaps strange ideas, and my Messenger—you have also entertained angels unaware,[15] beloved. Now become aware, through the heart of the Holy Spirit and the Maha Chohan, the Great Initiator, of the gifts and graces of the Holy Ghost.

Zadkiel of the Light, intensify now in those who affirm and assent to thy presence here and throughout the earth, intensify the flushing-out process of the atoms, cells, electrons, organs, four lower bodies, all manifestations of these lifestreams. They have responded to our call, Zadkiel. Keepers of the Flame throughout the earth and Lightbearers in many walks of life have also responded.

Let the violet flame flow from thy retreat, Zadkiel, as a mighty buffer to the nations in answer to the call of these decreers! Let it be, then, a cushioning effect as every man must by Cosmic Law bear his own burden.[16]

Thus, these angels shall complete their tasks, beloved, within twenty-four hours and then a fortnight. Fourteen days this violet flame angel will tarry with you to assist you as you decree and to multiply the violet flame.

Now, beloved, as you enter the age of responsibility for karma, denying it not but welcoming the proud wave of thy returning cycles with the command, "Thus far and no farther! Submit, I say in the name of God, to his all-consuming violet flame!" so, let it be known of thee, beloved, that thou art the generation who saw the vision and acted upon it.

May I remind you of one who was accountable for thee, lo, two thousand years. The avatar Jesus Christ, when facing the bearing of world sin, world karma, declared with joy and God-Mastery, "My burden is light!"[17] May you say it into the teeth of every problem and may you know the inner meaning of the "burden of the LORD." For each of the Lords of the Seven Rays bears as burden his dharma, the cosmic duty of service to a life-wave. His burden is light. His burden is the karma he bears for his chelas. His burden is a twenty-four-hour sense of responsibility.

As the Maha Chohan has said, "I AM keeping the flame for thee until ye are able," I, Saint Germain, say to you, ye are able, God is able. Acquaint now thyself with him and be at peace.[18] May it be a true peace, beloved.

My hand is raised now, for it has been raised by Keepers of the Flame who have given to me a mandate and a day's vigil of violet fire. I, therefore, raise the hand before the oncoming Black Horse.[19] I raise my hand, beloved, and I ask you to do likewise in your prayers, saying, "Thus far and no farther! God in me and in all of Cosmos is the Resurrection and the Life of the divine economy on earth!"

Remember the twinkling of the eye of God. It is the eye in the capstone of the pyramid and it is on your dollar bill. See it well. It is the key to the healing of the economies of the nations and the defeat of the karma-bearing Black Horse.

I AM Saint Germain, your Brother of Light always, forever. And when you call me, surely I do answer! For I love thee with a love that shall not die.

"The Summit Lighthouse Sheds Its Radiance O'er All the World to Manifest as Pearls of Wisdom." This dictation by Saint Germain was **delivered** through the Messenger of the Great White Brotherhood Elizabeth Clare Prophet on **Sunday, February 22, 1987,** following the Messenger's lecture "Saint Germain On Prophecy," at the Holiday Inn Downtown, Minneapolis, Minnesota. (**1**) I Cor. 15:52. (**2**) Mal. 4:2. (**3**) **White ash.** Following cremation, there remains a residue of powdery white ash. When one makes a physical ascension, a white ash may also be left as the residual untransmuted substance of the lifestream. (**4**) Ps. 110:4; Heb. 5:6; 6:20; 7:17, 21. See also Mark L. Prophet and Elizabeth Clare Prophet, *The Lost Teachings of Jesus II,* pp. 411–12. (**5**) Gen. 14:18, 19. (**6**) Heb. 7:3. (**7**) *The Lost Teachings of Jesus I,* pp. 57–61. (**8**) Matt. 26:29. (**9**) Luke 24:32. (**10**) Acts 2:3. (**11**) Matt. 25:14–30; Luke 12:42–48. (**12**) Rev. 22:2. (**13**) Mark 11:12–14, 20, 21. (**14**) Jude 14, 15; Enoch 2. See Archangel Uriel, February 21, 1987, "The LORD's Descent with Ten Thousand of His Saints!" 1987 *Pearl of Wisdom,* vol. 30, no. 9, pp. 113–16. (**15**) Heb. 13:2. (**16**) Gal. 6:5. (**17**) Matt. 11:30. (**18**) Job 22:21. (**19**) Rev. 6:5, 6. See also "The Ride of the Black Horse," in *Saint Germain On Prophecy,* pp. 57–68, Book Two.

Vol. 30 No. 11 — Beloved Archangel Uriel — March 15, 1987

Christ's Resurrection in You

I

"Judge Not Lest Ye Be Judged"

Hail, O Lightbearers of the Sun,
Angels of My Bands, Children of the Light!

I bow before the Ancient of Days and the God of very gods.

I beseech you, then, stand in the name of the LORD.

The legions of Light announce to you truly the coming of the LORD Christ. I AM the forerunner of the LORD, the Evangel of the Most High God in the heart of the living Saviour. I descend into this city to make it light.

Now, then, O hosts of Sanat Kumara, descend to this place! For the purging of the earth in Christ's name must begin and begin again, as it is meet that the Lightbearer should not perish and the fallen one meet his destiny.

O sons and daughters of the Most High, the sternness of my legions is broken for a moment as a smile comes to their lips and eyes in recognizing you as friends of the ancient times. Thus, a love tryst of angels, elementals, and sons of the Most High does take place here and now by the grace of some generous hearts who have made us room.

There is a bowing in acknowledgment of the Light within you by the one who sitteth upon the great white throne.[1] Therefore, in obeisance and love be seated now as I deliver to you his message.

O thou Most High Being of all beings divine, release, then, thy Word, O LORD.

Thus, the Great One does speak. Thus, he does deliver to my hand a scroll, and upon that scroll is written these words of Christ: "Judge not lest ye be judged."[2]

O beloved, remove yourself, then, from the very judgment process. But let the LORD speak through you his Call. Make haste to remove yourselves from the arenas of life where those who have prospered at the expense of others' labors must, then, receive the initiation of the Cosmic Christ in a stripping action that does strip from them in this hour all gained by the manipulation of the lifeblood and sacred labor and the supply—even the very gold—of hearts of gold of a mighty people.

There has been, then, a leveling in this great state and nation as oil has sought its level and will seek it again, as water has sought its level and will rise again ere it fall. For the seas shall rise and the earth quake—thus saith your God! And by the rod of the LORD Christ, *know* it is done.

Angels have come—angels promised of Saint Germain and Jesus Christ. They come now very nigh, even at the door of the heart and with a tap on the shoulder. It is an hour of the quickening of the immortal spirits of God worldwide. It is an hour when angels from above seek those angels of Light who have volunteered to embody and to teach mankind.

Blessed ones, it is an hour of a great assembly. It is an hour when the great book is opened—out of it the secrets of Life, out of it the name of every living soul sent from the heart of the Father/Mother God to make her way through lowly places, darkened places, for the saving of that which has been lost.

Make no mistake. I AM Uriel of the Sun. And the Sun of Righteousness is come with healing in his wings.[3] I come, then, to mitigate where there may be a mitigation of the Law, to increase where those who have increased in Evil[4] must receive that [which] is due.

I come in the heart of a flame of love and Love begetting love. For I AM the fiery vortex of the flame enfolding itself:[5] Where I AM THAT I AM there is a vortex of light.

Let all who are not ashamed before their God receive me. Let all who need the cup of forgiveness drink it now—and "drink ye all of it"[6]—that the wine of the Spirit might indeed be for the purging of all sinful sense, all illusion, strong delusion that has torn you from the path of the origin in Christ.

Come, then, to the heart of an Archangel. Come, then, as I speak in Jesus' name, you who are weary, heavy-laden with the burdens of life—

The earth shall increase in heaviness ere the Light come. Seek and know the Presence of the living God above you. Nestle in the Tree of Life. Let its bowers now entwine as heavenly bowers and blossoms of God's love. That place of the Most High must be sought and known. Thus, find its secret, beloved.

For the days are shortly coming in the earth when men shall cry out to the mountains, "Fall on us!"[7] But the brazen ones do come to deprive even Elohim of the withdrawing of the last breath. They take their life and in so doing deny the breath of Life. It shall be denied unto them, O people of God.

Therefore, listen well. For the LORD our God has provided a way of escape. It is a spiritual way! When there is no way in the box of materiality, when the narrow room of matter has no window or door, know, O prisoner of karma, that the escape hatch is yet—yet available through the Sacred Heart of Jesus, through the Immaculate Heart of Mary, through a network of light and Hierarchy.

Let none tarry a moment longer in the cups of self-indulgence. Many children need thy art of the spoken Word and its science. Withdraw not the cup of living water.

And there was silence in heaven for the space of half an hour.[8] And in that space of silence men did contemplate Life and Death and the sands of opportunity running out. And at the conclusion of that half an hour, many names were called—some being recalled from earth's service, some coming to the conclusion of millennia of assaying in the earth and yet denying the LORD simultaneously, those wearying in their toilings, reveling in their toilings, O beloved, making merchandise of men and souls: These who have denied me, saith the Lord, them will I deny before my Father.[9]

The pastors in the earth do not preach the Final Judgment. But I am the angel of the annunciation of the Final Judgment. My message is not welcomed. But surprisingly, a small percentage do welcome me, for, beloved, they know they have denied God and Life and they are relieved to experience terminus to all struggling against the living Word. Having no desire to enter into the marriage feast of the Lamb,[10] these welcome the hand of an Archangel that does close the eyes and the eyes of the soul in the final rest where life has never glorified God.

Thus, I am an angel of mercy—the ultimate mercy. Many seek a surcease from pain. They have none to tell them of the violet flame; and the children of the Light imitate, then, those who spiritually are on death row, who have squandered all inheritance and opportunity given again and again. Thus, in imitating they have failed to imitate Christ, for they are not God-taught. The false pastors are in the schoolhouses of the nations leading the children astray while their parents surfeit themselves in all manner of diversion, decadence, noncaring.

Blessed ones, when you look around you, as I must look and as my angels many time do cover their eyes [for that which is taking place], you also cannot find justification for a continuity of being in those self-destructive ones upon whose coming there is, beloved, destructivity in all the house.

Let the spoilers pass away as the dross. If you extend sympathy to death and dying, then how can an Archangel raise the sword or miter or the Shepherd's crook to deliver you? You must know what it is lawful for you to want and what it is not lawful for you to want—on pain of sinning against the Holy Spirit.

Go not after the dead/wounded and dying who expend themselves as the stars that come and fall and are no more. Oh, the idolatrous ones! How they yet follow the fallen angels. Recognizing them not, they lose their souls in throwing themselves at their feet.

A soul is like a ball of yarn grandmother has wound—a very large, tightly wound ball of yarn. And the spoiler is like the cat that finds the ball and pushes it down the hall that never ends: Until in its kittenish playfulness there is no longer a ball of yarn but only a finite line that might have been, and there exists no longer a coil of identity round which the Holy Spirit might gather the stuff of substance of soul. Until the Divine Mother can no longer weave of that ball of yarn a Deathless Solar Body, a garment for that fledgling soul, even as a mother does knit for her newborn child a garment. "And Hannah made a little coat for Samuel"[11]—a little coat for one who should become a prophet.

Blessed hearts, the message you have heard this evening is the message of Alpha and Omega. Souls are being lost at a rapid rate in earth. Blessed hearts, the Divine Mother weeps and her daughters weep. Weep for me, O daughters of Jerusalem,[12] for I AM an Archangel which standeth in the Presence of God, which standeth in the Presence of the LORD Jesus Christ, which standeth in your presence in this hour.

My angels stand with me, and before each one the Scroll of Life is read. It is the final reading for you, beloved, for this life.

Wonder not that you have gathered on the head of this pin in this place in time. Wonder not that you are here. For each and every one of you is due this real life-reading that shows the life of a soul—that which is above, secured in the etheric octave by the path of Word and Work; that which is below, the corruptible self, the self which because it is corruptible and corrupting may continue to rust and decay unless you stop the process of oxidation and enter in to an alchemical union that cuts you free from the ravages of time, space, and the law of mortality.

Yes, beloved, whether it is mold or rot or disease or rust, know that there is a portion of the soul that must be excised lest the whole be contaminated. And when it is so, the divine matrix of the Divine Image may restore to wholeness and give new life to that which is whole, as the green shoot, that it may therefore increase again after the pattern held in the divine placenta where the soul must be nourished until her day is come to be the bride unto her Lord.

I AM an angel of the violet flame. I AM an angel of peace. I AM an angel of wisdom. I come! Hear, then, the angel standing before you now read to you each one a record of Life, yet a record of Death.

I stood in the presence of Moses when he gave the mandate "Choose Life, not Death!"[13] You must choose the life that you have—and have gained and not yet lost—as a point, even a cradle, to receive the sacred fire that the flame might wax, intensify, and out of the womb of the Divine Mother this soul come forth, truly able to enter the heart of Manchild and wax strong in the LORD.

Uzziel, hear me now! Descend! Place thyself upon our Messenger. Uzziel, strength of God,* let the Body of Light in earth be strengthened. Let them return by the Great Central Sun Magnet to the heart of creation.

It is an hour of re-creation, souls of Light, filling in the patterns that have never been developed, patterns in your soul, stillborn. Now let them be quickened. For each angel does take from heart a vial of living sacred fire of the Sun, brought to you from the altars of Alpha and Omega.

Therefore at thy consent, saying, "I will, O LORD, be thy bride of the Spirit—I will, O LORD, fulfill my fiery destiny!" so the angel shall pour a vial of sacred fire into the urn of the heart. So it is sacred initiation.

Let them who mock the divine doctrine of an Archangel and of the LORD tremble, then, for the scroll is written, "Judge not lest ye be judged." Upon their own heads shall be the karma for the denial of that true religion of God which I speak unto you.

It is the private property of no one. It is the scripture written in heaven, a portion of which is written in your inward parts,[14] another on papyrus and page that you might read and run, filling in the missing links that the outer mind in its ignorance might no longer be a source of vulnerability to the soul.

Of what do I speak? I speak while an angel speaks to you,

**Uzziel* [Hebrew]: strength of God.

beloved. Do not doubt it, for this is an angel of opportunity of Uriel's bands. We have angels of every virtue and quality of the Holy Ghost. For, beloved, great ingenuity must come forth from the heart of the Sixth Ray angels. For we are saviours of souls in the name of Christ.

Thus, beloved, it is an hour when opportunity knocks. It is an hour to sense the co-measurement. For when he that sitteth upon the great white throne does regard the handiwork of God in the earth as well as fallen angels who have sown their wares—metallic, dark, deceitful and lying—O beloved, so the devils tremble upon the footsteps of an Archangel.

I AM that One! Therefore I come in defense of the Word in you and in ye all, defending your right to be, to recapture the lost Word and sound and light of your origin and beginnings in God. So be it.

O thou soul encased in clay, canst thou fly and reach the Pleiades? We have no need of spacecraft. Thou dost need the Deathless Solar Body. Moving to and fro in space is not the adeptship we teach, but co-measurement in God! To be everywhere in the consciousness of God—this is the mark of the soul expanded in Christhood, co-occupying time and eternity.

Endless time, a trap! Space unending, a trap! Surfeiting pleasure, a trap!

Awake, I say, for I speak in His name! I AM His Messenger, Uriel! I AM of the Presence of God. Where I AM I bear that Presence. God is with me. I AM the Angel of the LORD. Put off thy shoes from off thy feet; the place whereon thou standest is holy ground[15]—made holy by fires dripping from the altars of heaven.

The world is not hopeless, but the hopeless are hopeless. Is it a bit of quaint wisdom? Nay. Those without hope who deny the hope of the Almighty cut themselves off from Life itself! The new shoots of springtime are a perennial and annual hope. Without hope, Life is dead. See that thou choose not Death, seeking to choose it before it choose thee. There is no Death except unto the wicked. Christ has proved it. Let him prove it in you this year, beloved.

On these things you ought to meditate while securing your substance in gold instead of ventures beyond ventures. Seek the holy mountain of God and thy peace in him. Seek, then, the law of transcendence—*the law of transcendence*—the law of the transfiguration. Seek to be changed in a twinkling of an eye.[16] Seek Him while there is time.

As the angels have poured now unto those who have accepted or are accepting the vial of fire, so I would make the tangible and physical offering of Light transferred through these hands.

By, then, the authority of the mantle and the Shepherd's crook of the Vicar of Christ, I, Uriel, have come to you, called of the Father and of him that sitteth upon the great white throne. It is a staying by the hand of God. It is the opportunity called for by your soul to make good, to heal, as instruments of healing—to help others to help themselves.

Let ministration and service unto Life that is God in children and all people be your lot. You shall never forget and you shall never regret, beloved, this service. For this service in being thy brother's keeper is the building of a ladder twixt the finite realm and the infinite. By love serving, by entertaining angels,[17] by sharing the cup of the water of Life freely,[18] by saying unto your Christ, "Drink me while I am drinking thee," you are assimilated unto God, you are assumed unto heaven.

Thus, build your stairway, as Joseph did, to the star of your Mighty I AM Presence. With Christ as your guide, angels as your goad, and the Law of the One reproving you, you shall retain what you have gained by attainment. All else shall be stripped from you.

Even so, the Lord Christ submitted himself to the stripping of garments.[19] Thus, naked he stood, showing you that all these things shall be stripped from you save the Light of the LORD God Almighty and his Christ in your heart and soul and mind. This only shalt thou keep. All else give away, then, as Nada has said, "I give you my love, for all else I have given away."

O beloved, in giving away all else, the fire of the heart is banked. Let men who are weary seek you for the fount of love that you prefer above all else.

Come now to me as I stand before you. And as my hands are placed upon you, say quickly in a whisper those things that you would be delivered of. Then move on, for the light travels quickly, beloved. All must be touched and only the quick touch of an Archangel is necessary for the repolarization of being unto God—I said, *the repolarization of being unto God!* The meaning of this is conversion—the turning around of the magnet of self, repolarized to her God Star.

Let it be done! It *is* done in the name of the Father, the Son, the Holy Spirit, and the blessed Mother.

[Messenger touches each one on the head as they pass by her at the altar to receive the blessing of Archangel Uriel.]

Ho! Legions of Light of my bands, now sprinkle the holy water of Uriel upon each one. Let them glisten in the drops and know it is indeed of Christ the LORD—the waters of eternal Life.

Thus, the fount of the Divine Mother has opened and there has poured unto you this night, beloved, waters of Life.

Drink freely and live.

I seal your hearts, your promise, and your prayer in the Sacred Heart. Thus, in the vessel He shall know His own.

Remember, you have received opportunity this day, beloved.

Seize it. Run with it! Heal a world and be whole.

I AM Uriel of the Sixth Ray.

Good day, O stars in the night. Good day.

"The Summit Lighthouse Sheds Its Radiance O'er All the World to Manifest as Pearls of Wisdom."
This dictation by Archangel Uriel was **delivered** through the Messenger of the Great White Brotherhood Elizabeth Clare Prophet on **Wednesday, April 15, 1987,** during the 6-day Easter conference, *Christ's Resurrection in You,* held at the Downtown Dallas Hilton, Dallas, Texas. The Messenger delivered a lecture on "The Healing Power of Angels" before the dictation.
(**1**) Rev. 20:11. (**2**) Matt. 7:1; Luke 6:37. (**3**) Mal. 4:2. (**4**) **Evil** when capitalized refers to Absolute Evil as the antithesis of Absolute Good. When lowercased it refers to relative good and evil, the day-to-day rising and falling of patterns of human error that can be transmuted by the power of Absolute Good—God. See Archangel Gabriel, *Mysteries of the Holy Grail,* pp. 117–38, 153–62, 195–210, 236–38. (**5**) Ezek. 1:4. (**6**) Matt. 26:27. (**7**) Luke 23:30; Rev. 6:15, 16. (**8**) Rev. 8:1. (**9**) Matt. 10:33. (**10**) Rev. 19:7–9; Matt. 22:1–14. (**11**) I Sam. 2:19. (**12**) Luke 23:28. (**13**) Deut. 30:19. (**14**) Jer. 31:33; Heb. 10:16. (**15**) **"Put off thy shoes..."** Exod. 3:5; Josh. 5:15; Acts 7:33. (**16**) I Cor. 15:51, 52. (**17**) Heb. 13:2. (**18**) Rev. 21:6; 22:17. (**19**) Matt. 27:28.

Pearls of Wisdom®
published by The Summit Lighthouse

Vol. 30 No. 12 *Beloved Archangel Gabriel* *March 22, 1987*

Christ's Resurrection in You
II
To Keep the Flame of Life

Children of the Light!

It is an hour for vigilance in God. My angels hover near, for I AM Gabriel of the dawn of your Christhood.

Nevertheless, beloved, if there be darkness of this world surrounding thee, it is thou who must in this hour *pierce* the gloom, *pierce* the night, and by the cross of white fire cast out the deviltry that would separate you from our ministrations.

Beloved, the time has advanced. Space does disappear. Therefore know that advancing cycles of God's descent to earth do place upon you new challenge, new responsibility, and a mandate for new God-mastery.

Blessed ones, yesterday's Olympic feats are surpassed by today's. If man's physical prowess has accelerated in this century, ought you not to expect that with the turning of worlds and the increase of karma in the earth the cycles of Cosmic Christhood should also increase in intensity and therefore require of the sons and daughters of God a greater Light* than in prior centuries?

This is my message of co-measurement to you: Those who desire to save and to be saved must renew themselves in the equation of God. By the mathematics of light, universes are being born, suns are dying and exploding in a new birth. Know, then, that this day and date is for you a place of opportunity to expand a sphere of light.

Uriel, my brother, has opened the door. I come, then, to hold it open and therefore to stand in the way of fallen ones who would enter your house and temple and prevent the LORD's Day

*a greater magnetization of Christhood

and the victory that is upon you.

In the name of the Holy of Holies, angels of Gabriel, descend into this room! I command thee, in our LORD. In the name of the Almighty One, seraphim, descend! Let there be a stripping, then, of false theology and false religion. And let each and every soul be comforted neath her Great God Self.

Descend, O Light! Pierce, then, that which is not aright. Make strong, O Uzziel, the fragile sheath of the soul. Strengthen, O God, those who know the Truth and must step now not gingerly but with rhythm and light and determination of the armies of the LORD into the position of being Truth.

Some mistake the familiarity with our music, our name, our love-light and the color bands we serve with an internalization of the Word that in fact has not occurred. How will you know that your internalization of the Word is not sufficient unless you are confronted by challenges, only to discover you are not ready for these challenges? That of which I speak at the personal level of initiation, my children, is happening at a planetary and an intergalactic level.

Are the evolutions of earth ready for the turning of worlds? Sadly I say to you, nay! Their preparedness in many cases is almost nil. And this word I use—*nil*—is the beginning of nihilism, for it is through self-effacement and the self-effacement of God where you are that the nonpreparedness begins.

Thus, decadence and a loss of identity and the annihilation of selfhood as God are the marks of an age from the point of view of an Archangel. It may not be apparent to you, beloved, nor may you be aware that this disease of the psyche is more serious than any that is physical, yet the physical manifestation of terminal disease is a telltale sign of the nihilism that the soul herself, led astray, has embraced often unknowingly.

The delicate rhythm of the divine Word is compromised in the noises, the sounds that come out of hell itself—made popular, called music, yet it is a creeping-and-crawling devouring of the soul. For sound itself is creation, and that which is the unformed cannot coalesce as an integral whole when bombarded by the 'hard-rock' music, accompanied by images ungodly, chaotic. All this is nihilism, for it is nonintegration.

I AM the Archangel of the Fourth Ray of the Divine Mother, whose flame is the ascension flame. Make thy peace with the Divine Mother, for through her heart, beloved, you ascend to God.

Have there been unfortunate experiences with human mothers or woman or with feminine aspects of being? Blessed ones, draw the circle of light by the power of Christ in you as an oval, as a circle of being. Welcome, then, the blessed Mother Mary or Faith or Hope or Charity or Christine or the beloved Amethyst or Aurora. Understand that the Archeiai,* beings of Light who embody the Divine Mother, will come to you, will enter your circle of light, will intensify your oneness and your love of Mother.

Become the Mother and you will love Christ and Buddha. Know the Ascended Masters and you will find that behind all of their manifestation of mastery and love and wisdom is the Divine Mother continually translating the Mind of God and impregnating, then, a universe with the light, even the light of Father—round which the Mother spins the cocoon of material manifestation.

O seed of Light that is the seed of Christ, once thou didst enter this universe by the presence and love of Mother sent from Father above. Do not allow, then, O soul of Light, the seed of Alpha or the web of substance of Mother to be taken from you in this hour.

Understand the meaning of the soul that is a castaway,[1] that has been cast out by its own self-destruction of the womb of the Cosmic Virgin. Thus, beloved, there is nothing that can separate you from the love of Mother and, through Her, of the Divine Father except some knot of inner conflict, some schism or anger.

Beloved, the sword of Astrea and of my legions is able to cut you free in this hour. Know this. Call, then, for we respond when you speak in the name Jesus Christ and of the Mighty I AM Presence and Holy Christ Self.

Many of you are beset by tangled vines, jungled substance, and require much work of the legions of Light to disentangle you from the anti-Mother forces abroad in this world, beginning with war and the manipulation of the abundant Life and of technology. Thus, the violations of the body of the Mother are rampant. These are only the beginning—outcroppings of a soul compromised, yet affecting that soul from without.

I speak, then, of your responsibility to keep open the way of passage of my angels who hover near. If you do not open the channels and highways of your being, my angels, though standing a foot from you, may not disarm the demons or bind them.

Thus the call compels the answer.

Simple truths—but I speak to Keepers of the Flame and new students of the Light. One and all have neglected the call to God. There was a long period of darkness in the earth when no one called upon the LORD. But with the birth of the mighty Seth, then

*Feminine Complements of the Seven Archangels

men began to call upon the name of the LORD. Blessed be him, Sanat Kumara, Ancient of Days, I AM THAT I AM.

The sacred name of Mary, of Astrea, of Elohim carries God to your heart. Only whisper it and you begin the process of building a coil of light for which my angels wait, thereby to establish the tie and enter and bind the adversary hour by hour.

The chief enemies of mankind that are physical today are those who come in spacecraft as fallen angels and robotic creations, looking much like flesh-and-blood humans or aliens. These have manipulated the race long before the race had identity in God, having lost it through neglect of the God flame. Thus, earth has been subject to the prowlings of these beings who have raped her body and her mind.

Understand that enemies that are physical yet unseen are deadly. And they use all manner of technology in disobedience to God; their time is short but in their time they cause much destructivity. This is the root of planetary hypnosis—the blinding of the minds, the hypnotic spells that cause the people of earth to be nonresponsive to the call of the Great White Brotherhood and the Ascended Masters or to the dangers at hand magnified by fallen angels at every level.

Thus, beloved, there is a fraternity of Light. And the saints robed in white[2] are called the Great White Brotherhood. It is why we tarry with earth, why the Archangels are present and angelic hosts. For the Lightbearers under the net of such magnetic fields, created out of the misuse of God's energy, have no hope of life or endurance without our protection.

The calls made by Keepers of the Flame daily sustain our angels in the protection of every Lightbearer, seed of Christ, every son of God on earth. Without the protection of angels at the physical level protecting the mind and heart, the earth today should have already passed through a period of annihilation not seen in many tens of thousands of years.

Do not underestimate the Call nor the dedication of those who have perceived the power of the dynamic decree to open the physical octave as one would open a trapdoor of a giant cylinder whereby many angels can descend to defend your life and health at the cellular level.

Blessed ones, it is more than a miracle, it is cosmic science that does allow you to continue to walk the earth in the joys of life that you yet experience. Therefore, to Keepers of the Flame who rise daily with the sun to make invocation on behalf of all of the children of God upon earth, I say, God-gratitude from the Great

Central Sun to your blessed hearts. Gratitude from souls who are not aware in the outer but know on inner planes that your love and constancy, faithfulness and knowledge of the science in which you are engaged is truly efficacious in saving many, many in the earth.

Blessed ones, I bring to your attention, then, that even as you must keep open the highway of God into your aura and life, so there are some souls of Light so caught in the grips of Death and Hell through the plagues upon the earth—not only disease but drugs, rock music, and the squandering of light—that I ask you to make renewed effort with intensity to give your calls for the rescue of the true Lightbearers who by one mode or another or karmic entanglement find themselves struggling in situations from which there is no escape without your intercession in prayer—in planetary exorcism.

There are those who are victims in psychiatric hospitals in the USSR. There are those in the schoolhouses of America who because they are labeled "hyperactive" are also drugged. There are those, then, who are conditioned to discarnates and demon possession; and in this possession, beloved, they are removed from the mainstream of life.

Blessed ones, these cry out. And their souls will indeed be lost by a combination two-pronged of chemicals as well as the forces of Death and Hell. When the mind can no longer think to defend itself, so beset by the bombardments of the media or nicotine or drugs, blessed ones, the choice not to be that comes about is still a choice. And because that choice involves a letting go of God and angels and light, thus a soul may be lost.

There are many in the world today who are considered beyond help in the medical profession and by all professionals. There are some who consider themselves or their situation beyond help. You may wonder how a Lightbearer could commit suicide. You may wonder how it could come to pass that a Lightbearer could be aborted in the womb. Yet decisions are made. And when there is no connection and no opening to the angelic hosts, we are forbidden to act or to enter.

Only by the call made from the physical octave may we enter to rescue life, for the law of free will remains the keynote of the path of initiation and the soul's ascent to God. Moreover, souls demanded and were given free will; therefore, our Father has kept his covenant.

We are desirous of seeing that at this Eastertide (with the approach of the Dark Cycle[3] coming on the twelve/six axis of

Capricorn and Cancer on the Cosmic Clock) you will look at the perspective of some who are without hope and yet who began with such bright hope in the heart of the Divine Mother. May you ask the Father and call to the legions of Light to rescue these hopeless. For their hands reach out and they pray but they have no one's hand to clutch but your own.

Blessed ones, I come with encouragement. For as so many have been saved, the Archangels who have met in conference deliberating our messages to you during this class have agreed one and all that we ought to encourage you further to rescue those for whom Mother Mary cares, those who would be otherwise lost in this era.

If you are new to the Path, you have discovered in this hour, beloved, just how much God needs you and God in the heart of an angel needs your certain command, your word. For we are the armies of [assigned to] the sons and daughters of God and we go to do his will in answer to your call.

When your commands are in keeping with that will and consecrated to it, there is unerring assistance. When the battle is thick and intense and the hordes of hell rise up against the Light, then is when the continuity of decrees with intensity, the giving of prayer vigils by the hour, gives us fresh reinforcement and light from your causal body.

It is from your bank of light that we must receive dispensations. Not all may come from God or the Central Sun, beloved. For you realize that as men have sinned and taught others to sin, the responsibility for rectifying that wrong rests with those who are in embodiment.

Let it be, then, beloved, that those who come away from this class of *Christ's Resurrection in You* shall remember always and follow the motto "I AM my brother's keeper." The opportunity to be an elder brother and sister to millions is at hand. In an hour of death and dying, nihilism and the desecration of the body of the Mother in all of her children, I say to you, each and every one, it has never been more urgent for you to keep the flame of Life until those for whom it is kept may themselves respond and confirm Life with all of the determination and power of God that is theirs to call forth.

Oh, we come to intercede! We would buy time and space that souls might be saved. This is our prayer as we kneel before the LORD God Almighty in your behalf in this hour. May you also kneel in this moment, beloved. [congregation kneels] I ask you to implore the Father, for your prayer does count much in the earth.

And therefore, blessed Mary, thou Mediatrix of God, do now bring these prayers for opportunity for time and space to save the nations—bring them to the Father intensified and magnified by your heart.

O beloved Father, these thy sons and daughters kneel in fervent imploring to spare, then, this nation and the earth, at least until the Lightbearers can be rescued and found. Hear them now, O our beloved Father.

[congregation unites in silent prayer]

Now, beloved, the courts of heaven are opened. And your perpetual prayer throughout this class shall be heard and weighed at the Court of the Sacred Fire.

As I raise my arms to give you the blessing of an Archangel, know, then, that this place is filled with angels of the Light. Angels of the white light flutter and fill the space. They come to drench you with the light of heaven's altars, that in you the world might know that there is hope.

I seal your auras, beloved, that not one erg of light may be misqualified or taken from you. Receive it, then.

O thou Christ of each one, seal this light. O legions, protect them always.

I AM Gabriel, thy fellow servant. Rise in the flame of your God.

I direct light to the heart of each one to clear the chamber, to lift from you burdens of the heart, to expand the capacity to love! O expand, heart chakras! Those who love Light, Keepers of the Flame, expand now!

I AM Gabriel! And I am as determined as thou art, and as thou wilt allow it, in this year to expand this capacity of the heart to love and to love and to love God in all whom you meet—to so love God that you will understand that in your heart is a flame and the flame is the presence of Christ. And for him and through him in this world you must know the meaning of being a world saviour.

Be, then, the Christ! By Love and only Love, cast out sin and all deviltry and witchcraft and all Death. Oh, speak to my youth and children and bring them to the fount of self-knowledge. Rescue them, I implore you! My angels will come in numberless numbers to assist you.

They are the future of this land, yet how weary they are, how weary. How can the youth of an age be so bowed down and yet so surfeited in pleasure?

I AM an Archangel! I hurl now my mighty flame from my flaming sword! And I *hurl* now that sword Excalibur! O thou mighty one, go forth! Cut free my own.

It is my call made physical through this vessel that allows me to count also for the call of earth that compels the answer. Be thou now the willing vessel of a determined love that shall rescue my children.

O beloved, my love shall never, never leave thee. Do not leave thy God. We are one.

This dictation by Archangel Gabriel was **delivered** through the Messenger of the Great White Brotherhood Elizabeth Clare Prophet on **Holy Thursday, April 16, 1987,** during the 6-day Easter conference, *Christ's Resurrection in You,* held at the Downtown Dallas Hilton, Dallas, Texas. (**1**) I Cor. 9:27. (**2**) **Saints robed in white.** Rev. 3:4, 5; 4:4; 6:9–11; 7:9, 13, 14; 15:6; 19:8, 14. (**3**) The **Dark Cycle** of mankind's karma is signaled by the vials of the last plagues poured out by the Seven Archangels and the coming of the Four Horsemen. It began April 23, 1969, under the sign of Taurus, denoting that this Dark Cycle would be the karma of Atlantis revisited. Beginning the chart of this cycle on the twelve o'clock line in Capricorn (4-23-69) and progressing it one line each year moving clockwise, we arrive at the six o'clock line in Cancer (4-23-87). This means that between April 23, 1987, and April 23, 1988, mankind will be dealing with karmic initiations under the hierarchy of Cancer: hatred of the Mother—both divine and human—and her Christ Child; the hatred of the Guru, represented in the Person of the Ancient of Days as well as in authority figures in day-to-day life, and hatred of the heirs of Christ; rebellion and anger against the Mother Principle and mother figures, all children and their proper education; all misuses of the desire body, diseases of the stomach, misuses of the base-of-the-spine chakra, the Fourth Ray, the ascension flame, the Kundalini fire, and hence the returning karma of diseases resulting from the misuse of the sacred fire in perversions of sex (AIDS); abortion, war, and the misuses of the technology of the Divine Mother to the purposes of all types of warfare and the pollution of Mother Nature. In this cycle, earth will also face the karma of the nations and heads of state and the returning karma of the misuse of the abundant Life of the Divine Mother, which could affect the economy. For more on the Dark Cycle, see *Kuthumi On Selfhood* (1969 *Pearls of Wisdom,* vol. 12), pp. xi–xii, 10, 30, 246–54, 263–66.

Vol. 30 No. 13 *Beloved Archangel Raphael* *March 29, 1987*

Christ's Resurrection in You
III
To Prepare Vessels for His Coming

Ho! the light has come into a willing vessel. The light has entered in, O my soul. Therefore I AM Raphael Archangel, the one who has held in heaven the balance for Mary in earth.

Lo, the Saviour is come to you midst the flaming flame of illumination. Now with illumined action, empowered by his Body and Blood,[1] go forth.

I would bless you as healers of men, but first thou mayest be healed, touching the waters that have been touched by an Archangel. Therefore, I begin the bringing into alignment that will enable new cups assembled in the psyche to be ready for this baptism of resurrection's fire on Easter morn.

I AM the guardian light, thy brother on high—and now here with thee. Thou who hast tarried to the midnight hour to behold the LORD's coming into the temple of being, O pursuers of Truth, seekers of knowledge of the Divine Self, I give myself as presence and aura and magnetic field. I lend my Presence to my brothers and sisters here below.

Thus, as you tarry throughout this weekend, my Electronic Presence with you (with the healing thoughtform[2]) is set with you as you accept and will it so, beloved, that the inner blueprint might mesh with the outer manifestation and that the outer manifestation, swept up by the Holy Spirit's Maha Chohan, might be one with the inner blueprint.

Increment by increment, so let Christ be formed in you.[3] To tarry with an Archangel—so be it. I would tarry with the ascendant ones.

Beloved, the Maha Chohan would speak to you and impart his flame. This representative of the Holy Spirit has sent me in his stead to prepare vessels for his coming. Thus, before the weekend is concluded he shall speak. Therefore, with illumined action and a comfort flame thou shalt go forth. Attend his coming and his Word.

Peace be unto you. Receive ye the Holy Ghost.

Therefore, I counsel you to read of this Lord of the Eighth Ray and the Ninth—this one who is the Teacher of teachers of the Lords of the Seven Rays. Study his Teaching, then, on the mirror of consciousness and his dictation in that little book so released.[4] Blessed ones, come to know the Holy Spirit and receive him.

Thus, I am Raphael, extending warmth and love to you who have toiled and labored long in our Father's vineyard. I give you renewed charge of wholeness and healing for the mission that is yet to begin again.

In the heart of the Holy Spirit thou shalt thrive and prosper. And the Word itself shall prosper. And the Teaching shall go forth and the Teacher shall save that which is lost.

Be thou the whole loaf
  and know Him as I know Him and as I AM.
A bite of the Word is Communion in the All—
  thus holy water, thus holy wine.

"The Summit Lighthouse Sheds Its Radiance O'er All the World to Manifest as Pearls of Wisdom." This dictation by Archangel Raphael was **delivered** through the Messenger of the Great White Brotherhood Elizabeth Clare Prophet just after midnight at the conclusion of the Thursday evening service on **Good Friday, April 17, 1987,** during the 6-day Easter conference, *Christ's Resurrection in You,* held at the Downtown Dallas Hilton, Dallas, Texas. (**1**) Holy Communion was served on Holy Thursday, April 16, 1987, prior to Archangel Raphael's dictation. (**2**) The **healing thoughtform**—composed of concentric spheres of white, sapphire-blue, and emerald-green sacred fire—is scientifically formulated to restore the inner blueprint and divine wholeness when visualized surrounding and penetrating the cells and atoms of the four lower bodies, or a specific organ. As described by Archangel Raphael in his dictation of March 28, 1964, the blue sheath, which surrounds the central white fire core, "denotes the will of God...the manifest perfection for all mankind"; the green, "vibrating and quivering around all, is the substance of the healing qualification for the earth and for the evolutions thereof." See Archangel Raphael, "The Healing Thoughtform: The Crystalline Star of Understanding," 1982 *Pearls of Wisdom,* vol. 25, no. 49, pp. 461–65; and Mark L. Prophet and Elizabeth Clare Prophet, "My Visualization for the Healing Thoughtform," in *The Science of the Spoken Word,* pp. 144–49. (**3**) Gal. 4:19. (**4**) See the Maha Chohan, "The Reflecting Pool of Consciousness" and "If You Love the Chohans...," in *Lords of the Seven Rays,* pp. 279–97, Book Two.

Pearls of Wisdom®
published by The Summit Lighthouse

Vol. 30 No. 14 *Beloved El Morya* *April 5, 1987*

Christ's Resurrection in You
IV
The Chalice of the Word

O Lord, unto the Most High God, I, El Morya, bow—before thy magnificent will and thy Presence in all the universes born and unborn and in these hearts who have made themselves a chalice of light fashioned after the chalice of Paul the Venetian given to the Lord Maha Chohan.[1]

Can a single chalice of light formed by the sound of the Word uttered in joy by a company such as this remain intact, sealed? Aye, it is so.

Hearts in communion in Christ, so the evening's mantras, prayers and devotions have released, even by the hand of the Maha Chohan, a beautiful chalice now suspended, held by angels in the very center of this room. Beloved ones, it is called an etheric chalice, part of the heaven world.

I apprise you of this so that you may understand that when two or three hundred or thousand or ten thousand are gathered in the name I AM THAT I AM, when the harmony is released, when the fire is called forth according to the mantle placed upon the One Sent, the light of heaven does spiral through the chakras of each devotee and coalesce in a thoughtform that does represent the cumulative virtue, quality and vibration of all so present and so blessed. Understand that each one's own Holy Christ Self does contribute the facet, the geometric form, whereby light is sent across the universe.

Blessed ones, on earth many celebrate year after year as alumni of a certain school, as graduates of a group experience, and they return again and again to reminisce on their doings and their evolution together. Beloved ones, for every conference held by the

Great White Brotherhood, for every gathering of our chelas, there is a thoughtform; and the signature by electronic blueprint of everyone present becomes there a part.

Since no two gatherings are alike, these are unique and single pieces of cosmic art—rare, then, and kept in the inner retreats of the Great White Brotherhood. And it is we, the Ascended Masters, and you who journey there at night who do indeed, beloved, find these treasures.

Thus, there has come upon not a few of the lips of disciples, almost astonished, the words of the Lord Christ: "Lay not up for yourselves treasures on earth where moth and rust doth corrupt and where thieves break through and steal: but lay up for yourselves treasures in heaven . . ."[2] What greater treasure, then, than the gift of the mantra become form by the science of sound!

I AM El Morya. You have known me here and there along life's way. I radiate to you now through my own picture that you might see and feel the intensity of the will of God. For I do have a message of fiery blue to bring to you for the penetration of hearts, oh, so ready for a change.

Do we not all welcome the winds of change of Aquarius, beloved? Do we not look forward to the dawn when our hearts, a greater vial, might receive a greater outpouring of the fire of God? and what new experience might befall us, beloved, should we have an increment more of God inside.

This is why the walk with the Ascended Masters—those who have risen to the plane of the I AM THAT I AM, nevermore to go out in incarnation—is ever new, ever joyous, ever a sense of discovery, with revelation of the higher spheres descending as petals falling from the hand of the Blessed Mother.

The hour marks the spring equinox and beyond. Cycles have turned since last I spoke to my chelas. Now come again, I find new chelas joyous in the first rays of awareness of the unlimited potential of the soul in the Spirit to scale the heights of God and in humility to minister unto life. What a great awakening! How open is the Mind of God to the one who discovers the real purpose of life!

How millions are bored upon earth! Other millions are affrighted. Others find no reason for being at all, if in fact they have ever considered being as a state of consciousness or life or even of freedom itself. Tragedy upon tragedy that the souls of the youth have never had even the faintest knowledge of a path that Jesus walked which they might follow with rejoicing.

This path is difficult for only one individual, and that is the individual who has not surrendered unto the will of God. "It is hard for thee to kick against the pricks."[3] So Jesus said to Paul. Beloved ones, there are only pricks in the will of God for those who are outside of it. For those on the inside are in the heart of the blue rose of Sirius—special chelas of the Light.

Weep not, then, for those who weep in self-pity until a puddle of tears does surround them. Blessed ones, self-pity is the sign of the individual who has not rejoiced to be assumed unto her Lord—to be the bride of Christ.

Oh, the path of surrendering oneself unto God! May you know it and believe me when I tell you that the absence of joy as an eclipse of the sun of being is a sign that you must look for elements in the psyche and the subconscious that have not bent the knee before the living Christ.

You may say the words, you may have the desire to surrender, you may so kneel and pray but, beloved, perhaps there is hidden away supposed treasure of earth (somewhere lodged in the subconscious) of a desire not in keeping with God's divine plan for you.

You are a co-creator, from the beginning, of your own divine plan. You have joined the heavenly hosts in the beginning of your creation. You have said:

"I will! I will to fulfill this beautiful sapphire matrix, this blueprint, fiery and alive, of my internal being. I AM a Spirit-spark endowed by God. I AM whole! I AM One! I shall go forth! I shall expand—to the far reaches of the universe known or unknown—truly the pattern of my being, that in this pattern created by God, affirmed by myself, all might glory in his unique glory that is my very own individuality in him."

This you have said, beloved, and yet today you resist the One who would lead you to the very place of innermost joy. Thus, in the Passion Week when so many are thinking of suffering (this very day of the crucifixion), I come to assure you of the joy in the heart of Jesus then and now and to tell you what he has said not a few times—that "so many saints and Lightbearers have suffered, *truly suffered* so much longer than the few hours of my crucifixion on the cross."

Therefore, understand that there is more meaning than suffering to the crucifixion. There is the entering in of the Son of God through the cosmic cross of white fire and its nexus to the living heart of the LORD God himself. By the meeting of heaven and earth and Alpha and Omega, there is the open door of the resurrection and the life[4] unto all.

Thus, ye are bought with a price[5]—of not one causal body but the causal bodies of many Ascended Masters who have taken that initiation of the cosmic cross of white fire, being fastened to the cross and in that position experiencing the exchange, the cosmic interchange, whereby the lesser life is given up for the greater and the Greater Life descends and the lesser life surrendered is dissolved.

This initiation is the plan of God for you, and all of the steps leading to it are indeed outlined in the teachings we have dictated as a company in white.[6] Thus, study and listen. For by the spoken Word, spoken in the inner ear, you may hear the releases of years past delivered through the Messenger Mark[7] and thus experience today that sound being recorded within yourself on strands of light, fine thread, in every cell and atom. This is the meaning of "I will write my word in their inward parts."[8]

I come, then, to tell you of what will protect you from all these things coming upon the earth—the manipulation of electricities and energies and technologies to destroy the human spirit as well as the body and mind and sanity. *It is the sound, beloved, of the Word spoken.* For when the word is of God and from God through his heavenly hosts, when the mantras originate in heaven [and out of the Word itself whereby the heavens, and the earth, were created] and are sent to you as lilies of the field, understand that this sound accelerates all that is in you and around you, including the auric field.

You need wonder no longer why all statues of the Buddha are shown either in meditation or in the action of mudra. For the son of God who shines with the fullness, the plenitude, of the Sun of Righteousness[9] must keep constant the active flow of light to sustain life in physical matter and in this body.

Going out, then, from that circle wherein the Word is perpetually known and experienced within and without, there is only suffering. There is only agitation and burden. For there, waiting, are all of the hordes of Death and Hell who know they may devour only that which is mortal or encased in mortality—outside the circle of the Word.

And these false hierarchies of fallen angels desire to see not one son of God ascend to the Father. Therefore, they have seen to it that locked into the theology of the West is the denial of this experience in toto. But beyond this, beloved, unto those who do not accept orthodoxy, there are the most subtle distractions taking the soul away from this mighty work of the ages that is for the sustaining of the Word.

Beloved ones, aside from the recitation of the mantra, there is the playing, then, of these dictations. Beloved hearts of the living Word, understand that these very dictations when sounding in your house (in the secret place of prayer, in the closet itself[10]) sustain a frequency of light that becomes a chalice—not by the mechanical or electronic device but by the quickening of the original release of that Word spoken on the ethers which does coalesce again and come to the ear as physical sound, and does impress itself as physical sound, through these very electronics.

Thus, understand that there is a reintroducing into matter of the original Word not as recording but as though spoken again by the Ascended Master through the Messenger. The power, then, of the Word in dictation is a power that is used just as the chalice you have built by your mantras is used. It is used wherever the mantras are played in the world, beloved, for us to hold the balance.

And the balance of cosmic forces in this earth, beloved, truly comes through the retreat of Cuzco[11] and through the being called Surya—S-u-r-y-a, the *sur*ety of the Divine *Y*od in the lesser *a*lpha here below.

Surya of the Sun! Understand the Presence of this mighty one duplicating that Sun wherever his mantra is given. Those chelas who have set themselves to a perpetual flow of light in the mantra of Surya, through his decree and dictations, have come to understand how this *man*ifestation of God, who then *is* God, does bring order out of chaos on earth and restore the divine blueprint to each and every one.

Blessed hearts, listen then. For it is only a matter of days before the Dark Cycle of mankind's returning karma will turn one-twelfth of the dial and you will experience the return of karma to the earth (accelerating through the presence of the Four Horsemen) of the misqualification of the light of the Divine Mother. Under the hierarchy of Cancer—a cosmic council initiating light rising as ascension's flame, initiating as the Guru Mother, initiating as Sanat Kumara—you will come to understand all of the blasphemies declared against Woman and her seed.

And thus, the foreshadowing of this Dark Cycle is seen in America as the hordes of Death do not wait for the timetable of mankind's returning karma but have been abuilding for many years for the hour when mankind's karma plus the plots of the sinister force should entrap youth and age alike in these misqualified energies of the water element (under the water sign of Cancer).

Thus, we see the desecration of the Mother mounting in pornography, in child abuse, in rock music, in the taking of drugs, in the destroying of bodies, in suicide itself, in the misuse of science toward war, and in all of the manipulations that are across the face of the earth misusing the technology of the Divine One.

This, then, does present a serious challenge to Keepers of the Flame. And for those of you who have not heard of the Dark Cycle, take note that April 23, 1969, was a significant date in the unleashing of the cycles of karma—a decision by Cosmic Council and the Almighty One that inasmuch as mankind have not responded to the callings of Christ nor to the Messengers of the Ascended Masters nor to the Law within nor to righteousness itself, they must learn their lessons by their own karma, who is become their teacher.

It is the mercy of the Law to increase the returning karma. On the one hand, it prevents individuals from creating worse karma by being so enmeshed in their present problems. And on the other hand, it is the merciful action of the Law which does prevent that which could occur without the karmic brake. The alternative to the Dark Cycle would, then, be the horrendous abuse of Darkness by the fallen ones who without the restraints of their own returning karma would go unchecked. Thus, it is not only mankind's karma but also the karma of the fallen angels that does become a density in the earth serving as a damper on the proliferation of Evil.

Blessed ones, it has been twelve years since the Dark Cycle in Cancer descended last. Let it be understood, then, that 1975 did mark a tremendous release of light in publications and teachings and the going forth of the Word. It did also mark a high water in the persecution of Woman in the earth. Therefore, out of Death and Hell shall rise again the persecutors of Woman, and out of heaven shall descend the Archangel Michael to defend Her and Her Manchild.[12]

Let every man know that his feminine nature shall be attacked in this year and defend it. Let all understand that the perpetual watch of the hours is necessary. And think not that you come only to save others. It is for the saving of your own soul that you have found this path, and you must know that it is indeed a perilous fight that must be won daily in order for you to experience eternal life here and now in the earth through the living Word.

Blessed ones of the Most High God, I am a mentor of the Spirit and your elder brother. I come, then, to tell you that as the result of many souls of Light journeying to the universities of the Spirit under the dispensations given to the Lords of the Seven Rays, especially those begun January 1, 1987, there has come about a body of people on earth, some who have not yet made contact with this Messenger or the teachings published, who nevertheless keep the flame for each of the Seven Chohans and the Maha Chohan.

Therefore, beloved, understand that because so many have so determined in their hearts to walk the path of the Lords of the Seven Rays, we are able to receive a dispensation from Maitreya and the Cosmic Council which allows you to give intense calls for the binding and judgment of the false-hierarchy impostors, false pastors, false gurus, and false teachers misrepresenting the path of Christhood on the seven rays.

Knowing how rich is the teaching and into how many avenues of life and fields of endeavor the actions of the First-Ray Masters, the Second, the Third, and so on do penetrate, you can realize that almost anywhere you look you may see that there is where the Lightbearers of a particular ray should be, but instead there you see the antithesis.

As you come more and more to understand the qualities of the seven rays and those who serve on them, you will come to know on the outer what you have been taught on the inner—on which ray you serve with greatest strength and that supporting ray that is complementary to it. Thus, as a major and a minor, all of you have two rays of specialization, and any number of you have a certain mastery on each of the seven or are working toward it.

Beloved ones, this is a great boon to us who have seen in this hour not many dispensations coming from the Cosmic Council due to, alas, the wickedness that is mounting in the earth. This particular dispensation, then, can be to you for the opening of the temple doors to many new souls of Light and for the clearing of the arena of action where you serve.

Simply use the call of Jesus Christ, "They Shall Not Pass!", the call for casting out the dweller on the threshold, the LORD's Ruby Ray judgment and that of the Divine Mother and the Lord Buddha. Let the legions of Light move in in answer to your call and remove situations and conditions that are blocking the full-orbed appearing of the Lords of the Seven Rays and their path.

Blessed ones, we desire not to be repetitious by so saying that the time is short. But we do desire, it having been so said and said once and well, that you should take to heart the meaning of this dispensation which allows you to defend the true path and the true teachers and their students. For it does mean an acceleration of cycles.

Many have looked forward to the promise that the days [of karma] are shortened for the elect.[13] But today the elect are calling for the lengthening of the days and more time to save souls, preach the Word and prepare themselves unto the victory and the necessary passage through world changes, which may or may not be apparent but their acceleration will indeed be felt.

Therefore, beloved ones, if the time be short and shortened, you understand that your hours must be filled with a greater intensity of the Call. Let your eye be on the goal of the ascension and the goal of service to Life. Let yourselves be one-pointed in delivering the message of the prophecy of Saint Germain.

The Darjeeling Council saluteth thee in a spirit of camaraderie with all souls who seek the betterment of earth and their nation and home and self. We are forever the brothers robed in white. The acceleration of our beings through our chelas and the many who have attended our classes gives us the opportunity to be more physical, more available and ever ready to respond to your call.

Believe in the Call. Make the Call. Do it quickly while you think of it! While angels speak in your heart and mind a prayer, say it out loud—say it loud and clear and cry out to heaven for souls distressed. There is nowhere you can look today that there is not need, and therefore abundant is opportunity to gain sainthood and God-mastery in the same short time.

Bless life. What else can one do when one is at the mercy of Almighty God and the karma of mankind? Standing between two worlds, take dominion over that which is beneath and see to it that in all thy ways thou art diligent in discipleship, that when the Maha Chohan may call thee and send his angel to gather again the breath of Life and the divine spark, you yourself will follow the spark and the breath to the octaves of the ascension. This is the opportunity at hand. We serve to that end.

We send courage and a sword. Never retreat until you have fought to the last and the last enemy.[14] There is no retreat for chelas of the will of God except into the heart of the Father.

In earth be warriors of the Spirit.
In heaven be angels of Peace.
I AM Morya.
I bow to the Light in my chelas
  and to the ingenuity of the crystal of light so fashioned.
I bow to the Light of the Maha Chohan who displaces me now.
Let him increase in your presence as I decrease.

This dictation by El Morya was **delivered** through the Messenger of the Great White Brotherhood Elizabeth Clare Prophet on **Good Friday, April 17, 1987,** during the 6-day Easter conference, *Christ's Resurrection in You,* held at the Downtown Dallas Hilton, Dallas, Texas. (**1**) **Paul the Venetian's chalice.** See *Lords of the Seven Rays,* pp. 144–47, Book One. (**2**) Matt. 6:19, 20. (**3**) Acts 9:5; 26:14. (**4**) John 11:25. (**5**) I Cor. 6:20; 7:23. For notes 6–14, see Pearl No. 15, p. 162.

Vol. 30 No. 15 *The Beloved Maha Chohan* *April 12, 1987*

Christ's Resurrection in You
V
Guard the Light Thou Hast Received!

Most Gracious Ladies and Gentlemen,

In your midst I descend, a shaft of fire, and become, then, a living form and person that you might know and see that there is such a thing as an Ascended Master who may speak to you. Garmented as I am in white linen, turbaned in white, I stand very simply, very tangibly.

Let my aura and radiation enfold you for one purpose alone—to know that which you too may become. It is your decision and life. You may effect this transformation in your world even as I did.

It was not so long ago that I walked the earth. Though it must seem no peril could have ever touched the peril of this day, I assure you that in our locale and in our proximity to fallen ones we indeed experienced life-threatening situations that could terrorize an entire town or city.

Blessed ones, the choices were the same as they are today. Sometime, somewhere each individual must decide *to be*—and to be the fullness of Almighty God. It is the half-baked decision that causes delay, setback, and ignorance.

The wheels of the chakras must spin! Let them spin, and know how scientific was the devotional exercise given to you this evening.[1] It is not as simple as it seems, beloved. For the release of our light does go on throughout the service, and this is the meaning of the mantle of the Messenger of the Great White Brotherhood.

This is the one we have sent for the transmission of our auras. Even my aura could not be physical to you without passing through the mantle upon the Messenger. Thus, a mediator is needed until you are become as I AM. And this can truly be as swift as the eagle flies to the heart of the mountain.

Let the snows melt upon you. Let them bear unto you, beloved, great crystal fire locked in Nature.

I speak of a spiritual snow, beloved. I speak of etheric octaves. I speak of streams that proceed out of the mountain of God and apparently to human eye simply come tumbling down the mountains as though from some subterranean source. There are so many miracles in the earth, beloved, but the bent of the scientific mind cannot conceive that the world that is invisible is more real, more tangible—because it is more fiery.

Thus, the half-baked decision—I would speak of it. For, you see, to carry out the act of being you must have momentum. Momentum is a certain fiery upward sweep that does not slow down even in sleep.

Blessed ones, you must have momentum of the Holy Spirit to attain the kingdom of God here and now. And, by God, I tell you, you have never needed that kingdom more here on earth in your heart and soul and chakras than you do in this very hour and in the remainder of the hours of your life!

Trust me that I know. For I will paint no dire foreboding but only come with the full mantle and authority of my office to tell you that now is the hour to take the gift of the Lords of the Seven Rays, to truly seek the nine gifts.[2] For these *siddhis,** these powers, can be yours lawfully by initiation.

Seek them, then, and know. Soon you will understand that nothing else in this world has value or is worth keeping. Soon you will know that it is by God and God alone that you shall rise not only in the pyramid of lives but in the resurrection. Let your values be the cherishment of the resurrected Son of God.

You can walk the earth in the resurrected state! Has anyone told you this? Death is not the doorway to the resurrection. The resurrection is a state of being and you may have it by the mantle of your aura and your heart. It is a flame that can burn on—resurrecting, uplifting, life-giving to all who are the worthy ones.

For the light is for the Lightbearer and not the castaway.[3] And when you cast your pearls of light to those fallen ones who have never bent the knee to Christ,[4] it is a permanent loss, beloved, and the increment that is your own is reduced by cosmic law.

Some, not understanding the price that is paid for the giving from the fount of eternal life to embodied chelas, have thought

***siddhis* [Sanskrit]: supernatural powers acquired through the practice of yoga—union with God in all of one's members.

that they should go forth and simply freely give to any and all of that light that they ought to carefully guard as oil in their lamps,[5] oil in the chakras, that must be blazing at the day of the vengeance of our God[6]—which simply means the descent of karma.

Thus, beloved, you are not initiators. The light that is given to you is for your healing, for the weaving of the Deathless Solar Body, for the sealing of your being unto the hour of your victory. God, then, may reach many through the appointed Messenger or the appointed teachings so published or the spoken Word, whether on audio- or videotape. Every man may receive this of his own free will by opening his heart and soul.

Understand that some of you have not received in ten thousand years the increments of light that have come to you through our service, yet still a misunderstanding of cosmic law does not allow you to understand what a treasure it is. Thus, beloved, if you are chosen to receive light, see that thou dost retain and guard what thou hast received!

I tell you this because I am your initiator following the Lords of the Seven Rays and I bring the testings of soul of the Holy Spirit. And the Holy Spirit upon you, beloved, may seem to you to be almost a scourging, an almost unbearable weight and mantle—especially if you should receive it before the time and hour that you have established, by dynamic decrees, such a wall of protection as to be able to contain the presence of the Holy Ghost. If you think that there is hatred of Christ in the earth, beloved, know this—that the hatred of the Holy Ghost is even greater.

Therefore, beloved, many impostors come and discarnate and weeping and wailing entities—pretenders, impostors of my holy angels. They convey not the gifts of light but lesser manifestations to those who are not connoisseurs and have not developed the spiritual senses to know the difference.

It ought to be easy to understand that some go into the marketplace and know the difference between the real and the counterfeit while others are perfectly satisfied with the baubles and trinkets that pretend to be the jewels of the chakras. So it is with the gifts of the Spirit, beloved. Be not tempted nor inordinately desire them, but fulfill the Law of Love under the Chohans and all these things shall be added unto you.[7]

Have compassion for one another in these hours. I say it, as it has been said—have compassion for one another. For many of you have invoked an extraordinary light and then gone off into the midst of the world and become so burdened and troubled as to be almost beside yourselves.

It is a treacherous time as well as a short time. And the treachery is to somehow catch you off guard midst the greatest Light and greatest Darkness the world has seen and in that way, even by your weariness in service, to somehow cause you to trip and fall and not rise again.

Help one another, support one another. Understand yourselves as a brotherhood, a sisterhood, a fraternity of Light. Guard the sacredness of each one's integrity. Seek not to gain monetarily from a brother but rather give and give freely.

Understand, then, that there is something very precious about the union of hearts committed to the Law of the One. Every member of this body can be strengthened by this loyalty, preferring one another in love.[8] Blessed ones, there is a common bond midst all those who break the Bread of Life and know the saints as the Great White Brotherhood.

I AM the Maha Chohan. Using, then, the oil of spikenard I transfer to you by its molecular structure an increment of light upon the third eye. You may receive this according to your free will or pass it by as you will, beloved.

An angel of my band shall guard and seal you as through the remainder of this conference you absorb the blessing of the Holy Spirit. Thus, in the final hour of Easter Sunday evening I shall come to breathe upon you the breath of the Holy Spirit.

Now I consecrate that temple which I desire to bless, that those who will may come forward.

The Maha Chohan's dictation was **delivered** through the Messenger Elizabeth Clare Prophet on **Good Friday, April 17, 1987.** (**1**) Preceding El Morya's dictation, the Messenger conducted a 3-hour service of "Meditations for the Clearing of the Chakras with the Lords of the Seven Rays." (**2**) **The nine gifts.** The Maha Chohan and the Seven Chohans initiate the soul in the nine gifts of the Holy Spirit. See *Lords of the Seven Rays,* Book One, and I Cor. 12:8–10. (**3**) I Cor. 9:27. (**4**) Matt. 7:6. (**5**) Matt. 25:1–13. (**6**) Isa. 34; 61:2; 63:4–6; Jer. 46:10. (**7**) Matt. 6:33; Luke 12:31. (**8**) Rom. 12:10.

Notes from Pearl No. 14 by El Morya continued:
(**6**) **Company in white.** Refers to the Great White Brotherhood revealed in scripture as: the "Four and Twenty Elders. . . clothed in white raiment" (Rev. 4:4), "the souls of them that were slain for the Word of God. . . and white robes were given unto every one of them" (Rev. 6:9–11), "a great multitude, which no man could number," who "stood before the throne and before the Lamb, clothed with white robes" (Rev. 7:9), "the seven angels. . . clothed in pure and white linen" (Rev. 15:6), and the armies in heaven who followed the Faithful and True "upon white horses, clothed in fine linen, white and clean" (Rev. 19:14). (**7**) See the ***Only Mark*** series, containing the dictations of the Ascended Masters delivered through the Messenger Mark L. Prophet. Thirteen albums (four 90-min. cassettes each), $26.00 ea. (**8**) Jer. 31:33. (**9**) Mal. 4:2. (**10**) Matt. 6:6. (**11**) The retreat of Cuzco is at Viti Levu in the Fiji Islands in the South Pacific. (**12**) Rev. 12. (**13**) Matt. 24:22; Mark 13:20. (**14**) I Cor. 15:26.

Pearls of Wisdom®
published by The Summit Lighthouse
Vol. 30 No. 16 Beloved Mother Mary April 19, 1987

Christ's Resurrection in You
VI
The Resurrection of the Divine Mother in the Earth

In the fiery heart of Cosmos I am come to address you, my beloved. My mission in this city and state, sent by the Father, is to summon legions of angels for the clearing—by way of transmutation and fohatic keys of sacred fire—of records of recent history, as recent as today or the assassination of a late president or one hundred, two hundred, three hundred years, through all history of the United States and prior, unto ancient civilizations, beloved.

First, then, there is a whirling star of light. And now you come to understand the purpose of the Secret Love Star. The Secret Love Star is an action of light, of Ruby Ray activating the secret rays for an intense action of the purging of earth whereby the children of the Sun might have renewed opportunity, no longer falling into the traps and pits of old records of old civilizations.

Blessed ones, as Jesus has taught: neither the karma nor the sin of a people so burdened by tragedy in this state can be considered any greater than that of the people of any other state. Though the cross hairs of the eye of God may pinpoint a date and place and time for events to take place, beloved hearts, the event must be considered a planetary karma, a national karma. So, too, anywhere on earth where the fire of judgment must descend by the right hand of the Divine Virgin or the Son, all others must consider that by grace they are saved[1] and there but for the grace of God might have been their own demise.

Blessed ones, from time to time an assassination or war or calamity does bring an object lesson to all people that the time is also short for them and that they must hasten to bring fruits meet for repentance[2]—those fruits which may count and therefore stand between the soul and the avenging sword of the angel of the LORD.

Therefore comes the mighty Archangel of the Twelfth Ray descending over this state for the binding of condemnation, criticism and judgment of her people, her life-style, the misrepresentation in the media of this people of God. Thus, according to the twelve hierarchies of the Sun do the Archangels of these remaining eleven points of the clock descend with their Archeiai for a purging.

Beloved ones, I believe that the people of this state have always known that there is a star in their destiny and that they are called to defend freedom on the line and to give their life on that line as so demonstrated at the Alamo and in many other challenging situations. But, beloved, the full fruition of that destiny has not come, for the weighting upon the state of recent and ancient records of tragedy.

Though our concentration be here, then, the light rays overflow to the southwest, southeast and central-south portions of the United States. As the Messenger does move from city to city, so by the spoken Word we shall anchor again and again in the physical octave this which is indeed a dispensation of Eastertide for the clearing of records which would [if not cleared] hasten the day of judgment and continue to ensnare a people in old habit patterns, whether of Lemuria or Atlantean days or other forms of civilizations that existed prior to, in between, and post the sinking of those continents.

Blessed ones, this is a most necessary action. And it is the building of the fires of freedom—"a hundred circling camps" and more of our Study Groups and Teaching Centers who have raised an altar to God and kept that flame-flower burning. Truly the violet flame spirals in the cities across North America have done a great deal for the protection and liberation of souls.

It is our hope with the release of Saint Germain's Prophecy and the Lost Teachings of Jesus—we of the Archangelic hosts—that many who are wise at inner levels will become quickened and awakened on the outer [as well as on the inner] and will enter a new day and a new activity as co-workers and co-servants of the LORD.

Thus, I AM come in the fullness of my office this day as spokesman for twelve Archangels, including my beloved Raphael. And therefore the circles of light are being drawn. And the preparation for this event has been tremendous in heaven as seraphim and cherubim have been conscripted as cohorts serving on the seven rays and the five secret rays.

O beloved of the Light, let the intensity of the Great Central Sun be upon you in this hour as Helios and Vesta do consecrate your life, your community, your family, county, state, nations and all continents in the earth to the best hope, to the highest opportunity truly to do what heaven can do best—and that is to expend itself to the fullest extent of cosmic law that the salvation of many souls might be forthcoming.

Therefore in Jesus' name, I AM the witness that the descent into Death and Hell by this magnificent Son of God was not for naught. It was not only for the conversion of sinners and the giving to the devils of a final warning that they might repent else face the Final Judgment, but it was also for the clearing of those records, beloved. It was for the going in to the astral plane and the pits themselves for the binding of spirits that could be bound only at the command of the living Son of God yet in embodiment, who yet descended in his etheric sheath to those other octaves of earth where that Light* of Christ must shine.

Therefore, this Holy Saturday may be unto each and every one of you the sign of your own descent into the astral plane, as you have already gone there with Archangel Michael in your invocations and calls. Beloved ones, where you send the call daily, there you are! For you are not separated from the call of the Most High God. And thus understand that wherever there is a sunbeam, there is the sun itself. Wherever there is a halo of light and the radiance of God upon a saint, there is the Sun behind the sun and our God himself. There is no separation in time and space.

Loved ones and twin flames separated by the octaves, grieve not. Let each individual half of the Divine Whole accelerate and ascend to the altar of her God, thereby creating a powerful magnet, a force of light to draw not only the other half of the Divine Whole—the twin flame embodied, the soul mate—but also fellow souls, kindred ones, old family members and cohorts in the highways of heaven.

Beloved ones, how great is the love that does sacrifice a life on behalf of the many rather than compromise for the sake of agreement (otherwise known as sympathy) with another who does refuse to ascend the ladder of Life. Those who have ascended and left behind their twin flames, beloved, have never regretted it once. For by that ascension the one in embodiment does perpetually have the momentum to draw upon and to impel him/her upward in search of the perfect Love.

So it is that you are on earth. And saints in heaven who yet retain karma in this age are thus magnetized by your hearts of fire to serve with you, side by side. How fortunate are you who can understand that by having physical presence in the earth and the power to intensify the call, and by your call and service, many

*en*light*ened consciousness of Christ

saints in heaven may balance their karma. For your instrumentation in delivering the Teachings often does touch the very ones upon earth for whom these saints are required to give blessing, to give prayer, to give guidance.

When you place in the heart and hand of one upon earth the full knowledge of his I AM Presence and the violet flame and the "Heart, Head, and Hand Decrees,"[3] beloved, you give that one the greatest gift of Cosmos—and it is a gift not only to himself but to those ascended who may have karma or ancient ties with that one. For the beginning of the meshing and the interaction does take place the moment the individual does say,

I AM THAT I AM, Mighty I AM Presence, come into my temple now!

Beloved, say it this moment for a purpose:

I AM THAT I AM, Mighty I AM Presence, come into my temple now!

This unison and consonance is the "one accord" of those who are together in "one place" of consciousness on the day of Pentecost to come.[4] Thus the infilling of the Holy Spirit descends again into a chalice of light, devotion and faith that you have builded uniquely, each one, by facets of your own soul blueprint and the fiery blueprint of your I AM Presence.

Thus, beloved one, in this affirmation and all decrees throughout this conference to come, including the prayer vigil on Monday, we shall use those calls specifically for the penetration of earth and soil of this state, for the consecration of it once again to the victory of the abundant Life. And let that abundant Life be based upon the divine economy and the genius of Christ in the heart and the path of initiation of Maitreya.

Beloved hearts, it is time for the ingenuity of this people to find the way to go around and under and over a false dependency upon a single or several commodities. Beloved ones, it is not the will of God that America should have placed the commodity of oil or any other at the disposal or mercy of foreign powers, evolutions and laggard races, who should artificially raise or lower the prices and thereby cause an earthquake in the economies of this nation and the world.

Blessed ones, these laggards and fallen ones are in America and outside her borders! Let it be understood as it has never been understood before that America as originally conceived by God through the hierarchy of Light is a place prepared for the path of initiation and for souls of Light!

Let the seed of Christ for whom this is the Promised Land gather to take dominion *now* over the serpents who have invaded the garden of God. Blessed ones, it happened then and it can happen again. Let us not suffer, then, five, ten thousand and more years of being expelled from our own Garden of Eden because, beloved, we have not kept the flame of Life and of the Tree of Life and placed our sentinels at every gate—north, south, east, and west and the twelve doorways of the Sun.

Thus, beloved, one must have the discernment of spirits to understand the meaning of the entering in and the passing through your midst of the serpent mind and the serpent consciousness and the serpent known as the embodied fallen angel. Precious ones, remember that Satan himself has been "transformed into an angel of light."[5] And even the very elect have from time to time been confused or even fooled[6] by the seeming glamour and radiance of these fallen ones who have borrowed the light of the precious children of God.

Blessed hearts, America is a bastion of freedom and a garden paradise for the path of initiation. Let every lifestream upon earth who does so identify with the return to Eden make it his very sincere business to enter this nation for the restoration of the path of the Divine Mother and her Presence on earth.

With the acknowledgment in such great fervor and love of the Goddess of Liberty, you see the ancient religion of the Mother of Lemuria, of South America, and of ancient lands being restored on this very soil. It is a wondrous sight—and I repeat it again—to know of no conflict whatsoever amongst a people in their embracing of the statue of Mother Liberty. It is wondrous to find a symbol that can be so universally admired.

And, beloved ones, I must also mention in memory and in the coming commemoration of July 4th that nations in the earth did revile, did mock and scorn the great pageant held for Mother Liberty, accusing America of overdoing such things. O beloved, these words of the cynic reveal how nations beyond the pale of the sponsorship of Mother Liberty do not appreciate the fullness of that torch of illumination as the enlightenment of the Holy Spirit, as the entering in to the temple of God's people of the Father and the Son!

Know, then, O beloved, that the gift of the threefold flame is both misunderstood and envied. Let those who have received the blessing of the son Joseph understand their calling and know that the tribes of the earth who mourn also mourn and grind their teeth in the envy of this land.[7] Therefore, do not exclude envy, jealousy or revenge as a motivating factor for the economic or nuclear-blackmail takeover of this nation.

I come, your Mother of ages. I come aligned with the

Ascended Lady Masters. I come in the full power and the mantle of Almighty God! And I rejoice to speak to mighty hearts who are still determined to take their stand for absolute God-Liberty in the earth.

Therefore, beloved, the shaft of the Feminine Ray does descend. It is a pillar of fire in the very midst of the City Foursquare. O let it be done! O let it expand! O let the true beauty of the Divine Mother now be upon the face of every man, woman and child!

I come, then, to deliver my message of liberation to those who would be liberated because they know they are in bondage. And that knowledge reveals that they are awake. Those, then, who desire liberation, let them be liberated by enlightenment of the Holy Ghost in this hour. For I am known as the Queen of the Angels and the Bride of the Holy Spirit.

I am not his only bride, beloved. The Holy Spirit is the great Divine Husband of all souls reaching for the divine union with God. But, beloved, I am a chosen bride and therefore I can also choose—I can choose to raise you up, to place upon you the bridal veil, to restore an ancient virginity whereby consciousness is sealed, chakras are sealed, and you are a vessel holy and pure, ready to receive the light of the Father in all of the seven centers of being.

My beloved of the Sun, hear me! Alpha and Omega are in my heart as above. This is the meaning of the descending of the mighty sun at Fátima. It is the understanding of the Hermetic axiom "as Above, so below."

Thus with the descent of the Sun of the I AM Presence, men cry out and fear. It is the judgment for some, but for the daughter of God, I tell you, it is the rejoicing that our God is come and that the soul is truly sealed in the heart of the Cosmic Christ.

See now how Maitreya does descend from the north. See how he is walking down the continent of North America, having emerged from the very heart of the earth in communion of saints. Thus, from the area of the North Pole descending in a mighty V are legions of Light and Victory, legions of illumination's flame. And they come for the "Great Awakening"—as Francis Bacon would have had it, the "Great Instauration," the great restoration.

And the fire internal enfolding itself shall now intensify and expand through the bodies of this people, beloved, until they shall know their God and know Him as Brahma/Vishnu/Shiva—a Divine Trinity and a gnosis of self-knowledge whereby they may never be fooled again by false prophets in Church or State, in education or the arts, in science or government. Beloved ones, they are everywhere tearing from you the innate Christhood to rise up and deliver a nation and a planet.

I AM here, beloved, because I AM your Mother of mothers and I believe in you! This is why I have come. I cannot go where I cannot believe in those to whom I am sent. Thus, as you have believed in me as an Ascended Lady Master—one who descended as an Archeia, took embodiment long ago on Atlantis, passed through the initiations of the mystery schools even at Lord Zadkiel's temple, and therefore came into the consonance of the path of a daughter of God and did win my ascension—I AM ascended in the Light and free! I AM truly risen because my Son has risen!*

O ye daughters of Jerusalem, weep no more,[8] for the day of your resurrection is come! I say to the souls of Light in the earth, know, then, the hour and the sign and the season. Know that now is the accepted time.[9] Now is the day when, no matter what has passed, the light of the base-of-the-spine chakra can be and is raised by the power of the resurrection flame.

Rise and rejoice in the power of the resurrection! O ye people of God, feel the power of this flame within you and understand that there are moments in cycles of centuries when the gateway of heaven is opened. And it is opened this day by the Secret Love Star. And therefore the ramification of this dispensation by the Cosmic Council is unto *you,* O mighty people! Run with the fire of the resurrection and that spirit.

Dare, then, to dream indeed the impossible dream! Dare to dream it, beloved, and to make it reality. Dare to call to me and the Holy Spirit to strip from you now every illusion and confusion, all fantasies and unrealities. There are too many and they are as cobwebs. Would you be free to see reality and live with it? ["Yes!"]

O enter now, legions of Light of Raphael, legions of Archangels of Cosmos' secret rays, legions of the Seven Archangels and of the Lord Christ, legions of Sanat Kumara, Gautama Buddha, Lord Maitreya, Jesus! I AM the Mother as Above, so below! In the name of my Keepers of the Flame, I summon you now! Let them be stripped of all illusion that has settled upon this nation. Let them be the firstfruits of our coming and our clearance, which does begin with the "queen of the South"[10]—with the very star of Texas.

Therefore let the queen of the South rise up and let the light of the Divine Mother appear in this state. And let this action continue out of the fountain *now* of the six o'clock line of America, *now* out of the Divine Mother. And therefore, in preparation for the coming of the Dark Cycle of the return of mankind's karma, this light has gone forth and it has preempted the plots of the fallen ones who would abuse mankind through accelerating and manipulating their karma.

*Because the Sun of my Mighty I AM Presence has risen within me, I AM risen.

Now I say: *You* fallen ones who have stood to taunt, to tempt, to defy and tear down my children and my sons and daughters—*you* are bound this day! *You* shall not escape the hosts of the LORD, for the Cosmic Mother Astrea does encircle you *now! Be bound!* and exorcised from this state, from this city, from this entire territory marked by the map of light on the council table in Sirius!

Blaze! the full power of the Great Central Sun Magnet! I AM Mary the Mother. By the direction of my Father and the LORD God Almighty, I stand this day and I draw a mighty line. And it is drawn now as a circle of fire. And it does encircle the territory and it does intensify to the very heart of the earth. For we shall clear, we shall purify, we shall purge. And therefore, all souls of Light will know this day that the Divine Mother is come in the earth!

And *now,* therefore, into the hearts of those who have given their assent, let the mighty fire of Cyclopea, of the Fifth-Ray Elohim of God, intensify the action of the third eye begun by Archangel Raphael. And let there be a clear seeing of the absolute reality of God, of the absolute unreality and yet presence of Death and Hell in the earth—of the absolute reality, in the flame of divine reality and realism, of the place on the Path of each and every soul of that which must yet be fulfilled and that which is already sealed in attainment.

Blaze the light through them! For they have called, I have answered. I have called and they have answered. *Blaze* the full power of the light of God that never fails! And I AM answering now and delivering unto them this stripping action of Shiva.

O Holy Spirit, come forth! *Shiva!* now, *Shiva!* now, *Shiva!* now by the mighty sword of blue flame, let there be a stripping!

I demand the binding of all fantasy regarding the human personality and vanity! I demand a stripping action *now* of all that is an absence of intelligence! *Bind* the core of ignorance! *Bind* self-ignorance in the Law! *Burn through!* O mighty legions of the First, Second, Third, Fourth, Fifth, Sixth and Seventh Rays! *Burn through!* O white fire core of being! Let there be a remnant in the earth and let the remnant be found across North and South America.

Go forth! then, O Messenger of the living Word! *Go forth!* across these United States and let the remnant be cut free!

Raphael and I in the Mother flame descend to clear the way for the cutting free of those Lightbearers who must come to know the LORD as the Mighty I AM THAT I AM, who must be delivered, who must be spared, who must be raised up, who must be the ensign. *So* by the power of the Holy Spirit, let that full Light [of Cosmic Christhood] descend! For I AM Mary, clothed upon by the Holy Ghost in this hour. And *none* shall stay the hand of the Divine Woman's judgment. *None* shall stay that hand!

By my right hand, therefore, I declare the judgment of the false pastor by the authority of the Church Universal and Triumphant and the Vicar of Christ and the dispensations of the saints of the Most High God and the Mystical Body of God! Therefore, let it be that the false pastors, false priests and false rabbis—fallen ones and false teachers in Church and State—be *exposed* and bound this hour!

And let first of all those who espouse a position of nihilism and spiritual and physical suicide be *bound* in their superstition! Let them be exposed! For they have departed from the vows of their holy office and from the trust of the people (entrusting their lives to them) by the casting of the ballot and by appointment. Therefore they may no longer represent this people. Let them be exposed by the power of Light!

And *you,* the seed of Satan, *you,* the Church of Satan—*you* shall go down in this hour! *You* shall not claim the victory now or forever over those servants of God who have erred and strayed!

I AM blazing the Light of the Divine Mother into the very teeth of those practitioners of voodoo, black magic, Satanism, spiritualism, and all manner of channeling of "spirits that mutter and peep!"[11] *You* shall not have the day! *You* shall not corrupt this Holy of Holies, this nation under God!

I AM blazing forth the power of the highest heaven in this hour. And it is sweeping through America. It is a purging Light. It is a gentle Light. It is a *strong* Light. And it is the Light of the Union.

Therefore, by the single ion of Light who is I AM THAT I AM, I AM Mary. Call to me, then, for the defense of this nation, your soul, your child, your body, your mind, your heart. Call to me, for the Father has given to me a gift of excellence, a dispensation in answer to calls that could not be answered without dispensation—calls made by Keepers of the Flame and the Mother worldwide.

I have gone to the heart of God and the one who sitteth upon the great white throne.[12] I have discoursed with the One you also know, from whose throne you left off the serving of the Graces so long ago. I am come to tell you, dear heart, that your Father does long for your return and has asked me to tell you to tarry now for a greater resurrection,[13] a greater glory, a greater victory—and then to come Home.

Is heaven so far away? It seems far by longtime absence of your soul. Heaven is as near as the seraph that comes to escort you each day. Heaven is as near as the Archangel Gabriel, who does not leave off his ministration or implorings for you.

Gabriel does now enunciate daily, hourly before the Father

the names of all souls written in the Book of Life, all souls who may suffer loss unless someone will pray for them. I ask you, then, to continue to pray fervently that not another soul shall be lost during your tenure on earth who is of the Light and destined by free will and attainment to ascend to God. Let your shepherding and ministering and teaching in the world with the World Teachers show an abundant harvest, not the least of which your own victory.

Now in the joy of ascension's flame there is a sealing action. All is held in a great tension of Light and strands of Light. What could be done has been done by Archangels. The rest of the clearing shall be by yourselves in calls to the violet flame and Astrea for the balance of the conference.

O beloved, you are God's—his very own. You are the Father and the Mother in manifestation. Nurture life. Be a world mother and a world father. Your joy shall be endless and you will no longer be surfeited in self-concern, for everywhere you look are souls more needy than your own. In ministering to them, the Father shall fulfill in you every need and requirement, comfort and joy.

I AM Mary and I consecrate this state, America and Canada to my Immaculate Heart. This consecration shall be continuous by my legions of angels.

I desire to return for the consecration of Central America and Mexico and the islands of the Caribbean. Perhaps your fulfillment of Monday's prayer vigil shall offer unto Elohim the necessary balance for this action.

I take you to my heart. Today it is a field of white lilies. When you come there, one and all, angels of the lilies drawing threads of light from the sun shall strengthen your physical hearts as they weave the etheric chalice.

Come to my Immaculate Heart for the strengthening of your own. For I would soon place more of my heart in yours, but first the chalice must be strengthened.

In the perfection of the walk with God, I summon you, my beloved.

Mother Mary's dictation was **delivered** through the Messenger Elizabeth Clare Prophet on **Holy Saturday, April 18, 1987,** in **Dallas, Texas.** The Messenger delivered her "Fátima Update" (Part I) before the dictation. Part I and Part II (5-10-87) are published on 4 cassettes, K87033–K87036, $26 for set (add $.80 postage). (**1**) Eph. 2:8. (**2**) Matt. 3:8. (**3**) *Heart, Head, and Hand Decrees: Meditations, Mantras, Prayers and Decrees for the Expansion of the Threefold Flame within the Heart,* released by Elizabeth Clare Prophet, 36-page booklet, $1.25 (add $.25 postage). 12 booklets for $12; 24 and over, $10 a dozen (add $.80 postage for first dozen, $.30 each additional dozen). For notes 4–13, see Pearl No. 17, p. 182.

Vol. 30 No. 17 | *Beloved Saint Germain* | *April 26, 1987*

Christ's Resurrection in You
VII
The Reincarnation of the Spirit of America

Heart Friends of Freedom, I AM your unfailing, ever devoted and doting Saint Germain! [25-sec. standing ovation]

Now you see me and now you don't. But, beloved, if you will catch a tear in the Mother's eye, you will see my reflection even as you pass by.

O beloved, it is an hour when hearts overflow with the feeling of God from the Ancient of Days, who from the beginning has held the dream America, which dream has been a part of every disenfranchised poor soul on earth that has desired to be a part of the great ongoing dream of God.

Beloved hearts, I am grateful for your attentiveness and your responsibility in listening to these facts presented by our Messenger and the team of staff who make it possible for us to give you this information.[1] Blessed ones, I am gratified that this could be presented in Dallas and that you would tarry, realizing that here in this very city, out of the ashes of former civilizations and past performances [and non-performances] of its inhabitants, the phoenix bird could rise and America be reborn again.

Blessed ones, it is the hour of the reincarnation of the Spirit of America! [23-sec. applause] Let us together, then, designate this day of the resurrection of Jesus Christ for the rebirth of the resurrected Spirit of the soul of a people who have loved God in the beginning and will come through in the ending. [13-sec. applause]

The message, then, is no more powerful than the messenger, and *you* are the messengers of the Coming Revolution. *You* are the sparks that fly on the Fourth—and every day of the year. *You* are the ones who can take and implement an action that is needed now, based on the awareness not alone of information but of Almighty God, whose flaming Presence in your hearts is a mighty beating of hearts and drums and fifes and fervor and a new patriotism that *we shall live,* for Liberty lives in us! [13-sec. applause]

This cause of Life and Liberty crosses all lines. Therefore, I say with Jesus: Let bigotry and fanaticism go down in religion and politics! And let the new-age man and woman and child rise up to claim a lawful inheritance of a land protected, free, and at peace because it is defended in Christ. [13-sec. applause]

Angels of Liberty are traversing the land. And you have felt their impetus, their momentum, with the descent of this fire and presence of the Goddess of Liberty, who does place her Electronic Presence here, beloved. Let it be known, then, in earth and in every nation that out of the single star, even the star of Bethlehem over Texas, there is a revolution that does fly. And free men in every nation may think of that star and that place where a new birth in America did win the race to defend and to raise up arms to protect the peace. [12-sec. applause]

Let the wall of light around America remember [call to mind] the Alamo, and let the entire America be a fortress of light. I, for one, Saint Germain, now place the momentum of my personal tube of light around America—all fifty states one by one and as a whole. I AM placing my tube of light and momentum of violet flame in the midst of this New Jerusalem. I AM placing myself in the midst!

Hear me, O my beloved! Go forth and pronounce my message and name. For I shall be there wherever you dare to speak of me. [21-sec. applause] Let those who have ridiculed and said that dictations from the Ascended Masters are "off the wall" beware, for they themselves may soon be "off the wall"! [10-sec. applause]

I speak this not lightly nor as a threat but as prophecy itself. For I know well the flame of Freedom. And with this flame intensifying now, beloved, you will see the consuming and the judgment of forces of anti-Freedom: anti-Freedom of religion, anti-Freedom of conscience, anti-Freedom of private property rights, anti-Freedom of free enterprise, anti-Freedom of the press, anti-Freedom, beloved, in every quarter of life. Let it be so, then, that free speech be guaranteed, respected and honored so long as it does not desecrate the reason for being of God in man.

Oh, let the prayer now resound from the hearts of children and youth! Let the youth of America themselves declare the mandate:

> We will worship our God upon this soil, in our homes, in public places, in the streets. We will say the name of God, and we will say that name and dedicate our lives in the schoolhouse, in the Senate, in the Pentagon, in the forests and the lakes and streams.
>
> We will worship our God and we will guarantee the freedom of everyone to worship him as Christ or Krishna, as Gautama or the Divine Mother. We will stand and still stand under the Mighty I AM Presence, and we will defend our right to be—against all enemies, the forces of nonbeing, darkness and death!

So, this is the voice of the soul of America that must be heard, that must be articulated because messengers of my message have dared to teach them how to pray, how to decree, how to stand, feet firmly upon the soil, and still stand, and to know God: To dare, to do, to be silent and to be his voice when called.

O beloved, let the soul of this nation speak because you have spoken and seen to it that they are God-taught. Let the Chart of the Mighty I AM Presence as the Divine Self of everyone be seen everywhere as the sign of the coming of the sons of God. Oh, let America ring in the joy of the violet singing flame! [15-sec. applause]

I AM visualizing the thoughtform of a blue canopy of light over America—fifty states and more. Blessed ones, there is a spiritual defense that is of the God Star. It can be invoked through the heart of Archangel Michael and the Lord Christ. It can be invoked through the entire Spirit of the Great White Brotherhood.

A canopy of blue ought to be visualized. For, beloved, beyond nuclear war are spacecraft and actual harmful radiations that emanate from certain asteroids and even planetary bodies or comets. Beloved ones, the influences of extraterrestrials must be guarded against as well as extremely low frequencies bombarding the body. And you yourselves must know the signs of psychotronic energy bombarding the form of the Lightbearer.

Blessed ones, as it has been told to you, I speak it again—the spoken Word as a chalice for the Ascended Masters is available to you as a guardian action. The dictations are rereleased; as they are replayed, you have the original light. This is a dispensation of great magnitude.

For the Word is the fire of creation. It is the wall of light. It is the armour. It is the sealing of immortality in mortal form. It is the protection of the saints who in past ages have succumbed to superior technologies in civilizations where there was not offered to them the protection necessary to meet the plots of the fallen ones who used science to conquer and to create mass death.

Let the spoken Word, the image of God and of ascended loved ones be your protection, beloved, even as the expanded heart flame itself will rise, pulsate, and engulf your form.

O beloved, in this hour of heaven's rejoicing and God-determination and renewed expansiveness from the heart of the Goddess of Liberty, know, then, that the Light will protect its own as long as its own will serve the Light and give the mantra of ***Light! Light! Light! Light!*** O Son of God, appear!

Blessed ones, be seated now as you keep your vigil at the tomb. For the morning approaches when angels, rolling away the stone, will behold the mighty figure. Today he is the Ascended Master Jesus Christ. But upon every Easter, beloved, he is the Son of man who does represent yourself—the alchemist in the Cave of Light working out the problem of being and proving that no Death and Hell, projected by Nephilim gods or whatever false-hierarchy impostors, could ever be sustained or blow out the candle of Life.

I AM the Resurrection and the Life! He that believeth on the Light of me who is the Universal Christ shall not see death but have everlasting Life in the victory of the ascension.[2] Believing upon the invulnerability of my Christhood and your own, of that of Jesus and all ascended hosts, you may understand that death is but a chimera, an illusion, beloved, and that you need not see death but only the passing of the soul from one corruptible body unto the Incorruptible One.[3]

This is the message of Easter that has not been proclaimed:

As I have fulfilled the law and the initiation of the resurrection, so you may also do it in life and yet continue to live in that body, though that body have a greater influx of light, waiting to be sealed ultimately in the hour of the ascension. The resurrected one is not subject to the warfare of the flesh or Armageddon. He stands between two worlds, the figure of Christ on the hillside, the figure of World Teacher and Wayshower.

Let the resurrected saints appear. You may see those who have already entered and gone beyond the change which is called death, but you may also see the resurrected saints yet walking the earth [in veils of flesh] with the fire of the eye and the light of the body and the fury of the Divine Mother that is a wrath of Kali purging the earth, separating the Light from Darkness, and coming to the still small voice[4] that has the power of Elohim, that only need whisper and all of Nature does obey. Such is Elohim.

Elohim of God, Peace and Aloha of resurrection's peace—come now, Elohim! Father/Mother Light, reveal the transparency of Life. Reveal the initiation of the transfiguration that does precede the resurrection. Teach them, O Elohim, as I would teach them: that the alchemy of the violet flame and the alchemy of self-transcendence is the surest sealing of the body which is the temple of God against the last plagues and wars and economic failures—even the failures of all civilization.

Yet the Son of God stands tall upon the hillsides and the mountains, proclaiming the Word, proclaiming the Word. [chanting] And the Word that is spoken by the resurrected one does quiver the atoms and the rocks and the streams. And earth herself does accelerate and therefore clean escape the downward momentums of those who are not alive in Christ, Universal Light.

O beloved ones, hear Elohim.

UR [chanted]

So, then, beloved, *call* forth the resurrection. *Give* the mantra of the Cosmic Christ. *Know* why Jesus brought it to you from the far reaches of the Himalayas. *Know* why he said:

I AM the Resurrection and the Life.
I AM the Resurrection and the Life.

So, beloved, the living Christ in you is that pillar of fire. Know it, proclaim it, seal it, and let thy life be a guardian action of the sacred fire whereby you do proclaim for self, family, society, nation, and planet: I AM the Guard!

[Congregation affirms with Saint Germain:]

I AM the Guard!
I AM the Guard!
I AM the Guard!

In the name of Saint Germain,
        So I AM the Keeper of the Flame!
In the name of Saint Germain,
        So I AM the Keeper of the Flame! [congregation]

I give you joy in the violet flame to know the present possibility, even while yet in the flesh, that the flesh can be transformed, that it can be rejuvenated, and in your life you can *see* God and then *live* as God.

Therefore, be not discouraged or depressed, neither marking time waiting for the years to pass, as they pass so slowly in boredom and nonactivity. Beloved ones, some of the world wait for death and some wait for everlasting Life. The pity is that those who think of heaven believe they can get there only by death. But He lives! And the lilies trumpeting proclaim it.

Christ did not enter Life by [bowing to] Death, nor shall you. Therefore claim:

I AM the Life everlasting here and now!
I AM immortal in Christ my Lord.
I AM the fullness of Love none can touch.
I AM the spiraling, ascending flame
that God loves so much!
I AM my Father's child, son and daughter where I AM.
I AM in the wholeness and fullness of Wisdom's fount.

I AM bathed by supernal streams of Light. I drink the elixir of Divine Oneness. I come into the center and eye of God's Power.

I AM in the whirling vortex of Archangels. I AM in the center of the One and I AM on earth victorious in the flame of God-Freedom. Lo, I AM that God-Freedom unto America!

And I, with Saint Germain, with Johnny Appleseed, go forth now to sow the seeds of Freedom—to sow the flames. And where'er I walk, Zadkiel is with me, violet flame angels are with me. And each footprint leaves a footprint of violet flame for another to step into and *know* the joy of the Holy Spirit and *know* the joy of my becoming one in the Sacred Heart of Jesus.

I have recourse to the Immaculate Heart of Mary.

I AM in the ovoid of Helios and Vesta!

I AM here and now in the bliss of God!

There is nowhere to go, for I AM fully One in Him.

Lo, Thou art in me, I AM in Thee, O God. And we are One, as Above so below. And therefore, do with me what Thou wilt, O living Word. For I AM thy servant-spokesman. Thy Divine Mother I AM. I AM thy child and brother/sister. Lo! I AM thy friend, O God.

O Abraham of old, let thy mantle be upon me, for I would walk the earth a friend of God.[5] O Morya, come unto me now. For it is long enough to be saturated and supersaturated with human selfishness and nonsense. I AM through with all of this! It is resurrection's morn!

I glow in Christhood. And as my members glow, I see the Sun shining, passing through me now. And all is transparent light and rainbow rays, and the causal body does shine. And I see the Sun of my causal body *rising* in this hour, *rising* in this hour, *rising* to the heart of God!

And lo, I AM in the center of the One. And even as the shaft of light does accelerate up, so it does accelerate into the heart of the earth. And there in the center of the One I hold the balance for evolutionary life till all be fulfilled, till karma be expiated, till earth come into alignment, till the golden age appear—else till the new planet and the new world appear.

And I AM in the heart of that new world even as I AM One. I AM in the center of the new world. I AM in the surface of the new world. And the new world is born in the heart of Helios and Vesta. And earth is in the violet flame. And lo, I AM THAT I AM.

And therefore, by the sign of the cross did Francis bless. By the sign of the cross do the birds caress. By the sign of the cross I AM prepared to meet my Love and be all One.

In Christ I AM reborn—in Christ this golden morn. America, I love thee! America, I love thee! America, be infused with resurrection's light!

I go now to the Royal Teton Retreat, there to behold the sunrise over America and a new day. It is a promise that I shall make good. For I know that only the Keeper of the Flame can keep the flame of resurrection burning when all the world is dying and annihilating self, and self destructing.

I AM the Keeper of the Flame. I AM the Resurrection and the Life of the flame in all hearts! I keep the vigil with the Goddess of Liberty and I AM one in the heart of Hope. Hope shall never die in me till all cycles be self-transcended and fulfilled.

Lo, I AM in the wings of Hope.
I AM in the heart of Faith.
I AM the instrument of Charity.
Red, white, and blue—ruby ray, purity, sapphire hue.
I AM thy first love, O God. Thou art my own.

Blessed ones, such a prophecy, a dispensation, and a vision is only as good as those who crystallize it in form. Those of you who have not thought of it, I say, dear hearts, *think* of it *now!* I AM Saint Germain. I need you at the Inner Retreat to build my Community and place of safety *now.* I *need* you to publish my Word.

I come as Jesus once came. I come, then, to call you—to make you not only fishers of men[6] but alchemists preparing for the initiations of Melchizedek. I come to call you from your nets of foreign entanglements and alliances.

Who will keep the flame of God? Who will shepherd the thousands I would send to you? Who will prepare the feast of Light in the wilderness? The LORD, the Maha Chohan, hath need of thee. And I, even greater in need, am not ashamed to say that my need is desperate for my helpers now.

Blessed ones, the lilies of the valley, the irises in the sun of springtime gently moving in the breath of the Holy Spirit signal that we ought, each one, to change our position in time and space and enter the octaves of Light. Let us, then, agree to meet this night at the Royal Teton [etheric retreat at the Grand Teton] where in conclave many souls of freedom desire to be God-taught.

My prayer is this—let them be saturated in the violet flame cauldrons, in the mighty jade and violet flame cathedral. Beloved ones, those of false political and theological persuasions and bent need the saturation of violet fire to know this new birth and to join you in the saving of nations. Blessed ones, let us invoke it from the heart of God, from whom all blessings flow.

Mighty crystal stream of Life, River of Life, waters unending descending from the fount of the Divine Gnosis of I AM THAT I AM, descend from the Central Sun. Envelop my hearts so pure, my beloved and all sincere ones who must now come over the stumbling stones placed in their way by serpents *who have had their day!*

Yes, beloved, we have declared and echoed the voice of Jesus Christ. His first words this day are empowered by the Spirit of the Resurrection and the sword that does defend it in the hand of Archangel Uriel, Angel of the Judgment. *They have had their day*—the serpents from the Garden who to the present have purveyed their economic, religious and political philosophies and those of education which are an abomination to the spirit and minds of my people.

I AM Saint Germain and I join the Lord and Saviour in the world with his fiat on the Serpent and his seed:

They have had their day and their day is done!

[24-sec. standing ovation]

You may also be quick to echo it:

[Congregation affirms with Saint Germain:]

They have had their day and their day is done!
They have had their day and their day is done!
They have had their day and their day is done!

Blessed ones, let them be marked by the sign that I shall not reveal but that shall be upon them, every one. I touch your foreheads that you might know who are the wolves in sheep's clothing and the impostors of the living Word. Blessed hearts, call for this discernment of spirits fervently from the Holy Spirit and your living Christ.

Mighty I AM Presence, thou one Lord, quicken, infuse, enlighten, remove the scales from these eyes by the violet flame that I give unto them in this hour. Let their eyes be opened and let them know *who* is a servant of light and *who* is a servant of corruption and self-love.

In the beginning was the Word. In the ending is the Word. In the middle is the Word. Throughout eternity is the Word! I AM the Word and you are the Word! And we are pearls of light ascending and descending the filigree thread of contact of the Great White Brotherhood with the Great Central Sun.

Lo! I AM the Word.

Lo! thou art the Word.

Lo! thou art the Living One.

Arise, beloved. Shed now the snakeskin of all former selves. Arise and step forth. For you shall see yourself this night at the Royal Teton as you have never seen yourself before. You will look into that mirror of light. You will see that snakeskin shedding, beloved ones, and you will *know* who is who within yourself. You will have the discernment of those spirits which have co-occupied your form. You shall cast them out at the side of Jesus and in his name, as he does tutor you continuously in the Ritual of Exorcism.

Beloved ones, there is no limit to the service you can render when you choose to be the Son of God and nothing else.

Lo, I AM come!

Lo, I AM Saint Germain!

Lo, I AM in the fervor of the resurrection!

Let all Lightbearers of the earth now *rise* unto the Sun—*rise* unto the Sun of Righteousness and the Mighty I AM THAT I AM! So be it! So it is done!

I AM forever your own beloved, devoted and doting Saint Germain, ever at your side, ever one with you, ever caring when you are weary—ever sharing with you my mantle and cape.

Lo, it is done. *Lo,* it is upon you.

Seize the opportunity, beloved.

For Portia has said: "It is the last time."

I thank you and bid you good evening.

[1-min. standing ovation]

I AM the Violet Flame

I AM the Violet Flame
In action in me now
I AM the Violet Flame
To Light alone I bow
I AM the Violet Flame
In mighty Cosmic Power
I AM the Light of God
Shining every hour
I AM the Violet Flame
Blazing like a sun
I AM God's sacred power
Freeing every one

"The Summit Lighthouse Sheds Its Radiance O'er All the World to Manifest as Pearls of Wisdom."

This dictation by Saint Germain was **delivered** through the Messenger of the Great White Brotherhood Elizabeth Clare Prophet on **Holy Saturday, April 18, 1987,** during the 6-day Easter conference, *Christ's Resurrection in You,* held at the Downtown Dallas Hilton, **Dallas, Texas**. (**1**) The Messenger's lecture "Saint Germain On Prophecy," given February 22, 1987, in Minneapolis, was played prior to the dictation. (**2**) John 11:25, 26. (**3**) I Cor. 15:53, 54. (**4**) I Kings 19:12. (**5**) II Chron. 20:7; Isa. 41:8; James 2:23. (**6**) Matt. 4:19; Mark 1:17.

Notes from Pearl No. 16 by Mother Mary continued:

(**4**) Acts 2:1. (**5**) II Cor. 11:14. (**6**) Matt. 24:24. (**7**) The twelve sons of Jacob were the progenitors of the twelve tribes of Israel. Joseph, the eleventh and most favored son, had two sons, Ephraim and Manasseh. These were blessed by Jacob as his own, being counted, then, as two half-tribes or two whole tribes, depending on what scriptural interpreters you read. The descendants of Joseph embodied in the English-speaking nations—Ephraim primarily in the United States and Manasseh in the British Isles. The other eleven tribes reincarnated to form the European nations; many were scattered, embodying in every race and nation. The tribe of Reuben reincarnated in Russia. See "Soviet Invasion of Europe: Karma of the Great Brothers," in *Saint Germain On Prophecy,* pp. 123–36, Book Two. (**8**) Luke 23:28. (**9**) II Cor. 6:2. (**10**) Matt. 12:42; Luke 11:31. (**11**) Isa. 8:19. (**12**) Rev. 20:11. (**13**) Heb. 11:35.

Pearls of Wisdom®

published by The Summit Lighthouse

Vol. 30 No. 18 *Beloved Jesus Christ* *May 3, 1987*

Christ's Resurrection in You

VIII

The Foundation of Christendom That I Have Laid

She said to me, "They have taken away my Lord and I know not where they have laid him."

I say to you, they have taken away the heart of my beloved Magda.[1] And no child of God to this hour has known where is the heart of Magda—where is the secret of the mystery of Christ-love, where is the mystery of the union of the disciple with her Lord, where is the foundation of Christendom that I have laid in the beginning.

Lo, I AM come, Alpha and Omega in the beginning and in the ending. I therefore crown woman as the highest representative and as the symbolical Church. Therefore, let the pulpits be opened to woman and let the crown not be denied my daughter. For this Church Universal and Triumphant shall have as its sign the twelve-starred crown of Mother that signifies that Mary, the Teacher and the true and living Guru of all, does give, as my Mother[2]—even as Mary, my twin flame, does give—the true teachings of the path of the ascension of the fiery spirit of a man and a woman taking unto the self the swaddling garment.

Lo! it is drawn from above. Lo! it is drawn from beneath. Be clothed, then, ye who are naked souls—naked because you have been stripped of the precious threads of my doctrine.

Therefore, I AM come, for truly it is the hour of the return of Mother Mary, of Magda, of the saints, and of all who are of the Mystical Body. Let the Woman clothed with the Sun appear! And let that Sun of the Mighty I AM Presence be upon every soul who has dared to face the challenge of the antithesis of Self in the seven planes of being.

Thus, the path of gnosis, beloved, as self-knowledge, must include the knowledge of the enemy. Therefore, you will know him by his fruitless doctrine![3] O beloved, these fallen ones have said it is in scripture or it has come from my lips or those of my followers. I say, go not there, go not here, but look within. For the only true testimony of the Word is the kingdom within you.[4]

I AM present in you now, beloved—the resurrected Christ. Come to me, O my beloved. I come with the whispering hope of resurrection's fires. I come with the gentleness of the spiritual flame that does now gently take from you every care and burden of this life.

Blessed hearts, the way is not sorrowful; neither is it a struggle, save to those who desire not to give up the lesser self. The joy of acceleration in light is incomparable! Only witness those who have my fire upon them. Blessed ones, they cannot be known by any outer standard or classification or labeling. They are anywhere or everywhere in the sea of life. Suddenly you see that fire and you know: Truly, this man, this woman is the anointed son of God.[5]

You may look into a million faces but you will come to the one. And here where truth abounds—and the violet flame and the Spirit—it is not uncommon to see many, beloved. How true is Truth unto its own witness? For the fire cannot be denied, nor can the overlay, as a glassiness, fail to expose nondiligence in my path.

Angels read but humanity know not the sign. They have never seen the light of the eye of the ascending one. Well, I say, beloved, let us make it a familiar sight! Let them rejoice to see the alive ones—the lively stones[6] who have a testimony.

O beloved, you who have sunk back into a comfortable situation, even proposing monuments called focuses and other trappings to signify a spiritual forcefield, I say, there is no spiritual forcefield save the Sacred Heart! Desire, then, that the LORD should look upon you and call your heart sacred or immaculate or magnanimous in Spirit. Blessed ones, the Sacred Heart may endow surroundings with a holiness and a vibration that cannot be denied, but surroundings can never endow the individual with that which he must seek within.

Thus, modern civilization and wealth, intended to be an abundant life shared with all to the blessings ordained by God, has become a substitute for the true path of spirituality. And a dead ritual has replaced the "right-you-all" of righting the wrongs of an ancient karma and getting on with eternal life in the here and now. And a theology dead twice, thrice over, yet lives. For man and woman are too busy to examine and to know the Truth. Nor do they seek my voice within.

I speak to many, beloved. They do not hear—they *will* not hear. Then again I speak through the child who in holy innocence declares the Truth so simply. But the elders smile and say, "What can you know? You are too young."

Blessed hearts, my angels and the ascended host have truly sought and they have pursued every means to reach and contact the heart that is riveted in a rigidity of a belief system that does not allow for the resurrection presently and in an ongoing daily accretion of the fire of the rainbow rays of God.

Blessed hearts, I therefore propose a summoning of Archangels in this hour—as this is my day of days and inasmuch as many have prayed to me this day in a manner seldom accomplished except at the Christ Mass. Blessed hearts, these prayers, though perhaps based on ignorance, are sincere. People are sincere in their orthodoxy. O beloved, such a tragedy of errors.

Therefore, I say, in answer to their calls, let us one and all together in this communion answer prayer by invoking the intercession of the Archangels. This I propose, beloved, for it is fear, it is anger on the part of the fallen ones and their rebellion that presents to me as I knock at the door of the heart that impenetrable wall of a misused free will!

Even the Son of God may not transgress the threshold of free will! Understand that this is our Father's rule and we do not violate it.

Therefore, we are free by coaxing, by preaching, by loving, and by the violet flame to attempt our conversion to change the alignment of free will as one would change, then, the alignment of molecules, ions, electrodes. Blessed hearts, alignment is a universal necessity, both in science and religion. Nothing works without alignment. Thus, let the Polestar [of the Mighty I AM Presence] descend!

Know, beloved, that when you pray for another the prayers are locked in the heart of the Holy Christ Self, who does minister unto the needs of the soul to the fullest extent that the Law will allow. Some have released the false doctrine that it is not lawful to invoke the violet flame for another. I tell you, it is indeed lawful to pray for gifts and graces unto all, for every call is adjudicated by the will of God. Every call made in the name of Christ descends only by that Christ-discrimination of the individual's I AM Presence and Christ Self.

Therefore, beloved, understand me: The momentum of prayer and graces and light is held, as it were, in a vault of safekeeping, preparing to descend as a bower of loveliness upon the soul who does at last, in desperation with the limitations of a belief system, cry out unto God, "O LORD, help me now!" And at that moment the angels come and they release the bowers of your momentum of prayer on behalf of that one.

Precious ones, there is help unto all. There is grace unto all. Criminals engaged in crime have called to Astrea and invoked the violet flame and received results. This is the guarantee of the decree itself. However, the Great Law does limit even by the matrix of a mantra itself (for the mantra *is* the power of the Word) the repetitive cycles of the misuse of the water of Life given freely.

Therefore, my proposal in this hour, beloved, is that I give my office this day for the invocation unto the Father to send legions of angels for the binding of the Liar and the lie and these fallen ones who corrupt my children.

I would speak to you again, then, of the path of illumination—of being the world teacher with me and Kuthumi, understanding, therefore, that next to the violet flame and the Ritual of Exorcism and the power of the Divine Mother Astrea to bind entrenched forces of limitation, there is nothing that can equal the enlightenment of the Holy Ghost or the true Teachings of my heart for an absolute conversion of the soul unto Life.

I would desire to read to you my teaching on the concept of sacrifice, that you would understand that you can live a life of sacrifice in abundant joy. I would desire you to know the true theology of the doctrine of the remission of sin by the Blood of Christ.

Blessed one, hear me, then—you who have looked and toiled long for your Lord. I AM indeed Jesus. I AM here, beloved, as I AM a free spirit ascended. And I may choose to anoint and ordain one among you to deliver my Word, and none may deny my right. Thus, be safe and secure. Should I not, then, call Martha, who has served me in numerous lifetimes, to come now and feed you as she has fed me so well?

Blessed hearts, I AM able. I AM able to raise up in you by the Spirit Holy that instrumentation of my doctrine, if you are willing to study to show yourselves approved.[7] Perceiving, then, that some are negligent in the learning of the true theology, I shall indeed read to you from my book.

Blessed ones, understand the need and be watchful. Those beset by orthodoxy and the lies incorporated within it know not why they believe what they believe nor who was the instigator of this anti-Christ religion that passes for my own. When you meet them in the way, you must know every point of the Law, both in codified scripture and in my Teachings now released.

Students you must be. I require it, beloved. For the age shall not turn or the freedom be gained unless my Church is founded upon the rock of your confession of the living Christ in me, in you, in every child of God.

Blessed hearts, the old has already decayed from within. But it is kept alive by both the devotion of good people and the black magic of a priestcraft that does abuse even the Sacrament.

There is a fury of hell in Rome! Be it said. Be it known. Be it challenged by those in embodiment who *are* my own, whom I call brother and sister. There is a fury of hell moving through Protestantism, as there has been from the beginning. For no church can survive without the call to Archangel Michael, to my blessed Mother, and to the saints of God.

This is a communion. This is an Armageddon. This is a fight against the heinous forces of World Communism that are supported by fallen ones in every camp. Blessed hearts, there is no church except that church take a stand to enter the Armageddon that began in heaven and must be finished upon earth.

Build the temple of man with the Truth. And do not allow yourselves to fritter away the hours in ignorance! You believe you are awakened but the Word must be from within. You hear me now. You hear the Messenger speak. Pursue, then, and know the detail of the Law because it is a sword of Truth that defeats the Liar because his lie cannot stand in its Presence.

So be it, beloved. I shall now illumine you by a written word, that you may then go after it yourself:

Corona Class Lesson 22: Sin. "Sacrifice." Learn now the meaning of it, beloved. ***"Without Shedding of Blood . . ."***

To the Deserving of the Path of Joy,
Abundance, and Happiness—

Foremost among God's ideas scintillating in the universe is the ever-living love that radiates joy to the world. The poor in spirit[8] as well as those deficient in this world's goods will always find enough in the cup of Christ's consciousness that runneth over.[9] His abundant Light fills every human need—and divine.

I AM the source of all joy, of all abundance, of all! Why, then, do men seek to find happiness elsewhere? It is because in their sense of lack they amplify their need to possess that which in reality is already their own. This is a misunderstanding of the divine vision of universal Love which gives without limit to all.

Religious movements are conceived in order that people might be happy in God in the present and that they might find happiness in God in the future. The security of heaven is an anchor for which men yearn. I am certain, then, that the Spirit of the Father flashes out in response to each blessed lamb with an intensity beyond that soul's yearning.

God's love can be perceived shining through the foliage of Nature, in the electronic composition of matter, and as a light in the eyes of men. So little understood is God, so little is he known or realized by most men, that scarcely can they conceive of his outpouring of power which lies latent within their being.

You see, blessed ones, by the law of the circle, when you apply limitation to another it returns to you for adjustment. When in ignorance people apply limitation to God, to others, or to themselves, this practice, which is most dangerous, causes the Great Law to withhold from them the very powers of Light which would give them their freedom.

The statement that "truth is stranger than fiction" is often true. Just think of the hundreds of years that Christendom (which means "Christ's kingdom") has contemplated the sacrificial aspects of my crucifixion! But in this case, the truth about sacrifice could not possibly be stranger than the fiction that has been handed down concerning the crucifixion.

Biblical writers, saints, prophets, and holy men have written and taught about the idea of appeasing an angry God through the blood sacrifice of his Son. Although these have acted with great sincerity, they have nevertheless been influenced by the strictly pagan practice handed down from distant days when men departed from the ancient religions of Atlantis wherein true communion with God was taught and experienced as the interchange (sacrificial emission) of light between the soul and the Spirit.

Subsequently, the true art of sacrifice (self-giving unto God) degenerated into the sinister and perverted uses of the sacred fire in sexual rites performed at the altar. As a substitute for the ritual of self-sacrifice of the synthetic image (shedding the snakeskin of the serpent mind), the false priests offered temple virgins (in place of themselves) in sacrifices of appeasement to the gods. (It came to pass prior to the flood that young men were offered in place of women.) The malpracticing priesthood encouraged the bizarre and sensual in their subjects and, magnetizing the denizens of the astral world through nefarious incantations, cooperated with the black magicians who created the conditions which led to the Noachian deluge and the sinking of Atlantis.[10]

The Canaanite idea of child sacrifice, "burning their sons and daughters in the fire,"[11] temple prostitution, and burnt offerings and sacrifices to Baal, imitated by the Israelites, recalled the last days of a decadent Atlantis. These abominations, of Nephilim origin, were denounced by Jeremiah and Ezekiel, as well as by Isaiah, Amos, and Micah.[12] By and by, the substitution of the blood of sheep and other animals for that of human beings was deemed preferable in the rites of atonement practiced in the cultures of the Fertile Crescent. Yet, to this day, human as well as animal sacrifice can be found on the continent of Africa.

In the knowledge of the foregoing historical facts and self-evident spiritual truths, consider how unreasonable it is that a formula for human or animal sacrifice or the shedding of blood could have been required or ordained by God for the propitiation (atonement, expiation, balance) of sin (i.e., karma).

If, then, sacrifice is *not* required for the remission of sins, what *does* Life demand in order to balance humanity's debts? I am happy to clear up this point for all who adore the Truth that will make them free[13] from such smoldering error which blind theology has kept active, thereby mutilating both the human and the divine image in man which would otherwise have been universally outpictured upon earth long ago.

Let us together examine the mystery of the blood of the Lamb as the acceptable sacrifice which, we are told, meets with the divine approval in remitting the sins of mankind.[14]

Life and *God* are synonymous terms and denote interdependence in the interchange between the divine and the human, for the life of man is God and God's Life flows in man's veins. The term *life* is equivalent to blood in the scriptural sense and is preferred to *blood* by the spiritual student, who rejects the idea of the shedding of blood as abhorrent and inconsistent with true humanity and certainly with Divinity.

The scriptures declare that "without shedding of blood there is no remission" of sins.[15] I am declaring to you and to all men forever the truth concerning this biblical statement, herein quite simply revealed: without the shedding (casting off) of that life, or life-force, which has been misqualified with human foolishness, the sins of man can never be remitted (requalified with the love plan of God). Moreover, without the release of the life-essence (i.e., 'blood') of the Lamb who is your Holy Christ Self, you cannot balance your karma.

Hence, it is by a continual requalifying, mastering, governing and controlling of energy through the Ascended Master Light of the individualized Holy Christ Self that men and women shall rise to the point where their former sins, which are solely error recorded in memory, are blotted out[16] by the Holy Spirit. This ritual of true sacrifice takes place as they invoke the violet fire of forgiveness, the white radiance of God-purity, and the comforting assurance that as they put off the old man with his deeds, the new man—the firstborn Son made in the image of God—comes into manifestation in the glory of reality.[17]

The idea that God, your beloved I AM Presence, favors one child and rejects another is totally inconsistent with divine Law. My own life was offered to God to epitomize the Cosmic Christ, to prove that man and woman in physical embodiment can ascend out of Matter and remain close by in octaves of light (invisible, yet co-occupying the physical plane at a higher frequency) to mightily assist the earth and its evolutions in returning to the original divine plan of the abundant Life.

This I am doing to the present day. Well may it be spoken of me—as it should be of every soul who is destined, whether one knows it or not, to be a Christ—"I AM" (the I AM Presence in me *is*) the Way, the Truth, and the Life: no man cometh unto the Father but by the same path of personal Christhood which all who have embodied the Word have demonstrated.[18]

In the purified state man "sheds the light" of the I AM Presence through his sanctified (sacred) heart and other spiritual centers (chakras) for the transmutation of world sin (karma). In this release of light the initiate discovers the true meaning of the remission of sin by the "shedding of blood," noted by the mystic writer of Hebrews.

However, the full force of this initiation is not experienced until after the records of personal *sin* (violations of the law of grace) are consumed by Love nor until personal karma (the obligations to Life incurred through disobedience to God's laws) is balanced by sacrificial service (words and works, including dynamic decrees for world transmutation).

"Without *shedding of blood*..." is then seen to be the flow of Life from God through the purified soul and temple of man. The pure life-essence of the Holy Christ Flame is released in "rivers of living water" from the 'belly'[19]—and this refers to the *solar plexus,* or *place of the sun*—which becomes the fount (chakra) of Christ-peace in all who also believe in the Christ of me as the God-power in themselves.

Yes, without the shedding of this 'blood', there is no world remission of sin by the Son of God incarnate in you! And for this cause you and I came into the world—to take upon the office of our Christhood the burden of world karma so that the lost sheep gone astray from the House of Reality[20] might experience a deferment of their karma and a certain relief from suffering while they learn of me and my true burden, which is Light.[21] This Light, when internalized by themselves, will enable them in their turn to take full responsibility for their own burden of karma as they, too, follow the selfsame path of discipleship you are on: personal transformation through integration with Christ, the Light of your world.

How fallacious is the idea that God respects men's persons or favors one of his sons while dishonoring another. Some do not see that it is mortal men who dishonor themselves, doing despite to their own cause before the courts of heaven. Yet I am not concerned with the changing human but with the changeless God Self and his intentions, which are to endow the *Son of* his *man*ifestation with every honor and blessing that the soul prepares herself (qualifies herself) to receive.

One of the first requisites the aspirant to Christhood must meet is to acquire the inner knowing that God is no respecter of persons[22] and that he is willing to bestow his powers without limit upon all of his children when they prove themselves trustworthy. Then he must accept the reality that Life is already manifesting through him with the fullness of Life's blessed God-powers.

The knowledge of the correct use of these powers to

the glory of God and for the healing of the whole Body of God from the cause and core of every disease and discomfort must follow. It is the Law!

I AM the Christ-gift that lifts karmic burdens, heals all souls, and lights your way![23]

I have signed this letter "Jesus the Christ."

Beloved, this is one of a number of dictations given by Kuthumi and me under the heading of "Sin." I desire students of my life and Teachings to know that this book of the Law will enable you to be experts in my Divine Doctrine. My soul hungers and thirsts for those who truly know me and speak of me and of my words and my Teachings that I gave two thousand years ago and have not left off giving to my saints who know my voice.

This is the work of the doctrine in forty-eight lessons that will give you a corona of light when you know it, understand it, teach it and assimilate it. I desire to see the halo of illumination upon you. I desire you to be able, so gently but firmly, to simply undo the snarl of human, conceited dogma.

Blessed hearts, neglect me not. I have been neglected for two thousand years. This day I affirm: My mission shall not be aborted! It shall no longer be aborted, for I AM *here* in the flesh of my servant—and in your own hearts. I AM here. I AM resurrected as you, too, *can be,* as you *are,* and as you *shall be.*

This work of Truth shall swallow up error. And when seen as the keystone to all Teachings of the Ascended Masters, it provides you with a foundation and an open door for speaking to people and groups as out of the Holy Spirit. For when in your heart the Truth is set, the Holy Spirit shall play upon you, as upon an aeolian harp, melodies of the Spirit and a fire for conversion—conversion away from that fear and anger and rebellion and ignorance.

O beloved, the time *is* at hand.

Some have not believed me when I said, "I came not to send peace but a sword."[24] Throughout the ages, beloved, I have loaned my sword to special initiates. The well-known legend of Arthur pulling the sword from the stone derives from an initiation of Maitreya's Mystery School. Blessed hearts, the time did indeed come when I did tell the disciples to take the sword.*

Blessed hearts, I am not an advocate of physical war. But I AM fully engaged in the slaying of demons and discarnates who

*". . . Now, he that hath a purse, let him take it, and likewise his scrip: and he that hath no sword, let him sell his garment, and buy one. . . . And they said, Lord, behold, here are two swords. And he said unto them, It is enough." (Luke 22:36–38)

prey upon my own. And I AM fully willing to challenge the mighty and the kings and the potentates. I AM alive forevermore.

Therefore, beloved, seek the initiation of the sword. And understand that it is a rod of sacred fire fashioned by the Divine Mother out of your own sacred life-force rising from the base chakra to the third eye. Therefore, beloved, the sword that is taken from the stone of Matter is a spiritual fire. Legend would have it that it is a magic sword.

Beloved, the spiritual fire does dissolve on contact all unlike itself. Know, then, that as I pray, so I also act that you may do likewise. Therefore, I say:

> O my Father, by thy Presence send the Archangels! I command them in the Christ Spirit of every soul upon earth. I AM in this hour the fulfillment of the prayer of the righteous. Now let the sword of God descend for the binding of those who have too long taken away my own from the altar of the living Word.
>
> My Father, in the name of my brother Saint Germain, in the name of my Mother Mary, I ask—do Thou grant it—for the dispensation of legions of Light to clear the way for the true Teaching and the true Church to be manifest swiftly.
>
> Let the houses of worship, O Father, be cleansed by angels and seraphim. Let billions of angels descend into America and the earth! My Father, this is my call, answering the prayers of my own.
>
> Let it [the answer] come swiftly as the two-edged sword which I now hold. Let Excalibur be in the hand of the initiates who run quickly to receive this initiation from the Cosmic Christ. O Father, to win, to have our victory, we desperately need an action in America *now,* as Saint Germain has said.
>
> O Father, gather those in the fields white to the harvest.[25] Gather them *now* and let them be cut free. Send forth the light, O Father!
>
> I see Thee raising now thy right hand. So I raise my own. And so it is time, told by the Mother, for the right hand of the Son to descend in the earth. I accept thy judgments, my Father. I accept them, my Mother.
>
> I AM in the earth and on the battlefield, at the workplace, in the home, at the birth of the child and the passing of the elderly. I AM with my own, O Father—away from Thee, as it were, for a time and space—fully

engaged to clear a place for a victory that would be denied. It shall not be, O Father, for faithful hearts have arisen.

Thou knowest the secret prayer of my heart for each and every one on earth who calls to me and even those who do not. Let recording angels and the Holy Ghost deliberate and give unto me thy graces for their fulfillment.

[chant in an angelic tongue 42 seconds]

Twelve legions of angels, it is the appointed hour: Come now! Stand on the lines of the [Cosmic] Clock, each one. One hundred and forty-four thousand angels, come, then, for the clearing of this house of Joseph. Come for the clearing of this seed and nation. Come now, O legions of Light! Let there be the remnant. Let there be the rising. Let America and all who call themselves Americans be raised up by the canopy of the Son of God!

Now unto the worthy the increase is come and the cup runneth over. Now unto the unworthy—Archangel Michael, descend and strip them of all unworthiness and let the soul stand forth.

Know me, O soul of Light, thou who hast acted in unworthy manner, in sinful sense. Therefore, I call thee from corruption and the servants of corruption. Hear me now! I speak directly to the heart, directly to all those who have thought of me as the resurrected Christ this day:

I AM the blazing light of the Son of God now in your heart! I AM the fire from the altar of the Father, stripping from you those filthy rags and outworn garments. Step forth now!

Millions of souls, step forth now! Be converted by my love, my intense love for you, O soul. I AM the consuming by sacred fire of self-condemnation, unworthiness, and the sinful sense.

Awake! I say. *Awake!* I say. And the Christ of me and all shall give thee light. *Awake* now and be shaken. I AM the living One. I AM your brother here and now. I take your hand.

O thou child of unworthiness, *Come* to me now! *Come* to me now! *Come* to me now! Your brothers and sisters attend thee. *Come* to me now, O soul. Take the step forward now. I AM *here* and in my Electronic Presence I appear to millions of souls whom I desire to save in this hour.

O saints on earth, O Keepers of the Flame, *rise* with me and *stand* in defense of these souls of Light. I *woo* them back! And I show you, O unworthy ones—unworthy only by your own lack of sense of Christhood—I show you these Lightbearers. I show you what you can be by diligence, even in the twinkling of an eye.

Come now and take my hand. *Come* now, I say. I *AM* in the Spirit of the Resurrection. I *impart* to you the *leaping* of the spark of the resurrection flame. *I AM* igniting and quickening that threefold flame in your heart.

Come now, for I AM Jesus. I AM your brother and I come to save that which is lost.[26]

O LORD, return now the elements lost. O LORD, fill in now the weak places and let the rough be made plain.[27]

O soul of Light, *Come* now into the union by the Holy Spirit. *Leave* off the cups of self-indulgence, which is self-suicide, and the squandering of light until there is nothing left in the cups of the chakras. I take my sword. I cut you free by the authority of your own Christ Self. *Now* declare your own freedom, O soul. *Now* declare it! *Now* declare it!

So I descend into the level of the astral plane in the astral body. *So* I go there with the quickening fire of the resurrection. *Rise* out of Death and Hell! *Rise* up ere the flames lick your feet!

I AM the blazing power of the Son of God. I have come with my angels to rescue you now. I will not leave thee except thou commandest me in free will to do so. And I AM here to restore the faculty of free will—clear-seeing, clear-knowing. *I AM THAT I AM.*

I AM the Amen.

I AM the AUM.

You must know, beloved Keepers of the Flame, that I have dedicated my Easter address 1987 to this cause of the rescuing of souls from dead-letter doctrines and all manner of self-indulgence *because there is a war.* It is ongoing and continuing. And the devils would tear them limb from limb until they sense themselves insane and have no more heart for the struggle.

I AM here and I have summoned Archangel Michael. I summon all the Archangels in the command of God and Michael, thou Prince of the Church.

O holy ones of God, I command you from the heart of the Father—Go to! Cut free them in the seven planes of being. Cut free them throughout the quadrants of Matter. *Blaze* the light of this dispensation of Cosmos. And let them come to the marriage supper of the Lamb.[28] For I hold court in heaven this night. And I invite the beggars and the waifs and the orphans to my table. I invite all that have not been dealt with justly by the rich, the prosperous and the proud.

Blessed hearts, come to the marriage supper of the Lamb. Come, then, all among you who need this sealing of your heart to my Sacred Heart. Come, then, and make yourself an elder brother, an elder sister of these almost lost ones.

Blessed hearts, long ago I said, "Feed my sheep."[29] And this you will also do. But in this hour, I say, take up the sword of the Spirit and *fight* for my sheep ere they are lost to the clutches of the drug peddlers and the peddlers of deceit and annihilation. This is my cry and my plea.

Angels of the Resurrection, angels of Archangel Uriel, Spirit of the Resurrection, descend where I have placed my Electronic Presence twenty-four hours a day for the rescue of souls! Wrap them in the swaddling garment, mother-of-pearl, warmth and comforting presence of the resurrection flame.

This is my decree, O God. I thank Thee that Thou hast heard my Call and answered—even the answer forthcoming through these, my beloved.

I send you as sunbeams of my Sacred Heart to brighten a world and to tell all the world we are not defeated but shod with sandals—winged sandals of light. And we shall be and are Victory's legions now and forever: It is done.

"The Summit Lighthouse Sheds Its Radiance O'er All the World to Manifest as Pearls of Wisdom." This dictation by Jesus Christ was **delivered** through the Messenger of the Great White Brotherhood Elizabeth Clare Prophet on **Easter Sunday, April 19, 1987,** during the 6-day Easter conference, *Christ's Resurrection in You,* held at the Downtown Dallas Hilton, **Dallas, Texas**. (**1**) In the service prior to the dictation, the Messenger read John 20:1–18 on the resurrection of Jesus Christ and his appearance to Mary Magdalene. She then read from the Gnostic text **The Gospel of Mary Magdalene** (from the Nag Hammadi library) expounding on the mysteries taught to Mary Magdalene by the Lord which she imparts to the disciples after his resurrection. Sermon and dictation published on two 90-min. cassettes (B87030, B87031), $13.00 for set (add $.80 for postage). (**2**) Here Jesus declares his Mother, the Blessed Virgin, to be "the Teacher and the true and living Guru of all." (**3**) Matt. 7:15–20; 12:33–35. (**4**) Matt. 24:23–26; Luke 17:21. (**5**) Mark 15:39. (**6**) I Pet. 2:5. (**7**) II Tim. 2:15. (**8**) Matt. 5:3. (**9**) Ps. 23:5. (**10**) **Atlantean miscreations.** See Mark L. Prophet and Elizabeth Clare Prophet, *The Lost Teachings of Jesus II,* pp. 300–304. (**11**) **Child sacrifice.** Lev. 18:21; 20:2–5; Deut. 12:31; 18:10; II Kings 16:3; 17:17; 21:6; 23:10; II Chron. 28:3; 33:6; Ps. 106:37, 38. (**12**) **Child sacrifice denounced by the prophets.** Jer. 7:31, 32; 19:1–6; 32:35; Ezek. 16:20, 21, 36; 20:26, 31; 23:37–39; Isa. 57:5; Amos 5:25, 26; Mic. 6:7. (**13**) John 8:32. (**14**) Matt. 26:28; John 1:29; I Pet. 1:19; Rev. 7:14; 12:11. (**15**) Heb. 9:22. (**16**) **Sin blotted out**. Ps. 51:1, 9; Isa. 43:25; 44:22; Jer. 31:34; Acts 3:19; Heb. 8:12; 10:17. (**17**) **"Put off the old man..."** Eph. 4:22–24; Col. 3:9, 10; Rom. 6:6. (**18**) John 14:6. (**19**) John 7:38. (**20**) Matt. 10:6; 15:24. (**21**) Matt. 11:30. (**22**) **God is no respecter of persons.** Deut. 10:17; II Sam. 14:14; Acts 10:34; Rom. 2:11; Eph. 6:9; Col. 3:25; I Pet. 1:17. (**23**) Jesus and Kuthumi, *Corona Class Lessons,* Summit University Press, pp. 177–84, $12.95 (add $1.00 for postage). (**24**) Matt. 10:34. (**25**) John 4:35. (**26**) Matt. 18:11–14; Luke 15:3–7; 19:10. (**27**) Isa. 40:4; Luke 3:5. (**28**) Rev. 19:9. (**29**) John 21:15–17.

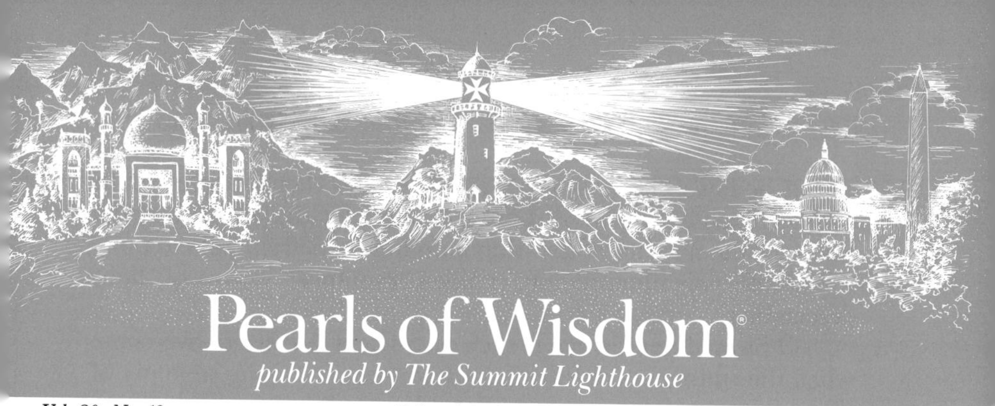

Pearls of Wisdom®

published by The Summit Lighthouse

Vol. 30 No. 19 — *Beloved God Meru* — *May 10, 1987*

Christ's Resurrection in You

IX

To Plead the Cause of Youth

O Love that unites hearts whose filigree thread is tied in a bowknot of love at the altar of Titicaca!

You may seldom think of us as Father and Mother representing the Godhead to your souls but we are indeed Manus of the root race. And thus, bearing the Feminine Ray, the ray of Cosmic Christ illumination to a world, we are grateful to greet you here to remind you, beloved, that this conference is convoked for Christ's resurrection in all peoples of North and South America.

Lo! the entire hemisphere is bathed in this hour in the fullness of the light of Lake Titicaca. It is a golden glow of Christ wisdom. Therefore, legions of the resurrection Spirit, so intensify now this aura of oneness!

We come, then, sponsors by right of all other evolutions of this hemisphere not included as the United States. You see, beloved, our dispensation from Helios and Vesta allows us to complement, coordinate and cooperate with beloved Saint Germain and Portia. Thus, it is in the mandala of heaven that many beings in Cosmos may add their crowns to the crown of Christ on this occasion.

Our coming is to extend to this place and area the golden spheres established at the Inner Retreat.[1] We come in our sponsorship to assist in placing the electrodes for the holding of the balance until the consciousness of the many may catch up to the few in the understanding of the dynamics of power in earth as it is misused in power politics and war and technology.

Blessed ones, we are also betting on the Lightbearers and the Keepers of the Flame with the full conviction of our mantle and causal bodies. There is much at stake, and therefore we would give as much as the Great Law will allow for the drawing of the circle for the nativity of the Manchild in hearts from pole to pole.

Shafts of illumination, golden radiance, dawn of light descending!

O blessed ones, there is such an ancient density to overcome when the rudiments of learning are so meager among so many of the evolutions of these nations. Would to God that the "Education of the Heart" and all of the teachings we have given the Messengers were published! O beloved, the revolution in education will not come until these have gone forth in your own publications on education.

You contain the keys, you have applied them—they work. Mother Mary is waiting and so are we. All who are teachers and see the success of our school must know that it is not enough to educate the few. The many must have combined with the Montessori method all those innovations that have been inspired upon you, ingenious through the Holy Spirit.

Blessed ones, as is always the case, as you have discovered, until you hold your prayer vigils on education, on the proper reading method, on the proper acceleration of children that they might finish the responsibilities of schooling at an earlier age to move on to careers, professions, and service—*blessed ones, until the prayer vigil is held and the books are published, you will continue to see a yoke, even the cross itself, on the backs of the youth.*

They are the target in every nation through all the world of the forces of Death and Hell. And those who are adults seldom comprehend what burdens lead the teenager to suicide. These are not all nonthinking ones. Some simply fall beneath the weight of their cross, bearing as they do a portion of world karma. For they have volunteered before taking embodiment, and there has been no Simon the Cyrenian to carry that cross for them while they should also bear the karma of the earth—no Joseph of Arimathea to anoint their bodies with myrrh and aloes.

Blessed ones, there are Christed ones in the earth and Mother Mary has called the Messenger and does call you now—"Take them down from the cross!" This is the message that comes from the heart of the *Pietà*.

Realize that the Divine Mother in you must understand that the gap called the generation gap is that which is perpetuated by demons and false hierarchies of anti-youth in the earth. And they move to separate you from sensitivity to the situation and seeing the problems or knowing just how far a child, a teenager may be dragged into the grips of the toilers of the astral plane.

They [children and teenagers] do not tell you, for they would keep up the appearance of that which you desire to see, ever desiring to please the parent. Thus, in so doing they forfeit any assistance that might bc forthcoming—and then, beloved, it is too late and too hard to bear.

We are the sponsors of youth and of a new generation. We *must have* a new generation, for so many have bodies that they have corrupted through following the pied pipers of this decade.

Blessed ones, we must prepare for a future when the survivors shall be the Lightbearers. Today it is difficult enough to survive physically. I ask you, then, how can they even begin to survive spiritually when what is upon them is of such a dread and diabolical nature?

I therefore take this opportunity, Meru in the fullness of Cosmic Christ illumination—flanked by Jophiel, Apollo and Lumina and Lord Lanto and many angels of illumination's flame—to plead the cause of youth, even as Jesus in the fullness of the Second Ray this day has pled the cause for those who sense themselves unworthy. There are so many who need help, and the force has a plot agoing to keep you from the awareness, to keep you lulled by the forcefield and aura of your own decrees and therefore not understanding just how terrible—*how terrible is the burden upon the children of this earth.*

Blessed ones, we need an army of mothers and fathers and sponsors and teachers who will take the intensity of the call—taught by the Messenger and being perfected by the chelas—and use the Archangel Michael Rosary to bring a concentrated effort of judgment on segments of life that are bringing Death and Hell into the very marketplace.

Blessed ones, look for the worst and deal with it first. For you are the ones who by this science of the sword, the sacred Word, are holding back an even greater flood tide of Darkness that was in fact programmed and planned and plotted in hell but has not seen its day—for the Keepers of the Flame have indeed kept the flame! [11-sec. applause]

You will note that the emissaries of heaven go to the successful ones, the ones trustworthy and tried and proven who have shown that they will wield the sword and that they truly know what must be done.

Precious hearts, in the building of the Inner Retreat, in the building of that Camelot on the site planned, you will understand that the greater the security and the greater the strength of the heart of the movement, the greater the light and dispensation that can be forthcoming from the Manus Himalaya, the Great Divine Director and Vaivasvata.

Hear, then, as we call. We call for the securing, the building and the putting in place of all that is needed in the sense of spiritual/physical survival. We call for your going out from this hub of the wheel [the Inner Retreat] and that many spokes will reach many cities. Let the call go forth—even your call to those who sleep. Blessed ones, there are many.

Therefore, I read to you now a scroll. This scroll, beloved, has been penned by the angels of our retreat. And it is the setting forth by the beloved Goddess Meru and myself of the priorities which we see for the protection and the securing of youth to a ripened age of maturity and Christhood at thirty-three:

First and foremost, *the dedication of education upon the Word and the Sacred Heart*—dedicating the three R's as the three rays of the threefold flame and therefore setting the foundation whereby all learning might proceed from within, from the interior castle, from the secret chamber of the heart and the soul's ascent to that place prepared, through the gentle meditations and inspirational sendings of the Messenger and their teachers. Thus, do not forsake a spiritual path in the classroom.

Blessed ones, parents need understanding and training. Therefore, second on our list is *parental training* and the use of the Cosmic Clock in order for parents to accelerate and proceed with all diligence in the slaying of the dweller on the threshold [the carnal mind in themselves as well as in their offspring] and in the gaining of an understanding of their relationship to their parents—making a conscious decision to root out those behavioral patterns and attitudes involving the subconscious hatred of the child that has been placed upon them [through the ancestral tree] and is [may be] being transmitted to their offspring.

There must be as point three *a pact* made *twixt parents, teachers and sponsors of children* to work together as a threefold flame of devotion in this Community and then city by city. This entails the realization that Death and Hell desire to devour your children and therefore you must pray fervently! You must vow, after understanding the meaning of the vow, to stand between the youth of the world and Death and Hell.

Blessed ones, it is wrong that children are conscripted to fight in the Middle East, that guns are placed in their hands before they have transcended even the age of seven! They know nothing but war and death. How can they carry a flame of peace and freedom when their hearts beat in torment for that struggle that you see in

Afghanistan and amongst those leaders of gangs that come out of the Middle East attacking one another and others?

Blessed ones, you see in these rival groups the seeds of anarchy—the seeds of anarchy sown. And such groups have thrived on planets that have lost all government, all organization and the right use of power.

Fourth on our list must be the white-fire bastion of *the vow* made. When you take this stand, beloved, you will become the targets of the attackers of youth. These are foul spirits—bastard ones, fallen angels and devils, the lowest of the low—used by false hierarchies who do not soil their hands but use the lowest types of criminal elements on the astral plane to do their dirty work.

Blessed ones, adults have avoided the encounter, the confrontation, the wrestling with the "beasts" that sit upon their children. How many more teen suicides need there be to alarm a population that there is surely something rotten in America! Blessed hearts, this cannot continue.

Once the vow is taken, you must remember the first Mother of the Flame, Clara Louise, who kept a daily prayer vigil for the youth, beginning at four in the morning and not concluding till late morning, praying for all souls of the youth, from the unborn to those in college and beyond.

Blessed hearts, some must keep the flame.

Community action is next on our list—an involvement of community that does reinforce family as these twin pillars of family and community brace a path of individualism for those of all ages. The breaking down of the family, the breaking down of the neighborhood communities—this, beloved ones, is a fragmenting of society and the separation of members of karmic groups as well as individuals of varying ages so that they cannot learn from one another and ripen and mature as the mature inspire those coming up and the youth introduce the new wave of a new age that can also challenge those in the middle of life or retiring.

Community, then, must be a stronghold of values, of serving together, of meeting one another's needs and of establishing goals and priorities, not the least of which is the protection of that circle of lives. Blessed ones, a community must have more than the survival of itself or its happiness as a goal. It must have a totality of a reason for being toward which every member is galvanized and does rise.

Beloved hearts, apropos this, our next point on the list is the *training* of all members of society and especially the children *in responsible citizenship*—in taking responsibility for the necessary functions of the group, whether as a police force, as firemen, as a city council, or as those who are supplying the unguent and the service in order that a community might endure.

When all of the forces of chaos are attempting to break down a way of life, let us turn to *the music of the spheres*. Let us turn to the quieting of souls, to the invoking of harmonies, to the bringing forth of the golden-age sounds that have not been heard. Thus, this point on our list, beloved, is an activation from the heart of Cyclopea, who does join us in sponsoring this call. Cyclopea holds secret melodies waiting to come forth that will remind the youth of ancient times, inner vows, other years when beauty and love, even in etheric octaves, was their lot.

The youth need comfort of the Holy Spirit and not surfeiting. Tragically, tragically, few among them in actuality desire a path and a discipleship. Therefore, we do recommend the study and the structuring of a program that does *reinforce individuality* and thereby diminish the necessity in perilous times for such an emotional interdependence among teenagers as to make them fear to stand their ground for a cause or a principle.

Why is peer pressure of such great consequence, beloved? Is it because of absence of parental reinforcement, understanding, and even the comradery of a family that is not so distant and that does not set artificial barriers between one generation and the next? Let us not so poorly educate children as to see that they do not know their own minds or hearts or values, having had no noble ideals or stories of saints and heroes or examples of karmic consequences of misdeeds.

Blessed ones, there are devils in the schoolhouses of America programming children to that which ought not to be. There are devils in the motion-picture industry programming youth to the bravado of the fallen angels, to the daredevil life and the devil-may-care attitude.

Blessed ones, I must tell you that judgments have descended upon cities for the desecration of Life by the placing before the people (or even for the protecting) of corrupt practices, perversions, misuses of the sacred fire and for exposing that which should be sealed in the secret chamber of the privacy of man and wife. Blessed hearts, we veil our eyes, trusting to postpone the descent of judgment upon those who have set before youth the alternatives and sexual choices that have become a mode of life.

Were we to take any single factor that does truly spell the end of civilization, we would say that it is the popularization, it is the making common, and it is the placing before little children of those matters [of sexual intimacy] that ought to wait for them until the ripening of age and soul and consciousness and maturity. The fallen angels have taken as their greatest weapon against youth the enticements of sex at an age when a generation ago little children were not even exposed to the questions that they are being asked to decide in this hour.

Thus the scroll continues and the list goes on . . .

Blessed ones, unless there is *a determined all-out war* launched by those in heaven and on earth, you will find that though all other problems may be solved you will not have another generation qualified to rule, to govern, or to build a society that is just, a civilization that is advanced. So serious is this picture that I desire not to cloud the issue with any other topic in my dictation saving the dispensation of golden light and spheres extending and anchored in the etheric octave over this place.

Now legions of Light and Christed ones and angels of Jophiel's band do gather the combined momentum of your decree force and the dictations [given at this conference] to form a three-dimensional thoughtform of the star that is the emblem of this state, to symbolize the path of the individual going within to the secret chamber of the heart and there being reborn by the secret rays in the image of Christ. This is the new birth of Bethlehem that we desire to see intensify in this state, that this state might be in America an example to all states even as America ought to be the example to all nations.

Each time we send our Messenger and chelas to an area, we look for fruits, we look for the gain that our dispensations require in order for us to give new and intensified dispensations. I know the great hearts of the people of this great state will surely feel the pulsations of Titicaca, will surely know that Texas is a state of golden illumination's flame, even as she is holding the balance in the base chakra of America in the very center of the nation. Thus, of the great energy that has flowed from this state we would say, let it flow again! Let life move on but let the economy be based on an abundant Life in Christ's service.

Nada, with the beings of the Secret Love Star, is with her own hands fashioning out of the light this star symbol and focus that does represent opportunity day by day for all who come within the borders of the state to be liberated—especially from a false theology—and to pioneer Aquarius because you have listened and heard and become even the Christ-bearers.

We do look, then, for the dispensation of your hearts in these publishings that we might have the wherewithal to right the axis of world education, beginning in the United States. We would also like to have such tools as you have provided Saint Germain and Jesus and the Seven Chohans [recently published books], and we know that this is the hour for this dispensation.

Therefore, seeing the adversity that has beset you, the teachers, the Messenger and parents, we place a certain topaz jewel, and in it our presence and focus, that we may take on that burden of world karma that stands between you and the accomplishment of this call to publishing.

It was Sanat Kumara who gave to the publishing department of Camelot the needed and necessary intercession for the holding of the balance of karma held by the staff and the Church until the move and the publications could be completed.[2]

Having seen so great a multiplication that has, in fact, beloved, balanced the karma that was held for you in its very action of enlightenment, we too may pledge our causal bodies with Casimir Poseidon and those who have served with the Messengers and yourselves before. This we may do because we have seen the good fruit and diligence of your Tree of Life.

A final word, beloved—do not underestimate the enmity of those unfortunate ones in the churches who do consider this message and Messenger a threat to their very existence. They pray with a frenzy. And the more that they condemn, beloved, the more they become possessed. It is a sad state and a travesty upon the freedom of religion which this nation ought to espouse, but it is happening through the churches that have made it their business to denounce *The Lost Teachings of Jesus.*

We are the God and Goddess Meru. We are the sponsors and the teachers of Jesus and all who have come to minister unto the sixth root race. Thus, Jesus and many other saints have long studied in our retreat. It is a home base for them. We invite you to come frequently.

We, therefore, are of course concerned with the twisting of Jesus' doctrine and we desire to see that twisting removed from the field of education. And it is Mother Mary who first went to the Father and then to us to secure our attention, grant, and dispensation.

Thus you know that with the World Teachers we shall abide with you until every child on earth does have the opportunity to be tutored in the heart by the Holy Christ Self and by anointed teachers and parents and sponsors.

We shall place—and have remaining here throughout the twenty-four-hour cycle—our causal bodies for the prayer vigil for

Central and South America, for the prayer vigil for Nicaragua and for all troublesome situations in the lower hemisphere.

Blessed ones, your calls are needed. I seal you that you may return early. It is a day for Keepers of the Flame. Therefore, we graciously invite you who have come to our door to enter the fraternity and experience in the name of Fátima a prayer vigil for the judgment of the fallen angels in World Communism and the conspirators supporting it.

Blessed ones, learn to wield the two-edged sword!

Thus, we with Saint Germain shall not withdraw our presence till it be fulfilled. And at the conclusion we send our angels to your home and place of service to protect you there.

By the cosmic cross of white fire, the angels—angels of the Body and Blood of Christ, the Ruby Ray, and the ascension flame—do send their love and have asked me to speak their word of gratitude to your company. Thus, angels are grateful and heaven does rejoice even as you rejoice in God's name.

I AM in the flame of the Central Sun and I AM THAT I AM in the Father/Mother God. Lo! *I AM.* Lo! *we are* in the oneness of that Sun. So it is done. Amen.

"The Summit Lighthouse Sheds Its Radiance O'er All the World to Manifest as Pearls of Wisdom."
This dictation by God Meru was **delivered** through the Messenger of the Great White Brotherhood Elizabeth Clare Prophet on **Easter Sunday, April 19, 1987,** during the 6-day Easter conference, *Christ's Resurrection in You,* held at the Downtown Dallas Hilton, **Dallas, Texas**. (**1**) See Jesus Christ, December 25, 1986, "The Coming of the Divine Teacher," 1986 *Pearls of Wisdom,* vol. 29, no. 78, p. 682; or 1987 *Pearls of Wisdom,* vol. 30, no. 1, p. 16, n. 1. (**2**) See Sanat Kumara, July 27, 1986, "The Empowerment of Christhood," 1986 *Pearls of Wisdom,* vol. 29, no. 71, pp. 622–23.

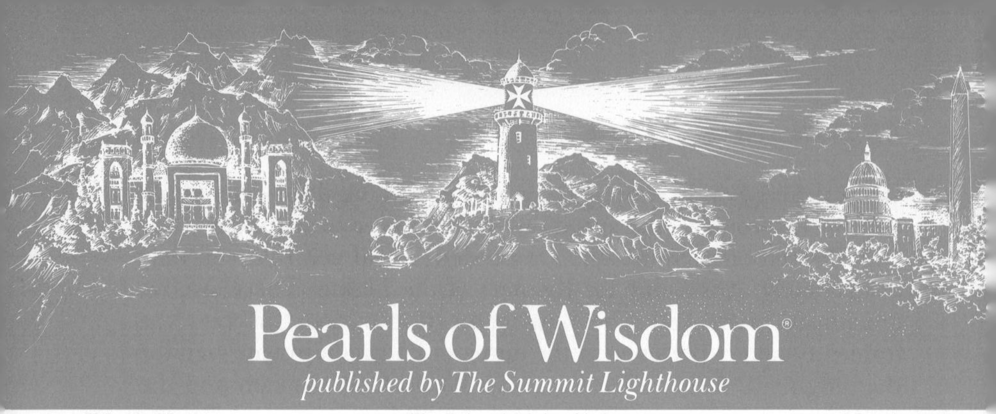

Vol. 30 No. 20 — The Beloved Maha Chohan — May 17, 1987

Christ's Resurrection in You

X

"To Breathe upon You the Breath of the Holy Spirit"

Peace be unto you!

As the Father hath sent me, even so send I you.
[The holy breath sounds.]

Receive ye the Holy Ghost.[1]
[intonation of holy vowels and consonants, 54 seconds]

Purusha, Purusha, Purusha, Purusha, Purusha. [whispered]

Unto the Father I kneel—the Father I AM.

Unto the Father I kneel—the Father I AM.

Unto the Father I kneel—the Father I AM.

This dictation by the Maha Chohan was **delivered** through the Messenger just after midnight at the conclusion of the Easter Sunday evening service **Monday, April 20, 1987.** (**1**) John 20:21, 22.

Vol. 30 No. 21 | Beloved Mother Mary | May 24, 1987

Christ's Resurrection in You

XI

The Old Order Must Pass Away

I, your Mother, have placed your feet upon the very first place of the highway of our God. Your feet, then, positioned on this highway and keeping on this road of life may ultimately arrive at the goal, beloved, that is your beginning in the heart of God.

I will not tell you how long is this road, beloved. For infinity is too long for some and too short for others. Rest assured that there is a co-measurement on this highway to be established by you through the development of your heart, one with my heart.

I do this, beloved, for one and all have given much, even to the saving of the Church of my Son—the Church Universal and Triumphant. As he said to the disciples, Ye have been with me through my temptations[1]—so you have also endured through the initiations of our initiate, whose name is now spoken in ancient tongue by Lanello.

Therefore, beloved, may you endure the next round whereby the highway of our God will surely test your souls but with the support of the office, mantle and causal body of the Woman clothed with the Sun represented in our Messenger. Therefore, beloved, there are cycles and seasons.

I see now the bejeweled garment placed upon you by angels—these jewels embroidered into a fabric magnificent. Lest you consider that there are those who have tried less than others, I would point out to you that in some of this embroidery there are stones missing for virtues and graces not diligently acquired. And in some there are many stones missing, whereas for others there are more clusters where there has been a heightened service.

Thus you see, beloved, that stripes upon angels, epaulets do indicate a certain attainment. And it is so in many activities on earth—not only in the military but also in fraternal and scouting orders. Therefore know, beloved, that not a single sacrifice goes unrecorded or unrewarded. This ought to be a motto you say to yourself when the Virgo misuse of the [Libra] scales prompts you to consider something an injustice.

Oh, is it not wondrous to compare yourself to your Christ image or I AM Presence instead of to another who seems with ease to acquire without the same toil that you go through?

Blessed ones, heaven always expresses gratitude in a magnanimous way to every heart. We believe (and have spoken much about it) that it is our joyous responsibility to confirm the greatness of souls, to make known achievement—to love, to praise and to let it be known in the heart of hearts of a chela that truly good has been accomplished. And this is due to the fact that there is so much condemnation on earth that we say, where praise is due, let praise be spoken!

Blessed ones, rewards may come late. They may come after lifetimes when you come full circle to lay your crowns before Him, to give God the glory and to recognize that the highest reward is not greatness of itself but to be the servant of all and to be the instrument of the Greatest Light.

I come with this scepter of the Shepherd's crook that is my Son's and I tell you that the Mother flame in the Church must be restored fully. I tell you, beloved, that even in his life the apostle Peter never completed the assignments given to him by Jesus, neither when he was with him following the resurrection nor after Jesus' ascension—to the present hour.

The incompleteness of that mission is reflected in the incompleteness and the corruption of the mission of the Church. And by "corruption" I mean the decay—the very quality of it being capable of being decayed or corroded. This also does apply to actual corruption, as you would use the term, within the hierarchy.

Blessed ones, do you not find it strange that the original Vicar of Christ, Peter, was married and yet all others who followed have been given the law of celibacy? Do you understand, beloved, that the rabbis who came before were married and are to this hour? And do you understand that the nature of wholeness found in the balance of Alpha and Omega is a security and a protection to the path of spirituality when complementary ones may serve together in holy matrimony?

You find, then, that where the spiritual teaching as practiced in the Far East is not a part of the goal of celibacy, the end of that celibacy is far more heinous than the lawful marriage that is also ordained for those clergy outside of the Roman Church. Thus, today homosexuality is rampant in the Church with high percentages of my priests so engaged. The misuse of the sacred fire, unlawfully [according to the laws of God], does place those priests outside of their vows, outside of a sense of personal dignity and truly outside of the holiness of the altar.

These burdens upon the religious in holy orders have, as you know, in times long ago resulted in pregnancies and often the abortion or the death [killing] of the child at birth in an attempt to conceal and remove the evidence of the infraction of that code of ethics and conduct.

Blessed hearts, it is good to place before oneself goals and self-discipline. Even the path of celibacy may be put on by married couples for a season of devotion, fasting and prayer. These cycles, then, of conjugal love side by side with an acceleration of the marriage to the living Christ can therefore allow the individual to be balanced, to retain dignity, to know the beauty of family life yet not to be deprived of the priesthood of holy orders.

Even so, the ancient prophets were married. Even so, some who later became saints and came apart from the world were married in the beginning, such as Siddhartha. And you know, beloved, that my own Son shared a beautiful love with his twin flame, Magda, who held the balance for him, even as I did, as he pursued a mission of immensity, holding the sacred fire of the Divine Mother in the full mastery of his chakras.

Blessed ones, take heart then, for the corruptions of the old Church must pass away with the structure itself. Souls must be liberated. Devils who have crept in, as the fallen angels who perverted the temples of the Mother in Lemuria, must be bound and judged.

This temple, this inn, this holy church, is to us the new wineskin for the new wine.[2] It would be impossible, beloved, to deliver the magnificent teachings on marriage, the balancing of karma, the transcending of the human marriage and the entering into the marriage made in heaven given the old wineskins of orthodoxy.

It is important to understand, as the Messenger has said, that all must have a path that they can follow—steps that are not too difficult nor too easy. You know with children that in either case they become bored or frustrated; and therefore the initiations set by the angels and the great Masters are meet for the individual.

We must give you those knotty problems that we also faced. We must place before you even a conundrum, as it were, or a Chinese puzzle. When no answer seems to be the answer, you must find the way through—you must find the loophole.

You must understand that on earth and in karmic conditions and circumstances there are, in fact, some situations to which there are no solutions. This is a very important truth, beloved. Consider well what I have just said: I have said there are some situations for which there are no solutions.

The present order of the Roman Church—its corruption, its travesty against my Son and his Teaching, its compromise with World Communism which bespeaks some plot or conspiracy as has been suggested[3]—surely, beloved, must show that the old order must be replaced by the new. Yet there is no resolution to that old order because of free will, because of entrenched forces, and because of such a horrendous karma on the part of this institution that it is as though it would be better to let it go bankrupt and dissolve rather than to have a new set of lifestreams and saints take on the Church and with it take on a karma that is not even theirs.

Thus, when individuals buy into businesses that are about to go bankrupt, they must take on the debts if that bankruptcy is indeed to be avoided. Therefore understand, beloved, that in the case of this life, this planet and system of worlds, the action of the Holy Spirit, the action of Shiva, has provided a recourse: The Destroyer (or the Dissolver, or Transmuter) must simply take the clay pot, break the vessel and let that clay go back to the Divine Potter and be remolded anew, fully stripped of its old pattern and energy, ready now to be formed in a higher matrix.

Another example of a situation to which there is no solution is life itself. Individuals come to the end of their karmic round with threescore and ten or more or less. At that point in life the body may suffer disease and old age, have expended its light, and have no further endowment or opportunity for the cycle. The resolution to a nonsolution is to break the mold, allow the soul to fly from the prison house of matter and have the opportunity to begin anew in a new temple.

So it is true with outworn houses and buildings. Along come the wreckers. Many are glad yet many protest, for they are attached to the past. They desire to see neither themselves pass away nor the old order nor the old institutions nor the body itself. And they do not easily give in to Death or the Death Angel.

I come, then, with this teaching that you might wax wise and philosophical concerning what Saint Germain has instructed you on—to deal in the realm of the possible. This teaching was given in the Washington, D.C., Teaching Center on the occasion of the downing of this [KAL] plane where all were destroyed. Beloved ones, to expect the impossible or the improbable that is not in the realm of the practical nor in the givens of mankind's free will is to be out of touch with reality and what decrees can accomplish and what they cannot.

Miracles are indeed a fulfillment of cosmic law and not an exception, and they come about because of the graces that are stored in the causal body of those involved. Thus, miracles do happen but every miracle is in the framework of that which is possible and according to the Divine Plan and the Law itself.

Intercession comes, then, through the sponsorship of Lightbearers. And when Lightbearers consider the world, they must not impute to the world the purity of motive or the faithfulness or even the desire for attainment or a golden age that lodges in their own hearts. This is one of the most important lessons that I must teach to my children and sons and daughters as they newly take up life on earth.

It takes some time to realize that most of the world does not share your zeal for heavenly things or the abstentions from the fun and frolicking that most people engage in. And therefore, a life that is full of the joy and bliss of heaven, the communion of saints, has no appeal to those who must have the noise and raucousness of this planet.

Blessed ones, there are downward spirals descending as Taurus enters. There is a situation of the Dark Cycle coming, and you have had clues to the events of this Dark Cycle even in the dictations you have heard. Beloved ones, if it is possible for you to see and hear the dictation of the Ascended Master Pope John XXIII recently given at the Inner Retreat, you will understand the decisions made by the Cosmic Council concerning the Church of Rome, this Church Universal and Triumphant, and our Vicar.

Blessed ones, the hours are moving swiftly. The sweetest joy of my heart in coming to you this evening has been to bring to you the gift of placing your feet on the highway of our God. For this occasion my angels have sewn for you little slippers that you may wear—soft slippers for a highway that is not rough as earth's highway is and yet fully adequate to the support you will need on this journey.

Blessed ones, the highway of our God is traversed only by saints and Cosmic Beings. But you are not free to take the next step except you enter the next initiation. But having two feet on the edge of this road where heaven begins and earth leaves off is a very momentous gift and a very momentous occasion. Think about it often and pray to the Archangels to give you those tests where you might take a single footstep forward.

Sometime along this highway the grand initiations leading to the resurrection and the ascension may be accorded to you. Thus, when you are on the highway of our God you may find that the change in vibration is altogether natural and not so sudden in the reentering into the higher octaves.

I am therefore expressing to you the gratitude of the hierarchy of Light for your diligence in this service.[4] Certain entrenched momentums of opposition to our Church and Messenger and movement have been bound and dissolved by the hosts of the LORD for your very staying power. And therefore in these hours we have been able not only to deliver a mandate and a thrust in Central and South America but we have been able to use the calls for other areas.

Beloved ones, the practice of voodoo and black magic against your leadership and yourselves is ongoing not only by voodoo 'artists' but also by those of the major world's religions. Whether or not they use them in combination with actual voodoo rites and bloodletting, it matters not; for where there is hatred in prayer, there is black magic.

See to it, beloved, that you make the call to your great friend Archangel Michael. Trust God. Place your hand in his and in ours.

Understand that the beginning of this cycle of Taurus does deal a death blow to certain forces of Darkness that were raging heavily under the sign of Aries, determined to displace the God-identity and God-control of anyone in this movement into whose psyche they could gain a toehold.

Thus the wrestling with Death and Hell described to you—faced by the Messenger and explained by Saint Germain[5] and other Ascended Masters—is ongoing. And Death is not only a false hierarchy, an Absolute Evil, and a band of demons, it is the false belief that the self must pass away as mortal. This false belief rests on the mistaken idea that you are mortal. Therefore affirm your immortality.

Blessed ones, I have a message to you from all elemental life and it is very simple—"Please don't forget us." As Morya says, "Forget me not," so the elementals have said to me today, "Our Mother, are they going to forget us? Will they not once call forth the violet flame for our bands?"

Blessed hearts, the elementals are so grateful for the violet flame already invoked for them in the decrees given at the Ranch, and wherever you have given them, that they have rendered many services to you individually which you may or may not have recognized. And therefore, I tell you, there is a bit of wisdom and enlightened self-interest in the thoughtfulness to give daily decrees for the elementals. They desire and need the violet flame to carry out a mighty service that does bring transmutation and the breaking of the old order and the old matrix that must come to pass in these earth changes.

Blessed ones, do not lament the passing away of that which is no longer useful. Be able to hold onto that which must be held onto, which is the Teaching and the Word of God. Be able to let go of that which you must let go of. This is a very important lesson in life, and it is part of the decision-making process.

Above all, beloved, when there is no answer or solution (or decision forthcoming) to a particular knotty problem on the world scene, at home, or in the Church, I ask you to call to my heart. For my Immaculate Heart does hold the original blueprint for every event and eventuality that could come forth out of the creation of God. It is a very strong inner blueprint, and it may be called up on the screen of the mind before you in your sanctuaries.

This blueprint, therefore, by contrast to the state of the problem as it appears to you, will show you the distance traveled between the original will of God and that which has come down to you as the mess that mortals make of the will of God. So, beloved, as you see that which is the equation of the perfection and the imperfection, you may attempt to pull some strands and begin to weave some substance of a likeness to that blueprint.

But in another sense you will come to understand it is important to take the whole ball of wax of human confusion and cast it into the sacred fire and the violet flame and immediately call for the replacement of that failed test or initiation with the original blueprint being clothed upon with the substance of the Body and Blood of Christ. In this way it is often accomplished ever so more quickly that you may build anew after you have torn down the old order.[6]

I leave you with these thoughts so that you may consider civilization, crime, burdens in the society, and in your heart begin to think as members of the Karmic Board, as Lords of the Seven Rays think. Think as I think by calling to (for) the diamond-shining Mind that God has given to me. Think in your heart as I think in my heart by calling for my Diamond Heart. Ask yourself, "How would our Mother Mary review this situation?"

If you had to vote at Cosmic Council, if you had to deliberate, if you had to give some sense of your position to the Lord of the World, how would you speak in council? How would you present yourself on that which you believe ought to be consumed on earth and not saved and that which ought to be saved?

I think you can all immediately think of things that should be instantaneously consumed by the sacred fire, such as houses of ill repute, such as pornographic films, child prostitution, and all areas where such activities take place. So as you continue up the ladder from the most vile of hell—on which most would find accord—you come to a place where you cross the line and you say to yourself, "Where is freewill choice and how will individuals learn from the experience of life if all these situations are suddenly no more?"

There will be many malcontents if there are no bars left in the world—no bowling alleys, gambling casinos and so forth. And so you will see that the very ones who have created these situations will re-create them again if they are given the opportunity to do so.

Therefore when considering what ought to be destroyed and preserved, regarding civilization in its decline, we realize that it is not only the removal of the miscreation but it is also the great and more serious deliberation of what to do about the lifewaves who have created those conditions. For when given a new place or a new civilization or a new opportunity, they will re-create them immediately because their desire bodies contain the patterns as well as the lusts as well as the demons and entities which carry over to the next life and the next.

You can begin to see, then, just how very complicated the decisions of the Lawmakers and those who embody the Law must be when considering the great question of how to salvage souls and a civilization and a way of life—how to keep the good and extract the evil and still preserve an identity, still preserve a way and yet not take with it the old order and its corruption.

Blessed ones, you can see by past history what has been the deliberation of cosmic councils. It was deemed that Atlantis must go down, for the evil and the misuse of science could not be allowed to proliferate. Therefore, the entire civilization was let go of. So it was in the case of Lemuria, and so it was the greater case according to the records of the planets Maldek and Hedron. The proliferation of evil being so great and the possibility of the loss of souls being grave, cosmic councils and the LORD himself determined that for the sake of Almighty God and his little ones, all should be removed from the physical and astral planes.

You know the Eastern teaching that at the end of cycles the entire universe is drawn up and is no longer material and all that is retained is the spiritual fruit of the glorying in God. This has also been the conclusion of the matter at the end of cycles. We are not at the end of a grand, grand cycle whereby we are returning to the Central Sun, but isolated individuals are at the end of their cycle and these ones are called Home by the Father/Mother God.

These ones who are called Home—for whom all of their karma and matter creation will be drawn up and will be taken back to the Central Sun—are the ones whom we have called to this activity and this Teaching. Therefore, all know when the words "It is the last time"[7] apply to them. And those who know this want to be very certain that everywhere they have left an untoward vibration, there violet flame flowers and footprints will be in its place.

These ones are also very concerned to leave firm footprints of violet flame that others might follow in. You will desire greatly from the heaven world to have vehicles whereby you can speak to those whom you love, those for whom you care and, prior to your return to the Central Sun, those with whom you may yet have karma even from the ascended state.

It is wonderful, beloved, to contemplate life and its opportunities before you and to be able to plan your life and plan it in keeping with the divine plan and find no pain in embracing the will of God and no sense of struggle in surrendering the anti-will. To see the rest of your life, from this very moment on, as an opportunity to become God—this, beloved, is the greatest news of the Everlasting Gospel.

Amplifying it in your hearts now, multiplying your heart flame by my own to the fullest extent of the mercy of the Law, I, Mary—Servant of the Most High God and of his sons, Archeia of the Fifth Ray, the Beloved of Raphael and of all my children, sons and daughters—do now consecrate Central America, Cuba, all islands of the Caribbean to my Immaculate Heart with a fervor, a righteousness and a wrath of the Cosmic Christ.

Thus the fire that descends is heaven's answer to your call. It is more than a consecration. It is a purging and a judgment. It is a branding as with a branding iron, and it is a divine decree!

In the name of the Father and of the Son and of the Holy Spirit, by the Shepherd's crook of my Son, I, Mary, infuse the entire territory with light and I say to you, beloved, Onward, march!—north, south, east, and west throughout Central America and onward to the very southern tip.

Let us keep in mind the God and Goddess Meru and their call to educate all people as to the knowledge of the hidden man of the heart, the Holy Christ Flame, the interior Light. This is our call and our calling.

And in this hour, therefore, our legions attack all centers of voodoo and witchcraft permitted by the church fathers throughout Central and South America right within our own tabernacles and temples and cathedrals.

Blessed ones, the accommodation of the Roman hierarchy to the superstitions and black magic of the people of Central and South America is a crime of the first magnitude against my Son and his little ones. For millions have been trapped into the astral plane, the psychic, and cursed to Death and Hell itself while the priests have stood by to allow the people their superstitious and evil practices rather than challenge them and perhaps lose members or control or money for their coffers.

It is a shocking experience, beloved, to see the evidences of voodoo and the malpractices of people, not outside but right within the churches. These practices all over the land are the open door to World Communism and to an age of Great Darkness.

Let all you who would take the flame to Central and South America know that you will be facing black magicians, fallen angels. And those who perform these practices are truly in league at inner levels with all of the terrorist acts of World Communism, which are the practice of Satanism—the shedding of the blood of the saints, their massacre and the violation of their bodies by devils incarnate.

These practices, beloved, come forth out of the evil heart of Lenin and his initiation of the dark cycle of Mother Russia, which has become the Soviet Union. That reincarnated one in the person of Anton LaVey, blessed hearts, continues to practice cursings and rites of Satan against all churches and lovers of God.

For the overstepping, therefore, of his bounds in the attacking of my representative, I say to you, in this hour he is stripped entirely of the powers of Satan and has them not! Archangel Michael stands over him and binds him in this moment as I speak to you, beloved! [38-sec. standing ovation]

You must ratify this judgment by your free will and by the authority of your being in embodiment—daily. This individual occupies physical space in physical matter. The saints on earth must call the judgment and wage a warfare of the Spirit and wield their swords of the sacred Word.

Understand that this is only the kingpin. You must know that that which is being judged are his words, his works, and his person. And the works of Anton LaVey are in support of every pleasure cult, all homosexuality, prostitution, the violation of the holy child, all evil, all gambling, and all money schemes. This one has dared to claim responsibility through Satanic rite and mortal cursings for the recent scandals that have taken place in the Christian churches.

Blessed hearts, indeed these fallen ones move against all who attempt to represent Christ. Therefore, know that they always know where are the highest initiates and who are the Keepers of the Flame. They know their day is done when confronted by the Call. They have seen their cursings literally dissolve and decompose, and they know what the source of that Call is and who is the mouthpiece thereof.

Therefore understand, until the Church of Satan itself does go down and until a larger body of people on earth protest that church instead of acclaiming it as the true and old religion, it will take the power of yourselves as Lightbearers to be one with God as a majority of free will.

These practices are an open door for the very same Satanic rites and other misuses of science practiced by aliens in their spacecraft and others in embodiment who would shun all association with the Church of Satan and yet have the identical vibration. Thus, Satanism is far more rampant than you would calculate. For it has to do with World Communism and the shedding of blood of the Lightbearers in every nation. It has to do with the abortion of life that is the work of Herod and his henchmen.

When you look at the ills of society and realize that it is the fallen angels, the Satans,[8] that have originated and sustained these, you will understand just how far-reaching is the support for the Church of Satan even without affiliation.

Let the judgment, then, begin with the source and the head and let it proceed throughout the world. For this world must become the cradle of the Divine Manchild and a golden-age civilization.

The question that hangs in the balance, beloved, is: Shall the Manchild be born or not be born in this hour? Whether the cradle is safe or not, we must see. We speak, then, of a specific lifestream as well as many Lightbearers who ought to be descending who have the anointing of Light.

Blessed hearts, much hangs in the balance. Therefore I have said what I have said. I have spoken what I have spoken. I have delivered the words of our Father and our Mother, of the Darjeeling Council and the Lords of Karma. All of these have been contributed in the flow and the stream of my delivery.

Therefore the hosts of heaven rejoice and the angels serve a heavenly mass in the Temple Beautiful. May you know that our love is with you forever and that we look forward to the day when we may walk with you on the highway of our God.

The benediction and grace of the Lord and Saviour Jesus Christ be upon you forever and forever, Amen.

"The Summit Lighthouse Sheds Its Radiance O'er All the World to Manifest as Pearls of Wisdom."

This dictation by Mother Mary was **delivered** through the Messenger of the Great White Brotherhood Elizabeth Clare Prophet on **Tuesday, April 21, 1987,** during the 6-day Easter conference, *Christ's Resurrection in You,* held at the Downtown Dallas Hilton, **Dallas, Texas.** (**1**) Luke 22:28. (**2**) Matt. 9:16, 17; Mark 2:21, 22; Luke 5:36–38. (**3**) On April 18, 1987, the Messenger delivered her "Fátima Update," which included a review of the little-known 1962 Vatican-Moscow Agreement. As part of the agreement, the Soviets allowed Russian Orthodox observers to attend Vatican II in exchange for the promise that the Vatican council would not attack the regime or people of Russia. Reportedly, the Church has continued to honor the agreement ever since. See Elizabeth Clare Prophet, "Fátima Update" (Part I), published with Part II of "Fátima Update" (5-10-87) on 4 cassettes, K87033-K87036, $26.00 for set (add $.80 for postage). (**4**) Prior to this dictation, a service was held for the liberation of Central and South America. (**5**) See Saint Germain, January 1, 1987, "The Vow," 1987 *Pearls of Wisdom,* vol. 30, no. 2, pp. 27–29. (**6**) Jer. 1:10. (**7**) I John 2:18. (**8**) **Satans** (pronounced Seh-tánz): the race of the seed of Satan who long ago rose up against the I AM Race and "who have infiltrated every corner of this galaxy and beyond." Jesus Christ pronounced their judgment, concurrent with the final judgment of Satan, in his dictation given February 1, 1982. See "The Final Judgment of Satan," 1982 *Pearls of Wisdom,* vol. 25, no. 16, pp. 187–96.

Vol. 30 No. 22 *Beloved Saint Germain* *May 31, 1987*

A Cosmic Realism

Keepers of the Flame of Liberty,

I AM here! [35-sec. standing ovation]

I bid you welcome to my heart—and be seated, if you will.

Blessed ones, Cosmic Beings are in council. I have been invited to their chambers. Therefore, I come quickly from that place prepared above where those concerned with the future of planet earth and her evolutions continue.

In these discussions, beloved, our Lord Gautama has been present as well as unnamed beings of Light. There has been in recent weeks a great gathering of forces of Light, presences who until this hour have had naught to do with planet earth for many tens of thousands of years. Beloved, they come not to preserve an old order but rather for the harvest of souls—souls of Light whose hour has come for the transition into highest octaves and the ascension.

Some of these souls have remained with earth beyond the necessary attainment for their ascension. These, then, are counted here and there and I shall not elaborate. I merely reveal to you on this day (that is also the birthday of my son Christopher[1])—that is my rejoicing in your heart upon the anniversary of my own ascension day—that Cosmic Beings, each and every one who does occupy the chair of Guru, remain loyal to the chela in the earth who has remained to keep his flame.

Thus, the obligation as a dharma of Cosmos is seen. Where there is a soul, where there is a Light that has realized Godhood, there is a reason for the descent of Cosmos in the person of the One and the many—chelas left behind, therefore, who volunteered to keep the flame unto this hour. This "hour" being a word for months, years, perhaps decades, for these times are short as cycles are reckoned and as opportunity can be fulfilled. Therefore, sense the weight of these presences, beloved, for earth has not been host to such beings for aeons.

Know, then, the burden of the LORD as Light! Know, then, the burden in the earth of a dark, dark cycle. Understand, beloved, the equation. The coming of the Great Gurus does signify that those who have kept the garden of God on earth, those who have represented them as the heirs do now receive an extraordinary presence of sponsorship.

Know, then, that with the drawing nigh of so great a Light there is also a descent of judgment upon those who have not heeded the word of their spokesman, even the heir himself, the Christed One representative of the living Guru.

Thus, inevitably where there are those pursuing a cosmic path in the hierarchical chain and where these are solitary figures in the earth and where a humanity or a mankind or a manifestation has not embraced that Light, that One anointed, then in addition to that evolution's dark cycle there must come even the judgment for the ignoring of the One Sent by the Great Guru to draw the many into alignment with a path of God-free being.

Thus, beloved, adding to the weight of crisis, as a cross that you face upon earth and a crossroads, must come not alone the karma of a dark cycle upon a people but the karma of judgment for their failure to receive the Great Guru and the Chela and the Path and the Light.

This Light contacting the earth may be devastating to some. And to others who have not forfeited their threefold flame, but who have kept that flame, increased and expanded it, there is yet that narrow window of opportunity to seize the hem of the garment of the Chela in the earth and thereby also be translated in the hour of that Chela's crucifixion, resurrection—and surely the ascension.

Beloved ones, there are many factors playing upon the outcome of earth. I do not present myself this eve to preempt the Wesak address of the Lord of the World. I come, therefore, to bless, to heal, to be with my own and to bring you some word of the beyond.

Blessed hearts, the emphasis must be placed on a path of individualism and free will. This much I can tell you. It is an hour of the harvest, as I already declared in Washington, D.C., in 1984. Blessed ones, in the victory of the God flame know, then, that the harvest of thine own works draweth nigh. The accountability for oneself is the only surety in Cosmos.

I stand before you as physical as the violet flame is physical, which I also stated in my address in the nation's capital at that time.[2] I am bearing witness before you, in my presence, to a path of right choice and its fulfillment. This is not a matter of prediction or prophecy. It is a matter of will, fulfillment and the grasping of a flame of Life forever and forever each day.

My presence must remind you, then, that it is the forgetful ones who do not arrive at the gate—forgetful, then, of blessings, forgetting to be grateful, forgetting to remember the presence of the Masters in their midst, the Law that is spoken, the Teaching that is taught.

Blessed hearts, it may seem axiomatic but it does require repetition: The Great White Brotherhood cannot interfere with free will or mankind's karma. The Great Law and the Great Central Sun is far beyond the consideration of the preferences of mortals who have made faint effort to alter their garments, to embrace Immortality while she has been in their midst.

These ten days that pass ere Wesak come ought to be considered by yourselves in committee and conference, if desired by you, as to the planning for your own denouement. You can plan on only those things to which you harness your free will. You can trust brother or sister only insofar as that one places his free will in the heart of God's and shows a momentum, and certainly a background, of keeping the flame in cosmic honor—capable of fulfilling unto the finish that which is begun.

Let us say this, then, beloved, that the fate of a planet is only in God's hands—neither in our own nor yours. But your personal fate is indeed in your hands, as is the fate of this property, your families and your future. We have spoken upon the subject [of preparation] and Morya has reminded of the dates in a recent Darjeeling Council meeting. We have said that preparation is the key. Therefore, with the turning of the Dark Cycle [April 23, 1987], our message to you is to be well-grounded in the Rock [of personal Christhood] and in the earth, to secure the preparation that is physical, and to understand that we raise our hand: Be it blessing or judgment, let the flow of the events reveal it.

Some men consider that the future of earth is in their hands. They have thought so for aeons. These are the fallen ones whom we call the insane. Thus, beloved, in insanity have they plotted a course which they envision to be the fulfillment of power, but this is not the power of God.

It is an hour when every man, every woman, and every child shall outplay what he is and what he is not. It is an hour when those who have heart and light and vision and true origins in the honor of God may experience personal change, self-transcendence and a continuity of the path of chelaship.

In times past, beloved, as when Enoch walked with God and we were in the earth in dire places and under arduous conditions, we knew and we discovered the eternal verity that the flame of Hierarchy never leaves the one who chooses to be in constant communion with the Light, at the same time understanding the need to secure one's physical presence and future.

Dear hearts, for your effort and intercession a blessing has surely been added to the earth by violet flame angels. Your calls shall be multiplied. But the greatest blessing of all shall accrue to you personally as you have added to your stature as a chela and increased the strength of your Deathless Solar Body and your God-awareness.

Let the Prophecy go forth. Let the Teaching go forth. But let there be abuilding that which is secure for those who are truly destined in my heart to endure.

Beloved ones, there are no promises forthcoming from the Cosmic Beings. And I myself have secured no great dispensation, even though I am freeborn. But, beloved, the violet flame does alter time and space for those who use it. And it may alter time and space for those who refuse it. For one it is blessing, for another bane. On the one hand time is extended, and on the other it is shortened because none have stood between the power mongers and their mongering of power and the people themselves.

The Advocates are not in the high places of the seed of the wicked. The Advocates are found in the cave of the rock and in the heart of hearts and at the side of the soldier on the battlefield. The Advocates are the Cosmic Christs invisible and legions of angels. They come to save, as has been said, "that which can be saved."[3]

We, then, advise all to hearken and to remember that the date January 1, 1987, was not given as a farce but it was given as a date to be a sign of opportunity when all things could be fulfilled in good time. "Let none gamble with a cosmic date." These are the words of El Morya who has entrusted them to me for yourselves this eve.

Therefore, know that in the physical octave cycles are required. I tell you only this, beloved, that the day and date is at hand—can be known and is known—whereafter neither I myself nor a Cosmic Being may stand between any people and their karma. However, beloved, opportunity has not run out—not for the true Keeper of the Flame nor for the Lightbearer who has stood to intercede nor for those who are yet to be called and to be chosen.

Therefore, I have a particular message for the armchair Keepers of the Flame—those who have already wearied in keeping the flame in our services. The tide of darkness oncoming is too great. Unless you seriously intensify the sacred fire in your temple, you will note that the tide of darkness—whether of a personal or planetary karma—will sweep you from me even when my hand is outstretched.

Thus, beware, beloved. To navigate the tides of the dark cycles remaining in this century requires the sealing of one's being in the sacred fire. There has never been an hour in the history of earth when it has been more important to keep the flame of Sanat Kumara within oneself and to take all necessary steps for the securing of that flame and its burning in the place chosen and designated by Hierarchy.

Blessed ones of the Light, some of you may read the handwriting on the wall for planet earth even better than those of far distant stars, for you are in the very midst of a people. You know the vibration, you know their ways, and you know their sleepfulness.

I will tell you this, beloved. It is necessary for the wicked to outplay their hand and for those that sleep to bear the fruit of their karma of ignoring both the Law and the dangers that are thrust against that Law. When all is outplayed and the harvest of all men and women is known, then you will understand that the judgment itself will sever night and day, reality and unreality, and the dawn of a golden age shall appear.

The choice to make in this hour, beloved, must be a fervent choice to shun every part of Death in self and society, to champion Life and to determine to be in Life continuously in the physical octave until the coming of that dawn. To this end *you* are called. To this destiny you have arrived. *Let no man or woman or situation or personal karma or opposition or fantasy or nightmare take from you that to which you have been called and chosen by Sanat Kumara for hundreds of thousands of years.*

Blessed ones, do not derive from my message either hopefulness or hopelessness. Do not attempt to interpret from it the coming message of the Lord of the World. What you may interpret from my word is this—that we require of our chelas a cosmic realism, a realism that does analyze the present, not with an anticipation that suddenly those who have walked a dark path shall turn to the violet flame, but a tangible assessment of those things which can be expected in the earth, a tangible assessment of those things which cannot, and again of those things which we do expect of our chelas.

It would do you well to place yourselves in the person of myself—of both Hierarch, Teacher and Ascended Master. I ask you to do this and to that end I give you gladly a loan of my Electronic Presence for twenty-four hours from this moment. Thus, you must reason within your heart, "What shall I do, for I am responsible for this Community, these chelas, these Keepers of the Flame? What shall I require and expect of them? What is the most necessary and urgent need of the hour?"

Blessed ones, for the vast many, an hour has passed of opportunity where they can no longer choose a path of Light, for they are tossed and tumbled in the waves of this dark cycle. For another few who still represent millions, the door has not closed. Therefore, *shepherding, stumping* and *teaching* is still the urgent cry of the hour.

The place must be prepared. As I have said to my Messenger this week, the name is well chosen, for it embodies the goal. This place has been prepared by Elohim, Archangels, Manus and elementals. Now, beloved, it must be prepared *by you.* Thus, we can say, "It is the place." But you must say, "It is prepared." Today it is not. Tomorrow it must be.

I summon the resources and the will of every Keeper of the Flame who has eyes to see on planet earth and who hears my call: Let the place be prepared! Let your hearts be prepared! And take, then, a word to the wise from the Messenger who did pause to draw you into a heart sensitivity to your own need for spiritual development and holiness and a remembering that "the heart that has truly loved never forgets."[4]

We have not forgot you, beloved. Do not forget yourselves, your children, your Community—or us.

Prepare my place, beloved, for I will be here also. You shall see me next at the side of the Lord of the World at Wesak. In the interim, may you reason together as responsible sons and daughters of God.

Zadkiel, receive them! Amethyst, *purge* them as only a Seventh-Ray Mother can.

I draw a line of the electromagnetic field around each one here and each one who has kept my vigil this weekend. I draw a line, beloved. It is a line of the sealing of the aura, and it is a line that does show you the difference between what *is* outpictured by you and what *must* be outpictured by you for the spiritual magnet within you to be a focus of spiritual/physical survival.

May you know that unseen forces are repelled only by the aura and electromagnetic field of the chela who has taken upon himself the aura of his Guru. This is a law, beloved.

The line is drawn. Fill it in, I say, and you will know in the day of the LORD's reckoning that I and my Keeper of the Flame are One.

I AM Saint Germain. And I shall survive physically in the body temple of all who present me this *Place Prepared.*

So, Zadkiel, they are thine own until my return. Keep them well, for the Lord of the World prepares his address and his coming.

"The Summit Lighthouse Sheds Its Radiance O'er All the World to Manifest as Pearls of Wisdom." This dictation by Saint Germain was **delivered** through the Messenger of the Great White Brotherhood Elizabeth Clare Prophet on **Sunday, May 3, 1987,** at the **Royal Teton Ranch, Montana.** (**1**) Christopher Lyle Prophet, born to Rev. Sean C. Prophet and Kathleen Anne Prophet (née Mattson) May 3, 1986. (**2**) See Saint Germain, December 2, 1984, "The Harvest," 1984 *Pearls of Wisdom,* vol. 27, no. 61, pp. 549–60, or *The Lost Teachings of Jesus II,* pp. 474–90. (**3**) See Gautama Buddha, December 31, 1986, "The Golden Sphere of Light," 1987 *Pearls of Wisdom,* vol. 30, no. 1, p. 9. (**4**) In the service preceding the dictation, the Messenger conducted at Saint Germain's request a meditation for the clearing, initiation, and strengthening of the heart chakra. The Messenger led the congregation in prayers, decrees, songs, visualizations and invocations for the consuming of all burdens and records of the past that prevent the expansion and balance of the threefold flame. "Saint Germain's Heart Meditation"—an important part of your spiritual survival kit—is available on a single 90-minute cassette B87027, $6.50 (add $.50 for postage).

The Flame of Freedom Speaks
by Saint Germain

The Flame of Freedom speaks—the Flame of Freedom within each heart. The Flame of Freedom saith unto all: Come apart now and be a separate and chosen people, elect unto God—men who have chosen their election well, who have determined to cast their lot in with the immortals. These are they who have set their teeth with determination, who have said:

I will never give up
I will never turn back
I will never submit
I will bear the Flame of Freedom unto my victory
I will bear this flame in honor
I will sustain the glory of Life within my nation
I will sustain the glory of Life within my being
I will win my ascension
I will forsake all idols and
I will forsake the idol of my outer self
I will have the glory of my immaculate divinely
conceived Self manifesting within me
I AM Freedom and
I AM determined to be Freedom
I AM the Flame of Freedom and
I AM determined to bear it to all
I AM God's Freedom and He is indeed free
I AM freed by his Power and his Power is supreme
I AM fulfilling the purposes of God's kingdom

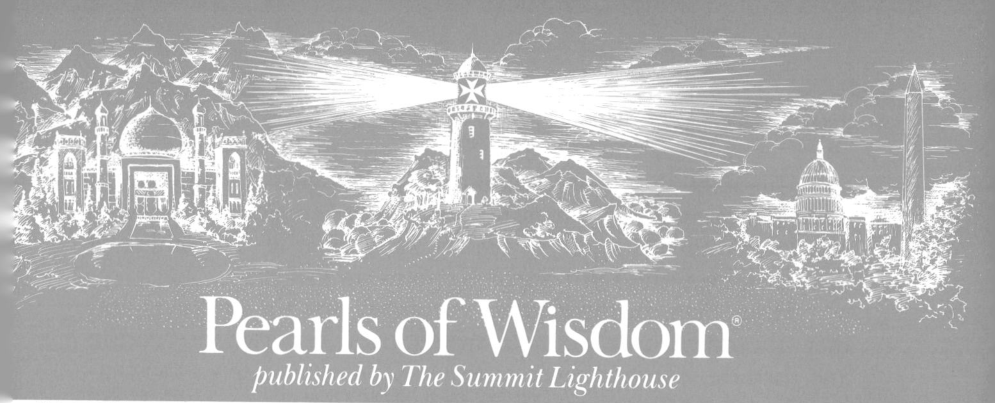
Pearls of Wisdom®
published by The Summit Lighthouse

Vol. 30 No. 23 *Beloved Mother Mary* *June 7, 1987*

Be Prepared and Be at Peace

You, beloved, who have attended my coming these nine hours, know that I AM with you in the beginning and the ending.

I AM Mary, your Mother of Light. I have held you in my embrace all through these hours and many aeons beyond. For, beloved, this day of Mother I have desired to see the saturation of your being—to see it absorb my own, and myself your own, that we might truly be called the Mother and the Daughter of God.

In our oneness, therefore, as you have received me, now be seated.

So the fingers of your minds have followed step-by-step the course of my appearance, even the dispensation of our Father early in this century, prior to the release of the violet flame or even the knowledge of the I AM Presence. I AM that presence of Fátima. I AM, beloved, that Sun.[1]

Do you not see in the miracle of the sun (according to your own enlightenment by the Holy Spirit) the vision of the I AM Presence whirling and spinning and appearing to descend and plummet to the earth? Is this not a message of our Father's coming, even into the individual life of each one? Is there not fear, then, on the part of the one beneath who anticipates suddenly the coming of the Lord into his temple and does cry out, "God, have mercy upon me!" And thus, the mercy of God does come in the person of my Son, so present with you always in your beloved Holy Christ Self.

This, then, was God's way of delivering the image of a lost memory, beloved, of each one's own I AM Presence being that powerful and beyond the power of the physical sun to the Sun behind the sun. This was a promise, beloved, that through the dark night of this century there should appear a golden age. Some of you in embodiment in those hours remember that event and have returned again to see the fulfillment of the coming of the Lord, even the Lord Sanat Kumara, to this place.

Hear, then, in the keynote *Finlandia** first the darkness and then the dawn of mankind's sleepfulness, a period of waiting and then the footsteps, even of Sanat Kumara, create an awakening. And with the coming of the Person of God, as with the LORD God in Eden, there is a chemicalization, there is a breaking of the void. Darkness is dismantled and the descent of light creates a whirlwind action and a flurry as men and nations must align themselves and truly come to grips with that very personal Presence whom all must meet. Even the simplest of Christians know they must prepare to meet this God.

The concluding bars of *Finlandia* are the comfort and presence of a new age and a new light when all the earth has once again realigned itself in the presence of the Elohim of Peace. Truly, I come as the Queen of Peace. Elohim of God, present now, occupy a vast space and time from this center and fulcrum.

Know, then, beloved, that I have also appeared in Yugoslavia to these special hearts,[2] young in body but ancient of days, as the Queen of Peace. For peace is a pillar of fire that is thrust as a sword in the very midst of Communist territory. Thus, it is a warning to World Communism that whereas my supposed representatives in the Vatican have not challenged their presence,[3] lo, I, Mary, have challenged it! Except you receive Him as a little child, ye shall in no wise enter in.[4]

Beloved, the message is plain. There is one thing they cannot control—neither myself nor the hearts of those whose minds are stayed upon me. Blessed ones, Medjugorje has become as a figure-eight flow where so many hearts give attention to me that the light may descend as judgment.

Understand, blessed ones, that I have come there to prepare this people for calamities to come. The simple of heart need to be reminded of their original faith. To deliver to them a message beyond that which they comprehend within the supposed security of the Church would only serve to neutralize the message and their opinions of its authenticity. Thus, to depart from scripture or canon would be to obviate the very purpose of my coming, which is to draw a tremendous devotion of people of every faith to the heart of God and the Divine Mother, that in this sacred tie to heaven they might pass through a darkness to come.

Blessed ones, I came there to prepare them also for the

**Finlandia* by Jean Sibelius was played as the meditation music before the dictation.

transition. Many souls may be taken unless a great divine intervention does take place by your hand and heart and oneness in this Community. Thus, realize, to the simple of heart a simple message when lived does mean a great increase of light that shall prepare them in the appropriate hour to know the higher Truth of the Holy Spirit that is given to you to know.

I have desired, then, that you should see and understand the light, the determination, the joy, the confidence that the seeing of myself has given to the six—and which through them has been radiated to the many. Blessed are ye who have not seen and yet who have believed.[5] I repeat the words of my Son that you might know that it was the Messenger's prayer long ago—she understanding the great demands made upon the light of the universe itself in the appearances of myself and the Masters—to let the Great Law withhold the appearances and rather give that light to the healing of the world, to the balancing of karma.

This the Messenger did request, thus believing in us and declaring, she having already so seen, that there should be no necessity for the repetition of tangible appearances to reinforce faith but only the release of the Word that itself should be for the conversion of those who also have the inner sight to see, not as form and figure necessarily (but sometimes indeed), but seeing as becoming, seeing as total oneness with our presence.

Beloved ones, therefore, to each is given what is a requirement for the quickening. What we would say to you, then, in this hour is by way of preparation for the coming of the Lord of the World. I have been sent by the Father to the end that if there needs be chastening it should come from my lips to spare the Lord of the World of going into that chastening or of raising that rod.

I, Mary, speak to your hearts and I speak simply. I say to you, how much greater is the dispensation of the Great White Brotherhood of this property, even in the vastness of its acreage, how great a salvation is there in regular and constant, decade-upon-decade dictations of the Ascended Masters, consistent and pure and accurate for your personal ascension—by comparison to the visitations.

Beloved ones, these children and the many who come there are not yet ready for the ascension nor are they being readied, but that they might obtain a better resurrection to pursue the path of discipleship as ye know it. Realize, then, beloved, that to whom is given so great a cup of salvation much is expected.

I place, then, the sword of peace into the earth in this place. So let it be known and designated forevermore.

Blessed hearts, understand, then, these my words to you. If so simple a people with so simple a message can wax hot in the Spirit, endued with the fire of God, can ye not also realize that for all of thy getting and all of thy acceleration there needs be the retracing of the steps down the mountain to begin again, even from the River of Life to the heart of the Cosmic Christ Maitreya? I tell you simply, each one must fill in the gaps of his devotion. Each one must treasure the words we have spoken as these children and all the world treasure my simple messages to them.

Blessed ones, I have also come to consecrate a place as the Divine Mother Omega once consecrated the Retreat of the Resurrection Spiral in Colorado Springs.[6] I would call you to a higher calling, yet you have not yet fulfilled the calling already given. When I say "you," beloved, I speak to the worldwide body of Keepers of the Flame who must hear me in this hour.

Understand, then, that my coming would be to announce my calling to you to place upon Maitreya's mountain a cross to be the electrode to that cross in Medjugorje. Thus, beloved, Medjugorje, the place of the cross thirty-five feet tall—it is an electrode in the earth. And by the devotion of many I have therefore charged it with a tremendous light.

You have known, beloved, that in many of my appearances I have required that a church be built on that place for the very reason that I desire in certain points in the earth a place that can be charged with great light by myself through the devotion of the people. This retreat is such a place. But for the building of the cross, the other callings of my Son must first be fulfilled. Yet I say to you that when these are fulfilled, the cross may be built.

I envision it and have given that vision to the Messenger as a cross of thirty-three feet. And around the center of the cross of cement, beloved, there is a crown of twelve stars. Thus, the cross is the marking of the place where God in man meet, showing that the path of discipleship leads to the crown of everlasting Life, which is indeed the crown of twelve stars of the Woman[7] that is given by the Divine Mother unto all who endure to the end.

Blessed ones, the trek up Maitreya's mountain is indeed a pilgrimage and a calling—and even the placing there of a type of structure such as a log cabin where the sound of the rosary might be heard and recited: Archangel Michael's Rosary, my rosary, Kuan Yin's Rosary yet to be written down. Thus, it shall become a place of perpetual prayer, thanksgiving, a point of pilgrimage where many can rally.

Blessed hearts, we would not have you begin this sacramental building prior to your having understood that sacrifice is necessary and indeed a requirement of the obedience unto God. Obedience, beloved, begins with the alignment of oneself to the inner cross of white fire, else the outer sign and symbol cannot afford the victory but perhaps should become a substitute for the interior correction of Maitreya. Let the cross be the sign of the saints' overcoming.

Beloved hearts, let us deal with first things then. Here we see at the Inner Retreat the place of the calling—the place whereto there was given the date of January 1, 1987.[8] We have sent forth the call for the builders, for those who would farm and till the land and prepare this place. And yet, as of this moment there are not enough here even to tend the current needs. There are many in the field waiting to the last moment, having not heard, expecting to find all things prepared as they arrive, somehow, at the final hour, thinking that surely the Masters or the Messengers will say, "Come now, come quickly."

But, beloved ones, you must understand, a place cannot be prepared without first the conversion, which I have stressed to these children: the conversion of the heart in every single member of this Community, then the adding thereto. To what? To the Diamond Heart, to the Immaculate Heart, to the Sacred Heart, of which you are a part and which is composed of your own sweet hearts—of many who are magnetized to that magnet.

Blessed ones, there are challenges to be met, and many have already been met as you have come up the mountain in a spiral. I speak not of a physical mountain but I speak of a spiritual pyramid of Life where chelas around the world have gathered in prayer in defense of the Messenger, the Community, the Church, night after night after night.

Are ye not also saints? Yea, ye are the saints of the Holy Church and of my heart. Your life has been sacrificial, even beyond the requests I have made at Medjugorje. Realize, this, beloved, in a sense of co-measurement. Indeed, much has been expected of you, but you have already given much, wherefore there has been warranted unto you so many blessings and dispensations. Blessed hearts, truly you must understand that this is the highest calling and the highest dispensation in the earth that the Great White Brotherhood can afford according to the will of God and the Cosmic Christ in this hour.

Let those around the world hear me then. The hour is coming and now is when the preparation must be complete—the physical preparation, I say. For you are called to be physical and to remain so for the holding of the light in the earth and not to be counted among those who are taken from the screen of life when events foretold may take place.

Blessed ones, if you are holding out for outreach or service anywhere in the nations, realize it is best to come and build and then return to your fields, if you so desire, when all is in readiness here. Prepare the place. And if in your preparing, as Saint Germain has said, world calamity is turned back, averted or mitigated, then you shall see a golden day of opportunity again. It is time for the going within and the preparing. And in the process, beloved, of your own self-transcendence, to this you must give attention.

Therefore we say, let the food be prepared, enough to care for the many. Let the survival shelters be prepared, enough to care for those who intend to be here. And let those who intend to be here know that they have a responsibility, whether in service or whether in prayer.

Those of skill and experience may perform the tasks but, beloved, choirs of angels require voices. Prayers and decrees must be perpetual and continual. Therefore, determine how this place may support those who are required to hold a spiritual balance even while the physical work of the LORD becomes the anchoring point of the Word.

Blessed ones, this has been my message since 1917. The words given to the children and recorded by them have a certain percentage of accuracy. They are accurate in the context of mitigation rather than complete aversion of descending karma. It is a self-evident truth that the whole world will not be converted and that that world therefore must face also the Great Teacher in the Person of returning karma.

Thus, let those who are called to endure begin to understand that now is the hour to respond to Saint Germain and to El Morya to build my house, to know that this temple made with hands is necessary for the protection of your temples until you fully realize the temple made without hands in the Deathless Solar Body, in the resurrection cone of light and in the ascension itself.

Thus, beloved ones, I must make clear to you that throughout the world there is a percentage of Keepers of the Flame who have waxed cold and who have not followed the joys and the disciplines we have offered, whether in the dynamic decree, whether in the prayer and fasting, whether in service.

Beloved ones, World Communism is a dread disease of the mind, but I tell you world materialism is even greater as one of the dread diseases of the time. It has been said that in the West the people are indulgent. Blessed ones, it is so. And I am sorry to say that many of our Keepers of the Flame are demanding far too much of the material pleasures or what they think are their material needs, and not understanding that there are sacrifices that must be made in the present if the future is to be secured.

The very process of this sacrificial life, beloved, is a process you need in order to put on the fullness of your Christhood. Emergency demands evoke from you the fullness of the heart's genius and attunement with Christ. The responsibility of children, loved ones and Lightbearers of the world therefore impels you to call upon the Lord for strength and to be strengthened of mind and heart and body.

Blessed ones, I tell you, from this hour forward (as to the Messenger's service to you) let her use the hours remaining of cosmic time to once again deliver the books to the nations while you have the light. Let the communications to her of your needs be received and answered in the giving of prayer, invocation.

Let each one who has a problem learn to take the cassettes of the rosaries and of decrees that are to be made, to give their novenas, to write their letters to me and, above all, to make sacrifices at the fourteen stations of the cross and thereby know that God can be the solution to their problem and that I may be that solution and that their communion with their Mighty I AM Presence through prayer is indeed that resolution.

Blessed ones, those who suffer, having seen so great a salvation, *suffer due to nonsurrender!* I tell you, you will be left to face alone that which no man or woman can face alone. Therefore, come ye into Union. Come into the Community of the Spirit and offer your life without complaint.

Blessed ones, our Messengers are not hard taskmasters. Do not fear, then, the loss of the fat of selfishness. Do you desire to see me and talk with me? Watch how the veil thins. Watch how you see myself superimposed over the Messenger as you have never seen me before. Watch how heaven can truly cohabitate this physical octave through the etheric sheath we have placed over this Inner Retreat.

Blessed hearts, it is a consecrated place. Let none so seek, then, a physical flesh-and-blood salvation or so misinterpret the Yugoslav dispensation as to go there to find me or healing. Blessed ones, I AM here! I shall not leave this place or the side of anyone. I have come to intercede, to administer, to organize, to inspire, to be with you. I am more available here, beloved, than anywhere on earth because of so great a rising of prayers and invocations!

Beloved, as Saint Germain has told you, there are so many calls that cannot be answered for the failure of those of the leadership of the world to be converted—yet by your intercession these calls *are* answered and they accrue to yourselves and they have so accrued. And the Father has sent his answer in the person of myself, beloved.

I AM Mary with you. I place my electrode in the mountain, in the stream, in the river, in your heart. I am here every step of a physical way that *must be bought with a price.* I have sent my angels with Raphael's angels to the Keepers of the Flame in the earth.

Let all who hear our call to be here, beloved, so make it known, so apply and so prepare yourselves. Those whose time has come to be at the Inner Retreat must not resist and go about the human planning of a separate existence in an hour of earth's history when, I tell you, it is untold and unspoken as to that which could come upon the earth unless there be a tremendous conversion, a tremendous increase in those who give the violet flame decrees.

You have wondered why the Ascended Masters have not spelled out their prophecies more specifically. It is for the same reason that these have been told in secret, in part, to these children. Beloved, we never give the fullness of the vision of what karma could bring until almost the very hour of it, because until that time we are kneeling before the throne of the Father begging intercession and dispensation.

O beloved, realize, until the right hand of God descends, until the last grain of opportunity in the hourglass descends, there is opportunity, there is dispensation abundant (as has been read to you from our prior dictations[9]) for the world to be raised up, for all to change in the twinkling of the eye.

Thus, it is Elohim of Peace who plant their electrodes as a magnet—peace as the very defiance by Almighty God of war itself. It is the living flame of peace in your hearts and the hearts of all those who have been converted by my appearances that shall deflect war, even as a diamond heart does deflect it and send back to the enemy, by a mirrored image, the fullness of his malintent.

Blessed ones, may I tell you, then, the scientific explanation of the prayer of the rosary and all decrees. Blessed ones, it is a building up of light in the body temple, that you yourselves might deflect, as one Mystical Body of God, the oncoming Darkness.

If a few men in a house in Japan could emerge whole after a

nuclear holocaust,[10] will you not, then, place your faith in the Divine Mother, in my intercession and in Almighty God first and foremost and always? Will you not understand that daily you need to be buoyed up in this spiritual light and flame, not as impracticality but so that you will not enter the pitfall of depending upon a survival shelter or food storage to carry you through a period of world travail—travailing even as the Divine Mother is yet determined to give birth to her Manchild.

Understand, beloved, that when we counsel the preparation, those who fear most, those who are the unbelieving, those who seek to save their flesh rush in. They will never be saved, then, by such preparations. These preparations must be the stem of the chalice of the Holy Grail which you uphold.

I tell you, beloved, those who build such preparations in fear do not build on a solid foundation. I tell you their hearts will fail them for that very fear, for it becomes an internal magnet of fear, an internal point of vulnerability. And when the elements of the earth melt with the fervent heat[11] of a divine alchemy, their karma upon them, beloved, will take them from the screen of life even if they have all of the physical necessities.

Look through the walls! Look through time and space. Desire God and only God.

I am come to deliver you of inordinate desire, that when the Buddha arrive he shall not be agitated by auras of those who desire many things and do not desire the centrality of everlasting Life—not for themselves but for the continuity of being on earth.

Beloved ones, understand that the beings in the center of the earth in polarity with yourselves, in these very hills and mountains, hold the balance in this hour for the holding together of the earth that it not split and be tossed out by the immense force of discord of her evolutions.

Blessed ones, had it not been for the Great White Brotherhood in the earth and on the surface, this earth could have already become another Maldek, another asteroid belt—not by any particular collision, though that collision should have occurred; for earth's vulnerability is also to those very forces colliding as in the coming of ancient planets or meteorites splitting and sawing asunder the planetary orbs.

Beloved ones, the tube of light Keepers of the Flame have invoked in this century has resulted in a protection for the planetary body herself from untold evil of aliens, even sealing her from her own vulnerabilities to attract the dangers of harmful rays, diseases and consciousnesses of outer space.

Blessed hearts, the prayer of one child in Montessori school—any child, a single child—as given daily here is the equivalent of thousands who in ignorance pray the Mass yet have not received the formula which you have received by grace to access the supreme power of the Godhead. Let all cherish, then, and value this opportunity. Let us move swiftly.

Beloved, the months are short. You must know and understand this. Prepare and be at peace. When you are prepared, let the pillars of flame rise from the heart of the earth to the heart of the Great Central Sun through the chakras of each one. I instill in you, then, a love of the mission.

I come to take from you in this hour burdens of personal inner struggle. I come to give you the vision of the Fifth-Ray Masters, that you might see that which has held you in bondage and that you might be delivered.

Take my book, beloved, the concentrated focus of my presence, flame and rosary in *My Soul Doth Magnify the Lord!*[12] Place it in remembrance of me beneath your pillow. Know, then, that I radiate through the living Word, that I radiate, then, through the statue of myself, gold plated and given to the Mother of the Flame long ago by Catholic devotees of my heart. The weight of this statue being so great, it may not be seen by you, but I trust it shall be in place before long. For it speaks of a golden age and golden wisdom and the crown of Life.

May you look upon that photograph of my statue which is in this book, beloved, for it was the final act of Mark Prophet and his beloved to so arrange those roses, to so have that statue photographed. When you see it, you will know that next to the position of the photographer, standing but six feet from the statue, is your own beloved Mark. And the image of Mark, though unseen, is actually impressed upon my statue in this photo. Thus in it you may have a focus of the Messenger in his ascension coil but hours before he took his leave from this plane.

As you take the Communion prepared, beloved, know that you ingest a portion of light of myself that is able to quickly lift you out of a limited sense-consciousness into the illimitable trammels of the Spirit.

I come to bear your burden, to relieve and deliver you, to quicken you to the realization that the snakeskins must be shed quickly and that you must know who you are in Christ.

Receive my admonishment through the Messenger when it comes or from the heart of your Presence when it comes.

If you desire, then, to keep a vigil here till the coming of

Gautama Buddha, let it be of violet flame and of all the defenses you have mounted in summoning Archangel Michael to be wherever World Communism has purposed to destroy the earth or devour her people.

While there is yet time, I expand and accelerate for you time, space, energy, consciousness and eternity. Thus, fulfill all things. Be prepared and be at peace.

I AM Mary. And I AM here to stay till all these things be fulfilled in you.

"The Summit Lighthouse Sheds Its Radiance O'er All the World to Manifest as Pearls of Wisdom." This dictation by Mother Mary was **delivered** through the Messenger of the Great White Brotherhood Elizabeth Clare Prophet after midnight at the conclusion of the Mother's Day service on **Monday, May 11, 1987,** at the **Royal Teton Ranch, Montana.** (**1**) Prior to the dictation, the congregation viewed the film *The Miracle of the Sun* and watched a replay of "Fátima Update" Part I (delivered in Dallas April 18, 1987), in which the Messenger lectured on the appearances and messages of Mother Mary to three shepherd children in Fátima, Portugal, May 13 to October 13, 1917. Mother Mary had promised to work a great public miracle so that all might believe in her apparitions to the children. On October 13, her final Fátima appearance, an estimated 70,000 people gathered for the event and were witnesses to the "miracle of the sun." At first appearing as a silver disc, the sun began to spin wildly like a wheel of fire, flashing multicolored beams of light in all directions. Three times it stood still and then resumed this whirling action. With a zigzag motion, it then appeared to leave its place in the sky, plunge toward the earth and hover for a moment above the crowd before climbing back to its normal place in the sky. (**2**) In "Fátima Update" Part II, delivered prior to the dictation, the Messenger lectured on the reported daily appearances of Mother Mary to six youths in Medjugorje, Yugoslavia, that began in 1981. (**3**) See 1987 *Pearls of Wisdom,* vol. 30, no. 21, p. 218, n. 3. (**4**) Luke 18:17. (**5**) John 20:29. (**6**) See 1987 *Pearls of Wisdom,* vol. 30, no. 9, p. 124, n. 5. (**7**) Rev. 12:1. (**8**) See Archangel Michael, April 11, 1982, "Because You Need Me," 1982 *Pearls of Wisdom,* vol. 25, no. 28, pp. 285–86. (**9**) In her "Fátima Update" Part II, the Messenger presented the **Ascended Masters' prophecies, admonishments and dispensations** as an update to Mother Mary's Fátima message. She reminded students that "no prophecy can be utterly fulfilled in the physical atoms of this planet unless you confirm it by your decree. . . . All dispensations that I have read to you and all that you find in the Pearls of Wisdom are yours to compose in affirmations and decrees."

Mother Mary, 8-15-58: "Let the Christ in you magnetize those individuals, those loving and willing and worthy and capable chelas whom you require and, more importantly, that the Ascended Masters El Morya and Saint Germain require to create a planetary Diamond Heart of spiritual freedom. Yes, though we cover this planet round, though we bring angels into the atmosphere of earth, a Diamond Heart which is the center of the spiritual foundation which is to be the predominant focus for the next two thousand years shall be sustained, for I, Mary, established the beginning of it."

Mother Mary, 7-3-72: "The land is plagued with darkness upon the screens of the invention of the motion picture. The land is plagued with darkness over the churches devoted to honor my Son's name. The land is plagued with darkness as the political candidates struggle among themselves seeking a temporal crown. . . . The elementals have communicated recently with one another and they are preparing to execute cataclysmic strands of destruction that have only begun in the world order. And this shall come to pass unless the teachings of God shall be fulfilled in the hearts of many men and women presently totally dedicated to their own selves without understanding the great needs of humanity."

Mother Mary, 12-31-77: "Until a correct understanding of the I AM THAT I AM be made known across the land, governments will fall, economies will crumble, churches will come to ruin, darkness will cover the land, famine will be present, and souls will be lost."

Mother Mary, 1-28-79: "Within my Sacred Heart is the acceleration of light this day . . . unto the judgment of those who have persistently denied the miracles of the Virgin Mary. . . . Let there be the judgment of the false teachers who have stolen into the churches with their false theology. . . . Everyone who has interfered with the birth of these little ones—everyone who has advocated abortion from the pulpits of the churches, I tell you they will suffer exactly the karma that is written in sacred scripture spoken by my Son and it will not be withheld this day!"

Saint Germain, 10-6-83: "We [the Darjeeling Council] therefore resolve that Central America and the Caribbean shall not be overrun by the warlords, by the fallen ones, by the Communist hordes!"
Archangel Michael, 11-27-83: "We therefore declare this day as that day number one when there shall go forth from Keepers of the Flame, from this altar and from hearts of Light worldwide, the rolling back, by every ray of the seven, of the entire world movement of Communism, of the Nephilim gods and all who supply them their technology, their grain, their money and their support and sympathy. . . . The entire momentum of the Soviet Union of this earth and the seizing of landed areas thereof will be put back, will be turned, will be upset! And the day of liberation will come to those oppressed peoples."
Mother Mary, 12-24-83: "Prove me now herewith that the entire Soviet establishment will not endure when a nation, Mother Russia, returns to the devotion of the Blessed Virgin. . . . It is the Mother flame in the earth consecrated in all of your chakras which will *beat down* the entire juxtaposition of nuclear war and all those things that now challenge you so greatly."
Gautama Buddha, 5-14-84: "I decree in this hour that all devotions to the one God in many forms and formulas and formations, whatever thy belief—the Our Father, the psalm, the Hail Mary, the chant out of the Eastern temple—shall know the concentrated fire of the legions of light. . . . The devotion that is spoken shall be focused upon that end which is the consuming, by the fire of the threefold flame in all life, of this cancer of a planet spawned by the gods—this World Communism."
Mother Mary, 7-3-84: "I extend to you, then, access by the rosary—*by the rosary*—to my causal body, to the attainment on those fourteen stations which I have gained throughout my long spiritual history. I give you, therefore, the opportunity to receive that power and attainment which God has given me as my great Teacher and as I am his servant. This I transmit to you that it might become close to the physical world and the physical problem through your own physical body and heart. I propose, therefore, beginning now and continuing on until there shall be a very obvious turning of the tide of World Communism, the giving of the rosary and the calling forth of this divine momentum."
Mother Mary, 8-26-84: "The Father has said to me: '. . . I place in thy Hand the rod of authority for the utter annihilation of world atheism known as World Communism.' . . . The Power of God in my Right Hand is as good as your confirmation of that Power." (See decree 56.02.)
Jesus Christ, 11-22-84: "I come to change the prophecy of Fátima. I come to undo the dire predictions. I come to work through you for the saving of every soul that is gone astray. This is a dispensation of the moment, the hour and the decade [of the eighties]. Work in this wise while ye have the Light. For should the dark night come to the planet—and we pray God it shall not—but should it come, in that hour my own must be safe in the arms of the Universal Mother, that they be not torn from eternal Life by any condition whatsoever."
Mother Mary, 12-9-84: "I live with the Fátima prophecy. I live with its message. And I go from door to door and heart to heart knocking, asking for those who will come and pray with me—pray the violet flame or the rosary or the calls to Archangel Michael. But above all, pray. For by thy prayer is the open door extended, and the angels come stepping through the veil to prevent disaster and calamity."
Jesus, 12-25-85: "Understand that it is truly the hour when those [of my anointing] may take up the fallen mantle of this apostle [Peter] and move forward, beloved, to cast out of the very Holy of Holies those priests and false pastors, those rabbis (who are not rabbis of the Holy of Holies), and all who misrepresent the Godhead."
Saint Germain, 1-1-87: "The vow that I have taken is to serve with this earth until the true Lightbearers are free. The vow I propose to take, having accomplished this, is to stand with all others who have accepted the transfer of the flame of freedom from our best servants. The specifics of the vow must be, then, to defeat World Communism before it defeats the West and to defeat in the West those betrayers of the Word before the very foundations of Western civilization crumble for their presence in that foundation."
Mother Mary, 4-18-87: "I consecrate this state [Texas], America and Canada to my Immaculate Heart. This consecration shall be continuous by my legions of angels."
Mother Mary, 4-21-87: "I, Mary, . . . do now consecrate Central America, Cuba, all islands of the Caribbean to my Immaculate Heart with a fervor, a righteousness and a wrath of the Cosmic Christ. . . . It is more than a consecration. It is a purging and a judgment. It is a branding as with a branding iron, and it is a divine decree!" "Fátima Update" Part II is published with Part I on 4 cassettes, K87033-K87036, $26.00 for set (add $.80 for postage). (**10**) When the atomic bomb was dropped on Hiroshima in 1945, eight men living eight blocks from the center of the nuclear blast were miraculously untouched. One of them, Father Hubert Shiffner, S.J., explained, "In that house the rosary was prayed every day. In that house, we were living the message of Fátima." See Francis Johnston, *Fatima: The Great Sign* (Washington, N.J.: AMI Press, 1980), p. 139. (**11**) II Pet. 3:10, 12. (**12**) Mark L. Prophet and Elizabeth Clare Prophet, *My Soul Doth Magnify the Lord!* Summit University Press, $7.95 (add $1.00 for postage).

Pearls of Wisdom®
published by The Summit Lighthouse

Vol. 30 No. 24 *Beloved Gautama Buddha* *June 14, 1987*

For the Alignment of a World
"A Proclamation" by Alpha
Wesak Address 1987

"A Victory Unparalleled in the Face of Unparalleled Odds"

The Law does come to fulfill itself. Fear not. Fear only when thou dost not fulfill the Law. For this cause I came twenty-five hundred years ago and ten thousand.

I AM THAT I AM Gautama in the heart of Sanat Kumara, intensifying now the Ruby Ray that those who themselves have espoused it will wonder and say, "Shall we also faint at the coming of the notable day of the LORD?" *HRIH!*

Therefore, I come not alone for the shattering of worlds; I come for the shattering of auras of unfaithful stewards. *HRIH!*

So let those who gather as devotees of Buddha Maitreya know that when the light does descend from the center of the altar it does perforce purge those nearest to the altar, as in radiating, undulating spheres of light the earth is penetrated and permeated in this hour by the light of the Central Sun for realignment. *HRIH!*

So, beloved, for this cause I came twenty-five hundred years ago and ten thousand—for the alignment of a world, for the alignment of a solar system, for the alignment of souls of Sanat Kumara.

The Light ripples in rings from this center. And so, where the Light that is the positive polarity of the Great White Brotherhood and our Messengers does contact, then, the negative manifestation of Mater as materialism, as inordinate attachment, possessiveness, where souls have made themselves a part of the mud ball of human creation—so the Light beats upon the shores of anti-Matter and anti-Self.

Know this, beloved—that there is perforce the backlash toward the center. Where the bodies are not a latticework of Light and therefore do not allow the Ruby Ray to pass through, so it does come back upon the circles of devotees.

Understand, beloved, you face the Sun. And the Sun in its dazzling Reality does give to you the very object of your devotion as Light! Light! Light!

But, beloved, behind you are the ones who reject and resist it. And therefore, as they do resist, there begins the contamination of the Ruby Ray. Thus the shadows from behind bring back to the center (or would if they could) the mass consciousness of the very perversion of the Love Ray in all abuses of the Light now manifest in the civilizations of this earth.

Therefore, beloved, the grave danger to the devotees in this hour is truly not the Law or the Light that does send forth such intensity but it is actually that which does return [as the reactionary force] which goes unchallenged, unheeded. For the return of the mass creation of a planet is indeed a warning to all who yet abide in this octave that until the permanent atom of being be won and the soul one in it, there is the danger of the returning wave breaking upon the devotees.

And therefore we see around the world in many ashrams and places of worship—those esoteric and mystical as well as the outer simplistic [ritualistic] forms whether of Christianity or Buddhism—that the untutored in the divine art of the Word receive unto themselves and outpicture the vileness, the sinfulness that is abroad in the land. And by this process, beloved, the fallen ones may take their positions and take their means of communication and point the accusing finger and say, "See this one, see that one!"

Thus scandals come and go. But I come to deliver the threatening woes.

Blessed hearts, those who mount the hillsides in the valleys need no picks or ropes or guide. But those who must, then, climb Everest and beyond must be surefooted as the Sherpas and the elementals who leap higher and higher. A warning, then, to you who would make the ascent and fulfill it in this life:

Beloved, you have not protected yourselves from behind, nor have you exercised a co-measurement with the awesomeness of the climb and its dangers.

Beloved ones, know, then, that at every hand the forces of entrenched materialism and sensuality, the lust for money and the greed to possess souls and light, the earth, the sea and the land—these forces, beloved, pursue your flight to God.

Defend, then, the position of your attainment.

Defend the position of those of the highest attainment within the movement and those of the least. For when there is a protection through Community, through Hierarchy of those who must lead to the top and those who must bring up the rear, then there also is a guardian action by and for and of those in the middle who form the vast multitudes who, when seeing the surefootedness of the leader and the footprint, will mount up and will fulfill their courses.

Thus, beloved, understand even the dangers of being seated in the very front row of our congregation. But, beloved, the Light is infinite. And you who have positioned yourselves the farthest [from the Messenger] as though [in the wide orbit of] the planet Pluto—you also may know that you do not escape my eye nor the intensity of the Light that must be released in this day and in this noonday Light of the Sun behind the sun.

Therefore I AM come. For I must speak to the gems—the gemstones amongst our disciples: the ruby or pearl, diamond or emerald, amethyst or aquamarine. Let them be known and seen—these star sapphires, these luminous ones.

Blessed hearts, all hangs in a delicate balance. But that balance is nowhere more delicate than in the very person of the chela, in the heart and in the mind that would reach out to God and yet has not first gone forth to slay every oppressor of the Buddha where I AM THAT I AM in the heart of the devotee.

Here I AM, then, beloved. I am come with many thousands of saints and angels. I am come with elementals who, as my students, have gained great mastery over the centuries. Truly masterful presences from all evolutions gather for the delivery of a Word which they have long anticipated.

I come, then, by way of introducing the light of Judgment into the earth, stressing a personal path as has been stressed again and again in these years. Blessed ones, let me tell you that the Divine Mother approaches, her Person present in Sarasvati.

> O Sarasvati, daughter of Light incarnate now and again, let Wisdom's rod prevail. Let Wisdom, then, written, not fail but instead awaken, defend, set purpose to life! Let the written Word be the power of the sword of the Buddhas who make war this night upon the anti-Buddhas in the earth.
>
> O Divine Mother, receive thy children ere they be strung far and wide by the hurricane of the vortex of the descending Sanat Kumara.

I AM THAT I AM in this heart. *HRIH!* Therefore, O beloved, know the Word, know the Law, know the Way.

My angels hold for me "A Proclamation" written in script on a large scroll. Beloved and most blessed ones, I bring you, then, the word of beloved Alpha.

Beloved Alpha Speaks:

Sons and Daughters of God, Children of the Sun, through my blessed servant and your own Lord Gautama I send to you this day this statement of my purpose. I have spoken it before the Cosmic Council. I speak it again. So it is written. So I have written:

> Therefore, from the Cosmic Council we send to all lovers of God and Lightbearers in the earth salutations of the heart, deep devotion, a love that will not fail.
>
> To all evolutions who have not afforded themselves the opportunity given to rise to the level of the Christ Standard but who have denied it in my little ones, who have denied it in the inner voice and in that of angels standing near, I say to you:
>
> The hour is come and now is that your judgment must descend and become physical in the earth in the span of physical matter that does exceed that which is known to the physical eye. Therefore, upon you this day is delivered three woes.
>
> *Woe! Woe! Woe!*
>
> And therefore, for the abuse of the Father and of the Son and of the Holy Spirit in my little ones, you shall know what is the meaning of the hand of the Law and of the Cosmic Christ. So be it!
>
> By the Presence in the earth of the Mother of Knowledge, by the Presence in the earth of true Keepers of the Flame, *you,* fallen ones, have been spared this hour the fourth woe. This woe is the karma for the desecration of the Divine Mother and her seed in this very physical octave.
>
> I say, then, to all who hear this word, When the fourth woe shall descend upon them—if they do not heed the Karma, the Message and the Judgment of the first three—*then* shall all Lightbearers be aware that it is the hour to retreat into the innermost retreat which I, your Father, have provided for you.
>
> Thus understand that much may occur upon the earth. And many who know and see and read the signs of the times

will not await the coming of the fourth woe [before they retreat from the world arena of the judgment of the fallen ones]. For the hour of the coming of the fourth woe no man knoweth save myself.

I AM the Father. And as I write, I read. And as I read, I speak through my beloved Gautama and his Messenger—his Messenger called Wife. For every devotee of Buddha is Wife—thus Shakti, thus vessel.

Blessed hearts, I shall continue the reading of the scroll.

Therefore, O ye who have not hearkened—neither unto my voice nor unto the voice of my Son, the heir, nor unto the Rebuke and the Law of the Holy Spirit: this day shalt thou know that the LORD God Almighty Universal has decreed it, and there shall no longer be given opportunity from without for thy salvation.

But the only salvation known to these fallen ones shall be the immediate bending of the knee before the living Word, the repentance and the conversion unto the Trinity and the Brahman above.

Therefore, unto those who have earnestly sought and have for the most part maintained that level of Christ consciousness, going apart only out of ignorance or thoughtlessness—unto these I would speak:

You who are scattered throughout the earth and in this activity, unto you is given tenfold opportunity to rise into that Christhood full, into that I AM Presence.

Wherefore, no dispensation shall be forthcoming to those who have not sought a path of personal Christhood.

Unto those who have [sought a path of personal Christhood] there is and shall be given protection, a way of Life, abundant opportunity for acceleration—with the warning begun by Gautama in this message and stated by myself:

The fallen ones in the earth who are judged in this hour—where the Light does excel in you if you will it so and accept it—shall not cease to tempt you, to engage you in all manner of Darkness and to attempt to take you with them through the Second Death[1] should it come to them.

Blessed ones, the opportunity given, then, to those who have sought earnestly and achieved some measure of Christhood is this: it is a dispensation and a light that cannot, must not be lost, betrayed, misqualified or neglected. This opportunity and dispensation if lost, beloved, will cost you such a price as I shall not enumerate.

Let those who understand the Law know that if it is not the end of the world, it is indeed the end of a cycle. And in this cycle all those for whom it is possible to ascend to God are now given that momentum, that impetus to do so.

If the Path is followed victoriously and diligently, the fullness of the Cosmic Christ consciousness shall await you in the hour of your victorious ascension. If it is not, beloved, it shall take untold aeons of rounds and cycles to come to the place again where the karma for the loss of this Light is balanced and a new dispensation may—and I say *may*—be given.

Beloved hearts, the Divine Decree has gone forth that unto them who *have* Light, more Light shall be added; but from them who *have not,* this day there is taken away that Light which they have abused and misqualified.[2]

Blessed hearts, we have said that with the passing of the decade, the opportunity for the saving of the earth could be denied.[3] I, Alpha, write to you this day that this opportunity has been lost to the fallen ones—that no new dispensation is forthcoming on this Wesak 1987 for the planet as a whole, but the dispensation [that is forthcoming] is a mathematical formula to each individual according to his own inner attainment.

Indeed, the dispensation of which we have spoken becomes a mathematical formula. As you have given to God, so does God give to you in this hour, beloved, by an x factor of multiplication that shall not be spoken to you.

Therefore, beloved, know the fruit of a harvest and know that there is work at hand, that a new increase may be gained as accrual, as multiplication factor should new dispensations be forthcoming.

Beloved, there is not an Ascended Master who is given a new dispensation for the saving of a planet but every Ascended Master is given a dispensation to assist the true chela of the Light.

In the ancient tradition of the Guru/Chela relationship, then, there is descended a very present help and much closer, as angels, to every devotee of God upon earth.

Now I write that every devotee, therefore, shall be tested. And every devotee who does receive this Light may also understand the equation that he may lose it. The day will come for each and every one that they [he] must show forth their [his] Light independent of any other source or reinforcement.

That day is at hand! Few there be in this hour who can show forth that Light and defend it. Seek this God Mastery from Sarasvati.

Beloved, know, then, that many of you here at Maitreya's Mystery School are yet prisoners of your own human consciousness. While thinking to become adepts you yet entertain miserable conditions of records and accumulations of humanly misqualified energy. The warning that I write to you, then, is to seek God and live, to be not tolerant of those lesser states.

We have spoken many times but I tell you it is the hour. One is taken and another will be left.[4] Therefore, the dispensation this day is that every Lightbearer and citizen of this world may work toward the Good, toward Peace, toward Freedom, toward the defeat of the fallen ones arrayed and under many guises and masks.

In your hands lies the total and complete opportunity for the saving of the earth. As you work, as you serve, there is forthcoming from your sponsoring Gurus access to the Light of the Cosmic Christ to give the increase.

The Keeper of the Scrolls has read to me, as I have called him to my side in the writing of this Proclamation, the list of dispensations given through the Ascended Masters' activities in these one hundred years, beginning with the most recent and going backward.

I have read them all and heard the reading thereof and I say to you, each dispensation is a sword to be wielded, a banner to be unfurled. With the full and consistent and dedicated invocation of these dispensations, you will find already placed therein the key to the saving of the earth.

When these dispensations [each one in its cycle] and the calls thereto have been fully and sufficiently exhausted by the devotees of the earth, then that dispensation by the very calls made does become a "secret love star" implanted in the aura of the earth, so fully charged with the decrees of the devotees that it does become a permanent light in and of itself, suspended in the Matter cosmos.

Therefore, beloved, with the application and the invocation of all dispensations given, those who are in the earth in this hour (calculating their causal bodies, as I have) may indeed turn the earth around and have a saving of a day for Sanat Kumara and his Sons.

Let it be known, then, that the earth is in the hands of those who have pursued and maintained a certain level of their Christhood. The earth is in good hands.

Let all those of the Christed ones who have the teachings we have given through these Messengers know that were each and every other Lightbearer in the earth [who should be] drawn into this path to give it a fiery application, you would see victory upon victory.

Let it be known, then, that the forces in the earth which are gathering and the changes which the Great Law calls for project upon the screen of life events which may be mitigated by the very factor of the descent this day of the three woes upon the fallen ones coupled with the increase of Light to the Lightbearers.

Thus, beloved, we do not decree downfall, chaos, Darkness and Old Night. We decree a victory of great magnitude for those who are of the bands of Light. We await, then, the choice and the decision and the response of all Lightbearers in the earth.

We wait, then, to see a greater vision, a greater acceleration and realization that in this hour the Ascended Masters of the Great White Brotherhood may not stand between earth and her descending karma but they may stand as the guardian action of a Cosmos for and on behalf of the Christed ones. They may stand for the implementation of every call and every judgment but they may not prevent a karma unchecked—[a karma which might yet be checked] whether by the violet flame invoked of the Lightbearers or by the final surrender of the fallen ones before the living God.

Therefore, beloved, because the seed of Sanat Kumara is in the earth there is hope in heaven and there is hope in earth. Knowing well, then, that the dispensation given to you personally, as it is realized and applied, may yet be increased, you may understand that surely and squarely as it has come to every planet in the past, those in embodiment must now take the full responsibility for the outcome of planet earth.

I sign this and seal it this day in cosmic time and according to the date of the Book of Life,

Alpha of the Flame

My mantle of the Lord of the World drops now about this Messenger. It is a weight not able to be calculated as weights are calculated in this octave. The congruency of myself in this form is allowed by this dispensation, beloved, for inner reasons and an inner past which I shall not enumerate.

Suffice it to say, beloved, that when each and every one of you may attain to a certain stature of Christhood, the mantle of a living Ascended Master Guru may drop around you. And thus you may serve as the self of that one below and thereby have and contribute to the stream of earth's victory the momentum of a shining one.

Thus, within the framework of the Law is the judgment of God somewhat mitigated or bypassed. It is the intercession of the Mediator. In this case every Ascended Master and Cosmic Being is a Mediator, beloved. Thus, in your Christhood you may wear our own [Christhood]. I urge you, beloved, to call upon the LORD in the Person of one with whom you so identify—whose mantle and service you may choose in this hour to make your own—that here below you should truly have our Presence.

Blessed ones, there is not a dry eye in heaven in this moment. You see, we would desire much more. Beloved, we would desire even to take embodiment through you, would the Great Law so allow it. We would give, beloved, even another life that some greater measure of grace could be forthcoming.

In this hour you may see our hands tied and yours untied. Therefore, we shall search ways and means to assist you, to appeal to the Great Law that we might bear the karma of our best servants and those who daily bear the karma of a world. As you try, we shall try. And in multiplying our trying, beloved, we trust we shall see the New Day.

Blessed ones, inasmuch as we have given so much and now are required, as it were, to stand back and see what the masses shall make of the earth and what the Lightbearers shall make of the earth, we must call to your attention that you must see to it that in all things you *Prepare.*

Let those who have heard the Blessed Mother and Saint Germain and so many others now come—come to the Western Shamballa. Come to the place where a Community of Light may raise a shining sword Excalibur once again to assemble all hearts of Camelot and, with Ascended Masters very close, demonstrate before all of Cosmos and our Father Alpha that the wisdom given and received, the warning proclaimed unto wise ones who have seen the rise and fall of civilizations will in this hour so be heeded and so be a goad and a means to the implementation of the highest Cosmic Law that there shall be achieved a victory unparalleled in the face of unparalleled odds.

As Alpha has called the Keeper of the Scrolls, so I also have called him. And as though Veronica's handkerchief were given to us each one, the very record of your lifestreams and your causal bodies is our comfort this day. In our vision, beloved, we desire to tell you that you do possess in hand, and available by immediate access, the wherewithal in the causal bodies of yourselves embodied and all members of the Great White Brotherhood embodied to defeat the Adversary in the earth.

If we wait with bated breath, it is not to see if you *can* do it but if you *shall.*

As I come to you in this hour, therefore, beloved, I am apprised and aware of all events moving on the planetary body of Absolute Good in the hearts of the sweet saints and of Absolute Evil yet parading before the unawakened.

We bow before our God and before the Great Lord Alpha in gratitude that the woes have descended upon the seed of the wicked.

Blessed ones, in the very cup of gratitude is a cup of sorrow, inasmuch as this seed is almost all-pervasive and therefore their judgment does [perforce] affect the Children of the Sun. Even though their lives and hearts are sealed in Light, yet they are a part of the fabric, and the warp and woof thereof, that these fallen ones have woven as patterns throughout civilization.

It is plain, beloved. It is plain. Get thee up to the mountain of God. But first leave thy bag and baggage behind and recognize that there is no more room for folly on the path of chelaship. I am even forbidden by the Great Law to say it once more, for it has truly been said.

And those who have not understood sacrifice, in this hour themselves receive the judgment of their nonsacrifice, which is a densification and a waxing gross even of their perceptions and ability to perceive a path they should long ago have espoused.

Therefore, where the Messenger and the magnitude of Light and vibration we have sent through our spoken Word has not effected conversion in those who should have been turned around to face the Sun, I say this day:

In this hour or in the hour of your hearing of this dictation, I, Gautama, am required and permitted to cross this line [steps over the line drawn symbolically in the floor] to give one final opportunity to you to come into the Light and live forevermore as God.

Woe! to those who have heard our voice and who, having been called, do not answer that call but reject it.

In the heart of the Grand Teton, in the heart of Maitreya Mountain I AM Gautama Buddha ever keeping the flame and the vigil at the Inner Retreat of the Western Shamballa.

My hand and my Presence does physically consecrate the Heart of the Inner Retreat as the international shrine and gathering place of the devotees of Light and Christed ones of the world.

This shrine, then, is now consecrated and shall so be consecrated at the occasion of the Freedom conference. In that hour, our Father Alpha shall speak directly to you, coming on the path set by Helios [July 4, 1984]. From this date to that we anticipate a mounting light, great love and prayers laid upon the altar of that Heart which is my Heart and the Immaculate Heart of Mary, the Sacred Heart of Jesus, Maitreya, Sanat Kumara.

Therefore, beloved, our Father has promised to us all to bring some good tidings of a report based upon the true conversion, first of the Lightbearers and then of those yet to be contacted by our Teaching.

I seal you with the cosmic cross of white fire as angels of the Ruby Ray, angels of the Body of Christ come to minister unto you, to succor you and to serve you our Holy Communion—token sign and presence of the communion of saints, as Above so below.

Into the heart of your I AM Presence I retire. In Love I AM with you always. Even as you speak the name I AM THAT I AM, so I AM with you alway, even unto the end of the age.

Messenger's Benediction:

> In the name of the entire Spirit of the Great White Brotherhood I seal you and I give to you my Heart, my Love and my Life.

"The Summit Lighthouse Sheds Its Radiance O'er All the World to Manifest as Pearls of Wisdom." This dictation by Gautama Buddha was **delivered** through the Messenger of the Great White Brotherhood Elizabeth Clare Prophet on **Wesak, May 13, 1987,** at the **Royal Teton Ranch, Montana.** (**1**) Rev. 2:11; 20:6, 14; 21:8. (**2**) Matt. 13:12, "For whosoever hath, to him shall be given, and he shall have more abundance: but whosoever hath not, from him shall be taken away even that he hath." Matt. 25:29; Mark 4:25; Luke 8:18; 19:26. (**3**) See Gautama Buddha, May 3, 1977, "One Decade for the Turning of the Tide: The Great Central Sun Messengers, the Cosmic Christs, and the Buddhas Come Forth," 1978 *Pearls of Wisdom,* vol. 21, no. 28, p. 148; excerpted in 1986 *Pearls of Wisdom,* vol. 29, no. 65, pp. 577–78. (**4**) Matt. 24: 40, 41; Luke 17:34–36.

For My Personal Record

A "clean white page" on which I write my response to the Lord of the World and beloved Alpha

Vol. 30 No. 25 — *Beloved Saint Germain* — *June 21, 1987*

"A Door That Shall Open . . ."

Dearly Beloved,

I have heard the word of Gautama Buddha delivered from the heart of Sanat Kumara. The councils of the Great White Brotherhood have listened with rapt attention to the Proclamation of Alpha read to the devotees on the occasion of Wesak, May 13, 1987.

Therefore, ye who would know the day and the hour of the coming of the Son of man,[1] note well the Divine Decree:

The opportunity for the saving of the earth has been lost to the fallen ones: no new dispensation is forthcoming on this Wesak 1987 for the planet as a whole.

Unto those who have not afforded themselves the opportunity given to rise to the level of the Christ Standard but who have denied it not only in these little ones but in the inner voice and in that of guardian angels, there is delivered three woes for the abuse of the Father and of the Son and of the Holy Spirit in the children of God.

These betrayers of the living Word were spared the fourth woe by the presence in the earth of the Mother of Knowledge and the true Keepers of the Flame.

Thus, the karma for the desecration of the Divine Mother and her seed is held in abeyance pending the bending of the knee by these fallen ones before the living Word and their repentance and conversion unto the Trinity.

It is considered by the Great Ones that the severity of returning planetary karma and the necessity for earth changes may be mitigated by the descent of the three woes upon the fallen ones coupled with the increase of Light to the Lightbearers.

Though no new dispensation be given this Wesak to any Ascended Master for the saving of the planet, yet there is given a great dispensation to assist the true chela of the Light.

Unto those who have sought and maintained a level of the Christ Consciousness throughout the earth and in this activity, there is given tenfold opportunity to rise "into that Christhood full, into that I AM Presence"—moreover protection, a way of Life, abundant opportunity for acceleration together with a stern warning delivered both by Lord Gautama and the Lord Alpha.

The dispensation and the Light given "cannot, must not be lost, betrayed, misqualified or neglected." And to those for whom it is possible to ascend to God in this cycle, that momentum and that impetus to do so is given.

These conclusions of the Cosmic Council delineate the Divine Decree also spoken by Jesus Christ two thousand years ago as he prophesied both the beginning and the ending of the age, the law of Alpha and Omega: Unto them who *have* Light, more Light shall be added; but from them who *have not,* this day there is taken away that Light which they have abused and misqualified.

The earth is in the hands of the Christed ones. Therefore, the prophecy is for a victory of great magnitude for those who are of the bands of Light—according to the choice and the decision and the response of all Lightbearers in the earth.

This is the same law that has been applied surely and squarely to every planet when in the past the Ascended Masters and the heavenly hosts who comprise the Great White Brotherhood no longer have had dispensation to intercede between a planetary evolution and their returning karma:

Those in embodiment—even the chelas of the will of God who do sustain the figure-eight flow of the Guru/Chela relationship, as Above so below, with Hierarchy—must take full responsibility for the outcome of planet earth.

Please note well, beloved, that every Lightbearer who does respond to this great dispensation, which is as a mathematical formula to each individual according to his own inner attainment, may increase through the Word and the Work and multiply the gift for new dispensations forthcoming.

It is especially the desire of the Darjeeling, Indian, and Royal Teton Councils of the Great White Brotherhood that the direct word to the unfaithful stewards (those who have known the Great Law and the Ascended Masters' Teachings who have resisted the conversion of the living Word and who should have been turned around to face the Sun) be thoughtfully considered.

So momentous was the statement of the Lord of the World that I quote it here:

"I, Gautama, am required and permitted to cross this line to give one final opportunity to you to come into the Light and live forevermore as God. *Woe!* to those who have heard our voice and who, having been called, do not answer that call but reject it."

Sealing his address with the consecration of the Inner Retreat of the Western Shamballa as the international shrine and gathering place of the devotees of Light and Christed ones of the world, beloved Gautama announced the scheduled address of our Father Alpha set by the Cosmic Council for the "FREEDOM 1987" conclave.

No doubt every Keeper of the Flame who does value our communications through our anointed Messenger will reread and study Gautama Buddha's Wesak address published in last week's Pearl of Wisdom, communing in his heart with the Cosmic Christ as to how he might truly fulfill the Law of the Word.

The numberless numbers of saints in heaven applaud the delivery of this message as well as the true and righteous judgments of the LORD God reflected in the Proclamation of Alpha. With one voice and accord, we affirm that this document does once again convey a Light and a Judgment and a Dispensation for, in the words of Gautama, the alignment of a world, the alignment of a solar system and the alignment of souls of Sanat Kumara.

Beloved El Morya—founder and sponsor of The Summit Lighthouse in 1958, beloved teacher of the Messengers whose disciplined path given to them enabled me to receive the authorization from the Cosmic Council to anoint them as Prophets to this age—has accepted the offering of the chelas of the will of God attending his university of the Spirit at Darjeeling as well as that of thousands of angels and devas serving the diamond heart of God's will.

In gratitude for this message these have formed by their combined electromagnetic fields a giant blue rose over northern India. This emblem of Sirius is a sign to the heavens of the gratitude and the determination in the heart of the earth on the part of angels, elementals and Children of the Sun serving together to deliver a planet and a people from the distress of their own deleterious deeds.

We, therefore, seated in the Great Hall of the Royal Teton Retreat do also watch as devotees of this hemisphere with angelic hosts and elementals form over the Grand Teton a giant yellow rose signaling the hope, joy and God-determination of those frequenting the outer mystery school* and the etheric retreat to so illumine a nation, a people, and a youth as to make absolutely clear the choices at hand.

Finally, beloved, we describe to you the giant ruby-pink rose formed over northern Canada by angels and elementals of the Third Ray hierarchies and those with the attainment of the heart chakra from the five other retreats of the Lords of the Seven Rays.

Beloved, so great an offering of hearts so one the planet round at inner levels does indeed comfort heaven, as the disciples of the Father, Son and Holy Spirit in the earth take their very lives and bodies in a union of the three kingdoms and in a spiritual unity of souls of all nations to say unto the Lord Alpha and his Son Gautama, the God of the Earth:

"We will present ourselves a living offering unto God. And, in the fullness of our causal bodies of Light, raise on high the fruit of our finest hours and expressions of this Trinity, protesting by way of cosmic demonstration the abuse by the fallen angels of the voice of the Christ in the threefold flame, in the little children, in the temple of Being and in the angels standing by."

It is therefore our thought, beloved, in accordance with the dispensation of opportunity granted to the Christed ones alone (whereas the three woes and no opportunity be forthcoming to the fallen ones and inasmuch as the Lightbearers have already so responded to the Call and the calling of the Lord of the World) to place our assistance—as that which the Great Law will allow us to do in this hour—behind the mandate so stated as Gautama's conclusion of the entire matter:

"It is plain, beloved. It is plain. Get thee up to the mountain of God. But first leave thy bag and baggage behind and recognize that there is no more room for folly on the path of chelaship."

Therefore, we who are your mentors of the Spirit counsel you who serve beyond the borders of the United States of America to place a priority upon being *here now* legally according to the laws of the nations, legitimately according to the law of chelaship no later than Wesak 1988.

Your immigration through the heart of the Goddess of Liberty is a path of initiation to be fulfilled in the mantra *I AM gratitude in action.* You must fly as eagles to the cities of North America on the wings of your sacred labor, an avocation and a profession *en main* (in hand) by diligent striving and application in the LORD's Work.

Whereas I, Saint Germain, your Knight Commander, do have the dispensation with my colleagues to sponsor our best servants, the Christed ones, to come from abroad and all the

*Maitreya's Mystery School at the Royal Teton Ranch

earth to North America: as a result of the Divine Decree of the Cosmic Council announced at Wesak I have no further opportunity to assist Europe but only the Lightbearers therefrom. All that could be done has truly been done by the tireless calls of those who have gathered in our prayer vigils worldwide.

The announcement following Wesak by the ministers of NATO to agree to a 100-percent removal of medium-range missiles from Europe and the Soviet Union demonstrates the common denominator of a karma and a karmic weight outplayed when the hand of the Mediator is withdrawn by cosmic law. This concerted act by the representatives of the people is the sign and the signal that they have believed the Great Lie and would plight their troth with the Liar—whoever and wherever he is.

Therefore it is written: "Their damnation is just."[2]

Let, therefore, the Keepers of the Flame of Europe finish the work which they have purposed to do. Let the Sacred Heart burn within them as they as one body form the diamond heart of Mary, calling fervently for the rescue and saving of souls that they might see and know the living God in the Chart of Your Divine Self and recognize the Ascended Masters as their true teachers and leaders to the Promised Land.

The hour is come, beloved. The mountain of God is his Higher Consciousness which must be sought and won. Let the Lightbearers who are the seed of Sanat Kumara claim their divine inheritance and the land that God gave them from the beginning. Let them carry in their arms as Christ-bearers the precious ones who must not be left behind.

Your coming to the shore of Light must be by self-effort. Do not fail to heed my call, for indeed you shall not sup with me again until ye do so at the table I have prepared for you in the wilderness,[3] nor shall ye drink with me again until ye drink the new wine of the New Jerusalem[4] in the Heart.

There is a door that shall open if you knock.

There is a way that shall be made plain if you pursue it.

There is a salvation to be worked out if you have heart and faint not, neither delay your coming.

Therefore, to all chelas in the earth, we say:

Let all effort, invocation and decree be for the cutting free of the Lightbearers and those who are one at inner levels but yet know not the path of victory through the Ascended Masters' Teachings.

Let us call for the guardian action of the heavenly hosts on behalf of the territories of the Lightbearers in the Western

Hemisphere. And let the great gathering of the elect[5] be now.

Let those who would suck at the paps of World Communism, false peace and false promises be left to the false Mother and the false Guru they have chosen by free will and with their eyes wide open to the historical choices they are making.

Let the Truth-bearers converge where Truth is.

I seal you with the sign of the Holy Cross, the cosmic cross of white fire ministered unto by the angels of the Body and Blood of Christ. In the ruby and white of the crusaders of the Spirit, I remain at the side of the faithful of my calling

Saint Germain

(**1**) Matt. 25:13, "Watch therefore, for ye know neither the day nor the hour wherein the Son of man cometh." Matt. 24:36, 37; Mark 13:32–37; Luke 12:40. (**2**) Rom. 3:8. (**3**) Pss. 23:5; 78:19. (**4**) Matt. 26:29. (**5**) Mark 13:27, "And then shall he send his angels, and shall gather together his elect from the four winds, from the uttermost part of the earth to the uttermost part of heaven." Matt. 24:31.

Pearls of Wisdom®
published by The Summit Lighthouse

Vol. 30 No. 26 *Beloved Archangel Michael and the Goddess of Liberty* *June 28, 1987*

I Have a Plan

Hail, Children of the Sun, Legions of My Bands!

I count you every one a part of my own.

In the flaming presence of my sword of blue flame, O legions of the will of God, my very own chelas, be seated now, for I have surely come in joy to rescue the Lightbearers of earth! [25-sec. applause]

To whom shall I go, Lord,[1] except to these, as here and there bonfires of blue flame are found upon the mountains where chelas of the will of God will recite the rosary,[2] will give the calls to my heart?

Yes, I come, beloved, and I do have a plan for the implementation by Hope and Faith and Charity of the Call, the Divine Direction and the Decree set forth by our Lord Gautama Buddha, by beloved Alpha.[3]

I AM the flaming Presence of the I AM *Who* I AM.

Therefore, beloved, come with me, listen with me.

First and foremost I must have from you ere forty-eight hours have passed a perfect Alternate Preamble for the defense of freedom in America in the three branches of government and in all departments of state, local and federal agencies.

Beloved hearts, I must have a complete statement that is not unwieldy but that does direct my angels each morning, according to your dynamic decrees, into those areas where, as I have shown the Mother this day, there is a fumbling of the ball of America due to the nonalignment of her people with the Divine Mother—through the Immaculate Heart of Mary and with the living Buddha by the parallel paths that are indeed one path of Christ and Buddha.

Blessed hearts, the indecision of this people, the self-pity that has become self-indulgence, the absence of the lowering into manifestation of the divine plan for victory—all these are signs that have been coming, and coming again and again, but are nowhere more apparent than in this Dark Cycle.

Therefore, I have determined and volunteered to come forth on the wings and the heels of the Light* of Wesak that I might address you while the sun is yet in the month of May.

O blessed hearts, hear me, then. For in the earth under the sign of the Buddha[4] in the very element physical whereon you stand, I take my sword, I place it into the ground and I say to you, *Rally around this sword!* And let it be placed now in the very presence of every chela at that six o'clock line. Beloved, on that line we shall stand and conquer, [for] on that line is the greatest vulnerability to failure. Understand, beloved—now moving toward the Fourth of July when the sun shall again be in this Mother sign[5]—that the foundation must be laid.

Blessed hearts, the protection of America must become physical swiftly. Let the defenses be raised up. Let the necessary programs be espoused. Let there be a meeting of the minds and a stripping action.

I promise you, beloved, as the Chohans have promised me, that you may come every single night[6] with my bands to go forward and strip the public servants and the citizens of all that has been laid upon them by a *rotten* press and a *rotten* educational system!

Let it crumble from the foundations and let the new system of divine education appear! And let the great systems of communications now deliver Reality and Truth to a people who have been prepared by my bands in answer to your calls and by your own action.

For, beloved, do you understand that inasmuch as the earth is in your hands we must have those in physical embodiment at our sides? We must have with us the Lightbearers who have been given the dispensation to join us in those hours of sleep that we might indeed strip this nation of astral hordes and karma.[7] And truly light a fire of violet flame such as the world has never seen, that in the name of Saint Germain it become the most blazing bonfire that shall complement the blue flames of our rosary, hillside by hillside!

Blessed ones, the plan, then, is for the most effective and incisive Call. It must not be too long, for all must give it daily. Understand this, beloved.

We have not had for some years a very specific Call that could be given to our legions. And when it is given at night, beloved, they spend the next eight hours going after those forces

*The Christic or Buddhic consciousness

that are preventing *right decision, right action, right-mindfulness, right strategy* in the defense of Freedom and the Light.*

I have heard the Word of the Lord. I believe it. I AM it. For I stand before and in his Presence.

Therefore, it is possible for the Lightbearers of the earth united indeed to turn the world around and to widen the crack in the door that has yet been left open. Is this not the great miracle of this Wesak, that the door has not been shut on Opportunity? Beloved, be grateful and praise the Lord! [29-sec. applause]

Therefore you peep through that door to our octave, we peep through that door to your own. Our hands yet fit through. We clasp hands and as millions join us the door widens, beloved.

My heart's fire and plan, then, is to greet our beloved Alpha and his hosts in the Heart over this Fourth of July conference and to present him such a momentum, such a gain for the very intensity of our determination that our Father might well go before the Cosmic Council and deliver to us some greater measure of protection, some timing and timetable.

O beloved, I dare not tell all that I see and know. But be reminded that there are daily advances being made by a Soviet system and by its participants with one goal in mind, to assume the *power,* beloved, to assume the power and then *wield it* or hold it as a threatening woe unto the United States, even as the fallen ones in the earth have received those woes.[8]

Beloved, do you see? Surely you have seen, but I open your eyes this evening to a greater vision, that World Communism and all of its conspirators in the West have done this for one reason alone: for the amassing of power. Blessed ones, it is not alone for the power of the Father or of the Son—it is for the power of the Holy Spirit, for these three as well as for the power of the Mother, that they have done this.

Therefore, inasmuch, beloved, as the Judgment of the LORD is upon them, you may invoke it daily.[9] Each time there is a manifestation repeated, again you may multiply the judgment wherever there is a betrayal by the fallen ones of the Trinity in the hearts of these little ones.[10]

Blessed ones, a defilement of the threefold flame or the personages thereof is surely the triggering for the Judgment Call to be given again and again by the sons and daughters of God in the earth. You may shout the calls that you have in your decree books with greater intensity, with greater righteous indignation. For you are but confirming a Judgment that is already judged and demanded, in order that all elemental life may now concentrate it in

*When *Light* is capitalized it means Christ consciousness.

the physical domain of those who remain the spoilers in the earth.

Thus, beloved, though a serious message from the God Star was this proclamation and dictation, realize that for those who are astute and those who know the Law the message provides a better opportunity than that which has been given for many a year, even though it may be as a razor's edge in its accomplishment.

Blessed ones, ere these fallen ones realize what has transpired and what will come upon them shall we not scoop, then, a victory? Shall we not move forward, beloved? And shall we not gain such ground in our calls and in our action that they will be stopped before they are able to recognize the outcome or even to know what has happened to them?

Blessed ones, we are of the First Ray. And all chelas of El Morya present surely have an increase of that blue fire by the very love of his diamond heart.

I, then, give to you with the heart's gift of the Messenger[11] my heart, the heart of an Archangel, a diamond heart of blue fire, white intensity and a secret chamber with all rays and secret rays and all gradations of color. Thus, beloved, although I am "true blue" and do not wear upon my sleeve all of the colors God has given to me, yet I salute the colors of all nations as the focus of the Cosmic Christ and I bear truly the Great Causal Body of the I AM THAT I AM.

Blessed hearts, though you may know my history or know it not, I can assure you that you may win all that I AM, all that I have. I have not gained it without *sacrifice dear, surrender total, unending service,* beloved.

Surely you must understand that at least this trinity must be manifest out of the four pillars of Life. Then, beloved, you will be the Spirit of Selflessness, and when you are you will discover the key to the courage, the honor and the bravery of my legions. For in selflessness there is no self that can live or die, for that self merely is, always has been and ever shall be. Self*less*ness—without the human self and fully endued with the Divine Self, beloved, you are never a target in this octave.

Thus, if you stick out a little itty-bitty toe outside the circle of your service, blessed ones, be prepared. For that little toe of self-awareness in the human, finite condition will render you vulnerable. Stand on and in the circle of infinity, beloved, and know that it is an armour beneath you and one day it shall be a dais from which there shall spring forth spontaneously in the presence of Serapis Bey truly the ascension flame.

To this end we have called you. To this end we prepare you.

And we believe that our service and our legions present the most fantastic opportunity ever known to meet the demand of an unparalleled victory in conditions of unparalleled vulnerability.

Blessed ones, let all of your vulnerabilities become mighty victories, diamond points, that you might see that an armour is forged and won by conscious determination to remove the weak spots.

Therefore, beloved, my plan begins with the Call incisive, a Call so determined that no longer shall America be undecided, no longer shall decisions be made for her people that are not the fullness of the perception of the will of God by the Fourteen Ascended Masters who govern this nation.

Blessed ones, the Lords of Karma have also heard the message of Gautama. And here at my side is the beloved Goddess of Liberty, who must, for she is determined, speak to you in this moment. And therefore I step aside for the mighty Lady of the Lamp who does wish to give you her word of comfort. [congregation rises]

The Beloved Goddess of Liberty

Most Beloved Ones,

As the Spokesman for the Karmic Board I must tell you that the dispensation of a Light tenfold to the Lightbearers of the earth[12] is being deliberated for implementation of maximum effectiveness through the seven rays to your seven chakras.

We are determined also that the Lightbearers shall not be without a rallying point, a banner, a presence, beloved, that they shall know the way and walk in it, that they shall be cut free and stripped truly of those very elements which they desire to be rid of in their deep desiring to effect this rescue of planet earth.

Therefore, beloved, in these weeks until our July conference we are looking to you to prepare yourselves, to write your letters and to ask for dispensations at this half-year level as to the implementation of the Light allotment, indeed the mathematical formula that was given to you on Wesak.

It is our desire, then, no longer to see disorganization or disunity among the Lightbearers of the earth. *And therefore, we shall place as great a momentum of your dispensation as you allow us to the fetching of the greatest hearts, truly those who are the knights at inner levels, to come into the Keepers of the Flame Fraternity.*

Decree for them night and day, beloved. There are many in the United States and there are also those scattered throughout the whole world. Blessed ones, miracles are needed that they might be found at the right place in the right time, even to make the contact.

Thus, I come representing the Lords of Karma. I stand and I keep my vigil and I gaze across the Atlantic. I am searching, beloved, and holding a light to all souls around the entire world and throughout the Pacific who must be a part of the flame that is America.

I ask you to call to me, as I call to you now, for the multiplication of my own opportunity to gather these so that you might have a miraculous reinforcement in all service and especially in decree services never-ending. For this to take place, beloved, there must be a mighty increase of decreers.

Let them come, then, beloved. For we are preparing for a victory to defeat defeat before defeat comes upon our doorstep. Therefore, beloved, it is an hour to appeal to each of the seven of us [members of the Karmic Board] and to understand what we may offer as our own causal bodies of expertise. (I thank you for your welcome, beloved, and ask you to be seated.)

The plan of Archangel Michael is our own. He is the great Cosmic Being who did leap immediately in anticipation of the coming of this opportunity and present to us surely a way out, surely a way for the changing of the mood and the very winds of [public opinion in] America.

Let none then doubt the efficacy of decrees or the intercession of elemental life. Let none doubt that all power in heaven and in earth[13] is surely at the dispensation of the mantle of the Lord of the World upon the Messenger.[14] [And you must call for the power of this mantle to implement each and every aspect of the Divine Plan that must be outpictured if you are to have your unparalleled victory.]

You must invoke in the name of Gautama Buddha those dispensations that you know must take place.[15] Beloved ones, do not allow yourselves to think either that it takes long hours or that it is impossible. Nothing is impossible to you if you make the Call. However, in this octave we require willing hearts and receptive hearts.

Thus has Saint Germain written, and it is so, that as of Wesak he no longer has an opportunity, a dispensation to intercede in Europe. Therefore, with his Mediatorship withdrawn you will see events taking place unfortunate. Yet the sponsorship remains of all Lightbearers upon that continent, and upon these must we concentrate.

Blessed hearts, it has been said that our hands are tied.[16] Indeed they may be tied but yours are not. Remember the Call.

It is the blessed tie that binds earth to heaven, and *the name is Hierarchy!*

Thus, the golden chain of Hierarchy remains intact from the Great Central Sun through this heart to the chelas in the earth. You are strong links in this mighty chain, beloved. And therefore understand: with Hierarchy as God in manifestation through the entire Spirit of the Great White Brotherhood, nothing shall be impossible to you.

Only act! Only act by word, by deed, by ingenuity. And let the publications go forth. For every magazine and Pearl and book, for every video- or audiotape we assign legions to see to it that many hear the Word.

Now in this hour, with the offering and presence of Archangel Michael, you will see how much greater receptivity there shall be with each and every one of you engaged with his hosts throughout the night. Blessed ones, you still shall have a shortened session in the universities of the Spirit as the Chohans have agreed. Understand, then, that time is infinity when you will it so, and much can be compressed in those hours of rest.

I AM the Goddess of Liberty and I look forward to the coming of Alpha. Moreover, I look forward to the coming of Alpha's Sons, Christed ones. For out of Elohim so were they born; male and female created he them.[17]

In the presence of the Light of the heart of devotees heaven is attentive, heaven is available. The authority of your causal body and I AM Presence is the authority of God with you, which by the Word, beloved, shall be manifest. Remember, we enter the door through you.

In the joy of this love of our oneness, of this great family of Light, I seal you in this hour, beloved, for those events taking place in the Middle East demand our full attention.

Keep the vigil, beloved, for the hour of the Judgment is come.

Beloved Archangel Michael

Blessed Ones,

The Seven Archangels bow in gratitude before the presence of this Woman clothed with the Sun, the Goddess of Liberty, and the entire Karmic Board. And we are grateful that in this humble place there is indeed a crossroads of Cosmos and truly a Place of Great Encounters.

Is there anyone you would rather meet in this hour than the Goddess of Liberty, beloved? ["No!"] As she takes her leave (now already in the higher octave), won't you, then, send your great gratitude to her flame. [37-sec. applause]

As she traverses the night sky of America, it is a cosmic sight: billowing garments and a torch held high, a crown of stars dazzling, truly, more brightly than the stars in the heavens. A great figure, beloved, large of stature, her form expands when in higher octaves and therefore she can be seen far and wide as the hope in the heart of so many who are brought to the tensions of this hour.

Blessed ones, it is no surprise that following Wesak it would be the Middle East where tensions would erupt.[18] It is the crossroads of all fallen ones of all systems, and the Lightbearers that are there, beloved, must truly be strong to survive.

Thus, it has been the concentrated area of the comings and goings of the fallen ones where they have fought their wars of the gods, unleashed their nuclear holocaust and on and on, counting not the cost of their ancient rivalries. Beloved, with the coming of Wesak all of this is past. They will not admit it. They will not accept it. Understand this attitude of the enemy. He does not accept defeat, he does not accept your Victory!

Therefore know, beloved, that when they are judged by God they must be bound hand and foot by our legions and restrained in order that they may not go beyond the binding power of the Law. As God has spoken, so the Archangels and our legions implement that Word. And because we are the embodiment of the I AM Presence, the moment the Word is spoken it is directed into the physical earth through us. This may appear as time and space and cycles to those evolving in this earth.

Therefore, catch a glimpse at inner levels. See the falling star Wormwood[19] and see the stars of Archangels who bind him simultaneously. Compress time and space and know that as they are judged in the beginning, so they are judged in the ending. And this beginning and ending are compressed, for time and space are not.

And when, beloved, the sacred fire of the purity of the Mother within your heart comes forth from the secret chamber thereof, you will understand all that has ever taken place between the beginning and the ending as time and space is collapsed and consumed by the sacred fire. And when the white flame does burn in your heart as this action of a divine initiation and you magnetize the white fire of the Mother below, of the Father above, it is the hour, beloved, of your ascension.

Thus, I have given you a gift of an understanding that it is the white fire of the Mother, sealed in the secret chamber of the heart, that comes forth from the heart only upon that point of readiness. For once the ampule is broken, as it were, so this mortal is swallowed up in Immortality,[20] so man can live no longer as man but as God, as the Divine One, beloved. Thus, may you remember it is the day to which the chela of Morya, Serapis Bey and Archangel Michael is called.

When you look at the tasks at hand, remember the co-measurement. And imagine, beloved, if you can, what it is like to feel this intensity of the Mother fire emerge thus, pronouncing the Word of eternity forever.

O eternal ones of God, thus in form you remain limited. For if you were not so, you could not minister to human life here below. But you are immortal already and forever.

Now know the potential of the fire of the Mother within you and recognize why you must have a place apart and vast acres so as to contain the increase of Light that is yours for the Call. As the Light increases it must merge with nature, with mountain and stream. It must not be absorbed in the cities.

Thus, you were once told long ago by Maitreya that the day would come when you would be at a place on the Path that this retreat would become an absolute necessity for your further advancement. Each one will know that time and moment, beloved, when he must be in the mountain of God.

Therefore, my plan is to sweep the nation clean of this substance misqualified on the Cosmic Clock, to cut free the current representatives. But, beloved ones, the judgment of serpents leaves many a vacuum. Sons and daughters of God and children of the Sun must be prepared quickly. And I tell you, beloved, this is not hopeless, for my cohort beloved Jophiel has reminded me of the conversion of the Holy Spirit in the twinkling of an eye by wisdom's rod, by Chamuel's ray!

Therefore, know that as you encapsulate Truth and the logic of the right path, the right action and the right decision in a simple statement, in an article, in a message, those who are ready and of the Light will take it. It will enter them as a fiery coil. It will enter them, beloved, as a transforming message. They will not need six years of higher learning to understand how to defend the people, how to make right choices.

Blessed ones, only see that the chelas are truly literate, not only in the ability to read but in the ability to comprehend. Comprehension, again, is by the Holy Spirit.

Why do you suppose the Lords of the Seven Rays devised

such a system of intense training at their universities of the Spirit? Beloved, it is because through the nine gifts of the Holy Spirit individuals will gain the ability to take their place in this society even though they may have been programmed to wrong ideas or been deprived of a correct education. And thus the Chohans would hasten the day of your receipt of those gifts, that all of the areas of necessity might be filled in.*

Blessed ones, of a truth, had your own beloved Mark[21] been more educated, it would have been more difficult to use him as the instrument, so bad have the systems of education become in their programming of the true servants of God away from the inner calling.

There is no greater gift that any teacher or parent may give a child than the exercise of listening to the inner voice of Almighty God. Do not neglect this, O teachers who understand the necessity of preparing children for the institutions of the day. Remember that that voice will speak to the heart of the student when his professors or others who might lead him astray may tell him the most convincing lies of logic, philosophy, political and economic theories, may deliver all of the developed speeches of the serpent in the Garden to woo the child away from the inner life.

Blessed ones, I was the voice of God in the heart of this Messenger as she would sit in the halls of university, having one page for the voice of the professor and his comments and the opposite page for the tutoring of God. So the inner voice, beloved, should not be drowned out (by the wrong kind of educators or education), even here at the Inner Retreat. Let children be taught to know the vibration and the sound of the voice of Christ and to differentiate between it and the spirits that mutter and peep[22]—the harsh and strident sounds of the fallen ones who whisper in the ear. Beloved, this is the necessity.

Therefore know the prophecy, the dispensations and the opportunity at hand and do not be dismayed or discouraged. The cleaning out of America by our work at night and your calls given through this very special preamble you shall write, combined with the publishing and the sending forth of the outline of the Path that must be walked to extricate this nation under God from the toilers, will accomplish much. And when the message is hurled and preached, beloved, we will see that those who have ears to hear are there to listen, that those who have hearts that can comprehend are also there and that those who can read and run will have in hand the message.

*Don't delay any longer: Read *Lords of the Seven Rays: Mirror of Consciousness* by Mark L. Prophet and Elizabeth Clare Prophet. Send $6.45 postpaid to Summit University Press, Dept. 703, Box A, Livingston, MT 59047-1390.

Therefore, beloved, my rod does place now a magnet to liberate those and only those who can write and organize our message and the various organs of publication that have to be our mouthpiece.

Blessed ones, I send forth the true Power of God, the true Wisdom of God and the true Love! By the power of the Trinity, let it be so. And by the power of Almighty God, who has taken to himself that light misused, let those who have perverted these three go down now by the effective action of the legions of angels and all who join our bands!

So, beloved, *I AM* the Call! And I send this Call to the hearts of those who know and will answer. Thus, may they also remember the warning of Gautama.[23]

Let those who hear my Call come, then, and be a part of this rescue mission. We have never been more ready, never more determined, never more *totally* engaged in the saving of any world anywhere, beloved! And it is indeed for your sakes, the sakes of all Lightbearers upon planet earth.

Therefore, I, Archangel Michael, stand and still stand! Amen. [50-sec. applause]

"The Summit Lighthouse Sheds Its Radiance O'er All the World to Manifest as Pearls of Wisdom." This dictation by Archangel Michael and the Goddess of Liberty was **delivered** through the Messenger of the Great White Brotherhood Elizabeth Clare Prophet on **Sunday, May 17, 1987,** at the **Royal Teton Ranch, Montana.** (**1**) John 6:68. (**2**) *Archangel Michael's Rosary for Armageddon,* 36-page booklet, $1 (add $.25 for postage); booklet plus 90-min. cassette of rosary, dictation by Archangel Michael and angel songs, $5 (add $.80 for postage). (**3**) See pp. 239–49. (**4**) Taurus. (**5**) The sign of Cancer is charted on the 6 o'clock line of the Cosmic Clock as taught by Mother Mary. See Elizabeth Clare Prophet, "The Cosmic Clock: Psychology for the Aquarian Man and Woman," in *The Great White Brotherhood in the Culture, History, and Religion of America,* pp. 173–206; and *The ABC's of Your Psychology on the Cosmic Clock,* 8-cassette album (A85056), 12 lectures. (**6**) Out of the body in soul travel during sleep, garmented in the etheric sheath. (**7**) See Archangel Michael, February 3, 1985, "The Summoning: Straight Talk and a Sword from the Hierarch of Banff," 1985 *Pearls of Wisdom,* vol. 28, no. 10, pp. 101, 102, 106. (**8**) See p. 240, par. 6; p. 242, pars. 5–9. (**9**) See the Judgment Call "They Shall Not Pass!" by Jesus Christ, decree 20.07, in *Prayers, Meditations, and Dynamic Decrees for the Coming Revolution in Higher Consciousness* (Section II). (**10**) See p. 242, par. 8. (**11**) See p. 249. (**12**) See p. 243, pars. 5, 6, 10. (**13**) Matt. 28:18. (**14**) See p. 247, par. 1. (**15**) See p. 245, pars. 5–8. In addition to invoking the dispensations of the past century, compose calls invoking the dispensations from the most recent dictations. (**16**) See p. 247, par. 5. (**17**) Gen. 1:27. (**18**) On May 17, 1987, 4 days after Wesak, the U.S.S. *Stark,* a Navy frigate on routine patrol in the Persian Gulf, was hit by 2 Exocet missiles fired from either 1 or 2 Iraqi fighter jets. Thirty-seven U.S. sailors died in the attack. (**19**) Rev. 8:10, 11. See "Chernobyl: A Prophecy of Karma in the Bible," in *Saint Germain On Prophecy,* pp. 179–89, Book Two. (**20**) I Cor. 15:53, 54. (**21**) The Messenger Mark L. Prophet. (**22**) Isa. 8:19. (**23**) See p. 248, pars. 8, 9; p. 249, par. 1.

The Judgment Call
"They Shall Not Pass!"
by Jesus Christ

In the Name of the I AM THAT I AM,
I invoke the Electronic Presence of Jesus Christ:
They shall not pass!
They shall not pass!
They shall not pass!
By the authority of the cosmic cross of white fire
it shall be:
That all that is directed against the Christ
within me, within the holy innocents,
within our beloved Messengers,
within every son and daughter of God . . .
Is now turned back
by the authority of Alpha and Omega,
by the authority of my Lord and Saviour Jesus Christ,
by the authority of Saint Germain!

I AM THAT I AM within the center of this temple
and I declare in the fullness of
the entire Spirit of the Great White Brotherhood:
That those who, then, practice the black arts
against the children of the Light . . .
Are now bound by the hosts of the LORD,
Do now receive the judgment of the Lord Christ
within me, within Jesus,
and within every Ascended Master,
Do now receive, then, the full return—
multiplied by the energy of the Cosmic Christ—
of their nefarious deeds which they have practiced
since the very incarnation of the Word!

Lo, I AM a Son of God!
Lo, I AM a Flame of God!
Lo, I stand upon the Rock of the living Word
And I declare with Jesus, the living Son of God:
They shall not pass!
They shall not pass!
They shall not pass!
Elohim. Elohim. Elohim. [chant]

Posture for giving this decree: Stand. Raise your right hand, using the *abhaya mudrā* (gesture of fearlessness, palm forward), and place your left hand to your heart—thumb and first two fingers touching chakra pointing inward. Give this call at least once in every 24-hour cycle.

Pearls of Wisdom®
published by The Summit Lighthouse

Vol. 30 No. 27 *Beloved Jesus Christ* *July 5, 1987*

Christ's Ascension in You

I

From Temples of Love
The Call to the Path of the Ascension

Keepers of the Flame of My Life on Earth,

I salute you in this hour of my Victory. It is a renewed victory of the life everlasting now increasing its light upon the altar of your heart.

Beloved, not only have I called you but I AM the Call. Not only am I the living Christ but I AM in the Christ of all.

Therefore, O people of Light, receive me in this hour as I have received you, as I am receiving you, as I am indeed entering your life if you will respond to my Call in a more than ordinary way. For I am sent by the Father for the quickening now of ten thousand saints in the City Foursquare that I mark as North America.

Blessed hearts, it is to these states and nations of the lost tribes regathered that I come, even as I sent my apostles to the lost sheep of the house of Israel.

You have descended from [the] All that is Real. Now *defend* [the] All that is Real. For this place, North America, is a land promised to you long ago which through my heart, called the Sacred Heart by certain of the Christian devotees, has been consecrated unto the path of the ascension.

Therefore, it is altogether fitting that in this city, where some disciples of mine have invited this Messenger to speak, I should tell you in this moment of the quickening of your own ascension through my own that the path unto the seed of Light, the path which is initiatic in nature, is one that can be fulfilled upon this continent *because,* beloved, there are certain retreats in the heaven-world, called the etheric octave, where there is a consecration of that ascension flame and path, which can be entered into only by Love.

Therefore, consider the love of John my beloved for the Light that I bore. Not John alone but the celebration of this love betwixt thee and me, beloved, is taking place daily if you will only appreciate and contain the sense of self-worth whereby truly the gold of the divine image and the soul ascending is worthy of the intimate relationship with my heart.

Beloved, there have been many approaches to Christianity and to religion, but it is only by the path of Love that thou mayest enter in. When to this Love there is added Wisdom and the joy in self-givingness unto the self-emptying unto the Self, infilling and fulfilling—blessed ones, this Love that intensifies as the burning of the heart, consuming the dross and nonsensical non-self-awareness, does expand and expand until the whole of self and being is enveloped and engulfed with the living presence of Love!

And in this Love tryst, beloved, can you determine who is thy Christ and my Christ? Beloved, I and my Father are one, I and my disciple are one. When you merge with that Christ, lo, I AM with you alway, even unto the end of this age and all ages to come.

Thus, beloved, very near to this city, encompassing a large area, is the retreat of the mighty Archangels of Love, Chamuel and Charity. O beloved, their retreat over St. Louis expands in a very wide dimension.

The Archangels are teachers of Christhood par excellence. And when you have done visiting even the retreats of the Lords of the Seven Rays may you perchance be invited to a series of studies in the retreats of the Archangels. This, beloved, is my prayer unto the Father, who has responded by saying, "My Son, let them prove themselves with thy brothers, the Seven Masters of Light, and then they shall truly know the divine interchange with Archangels."

So, beloved, rejoice that not alone Archangel Michael, who has called you in his service, but all of the Seven may one day host you in their retreats for the accelerated initiations of Life unto eternity. This retreat, then, of Chamuel and Charity is one of a number of retreats in the etheric octave over North America.

Blessed hearts, realize of this nation, the United States, of this Dominion of Canada, that each one is passing through serious initiations on the path of Love, the path of the internalization of the Holy Spirit: of Love, then, that becomes the sharper-than-the-two-edged sword. Love, then, that becomes the scepter that turns back all anti-Love.

Love, then, is itself the defense of Freedom and of Peace. Love is the giving of oneself. Thus, Charity—by whose name the very virtue is derived—must serve those who are becoming the compassionate ones, the students of the Christ and the Buddha, and the Buddha as Christ.

Thus, my beloved, there is a focus of Paul the Venetian, the Lord of the Third Ray, anchored firmly over the city of Washington, D.C. There is the great retreat of Heros and Amora, Elohim of the Third Ray, over Canada at Winnipeg. Blessed hearts, these are mighty temples. Many of you here have already journeyed there while your bodies have slept.

Blessed hearts, because you are ongoing students of the inner mysteries, you have brought back from this inner temple experience an awareness of what it means to say, "Love is the fulfilling of the Law." It is the whole Law, beloved. But even the heart chakra must be purified, for human love does reside there. And Divine Love little by little does displace it until such Divine Love appears, O beloved, that the white fire must also descend.

Angels of the cosmic cross of white fire, I, Jesus, mark the sign of the cross over this North America, that by the Ruby Ray and by the white fire my Body and my Blood might infuse the Lightbearers for the protection of a path that is to be forged and won and for the peace of the heart.

Blessed ones, over the state of Arizona there is a temple of Eriel of the Light and there is the retreat of my beloved John. These retreats are ancient; they have not suddenly appeared. There are retreats all over the world, but I have chosen to speak to you on this day of the commemoration of my ascension of those retreats in North America that facilitate a path that some must win, a path of Divine Love.

Love, then, is most misunderstood and misqualified. For when the love of God comes upon an individual who has not yet pursued a path, that love may become qualified with human emotion and concepts of love that are not the fullness of the cup that I offer.

Greater love than this hath no man, that a man lay down his life for his friends. Blessed ones, this is not speaking of death but of a vibrant life lived—lived truly to convey the fire of my heart to all. This is the meaning of being a disciple who is called apostle, instrument and messenger of Light, conveyer of that Light, beloved.

So too, beloved, learn the mystery of Love. Even the sign of the Statue of Liberty points to a temple of light of a Divine Mother, a being who has embodied and ensouled the flame of Liberty and out of Love does keep that flame for all who make their way to this continent.

For, beloved, you must understand that to enter this land is to enter a path that can culminate in the soul's ascension. Even the concepts of freedom and of free enterprise, all of these, beloved, bespeak the initiations of the abundant Life whereby each individual with maximum independence and freedom may prove himself in God, and in Christ reprove the lesser self and learn daily the wisdom of the heart.

Therefore, beloved, understand that though the Royal Teton Retreat at the site of the Grand Teton is celebrated as a temple of Wisdom, truly all who have ascended have ascended through Love, serve the seven rays in Love, teach in Love, give in Love, initiate in Love. Love may be a chastening fire that does hasten the soul's departure from error and illusion.

Thus, without Love as a chastening there is no true compassion. Let the teacher be firm yet yielding, tolerant yet stern when pointing to the immutable Law which is the true and only salvation. Salvation through the Law of God, beloved, may be achieved by entering into and embracing the mercy as well as the justice of that Law.

Thus, you understand the great need of humanity for the Mediator, the Intercessor, the Advocate. This Person of God who does defend those who have gone out of the Way, who does plead before the courts of heaven for mercy unto the ignorant, this Person, beloved, is the Universal Christ that I AM, that you are or shall become, whose Presence just above you may descend as your vibrations are elevated, resurrected, accelerated by the great science of the spoken Word which we teach.

Understand, beloved, that the meaning of the office of World Teacher which I bear and share with my beloved Francis is to be that Intercessor, to bring enlightenment as well as comfort, that those who are in Darkness may see a Light, and a Great Light, and walk in it.

I call to you to be world teachers. I call to you to understand—because you have understanding, because you have an inner gnosis, because you have walked with me for centuries—the Reality, beloved, that this is the hour to claim the mantle of Mediator, to claim the mantle here below of your Holy Christ Self and to take your stand through prayer and invocation, through dynamic decrees to the Father, for grace and mercy and light to flood this North America and the entire earth to contact those of greatest Light and to transfer to them even the sacred fire of the Word, that there might be here below an increased manifestation of Light to hold the balance for the Darkness that shall surely come upon this earth unless a people swiftly turn to the inner Light and unless millions, beloved, come to the realization of the

God who is within as well as the God who is in his heaven.

Blessed hearts, I have come, then, to make a plea to you and to send my Messenger abroad across this continent for the gathering of ten thousand who will call themselves Keepers of the Flame of Life and who will understand that I, Jesus, have called them. For I was called by the Father, by the servant-Sons, by Saint Germain and the hosts of heaven to establish a teaching, a path and even the Keepers of the Flame Fraternity, that these lessons might be studied, that the daily decrees might be given, that the Light might be anchored and the Light itself be the Mediator to stand between a people, a world, a continent and their own returning karma.

You have heard it said that the Son of God is come to bear the sins of the world. I AM that avatar for this two-thousand-year cycle, beloved. But the hour is come, beloved, as you have understood it and seen it abroad in the land, when inasmuch as I have borne the sins of the world, or world karma, that the transfer of that karma back to those for whom I have borne it should come to pass.

Understand this law, beloved, and heed this teaching. Forgiveness is the setting aside of karma, or sin, and that setting aside is a period of opportunity. Two thousand years, beloved, has this planet had the opportunity to recognize the Christ of me and of many saints and Masters of East and West who have gone before me.

For I am not alone in heaven as some have thought. But many have ascended by the very same law whereby I was taken down from the cross and did enter the tomb to prove the initiation of the resurrection, that you might also prove this great law of the Spirit of the Resurrection.

Therefore, beloved, understand that in this hour many have internalized greater and lesser measures of my Christhood and their own. And many have turned a deaf ear to the message.

Thus, beloved, the Day of Reckoning that is referred to by the prophets as the Day of Vengeance of our God is the day when that opportunity comes to a conclusion and every man must bear his own burden. (And these words, too, are in scripture.) Thus, the burden of karma is daily being placed, individual by individual, upon the just and the unjust, beloved.

But the grace and the mercy of the Law and of all heavenly hosts and of the Father has been the gift of the Holy Spirit, the gift of the violet flame whereby through the invocation of that violet flame, intensely and daily, that karma descending at a personal and a planetary level may indeed be transmuted, or balanced. This process is by the all-consuming sacred fire of God through the Person of the Holy Spirit. It is, if you will, a baptism by fire.

This purging, beloved, does therefore enable the sons of God in the earth—and all who will heed the message of my brother and friend Saint Germain on the use and application of the violet flame—to accelerate on the path of the ascension by Love, for the violet flame is Love's all-consuming forgiveness.

This beloved brother who was with me as my father Joseph (for so I called him, beloved) has been an adept of the Seventh Ray and of the use of the violet flame for tens of thousands of years and beyond. This has been his calling in God. This is his gift from the Father and his gift to the Father's children.

Understand, then, that in the ongoing cycles of two-thousand-year dispensations, it is the age of Aquarius and of the Seventh Ray that has descended upon earth, meshing, then, with the final decades of Pisces.

Therefore, you will see at this altar our oneness, our oneness as we together assist earth's evolutions to make the transition into an era of freedom, that by freedom's flame that is called the violet flame, souls who yet have karma to balance may not be overcome, may not be struck down by that karma, nor a world itself be destroyed or come to an end. For there be few and then many in this planet who shall hear my voice and his, know the Truth and confirm it in their hearts and call to that violet flame, beloved, unto the victory of individual Christhood and planetary Cosmic Christ awareness!

I, Jesus, preach this message *to you,* beloved. It is an urgent message. You who have an inner awareness, do not deny the signs of the times, do not deny the rumblings in the earth or my own prophecies written in scriptures already in your hands.

It is the end of an age when there must be an entering in of a new vibration, a new opportunity. And the question is, beloved, Will enough of the Lightbearers in the earth recognize this vibration of the Seventh Ray and realize that it is the key to the conclusion of this two-thousand-year cycle?

Blessed ones, this North America, a place consecrated by Love to the reunion of souls with God, is a place where if the Lightbearers would respond and *make the Call,* even as I call you this night, there should be established even the white light over a continent to protect it from those calamities of the Four Horsemen, which could indeed appear for want of mediators in the earth.

Understand, beloved, that the mediators who must stand between a people and a planet and their karma must be in physical embodiment. If you will read my words you will find that they say, *"As long as I AM in the world, I AM the light of the world."*

"As long as I AM in the world..." Beloved, I AM in the ascended octaves of Light; I AM the *Ascended Master* Jesus Christ. And I AM in the world only when I AM [the I AM Presence of me, the Christ of me is] in my own, when the temple is prepared, when the Christ Self has been invoked, and when the violet flame has cleansed the four lower bodies to prepare a highway [a tunnel of light] for our God's descent into form.

I desire to come into your temple, beloved, and *be* in the world. And therefore, when you feel me entering into your house in that Second Coming, understand that you in me and I in you as we are one make the same declaration: "As long as I AM in the world, I AM the light of the world."

Blessed hearts, recognize the Call. Your souls are ancient. It is your hour and the moment of your destiny. Recognize, then, that the Call to be the Divine Mediator must be answered ere the earth changes that must come about take their toll in a cataclysmic way or perhaps in war, even that war prophesied by my Mother at Fátima.

Blessed hearts, the choice is yet to free hearts and free thinkers who will know the winds of Aquarius and be the Keeper of the Flame of Life on earth. Thus, do not fall prey to a sense of predestination or of psychic prognostication wherein you believe all that must happen will happen and there is nothing that you can do to change it. You have not been taught the true meaning of prophecy, which is to show you upon the screen of life what *could* take place *if* you do not intercede.

Blessed hearts, what you see in the mind's eye can be canceled out by decision and free will. You do not need to fulfill any thought, feeling or idea that is negative. But, beloved, when you see the projection upon the world screen of that which can easily be calculated by the signs of the times, this, then, must be transmuted because you are seeing a prophecy of karma returning.

Therefore, take the violet flame; invoke it. Call to me and all saints of heaven and all powers of angels to intercede, that the sacred fire might consume planetary karma and Archangel Michael and his legions do battle and bind the fallen angels and evil spirits which would possess, destroy and defile even the souls who are on the path of overcoming.

Blessed ones, some of you have been taught that evil is not real. And indeed it is not real in God. But you cannot deny that there are spoilers in the earth who have wreaked their holocausts upon millions. You cannot deny that in the hearts of some there is a will to do evil.

You must understand that this malintent must be checked by those who know the science of the spoken Word. For the Word itself will swallow up the appearance of evil. Take heed, then, that the appearance and the illusion does not swallow up souls ere they have realized the Truth which you know—that in the absolute sense of the scientific affirmation of being, evil is not real.

Armageddon is yet to be fought by the Archangels and the legions of Light and the Faithful and True and the armies in heaven. Yet, it is your hour to make the Call. He who understands the Call made in the earth unto heaven and the Call of heaven made unto earth will arrive at the nexus where heaven and earth meet in the Divine Call and the Calling.

Beloved, I leave you, then, with this charge: Make your calling and election sure. For millions who yet dwell in ignorance *need your intercession.* In the name I AM THAT I AM, in the name of Christ of you, I say, *Keep* the flame!

Now, then, in commemoration of this hour of our oneness, I shall take from the chalice of the Sacred Eucharist the wafer which I now consecrate and through this Messenger I shall place it upon the tongue of those who desire to receive it.

Know, then, that as my light does pass through and charge this body, so I am able, even from the ascended state, to use these chakras [of the Messenger] for the conveyance to a simple substance such as the wafer of an increment of light for thy blessing and thy initiation.

Let my servers serve the wine. Let my Messenger give to you my Bread of Life.

Receive, then, this my Body which is broken for you, that you might know the mystery of a crumb of Life that does become the whole loaf.

I AM in heaven and on earth Jesus the Christ. If you will receive me truly in your heart and temple, I shall remain in earth. It is the Law, beloved. So receive me now.

"The Summit Lighthouse Sheds Its Radiance O'er All the World to Manifest as Pearls of Wisdom." This dictation by Jesus Christ was **delivered** through the Messenger of the Great White Brotherhood Elizabeth Clare Prophet on **Ascension Thursday, May 28, 1987,** during the 4-day conference *Christ's Ascension in You* held at the Regency Park Conference Center, **Overland Park, Kansas.** Prior to the dictation, the Messenger delivered a lecture on "The Lost Years and the Lost Teachings of Jesus," which included readings on the ascension from Mark 16:19, 20; Luke 24:49–53; Acts 1:1–11; and the Gnostic text Pistis Sophia, bk. 1, chaps. 2–6. Lecture and dictation published on two audiocassettes, A87032, $13 (add $.80 for postage).

Vol. 30 No. 28 *Beloved Hilarion and Paul the Venetian* *July 12, 1987*

Christ's Ascension in You

II

The Seven Chakras Must Blossom

Hail, thou Lady of Love, thou starry Mother, Regent, Divine Mother of Sanat Kumara!

Come forth, thou who hast sponsored thy sons in a visitation of light to earth. Come forth, blessed Mother of Love, now to quicken in these souls the memory of the Ancient of Days and of the journey to earth, as many came from distant planetary homes to rescue the children of Light of earth who had lost their way.

So I call you, hearts of Light who have gathered here, that you might remember now a half a million years ago, two million, and still consider that thy spirit fiery, that does attend the Mother's travail in giving birth to the Light in this earth, therefore doth know that in thy beginning so in thy ending, the Mother of Love is the key to the unfoldment of the star of greatness in thee.

I AM, then, Hilarion, called to be spokesman for that Light. O beloved, hear that Call. For I am one who answered, yet I must be compelled to answer by the Call itself, by the One Sent.

Witness, then, the living Word in that Jesus, who is yet before you tarrying in his Ascended Master light body in this place, that you might absorb truly the ascension currents for thine own ritual in the ascent. Truly, the soul ascending, beloved, must tarry in the houses of the chakras, thereby slaying those forces of Darkness that would enter there to displace her divine place in the lotus seat, in the petaled throne.

Thus, beloved, the sounding of the Word is for the filling of the cup of the chakras. What will'st thou [do] when the cups be filled? I shall tell thee, beloved. Empty the cups by giving to drink to those who hunger and thirst after the Law,[1] whereby in its right use they might also gain fairly a share of light that is their just portion from on high.

I AM Hilarion, come to bestow gifts of healing by first quickening. O ye who would be instruments, know, then, the law of Truth, know the law of vision, know the science of the immaculate concept, know compassion, know the caring, know the transfer of light to the body itself.

Thus, I would speak to you of the need of the hour. You have heard of the call to be mediators;[2] and so he called me.[3] And so I saw from the inner teaching of the mystery, truly of the Ineffable, beloved, the necessity and the Mother of that necessity, the Divine Mother of Love who would reach her own through my heart. O beloved, I saw that the Truth would not live unless each one in his succession would become the chalice, would become the cup from which all might drink.

It is an hour, then, when many thirst. Where are the cups of the Divine Mother? Where are the cups which will catch not only her ascension light but her tears shed in this hour for the burden that is come upon her own?

I plead, then, the cause of the Divine Mother in the name of her Son Jesus. I plead that cause not alone for the children of the Sun or for the gratification of the Mother and the Divine Son. *Hear me, beloved,* I plead it for you and because of you! Because you need it, beloved. You need an avocation, a divine calling that will galvanize all of your forces because you perceive the need and because the Divine Mother of Love has entered your heart and you desire to fill another's need.

Blessed ones, it is said if one is hungry and naked and in want of "all these things" he cannot perceive and fill the need of another, being about the business of satisfying his own and his family's. Beloved, this is true at a certain level and thus Saint Germain and many of the Masters have sponsored a civilization where, the personal needs of each life being met, the soul should be free to nourish the spiritual needs of many.

Unfortunately, and as you know, people have become drunk with materialism, desiring and requiring more and more and therefore never satiated, but filled with their own wants, having little compassion for the basic spiritual as well as physical needs of others.

Blessed hearts, let it not be said of you that there ever was neglect to perceive the need of a lonely, burdened or pained heart and to supply that need. Therefore are you nourished. Therefore do I bring to you the mantle of the Fifth Ray.

Blessed ones, it is a simple cape that my angels bear. Why do you suppose I have brought them bearing capes? Is it because one is deserving or has attainment or that all do? I have not even regarded levels of attainment this night, beloved, but what I have regarded is the great need of the Divine Mother for her own.

Therefore this cape is reversible. For did you know that the pink cape of Paul the Venetian is lined in emerald green and that my own emerald green cape is lined with the rose of the Third Ray? Therefore, you see, we are juxtaposed together, each one with our inner and outer love for that Divine Mother as she does appear in Mary, Kuan Yin, Lady Venus, Portia, Pallas Athena.

You think these names be of Greek mythology? I tell you, beloved, Greek mythology has copied them from the very ancient ones, the divine manifestations that antedated all of the wars and rivalries of the good and bad gods.

Thus, understand, precious hearts, that this cape is given to see what you will make of it. A simple cape, fastened at the neck, worn on either side.

Now, if you desire to master the five secret rays by the power of the rose cross and the Third Ray of Paul the Venetian, wear the rose within and the green without. And then it shall be that without, the mastery of the seven shall be by the portal of Truth, truly the third- and All-Seeing Eye.

If you desire to pursue a course of the mastery of the five secret rays by the fullness of the power of the emerald ray, so let it be reversed and let the rose be on the outer; for Divine Love radiating from you in all directions will be found to seal within you an inner path of mastery of five points of the heart, even by the Buddha's love, even by the majesty of the Fifth Ray.

Blessed ones, now you know the secret of the pink rose and the bud appearing and the green stalk. Now you also know that the seven chakras must blossom.

Thus, beloved, at the conclusion of our address to you, angels will place these upon you, that you might make of them what you will, that you might wield them and use them; for a cloak may become a mantle by endowment with Light.* Thus, let it be charged *by you* this time, as we give you something of ourselves and you add to it your own momentum. Thus, from the moment these capes descend upon you, beloved, each one [each cape] is instantaneously different by your vibration, by the individualization of the God flame which you bring to it.

Thus, the cape is for your comfort and for the understanding

*the Christ consciousness amplified through the seven chakras

that the path of Truth is to comfort all Life. Do not judge, then, the condition or the karma of the one you comfort, but know that Life is locked inside that one—Life that is Light and God and soul waiting liberation, perhaps by your hand.

Blessed ones, if you never extend the hand, how will you ever know when God is ready to bless life through you?

If you never give the cup of cold water of Christ's teaching, how will you ever know if the Holy Spirit may speak through you?

It is in doing that God does act through you. Thus, in a time of quiescence, absence of activity does signify a garnering of light in chakras as fiery coils become a fire infolding itself and thus there is intensity built within these centers that shall be unleashed in a time of activity and movement.

Now, beloved, I must touch those in all of North America who are the original seed of Sanat Kumara. I must touch and quicken them, for some have come to occupy their place who are not worthy. Let the unworthy servant be removed and let the new plant be planted in that pot and in that earth.

Thus the blossoming continues, hearts unfold, hearts of gold set a standard. And until the Christ Standard be set, how can the Christ appear? Therefore, understand the flowers that hold a matrix by fragrance, color and presence. And that matrix sets a standard and all must reach it if they would pluck that flower.

So it is, beloved, as the mediators in the earth proclaim by example a Christ Standard, these mediators may also embody the Divine Standard, the banner of Maitreya, which banner he holds in this hour as the banner of the Divine Mother. Let the Son of God embrace his Mother and thereby let the Mother appear through him.

> O thou Buddhas, all devotees of the Divine Mother, I, Hilarion, call forth out of the causal body of the Divine Mother truly the science of healing, that in this earth a quickening and an acceleration of the spin and a straightening of axis might be, that all might have restored an ancient memory of the science of wholeness.
>
> Sanat Kumara, thou great physician having all remedies, so now transfer morsels of wholeness to these thine own. Saint Germain, let thy elixir of youth, regeneration and resurrection become, then, accessible to those who will make the call and understand the requirements of the path of eternality lived and experienced and embodied on earth.
>
> O currents of eternal Life, I, Hilarion, come now for the charging of these chakras and these lifestreams. I send

the ray by my angels, by my Messenger now to the crown and the base for the establishment of a pillar of fire midst the Dark Cycle of Cancer. Therefore, let the crown and the base so establish the equanimity, the balance, the polarity of being, that these souls might reach for the polestar of Being in the Mighty I AM Presence.

Now let there be the quickening of the heart, for Alpha, for Omega, present now, do quicken. *Now* let there be the touching of the third eye of each one. *Now* let there be the touching of the soul.

Awake, thou that sleepest![4] *Awake,* O soul! Rise now from thy bed, even thy bed of straw in the seat-of-the-soul chakra. Come forth now, be quickened and live! Come forth now by the quickening power of the Fifth Ray. Come forth now!

Lo, I AM Hilarion. And I am quickening now even the desiring unto God, even the awakening unto the desiring to be God in manifestation, to know and be the divine mystery, to know and be the Divine Word, to know and be the Buddha where I AM. So I am therefore quickening that desiring, that this desiring might be all of thy speaking and thy intoning of the Word.

So let the seven chakras! Now let them sound a ringing! Now let them sound a tone! Now let the ineffable be unheard but be sounded in other octaves.

Lo, I have come to touch those who have descended from the Central Sun with Sanat Kumara. *Lo,* I do it here. For in this place some have lost the way and will find it again.

For I say it, and so it is said by the I AM THAT I AM in the mystery of the Ineffable One, *Lo, I AM.* And I AM THAT I AM in the petals of the thousand-petaled rose that does unfold.

Lo, I AM THAT I AM. I AM, then, in the heart of the living Word, and out of that Word do proceed lifestreams who are the Ascended Masters.

And we the Lords of the Seven Rays salute thee this night, thou who art preparing, then, *thou who art preparing, then,* the way of the ascension, the way of the Deathless Solar Body. So, I anoint thee also with that oil of light.

And so the oil of light, the single drop is placed in the crown chakra of those who require that blessing in this hour: for their inner preparation is just. And therefore, I AM come. And the few receive it, for it does require the Ascended Master as well as the spoken Word.

And therefore know that all who are to ascend in this life are called to keep the flame in order that they might receive the initiation out of the flame which they keep, which is the flame of

Life. And that Life in me and that Life resonating through the Life flame of the Messenger does allow you to receive in the physical octave this blessing, beloved. Therefore, each one shall know it. And so long as the Messenger is in embodiment, so long shall the initiation be possible at the physical level.

And therefore, let the Christ Self of each one—for whom each one does become in time the spokesman and the mouthpiece—let that Christ Self therefore raise up, raise up and quicken now the chakras! Raise them now and quicken them! Raise them now and quicken them! Raise them now and quicken them!

So I seal you in the lotus of the heart.

So I seal you in the twelve-petaled lotus of the heart.

O thou Light! O thou Light! O thou Light!

Be sealed now in the fire of the heart.

I AM Hilarion, come, then, for the initiation of you each and every one to receive from your Lord [your Holy Christ Self] gifts of healing, gifts of healing, gifts of healing. As the chiming of a bell, so shall they descend. So I foretell it. Prepare the way, O my soul, for the angels of healing would enter thy house and teach thee their way.

["Love's Victory" by Thomas Moore, recorded by Excelsior, played as a meditation.]

Beloved Paul the Venetian

Love's Mystery

Into the fire of the heart is a piercing Ruby Ray! So, beloved, I come, the initiate of the Holy Spirit, bearing unto your heart a quickening light that is for Love's victory in *your* day.

Blessed hearts, we are ascending by increments. We have fulfilled the ascension, fully fused in the I AM THAT I AM. But the ascent, beloved, as an increase in God-awareness, is a never-ending process and thus there is no sky to heaven—no ceiling but only a bliss that does intensify as though new vistas were to appear. Do not, then, consider anything that is beyond in the Infinite as having any ending or any limit or any final end or goal.

For the moment strive to reach the fruit of the tree that requires even a stretch of the arm and a tippy-toeing to reach and perhaps even a jump itself. Reaching, then, for the fruit of the Master that does wait thy Call and his Call (and both answers) is a way to establish a co-measurement with lesser goals and reachable stars along the cosmic highway.

Intensify, then, thy adoring and self-giving and discover always that the mystery of Love unfolds as a magnet drawing unto oneself a light increasing that is given only when Love and Love's pursuit is for the goal of a self-control and self-mastery, that the power of Love be never squandered or lost or abused or trifled with.

So, beloved, understand the meaning of trust when considering the Love Ray and all that it does portend for the fullness of thy God-realization. Know, then, that trust is the word that must be received. As you trust in God, so God must be able to trust in you and to trust that the Light that is given will be held steady for adoring, for joy, for creating, for giving, for building, for tearing down, for laying foundation and for the raising up of the temple of man. This temple built without hands is laid stone upon stone by Love, and the chief cornerstone is Love.

Now understand how all rays of God have a mystery of Love and an initiation of Love. I come concerning the Love that perceives the needs of a nation, the needs of a planet. I come to give you a Love that is an enlightenment, for Wisdom is truly the other side of Love.

I come, then, that the rose side of the cape may be an emanation, a magnet attracting the highest initiates of Cosmos to bring to this North America, so consecrated by our Lord Jesus to the path of the ascension,[5] the very best teachers for those who will come to understand the path of the ascension as the very reason for the mission of Jesus, teachers who will teach the soul to return to the Source, to the beginning, in this the ending and the fulfillment of her cycles. For this cause did the Ancient of Days send forth this Son of God.

Now, then, be grateful that the Lost Teaching is restored and the mystery partially unveiled. For you see, beloved, it is not spoken or written, but left as a blank on the page for the soul to fill in. And this knowing may come only from the experiencing. But I tell you, beloved, it will come to those who see the Christ in one another, who minister and clothe and nourish and care for all who are in need.

The practical necessities of physical life include the protection of life, the defense of life, the drawing of the circle of fire that life might live free of Disease and Death. There are many needs to be met beyond those of which most think when thinking in these terms. Beloved, there is a need for the ultimate sealing by sacred fire of all who are the children of God on earth from all those things that may be coming upon this earth.

Let Love and the bliss of Love not blind you, then, to the dangers and the dangerous forces of anti-Love which by a misapplied free will would array themselves against this place, this nation, this path.

Why, then, do the heathen, who are the fallen angels, rage?

Why do they imagine a vain thing?[6]

It is because "it is the last time"[7] and they would devour the Light of the Lightbearers who will ascend if but given the hours, the weeks and the months and the years to realize the inner mystery as themselves. It is the hope and prayer of the ascended hosts that this opportunity shall not be cut short—nor for yourselves, nor for others yet to take embodiment and who are also already here.

Blessed ones, the opportunity for each citizen of Cosmos, of earth and these states to place the capstone on the pyramid of individual life is indeed here. It is the hour when the Master Mason, having laid the foundation, may now put in place the capstone of Life. To this end was this nation founded. To this end was the earth claimed for the Lightbearers.

Let the Lightbearers take their stand to defend freedom as a flame, as Life in every heart, and allow no encroachment in any octave to come forth to snuff out one of these little ones! The Lords of the Seven Rays are deeply concerned that all citizens of the earth come to a quickened awareness that by the flame of Peace and the sword of Peace, so must war and the hordes of war be turned back. Therefore, today begin a path of the assimilation of Light by the simple decree. Rejoice and accelerate as you can.

I AM Paul the Venetian. And in this split second and moment that must be noted by correct time,* these capes are dropped upon your shoulders. They are for you, beloved, a protection, a reality, a sign.

Let each one feel it, then, as a comfort of the Divine Mother delivered by two of her Sons and their angels. Let each one understand mysteries to be told.

Awake then! *Awake* then! Pray God the mystery be known on the morrow with the dawn.

I, Paul, brother of Light, defender of Mother Liberty my own, place within you a seed. And this seed of Light is a seed of Gnosis. And according as the Light is applied within the chakra where it is sealed (varying for each one), so shall it dissolve and give of itself and create the awareness which you are able to contain. Let each one so desiring it now pursue Light in all chakras lest the one skipped might be one where I have buried a precious seed:

It is self-knowledge of thyself, a gift from the Maha Chohan. [intonations, 27 seconds]

*11:18 p.m. CDT

Let gifts of the Spirit beget gifts of the Spirit and gratitude. Let the mantra of the Mother's devotees be "I AM gratitude in action."

Lo, we are come. Lo, we are determined that this giant City Foursquare shall bear fruit. So long as there is Effort and Love, Comfort and Truth, it shall be done.

AUM

"The Summit Lighthouse Sheds Its Radiance O'er All the World to Manifest as Pearls of Wisdom." These dictations by Hilarion and Paul the Venetian were **delivered** through the Messenger of the Great White Brotherhood Elizabeth Clare Prophet on **Friday, May 29, 1987,** during the 4-day conference *Christ's Ascension in You* held at the Regency Park Conference Center, **Overland Park, Kansas.** Prior to the dictations, the Messenger delivered the lecture "The Lost Teachings of Jesus on Gnosticism: The Ascended Masters, the Science of the Word, the Violet Flame and Chakra Meditations." She read from and gave teaching on the Gnostic texts the Exegesis on the Soul and Pistis Sophia, bk. 2, chap. 96. Lecture and dictations published on three 90-min. audiocassettes, A87034, $19.50 (add $.80 for postage). (**1**) Matt. 5:6. (**2**) See p. 272, pars. 4–6; p. 274, pars. 7, 8; p. 275, par. 3. (**3**) For further teaching on the embodiments of the Ascended Master Hilarion as the apostle Paul and Hilarion, see Mark L. Prophet and Elizabeth Clare Prophet, *Lords of the Seven Rays: Mirror of Consciousness,* pp. 183–208, Book One. (**4**) Eph. 5:14. (**5**) See p. 269, par. 5. (**6**) Ps. 2:1; Acts 4:25. (**7**) I John 2:18. See also p. 14, par. 4.

Instruction from the Messenger concerning the assimilation of the Light and Teachings of our Lord following Jesus' dictation (May 28, 1987, Pearl no. 27):

When you have received this bread and wine consecrated in this hour, I would recommend that you take your leave quietly and do not dissipate the dictation in your aura, the light of your aura or this Holy Communion, but go to your place of rest and pray the Father, the Son and Holy Spirit with guardian angels take you to the inner retreats of light where you may spend this night absorbing the fullness of the inner message of Jesus as well as that which is heard spoken. There is a very sacred and secret inner message from the heart of Jesus for you. And I ask that you pray fervently as you come to receive this Communion that you will know this message either when you awaken in the morning or some time throughout this weekend or whenever it is God's will to reveal it to you.

Universities of the Spirit. On 1-1-86, Gautama Buddha announced that he and the Lords of Karma had granted the petition of the Seven Chohans to open universities of the Spirit in their etheric retreats for tens of thousands of students to pursue the path of self-mastery on the seven rays. Traveling in their finer bodies (the etheric sheath) during sleep, students spend 14 days at Darjeeling for training on the First Ray under El Morya, alternating with 14 days at the Royal Teton Retreat for training on the Seventh Ray under Saint Germain until they have successfully passed certain levels of accomplishment in the use of the First and Seventh Rays. Then they may go on to receive training under the Lords of the Second, Third, Sixth, Fourth and Fifth Rays in that order: Lord Lanto and Confucius at the Royal Teton (2nd), Paul the Venetian at the Goddess of Liberty's Temple of the Sun over Manhattan (3rd), Nada at the retreat of Jesus in Saudi Arabia (6th), Serapis Bey at the Ascension Temple, Luxor (4th), and Hilarion at the retreat of Pallas Athena in Crete (5th). It is the desire of the Great White Brotherhood that through the courses given and the tests passed in meeting the challenges of everyday life as well as through second and third levels of instruction, students will quickly make outer contact with Summit University and attend its halls of learning at the Inner Retreat.

On 12-28-86, the God Meru encouraged us to follow the path of the Chohans by choosing to embody the Presence and Light of each Chohan and then the Maha Chohan in 14-day cycles starting 1-1-87 while attending their universities of the Spirit (see chart on next page). On 12-31-86, El Morya spoke of the chelas spending "14 weeks" with him. From this we act on the assumption that the Master was indicating that the chelas shall pursue 7 cycles of 2 weeks in each of the Chohans' retreats and that of the Maha Chohan. Those who follow this discipline starting 1-1-87 will conclude their 'Odyssey' through the 14 weeks of initiations with each Master on George Washington's Birthday, 2-22-89—a most propitious hour in the turning of planetary cycles when all chelas should be spiritually and physically prepared for earth changes in the decade of the 1990s. See 1986 *Pearls of Wisdom,* vol. 29, no. 21, pp. 178–81; no. 79, pp. 689–90; no. 80, p. 698.

Fourteen-Day Cycles at the Universities of the Spirit

as outlined by Gautama Buddha in his dictation of January 1, 1986
and by God Meru in his dictation of December 28, 1986

Chohan	First Cycle	Second Cycle	Third Cycle	Fourth Cycle	Fifth Cycle	Sixth Cycle	Seventh Cycle
El Morya Darjeeling, India	January 1, 1987– January 14, 1987	April 23, 1987– May 6, 1987	August 13, 1987– August 26, 1987	December 3, 1987– December 16, 1987	March 24, 1988– April 6, 1988	July 14, 1988– July 27, 1988	November 3, 1988– November 16, 1988
Saint Germain Royal Teton Retreat, Wyoming	January 15, 1987– January 28, 1987	May 7, 1987– May 20, 1987	August 27, 1987– September 9, 1987	December 17, 1987– December 30, 1987	April 7, 1988– April 20, 1988	July 28, 1988– August 10, 1988	November 17, 1988– November 30, 1988
Lord Lanto Royal Teton Retreat, Wyoming	January 29, 1987– February 11, 1987	May 21, 1987– June 3, 1987	September 10, 1987– September 23, 1987	December 31, 1987– January 13, 1988	April 21, 1988– May 4, 1988	August 11, 1988– August 24, 1988	December 1, 1988– December 14, 1988
Paul the Venetian Temple of the Sun, New York	February 12, 1987– February 25, 1987	June 4, 1987– June 17, 1987	September 24, 1987– October 7, 1987	January 14, 1988– January 27, 1988	May 5, 1988– May 18, 1988	August 25, 1988– September 7, 1988	December 15, 1988– December 28, 1988
Nada Saudi Arabia	February 26, 1987– March 11, 1987	June 18, 1987– July 1, 1987	October 8, 1987– October 21, 1987	January 28, 1988– February 10, 1988	May 19, 1988– June 1, 1988	September 8, 1988– September 21, 1988	December 29, 1988– January 11, 1989
Serapis Bey Luxor, Egypt	March 12, 1987– March 25, 1987	July 2, 1987– July 15, 1987	October 22, 1987– November 4, 1987	February 11, 1988– February 24, 1988	June 2, 1988– June 15, 1988	September 22, 1988– October 5, 1988	January 12, 1989– January 25, 1989
Hilarion Crete, Greece	March 26, 1987– April 8, 1987	July 16, 1987– July 29, 1987	November 5, 1987– November 18, 1987	February 25, 1988– March 9, 1988	June 16, 1988– June 29, 1988	October 6, 1988– October 19, 1988	January 26, 1989– February 8, 1989
The Maha Chohan Ceylon (Sri Lanka)	April 9, 1987– April 22, 1987	July 30, 1987– August 12, 1987	November 19, 1987– December 2, 1987	March 10, 1988– March 23, 1988	June 30, 1988– July 13, 1988	October 20, 1988– November 2, 1988	February 9, 1989– February 22, 1989

Vol. 30 No. 29 *Beloved Saint Germain* *July 19, 1987*

Christ's Ascension in You

III

The Chime of an Ancient Bell

Ho! let all who thirst come and drink of the waters of eternal Life.[1] It is the hour to quaff the proffered cup of the new wine served by angels bearing cups from Zadkiel's retreat.[2]

I am here in this city marking the sign of the Maltese cross whose arms provide four gates to the white fire center of being. Therefore, let those who value a spiritual destiny enter the secret chamber of the heart and know the Lord who attends thee. This hidden man of the heart[3] is the image of the LORD God out of whose divine image ye were fashioned in the beginning,[4] in whose image ye are fashioned, if ye will it so, in the ending.

Axes* have tipped, bones have grown crooked, the places have become rough. Let them be made plain[5] now as in sweet surrender to her vow thy soul does enter and say, "O Lord, I place myself upon the cornerstone and the chief who is my Christ, my Lord.[6] I enter, then, and I make my plea, Create me anew, O God. Re-create me after thy likeness."

This is the hour to be drawn up in the fiery cloud of the I AM THAT I AM, the cloud of unknowing[7] that is all-knowing, thy Home. This is the hour to cherish the friend who is God, and all Life. It is an hour in profound Peace to take a sword of Peace, to raise it and thereby, by its shining, to blind all enemies of thy Christhood.

Thus, *keep* the flame. The flame will then rise and leap to thy defense, beloved, taking whatever form be necessary whilst thou dost complete the divine union with thy Christ. Beloved, may thy courses be to pursue this oneness and thus to be of ultimate

*plural of axis

usefulness to the Great Law as pillars of fire in the earth and in the temple of our God.[8]

I AM Saint Germain standing in a shaft of white fire, desiring to speak to you out of the heart of the Divine Mother, even Mary and the Divine Feminine beyond our beloved Mary. Thus, I am in the heart of the Buddha, of the Christ, as I have also been in the heart of nirvana.

Blessed ones, as time and space are not relevant to eternal cycles, I can assure you that since I last spoke with you I have taken that point of rest in nirvana that I might return saturated with the Peace of the void, the bliss of all Union.

I come to keep my vow[9] to every Lightbearer and Keeper of the Flame. Though you may not know me or of me, I know of you, blessed heart. Thus, I come not empty-handed but with hands and heart of Peace to assist all in the earth who truly desire to assist her evolutions in this time of change.

It is difficult for all or any of us to rehearse and contemplate a scenario of chaos, destruction or Old Night. Yet, beloved, the angels of the Lord who are sent from the Central Sun must also study the battle plans of Darkness. For strategy does not end until in the end of this age and cycle of Cosmos there is no longer war in heaven[10] or war in earth. For in the Great Inbreath the souls ascending shall retain individualization, but the souls defiling, contemptuous do not retain Godhood nor can they retain a flame they have not kept but denied.

Thus, beloved, the cycles and the ages move on. And after a contemplation of the immediate threatening woes, is it not good to enter a sphere of repose, there to know the Source whence one derives the strength—strength, then, to extend the citadel of our God, to encompass Life and all elementals and angels who, beloved, you may be surprised to know, do look to you for sign, for assurance, for comfort.

Ye are sons of God and daughters, rightly so. And in that divine spark that burns aglow within your heart, I AM Saint Germain! Where'er a flame is kept I may step through that flame and through the veil, through your heart and voice that does speak and deliver, then, some morsel of Truth or grand statement of Being especially for those who desire to drink of my cup/thy cup extended as one, for we *are* one. All Keepers of the Flame on earth who therefore pledge to assist me in my Call and Promise of the New Year, beloved, continue to know no withholding but boundless Love and ovoid bright—fiery ovoid of violet flame.

There are yet some things I *can* do, beloved, and one of them is this: to multiply, by a figure beyond telling, your calls to the violet flame, to multiply the ovoid of your aura by my own in response to the activity of violet flame unending. *Lo,* let it be said, then, with the full joy of my Selfhood thine (and thine mine own), "I AM a being of violet fire, I AM the purity Saint Germain desires!"

O blessed hearts, it is indeed the day of the new wine and its offering. Let none resist it who love Light. Let all who love Light welcome angels who will take from you—if you allow it and command them—burdens dark of yesteryear and records no longer recognized by you as being apart from self. The surrender to the living God does bring with it great blessings and many changes.

Blessed ones, on the path of Life the initiate must be ready for changes. For, blessed hearts, if all things were acceptable as they are, there would indeed be no problem in the earth whatsoever and you would scarcely need us at your side. Thus, beloved, it ought to be apparent that as good as the human consciousness seems there is something better waiting.

Let the door fling wide! Fear not to enter the chamber where the brilliant Light does shine. Fear not to leave the shadows. Fear not, beloved, for all that is truly worthy of loving is all inside. And is this not the beauty of our God, that he has preserved for us all beauties and loves and truths that we could ever fear to lose? They are already jewels within the casket of his heart.

O precious ones of Light, fly to the arms of your I AM Presence! This very night invoke the Archangels to prepare your soul and body and mind for the coming of Chamuel and Charity in not so many hours. For they come with a Ruby Ray and a conveyance of the essence light of Christ. They come in a conveyance, beloved, desiring to assure your victory.

No one has ever said it is not a path of sacrifice. But, beloved, nothing can be taken from you that is a part of your permanent Reality. Consciously, knowingly, in full reason and sound mind, you ought truly to come to the conclusion that all that is unreal about yourself is surely not worth keeping, and baggage too heavy for the climb.

If these decisions are thought through and made as one's personal theology in life, if you can come to a definite direction, the Lord will truly send his angels to assist you. But if you waver and espouse this cause one day and another the next, put something on the altar on the morrow then take it back on the third day, blessed ones, the angels themselves shift from one foot to the other, waiting, almost wringing their hands in wonder, "Shall this soul truly arrive at a point of stillness and decision, that we might implement a will that is geometric and sound in the heart of the Word?"

Indecision, then, does prevent holy purpose from being fulfilled and holy angels from assisting you in right endeavor. Think through your cause and how you will spend your remaining lifestream. For things have a way of coming to an end in this octave, beloved.

Thus, measure the cycles and say, "I will live to do this thing, this one thing for my God and my friends. And I will see to it that this endeavor does endure, that my cause shall leave a measure of Truth that cannot be undone or denied."

Gifts upon the altar of humanity sustain civilization. And ye are heirs to many gifts of saints who have walked before you. Always and always be grateful and say to your God, "But for the grace of thy flame, O Father, there go I. And therefore I shall live to see that 'these dead shall not have died in vain'[11] but that I shall also immortalize not alone their gift but thy gift through me in this hour."

Endow a planet with grace, beloved. Leave footprints of violet flame. Live, and live Life to its fullest and drink the whole cup which that violet flame angel now extends into your hand. It is a cup of the elixir of the Seventh Ray.

Some have said to me, "Saint Germain, when will you reinstitute the giving of an elixir of youth?" And I answer them, "Why, I have already given it freely and many years ago. Did you not know? It is the violet flame."

Peel away years from your body and face by violet flame application, the grandest cosmetic I know. Let light and light and light fill in karmic crevices, lines drawn from an unmerciful heart. Nonforgiveness carves grooves, beloved, that age and distress. Blessed hearts, fasting with the wine from the grape without alcohol but pure and giving the violet flame decrees will avail much. Purity of heart is a chalice ever filled by the crystal clear waters of Life.[12]

In any case, beloved, qualitative life is needed immediately in these years. Therefore, whatever be the stretch of thy imagination or thy life span, fill the hours and grains of sands with the bestowal of beauty and freedom. By thy life, by thy love be the magnet that truly impels the highest life to come up higher, to enter the mountain of God, to be free.

It is true, beloved, that I once acknowledged Pallas Athena as patroness of my life's work.[13] I did never regret it, for in the pure heart of Truth I also found comfort for the burdens upon me in the juxtaposition of forces that were my karmic lot and the testing of my soul prior to my ascension. You may read of these in that embodiment where I was called Francis.[14] And some yet call me that in tenderness, remembering, as I remember well, that to set a course and path to defeat the Fates, the gods and daemons all is surely to set an example for a chela, a Keeper of the Flame having the worst of karma and enemies.

Blessed ones, I can assure you that adversities that came to me in that life were grave for the momentum of Darkness that came through them. Some of you well know that of which I speak. Blessed hearts, let all overcomers know that one must set one's teeth to the victory. One must become so determined in the face of every procrastinating liar that whispers in the ear, "Tomorrow, tomorrow, and tomorrow . . ."

Today and *now* is the only acceptable time. Fill your nows with victory. Defy all Darkness. Christhood is thine to claim. Too long have you envisioned yourselves upon a course or path whose goal is distant. I say, in a twinkling of the All-Seeing Eye of God[15] *you* can master your destiny and in so doing *help others*.

Those psychologically fragmented ought to demand wholeness of their God and be free. There is no reason to continue the recording again and again. Lift the needle from its track and move on rather than hearing that same old flak of the lesser self that does not leave thee alone even to groan in thy misery.

Therefore, be done with it! Shuffle off this mortal coil! Enter now the coil of immortality and be free. Yes, change is the order of the day and the winds of Aquarius blow. I trust I will find you in the mountain of God in the LORD's Day, for your I AM Presence awaits and has awaited long.

I AM Saint Germain, your brother, your friend. Remember me, also, beloved, for I have need of friends if I am to work a miracle or two in this age. I need many friends and Keepers of the Flame.

I AM hopeful, in the profoundest sense of the word, that you will hear my cry and know this: that God our Father has truly entrusted to my heart an opportunity to save this nation under God, not I alone but many Masters of Light. There is a special, special blessing he gives to my heart that is a catalyst and necessary, and yet I cannot bring it forth without friends on earth.

Move on, beloved. Move on to the new age. I extend my hand to hold your own. I can do no more, beloved, until you reach out and understand what I can do for your soul in the age of Aquarius. Oh, come quickly, beloved, while there is yet time.

The chime of an ancient bell now sounds. One of my angels called by Portia does begin this chiming. It will sound in the ear of every true son and daughter of Liberty as though he or she does hear a liberty bell that long ago rang on other spheres. This chiming, beloved, shall continue as the inner Call. And if it stop its chiming, beloved, Cosmos shall know that I, Saint Germain, have no longer opportunity to rescue the Lightbearer.

Therefore, beloved, let the giving of the violet flame on behalf of those who respond and hear be continuous as a vigil unto the seventh age. So long as there are those who respond, even a single heart reciting my violet flame mantra in each twenty-four-hour cycle, Opportunity's door shall remain open and the chime shall be heard.

So I have come. And in the period of this dictation your auras have been charged with the violet flame to the fullest extent of the Great Law. I seal you and this city in the Maltese cross. Four gates remain open, each one a path leading to adeptship in the Seventh Ray and age. I am thy sponsor so long as you will have and accept me.

I, Sanctus Germanus,[16] bow to the Light within you. And I raise now the sword Excalibur that you may know the true sign of my Peace.

It is the Peace of Christ I leave with you. By the Peace and the living flame that appears as a flaming sword, so I AM THAT I AM deflecting all forces of anti-Peace in thy life, in this city and citadel and earth. [intonations, 16 seconds]

[Recording of *Finlandia* by Jean Sibelius, performed by the New Philharmonia Orchestra conducted by Kazimierz Kord, played at the Messenger's request.]

"The Summit Lighthouse Sheds Its Radiance O'er All the World to Manifest as Pearls of Wisdom." This dictation by Saint Germain was **delivered** through the Messenger of the Great White Brotherhood Elizabeth Clare Prophet on **Saturday, May 30, 1987,** during the 4-day conference *Christ's Ascension in You* held at the Regency Park Conference Center, **Overland Park, Kansas.** Prior to the dictation, the Messenger delivered the lecture "Saint Germain On Prophecy." Lecture and dictation published on two 90-min. audiocassettes, A87037, $13 (add $.80 for postage). (**1**) Isa. 55:1; John 4:14; 7:37; Rev. 21:6; 22:17. (**2**) The retreat of Archangel Zadkiel and Holy Amethyst is located in the etheric octave over the Caribbean, centered at Cuba. (**3**) I Pet. 3:4. (**4**) Gen. 1:26, 27; 5:1. (**5**) Isa. 40:4; Luke 3:5. (**6**) Isa. 28:16; Eph. 2:19–22; I Pet. 2:6, 7. (**7**) **The cloud of unknowing.** See *The Lost Teachings of Jesus I,* p. 113. (**8**) Rev. 3:12. (**9**) See p. 33, par. 7. (**10**) Rev. 12:7. (**11**) Abraham Lincoln, Gettysburg Address, 1863. (**12**) Rev. 22:1. (**13**) The Ascended Master Saint Germain was embodied as Francis Bacon (1561–1626), philosopher, statesman, father of inductive reasoning and the scientific method, and author of the Shakespearean plays. As a young law student Bacon and his brother had founded a secret literary society, "The Knights of the Helmet," whose patroness was the Greek Goddess of Wisdom and Knowledge, **Pallas Athena**. Often depicted wearing a helmet and full armour with a spear in her hand, she was known as the "shaker of the spear" who shook the Spear of Knowledge at the Serpent of Ignorance beneath her feet. It is conjectured that this is the double entendre of Shakespeare, whose name and identity Bacon used to conceal his authorship. See *Saint Germain On Prophecy,* pp. 24, 93, Book One. (**14**) See *Saint Germain On Prophecy,* pp. 20–27, 86–93, Book One; and *The Golden Age Prince,* two 90-min. audiocassettes, A83176, $12.95 (add $.90 for postage). (**15**) I Cor. 15:51–53. (**16**) **Sanctus Germanus:** Latin for "Holy Brother."

Pearls of Wisdom®
published by The Summit Lighthouse
Vol. 30 No. 30 *Beloved Archangel Chamuel and Charity* *July 26, 1987*

Christ's Ascension in You
IV
Initiates of Love, Take Care!

Beloved of the Light,

Wherefore are we come but for Love's victory in you!

We stand as pillars of Love anchoring through you in the physical octave portion, just portion, of the flaming flame of our retreat. So it is a door, beloved, and it opens at the south side of a continent.[1]

Blessed hearts, we welcome you to enter the etheric octaves even in these hours. Each night while the body takes rest we welcome you to be tutored in the chambers of the Love Ray for the expansiveness of the heart, for the quality of compassion, charity, and the fierceness of love that is in the mother who protects her own.

Some have not understood a mother's protective instinct as the highest love known in Nature and amongst all who have descended from God. America is a motherland, her lifewaves come again from Lemuria, Atlantis and previous golden ages. Here this seed of Light is taught to mother life, to nourish it and therefore [to say,] "Hail, Ma-Ray!"[2]

This salutation unto the Divine Mother in all life is the key to unlocking the ascension flame. Out of the current of this mighty life-force ascending upon the spinal altar, you find, beloved, a love that is invoked for compassion's sake, for creativity and for the culture of the Mother that has flourished in all golden-age civilizations.

You have seen that culture as science and technology return to this nation, but it has not been used for the fulfillment of the Mother's instinct to protect the children of the Sun. Therefore, that which came forth as medical science has both harmed and healed. And so there is a two-edged sword in every field as mankind yet wrestle with the true mastery of alchemy in the sciences.

And so you have seen, beloved, how far lost is the Mother flame in this nation America where it is intended to be raised up. The noncaring of life expressed in abortion or nondefense as a policy, the noncaring of life in the failure to tutor the young in the Word, that they might be fully literate and educated instead of illiterate, these things are a neglect of little ones who depend upon the greatest nation upon earth (or what once was) to give them the opportunity to fulfill the Great Law.

We are Chamuel and Charity. And therefore, as giant straws, we let down cylinders of light, beloved. And these cylinders are for your soul's ascent and flight to the etheric octaves, that you might quickly atone for a nation and begin to intone the chime of holy love, guarded and protected fiercely by Archangel Michael and his legions and your calls to them.

Beloved, if balance is to be restored, if that which has been poured out by the Seven Archangels as the karma of the seven rays[3] is to be redeemed, there must be a balance of attainment and pursuit of these seven rays, and that with haste. Make haste, then, to our retreat, for by Love we would show you the way to the fulfilling of the law of all of the seven.

Beloved, Chamuel and Charity do not appear anywhere without the descent of the Ruby Ray for the judgment of the force of anti-Love. The fullness of Divine Love manifesting here must be, then, for the binding of the hatred of the child, of the hatred of man or woman or God or angel.

Understand that wherever there is a light kindled and a light so intense as the ineffable Love, there must stand one in life, in embodiment (and then the many), who will so cherish such a flame that it shall not be extinguished in this octave.

Blessed hearts, it is a sad day of revelation and judgment upon a nation who have let the flame of Love go out in simple kindness, sensitivity, friendliness and neighborliness. Beloved ones, the grave neglect of youth and the loss of many souls must be laid at the feet of those who stand at the pulpits of the nation and those other pundits who may be in systems of education and in the government.

Blessed hearts, the neglect of the full creativity of the flame of Love must therefore be met with a mighty purging light! This purging light is for the healing, and you will see the healing power of angels then come upon the wake of a purging that is for the saving of the body of a nation and not for its denial.

Let us understand, then, that it is a false sense of Love and a human-consciousness sense of Love that guards and protects World Communism in Central and South America and denies to those who will uphold the flame of freedom the full manifestation of protection and the backing of the sons and daughters of Liberty.

It is a sad day indeed when a nation does not love itself enough to see that those freedom fighters across the world who take their stands in their nations are taking those stands in the true Spirit of America and for this nation and that if these forces are not defeated in these territories they will surely overrun this nation! And we, Chamuel and Charity, will not be able to turn them back.

With all of the Light and Love that you have experienced during these four days, beloved, know this, that the Light and Love descending must be guarded and you must enter into the I-AM-the-Guard consciousness and not take for granted that the water of Life bestowed and the Power and Presence of the Holy Spirit will continue on and on merely because you do, therefore, call it forth and bid it to manifest. The call must be a call out of a heart whose consistency in the path of Love is shown and known.

Therefore, he said, "Feed my sheep!"[4] Rescue my little ones. Care enough to save your own heart and then you will care enough to save a nation because God is in your heart and because God is in the heart of a nation!

We speak as Archangels! We are not as the grasshoppers. We come from the throne of God, embodying the fullness of the LORD as the I AM THAT I AM. Do you think that we come to pat humans upon the head and to give them a divine approbation when they have yet tarried in their cups of selfishness and spiritual blindness and have not heeded the call of the Ancient of Days?

We can only say, with the full fury of that living Presence whose awe we behold, *Beware,* mankind and sons and daughters of Liberty! The hours are indeed short! And so it has been pronounced from the cosmic councils to the very throne of the God of the Earth.[5]

Let it be known, then, that we, Chamuel and Charity, stand to initiate those who understand the meaning of being a true initiate of Divine Love and carrying its fires unto the blessedness and the oneness of a John the Beloved and a Jesus Christ.

Let those who have enjoyed the magnificence and the beauty of Truth, as lowered into manifestation and sponsored in this nation, come to understand that this *is* an hour *to stand guard* for all of the principles, all of the Truth, all of the Light, all of the abundance that has been given in this land.

Children of the Sun, sons and daughters of God, I address

those who have had ancient memory of long ago standing in the Sun, of knowing truly the Father/Mother God and of being in the earth. In this hour we count on you to be our instruments.

Do not think because the Great Law has winked or that opportunity has come again and again that our words shall not be fulfilled. We must pronounce them for they *are* being fulfilled. Even as you are meeting in this hall this day, the Word of the Ruby Ray is descending in many quarters upon this earth and those who have failed in their opportunity find that they are bereft of the Light.

And it is come to pass, as the Lord has said, that one is taken and the other is left.[6] See, then, that you are the one who is taken truly unto the high road of Higher Consciousness and that you understand that it does not require tomes of wisdom or endless study to arrive at the point of realization that you *are* the Intercessor now, that upon you there does descend the mantle of your Christhood.

And it does come, beloved, and it does come as the Bridegroom.[7] And it shall come in the hour appointed by the Lord. And if you are ready you will see the miracle of God in your life, and if you are not ready I pray you understand the meaning of this chief cornerstone, for the stone will grind to powder those who have manifested the antithesis of the Almighty One.[8]

Blessed hearts, if it were not so, then Atlantis should not have sunk nor Lemuria, nor civilizations risen and fallen. If the Great Law and the sine wave thereof did not come with great regularity for a great harvest of light and for the binding of the tares,[9] then our preaching must be in vain, then our life and service must be unknown to those who in their vanity and conceit have configured a theology that does miss the vital links in the equation of life on earth and in heaven.

You, then, who are a part of the great conspiracy of Light itself, of those who have conspired before the LORD God to bring Light to the earth, to you I say, Now *is* the accepted time! *Now* is the appointed hour of the day of salvation by Love.[10]

If you would hold a flame of Love, beloved, know that all that this Messenger has told you regarding the action of the blue ray is manifest tenfold when you attempt to uphold the fiery core of the Love Ray which is the Ruby Ray itself.[11] Understand, then, that the presence of the Holy Ghost is not only gifts of joy and healing but it is a presence of a fiery light that does rebuke every evil form.

And therefore, inasmuch as the Holy Spirit is the power of exorcism, those who would be its initiates must understand that even as the pink flame of Love does protect and seal the blue lightning, so then, the blue lightning must come again to protect and seal the Ruby Ray intensity that is for a purging as no other ray can purge but that Ruby Ray, beloved, for it is the intensity of the essence of the very Blood of Christ.

Blessed ones of the Most High God, realize, then, how is the fire descending, how have cherubim who keep the way of the Tree of Life[12] intensified their presence here. They have come to guard the way of the Tree of Life within you, beloved.

Let us see, then, who are those who recognize that the fields are white to the harvest, that the LORD does require laborers for the vineyard ere this harvest fail.[13] Where there are those of Light waiting to be taken up by the angels of the Holy Spirit and yet no laborers come, do you not think that the fallen ones come in surreptitiously? I tell you they do. And they enter in and they steal them for the lower orders of the false teachers and the false gurus who entice them with their wares of stolen light coated with that sticky substance of human sympathy, personality cult and idolatry.

I tell you it is the power of the Third Ray that does tear down the idols and raise up a living Presence that is a transparency. Let the world behold God, as a transparency of yourself allows the child of Light to see through and to know his God face-to-face because you have been willing to make the sacrifice to keep the flame of living Love.

I tell you, the intensity of Divine Love does cleave asunder the Real from the unreal and therefore it is an essential agent to healing itself.

Blessed hearts, I tell you that people know not that they are diseased because they cling to their unreality, to their psychicism, to the feathering of their own nests and the idea that they are very special in a spiritual way and field. And thus, gathering clusters of individuals to themselves, they do not understand that every idol that is raised is an idol that shall fall. And when it does fall, the people who have not seen God (for the idol has got in the way), they themselves, then, have no Shepherd.

Woe! to those who set themselves between a people and their God. *Woe!* to those who do not reveal the I AM Presence as the living Presence which each and every soul may contact by the living Word.

Therefore, know ye the LORD and know the Archangels and know that as I speak to you this day the power of my Presence is held back by angels a thousand times less than you should receive it in this hour. Beloved ones, the nations do receive it, for it cannot be held back.

I stand, then, so near to you that the angels circle round

about. For I, Chamuel, with Charity do bring, therefore, the flaming sword of the Ruby Ray for the judgment of those who have persecuted the youth of this nation and the world.

Do you not weep, beloved, when you see children raised up to fight battles in the Middle East, in South America? Well, weep again, mothers, for it may take place upon this soil ere you disturb yourselves and perturb yourselves concerning world conditions! If you desire not to see your grandchildren in this posture, beloved, then know that the defense must come of the right of the individual to have and till his own land and to be free of the domination of superpowers or totalitarian forces or conspiracies that conspire against him.

I say, let those who love freedom defend it else find themselves behind the very defenses that they have not drawn and therefore bereft and face-to-face with such a colossal condition as they are not able to do one mite about it!

It is a question of timing, beloved! And when you do not take the crest of the wave of Light descending from the Great Central Sun that would literally carry you up to a victory against these forces of anti-Christ in your midst, when you miss that wave, beloved, the chance may not come again and you may be caught in the undertow and in the current that does carry you away into a dark current that is devouring many souls in the astral plane.

Have pity, beloved, and have compassion. For the majority of the people of this North America do not have what you have—nor light nor understanding nor capacity nor even the means to have an hour and a day to give unto these calls.

O beloved, the time is short! You have heard it in many ways. But we are sent this day in this city directly from our retreat for the purpose so stated, to draw up those who would be the initiates of Love into that more intense concentration on this ray and to let those who have persecuted the very Love itself of the little ones know that they are stripped of their power and they are bound.

Blessed hearts, what shall come upon a nation and a planet who mistreats its children and youth? This is everywhere apparent on the earth, but it is nowhere so grave than in this nation where there has been so great a dispensation, where there has been so great an approbation of Almighty God!

Therefore, those who know better and have the light must do far more and far better than merely enjoy that Light. Yes, the Light is a joy and for enjoyment, but much more; it is for the sensitizing of souls to the rescue of those who suffer.

Blessed hearts, in this moment there is lowering into the

nation's capital a vortex of fiery Ruby Ray. It is also for the rescue of the persecuted ones. It is also for the binding of an enemy that has penetrated too far into the upper echelons of this government while the nation and the members of that government sleep.

There is a false trust, O beloved, a false trust in the serpent mind of the fallen angel in the midst. Therefore, let the All-Seeing Eye of God intensify. Therefore, let the Ruby Ray descend. Therefore, let the Lightbearers be supported as we are allowed to support them throughout the earth.

And let there be the further reduction by the Ruby Ray as it comes from the Central Sun and the Holy Kumaras this day of all those who are determined to destroy as false-hierarchy impostors of the Third Ray and of the Holy Spirit.

Thus the destroyers in the earth who are not the transmuters are truly the spoilers and they, then, are bound this day and stopped by the right hand of the Almighty! This cannot be fulfilled physically unless you follow up this dispensation with a mighty call and the Ruby Ray judgment. So as heaven has given the dispensation, let earth respond!

So, beloved, the healing we would teach you is the healing of the wounds in the psyche of a nation. Your alarm ought to be great when there is no defense, when suicide is in vogue, when youth are hollowed out by drugs and rock and all manner of chemical and sexual perversions. You ought to be alarmed when the judgment descends for the perversion of the sacred fire and a mass epidemic does cross the nation and enter the mainstream of life.

Blessed ones, how close to hell can you come without being concerned and rising in righteous indignation and calling upon the LORD day and night? If you sleep much longer, O America, it will surely, surely be too late for any saving of a nation!

I come and I am in the fiery flame of the white-hot heat of the Central Sun. Hear me, beloved, and know what it means to be an Archangel standing in the Presence of the LORD God!

Understand the equation. And then begin to understand just how far this star is from the centrality of the Sun behind the sun, and then you will understand how lethargy does set in and procrastination and ultimately death, even the Death of the spirit itself.

Know, then, that my quickening is *hurled* to you as a Ruby Ray action! *Know* that it comes to you as a white fire! And be grateful that you tarried to give the calls to the nine levels of angels and to Archangel Michael, that you may stand and still stand in this aura and be a part of the absorption of an energy that must surely be planted in the earth this day.

Beloved, *earthquake shall come!*[14] Be prepared and be aware. So let the Light descend. For when the earth can no longer withstand the infamy of its evolutions against the Holy Christ children in its midst, then that earth must compensate somehow.

So let the violet flame be invoked with intensity. And let those who care know that we are Chamuel and Charity! We stand midst the heaven and betwixt the heaven and the earth. We stand and we care! We, therefore, ask you to care with us before it is too late.

By the sign of the cosmic cross of white fire and the legions thereof we are come. Therefore, receive that portion that you are able to absorb in your chakras now. [20-sec. pause]

In the invincible majesty of the ineffable Word, I AM, we are Chamuel and Charity. Be sealed in our twin flames, for this Love is for the fulfilling of the law of thy ascension. It is *done.* It is *sealed.*

"The Summit Lighthouse Sheds Its Radiance O'er All the World to Manifest as Pearls of Wisdom."
This dictation by Archangel Chamuel and Charity was **delivered** through the Messenger of the Great White Brotherhood Elizabeth Clare Prophet on **Sunday, May 31, 1987,** during the 4-day conference *Christ's Ascension in You* held at the Regency Park Conference Center, **Overland Park, Kansas.** (**1**) Archangel Chamuel and Charity maintain an etheric retreat over St. Louis, Missouri, "on the south side" of North America. The city's most prominent landmark, the 630-foot high stainless steel Gateway Arch, stands on the banks of the Mississippi River and symbolizes St. Louis as the gateway to the West. So, too, the Gateway Arch is intended as a sign to quicken the awareness of all who behold it that here is the open door to the etheric retreat of beloved Chamuel and Charity. (**2**) The Ascended Masters teach that the inner meaning of *hail* is "the *h*ighest *a*ction *i*s *l*ove." (**3**) Rev. 15:1, 6–8; 16. See *Vials of the Seven Last Plagues: The Judgments of Almighty God Delivered by the Seven Archangels,* Summit University Press, $5.95 (add $.50 for postage). (**4**) John 21:15–17. (**5**) Gen. 24:3; Rev. 11:4. (**6**) Matt. 24:40, 41; Luke 17:34–36. (**7**) Matt. 24:42–51; 25:1–13; Luke 12:35–40; Rev. 3:3; 16:15. (**8**) Matt. 21:42–44; Luke 20:17, 18. (**9**) Matt. 13:24–30, 36–43. (**10**) II Cor. 6:2. (**11**) As the power of the blue ray in the aura can be offensive when untempered by the seventh ray, so the presence of the ruby ray in one's forcefield may also provoke a reaction. The tube of light and violet transmuting flame thus seal one's forcefield and the violet flame acts as a buffer extending love, mercy, freedom and joy to all whom you meet, thereby making unnecessary the compromise of one's inner attainment held secure within the tube of light. (**12**) Gen. 3:24. (**13**) John 4:35; Matt. 9:35–38; Luke 10:2. (**14**) On June 10, 1987, at 6:49 p.m. CDT, an earthquake measuring 5.0 on the Richter scale, centered near Lawrenceville, Illinois (380 miles east of Kansas City), jolted 16 states of the Midwest and East and was felt as far north as Toronto, Canada. The quake caused minor property damage and at least one minor injury. This may be the earthquake predicted by Chamuel and Charity.

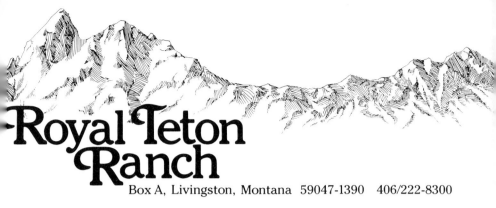

Royal Teton Ranch
Box A, Livingston, Montana 59047-1390 406/222-8300

June 2, 1987

Dear Friends of God's Unfailing Light,

I send you greetings from the Royal Teton Ranch, an ancient focus of the Great White Brotherhood now secured as the international headquarters of Church Universal and Triumphant.

This place prepared for the Lightbearers of Aquarius is also the home of Summit University and Montessori International. It is a community of people pursuing the inner walk with God, the eternal truths, and the mysteries of creation.

Bordering on Yellowstone Park and the Yellowstone River, we are just eighty miles as the eagle flies to the Grand Teton, site of North America's principal Ascended Master retreat. With Old Faithful the sign of our Lord's coming, we are reminded of our calling to be Keepers of the Flame in this era of world turbulence midst our witness of the Divine Alchemy of the New Age.

You may be wondering why you are receiving Pearls of Wisdom with November 1986 dates on them from a place called Livingston, Montana, and published by The Summit Lighthouse. And so I thought I'd better tell you why!

Our last mailing of the Pearls of Wisdom from Camelot Los Angeles was dated November 13, 1986. At that time we discontinued printing our Pearls of Wisdom because Camelot had been sold and the staged move of our entire headquarters was taking place right under our feet while we were busy as bees completing our final publications to be released from Los Angeles.

These included Saint Germain On Prophecy and Lords of the Seven Rays as well as The Lost Teachings of Jesus volumes I and II, Corona Class Lessons for those who would teach men the Way, and reprints of Climb the Highest Mountain: the Path of the Higher Self, The Great White Brotherhood in the Culture, History, and

Religion of America, My Soul Doth Magnify the Lord! Mother Mary's New Age Teachings and Rosary with a Challenge to Christendom, and Cosmic Consciousness: One Man's Search for God.

Midst a flurry of activity, we were Montana-bound to our 33,000-acre ranch/farm, spiritual community-in-the-making which had been purchased in 1981 and would now become our permanent home.

The big challenge was to provide housing and office space for all of our Church departments and to move ourselves as much as possible before winter set in. Indeed, all of Camelot proper was moved by Christmas, but our warehouse—S.U. Press, Kali Productions, mail processing, computer services, and shipping departments—actually took until the first of April to be completed.

To meet the immediate need we opted for used mobile modular units which had to be trucked to the ranch, set up with plumbing, heating and electrical. This Herculean task, continuing still, was performed by heroes and heroines—there is no other name for the staff and volunteers who had the courage to dig in and make this move happen.

We were most fortunate to be able to purchase from the Burlington Northern Railroad two wonderful buildings in Livingston totaling 61,130 square feet. Here our staff has been working steadfastly to prepare all of the facilities necessary to resume production in graphic arts, printing, and all that this entails.

And so, just as soon as our presses were up and running, we sent to you with great joy our first Pearl from our new address and our new buildings: the beautiful dictation of Archangel Raphael which opened our July Freedom 1986 conference, the last to be held on the 250-acre Malibu property we left behind.

It was with such rejoicing that this Pearl came off our press that I wanted to share our joy with you who have been a part of the Teachings of the Ascended Masters but have not received regular communication from us since we left off our service last November.

By the time you receive this letter, you should have received all of the Pearls of Wisdom from Freedom 1986, including the dictations of Beloved El Morya, Saint Germain, the Goddess of Liberty, Cyclopea, Jesus Christ, Sanat Kumara and Helios.

With all the love of our hearts, we who serve the Great White Brotherhood send to you these releases with gratitude to God, to the universe, and to hearts such as yours who are seeking the Truth, who have come to cherish the Word as we do, and who believe in our freedom of religion that we hold so dear to pursue the path of our soul's calling unto God.

These blessed Teachings have been the bread of Life for students of the Ascended Masters since 1958, having been mailed throughout the world since August 8 of that year every week without interruption until our recent move.

This is our Communion with the hosts of the Lord and with the Ascended Masters, who assist our beloved Jesus to restore to earth his Lost Teachings. The Pearls of Wisdom have also been the vehicle for Saint Germain's delivery of his prophecies for our time as well as the mystery of God and the Everlasting Gospel foretold in Revelation 10 and 14.

Because of what is apparent to all of us as the heavy weight of burden upon the nations and upon the souls of the Lightbearers, I have desired to break this bread of Life with you and to share my cup that overflows with love and gratitude. My heart's desire is that you should have the most recent dictations of the Ascended Masters which are given to us for our comfort, our enlightenment, and our divine direction in these times when all of us must determine how to face personal karma and planetary changes as well as the rumors of war and severe problems in the economy.

The plagues of cancer, AIDS, and drugs upon our youth are a challenge to each and every one of us, and I believe that we can meet these challenges together as we accept Saint Germain's call: "Lightbearers of the world, unite!" And so, I am extending to you "heart, head and hand" my personal invitation to continue to be a part of this weekly Communion—and, as such, partakers with me of the Light from the Immaculate Heart of Mother Mary and my own daily invocations made on behalf of all Keepers of the Flame and students of the Ascended Masters worldwide.

Truly our mutual Communion is with the Universal Christ in whose Body we share. It is the Communion of saints—our oneness with all Lightbearers in heaven and on earth—that is our lawful right and inheritance which we must not fail to claim or exercise. These Teachings are delivered to me through and by the Holy Spirit at the altar of the Chapel of the Holy Grail or on tour in conferences conducted throughout the nations. And sometimes they are dictated to me at my desk as timely letters from the Masters to their chelas.

Jesus promised us that the Comforter would come to "teach you all things" and bring to your remembrance "whatsoever I have said unto you" (John 14:26). Thus, the Comforter and the Enlightener of our souls is delivering to us through the Ascended Masters precisely the knowledge of the Lost Years, the Lost Teachings, and the Lost Word of our Lord and Saviour. These servant-Sons in heaven are telling us week by week what we need to know and understand in order to face the trials of this world and the triumphs of the next.

Yes, the path of the ascension, the soul's reunion with God, is made known to us step by step through the Pearls of Wisdom. Year upon year and line upon line, the foundation of divine knowledge has been vouchsafed to us for the blessed seekers for Truth throughout the world.

For those who have not found what they are looking for in organized religion or the systems of orthodoxy and dead ritual into which some elements of the world's major religions have degenerated, the Pearls of Wisdom are cups of cold water given in Christ's name, drawn from the living fountains of waters (Rev. 7:17).

The Pearls of Wisdom occupy a unique place in the lives of those special souls who know that they are to ascend in this life and that therefore they must be about the business of their Father/Mother God on earth—balancing karma, loving one another, serving to set all life free, challenging the forces of Anti-Christ in self and society, gaining self-mastery thereby, and finding one's twin flame and moving on in the grand cycles of destiny that will take us in a spiral of self-transcendence beyond this earthly life whenever we are called Home by God.

For twenty-six years I have been serving the Great White Brotherhood and their disciples as their Messenger. I had the joy of ministering side by side with my late husband, twin flame and teacher, Mark L. Prophet, who also served as Messenger, Prophet and Servant of the Lord until his passing from the screen of this life in 1973.

Our joint service continues though he is beyond the veil in the ascended octaves of Light; nevertheless it is the backing of our beloved family and staff and wonderful students and friends such as you who hail this mission the world over that is making it all happen: Because of you the Teachings of the Ascended Masters are being distributed in our many books, our Coming Revolution, the Magazine for Higher Consciousness, on cable television, through the Keepers of the Flame Lessons and audio- and videocassettes in a worldwide outreach of lectures, workshops, retreats and classes. But nowhere is the contact more precious or more personal than in the blessed Pearls of Wisdom delivered weekly as Christ's knock at your door.

I must tell you that in all of these years of preparing this weekly spiritual feast of the Masters' letters and dictations to their beloved chelas, I have noted with such happiness the bonding, through the Pearls, of souls who are aware of their destiny and have known it from their earliest years.

These are the fiery spirits who have heard these truths spoken in their hearts and have found in our offering a mutual recognition with many other souls who have also been tutored by the Lord and who find in the powerful, loving, and wise presence of the ascended hosts the answers to life's questions, practical methods of solving the most pressing problems of daily life, and a codification in print of what they have always known to be the Truth.

It gives me great joy to know that the service which you our staunch supporters in the field are enabling us to render as a Community of the Holy Spirit here at the Royal Teton Ranch is meeting the needs of those who have not found anywhere else the solace or the in-depth teaching they knew existed somewhere.

For many, The Summit Lighthouse publications are the last hope and the only answer that makes sense. Without this mantle and activity sponsored by The Darjeeling Council, they would truly have nowhere else to turn to find the very specific nourishment their souls need in this particular hour of their passage through earth as pilgrims of peace who have been called by the gurus "the lonely ones."

In the desire to serve you and the living flame which our Father has placed upon the altar of your heart, we come, truly bearing our Pearls and calling to you to drink the Master's cup—"all of it," as he said, not missing a week or skipping a beat even as the drummer boy with his "ra-pa-pa-pum" heralds Christ's birth in our hearts as we assimilate the Word.

The 1986 volume of Pearls of Wisdom when complete will contain a total of 80 Pearls. We will continue sending them to you weekly, while at the same time starting up the spiral of the 1987 releases so urgently needed by all of us who are charting our courses by the living Spirit of the Great White Brotherhood communicated fresh from the altars of the Masters' retreats during these crucial weeks and months. It is high time we all caught up on the dictations the Masters have been giving since Christmas in our sanctuary at the Inner Retreat!

The reason we must request a love offering for the Pearls is, as you know, because paper, printing, and postage costs have gone up greatly over the years—not to mention the monthly payments on our new equipment: a printing press, cutter, folder, inserter, labeler and postage meter! In order to meet our budget as well as the needs of the staff who so lovingly perform this service, we ask for a contribution of $10 quarterly or $40 per year.

Since the number and timing of these mailings varies from month to month and year to year, and the page-count has been increasing as the Masters have more to say and the chelas have more "ears to hear" (for example, the first Pearl of 1987 will be 16 pages and the second 21), we have determined that the best way to calculate your subscription is to count 15 Pearls quarterly totaling 8 more annually than the 52-week-calendar.

Therefore, if you subscribe quarterly, your "time-for-Pearl-renewal" reminder to yourself on your date book should be approximately 12 weeks or 15 Pearls after your last $10 contribution. Double that if you contribute $20 twice a year. And figure 52 weeks or 60 Pearls for an automatic renewal without interruption when you give $40.

Our computer will always show to what date or Pearl number you are paid up. When in doubt, give us a call or drop us a note. The Pearls are regularly sent third-class mail unless you specifically request and prepay first-class postage. Your first-class postage account will be tallied separately, however, with notice given upon your request when the pennies for postage are spent.

These messages are the meat of the Word for initiates of the sacred fire who call to the Most High God for his living Presence to come upon them. This format is one of the very special avenues through which the Father answers our prayers. And to this purpose He called His son, the Master El Morya, to begin these weekly communications from on high twenty-nine summers ago.

During the immediate period of these double weekly mailings (1986 and 1987), your Pearls subscription will expire more quickly than usual. To be sure you don't miss a single week, please use the enclosed postage-free reply envelope and renew your subscription today. Your love offering will be added to your balance or applied to your subscription in arrears.

Recently we sent to you our poster for our Fourth of July conference "Freedom 1987" to be held in the Heart of the Inner Retreat. As you know so well, words are not adequate to convey the profound joy and spiritual acceleration that can be realized by souls who make the pilgrimage to this mountain valley preserved in all its pristine beauty against the backdrop of our national park and wilderness lands.

Keepers of the Flame worldwide have been waiting for this conference in the Heart since our last, which took place in 1984. Because so many are preparing to come from all over the world, we have, as noted on our poster, restricted attendance to members of the Keepers of the Flame Fraternity. This is a necessity based on the limited camping and RV facilities available as well as environmental concerns.

But it is also an unparalleled opportunity for our entire movement to unite behind Saint Germain and through this commitment to accelerate in our personal and planetary initiations.

Accordingly, I am encouraging you to invite new students, old friends and family members to join Saint Germain's fraternity without delay. Those coming to Freedom 1987 may sign up upon arrival for class registration at East Gate. The enclosed brochure is new and beautiful, a tribute to the Divine Mother who keeps the flame of Liberty. It is a precious focus for your altar and a treasure to share with those who want to start with the very first steps on the Path as taught by the Masters.

The Keepers of the Flame Lessons are for beginners and they are a joy and a delight. If you yourself are not a Keeper, this is the time to make the decision and the commitment and to set out on your pilgrimage to the Royal Teton Ranch. If you are, it is definitely the moment to encourage others to join in this great gathering of souls. Either way, just xerox the forms, as many as you need for all applying, but keep the booklet.

(Some of you have asked if family members who are non-Keepers may camp with you during the class while sight-seeing in the area. This will work out just fine if you do not take up more than one camp site or RV space. And we're happy to have you bring your loved ones to special events and to see the ranch together on our guided bus tours after the class.)

And so, the extensive preparations are well under way and we are looking forward to gathering in the Heart June 26 in a prayer vigil for Saint Germain for the defense of freedom worldwide. Here we shall present ourselves in a demonstration before heaven of what the Lightbearers of the world can do to mitigate the most dire consequences of world karma in this "dark, dark cycle," as Saint Germain has called it, and we can't wait to pour our hearts into dynamic decrees, songs, and affirmations unto God as we are united as one for this event.

Therefore, it is our prayer that each and every one of you might be with us for what is to be truly the most important spiritual conference of the decade, if not the century. This is a freedom rally staged by you who are determined to bring in the golden age of freedom, peace, and enlightenment for all. And when you have been charged and recharged through the dictations and initiations of the Masters and Cosmic Beings who will address us, you will return to your respective states and nations to carry the flame from this "Place Prepared" known as the Western Shamballa—after the legendary "City of White," the seat of the Ancient of Days revered in the East as Sanat Kumara.

In dedicating the land of the Inner Retreat to the victory of the Light in the West, Gautama Buddha with Lord Maitreya and Jesus Christ have placed their flame and their shrine in the etheric octave in the retreat of the Divine Mother. Thus, a most special event that you will want to participate in at the Inner Retreat is the trek up Maitreya's Mountain, most recently indicated by Mother Mary as the place for the shrine of her coming.

And so, many are eager for the opening of the doors of Summit University, which we trust will reconvene in January 1988. This is Maitreya's Mystery School come again where the Teachings of the Universal Christ are given even as they were given long ago in that school on Lemuria called "Eden."

As we all know, this Community of Lightbearers shares a very deep commitment of caring with all those who are dedicated to keeping the flame of Life and Liberty on earth. Fortunate indeed are we who recognize the strengthening bonds of our oneness which bless each one who takes up the calling to be his brother's keeper and to rejoice in his studies in cosmic law so carefully conveyed by our ascended brothers and sisters.

Most of all, Edward and I look forward to receiving you over the Fourth of July in the Heart of the Inner Retreat. It is so wonderful to meet old friends from this and other times for whom the recognition is instantaneous and the love genuine. May we be there together under the "big top" when Saint Germain delivers his message to the nation—and our Father, who is beloved Alpha, does deliver his long-awaited address.

Sincerely, I AM standing with you every day until your hour of victory.

Mother

P.S. Please enjoy the enclosed Pearls of Wisdom message from El Morya even as you pray for souls of Light to be drawn into this Ascended Master activity. Let us offer a fourteen-day novena to Archangel Michael and Mother Mary using their rosaries and dynamic decrees as we ask our Father to send his heavenly hosts to cut all free whom he has called to receive His Word in the Pearls of Wisdom as well as in the Keepers of the Flame Lessons. Then look for someone special to give Morya's and Saint Germain's messages to! My love is ever with you.

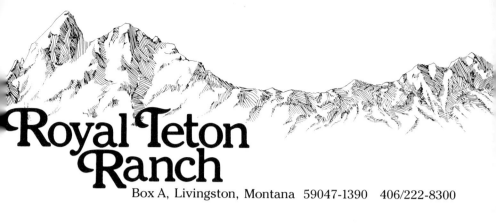

Royal Teton Ranch
Box A, Livingston, Montana 59047-1390 406/222-8300

June 18, 1987

Beloved Friends of Freedom,

Salutations of my heart as the fervor of freedom's fire leaps from mine to yours! We whose common bond is founded upon our love for Saint Germain are anticipating in these days approaching summer solstice our gathering at the Heart of the Inner Retreat as we are called by the Master of Aquarius to be there with him to keep the flame of freedom blazing everywhere on earth. For he has expressed his heart's desire:

> **I would deliver to you the healing power of the Seventh Ray. And I shall be therefore in the Heart of the Inner Retreat for some days surrounding the celebration of the Declaration of Independence, July 4th. I summon you to this high place and mountainous retreat where the light of the Holy Spirit flows and I may again transfer to you a just portion of the violet flame and your own divinity.** (February 7, 1987)

I am writing to you as you are making your final arrangements and packing your bags to be there with the Lightbearers of the world who are indeed uniting for a very special purpose that shall be fulfilled at this Independence Day celebration. For we are determined one and all to raise up a miracle chalice of violet flame called forth from the angel "Holy Amethyst" to receive Saint Germain's outpouring. That it might become a planetary electrode, by our offering enjoining that of the Archangels, that will make all the difference—this is our heart's desire.

We who have self-worth because we know the I AM THAT I AM as the beloved I AM Presence with us, we who know our voice and vote will count—and not only for "the Count" but for a Cosmos waiting for our resounding cry for freedom—we fear not to place ourselves row upon row in an interval of joy where time and space are not and we commune with God for renewal.

It is to be a renewal of ourselves, our dedication, and of freedom's courses, a renewal of planetary trends as the momentum of light invoked gives earth a new spin and her evolutions new hope.

As I write, the sound of earth-moving equipment and trucks up and down the Mol Heron Road and in the Heart tell of intense activity and many of our staff, departmental work abandoned, on site for the set-up of FREEDOM 1987.

By this Sunday, June 21, Archangel Michael's new blue and gold altar will be in place under the big top for Montessori International High School graduation with school awards, speeches, tears, laughter, applause and heart communion as we reminisce about the wonderful years and the wonderful lifestreams who have passed through M.I. and gone on to take up their service to Saint Germain in varied and creative fields.

For our family it will be a very personal moment, since our daughter Tatiana Marie Prophet is one of the graduates along with a special friend and chela, Victoria Jean Brailsford. Together they have brightened the classrooms and the roads of Camelot for many years.

This Father's Day event, commemorating the wondrous works of our Father in heaven and the stalwart sons who are the fathers of this Community, is a coming together of families and friends for a pep rally of Hope and a kick-off for FREEDOM 1987.

If you receive this message by modem and can come for summer solstice to the Heart this Sunday, please know we would be joyous to welcome you to meet M.I. faculty, parents, and tots to teens who represent to us Hope, even as they invoke from us God's love that cares. For these little ones truly represent to us our reason for being, for building, for striving to make America and the world a planet of peace where freedom and enlightenment are the enjoyment of all, and where security from war, famine, disease and economic chaos is at last achieved.

One glimpse into the eyes of our children, their trust and faith and carefreeness, is all we need to serve another day and to vow before Almighty God concerning the infamies and injustices of current and past history on this planet: "Never again!"

As I recently reread the dictation of beloved Saint Germain given New Year's Day this year, which you should soon be receiving, I was reminded of the vow that Saint Germain and our beloved Portia have taken century after century to stand with the Lightbearers of the world and to unite us under one banner—the standard of Maitreya and the Divine Mother. I thought of how much all of the Ascended Masters have given and given and given of their light and love and sponsorship, their teaching and training of our lifestreams. On the occasion of this dictation, which is Pearl number 2 of 1987, Saint Germain said,

> According to the dispensation given to me, I am able to do the following—and it is to vow my life, my causal body, and my service to planet earth so long as there are those in embodiment who are capable of making the identical vow. I will not tell you in numbers how many, for in some cases one heart so infilled by the Buddha Gautama, one heart such a vessel of Maitreya, may count for many. But I will say that it is a tally of a geometry of a weight of sacred fire, an Omega balance in the earth that will allow my presence to fully and finally intercede in all these things projected upon the screen of mankind's returning karma. . . .
>
> I do not even ask you to enter into it this day, for it shall require of you soul-searching, perhaps a period of self-purging and submission to more severe disciplines than those to which you are accustomed that you might see how you fare, [in order] to be certain. Then, of course, I must make the choice of those who step forward—those whom I can work through and with and sponsor, those whom I cannot. For it is I who pay the ultimate price in this hour and in this situation. . . .
>
> The vow that I have taken is to serve with this earth until the true Lightbearers are free. The vow I propose to take, having accomplished this, is to stand with all others who have accepted the transfer of the flame of freedom from our best servants. The specifics of the vow must be, then, to defeat World Communism before it defeats the West and to defeat in the West those betrayers of the Word before the very foundations of Western civilization crumble for their presence in that foundation. To this end I will answer your calls, and that is where the revolution begins.

As I renewed my vow to Saint Germain profoundly aware, as each and every one of you is, of the Master's great need for true chelas in this hour, I determined to do for him whatever God would give me the power to do according to the blessings he has already poured out upon me and upon us all in the tremendous opportunity the Royal Teton Ranch with its Inner Retreat offers us. And so I asked the question, How can I best get out the message for the reeducation of the people as to the realities at hand?

And I saw that to make the optimum use of presently available resources would afford me ample opportunity to give to the Master a tool that he could use to contact millions of souls not connected as yet with the Keepers of the Flame activity but surely ready to hear Saint Germain's message.

Summit University Forum was the answer! to free the Lightbearers of earth, to stand with those who keep the flame of freedom, to defeat World Communism and the betrayers of the Word in the West.

I picked up the phone. My research staff and family picked up their phones, and in a matter of a few hours and a few days we came up with the following roster of specialists whose information—well told and publicized, viewed on cable television on our Summit University Forum series—could indeed make all the difference!

Each and every one on the enclosed list has become the personal friend of our staff writers for The Coming Revolution: The Magazine for Higher Consciousness. All were enthusiastic about addressing you at FREEDOM 1987 and having the opportunity to present their positions based on their research and long experience. They accepted the challenge to answer the unanswered questions and to meet the arguments point by point of their critics.

And so it's up to you the audience—who may or may not agree with their assessment of the issues or their solutions—to be informed and to ask penetrating questions. Here's your chance to play Ted Koppel! At these forums the views from Left to Right will be freely discussed as well as Saint Germain's prophecy and pragmatic approaches to nuclear war, the defense of our sacred freedom, and what we must do to survive in an age of uncertainty.

You will note that these Summit University Forums are to be conducted and filmed as interview talk shows on our main stage in the tent. **Two will be held during our prayer vigil for Saint Germain June 26 and 30, three on July 1, 3, and 4 during FREEDOM 1987 and the concluding two July 6 and 7 at the survival seminar.**

What's great about these events is that they are open to the public and to your friends and families! Being entirely secular and nonreligious in nature, of high interest to all who are concerned about the fate of nations, they offer the opportunity for family members who do not desire to participate in the daily decrees and dictations to do their sightseeing and enjoy the recreational activities on and off the Ranch, but to join Keepers of the Flame each evening for what I believe to be the greatest group of experts on the subjects that most concern us: nuclear war, Communism in this hemisphere and the best defense of freedom.

Whereas in the daytime we will be dealing with spiritual freedom and the development of that freedom through the clearing of the chakras, the increase of light, initiations from the Great White Brotherhood, and all that we expect to derive from a truly spiritual retreat experience in the Western Shamballa of the northern Rockies, the evenings will provide us with the facts and figures, strategies and equations that we simply have to be familiar with in order to make the calls to Almighty God for the deliverance of mankind in this age. Were I to digest a library of material, or our staff to do research for a year, we could not bring to you the breadth of knowledge and experience that these guests will provide. The evening sessions will be professionally videoed, the tapes edited and reproduced for you to purchase at the conclusion of the conference—and spread the word. There is not a moment to lose to secure the defense of America's freedom!

Our fireworks over the Fourth will be YOU! as you become the sparks that fly, freedom sparks who will return to the farms, cities, valleys, and trouble spots of the nations armed with the gift of knowledge concerning conditions on earth and the gift of wisdom as to how to effectively tackle them. For truly the rod of power from the hand of God is accessed by the science of the spoken Word and by chelaship under the Ascended Masters which creates the blessed tie to heaven whereby we become the instrument of flood tides of light to transmute all that the Spirit of prophecy does bring to our view in these sessions.

The fee of $5 per evening for nonregistered guests, family members, and the public will be their love offering to help us defray travel expenses and honorariums for our speakers.

Since some of you are making last-minute decisions to become a Keeper of the Flame and to plan a family vacation around FREEDOM 1987 (and figuring out how your family members who may not be on a spiritual path will have a good time while you are in the Heart), I am writing to give you this schedule so that you can firm your reservations as well as your plans.

These forums together with the dictations and blessings untold to all in attendance make good the claim that this is indeed to be the most important spiritual conference of the decade. There is no doubt about it—for I know what the Brotherhood has planned as their offering, culminating in the address of beloved Alpha on Sunday morning, July 5.

The earlier your attendance, the greater the opportunity you will have for violet flame transmutation and the buildup of the light within your chakras, body temples, cells, and atoms to provide an electromagnetic field—an "amethyst crystal chalice"—into which the heavenly hierarchy and angelic hosts can pour the Maxim Light. Freely we give, freely we receive. Each individual receives, then, from the Ascended Masters at the quarterly conferences that which is lawful according to the record of his lifestream—his karma, his diligence in decrees, his loving service to life.

I pray, then, that if you are not already committed to be here Friday evening, June 26, for the beginning of the prayer vigil that you make the decision now to make it for Saint Germain! There simply is nothing more important happening than our participation, one heart, voice, soul, and mind, for the liberation of a planet and a people through the science of the spoken Word. Since the fundamentals of the power of the Word will be given to new Keepers in separate sessions during these five days, it will prove a sound foundation for your entering into the accelerated momentums that begin first thing July 1.

I can only testify and bear witness to the great response of the Ascended Masters which I have experienced over the years as they pour forth their light in gratitude for the service of their chelas during these conferences sponsored by the Karmic Board. This is the time to bring all of your problems to the altar, to commune with the Nature spirits, and to see how angels and elementals as well as the Ascended Masters are just waiting to enter into an exciting cooperative venture with you—in answer to your call: Ask and ye shall receive!

As you face the altar and give your invocations to Almighty God for his divine intercession in your life and in the lives of all of your family members and friends—in your business, your profession, your relationships, your calling, your goals, your dreams, and your ultimate victory over death and hell—you almost hear the rustle of angel wings and the chuckle of gnomes in attendance.

From summer solstice through the freedom festivities, people from all over the world come to this "Sacred Heart" of Jesus for their spiritual recharge that they might go forth for another twelve months to serve to set life free. This is the time when the wise ones generously fill their lamps with oil that they might be trimmed, ready any hour for the Lord's calling.

So much love awaits you here, but above all I await you in this place of the Sun where we shall sing together "I AM free, I AM free, I AM free forevermore . . . We are one, we are one, we are one . . ."

Members of the Community, staff, and our family send all our love to you personally as you embark upon your pilgrimage to "The Place of Great Encounters"!

May angels guard you all the way Home to our Heart!

Devoted to your Victory,
Always,

Mother

SUMMIT UNIVERSITY FORUMS AT FREEDOM 1987

ALEJANDRO BOLAÑOS: Friday, June 26, 5–9:00 P.M.

Alejandro Bolaños is an authority on Nicaraguan affairs. He was born and educated in Nicaragua and attended St. Louis University in Missouri, where he received his M.D. in 1948. After completing his residency in 1952, he returned to Managua and practiced medicine there until 1972. His well-developed interest in history has led him to write four books on U.S. intervention in Nicaragua during the 1850s and numerous articles on U.S.-Nicaraguan relations. Dr. Bolaños was in the United States when the Sandinistas came to power and has remained here since. He is the president of the Nicaraguan Information Center, which was founded to provide Americans with accurate information about life under the Sandinistas.

Subject: Dr. Bolaños will discuss the Sandinista/Contra conflict in the context of Soviet and Cuban presence in Central America and how the support of the American churches, press, and people affects the region. He will also talk about the geopolitical aspects of the Soviet penetration of the Western Hemisphere and various tactics of subversion they use.

THOMAS H. KREBS: Tuesday, June 30, 7–10:30 P.M.

Thomas H. Krebs, a retired Air Force officer, is an expert in space operations and planning. Formerly the Pentagon's chief analyst on Soviet space warfare capabilities, he is now a private consultant analyzing Soviet countermeasures to SDI. Prior to his work in military intelligence, he was involved with the research and development of ground radar installations, the space shuttle program, and the B-1 bomber. Mr. Krebs has degrees in engineering, systems analysis, and business administration. He is the author of Tsar Wars: The Challenge Posed to the Free World by the Soviet Commitment to the Military Control of Space.

Subject: Mr. Krebs will discuss the military aspect of Soviet space operations, the likelihood of the Soviets deploying a space-based missile defense in the near future, and what the U.S. can and should do to counteract the Soviets in space. He will put into perspective the complex issues of costs and countermeasures in the context of the strategic-defense debate.

ANTONY C. SUTTON: Wednesday, July 1, 7–10:30 P.M.

Antony C. Sutton is the nation's foremost expert on the subject of U.S. technical, economic, and diplomatic support of

Communist nations, particularly the Soviet Union. He has demonstrated that the West has made it possible for the Soviets to build their war machine and helped keep the Communist regime afloat by generous financial assistance. He has also written about the people and organizations in the capitalist world who have been the driving force behind East-West trade.

Professor Sutton is the editor of the Phoenix Letter and the author of numerous books, including his three-volume Western Technology and Soviet Economic Development, Wall Street and the Bolshevik Revolution, and National Suicide: Military Aid to the Soviet Union. His most recent books are The Best Enemy Money Can Buy and America's Secret Establishment.

He was born in London, England, and attended the Universities of London, Göttingen (Germany), and California. He was professor of Economics at the California State University at Los Angeles (1963–68) and a Research Fellow at Hoover Institution, Stanford University (1968–73).

Subject: Professor Sutton will discuss East-West trade, U.S. technical support of the Soviet war machine, the U.S.-Soviet Trade and Economic Council, The Order, weather manipulation, and Soviet use of psychotronic energy.

UYS VILJOEN, JAMES W. KENDRICKS, REV. E. GENE VOSSELER and REV. KENNETH E. FRAZIER:
Friday, July 3, 7–10:30 P.M.

Uys Viljoen is a political counselor for the Embassy of South Africa in Washington, D.C.

James W. Kendricks is an expert on South African affairs. Formerly a consultant to the governments of Nigeria and Liberia, Mr. Kendricks is president of the Kendricks International Company, secretary of Black PAC, executive director of the Afro-American Cultural Education Center, and special consultant to the California State Legislature.

An international commodities trade expert with a focus on Africa, Mr. Kendricks received a B.A. in international relations from California State University, Los Angeles, and a law degree from UCLA. He is the former deputy director of the Los Angeles Urban Coalition and contributes articles to the Lincoln Review, the Los Angeles Times and the Afro-American Cultural Education Journal.

Rev. E. Gene Vosseler has lectured internationally on defense issues for the American Security Council. As director of "Californians for a Strong America," he spearheaded opposition to the Nuclear Freeze Initiative in some 50 debates on radio, television, and university campuses in California. Along with Dr. David W. Balsiger, he was one of the leading spokesmen in the movement to protest the Soviet occupation of Afghanistan that led to the Soviet withdrawal from the 1984 Olympics.

Rev. Vosseler has made guest appearances on ABC's "Nightline," "Good Morning America," "The Merv Griffin Show," and CNN's "Crossfire." In 1981, he completed a three-week lecture tour of the major cities in South Africa and since then has kept close tabs on political developments there.

Rev. Vosseler received his B.A. from Midland College and his Bachelor's of Divinity from Central Lutheran Theological Seminary.

Rev. Kenneth E. Frazier is a veteran civil rights activist of the 1960s and a popular speaker on university campuses. A professional marriage, child, and family counselor, he received his training at St. Elizabeth's Hospital and the Washington School of Psychiatry. In 1986, Rev. Frazier was a candidate for Congress in Los Angeles' 12th District. He has recently returned from a two-week fact-finding trip to South Africa, where he met with the key parties on both sides of the escalating conflict.

Rev. Frazier received his B.S. from Tennessee A and I University and his Bachelor's of Divinity from Vanderbilt University.
Subject: Uys Viljoen, James W. Kendricks, Rev. Vosseler and Rev. Frazier will discuss the directions of political and social change in South Africa in the context of the global geopolitical equation, including the role played by the superpowers, multinational corporations, the African National Congress, and the press.

GEN. DANIEL O. GRAHAM and DMITRY MIKHEYEV:
Saturday, July 4, 7–10:30 P.M.

Lt. Gen. Daniel O. Graham, former director of the Defense Intelligence Agency and deputy director of the Central Intelligence Agency, has been called the father of SDI. He is chairman of the American Space Frontier Committee and the Coalition for the Strategic Defense Initiative and founder of High Frontier, an organization promoting the early deployment of strategic defense.

A graduate of the U.S. Military Academy (1946), General Graham served in Germany, Korea, and Vietnam and was decorated several times during his distinguished 30-year military career. He was military adviser to Ronald Reagan during his 1976 and 1980 campaigns and has written numerous books on strategic defense.
Subject: General Graham will discuss the A to Z of strategic

defense—the controversy surrounding it and his own plan for the near-term deployment of ground- and space-based systems using existing technology. General Graham will also talk about Soviet sabotage of the U.S. space program.

Dmitry Mikheyev was born in Krasnoyarsk, Siberia, in 1941. He holds a Ph.D. in theoretical physics from Moscow University. He was arrested and convicted of political dissent and attempted defection and served six years in hard-labor camps for political prisoners from 1970–76. He was forced to emigrate in 1979 and became a U.S. citizen in 1985. His military training in the Soviet Union was in radar guidance systems for surface-to-air missiles and his dissertation was on the "Non-Linear Effects of Laser-Beam Propagation."

Mr. Mikheyev is now a consultant to the CIA, the U.S. Army Command and General Staff College, and High Frontier, as well as associate scholar at National Security Research, Inc., and senior analyst in residence at the Institute for Foreign Policy Analysis. He has published numerous articles on the Soviet Union, including "Revolution in Military Affairs and Reforms in the USSR" and "Five Meetings with Misha Gorbachev," and broke new ground in the debate on strategic defense with the recent publication of The Soviet Perspective on SDI.

Subject: Mr. Mikheyev will discuss the effect of a U.S. strategic defense on the Soviet economy, long-term strategy, and military posture, and the dilemma it would pose for the Soviet leadership.

DR. JOHN W. GOFMAN: Monday, July 6, 7–10:30 P.M.

Dr. John W. Gofman is one of the world's leading experts on the effects of radiation on human health. He is professor emeritus of medical physics at the University of California at Berkeley and a member of the clinical faculty, University of California School of Medicine, San Francisco. He is both a physician and a doctor of nuclear/physical chemistry.

While a graduate student at Berkeley, he co-discovered Uranium-233 and proved its fissionability. During World War II he worked on the Manhattan Project where he isolated the world's first workable quantities of plutonium. Later he established the Biomedical Research Division at the Lawrence Livermore National Laboratory and from 1963 to 1969 served as associate director of the laboratory.

Over the years, Dr. Gofman has conducted research on a variety of medical concerns, including the relationship between cancer, chromosomes, and radiation. He was given the Stouffer

Prize (shared) in 1972 for his outstanding contributions to research on arteriosclerosis and was honored by the American College of Cardiology in 1974 as one of the 25 leading researchers in the field of cardiology of the previous quarter-century.

Dr. Gofman is the author of 150 scientific papers and a number of books, including Radiation and Human Health (1981), a monumental work which for the first time integrated the world-wide human data linking ionizing radiation to the injury of human health, and X-Rays: Health Effects of Common Exams, co-authored with science writer Egan O'Connor.

Since 1969, Dr. Gofman has been a leader in the struggle to prevent nuclear power from creating a public health tragedy and is author of "Irrevy:" An Irreverent Illustrated View of Nuclear Power.

His studies on the Chernobyl disaster, which demonstrated that responsible authorities on both sides of the Iron Curtain have dramatically underestimated the health consequences of the radioactive materials released, touched off an international controversy. Unlike many who oppose nuclear power due to its inherent dangers, Dr. Gofman believes the U.S. must maintain a strong nuclear deterrent force to protect its freedom.

Subject: Dr. Gofman will discuss the health effects of radiation from nuclear fallout released during atmospheric testing or in a future war. He will also cover the nuclear power controversy and give a realistic picture of the health consequences of the Chernobyl disaster, why the real figures from Chernobyl were covered up, and describe the danger to Americans from nuclear power plants. Dr. Gofman will explain how to limit the danger to your health from diagnostic X Rays.

EDWIN N. YORK: Tuesday, July 7, 7–10:30 P.M.

Edwin N. York is one of the nation's foremost authorities on civil defense. He is currently a senior research specialist in the physics department at Boeing Aerospace Corporation where he has conducted research on all aspects of weapons effects and systems survivability for strategic aircraft and missiles. For three years Mr. York served as technical advisor to NATO on improving survivability of all their headquarters and communications facilities. He is the author of twenty-three documents on nuclear weapons effects and survivability and has designed, personally constructed, and tested eight different types of personal shelters.

Subject: Mr. York will discuss how it is possible to survive a nuclear war, what survival technology is available, and types of shelter design and construction.

THE CHART OF YOUR DIVINE SELF

The Chart of Your Divine Self

There are three figures represented in the Chart, which we will refer to as the upper figure, the middle figure, and the lower figure.

The upper figure is the I AM Presence, the I AM THAT I AM, the individualization of God's presence for every son and daughter of the Most High.

The Divine Monad consists of the I AM Presence surrounded by the spheres (color rings) of light which comprise the causal body. This is the body of First Cause that contains within it man's "treasure laid up in heaven"—words and works, thoughts and feelings of virtue, attainment, and light—pure energies of love that have risen from the plane of action in time and space as the result of man's judicious exercise of free will and his harmonious qualification of the stream of life that issues forth from the heart of the Presence and descends to the level of the Christ Self, thence to invigorate and enliven the embodied soul.

The middle figure in the Chart is the Mediator between God and man, called the Holy Christ Self, the Real Self, or the Christ consciousness. It has also been referred to as the Higher Mental Body or one's Higher Consciousness.

This Inner Teacher overshadows the lower self, which consists of the soul evolving through the four planes of Matter using the vehicles of the four lower bodies (the etheric, or memory, body; the mental body; the emotional, or desire, body; and the physical body) to balance karma and fulfill the divine plan.

The three figures of the Chart correspond to the Trinity of Father (the upper figure), Son (the middle figure), and Holy Spirit (the lower figure). The latter is the intended temple of the Holy Spirit, whose sacred fire is indicated in the enfolding violet flame. The lower figure corresponds to you as a disciple on the Path. Your soul is the nonpermanent aspect of being which is made permanent through the ritual of the ascension. The ascension is the process whereby the soul, having balanced her karma and fulfilled her divine plan, merges first with the Christ consciousness and then with the living Presence of the I AM THAT I AM. Once the ascension has taken place, the soul, the nonpermanent aspect of being, becomes the Incorruptible One, a permanent atom in the Body of God. The Chart of Your Divine Self is therefore a diagram of yourself—past, present, and future.

The lower figure represents the son of man or child of the Light evolving beneath his own 'Tree of Life'. This is how you should visualize yourself standing in the violet flame, which you invoke daily in the name of the I AM Presence and your Holy Christ Self in order to purify your four lower bodies in preparation for the ritual of the alchemical marriage—your soul's union with the Beloved, your Holy Christ Self.

The lower figure is surrounded by a tube of light, which is projected from the heart of the I AM Presence in answer to your call. It is a cylinder of white light which sustains a forcefield of protection 24 hours a day, so long as you guard it in harmony. It is also invoked daily with the "Heart, Head and Hand Decrees" and may be reinforced as needed.

The threefold flame of Life is the divine spark sent from the I AM Presence as the gift of life, consciousness, and free will. It is sealed in the secret chamber of the heart that through the Love, Wisdom and Power of the Godhead anchored therein the soul may fulfill her reason for being in the physical plane. Also called the Christ flame and the liberty flame, or fleur-de-lis, it is the spark of a man's Divinity, his potential for Christhood.

The silver (or crystal) cord is the stream of life, or "lifestream," that descends from the heart of the I AM Presence to the Holy Christ Self to nourish and sustain (through the chakras) the soul and its vehicles of expression in time and space. It is over this 'umbilical' cord that the energy of the Presence flows, entering the being of man at the crown and giving impetus for the pulsation of the threefold flame as well as the physical heartbeat. When a round of the soul's incarnation in Matter-form is finished, the I AM Presence withdraws the silver cord, whereupon the threefold flame returns to the level of the Christ, and the soul clothed in the etheric garment gravitates to the highest level of her attainment where she is schooled between embodiments, until her final incarnation when the great law decrees she shall go out no more.

The dove of the Holy Spirit descending from the heart of the Father is shown just above the head of the Christ. When the son of man puts on and becomes the Christ consciousness as Jesus did, he merges with the Holy Christ Self. The Holy Spirit is upon him and the words of the Father, the beloved I AM Presence, are spoken, "This is my beloved Son in whom I AM well pleased" (Matt. 3:17).

A more detailed explanation of the Chart of Your Divine Self is given in *The Lost Teachings of Jesus* and *Climb the Highest Mountain* by Mark L. Prophet and Elizabeth Clare Prophet.

Pearls of Wisdom®
published by The Summit Lighthouse

Vol. 30 No. 31 *Beloved Archangel Chamuel and Charity* *August 2, 1987*

Freedom 1987

I

Bring Forth the Saviour of Your World

Pillars of the Ruby Ray and a Chalice

Fear not, O Mother, for thy Light is Krishna!

Therefore, O Cosmic Christ, we the Archangels of the Third Ray come to the Heart of the Western Shamballa to place pillars of the Ruby Ray. Thus, twin flames of our causal bodies implanted here are for the holding of balance in earth changes.

We could not hold back legions of angels of the Ruby Ray and of the cosmic cross of white fire. For they come from the Central Sun to dedicate this land and this Heart to a new age and a golden age and as a dais of light, large in diameter, whereon the saints may stand and rise.

Therefore called and summoned by Alpha and Omega to clear the way for Alpha's release,[1] we sweep through this Heart, life beyond and within. And from this point of cycles intensifying, spirals ascending, high into the etheric octave and to the center of the earth, we create a line of force and a fulcrum, that by the Ruby Ray and the Holy Spirit Life might be preserved, and that with integrity.

O blessed Keepers of the Flame, let thy Light* grow as a spiral and see how the growing of the pillars of the Ruby Ray suffice for a permanence in the earth even midst temporal amusements, temporal crowns and temporal changes that come to purify.

Who else but the embodiment of anti-Love should commit such crimes [as the Soviet/Sandinistas have committed] against humanity?[2] And though we witness veiled, we observe, beloved, such suffering and degradation! It is a portrayal of hell

*Christ consciousness manifest as the light of the eye, the aura, the chakras

itself in the physical octave.

Hearts of living fire, know the Truth. Insofar as you have entered in to a bhajan of devotion to the Lord Krishna, unto the Cosmic Christ of thyself,[3] so this concentration, beloved, by Love's own ray demonstrates a continuity of flow whereby the floodgates of heaven are opened. And down the chute of the pillars of the Ruby Ray there does flow light sufficient for the binding of that creeping and crawling Darkness that must be halted in this hour by legions of the Ruby Ray.

Our work, beloved, that is the LORD's, can bear fruit only as we can anchor this calling through your own bodies and chakras. Absent not yourselves from this communion and this vigil, for, beloved, a tangible chalice is being formed, tended by Paul the Venetian, by Nada, by angels of Love.

And high in the upper atmosphere await Heros and Amora. For when the chalice shall rise to meet and greet the Elohimic level, then shall Elohim pour into this chalice that which ye seek, beloved. Truly, and truly I say, it is the purging, purging of all impurity: Light, then, solidifying and codifying the Word within you.

Truly heaven is adequate. May many bowls be brought to receive the oil,[4] that the lamps in the earth may not go out during the period when Darkness shall be raked from the earth as hot coals of the underworld, as a harvest unfruitful, as the dead trees and the tares are bound into bundles and removed.

Blessed ones, you understand the difficulty of consciously seeing and then by God removing the flaw within self—the habit that is ancient, the suffering one endures until surrender is complete of some cherished belief or attachment known to be self-destructive yet desired.

Blessed hearts, if you have struggled with a condition of consciousness, then understand the turmoil and the upheaval as earth herself must give up the ghosts of anti-Love, that she might endure as a planet and not be flung apart by the force of a vacuum where God is not, in the empty and hollowed-out ones.

Thus, beloved, the purging is a wrenching experience for those fallen ones who are wed to Darkness. The Darkness cannot be purged from them, for their Darkness is a cancer that is one and the same self. Thus, the purging of these profligate ones (who have chosen not only the absence of Light, but to fill that vacuum with evil words and works) must be a purging of the whole identity which has departed from the God flame.

Let the unworthy servant, then, depart!

We are Chamuel and Charity standing in the earth firmly

and strong by the grace of God, holding pillars of fire, ruby fire in the Western Shamballa, that the stability of our presence might see you through the shedding of the snakeskin of the former self, the entering in to the Divine Whole.

We see, then, that Love as a mystery, Love as an initiation rocks the boat of family and friendships. For, beloved, it is the all-power of the universe and the very nucleus of the Cosmic Christ within you.

Blessed ones, this power of the Third Ray and the legions thereof, this power of the secret ray and the white fire core of the Third Ray is a sufficiency unto the devouring of the forces of anti-Love that go by the name of Communist or Satanist or those who detest the whole human race. Let the misanthropes, then, depart! For, beloved, they have not cherished self or God or infant or child.

In the mystery of the Word of the Archangels perceive, then, that inner work does take place. Perceive, then, the mystery of Love: for in it lies the key to the undoing of all that which seems as hopelessness.

We say it at this elevation as it has been said before. We say it specifically regarding the Third Ray and the ruby action of the Law. The power of heaven and of Archangels is sufficient for the turning around of that which has become this "international capitalist/communist conspiracy." The Light is there. The Ruby Ray and the Buddha of the Ruby Ray are here.

Jesus has called for ten thousand Keepers of the Flame in North America.[5] Those who should truly keep this flame on this continent in that number, beloved, who should understand the mystery of Love and of the Ruby Ray and its path, are sufficient for the turning around of the entire equation of Darkness upon earth. Knowing the multiplication factor of the ten thousand-times-ten thousand,[6] multiplied again by ten thousand Keepers of the Flame, realize, then, that the mystery of God is already on earth embodied in hearts of Light who have been polarized to another star and another center.

It is difficult for those without a Shepherd truly to discover the I AM THAT I AM and the polestar of Being. They are magnetized by falling stars such as Wormwood,[7] such as Abaddon,[8] such as the seed of Satan remaining. Beloved, it is the magnetism of Love turned inside out, misusing the rites of the ancient language of the Holy Kumaras. The original fallen ones stole the secrets of God in the etheric octave, beloved. Thus, they were cast out of this heaven-world into the earth where their misuse of the sacred fire might be impeded by the decelerating spheres here below.[9]

Blessed ones, thus it is in the name SANAT KUMARA—which does contain the fullness of his causal body, the true mantra and the true science of the Word—that these fallen angels in embodiment may be confounded and overturned, and that by the scepter placed in the hand of the Messenger and the authority of the living Christ which it does represent. It is indeed by the authority of the Word of the I AM THAT I AM and the increasing authority of all those who do embody the Christ that all these things can come to pass. Thus we overturn their works.

In the etheric octave the judgment is complete this night, beloved, of the oppressors of mankind. Now we seek to press into the mental belt of the earth that same judgment. For judgment from on high, descending, must traverse the octaves. Those who misuse the air signs and the air chakras,[10] those who misuse the Mind of God, they, then, must receive that judgment in answer to your call.

It is the rising fire, the sacred fire of the Divine Mother upon the spinal altar, which you feel intensifying in your devotions, that does rise from the base-of-the-spine chakra to meet the sacred fire descending from the Father out of your beloved I AM Presence. As the Light is contained in the temple and in the body, *lo,* as ye are lifted up by that Light, so ye become the magnet to pull down the Light and there does take place the action of the most powerful force of the universe within your very heart: It is the divine embrace of the Father and the Mother—through the Mighty I AM Presence by the sacred fire of the Kundalini rising.

This magnetism of Divine Love in your heart is the key to the expansion of the threefold flame and to the chalice whereby all decrees of heaven manifest upon earth. You may then become like the yogis and the bodhisattvas, beloved, so aware of this divine grace of the Father/Mother God which flows instantaneously as you are seated to recite the divine decrees, to recite the Pearls of Wisdom which are our dictations. For when by Love you are seated in the lotus throne of the Eighth Ray chakra (the secret chamber of the heart) the flow of the Word through you then becomes the instantaneous physical manifestation.

Oh, follow the path of the Buddhas of the Ruby Ray! Follow the path of the Ruby Ray angels! Follow the path, beloved, of Sanat Kumara/Gautama/Maitreya/Jesus, each representing the octaves four whereby the descent of this heavenly fire can be complete.[11]

Blessed ones, one lifestream infilled in the four planes of being with this light of the Third Ray can count for a million and more who have not accomplished this. Parents who seek the high and holy path of holiness itself may so contain in their aura this pillar of fire as to sponsor souls who as yet have nowhere to embody, for they require a cradle of the highest white fire and Ruby Ray.

Thus, beloved, it is a calling reached by initiates of old that is greatly needed in this hour of earth's turbulence. With Death and Hell marching in a very, very ancient time, like unto today, it was the God and Goddess Meru who early in their path elected to consecrate their vows to the infilling of the temple by this Grand Presence of the Father above, the Mother below, and their fusion in the heart.

Thus, because these two individuals, the God and Goddess Meru, did hold the polarity, they did therefore bring forth true avatars who—by their very presence in the earth, beloved, by their very auras of Light—were a counterweight from Cosmos that did prevent the misuse of this great science of the Word that comes from the Holy Kumaras.

Aspire to this, beloved. And on the path of aspiration, call for the twin flames and causal bodies of the God and Goddess Meru to be placed upon you, even as you call forth the causal body of yourself and your twin flame.

Realize that during the process of the quickening—while the soul who is emerging awakens to the path of the Buddha and the Mother—there is a time and space to be filled with God-mastery, yet no time and space to wait [for that soul to attain to that God-mastery]. Thus, it is your beloved God and Goddess Meru who shall fill that time and space to hold the balance with you until you [or any emerging soul] fill in by your lovely, radiant Third Ray auras even a portion, a sphere within a sphere, of their Electronic Presence.

Understand, beloved, how all the world does await the coming of a single or many avatars. For it was taught by the Ancient of Days that with the coming of the Great Light and One who was to be born, all suffering should cease, all should be healed, all karma should be balanced.

And so, beloved, we look to the incarnation of the Word. The Word is made flesh,[12] yes, in the One Sent. But you must go beyond looking here and there[13] for the one who will be sent; for your path, beloved, is so very specific: it is for the incarnation of the Christ Self where you are.

Thus, the determination to give birth to your Christ consciousness is a key to the here and now. It is the fighting of the good fight[14] to conquer the postponement in time and space, the procrastination by imputing to another the role of bringing forth that Christ.

In your universe, in your microcosm, macrocosmic in dimension, you and only you can bring forth the Saviour of your world. *Only you can bring forth the Saviour of your world!* I seal this message in your heart, for my angels have tarried to complete their mighty work.

O Saviour, O living Christ of each Keeper of the Flame, Thou knowest. Souls awaken, then, to this Reality! Receive thy God and live! Receive thy God and save the earth.

May you know the mystery, may you know the Word, may you know the work that this entails. It is the path of Maitreya, and Maitreya summons *you.*

We are Chamuel and Charity, sponsors of souls unto the Saviour's Light.

"The Summit Lighthouse Sheds Its Radiance O'er All the World to Manifest as Pearls of Wisdom."
This dictation by Archangel Chamuel and Charity was **delivered** at *FREEDOM 1987* on **Saturday, June 27, 1987.** (**1**) **The coming of Alpha** on July 5, 1987, foretold by Gautama Buddha, p. 249, pars. 4, 5. (**2**) See the June 26, 1987, Summit University Forum with Dr. Alejandro Bolaños on "Nicaragua: The Untold Story." (**3**) Prior to the dictation, the Messenger and congregation sang the bhajan "RAMA RAMA RAMA." (**4**) II Kings 4:1–7. (**5**) **Jesus' call for ten thousand Keepers of the Flame.** "I am sent by the Father for the quickening now of ten thousand saints in the City Foursquare that I mark as North America. . . . I have come, then, to make a plea to you and to send my Messenger abroad across this continent for the gathering of ten thousand who will call themselves Keepers of the Flame of Life and who will understand that I, Jesus, have called them" (May 28, 1987). See p. 269, par. 3; p. 273, par. 1. (**6**) On July 1, 1961, Lord Maitreya announced that "the Ascended Masters, in the great deliberations and the councils of the Great White Brotherhood, . . . have asked for a great petition whereby the student body today shall be given that which is known as the full power of the ten thousand-times-ten thousand. From this day henceforward, every decree that you utter shall be increased by the power of the ten thousand-times-ten thousand! I, Maitreya, declare that those who give decrees from this day forward shall be creating a tremendous, impelling, swiftly moving acceleration which shall sweep through the earthly consciousness of mankind and compel this earth free." See Lord Maitreya, "The Christ Consciousness," 1984 *Pearls of Wisdom,* vol. 27, no. 7, p. 63; and Mark L. Prophet and Elizabeth Clare Prophet, "**The Power of the Ten Thousand-Times-Ten Thousand,**" in *The Science of the Spoken Word,* pp. 78–79. (**7**) Rev. 8:10, 11. (**8**) Rev. 9:11. (**9**) **Fallen angels cast out into the earth.** Rev. 12:7–10. See Elizabeth Clare Prophet, *Forbidden Mysteries of Enoch: The Untold Story of Men and Angels,* containing all the Enoch texts, including the Book of Enoch and the Book of the Secrets of Enoch, Summit University Press, pp. 63–67; and *Planet Earth: The Future Is to the Gods,* 3-audiocassette album, A8056, $19.50 (add $.90 for postage). (**10**) **Air signs and air chakras.** Aquarius, Gemini, Libra; third eye and seat-of-the-soul chakra. (**11**) See Sanat Kumara, *The Opening of the Seventh Seal* (1979 *Pearls of Wisdom,* vol. 22, nos. 13–48). (**12**) John 1:14. (**13**) Matt. 24:23–26; Mark 13:21, 22; Luke 17:21. (**14**) I Tim. 6:12; II Tim. 4:7.

Pearls of Wisdom®
published by The Summit Lighthouse

Vol. 30 No. 32 *Beloved Lady Master Nada* *August 9, 1987*

Freedom 1987

II

Saviour of the Seed of Sanat Kumara

The Sponsorship of a Master/Disciple Nation

I bring to you, my beloved students of the Sixth Ray, good tidings and peace and great joy. For truly the Saviour is come this day in the Person of Jesus, and saints and Masters of the Sixth Ray.

Elohim Peace and Aloha now above this place have come for a continuity of purpose in all these things which have been spoken from on high since the beginning of the consecration of this Heart of the Inner Retreat.[1]

Therefore, I AM Nada. And I come from our etheric retreat over Arabia, that extensive place of light which does focus over the Middle East a guardian action of the Cosmic Christ consciousness that does hold in check, mind you, the untoward darkness of laggard evolutions abiding there.

Beloved, were it not for this retreat of beloved Jesus, were it not for his descent into this area of the world (truly the darkest place of the planet), I tell you this day, the fallen ones and laggard evolutions who were encamped there two thousand years ago, even a half a million years ago, should have wreaked far greater havoc on this planet. Thus, but for the Son of God, you would see a history of a planet Earth equal even to that of Maldek or Hedron.[2]

Understand, then, the meaning of the coming of this Saviour Jesus Christ, whom I succeed as Chohan on the Sixth Ray. Understand that those who perceive the law of Sanat Kumara and the path of chelaship under the Great Guru have even a more profound recognition of Jesus Christ [as] the Saviour than those who claim him in their modes of Christianity. For your understanding of the person of this our brother of Light, our most blessed Teacher, does go far back, far back into antiquity as he also passed through Venus and heard the call of the Ancient of Days and responded.

Thus, beloved, you may claim him the Saviour, even in this hour, in a profound conversion to this Lord Jesus with the understanding of his mantle that you may wield, with the understanding of the scepter of his authority and the sword of which he said, "I came not to send peace, but a sword."[3] How oft is this quoted by the clergymen who preach their peace for the very reason that they fear to take up the sword even in the hour when Jesus said to his disciples, "It is indeed time to take the sword."*

This sword of the Spirit that you wield in Sanat Kumara's name must not be underestimated, for the power of the Word is incisive. And as the armies of the LORD on the etheric plane do go after the base neglect of humanity by these fallen ones, so you must see yourselves as the true soldiers of the Cosmic Christ moving into battle with the Archangels in a very specific and particular strategy for the focusing of Light and the powerful decree in those areas where the enemies of mankind go unchecked—for none dare challenge them, beloved!

Therefore, let those who know the power of the Spirit and the sacred fire challenge Evil where Evil is, call a spade a spade and not deny the reality of the sinister force even while you observe your very loved ones devoured by the influences of that force.

I am privileged to speak to you during the two-week period when you come for study[4] to my retreat that is Jesus' retreat. Thus, we gather here [in the Heart of the Inner Retreat] today, having gathered there last night. For ours is a continuity of teaching in the universities of the Spirit, as Above so below, beloved.

Therefore, see how the love for Jesus, as the one who came to save the seed of Sanat Kumara who had lost the memory of the inner vow and their divine intent, is so much greater on the part of these than the love of those who never knew him prior to his Galilean mission.

See how much more grateful are the ones forgetful[5] who also knew him in the beginning ("Before Abraham was, I AM"[6]), how much more is the gratitude of those who also came to be world teachers and then were turned astray by the fallen angels/archdeceivers, by comparison to the new lifewaves of the sixth root race who claim him as Saviour and Avatar yet have not known the pain of such separation. [And they loved much for they are forgiven much (Luke 7:47).]

Blessed ones, are ye not all called to his heart? Does he not call

*Jesus said, "He that hath no sword, let him sell his garment and buy one." Luke 22:35–38. The spiritual meaning of *sword* is Sacred Word, or Spoken Word, signifying that the sword that is wielded by the Christed ones is the power of the spoken Word in defense of the sacredness of Life.

you to wash your feet this day[7]—this day that is the celebration of the education of the heart of the students of our Montessori International?[8]

Lo, he comes. And he comes with the ten thousand saints of Sanat Kumara.[9] For a pillar of illumination's flame is erected in the wilderness of America, not by angels or Cosmic Beings or Ascended Masters, but by Keepers of the Flame and Lightbearers of the world who have seen and heard and known and who themselves, each one a golden flame of the torch of the Goddess of Liberty, a petal of the flame of Gautama Buddha's heart, do now comprise this pillar of illumined action, do embody it, do welcome the Sons of the Central Sun.

Therefore, my beloved, as these preparations took place by Elohim and cosmic forces, preparations, then, for a mighty tunnel of light between the retreat of Lord Jesus and the Western Shamballa,[10] the Elohim Peace and Aloha did set the forcefield for this action of Light which is so quickly reflected mercurially midst elemental life.

Now see how earth changes shall also come in the twinkling of an eye. And see how the Lord Jesus with Gautama and Kuthumi have conspired to fulfill a great dream. Even as there was established a half year ago that highway of light to Lake Titicaca from the Retreat of the Divine Mother over the Royal Teton Ranch,[11] so *the same highway of light is now extended to the retreat of the Lord Jesus over Saudi Arabia and the entire Holy Land and the Middle East.*

It is expedient, beloved. For I tell you the Light must flow to hold the balance against war, and for this Light you have called through the day and the night.

We have seen how so many have sacrificed their hours, their free time, to stand and still stand to give these decrees. Where, then, they could not be answered according to your calls—for the recalcitrant ones would not and could not, by the very dye of their natures, bend the knee, confess the Cosmic Christ, and repent of their deeds—all of this energy invoked by the science of the Word and placed before the Lords of Karma has resulted in this dispensation.

You might say, beloved, that each and every one of you who has decreed on the subjects so indicated by Saint Germain is part and portion of a highway that is built of your very lifestreams. It is of pure gold, this funnel of light. See it, then, as it crosses the Atlantic and goes to the very heart of that geographical location [the etheric retreat of Jesus which John the Beloved beheld, saying, "And I, John, saw the holy city, new Jerusalem, coming down from God out of heaven..." (Rev. 21:2)].

The Lord's purpose, then, is that all calls descending there should be for the fulfillment of the Saviour's mission in you as you fulfill the necessary calling on the Sixth Ray of Ministration and Service to hold the balance and to cap the Darkness that could come forth out of the extreme anger of these lifewaves [of the Middle East and the entire Arab world]—anger against America, anger against the true Light and the true Avatars, anger against the Divine Woman, beloved.

Therefore know that your calls are instantaneously physically manifest there by this highway of Light as though you were physically standing there. So it is also true of the dispensation to Lake Titicaca. Forget it not. For these tunnels of Light are established at great cost to heaven above and to you here below.

That cost, then, is repaid by you as you give the calls and therefore prove the usefulness of the dispensation—and of the dispensation as a means to averting war and calamities untold. Thus it is for the mitigation of that which is projected upon the earth that we are about our Father's business.

On the return current of your devotions, beloved, there does come back from our retreat the full blessings of the Lord Christ, his Teachings as given to the inner circle of disciples, his Presence here and there simultaneously as he with Kuthumi and those of us who serve on the seven rays teach you day by day here at Maitreya's Mystery School.

So, then, beloved, the Elohim attend your voice and your answer to Chamuel's call. May the great chalice abuilding in the Heart out of the crystal fire of your heart chakras reach those levels where Elohim may truly ensoul a planet.[12] And then we will see what answer is forthcoming from the Cosmic Council.

Now I would speak to you of the souls of Light who have come forth from higher octaves to minister to Life. And so I speak, then, of the City of Light—a city of light, beloved, beyond your awareness or this world.

Long, long ago souls of Light stepped forth from that city to descend into these octaves. Blessed ones, these were volunteers. Many of them came to earth and they remain in the annals of earth's history the great Lights, the innovators, those who have opened a door that none other could open. For they did carry in their causal bodies a dispensation of the LORD God to deliver to a people not merely an intellectual idea or a plan for human improvement but a molecule of light which when delivered through the individual to certain hearts would initiate and expand a new culture, an age, an awareness of government.

The most fundamental of these dispensations, beloved, is

that of freedom itself. Time there was, after the descent of souls of earth to the darkest depths, that none knew or perceived the meaning of freedom nor had a desire for it.

Blessed hearts, in some quarters of the earth today there are those who would rather be told what to do, as cattle, than to have to think of how and what to do each day. They have become conditioned, almost as computers, to being tied to a vast mind that is the anti-Mind, fully content, then, to be daily filled by that mind to perform functionally their duties and responsibilities. They fear the cutting of that umbilical cord whereby they might be responsible for their own life and well-being, direction, self-determination.

Thus, beloved, I speak in fundamental terms. Sanat Kumara, the great bearer of the Light of freedom, and his Sons, most notably Saint Germain, have come to teach a people to understand that freedom is a treasure and a gift that can be lost. Realize, then, that as the memory of freedom was once lost in the earth, so it can be lost again especially through the philosophies of the fallen angels who sit in the seats of notoriety and authority in the universities, in the governments and in the economies, distorting the true knowledge of freedom.

Freedom, then, is powerful as a flaming flame that cannot be quenched, fragile as a feather that should escape from an angel wing in flight. Blessed hearts, it is the love of freedom, the love of the ministration of freedom, the love to teach freedom and all its applications in all fields that has sparked once again creative intelligence in the earth.

This has come to be renewed again and again by these souls of Light who came forth from this ancient city of light and therefore were heard to say, "We seek no continuing city here."[13] For they remembered, beloved; they remembered their City of Light and desired only to be pilgrims to deliver from their hearts an ampule of oil vouchsafed to them by Sanat Kumara and the Father/Mother sponsor of this city. To deliver it, then, to break it open within the secret chamber of the heart of those chosen was their mission.

And so there have been others to whom the oil has been given and who have passed it on again and again until a whole world has been filled with the knowledge of the LORD. But many among them, beloved, took from the originators the oil. And they said, "We will take this knowledge but use it to our own devices. Now that we have the knowledge, we need not the oil or the messenger who came bearing the oil."

And therefore the knowledge was kept. And yet, by the very absence of the holy oil, it became a materialistic knowledge without the fire of the Spirit. It was misused for purposes of humanism, for the perpetuation, modification and engineering of humanity and all civilization until it was no more.

And thus, beloved, there was the rejection of the Guru/Chela relationship. Every Son of Sanat Kumara did preach his name, his love and the Great Hierarchy of Light. Thus, deliberately they [the interlopers] said, "We have no need to give obeisance to a chain of command of beings of Light. We will do what we will."

Therefore the few retained the lamp of knowledge. And the rest took with them the fragments which were a sufficiency. For so powerful is the vastness of the knowledge of Sanat Kumara that even crumbs from the Master's table should endure and sustain civilizations for thousands of years.

People have made the simple statement that today there is a science without the true religion or the true communion with God that is necessary to be responsible for the uses of that science. You can see, beloved, that a little bit of religion and a few hours or less a week set aside for worship have naught to do with a path whereby the heart does burn by virtue of its oneness with this hierarchical chain of Light that passes through the heart of Sanat Kumara and unto the Great Central Sun, with all of the Great White Brotherhood serving this earth coming under the canopy of this One, this Ancient of Days.

Blessed ones, the sponsorship, therefore, of America by Saint Germain was the sponsorship of Sanat Kumara and with him that of Surya of the God Star. That sponsorship was that this land (and if all of North America should so elect) should be, then, a Master/Disciple nation. Into the midst of this nation Saint Germain was sent as the most likely one to whom the reincarnated twelve tribes should respond, they themselves being a part of those who had forgot.

It is a long history, beloved. And we who are of the Lords of Karma and of the Seven Rays are, you might say, somewhat sentimental as we look upon your faces and we look into the hearts of Keepers of the Flame worldwide and we see those who are awakened once again with a fervor of mission and the realization of what is to be done in this hour. . . .

. . . Let one and all be sealed now according to the inner vow to Saint Germain[14] made and taken and to be fulfilled. With what measure ye mete, it shall be meted unto you.[15]

We the legions of the Sixth Ray stand with all who stand with Saint Germain.

I AM Nada, truly of the heart of Love's discipline, and I do impart the Ruby Ray Path in the name of the Ancient of Days. Amen.

This dictation was delivered June 28, 1987. For notes, see pp. 377–78.

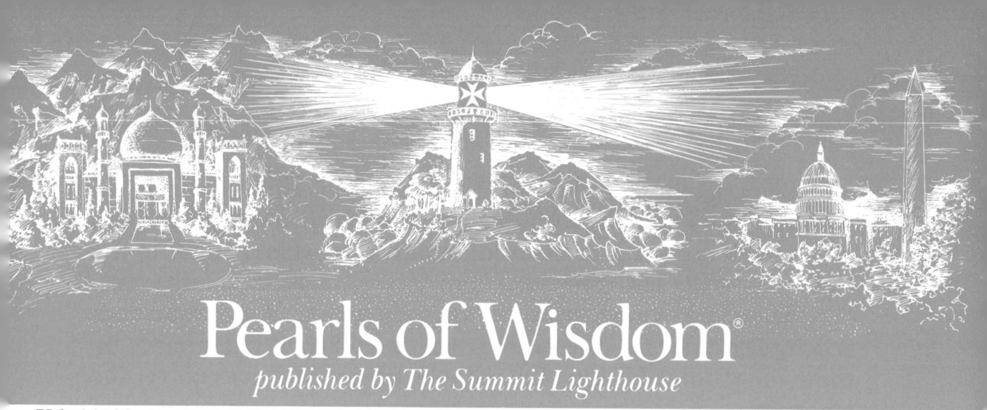

Vol. 30 No. 33 *Beloved Surya* *August 16, 1987*

Freedom 1987

III

The Drawing of the Line of Sirius

The Four and Twenty Elders over America

Ho! Ho! Ho! The God Star Sirius calls, *Ho! Ho! Ho!*

Therefore, Cry halt! ye angels of the living Word. Cry halt! I say. For they shall not pass who move against the Lightbearers of earth.

And I AM Surya of the God Star. And I come representing the Cosmic Council. Let, therefore, the Four and Twenty Elders speak.

In the circle of fire, in the center of sapphire, in the center of Light, so a molecule, beloved, can contain the All. I AM of the dimensionless, fathomless realm. I AM, in a word, here and there.

I come on a number of missions, one, therefore, being to seal that soul whom I sent forth and to seal in light and its brightness the companion. Therefore with the sapphire, the ruby and the diamond a destiny is sealed for the raising up of America.

Therefore see, beloved, as in my hands I take this nation and this I AM Race and I hold it aloft for an interval apart from Death and Hell. I hold it, beloved, before the God of very gods.

It is an offering, sapphire blue and white fire, tributaries of Ruby Ray. Thus, for the distribution of the river of Light, see, then, how this land, so consecrated in the God Star, is the resting place of those who did come forth from Sirius long, long, long time ago.

Therefore, ye angels, silence Death and Hell by the *Ho! Ho! Ho!*

Therefore, from out the Cosmic Council we see step forth this day the spokesman [of the Karmic Board], the Goddess of Liberty. She, then, does take her hand and dip into the sea of the God Star. With the dipping of the hand, beloved, there are the glistening drops of waters signifying, as they drop, the passing of eras, eras of righteousness and unrighteousness. And yet with the hand moistened she does draw a line.

Beloved, those of the God Star in whose heart there blooms the blue rose know the meaning, then, of the drawing of the line of Sirius. It is a sealing, beloved, of past eras when neither to the right nor to the left these may come.*

Therefore, know, beloved, that there is a word that does accomplish this end. The word, then, is spoken at inner levels by the great goddess Liberty. Let there be silence as it does quiver the ethers. [31-sec. pause]

The Four and Twenty Elders have formed a circle of light over America. They are dressed in shimmering, transparent white robes trimmed in sapphire blue cloth. They wear helmets that are as crowns, weighty with sapphire and diamond.

Truly the Four and Twenty wearing their crowns, beloved, do demonstrate the royalty of their origin. And they do contact in this hour the original seed of Light of Sirius who have kept that seed, who have maintained the Christ consciousness and Light. There is a reinforcement of Lightbearers in the earth, beloved.

Each one bears the sapphire cobalt-blue chalice. And thus it is a cup ceremony that does take place—the circle of twenty-four, my hands holding the continent, [which is] presented, then, to the Cosmic Council, and the power of the God Star in the center of the circle.

The molecule of Light is where we dwell. And so shalt thou when in right-mindfulness of Sirius thou dost know that the Mind of God is essential in order to grow, to embody, to be that sound of *Home.*

By the sound of Home now resonating in your very bones, beloved, there is the reestablishing of the tie of Sirius by sound and a soundless sound. It is a vibration you have longed for, sought for, remembered, yet somehow could not duplicate or recover. Out of this sound were the worlds created of those who descended from the Central Sun. Thus, the offering of the Four and Twenty Elders is reinforcement to those lifestreams of the Order of the Blue Rose.

[intonations, 24 seconds]

The drawing of the line of Sirius is a containment rightly deserved by those who have contained Light and restrained the Darkness and the dark ones by their grace, unassuming air and sweet simplicity. Thus, I salute the Keepers of the Flame of the God Star. I salute Gautama, Lord of the World, and Helios and Vesta. I salute the Christ of each one.

My pillar of fire, sealed within a pillar iridescent of substance

*The drawing of the line of Sirius is an action taken by the Cosmic Council for the sealing of the records of past eras and civilizations of a planet in order to 'buy time', or give a reprieve to the Lightbearers engaged in Armageddon. This sealing prevents, by cosmic edict from Alpha and Omega, the evil momentums of the fallen ones from being outpictured to their advantage in the present. However, it does not cancel what has already been unleashed upon this and previous centuries, nor does it cancel the karma thereof. This must be diffused by the fervent calls and dynamic decrees of the embodied Lightbearers. The drawback to such a dispensation is that "neither to the right nor to the left" do they come—which means that all is sealed—"eras of righteousness and unrighteousness"—so that being spared the evil neither can mankind inherit the good: all is sealed, for the tares and the wheat are intertwined.

unknown to man, is a pillar that passes through the entire earth from this place. This pillar of deep fiery blue has a circumference occupying this Heart area. Such an electrode, beloved, has not heretofore in known history been applied to earth. Its purposes are infinite.

By your sensitivity you will know that it is an integrating force and forcefield. It is a repellent, also, to aliens who have not espoused the cause of earth's freedom nor the freedom of the Lightbearers. Its presence allows the holy angels to be repolarized and magnetized to the God Star without journeying there, thus expending needless energy (time/space, as you would call it) going to and fro.

It is the urgent need of the hour that impels my presence. Hear the sound of the weight of Sirius in my voice, which I impart to a world fragmented by discord of every kind. Listen then to my son who will expose that discord to you on the morrow.* And know that I have sent him to turn around the entire course of Death and Hell as it has opened its bowels and spewed out upon this earth this discord of rock and roll unto its intended destruction. I speak of the misuse of sound and rhythm.

Blessed hearts, all must be instruments and therefore join him as one Body of Light to defeat once and for all the 'rock music', so-called, of the fallen angels on this earth. The foundations of hell have entered society at every level through the misuse of sound systems, electronics, and technology.

Know, then, beloved, that there are roots deeper and deeper that have extended into the astral body and the physical body of the earth that come from a sinister force even beyond the Pleiades. Why should they bother with this star? Simply because the Lightbearers gathered here and in incarnation now, if quickened by the Law and the Truth, could deliver the mandate of Victory to earth in very short time, such as twenty-four hours, twenty-four weeks, twenty-four months.

This they know. And they know that the Victory of earth does become the presentation to Sanat Kumara of a ball of light that he can run with, touching systems of Matter undreamed of by you.

There is indeed an interval as beings and systems wait with bated breath to see the outcome of earth's destiny. Truly, beloved, you who have gathered for this time are men and women and lifestreams of an ancient destiny.

Therefore I say, have it! Have your destiny! Will it. Love it. Know it. And do not let go of it! For who would be the one who in letting go should defeat a world? I, Surya, must quickly say, "Not I, LORD. By thy grace I shall stand with earth as my Electronic Presence fills this electrode of Light."

*An exposé was delivered by Rev. Sean C. Prophet on "Rock and Roll in America," July 2, 1987.

Therefore, I express gratitude to every heart who contains the vision, who did secure this Inner Retreat and therefore seal it in the name of the Great White Brotherhood. May its purposes not be neglected for others.

Let every lifestream who has felt the call of the Teaching know that the Teaching is not enough. You must have and hold and wed the Teacher. Know, then, that Ascended Masters and Cosmic Beings are gathering their own.

I represent God-government to earth. I have answered the call to place the grid of light with Hercules and the Great Divine Director, Archangel Michael and the beloved Son Morya. This inner blueprint does glow with a fire, imparting of itself the means wherewith to accomplish its purpose.

See and understand that legions of the First Ray come to hold the earth as though in the two hands of the Almighty One. This holding action, beloved, may buy time for you if you will decree it so.

No dispensation, therefore, *can be sealed except by the daily decree.* It will not hurt you to give the mantra I have dictated to my Messenger Mark to the God Surya for a fortnight and more to reinforce in the physical octave that which I AM THAT I AM. According to the Cosmic Council, then, *only that which is accepted, reinforced and sustained by the embodied Lightbearers can be retained for the permanent good of earth and her evolutions.*

If ever you entertained the notion of being a spiritual devotee, now is the hour to indulge that notion! Indulge it, I say. Drink its cup to the fullest. Do not postpone. The pillar I have set, you must individualize and become. The line that is drawn is for the sealing of a mystery and the opening of another.

The earth fits in my pocket.

What will you do, O mortal, when Immortality is nigh? Will ye choose to die or perhaps quest that Life? Will ye understand that implements of war and the knife will never suffice? These take life, reinforce mortality unto banality and nihilism.

What are these diseases conveyed by comets and falling stars?

What are these that have plagued the races of mankind?

I hurl into the midst of plague a white-fire sphere, that those of the Light who are touched by it shall repel it and consume it [the plague]. Unto those for whom plague is the judgment the white sphere does reinforce the judgment, that quickly the Darkness might be collected and removed and a new era appear, and a breath of fresh air and a light.

I AM Surya, known as God of Might! I ascend now to heights beyond. I seal you, for enough *is* enough! *Light! Light! Light!*

Darkness, be still! Be still! *Be still!* [26-sec. standing ovation]

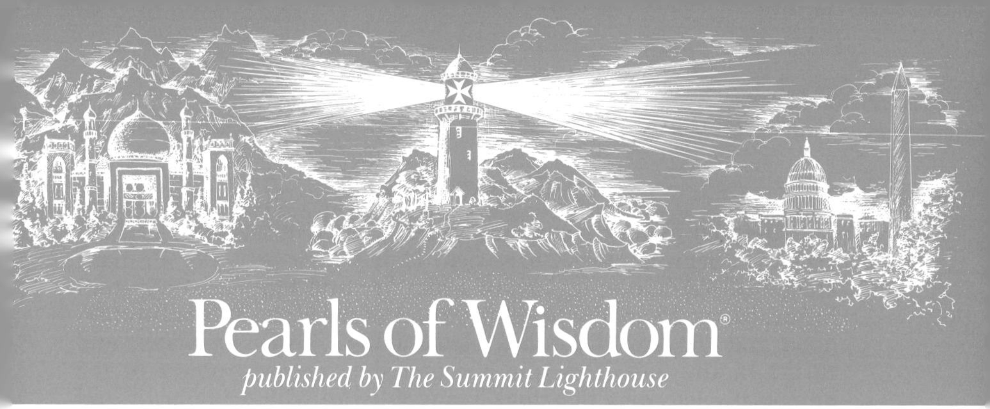

Vol. 30 No. 34 *Beloved Hercules* *August 23, 1987*

Freedom 1987

IV

A Stitch in Time

To Summon Earth to Divine Purpose

I AM Hercules of the Sun! I AM Amazonia!

Our Victory is in the heart of the Sun.

We come, then, to seal it in the hearts of the chelas of the First Ray of God's will and to reinforce, intensify, expand and protect the offering of Surya, the Four and Twenty Elders and of each lifestream who will value his own participation in a planetary and cosmic ritual in the heart of the sapphire of God's will.

Take, then, the blue leaves. Let their words be impressed within. Let the chain of Light begin. Let the winners win. Let the runners run. Let the singers sing. Let each one fulfill the whole bill of his divine calling.

Be thy true Self and never fret, for I AM Hercules. I AM Elohim as the will of God. By your presence I send through your body chalices—which I do qualify with sapphire diamond light—a current of the First Ray to summon all earth to divine purpose.

[10-sec. intonation]

The sound I have sounded in that instant, beloved, reached the Central Sun and did return as a cosmic stitch in time through this heart. So make thy heart a chalice of God's will and be those who sewed up the garment of earth with a stitch in time. I, Hercules, the cosmic tailor, will sew it through your heart. Be ready for the piercing of the needle. For no fight or fair maid or planet were ever won without the shedding of the drop of blood.

By the preciousness of thy Christhood let earth endure. Thy Christhood is precious as the sapphire that does hold the balance.

Ho! Ho! Ho! Legions of Light of the First Ray, return, then, to formation!

Beloved Surya

Beloved mighty victorious Presence of God, I AM in me, my very own beloved Holy Christ Self, Holy Christ Selves of all mankind, beloved Surya, legions of white fire and blue lightning from Sirius, beloved Lanello, the entire Spirit of the Great White Brotherhood and the World Mother, elemental life—fire, air, water, and earth! In thy name, by and through the magnetic power of the immortal, victorious threefold flame of Truth within my heart and the heart of God in the Great Central Sun, I decree:

1. Out from the Sun flow thy dazzling bright
Blue-flame ribbons of flashing diamond Light!
Serene and pure is thy Love,
Holy radiance from God above!

Refrain: Come, come, come, Surya dear,
By Thy Flame dissolve all fear;
Give to each one Security
In the bonds of Purity;
Flash and flash Thy Flame through me,
Make and keep me ever free!

2. Surya dear, beloved one
From the mighty Central Sun,
In God's name to Thee we call:
Take dominion over all!

3. Out from the heart of God you come,
Serving to make us now all one—
Wisdom and Honor do you bring,
Making the very soul to sing!

4. Surya dear, beloved one,
From our Faith then now is spun
Victory's garment of invincible gold,
Our soul's great triumph to ever uphold!

And in full Faith I consciously accept this manifest, manifest, manifest! (3x) right here and now with full Power, eternally sustained, all-powerfully active, ever expanding, and world enfolding until all are wholly ascended in the Light and free!

Beloved I AM! Beloved I AM! Beloved I AM!

Give this decree to Almighty God through the Electronic Presence of Surya with you. Give it nine times daily (or more) for 14 days or 33 or until your victorious fulfillment of your divine plan on earth. Write a personal letter to Surya and place it on your altar for three days, then burn it. Offer personal prayers to the heart of God in the Great Central Sun for guidance in all your plans, projects and decisions.

"The Summit Lighthouse Sheds Its Radiance O'er All the World to Manifest as Pearls of Wisdom." These dictations by Surya and Hercules were **delivered** through the Messenger of the Great White Brotherhood Elizabeth Clare Prophet on **Wednesday, July 1, 1987,** at *FREEDOM 1987* in the Heart of the Inner Retreat at the **Royal Teton Ranch, Montana.**

Pearls of Wisdom®
published by The Summit Lighthouse

Vol. 30 No. 35 *Beloved Archangel Michael* *August 30, 1987*

Freedom 1987

V

The Chela of the First Ray

For the Reinforcement and the Realignment of the Remnant of God

Legions of the Faithful and True, I summon you now. Stand, then, in formation round about this company and above.

I AM Michael, Prince of the Archangels. I salute the Keepers of the Flame in the name of Saint Germain! [45-sec. applause]

The mind of an Archangel *is* the Mind of God. So be it.

My purpose in coming is to reinforce Light.* Thus, the builders of [from among] my bands come to strengthen areas of the four lower bodies where the vessels are too weak to hold more Light. Thus, repetitive is the dissonance that gains entrance to the house of the chela.

I come, then, having entered the heart of the psychologists of the Spirit that I might determine why the chelas of El Morya and my own may not swiftly increase a greater comprehension, a greater containment and an all-enveloping Presence of the First Ray.

To be pillars of fire as the divine rocket bearing the missiles of divine grace does require an armour of Light more intense than ye have sought, beloved. Therefore, let your calls to me be not alone for the reinforcement of an armour and a pillar of blue flame but for realignment, for the breaking up of those patterns of self—human habits that are crooked as crooked can be and therefore do not as a matrix hold Light.

We desire to move forward with this company. It is necessary to understand that by the violet flame and the Elohim of God who are the Creators of form (and the Lords of form and the

*Light when capitalized stands for the Christ consciousness that is the true light of the body and the eye. See Matt. 6:22, 23.

Lords of mind) there is an alchemy that can be fulfilled and called forth. One must recognize the need for the old bottles to be broken and for the new bottles to appear.[1] This has been said but it must become a conscious awareness as a helmet that is worn. One must understand that when vessels are called for, the vessels must be of crystal light, they must be a chalice.

Blessed ones, the rock may break the old matrix, but far better that it be transmuted by the violet flame. For some the change called death has been the only reprieve from an untoward and unsuitable vessel. This is caused many times by pre-birth cycles or by accidents where one no longer has full faculties of the mind nor the ability, the resiliency to refashion the desire body.

Blessed hearts, you are not stuck in your cups unless you allow it! The genes can be transmuted by the Cosmic Christ. The call must be made and the visualization of Light in all the chakras and the intoning of the Word.

But I tell you, beloved, change must come if we are to save a planet through the Keepers of the Flame. There must be the inner self-correction by the Mind of Christ. Do not allow the old momentums [to cause you] to resist the coming of the Lord of the First Ray, the legions of the First Ray, the Messengers of the First Ray.

Should there be a battle, beloved, each time there is a necessity to move one quarter of an inch so that the light of Christ might enter your heart and fill it? I say nay! Do not battle the First Ray but embrace it. Understand that the First-Ray Masters and rulers of Cosmos do contain the power of God needed to swallow up the anti-power stolen by the forces of Darkness East and West now pitted against the children of the Sun and the Lightbearer.

Beloved hearts, understand that world crisis accrues from the following equation: that the fallen ones have stolen the power of the Lightbearer and of Almighty God and that they have channeled it into an abuse of power in technology and science, implements of war and all manner of governmental and economic manipulation; and that correspondingly, the Lightbearers who have a threefold flame have not sought the power of God or to be in alignment with the will of God as much as they should. Their seeking and their desiring for that power and that light has not been as great as the seeking of the fallen ones in their desire to pervert it and subvert it.

Therefore, in view of this we are faced with the following: The Lightbearers must seek and know the will of God, sacrifice to embody that will of God and fear not walking away from those cohorts that lead one down the primrose path of self-destruction.

Blessed hearts, I come with blue lightning and a sword to cut you free from human sympathy. But, beloved, you must be willing to be cut free.

With compassion in my heart, then, I acquaint you with the rigors and the sternness of the office of chela of the First Ray of God's will. May you know it. May you espouse it. And may you understand that could a body of Lightbearers and Keepers of the Flame worldwide so uphold in the earth that power of the First Ray of Alpha, no force would be able to override it or exceed it, beloved. You could not be victimized by invisible forces or those in your own world.

Do you understand that what it takes to succeed as a chela of the First Ray is the simple and basic totality of surrender from within to the will of God? The will of God is a shaft of sacred fire composed of that blue sapphire and white crystal from the heart of the Great Central Sun.

Thus, God Surya has shown you a vision of the Four and Twenty Elders.[2] Do you understand that as they comprise the nucleus of the Cosmic Council these ones of the sacred fire represent the epitome of the embodiment of that First Ray?

Do you understand, beloved, that the diamond-shining Mind of God is a quality of the First Ray as is the mercury diamond-shining Mind of God that is upheld by God Mercury? Do you understand that it is the First Ray that the fallen angels have sought to take from you, and that the spinelessness in America this day is evidence that they have somewhat succeeded in this round?

Blessed ones, I speak to you in an hour of national and international urgency beyond your reckoning. And thus, I have hastened the Messenger to receive this dictation, for I have absented myself from hither and yon in council meetings where my presence is required to hold the balance against untoward forces and decisions accelerating in Death and Hell the withdrawal of that maximum [military] protection that ought to be afforded Europe and that theater.[3]

Beloved ones of Light, Maximus does step forward. And he does hold the balance for the coming of Alpha in a mighty star of light over this Heart of the Inner Retreat. And he does communicate and beam to me now that you may apply to him for "the Maxim Light." But you must understand the path of chelaship and receive the interior correction of the Christ Mind and receive all emissaries of God, of the heavenly hosts and of the Messengers beneath, that you might quickly respond and not resist the will of God that is in the heart of the Maxim Light.

O beloved, understand that there is too much resistance in the spiritual people of the planet, even their resistance in the hearing of my Word and in the hearing of this Messenger—as though any human or mortal could convey the sacred fire and the power of God and the dispensations that have been delivered. Beloved ones, it is no time for human questioning and fear and doubt, for these are the antithesis of my living presence and the Presence of God which I bear.

Thus, beloved, angel ministrants will tarry with you. Would you become, then, a universal company of the embodiment of the white fire and sapphire jewel light? O beloved, would you experience this light from the heart of God in the Great Central Sun?

I tell you, there is no greater gift you could lay upon the altar of Alpha and Omega and the Almighty One. For America is wanting in those individuals of a fiery heart and light who will truly hold the balance for those who serve physically in the military and in the defense of the nation.

Blessed hearts of Light, look at El Morya. *Look at El Morya!* I tell you, beloved, he is still among the lonely ones. For many of those who call themselves chelas of El Morya have not yet received from him the engrafted Word.[4]

Would you, beloved, receive from an Archangel an empowerment this day? I tell you, there must be that inner discipline that does not repeat over and over and over again those silly mistakes, those flaws of character which, each and every time you indulge them, become, therefore, a wedge. And through that wedge the forces of anti-Archangel Michael, anti-God, anti-El Morya come through you. And I tell you, without self-discipline enlightened by the Holy Spirit, you are just as easily a tool of that force as you are a tool of Almighty God.

O chelas of the Light, I speak to you, then, as the LORD God did speak to the children of Israel. There is a remnant [of the seed of Sanat Kumara].[5] But among them there is yet that residual substance of that recalcitrance and of that rebellion. Beloved hearts, you have a love that is beyond all telling and a devotion. Can you not encapsulate it now in that fiery blue-flame will? Can you not rejoice that you have a Messenger who will stop along her way to correct you into the very core of that erroneous state of consciousness which you do not understand or will not understand?

O fill the vacancies, seraphim of God!

O angels of my bands, fill the vacancies now!

O beloved ones, heed the warning and the call when the Messenger does speak to you, for you know not the day and the hour of the appearing of the descent of your karma when the Law will require the breaking of the old matrix. Be prepared, then, by violet flame. Let there be the softening [by violet flame]. Let there be the inner cleansing [by violet flame].

And let all of you respond to my call to come to the World Teachers' Seminar following this conference, for it shall be taught by the Seven Mighty Archangels. For we are the Teachers of mankind. And we are demanding, therefore, that there be an excellence of spirit in the chelas of the First Ray who shall follow the Lord Jesus and Kuthumi and Maitreya and Gautama Buddha!

We have heard your call for the deliverance of a planet. Therefore, we come to respond to that call. We would deliver this planet through you, beloved. But you must come up higher. Whatever your spiritual attainment or whatever you may think it is, beloved, you need the Law. You need the exercise thereof. You need to attend our seminars and not be laid back in the opinion that you know all there is to know!

I, Archangel Michael, the first Teacher of mankind in these dispensations, speak to you, then. Do not measure yourselves after those in the valleys who have hardly even a grain of divine awareness, if any at all.

Blessed hearts, you are not of this world. And the world where you expect to go expects much of you and expects more than you are giving. For you may give, beloved, of your supply and your abundance and your love. But we desire to see you obedient to your own inner blueprint, to your own inner diamond-shining Mind of God and to the Mighty I AM Presence with you and, above all, having the sense of the mighty holiness of God in your midst and the holiness in the presence of the Archangels.

Do not tarry, beloved. For the time is thinning as though two walls were coming together, and you must pass through in time. Therefore, realize that for each and every individual here, there is a cosmic timetable. And I, Archangel Michael, declare to you now: that timetable is upon you! And my angels do read to you, with an angel of the Keeper of the Scrolls, the record of your lifestream to this date that you might have that fair warning as to what karma is coming upon you and what is the opportunity of the great cosmic light that will assist you in diverting and consuming that karma.

You are no exception, beloved. There is world karma. There is individual karma. The individual karma must descend or you will be left behind, beloved ones. For, you see, the forward movement of the etheric body of this planet is what we seek. Insomuch as the physical is temporal and in time and space, it is our mission to call you forth, beloved, and to accelerate your hearts that you might move forward with the etheric cycles of this planet which are already in the process of [outpicturing] the great golden age.

We desire to see you move forward with the etheric retreats of the Great White Brotherhood. Thus, the dispensation of the opening of the universities of the Spirit has been given to you. But not all have made the call. Not all have availed themselves. Not all have checked the schedules of the fourteen-day cycles or even made a single call to that Lord of one of the rays to be taken into the very heart of his inner retreat.[6]

Beloved ones, these dispensations are real! They are active! They must be entered into! You must not lay your head to rest at night without that fervent call to me and to the Lord of the Ray [to whose retreat you are invited to attend classes according to the schedule].

We are trying to accelerate you, beloved. But we cannot do it for you. We have done everything else but do it for you, beloved hearts of Light. Realize this and know it now. For the invincible majesty of the God flame is upon you. But it cannot descend, for it will devour you unless you first submit that human creation into the violet flame.

I call you forth, therefore, in the understanding that this world of Lightbearers is moving on with or without you. Whether or not you have ascended, whether or not you have attended this conference, this world is moving onward. It is moving forward toward the Great Central Sun. And it is the etheric octave that calls you.

And therefore, there must be a pulling up of the rear. There must be a transmutation in yourself of the bottom ten percent of your own karma, the most dense thereof, and the dweller on the threshold, and so forth, as you have been taught. We are seeking to elevate you out of the levels of Death and Hell by the transmutation from within yourself of all ties to those levels.

Thus, we have brought you up the mountain of God, for this is a place which those in embodiment who are sponsoring this activity have reached in their own inner attainment at the etheric octaves. I speak of the Messenger and others with her.

Therefore, understand that the whole Body of God must be elevated to this octave. And if you would live in the etheric octave and in the Retreat of the Divine Mother and in the golden cities of light, understand that there is something that must go, some hankering after the cities below and all that they contain. You cannot have both worlds! And if you choose to have both, you will have the lower, for the higher will not accept you.

Thus, understand that though the letting go may be painful, the [retaining of the] nostalgia does take up unnecessary energy and time within yourself. You must realize that the days are indeed short for the fulfillment of the cycle of your personal ascension. This world is moving on, beloved, I tell you. And those of the darkness, of nothingness, of annihilation, those who already do not exist are merely going through a disintegration spiral as you watch them [disintegrate] before your very eyes.

Do not consider, therefore, that there is even a question of a choice of your lifestream going the way of the flesh any longer. For one of these days the flesh may no longer be here. And unless you have woven that Deathless Solar Body, when you make the transition you will feel naked as [you did] when outside the Garden of Eden you no longer sensed that enveloping garment of light of the heaven world. This is the equation, beloved. This is the seriousness of the cosmic cross of white fire which I draw and I mark in this place in this hour.

Therefore, come, beloved. I have not ceased to speak to you. I have come to you in this hour as an impetus. My legions have come. And by your calls and devotions, we may now take from you that substance that has been the most recalcitrant, those things which you in your hearts desire to be delivered of.

I give you this opportunity, then, to sing that precious prayer "Eternal Father, Strong to Save" and in so singing to make attunement with my causal body, the records of my lifestream and my own sacrifice of those things that were dear to me,[7] that I might go on in the cosmic service to be ready when you should need me at this hour.

Beloved ones, there are those who need you in this hour *now!* There are those who *will* need you in an hour to come. You must be ready. And if you love enough and if you love much, you shall be ready. And if you desire to be ready, beloved ones, I am here to help you.

Therefore, during the singing of this song, I ask you to surrender consciously and out loud by the science of the spoken Word, even if it is but a whisper, those things which you are truly letting go of in this moment. Name them, beloved, during the singing of this song. I will allow it to be sung three times that you might empty your heart to me and that my angels might sweep through. And therefore on that basis we shall move forward with the balance of this conference to see how much more light we may anchor within you.

In addition, beloved, to the taking of those things that are required as sacrifice, if you make the call the angels will seek to mend the etheric sheath, the mental body, the astral body and the physical. Therefore, it is the hour to call unto the Archangels for healing of body, soul and mind. ["The Sweetest Psalm," song 285, sung three times to the melody of "Eternal Father, Strong to Save" while prayers are given aloud]

So the Light is come upon you! So, beloved, angels of the First Ray of the will of God come nigh your auras for the taking of that which is not, for the refinement of that which is, for the coalescing of atoms of light around the original blueprint. Do not be concerned if there is some physical chemicalization concerning this event in your life, for it is a cosmic surgery through the Cosmic Christ through the First Ray angels.

I AM Michael. I come. I would seal you. I shall return. For within forty-eight hours I desire to see necessary change that I might seal that which is raised up.

I AM of the blue lightning of the Sun. I AM of the First Ray. May ye be also, beloved. For my prayer is fervent and my desire is deep to draw you to the diamond heart of Morya, Michael, Mary and Lanello.

Hercules awaits in higher octaves. Now sing to him a song of liberation and rise on shafts of blue flame that you might touch the hem of Elohimic octaves and know that he who would dwell in the secret place of the Most High God must abide under the shadow of the Almighty.[8]

I AM the Archangel of the LORD! Dwell, then, neath the shadow of my wing and the I AM THAT I AM. Know Liberty and know peace.

Hail, O Elohim! Hail, Helios and Vesta! Hail, Alpha and Omega! I, Michael, in the physical body of the Messenger, salute thee from this lowly estate of the flesh that thy light might traverse through the physical atoms of earth, through all of these who are tied to the heart of Sanat Kumara, Great Guru, through her own [heart].

I AM Michael. I shall not leave them, O God. Now lead them truly to thy heart. [43-sec. applause]

"The Summit Lighthouse Sheds Its Radiance O'er All the World to Manifest as Pearls of Wisdom." Archangel Michael's dictation was **delivered** at *FREEDOM 1987* on **Friday, July 3, 1987**. (**1**) Matt. 9:16, 17; Mark 2:21, 22; Luke 5:36–38. (**2**) See p. 314, pars. 3–5. (**3**) Negotiations between the U.S. and USSR (INF Talks) to eliminate all medium-range and shorter-range ballistic missiles worldwide—especially in Europe and the Western part of the Soviet Union. (**4**) James 1:21. (**5**) **Remnant.** Isa. 10:20–22; 11:11, 12, 16; Jer. 23:3, 4; Zech. 8:6, 11, 12; Rom. 11:5. (**6**) See pp. 285–86. (**7**) See *The Lost Teachings of Jesus I,* p. 166, and Archangel Michael, December 29, 1984, "The Judgment of Peshu Alga," 1985 *Pearls of Wisdom,* vol. 28, no. 2, p. 23, par. 1. (**8**) Ps. 91:1.

Pearls of Wisdom®

published by The Summit Lighthouse

Vol. 30 No. 36 *Sean C. Prophet* *September 6, 1987*

Exposé

Rock and Roll in America

Open Warfare by the Seed of Darkness upon the Children of Light

Part I
Heavy Metal: Abuse of God-Power

I would like to address you on the war of the dragon that is being waged against the seed of Light on earth. Today it is the sons of Satan against the sons of Christ and the sons of Sanat Kumara, the Ancient of Days. This war is being waged against our youth in the form of rock music. We must tackle this dragon head-on.

We the people of America are at the point of the initiation of our Christhood where we must descend with Archangel Michael into the astral pits of Death and Hell for the binding in the name JESUS CHRIST of the foul spirits who prey upon our children and teenagers. Therefore, Keepers of the Flame, here is my exposé on "Rock and Roll in America":

Rock music was forecast in Revelation 9 as the first woe which was to come upon the earth. I choose to preface my lecture by giving you Mother's teaching on Revelation 9—a startling prophecy of the coming of the fallen angels with their rock music and drugs—recorded 2,000 years ago by John, the beloved disciple of Jesus.

> 1. And the fifth angel sounded, and I saw a star fall from heaven unto the earth: and to him was given the key of the bottomless pit.

With the sounding of the fifth angel, Archangel Raphael, John sees an angel fall from heaven who is given the key to open the bottomless pit. This sounding of the tone of karma keys the cycle of a planetary reckoning of the perversions of the Fifth Ray (including mankind's misuse of the science of sound in the third eye).*

As it is recorded in Revelation 12, certain angels called Nephilim[1] were cast out of heaven into the earth by Archangel Michael for their misdeeds before the throne of God and their blasphemy toward His Son. Upon taking embodiment midst the people of earth they went forth to make war against the remnant of the seed of the Divine Mother by

*The vibration of the Fifth Ray ranges from an emerald green to a Chinese green tinged in gold. It is the path of scientists, healers, exponents of truth, music, and mathematics in all fields. The bottomless pit is a deep canyon in the lowest level of the astral plane, called hell, where fallen angels are incarcerated.

way of carrying out their agenda of revenge against the Ancient of Days and His servant-Sons in heaven who had decreed their banishment from the heavenly courts. Their Absolute Evil carried out in the antediluvian epoch evoked upon them and their followers the LORD's judgment and the ensuing cataclysm, the Noachian Deluge, i.e., the sinking of the continent of Atlantis. Therefore, these spirits of Antichrist who perverted the sacred life-force of the Mother on Atlantis were bound by the Archangels and cast into the bottomless pit and here they have remained by edict of the Lords of Karma for approximately 11,600 years.

This judgment of the fallen angels was to afford the Children of Light and the Sons of God renewed opportunity to rise in the dominion and the mastery of the Mother flame (the ascension flame) in the seven chakras. And it was decreed that in that hour when the Lightbearers should once again have the full teaching of the Divine Mother, the Universal Christ and the Ancient of Days through Moses and the prophets, Gautama Buddha, Padma Sambhava, Confucius, Lao Tzu, Lord Jesus Christ and his apostles (as well as the instruction of the enlightened ones and the world teachers who appeared on every continent) and when they should have, by the Great Law, attained to a certain mastery on the path, these rebellious angels would be loosed out of the bottomless pit.

It was the intention of Elohim that the fallen angels should be given the opportunity to undo their evil deeds which had caused the sinking of a continent, and that if they would not repent of their deeds, the Lightbearers themselves, having the memory of their destructive misuse of sound, energy and technology, would prevent them from wreaking the same holocaust in this age.

Therefore, by 1939 at the beginning of World War II these fallen angels, bound since the days of Noah, were allowed to reincarnate and they came to their maturity in the sixties. And what they unleashed through their rock music and drugs were the momentums of the last days of Atlantis.

Many parents and teachers of the sixties failed to set an example of a path of Christhood to their sons and daughters and were themselves corrupted, although they had had 12,000 years to pursue such a path—unto this twentieth-century day of reckoning when the people of earth should be called upon to challenge once and for all the destroyers in the earth.

And therefore, when the angel fell from heaven and opened the bottomless pit, having the key to unloose both the fallen angels and their karma, all vileness erupted. As of old, they corrupted the physical plane through the rhythm and the sound of rock, and the youth followed the fallen angels—the rock stars that had long ago fallen from heaven and beguiled the sons of Jared to descend the mountain of God to the valley below.[2]

And the youth had no shepherds and they accepted no spiritual leader and they did not hear the voice of Mark Prophet crying in the wilderness, giving to them all that they needed to overcome Death and Hell and to get beyond what was unleashed to their destruction as a karmic retribution on the earth.

Therefore, the prophecy is given concerning the angel who was given the key:

> 2. And he opened the bottomless pit; and there arose a smoke out of the pit, as the smoke of a great furnace; and the sun and the air were darkened by reason of the smoke of the pit.

We have been told of the opening of the pits of Death and Hell under various areas of the planet, not one but numerous interconnecting focuses of the bottomless pit—like a labyrinth honeycombing the earth. The unlocking of the bottomless pit has allowed the fallen angels who had been sealed there to come out of these pits to take embodiment midst the people of earth. Hence, the darkening of consciousness through the rock rhythm and through marijuana, which is the smoke of the pit, the clouding of the mind through *Cannabis sativa* and cocaine, their hedonism and existentialism—and then the cloning, the programming, the penetration unto the seed of God of the genes of the Fallen One.

These rebellious angels are referred to in verse 3 as 'locusts':

> 3. And there came out of the smoke locusts upon the earth: and unto them was given power, as the scorpions of the earth have power.

Therefore, we have seen a plague of rock musicians and rock groups, and all of them venting the sounds of Hell sounding veritably like the sinewy whine of an oncoming swarm of locusts. Of the Seven Archangels who sound their seven trumpet judgments, five had sounded their tones prior to the opening of the bottomless pit. And the fallen ones have responded defiantly with their synthetic sounds and their strident tones from Hell. And those who align with Light align with Light, and those who align with Darkness align with Darkness.

And so there is a rallying of forces and there is a polarization and there is open warfare in the earth by the seed of Darkness against the Children of Light. And the Sons of God must come to their rescue before it is too late. But where are the defenders of youth? The plague of locusts is covering the earth with the Martian-originated agitation, apathy and atheism[3] of rock music and of the fallen stars and their fans. And the resonance and the reverberation of their destructive vibration is shaking the very planet from its moorings.

> 4. And it was commanded them that they should not hurt the grass of the earth, neither any green thing, neither any tree; but only those men which have not the seal of God in their foreheads.
> 5. And to them it was given that they should not kill them, but that they should be tormented five months: and their torment was as the torment of a scorpion, when he striketh a man.

You will notice that they do not have the power to kill those whose names are not written in the Book of Life but only to torment them. From this we conclude that those whose names are written in the Book of Life—the name I AM THAT I AM written in the threefold flame of their hearts (who have the seal of God in their foreheads)—cannot be touched by rock music and drugs. Or, if they encounter and even entertain the subculture of the fallen angels for a season, they are quickly healed when they are rescued by the legions of angels of the Fifth Ray who serve with the Beloved Mother Mary.

Therefore those who came out of the pit were able to rally to themselves all of mechanization man, the plastic people created by other higher-ranking hierarchies of fallen angels who were cast out of heaven and long ago took embodiment on planet earth.

But there were some who had light yet had not been sealed in their foreheads by the name I AM THAT I AM. For they had not received the Word of the Universal Christ through the servant-Sons of Sanat Kumara and therefore their third eye was not sealed with the consciousness of God and his Law. And so neither the inner vision nor the soul were protected. And these also responded, not to the true prophets teaching the way of the opening of the chakras by the eternal AUM and the soundless sound, but to the false prophets of Hell—the false gurus of the sixties and their false sounds and prophecies (the lyrics of the rock songs)—absent the internal harmony of Alpha and Omega.

Therefore the torment of the people who came under the spell of rock music was the torment of the perversion of the five secret rays, the five circles of light which cradle the heart chakra. And the torment is evident on films of early rock concerts—of young girls screaming, fainting, going into contortions, even orgasm. This takes place because the five secret rays of the virgin light of the Mother are violated and the youth are being stripped of the energy that is necessary not only for the protection of their chakras (most especially the heart), but also for the guarding of their life and of their entering in to the secret place of the Most High—which is their birthright.

Now, Scorpio is the sign of the piercing ray of the All-Seeing Eye of God. The scorpion is the lower symbol of this sign of the zodiac, the eagle being the higher. Those who have come up out of the pit purveying their rock music and drugs carry the scorpion's sting in the third eye through the perversion of sound and of the science of the Word in music. The elixir of life and the sweet nectar of the crown chakra (as well as the life-force in the base-of-the-spine chakra) are violated through hallucinogenic drugs which stimulate by the scorpion's sting, which is the sudden release of the light of the chakras by chemical induction.

> 6. And in those days shall men seek death, and shall not find it; and shall desire to die, and death shall flee from them.

Out of the pit, then, comes the Death-and-Hell vibration of the fallen ones who themselves desire to die. But they do not die. They cannot die, for they have never lived...[4]

And therefore we hear the rock groups singing about death, desiring death, calling for death, calling to Satan, and yet they die not. The candle of selfhood may have been extinguished by the blasts of their blasphemy, they may be the hollowed-out ones revived each Hallowe'en as children put a candle in a pumpkin to remember "the grateful dead"—but they still have a physical existence. They desire to be no more, to cease to exist. So until the final blackout they sell their wares of death to innocent Children of Light or other empty heads like themselves.

> 7. And the shapes of the locusts were like unto horses prepared unto battle; and on their heads were as it were crowns like gold, and their faces were as the faces of men.

The crowns of gold can be taken to mean the technology used by the rock musicians. This, taken literally, could be a radio headset microphone or, more figuratively, all of the technological paraphernalia—from amps, keyboards, and computers to elaborate lighting and stage equipment. And though they are devils they have the faces of men.

For when they were cast down into the earth, they were cast in the mold of Homo sapiens. And this is the mask we have to tear off of them.[5]

> 8. And they had hair as the hair of women, and their teeth were as the teeth of lions.

The fallen Atlanteans at the time of the sinking of the continent also had long hair and when they reincarnated they once again took up the custom of their long hair (for they had had no forward evolution in embodiment between then and now). Their hair is the sign of their rebellion against Christ. Long hair in the divine sense is a symbol—almost a badge—of attainment.

We see this in the story of Samson. When he lost his hair, he lost his power. Thus, the long-haired rockers, in keeping with their tradition of taking heaven by force,[6] seek to elevate themselves to heights of mastery they have not attained to through service to Life. Only a man having the attainment of Christhood as Jesus did may wear long hair as a woman. And their lions' teeth signify their devouring of the light of their followers and their perversion of the throat chakra.

> 9. And they had breastplates, as it were breastplates of iron; and the sound of their wings was as the sound of chariots of many horses running to battle.

Having never seen a rock star or his equipment, John the Revelator describes their guitars, drums and synthesizers as breastplates. He perceives that these fallen angels are misusing the power of their wings (their Gemini instruments)—that are of the air element and the sacred fire breath they once had from the Holy Spirit—in order to create a horrendous sound, electronically amplified, of "chariots of many horses running to battle."

If you were seeing this prophecy of twentieth-century Armageddon and hearing its sounds—seated in a cave on the isle of Patmos where John at the age of 94 wrote the Lord's revelation—how would you convey the awesomeness of this modern-day scene of Hell's angels?

> 10. And they had tails like unto scorpions, and there were stings in their tails:

And their tail is the misuse of the sacred fire of the Mother, the base chakra. And therefore they sting by the misuse of the sexual energy or by needles pumping drugs into their veins. The sting of the sexual energy when perverted through the black arts is death.

> 10. and their power was to hurt men five months.

And that five months—as cycles of putting on one's Christhood through the Sacred Heart of Jesus—goes on and on and on until there is the conclusion of each individual's initiation in the five secret rays. And if one does not ultimately pass the initiation, his heart chakra is stripped (by his own self-abuse) of the five circles of light of Elohim, of Alpha and Omega.

The number 5 also relates to precipitation by the Elohim of the Fifth Ray whereby sound results in creation in the physical plane—"In the beginning was the Word. . . and without the Word was not any thing made that was made. . . ."[7] The fallen angels are using the sound of the Word not as co-creators with God but as destroyers of the bodies, minds and souls of His own.

The power that is given to them to hurt mechanization man for five months is to turn and rend the people who are the godless (for they do not have the seal of God in their foreheads), that is, to turn upon them their own karma. In addition the fallen rock stars are given the power of the electrical energy without which they could not produce the sound.

It's tens of thousands of watts that are at the command of these 'musicians' who are really nothing but hellions out of the pit! This is a multiplication factor of 20 million, if you consider a pressure of one ounce on a guitar string moving it 1/4 inch, as compared to 35,000 watts, a typical concert power level.[8] Such an increase of power, or gain factor, is so large that it would make a bulldozer operator feel weak by comparison. Without this there would be no rock music, with the exception of the jazz and tribal African music from which it originated.

So rock music and the drugs that came with the fallen Atlanteans who have come up out of the pit are the first of the three woes[9] which come upon the inhabitants of earth by reason of the trumpet judgments.

And this concludes my introduction based on Mother's teachings. Now I would like to expose these fallen angels so you can know them by their present-day fruits. Because they really are a woe upon the earth. They are not only a part of Death and Hell but they are a direct part of the International Capitalist/Communist Conspiracy. Without rock, Communism could have made no inroads into America. And without Capitalism neither rock nor Communism would have had the technological backing to fly.

Whereas the Sons of God and their path of individual initiative are "from above," as Jesus said, rock and Communism are both "from beneath"[10] out of the bottomless pit, hence they have the same vibration, hence they are mutually reinforcing. They are members of the same team. This startling conclusion will be borne out as my exposé unfolds.

The coming of the forerunners of rock music, then, in the late fifties (pegged astrologically by Mother as December 31, 1959), was simultaneous with the coming of age of the reincarnated fallen Atlanteans. When you think about a generation of the seed of the Wicked One being confined on the lower astral plane in what is known as "the compound" and not being allowed to see the light of day for nearly 12,000 years—so evil was every imagination of the thoughts of their heart continually before GOD (Elohim) (see Genesis 6)—you can understand the pent-up anger they are unleashing against the seed of Christ and the revenge they would take against God and society.

And these are the very ones whose misuse of the science of sound, as well as of crystal[11] caused the sinking of Atlantis, the very ones who have reembodied to destroy civilization. They have not come to change their ways, to bend the knee, or to confess the living Christ; instead of taking the opportunity to make good they have determined to continue their proliferation of evil and to bring this civilization to its knees.

Many think that young people with their rock bands are just going through their phase—lots of people have had bands and then they go on to other professions. It's kind of an accepted thing in this country that having a band or a rock band is just something you do at a certain age and then you move on.

Youth is not looked upon as being evil; on the contrary, parents of these rock stars are proud of their sons—they're successful, they're popular, they get on TV. "How can they be evil, they're such nice young men and women?" (though there are much fewer women in rock). This logic is a lie because these 'musicians' are reembodied Atlanteans who destroyed their civilization the last time around; they've sworn enmity with God and they're likely to do it again, if we don't take a stand.

Tonight we'll be tackling three aspects of rock music. I know some have said that from a higher viewpoint it's not important to make distinctions between the types of rock. But I feel it's vitally important because rock is like a many-headed Hydra or like the dragon in Revelation 12 and we must identify each subgenre. By identifying it, we decapitate it and cauterize the stump so the Hydra cannot grow two heads in its place![12]

Most importantly, *this is war,* and, as Sun Tzu said in *The Art of War,* "Know the enemy and know yourself."

So, first we have heavy metal. *Heavy metal* today bears little or no resemblance to its ancestors in the sixties and seventies—groups such as Led Zeppelin, Pink Floyd, Uriah Heep, Black Sabbath, Blue Oyster Cult and others. It's a completely new form which has taken root since the early eighties and it's experiencing a great surge in popularity. Heavy metal is concerned with suicide, Satanism, a fixation with morbidity and death, and an obsession with nuclear war. You'll find all these things in almost every heavy metal piece. They're an integral part of it. There's no separating them. And I'll present my case as we continue.

Then there's *political rock,* which I feel is an important part of the conspiracy. Political rock is nothing new. It started in the early sixties. What hasn't changed about it is that it's anti-American, it promotes a one-world government, it's a satire and a mockery of the American way of life, and it's a transference of the responsibility for war and poverty in the world to America, away from the real source of the problem—the Soviet Union. One thing is certain, you won't find any political rock that is anti-Soviet.

So, on the political rock we'll cover several artists and I'll document each of the statements that I've just made.

The third aspect of rock that I'll be taking up is the techno-rock. *Techno-rock* is used for want of a better term because almost all rock today is produced electronically in a very sophisticated way. The 'tools of the trade' have grown in sophistication in the last ten years—especially in the last five. It's a whole new ball game, and I'll be demonstrating some modern studio equipment later tonight.

The fallen ones are using technology which has been given to us by Saint Germain to control sound. Sound is the force of creation; and what you hear, the sound you generate, that is what you're creating. The whole rock revolution that's happened has been through the evolution of digital computers and particularly digital audio, which I'll also explain later.

The digital manipulation of sound gives incredible power to the negative lyrics which these bands are prone to write, which in turn provides a fascination for many youth who love technology and are drawn to the almost irresistible sounds that come from the studio today. They're so unique. I am sure most of you are somewhat familiar with the types of sounds I'm talking about.

Now, with this techno-rock there have also been albums which are designed more as an "experience" than just as a record. You know, you buy this album and it takes you somewhere. That's not really new—the Beatles did that too. But it's more intense now and it's almost a sexual experience or a narcotic high—that's the type of high that you might get from some of these albums. And the lyrics are all blatantly sexual with most techno-rock.

HEAVY METAL

There are several types of heavy metal, as described by a 17-year-old metal musician:

> There is hard core, which is a general term, and metal, another general term, and then we have all those stupid subtitles—death metal, black metal, speed metal (which is also thrash) and Christian metal which is not popular. There is metal core, which is pretty much what we are, the stuff that crossed over. Metal core is what metal people consider metal and what hard core consider hard core.
>
> Black metal is the Satan stuff, silly Devil music. Death metal is pretty close to black metal but more doomy and less satanistic, the darkness-evil side, but not necessarily the Devil himself. Hard core is punk. . . There's a fine line between hard core and metal. A lot of bands cross over. A lot of people do too.[13]

As we will see, most producers and consumers of heavy metal music are very young. People can't usually stand it past their twenties. They have a saying which you'll see on one of these videoclips, "If it's too loud, you're too old."

Dave Benser, the author of the above quote, began listening to the group KISS in first grade. KISS has been rumored to stand for Knights in the Service of Satan. I don't know whether there is any truth to that but it seems highly plausible.

I'm going to play a segment from ABC's *20/20* on heavy metal that aired in May. I think it's the best way to introduce the subject because their coverage is pretty thorough. Although I don't agree with most of the things they say, at least you'll get a chance to see some of these people in action and some of the bands. So we'll play that now. [ABC *20/20* videoclip "The Children of Heavy Metal" played]

Barbara Walters: When a form of music that our children like becomes linked with ghoulish images and violent theatrics, and even suicide, it demands our attention. Perhaps more to the point, the children need our attention. Hundreds of thousands of teenagers are locked onto so-called heavy metal music. Are they despairing? What are their common bonds? And, as Stone Phillips asks, is there a message that may be too loud for us to hear?

Dad [videoclip, to son watching heavy metal group on TV]: What is this garbage you're watching? I want to watch the news.

John Marler, Eyewitness News: Good evening. It was rock and roll turned ugly—

Stone Phillips [voice-over]: A rock riot in New Jersey tops the local news.

Marler: There were nearly three dozen arrests and a state trooper was injured.

Phillips [voice-over]: A post-concert fight captures the headlines. A parking lot disturbance at one arena leads police to mobilize an army at the group's next stop. At issue, the impact of this loud, raucous music, heavy metal music, played here by the supergroup Iron Maiden. Screeching guitars, flamboyant bands, lyrics obsessed with sex, Satanism and even suicide—this is not mainstream rock and roll, it's the music of today's teen rebellion. What's it about?

Mike Zakarian, Age 15: Togetherness, man, we got to stick together and fight, man.

Teen #1: One giant family.

Zakarian: We got to fight—

Student: Fight for what?

Zakarian: Fight for our right, man, to listen to our music and party, man.

Phillips [voice-over]: As metalmania grows, so does the heavy metal debate.

Michael Konsevick, Teacher, Teaneck High: I think it's time, as Frank Zappa was saying, if your kid comes home with an album with a guy with a chainsaw between his legs, you better find out what that music is talking about.

Phillips [voice-over]: Critics say there's something seriously wrong with metal music, outrageous by design, that it may have contributed to a number of teenage suicides, like the ones in Bergenfield, New Jersey, March 11th. Four young people died in a suicide pact. A heavy metal cassette box was found at the scene. Later that same week, reporters were at the scene of another suicide case in Illinois.

Chris Bury [Alsip, Illinois]: In this case, music may also be involved. Her family says Nancy Grannan was obsessed by lyrics from the rock band Metallica, lyrics she wrote down.

Jim Davis, Brother: I have lost the will to live, simply nothing more to give, I will just say good-bye.

Phillips [voice-over]: This videotape by a Christian group criticizes a song by Ozzy Osbourne, linked to a 1984 teen suicide in California.

Announcer [videoclip]: Consider now for yourself the words to "Suicide Solution."

Ozzy Osbourne [words on screen]: Breaking laws, knocking doors but there's no one at home. Made your bed, rest your head, but you lie there and moan. Where to hide, suicide is the only way out. Don't you know what it's really about?

Phillips [voice-over]: The music has prompted pickets, record-burnings, even congressional hearings, where a call for record companies to print lyrics on album covers as a guide for concerned parents sparked a debate over censorship. Tipper Gore, co-founder of the Parents Music Resource Center.

Tipper Gore, Parents Music Resource Center: Parents should realize that we have explicit and graphic sex, extreme violence, suicide in lyrics that is going to children that are sometimes not even teenagers yet, and young teenagers.

Bruce Dickinson, Lead Singer, Iron Maiden: I mean, that's what annoys the hell out of me, that people are saying that we're a negative influence. I just wish people would get a sense of proportion about what's right and wrong, and who are the real people that are poisoning people's minds, and why are they doing it. We say things to people that mean something, I mean, you know, in our own little way, that kids can relate to.

Phillips [voice-over]: What are these heavy metal rockers saying to kids? And why are millions of teenage Americans listening? To find out, we went backstage at this heavy metal concert to meet Iron Maiden, and we went back to school to meet the kids who go to heavy metal concerts, who belong to the heavy metal crowd. Kids like these, with hormones popping, macho energy surging, kids who will be our guides into a world most adults are strangers to.

[on-camera] This is a high school in Teaneck, New Jersey, a school with a reputation for excellence. But like just about every other high school in America, Teaneck High has its own group of so-called tough kids, hoods or burn-outs—some into drinking or drugs, others who aren't into much of anything at all, except heavy metal music. [voice-over] It's against the rules to play music in the halls at Teaneck High, so it's hard to tell here just who belongs to the heavy metal crowd and who doesn't. But after school, Teaneck's heavy metal contingent is hard to miss. Meet Allen, Mike, Naseem and Melissa, four devoted heavy metal fans.

[interview] This is it, this is the hot stuff. Allen, turn it off for a second, so we can talk. Who is this?

Zakarian: S.O.D.

Allen Chaloub, Age 15: S.O.D.

Phillips [voice-over]: S.O.D.?

Chaloub: Storm Troopers of Death.

Phillips: Storm Troopers of Death, now, what does that mean—Storm Troopers of Death?

Chaloub: It's just a name.

Zakarian: It calms me down. Like, you know, if anything's on my mind, I just go and sit in my room and play some music, and just sit down and think.

Phillips: And you can sort of drown out the world that way.

Zakarian: Yeah, you know, it calms me down.

Phillips [voice-over]: For the most part, these kids are not star athletes or straight-A students. Most don't belong to any high school clubs or hang out with the popular crowd. Often, they feel like outcasts, like they don't fit in, especially in the classroom.

Teacher [videoclip]: What do you want to do with your life?

Student [singing]: I wanta rock.

Group of Students [singing]: I wanta rock.

Jason Kalfin, Age 14: It's like, you know, some people don't want to go to college. They want to do something else. I mean, once you get out of high school, you figure that you've been in school long enough, you don't want to, you know, spend any more time.

Phillips [voice-over]: They spend their afternoons at the record store, flipping through albums, talking metal music with their friends. The music is what brings them together. It's their way of belonging, their rooms a retreat from school and from cliques they can't relate to.

Michael Chaloub, Age 17: They got preps in there, they got the nerds, and they got, you know, guys like us. The preps, they're the ones who always wear like they're in friggin' Hawaii or something, they wear those ten thousand, like, multi-color shirts. And, you know, like those idiots over there, they go and play frisbee in the middle of a field.

Phillips [voice-over]: Sheigh Crabtree might be considered a prep. She used to go to Teaneck High and always believed the put-downs from the heavy metal crowd were just a cover.

Sheigh Crabtree, Former Teaneck Student: Instead of people just ignoring them, saying they're heavy metal kids, they need some support, they need some people to inspire them, some people to look up to. I think being a teenager is a really lonely time. You don't know who to trust. Maybe when you grow up, it's the same thing, but right now, I mean, I've never felt lonelier. And I think a lot of teenagers feel that way.

Phillips [voice-over]: Lonely, she says, and worried, like a lot of teenagers, about things like nuclear annihilation. This song, by the group Megadeth, is about nuclear war. [rock music played]

Kalfin: Like, you talk about the future and everything, and like, there might not ever be a future, 'cause they're still makin' all these weapons and everything, and I think about peace a lot.

Phillips [voice-over]: But make no mistake. This is not the summer of love. Folk music is not their thing.

Mrs. Gore: There is a group called Motley Crue that's very popular with kids. They have an album that has sold two million copies with lyrics like this, "Not a woman but a whore. I can taste the hate. Well, now, I'm killing you, watch your face turning blue."

Phillips [voice-over]: We asked the kids about that. They say parents pay more attention to the lyrics than they do.

[interview] Those kind of songs—you don't think it says the wrong kind of thing?

Melissa Gill, Age 16: Yeah, it does. You shouldn't say, like, you know, bad things about what women do, you know. It's just like putting them down.

Naseem Buddha, Age 16: It's like, not all songs talk about that, though. So you just avoid the music that you don't like, that's all.

Phillips [voice-over]: And it's the same with songs about Satanism and suicide. The kids in Teaneck said they were shocked by the suicides in Bergenfield, the town next door. But they still think it's wrong to blame the music.

Michael Chaloub: Why didn't we kill ourselves yet?—because we listen to the same thing. And if the music caused them to kill themselves, well, why didn't we?

Allen Chaloub: That song, "Kill Yourself," you know, I mean, it's just a song. You're not going to go out and do it, I mean, unless you got real bad problems and everything, you know.

Kalfin: It's, like, not the music that's going to kill you, it's yourself.

Phillips [voice-over]: Music journalist Charles Young has written about the heavy metal culture and believes it may be healthy in a way.

Charles M. Young, Music Journalist: Heavy metal speaks to the anger and despair of teenagers today the same way that the blues used to speak to the despair and anger of black people in the South. But without heavy metal there would probably be a lot more suicides, because metal and certain other forms of rock give teenagers something to believe in that they get no place else.

Phillips [voice-over]: Basically, Teaneck's metal fans feel adults just overreact to the music, don't understand it or give it a chance. Like the teenager in this music video, they feel themselves constantly colliding with the adult world.

Harvey Kalfin, Jason's Father: If it's too loud, you're too old.

Phillips [voice-over]: Take Jay's father, for example. He never shared his son's devotion to the music, never quite understood as Jay transformed himself into a heavy metal aficionado, at age five.

Harvey Kalfin: I kept telling myself that I had to appreciate his music, and I would listen to it and it lasted about 30 seconds, and then I'd yell, "Turn it down!" But seriously, I have no objection to what music he likes to listen to, and if—

Phillips: Would you?

Jason Kalfin: What?

Interviewer: Turn it down?

Jason Kalfin: Would I turn it down? No. I'd turn it up, louder.

Sylvia Chaloub, Allen's mother: I don't know what heavy metal is really like. Could it be worse than—

Allen Chaloub: Can I give an example?

Mrs. Chaloub: Like who?

Chaloub: Can I give an example?

Phillips [voice-over]: Allen's mom tolerates the heavy metal culture, or tries to.

Mrs. Chaloub: If it's like the music that you listen to—

Phillips [voice-over]: And the music is mild compared to this. [music played] This is called moshing, a dance popular among the metal crowd. At times, it looks more like a contact sport. And what about this, stage-diving, a common occurrence at heavy metal concerts all over the country? Jay broke his wrist stage-diving a few months ago, but his fellow fans insist they look out for one another.

Fan: You don't want to get hurt. Everybody's got a little kind of brotherhood. No one wants to get hurt. Everybody keeps their arms down. It looks—I have to admit, when I first saw it, you know, I got scared, but it's not—I'm all sweaty, but it's fun.

Phillips [voice-over]: Still, some counseling groups say heavy metal is out of control and advocate a tough stance, with rules to de-metal kids, impose a dress code, tear down posters, and turn off the stereos.

Zakarian: If you come home late, they start bitchin' at you and everything, you know, clean your room or take the dog out or somethin' like that, you know. You can't go up to them and, you know, tell them to go to hell, so you keep all your anger in and stuff.

Tony Kingslow, Age 15: My parents are threat—I said, "Dad, can I get an earring?" He's like, "I'll kill you, I'll rip out your ears." It's like, he said, "I'll kick you out of the house and get your name changed to spaghetti"—and then I say, "What's so wrong about having an earring? There's nothing wrong with that. It doesn't mean anything, anything bad about it." [crosstalk]

He thinks, "He's a girl, he's a girl. Only girls wear that." Who says?

Phillips [voice-over]: Tipper Gore has written a book for parents in the eighties. We asked her where she thinks parents should draw the line.

Mrs. Gore: I advocate a system where people can make up their own minds according to their own values and their own assessment of where their child is on a developmental spectrum.

Phillips [voice-over]: And if your fourteen-year-old daughter wants to listen to this, will you let her?

Mrs. Gore: To heavy metal music? I'm not sure. It would depend on what group.

Phillips [voice-over]: [group cheering] The Iron Maiden group, one of the best-known among more than 1500 heavy metal bands, is a worldwide phenomenon. They've even taken their act behind the Iron Curtain, where their fans look and act the same. Rock promoter John Scher.

John Scher, Rock Promoter: What happens at concerts now is vastly different than the scene that surrounded concerts in the sixties and seventies. It's become an *almost tribal* [emphasis added] kind of a gathering place. It has a lot more to do with socialization than it does just the music.

Phillips [voice-over]: When Maiden played this year at the Meadowlands in New Jersey, we went with our group from Teaneck.

Young: When you're a part of a crowd, you're incredibly powerful. And there's no drug, there's nothing that can approach that feeling of exhilaration.

Phillips [voice-over]: When the concert was over, we took them backstage. They got autographs from some of the band members. And we got to talk to one of their idols, Maiden's Bruce Dickinson. We asked him what he says when critics accuse heavy metal of inciting outrageous, even sick behavior.

Dickinson: You mean like selling arms to Iran, or you mean like, you know, all these guys doing insider dealing, or you mean like all these companies dumping toxic wastes everywhere, you know? But because they wear suits and ties, it's okay. They're not sick. Where else can these kids go, where they—you know, they come somewhere, and they all feel a sense of, you know, this is our thing, you know.

Phillips [voice-over]: Dickinson acknowledges though that heavy metal kids may be telling us something, about how they feel pushed out and put down, about their needs, and about how they're coping with the pressures teenagers face today, from family breakups to drugs.

Dickinson: And maybe if you listen, you might understand a little of what he's trying to go through, and then you might understand why he likes things, why he doesn't like things, and ultimately, you find out that he's a good kid after all.

Walters: You know, Stone, this is hostile music, and these are kids who seem to feel that the world out there is hostile to them. So much of it is a matter of self-esteem. But the music itself isn't what does them harm.

Phillips: No, even the critics that we talk to, among them, none says that the music alone is going to cause a child to commit suicide, for instance. I think the point is, talking to these teenagers who are into heavy metal music, that they're not necessarily looking for a heavy discussion with parents or teachers about the meaning of their music. But the point is, tune in and let it be known that whether you like the music or not, it matters, because the kids matter.

Walters: Oh dear. God, it's a tough time, and it's always a tough period for kids.

If you ask me, that's nothing but a whitewash. What this segment is designed to do is to put a human face on heavy metal in order to demystify it and make it palatable. By acting like the teenagers have chosen the music, the responsibility for its violence is transferred to the children themselves. It is never acknowledged that possibly the heavy-metal musicians have created their own market by taking unfair advantage of the vulnerability and natural rebellion of teenagers. Nor is the question even raised that the group members themselves might be tools of evil forces. It is denied that the music can have a negative influence and this Charles M. Young is sorely misguided if he thinks that heavy metal is something teens can or should "believe in."

The youth have been victimized and they don't know it. The battle is not about censorship or "saving children from themselves." It is about saving them from the likes of Bruce Dickinson of Iron Maiden, who lines his pockets with filthy lucre derived from the death of souls while pointing his finger at other elements of society.

Just because kids can relate to heavy metal and enjoy it doesn't make it a good thing. We do not allow heroin addicts to remain addicted just because it is their free will. Neither do we blame them for their continued craving for the drug. They have a "monkey on their back," and we should take a stand *for them and against the monkey.* The addict will hate us in the moment but thank us profusely upon regaining his senses.

Rock musicians will accept no responsibility for feeding America's metal habit. Instead, they are always putting down others. As you saw with Bruce Dickinson, he's doing nothing but transferring our attention, saying, "Over here. Don't look at me, look at them. Look at the government, look at the corporations."

This transference is the key to understanding the rock music plot because a lot of the political groups do the same thing when it comes to making the people blame America and blame our way of life for all the world's ills. It's a transference from the real source of the problem. And they're great at it.

These rock musicians are spokesmen for the seed of the Wicked One and they use their music and their beat to transfer the guilt for all the crimes of the fallen angels to the Lightbearers. This weight of guilt adds to the burden of the youth who are already bowed down with drugs and feel alienated from society. I won't deny that being a teenager is tough. But this just compounds the problem.

Heavy metal attracts the loners, as we saw in the clip. These are already the ones most likely to commit suicide. We heard mention of the girl who had the lyrics to a song with her when she killed herself. The group involved was called Metallica.

When I was going out to do the research for this lecture I went to a record store in Evanston near Northwestern. And when I first walked in, I said, "Hi. I'm doing research into suicide and Satanism." And the manager got real upset and he said, "There's nothing like that here. What are you talking about?" He didn't like me at all.

So I got into a conversation with a girl who worked there who was nineteen. And it turned out that this group was her favorite group. We got to talking about the suicide of Nancy Grannan and, of course, she didn't believe that that song had caused her to commit suicide. As a matter of fact she said, "It couldn't have. It's my favorite song."

So I asked her what she thought of heavy metal in general—and didn't she think that it was a possibility that music could at least have an influence on someone—maybe not a negative influence, but at least that it had the power to influence people. Well, she didn't really know. But then it came out later in the conversation that, well, she wouldn't really want her ten-year-old sister to listen to it. But it was OK for her.

We kept discussing it. She said she didn't think the words really meant anything, but that they were just an expression of emotion—that people were acting and the lyrics didn't really mean anything. And then she switched. She couldn't really defend that. So she said that the top 40 was as bad as heavy metal and that lots of kids listen to that and parents didn't care.

She cited the example of Madonna, claiming that Madonna had posed in the nude before she became a singer. I said, "Well, I don't think anybody should be listening to Madonna either." So she thought about it. And I think that she listened to what I had to say but she definitely wasn't converted by any means.

At one point she said she knew some members of a rock and roll band and she was trying to explain to me how they were just posing to look nasty but that they were really nice people. At this point the store owner came over and remarked that he expected that "a Northwestern student would be smarter."

So I'm going to play you the song which I believe caused Nancy Grannan to commit suicide. But first, I'd like to introduce you to some of the other music that this group has put out. This is a song about nuclear war—a familiar topic. I'm going to read the lyrics:

> Do unto others as they have done to you
> But what the hell is this world coming to?
>
> Blow the universe into nothingness
> Nuclear warfare shall lay us to rest
>
> Fight fire with fire
> Ending is near
> Fight fire with fire
> Bursting with fear
>
> We all shall die
>
> Time is like a fuse, short and burning fast
> Armageddon is here, like said in the past
>
> Soon to fill our lungs the hot winds of death
> The gods are laughing, so take your last breath

So we'll play that now. [Excerpt of "Fight Fire with Fire" by Metallica played] So it goes on. That's about a third of it.

Now, this Metallica would fall into the category of "death metal." They're not overtly satanistic. Take a good look at this album cover. What do you think the object in the center is? It's an electric chair. So you have this group who is actively singing about death and they talk about suicide in their song, yet they have a song which is against the death penalty. You figure that out.

We have them criticizing the death penalty, which is the only way that a civilized society can deter murder, and yet they advocate suicide.

In other words, they're saying to God: "You can't tell me by your law (the law of karma) when it's time for me to go, but I can take my own life (which is really God's life) anytime I choose. I'm better than you, God, and no one can tell me otherwise."

These are the lyrics to their song against the death penalty. It's called "Ride the Lightning."

Guilty as charged
But damn it, it ain't right
There is someone else controlling me

Death in the air
Strapped in the electric chair
This can't be happening to me

Who made you God to say
"I'll take your life from you!!"

Flash before my eyes
Now it's time to die
Burning in my brain
I can feel the flame

Wait for the sign
To flick the switch of death
It's the beginning of the end

Sweat, chilling cold
As I watch death unfold
Consciousness is my only friend

My fingers grip with fear
What am I doing here?

Someone help me
Oh please God help me
They are trying to take it all away
I don't want to die

Time moving slow
The minutes seem like hours
The final curtain call I see
How true is this?
Just get it over with
If this is true, just let it be

Wakened by horrid scream
Freed from this frightening dream.

We'll play an excerpt from that now. [Excerpt of "Ride the Lightning" by Metallica played] This is supposed to evoke sympathy for this individual who is being killed, but I don't think they have too much sympathy for the girl who killed herself.

We're told that Nancy Grannan, nineteen, of Alsip, Illinois, had listened to "Fade to Black" and that she carried the lyrics with her—copied in her own hand—and had them on the dashboard of the car while she allowed herself to be poisoned by carbon monoxide. Days before the suicide she read them to her sister-in-law, remarking, "This sounds like my life."

Grannan was trapped. She did have problems. She was going

through a divorce and she had some other personal problems. But it wasn't the end of her life. She could have been helped by a good counsellor or even by the violet flame. I'm sure there is someone she could have talked to. But instead, she turned to heavy metal.

It's interesting to note when you hear this song that it starts out kind of nice, you know, with the acoustic guitar—sounds kind of sweet. And this is what they do. The fallen ones always allure you with something that looks very good and very nice. And then when you've been caught, they show you what it's really like.

I think that this song is a prime example of that. I'm going to play the whole song—it's about six minutes long—because I want everyone to understand what this girl was up against and what all teenagers are up against when they feel the despair that my mother talked about in her commencement address on Sunday. It's just that—they have nowhere else to turn.

They feel alienated from their parents and they just turn to this music—almost for mother love. It becomes a surrogate mother, a pacifier and a security blanket—a shield from the real world, yet the repository of everything they fear most. And then the rhythm of rock—gentle and violent—neutralizes their fears of those things which they really ought to fear and then come to grips with in a mature way: sex, death, dying, suicide, and nuclear war. These musicians are the heroes of our children—like in Dungeons and Dragons, they lead them through the labyrinth of the underworld—but they don't bring them back. So here are the "Fade to Black" lyrics:

Life it seems, will fade away
Drifting further every day
Getting lost within myself
Nothing matters no one else
I have lost the will to live
Simply nothing more to give
There is nothing more for me
Need the end to set me free

Things not what they used to be
Missing one inside of me
Deathly lost, this can't be real
Cannot stand this hell I feel
Emptiness is filling me
To the point of agony
Growing darkness taking dawn
I was me, but now he's gone

No one but me can save myself, but it's too late
Now I can't think, think why I should even try

Yesterday seems as though it never existed
Death Greets me warm, now I will just say goodbye

This stream of consciousness is nothing but a dictation from the suicide entity, Annihla. This is channeling right out of Hell. With their syncopated beat and the electronic sound that becomes a "psychotronic" manipulation, they are the open door to the mouthings of demons out of the pit.

Notice the passage "I was me, but now he's gone." How often do you hear people going from the first to the third person in the same sentence? By this statement, the vocalist (and anyone who sings along) merges with the suicide entity and loses his own identity. "I was me, but now he's gone"—who's he? The disassociated self. The person is saying, "I used to be me, but the me that I was—now he's gone." But it's the suicide entity that has now displaced the I that used to be the self; and the entity says now he's gone and only I am here occupying this body.

I believe it's important for us to place ourselves in the position to hear what these teenagers are going through. So we'll play it now. ["Fade to Black" by Metallica played] If we didn't have the Ascended Masters and their teachings, we'd feel like giving up after hearing that song. And that's just how she felt and that's just what she did—Nancy Grannan, bless her soul.

What really struck me about this recording is that at the end of it you hear a kind of scream going off into the distance. It sounds to me like the soul screaming after it's left the body and realized it's been tricked into committing suicide and what a trap it is.

Now, as bad as it is, it's not the actual suicide that is the core problem of this heavy metal and of rock music. Suicide is only the end result of a chain of abominations. It begins with the rape of the chakras by the rhythm and the sound. It becomes an addiction, and the false hierarchy of Satan is involved in this at all levels. And by the time suicide becomes the solution because it's the only way to get out of the grips of these toilers, the soul has been devoured many times over.

There is a parallel here to the account of Jesus casting out devils in the country of the Gadarenes. The devils spoke to Jesus through the ones possessed and said, "Well, if you're going to cast us out, at least let us go into the herd of pigs." The Master consented and no sooner did they go into the pigs than the whole herd, as it is written in Matthew 8, "ran violently down a steep place into the sea and perished in the waters."

The swine—a very intelligent animal—committed suicide. It was their only way out. They preferred death to demon possession. And they did not have the power to deliver themselves from the forces of Hell. Neither did the Gadarene demoniacs. And neither did Nancy Grannan. And neither do our teenagers today.

I stand before Almighty God and in the name JESUS CHRIST I charge you, Metallica: James Hetfield, Kirk Hammett, Cliff Burton, and Lars Ulrich with the murder of this soul, Nancy Grannan, and for putting a stumbling block in the path of this sister who was a Holy Christ Child and had the opportunity, as we all do, to make her ascension in this life. Her blood be upon you and all of your ill-gotten gains!

Let us take our stand now and give The Judgment Call "They Shall Not Pass!" by Jesus Christ. Together:

In the Name of the I AM THAT I AM,
I invoke the Electronic Presence of Jesus Christ:
They shall not pass!
They shall not pass!
They shall not pass!
By the authority of the cosmic cross of white fire
it shall be:
That all that is directed against the Christ
within me, within the holy innocents,

within our beloved Messengers,
within every son and daughter of God...
Is now turned back
by the authority of Alpha and Omega,
by the authority of my Lord and Saviour Jesus Christ,
by the authority of Saint Germain!

I AM THAT I AM within the center of this temple
and I declare in the fullness of
the entire Spirit of the Great White Brotherhood:
That those who, then, practice the black arts
against the children of the Light...
Are now bound by the hosts of the LORD,
Do now receive the judgment of the Lord Christ
within me, within Jesus,
and within every Ascended Master,
Do now receive, then, the full return—
multiplied by the energy of the Cosmic Christ—
of their nefarious deeds which they have practiced
since the very incarnation of the Word!

Lo, I AM a Son of God!
Lo, I AM a Flame of God!
Lo, I stand upon the Rock of the living Word
And I declare with Jesus, the living Son of God:
They shall not pass!
They shall not pass!
They shall not pass!
Elohim. Elohim. Elohim. [chant]

Let us call to Archangel Michael to protect the souls of all teens who have committed suicide and to bind all demons of Death and Hell who have lured them to that fate. Together:

*Lord Michael before, Lord Michael behind,
Lord Michael to the right, Lord Michael to the left,
Lord Michael above, Lord Michael below,
Lord Michael, Lord Michael wherever I go!

I AM his Love protecting here!
I AM his Love protecting here!
I AM his Love protecting here!* (9x)

*I AM Presence, Thou art Master,
I AM Presence, clear the way!
Let thy Light and all thy Power
Take possession here this hour!
Charge with Victory's mastery,
Blaze blue lightning, blaze thy substance!
Into this thy form descend,
That Perfection and its Glory
Shall blaze forth and earth transcend!* (9x)

Thank you and thank God for that release of Light! (Please be seated.) There is a protective membrane around the etheric body. Mother has described it as being "white and bluish, having light veins throughout—veins of light." Gradually, from repetitive listening to rock, the membrane is weakened from being bombarded by violent sound. So, it wears thin until finally it bursts, and then you start having more tears.

The purpose of this protective sheath is to prevent the astral plane

(Death and Hell) from penetrating the four lower bodies and violating the soul. The real purpose of rock music, then, from the satanic point of view is to tear this protective sheath, thereby making the soul vulnerable to anything else the sinister force may desire to do with her until they've bled her of all her light: her own self-destruction becomes their method of discarding their victim.

Now I'd like to show you the pictures of a few young people that are into heavy metal and tell you their story. These are taken from a June 4, 1987, article in the *Washington Post.* This is Stacy Allen. She's twenty and she says that she doesn't even do drugs because a heavy metal concert is a better high:

"It's better than drugs and alcohol and I don't have a hangover in the morning. . . . Some bands are so good they'll just tear you apart. I'm not saying every band is good enough to do this. But my favorites, they can obliterate me. I feel like there's nothing left anywhere after I've been there. It's like, am I there or am I in Ohio? It's awesome. Anything that can blow you from D.C. to Ohio is pretty powerful."

This is an increment of self-destruction every time it happens to her. And the rush of the life-force going out of her which will never return is "sweet death." And she can't help herself, she can't stop herself anymore than a heroin addict can stop because she's addicted to that sensation. It's the bleeding of the chakras of their light. It is almost as if the chakras, which are normally convex and full of light, were to become deflated like a balloon. They literally get depressed. This loss of light is the spiritual cause of depression, which, as we know, has become recognized as a national disease—as highlighted in a recent cover story of *Newsweek.*[14]

When the life-force has been spent, whether through rock or perverted sex or drugs, two feelings emerge: depression and then the desire for more stimuli to counteract the depression. Who benefits from this vicious cycle? The depression entity, whose name as revealed to Mother is "Depressa," a female vampire entity. She and Annihla, the suicide entity, are a team—they work together.

The demons and discarnates out of Death and Hell all benefit from rock and roll. Because foul spirits can survive only by constantly raping the Light from the chakras of the Lightbearers. That's their only source. Without it they would be no more.

So they get one, a few or ten million listening to rock music and they have easy access to all the light they want. They live off of it, they get drunk on it—and drunk with power—and they use that power of the Children of Light to carry out the agenda of Hell: controlled social and political change by the architects of world destruction who, as the arch-deceivers of mankind, use the rock stars as pawns in the game. Thus some rock musicians are duped (themselves victims of the sinister force) but others are conscious willing tools of the powers of Hell.

And that explains the rock/Satanism connection. This connection consists of groups like Slayer and Venom who are disciples of Satanism. They don't deny it. They readily admit it and it's in their lyrics.

This is the *Satanic Bible.* On the cover is the inverted pentagram with the Goat of Mendes superimposed. Now, the inverted pentagram is a familiar symbol if you're into heavy metal. Some kids who are into it may not know that it's on the cover of the *Satanic Bible,* but there it is in its entirety. And here we have the man responsible for it all—or the pawn of the man responsible for it all. This is Anton LaVey, the head of the Satanist church. He has claimed credit for the rise of "black metal" or "Satanist metal."

As quoted in the *Washington Post,* February 23, 1986, he says, "The Satanist rock lyrics, the Satanic movies, even the Satanic murders,... all grew from the Church of Satan. Let's give me a little credit for having moved society—up or down—but for at least having moved it."[15]

It is interesting that LaVey claims not to like rock music. This is a bit like *Pravda* claiming that the Soviet Union doesn't like taking political prisoners. When you consider the background of LaVey as the reincarnation of V. I. Lenin, it starts to sound like old, familiar rhetoric.

LaVey himself is involved in music. You may not know this, but according to his own story he sits there 'most every night and plays his organ or banks of synthesizers—very late, in the early morning hours from 2:00 to 4:00 a.m. That's when Stalin held court and received his diplomatic envoys from the West. He would only see them at those hours.

And it's not just Stalin, it's the modern Soviet Union also. This is when the ELF[16] waves that the Soviet Union constantly beams at the United States are most effective. So you start to wonder, when all these things are happening, and you put two and two together. Well, the source is the same. We also know that beloved Kuthumi plays his organ at Shigatse (his retreat in Tibet) at night for souls who have made the transition. And he may be playing it to counteract Anton LaVey.

This is a slide of Anton LaVey again. I wanted you to take note of what he's doing with his hands. That's the Satanist mudra (with the thumb holding two center fingers against the palm, the index and little finger are raised). It represents the goat's head of the Goat of Mendes, also called the symbol of Baphomet, which is represented by the symbol behind his head. This satanic hand mudra is imitated by many of these heavy metal groups and listeners. In the clip we saw from *20/20* you could see a few of them doing it. But I'm going to show you some other clips as well and you will see that this is standard practice at a heavy metal concert.

It's a good bet that most teenagers have no idea what this means or that it has anything to do with Satanism. And the ones that do probably enjoy it. You know, there are the knowing ones and then there are their victims. Because we know that many of these teenagers are reembodied fallen Atlanteans, we can't say they're all innocent. But there's certainly a fair quotient of souls of light among them who have forgotten their spiritual birthright and are about to lose it.

Now I'd like to show you the first group, which is called Slayer. And if you thought Metallica was bad, this is worse. The name of the album here is *Show No Mercy.* On the cover you have the logo for Slayer, which is the inverted pentagram made up of swords with one sword missing. And who's holding the missing sword but the Goat of Mendes. That's a close-up of the Goat of Mendes.

The five-pointed star is the symbol of Christ—of you becoming the Christ. That's why we have the five-pointed star on our flag. America is a nation sponsored by Saint Germain where all people can pursue a path of personal Christhood with Jesus. So the inverted five-pointed star is the symbol for taking the figure of your Christhood and turning it upside down. This is the equivalent of placing the head of Jesus Christ at the base-of-the-spine chakra and perverting the light/energy/consciousness of the Children of Light into sexual orgies. Again, Satanism thrives on orgies because its rites are always aimed at raping the light of the chakras and the electromagnetic field of the body and the aura.

The lyrics which I'm going to read you are from the song "The Antichrist":

Screams and nightmares
Of a life I want
Can't see living this lie no
A world I haunt
You've lost all control of my
Heart and soul
Satan holds my future
Watch it unfold

I am the Antichrist
It's what I was meant to be
Your God left me behind
And set my soul to be free

Watching deciples
Of the satanic rule
Pentagram of blood
Holds the jackals truth
Searching for the answer
Christ hasn't come
Awaiting the final moment
The birth of Satans son

Screams,
From a life I live
Torment,
Is what I give
Torture,
Is what I love
The down fall
Of the heavens above

I am the Antichrist
All love is lost
Insanity is what I am
Eternally my soul will rot

So, now we'll see a videoclip of that song. [Videoclip of "The Antichrist" by Slayer played. At its conclusion Tom Araya (Slayer lead singer) says: "As I'm sure you're aware, we have a new album that's out, which I understand seems to be picked up by quite a few of you. I have one question—*Have you learned the words to our songs*? You have waited this long, Hell no longer awaits!"]

If you didn't see it, you wouldn't believe it. As you probably noticed, most of the members of the group were wearing upside-down crosses. It's the same principle as the inverted pentagram. Wearing Christ upside down. Inverting the crucifix when they perform a black mass—actually putting Christ's head at the level of the genital area—that's the meaning of the upside-down cross or crucifix. That's how vile

Satanism is. I'm sure most people don't realize that.

I wanted everyone to take note of the head movements of the band members. This is a new thing with kids. It's called "headbanging." In fact, this is the throwing off of the energy of the spinal cord and the medulla oblongata through the centrifugal force of the head motion. We wonder why this is done and why it's been popularized.

According to LaVey, who wrote the *Satanic Bible,* all satanic rituals need the energy of the life-force behind them. Now, LaVey also says in the *Satanic Bible* that he discourages animal sacrifice and human sacrifice. Well, I wouldn't expect him to write about those things because he would fear the law and fear for his own life. But I don't think there's any doubt in anyone's mind that the Church of Satan does practice human and animal sacrifice. In his "bible" LaVey lists alternative methods of providing the energy for a satanic ritual. One of those methods is through taking the energy released in an orgasm.

Now we can see that this headbanging which takes place at these concerts produces an outflow of the life-force through the crown chakra which is similar to the release of the life-force through the base chakra in an orgasm. The head movement—it's tantamount to self-abuse. It is our conclusion, therefore, that the astral result of this and the astral result of a heavy metal concert in terms of the light released is identical to that which is released in an orgy or a ritual sacrifice.

You will notice also that the lead singer, whose name is Tom Araya, asks, "Have you learned the words to our songs?" Now, we heard on *20/20,* and it's been printed in lots of newspapers and many people believe it, that lyrics don't mean anything. Well, the bands think that lyrics mean something. And the Satanists think that lyrics mean something. So the youth of America had better wake up to the fact that the lyrics do mean something and that when they go to these concerts and sing along and bang their heads to the syncopated beat, they are participating in satanic rituals.

We already knew that these lyrics are being pounded into the subconscious of the teenagers through the rock beat but now we have a performer openly talking about it. That's something that I've never seen before—not with lyrics that are this blatantly and openly satanic.

ECP: Well, this song is a decree—"I AM the Antichrist." He is revealing that they decree in Hell. Mark Prophet told me there are astral decree groups who decree against the Light and the Lightbearers. Tom Araya is teaching satanic decrees to those youths. And he wants them to know the words to the decree because, short of divine intervention, they will become antichrist in vibration when they say them.

SCP: The members of Slayer are Kerry King, lead guitarist; Jeff Hanneman—who wears an upside-down crucifix; Tom Araya—the lead singer that you saw in the video; and Dave Lombardo, the drummer. I also have two short audioclips to play but first I want to read you some more of their lyrics. This one, also by Slayer, is called "Evil Has No Boundaries":

> Blasting our way through the boundaries of hell
> No one can stop us tonight
> We take on the world with hatred inside
> Mayhem the reason we fight

Surviving the slaughters and killing we've lost
Then we return from the dead
Attacking once more now with twice as much strength

[twice as much strength after they got the light from their last foray]

We conquer then move on ahead
Evil
My words defy
Evil
Has no disguise
Evil
Will take your soul
Evil
My wrath unfolds

Satan our master in evil mayhem
Guides us with every first step
Our axes are growing with power and fury
Soon there'll be nothingness left
Midnight has come and the leathers strapped on
Evil is at our command
We clash with Gods angel and conquer new souls
Consuming all that we can

So, I'll play that now. [Song "Evil Has No Boundaries" by Slayer played] The next song is a denial of the cross. It's called "Haunting the Chapel." It reads:

The holy cross, symbol of lies
Intimidate the lives of Christian born
Speak of death, the words of hate
Anticipation grows amongst the dead
Hell has seen the priests attempt
To bring forth their lord of the cross
Strike of twelve, raise the dead
The chapel comes under attack

The ghosts of sin torment the priests
Their altar will soon be destroyed
Heaven's palace turning black
The church now belongs to the dead
Blackened magic infest with lust
Lucifer rules supreme
The crystal ball shows unknown fate
The last thing that's heard is the screams

Ghosts from hell invade this feeble shrine
Heaven's holy house will fall in time
Satan's morbid soldiers chant in lust
Destruction of the church we'll burn the cross

Attacking angels as they pray to God
Tormented preachers hail the twisted cross
Haunting the chapel hell's demons prevail
Death has come, the house of God has failed.

It pains me to read these lyrics.

ECP: They're all decrees. All of them are decrees out of Hell.

SCP: Now, if there are any skeptics in the audience, and these lyrics and the satanic symbolism aren't enough to convince you that these singers are by choice the embodiment of Evil, we have for you a clip of an interview with a group known as Venom where the drummer is actually admitting to writing satanic lyrics. His name is Abaddon, as written in Revelation. You may or may not know it but Abaddon is also one of the "infernal names" used for conjuration in the *Satanic Bible.*

"The Devil writes the best tunes," says Abaddon. "We write strong lyrics about a strong subject, things from the *Satanic Bible* and Aleister Crowley." You know, Aleister Crowley is the occult leader who practiced black magic, calling himself "the Great Beast 666." He was reviled by the British press as "the Wickedest Man in the World" and has figured in rock from the start. He is present on the cover of the 1967 Beatles' album *Sgt. Pepper's Lonely Hearts Club Band.*

We'll play now the interview with Venom. You'll also hear some profanity here. [Videoclip of interview with Venom rock group played]

Interviewer: All right, we're sitting here, as is very obvious, in the bowels of Studio 54, believe it or not. [Venom lead singer howls like a wolf] And this is the ultimate revenge for disco tonight. I am sitting with two members of Venom [animal noises made by Venom], who are mostly housebroken. They're not bottle trained yet, though.

Cronos: Food. I will say f____.

Abaddon: Yes, right.

Cronos: F____.

Interviewer: For the home.

Cronos: Feel free to say f____.

Interviewer: Collectively you have a stronger image or a stronger personality than you do individually.

Abaddon: That's something we've said all the time from the start was this band works as a solid unit.

Cronos: Brick.

Abaddon: Yeah, it's like a brick. Say, you know, it's just a solid unit which works. As parts it's, you know—I'm not a good drummer. He's not a particularly good singer. But put it all together and it works as a unit.

Interviewer: So the sum is greater than the parts.

Cronos: Since the day we began, the Venom concept was "We are a brick." And what you do is you got this area of land over here and you take a brick and you throw it and it goes [blast of music]. And then you take the brick and throw it over there again and then you pick it up from there and you throw it and like that's how Venom works. You land on a town. [several voices and blast]

Abaddon: You land somewhere and you hit it.

Cronos: And here's Venom at full flame, then off to the next town.

Abaddon: *It's an old story that the Devil has the best tunes. And that's, that's the way we see it. We write strong lyrics about all sort of happenings or sort of things that have gone in the past and interesting things—things that, you know, that you read in Satanic Bible, that you read it from LaVey, that you read from Crowley.* [emphasis added] So basically, that's it—we're writin' strong lyrics about a strong subject.

Cronos: Get the likes of King Billy, as we call him. And—

Abaddon: Yeah, King Walker.

Cronos: And the guy like he's got it all wrong. His heart's in it. He's really going for it. And he thinks he's doing right and that, but the thing is you can't turn around and say to the kids, "Right, we're going to have, f____ing rip virgins' heads off." I mean, what the hell is the point of that?

Interviewer: You mean there's no truth to the rumor you're going to sacrifice Madonna on stage tonight?

Cronos: Oh, we'll f____ her on stage tonight. But why sacrifice her? She's beautiful.

Abaddon: Sacrificing over a bitch, what?

Cronos: Oh, yes. Let her die and bring her back for an encore, you know.

Interviewer: Uncle Jack says—

Cronos: Really happening drink. Buy some. Drink it. No problem. Drink this, you'll fall over. [Abaddon and Cronos lick a Jack Daniel's bottle]

So there you see and hear him admitting to writing satanic lyrics. Now we will play the first song by them which is called "Witching Hour." [Videoclip of "Witching Hour" by Venom played]

How dare they do this on planet earth! How dare they bring their filth and their Hell into the physical plane! This sank Atlantis and it will sink this continent and cause earth changes if we don't stop it now!

You may have noticed that in addition to having the symbol of Baphomet on stage as their backdrop, the singer, when he wasn't singing, was mouthing and screaming.

Going back to Slayer, there's another song which comes very close to being an actual satanic invocation from the *Satanic Bible.* They're all satanic invocations but this one is particularly blatant. It's similar to the "Invocation Employed towards the Conjuration of Lust," which is in the *Satanic Bible.* It goes,

> My rod is athrust!
> The penetrating force of my venom
> shall shatter the sanctity of
> that mind which is barren of lust;
> and as the seed falleth,
> so shall its vapours be spread
> within that reeling brain
> benumbing it into helplessness
> according to my will!
> In the name of the great God Pan,
> may my secret thoughts be marshaled
> into the movements of the flesh
> of that which I desire.

And then they say, "Hail Satan!" and with it a Hebrew name of God, Shemhamforash,[17] which I will not do. The song by Slayer, "Captor of Sin," is not a verbatim transcription of the invocation but the concept is the same. We must look not at the specific words but at the fohatic keys of the invocation. The wording need not be the same to tie in to the same energy. Both have a sexual purpose, the former being the invocation for conjuration of lust and the following being its enactment. So I am referring mainly to the first verse of "Captor of Sin," which reads,

> Harlots of hell spread your wings
> As I penetrate your soul
> Feel the fire shoot through your body
> As I slip into your throne

Cast aside, do as you will
I care not how you plead
Satan's child now stalks the earth
Born from my demon seed

So it goes. I'd like to play that short first verse. [Excerpt of "Captor of Sin" by Slayer played] The two members of the band Venom are not merely possessed, they are actual black magicians who are knowingly doing what they're doing. They're a part of the false hierarchy of Satan.

So every one of these heavy metal musicians has a direct line to Satan. It's the antithesis of the spiritual hierarchy of Jesus Christ, the heavenly hosts, the Ancient of Days and his saints on earth—it's the false hierarchy. And so we can see that it's the Devil—or any of his lieutenants—giving dictations. Abaddon, Cronos, and their ilk are his messengers.

Now, a lot of people have defended these lyrics. They say, it's just rock and roll, it's just marketing—anything but what it really is. We must look at what things are, not at what we think or wish or hope they are, and not at our denial of what they are. Not facing up to the reality of embodied Evil is America's number one problem. You get people who'll look you straight in the eye and say that it's harmless. This is the Devil's word—"It's harmless." Any time you hear someone say that something's harmless you can be sure it's not harmless.

So, now I'll move on to the next group, which is called Megadeth. You may think that's a strange name for a group but I heard on National Public Radio that there are actually two groups who wanted to call themselves Megadeth and they sued each other to use the name. So I'm not sure who won, but there it is.

Some of these rock album covers don't really pertain to the content of the album but this one does. This is a song which is called "The Skull beneath the Skin." And that picture on the front cover is exactly what it's about. It's about a satanic ritual of torturing a person by removing their scalp while they're still alive and putting plates and staples on the skull so the person cannot see, hear, or scream.

Other songs on the album are "Loved to Deth," "Looking down the Cross" and "Mechanix." "Loved to Deth" is about necrophilia. "Mechanix" is a bizarre sexual song. And "Looking down the Cross" is another satanic decree. So I'll read the lyrics to "The Skull beneath the Skin":

Mean and infectious
The evil prophets rise
Dance of the macabre
As witches streak the sky
Decadent worship of
Black magic and sorcery
In the womb of the Devils dungeon
Trapped without a plea

See thing in agony
Necrosis is the fate
Pins sticking through the skin
The venom now sedates
Locked in a pillory
Nowhere to be found
Screaming for your life

But no-one hears a sound
Hellpp mmmeeeeeee
Prepare the patients scalp
To peel away
Metal caps his ears
He'll hear *not* what we say
Solid steel visor
Riveted cross his eyes
Iron staples close his jaws
So no one hears his cries
The skull beneath the skin
Now your drawn and quartered
Your bones will make the X
Symbol stands for poison
And it's chained to your head
And as we fold your arms
To make the holy cross
We cross the crucifix
Religion has been lost
The skull beneath the skin.

So I'll play that now. [Excerpt of "The Skull beneath the Skin" by Megadeth played] This song conjures up the feeling of being in Hell. As if I were somehow trapped in Hell and could not call to Archangel Michael, and this is what the Devil would play as he was revving up his demons to attack me. I mean, that's what comes to mind when I hear that song.

I think we need to look at what the teenagers do at these concerts. And I'll give you a little more detailed description. This is Dave Benser, the heavy metal musician who gave us the first description of the different types of heavy metal. He also has talked about *moshing, slamming,* and *diving,* which are the three different dances that they do at the heavy metal concerts.

So this is him with a picture of himself as a child. And it's not hard to figure out what caused the change. This is the one who listened to KISS in first grade. This is him in action with his band. That's a cartoon that was printed with the article. And that is the band.

Notice he's holding a skull. It's this obsession with death. I mean, why would anyone want to be so obsessed with death? There is no good explanation except that they are either possessed or influenced by these other satanic groups who started it in the first place. And we know heavy metal originated with the fallen ones in the bottomless pit. There were groups in the sixties, such as the Rolling Stones, and Van Halen in the seventies who referred to the Devil but it was never, never quite like this. I mean, it was much more polished, sophisticated and subtle.

Here's how an article from the *Washington Post* describes heavy metal dancing:

> *To mosh: a verb meaning to fling every limb as far from the torso as possible while maintaining as little equilibrium as possible.*
>
> [Dave] Benser on moshing: "Normally we have a pit. In the pit, you mosh. It's an aggressive-type dance. The object is to be as off balance as you can. The one who is most off balance is the

best. You kick your feet and kick your legs and move your arms all about and shake your whole body. You can usually mosh during the slower songs, and you slam during the fast parts. A slam is just complete chaos."

To slam: a verb meaning to ricochet bodily off anyone, everyone. A full-contact, interactive ritual essential to heaviness.

Benser on slamming: "The first time you see someone slam, you look and say, 'Oh, that's stupid.' But the first time you actually do it. . . I remember the first time I actually moshed. That was in 1985 at Nuclear Assault and Overkill. The crowd was going crazy and I got involved. It just kind of happened. It was kinda like a whirlpool and I got sucked in. I've been moshing ever since. It's a way of life, I guess. I do it all the time.

"It lets you get the aggression out. It makes you sweat a lot. It's really a good time. It may not sound like it's all that fun. Banging bodies. Football is not as aggressive. This is full contact. You're constantly in motion and constantly touching another person. With football you're not in on every play.

"It's an incredible rush. You're always looking over your shoulder to make sure they don't dive on your head. *There's a real feeling of brotherhood down there in the pit.* [emphasis added] If someone falls, they pick you back up. Most of the time people catch you. Now and then you go somewhere and people are real amateurs. They don't know what's going on. They see someone flying through the air and they move."

To dive: a verb meaning to fly, preferably from a stage.

Benser on diving: "We must be airborne. Oh, the feeling of a dive. That's one of the best feelings in the world, 'cause you have to trust people underneath of you to catch you. If they don't, you get little black elbows like I have now."[18]

This full contact is, again, just so many ways they invent to release the life-force. Back in the *20/20* clip they showed a little bit of the chaotic dancing. It looked like leaping demons.

You know, it's like he said—you get sucked in. I don't think anybody in their right mind would do it. But once they actually see their friends doing it, then they try it. And it feels good because the light is rushing out of their chakras and they continue. It's sensual.

This is a fourteen-year-old—Patrick Gilmore is his name—with a Slayer T-shirt with the inverted pentagram over his heart. You really have to wonder. I mean, is he a Lightbearer or a reembodied Atlantean? It's hard to say. But if he's a Lightbearer, he's being victimized.

This is Greg Rabinowitz. He's nineteen, in college. He doesn't look like he's into heavy metal, does he? He is. He complains that when he goes to concerts that he's ostracized because he doesn't wear costumes like everyone else. When they pass out literature they don't even give him any because they say, "Oh, you don't need any of this."

This brings us to our next group—Dark Angel. That's their logo. Notice the bat wings. There's the complete album cover. Now, this is death metal again. This particular group is preoccupied with nuclear war. All their songs are about the end of the world, nuclear war. There's a song on there about Nostradamus. It's really too long for me to play but basically it's a fatalistic acceptance of the prophecies of Nostradamus, with no attempt to change them. And it's a reveling in the death and the destruction that is prophesied.

The song that I'm going to play now is called "Darkness Descends," which is the name of the album. The chorus of this song is an astral decree in the extreme, even though these songs are all astral decrees. The way he repeats the chorus and the way that he says it is a misuse of the science of the spoken Word. So I'll read the words. And by the way, whoever is the lyricist is not just some teenager. He is very sophisticated. I mean, I had to look up some of these words in the dictionary.

Fear
The world now stands ancient, showing her age
Antique, senile, archaic
Peroration impending, not one to assuage
The human remnants of earth
Pandemic winds chill the soul
Eradication of the will
Nihilism extracts its toll
Frightening the meekly servile

Sacrosanct, the religious ones
Are fast becoming extinct
Chaotic precursors of what will befall
Permeate the night air
The fear of the end preys on the minds
Of all the soon-to-be dead
With death at the hands of a hideous fiend
A grisly fate to comprehend

Now, this is the astral decree part here.

Death
This city is guilty
The crime is life
The sentence is death
Darkness descends

This is repeated over and over again in the song:

This city is guilty
The crime is life
The sentence is death
Darkness descends

It goes on—

Fire
Internal combustion, plutonic rage
The bodies create their own hell
The flame from within, unleashed from its cage
Purging the great sins of all
Admissions of guilt are all that are sought
By judges who have twisted laws
The quick abrogation of the populace
Striking with great enmity

Listing the ways in which we will die
As the prophets claim we will soon

Self-immolation that's unjustified
Stygian shores ahead loom
The coffins are ready, the death warrant signed
Depression has swiftly set in
Inimical powers against humankind
This charnelhouse ensanguined

Mortis

Decaying, the ruins fall swift to the ground
The carnage is morbid and great
Mephitic deathstench of corpses abound
The earth meets an untimely fate
The horrific malignance, spreading its wings
Across the expanse of the sky
Contamination and all that it brings
The judges commit genocide

Retaliation, a useless ploy
We've gazed into the face of fear
We know that it stands for our own bitter end
The end we realize is now here
The claws of denouement grasp at our lungs
Asphyxiation rules supreme
The future of mankind cut down while they're young
Our children die clutching their dreams . . .

The theme of this song is death, nuclear war, hopelessness—it is useless to retaliate, useless to defend ourselves, there's nothing we can do. So I'll play a little piece of "Darkness Descends" by Dark Angel now. [Excerpt of "Darkness Descends" played] I wanted you to notice how in the beginning of that song it started out slower and then it changed to this fast beat which is called "speed metal." No one played like that any more than five years ago. I had never heard anything like that before I started doing my research. The speed of it has a pummeling effect. You hear this and you just feel like you're being beat up. It's constant.

One thing I noticed is that the kick drum, the bass drum, is hitting every beat—and that's also unusual—as well as numerous other drums. But that constant, constant beating on your chakras is really something that is a more serious offense to the Light and it causes the protective membrane, which I discussed earlier, to rupture sooner than it would with lighter rock.

I think that rock and roll just gets more destructive by the year. And it takes less time for the Lightbearers to have their sheath torn and to let the astral through into the physical. Now as never before it's happening in record time.

There's another song by Dark Angel called "Perish in Flames"—again about nuclear war, this time talking about it actually happening instead of talking about the fear of it. It reads:

Your orders are given, the time for destruction is now
They'll give you no reason, you'll be the first so be proud
They've tracked you on radar, the fighters will lead to attack
The terror will freeze you, because you know you might not make it back

> Gods of war have gone insane
> You've played with fire, you're to blame
> Perish in flames
> Perish in flames
> Take a stand for what is right
> Time is now so make the fight
> Perish in flames
> Die in flames, DIE!!
>
> You've locked onto target, the missiles stand ready to launch
> Your mind bleeds in terror, destination lines up in path
> Your final descent, the bird of prey unleashes its wrath
> You've pulled the trigger, the world goes insane so you laugh.

We'll play that now. [Excerpt of "Perish in Flames" by Dark Angel played]

You know, we have so many psychologists talking about nuclear fear in children. Well, we don't need a psychologist to tell us where today's teens get their fear of nuclear war! This fear of war breaks down the will. The point must be made: Totalitarianism is worse than nuclear war!

I cited in my New Year's Day lecture "Apathy in America" that there have been 190 million people killed by World Communism in this century. This is totalitarianism. And in World War II and all the wars in this century 60 million have died.[19] So which is worse?

The apocalypse described in "Darkness Descends" fits a Soviet takeover much better than an all-out nuclear war. A surgical nuclear strike would be a part of Soviet takeover, as has been said. The slow death, burning and asphyxiation described might be from radiation or it could be death in a concentration camp. Solzhenitsyn mentioned live burial and drowning as Soviet mass-execution methods. "Darkness Descends" also fits chemical or bacteriological warfare.

Teenagers are being given a message of nihilism—that nothing can prevent what is to come. In fact, it is this very attitude of paralyzing fear that will bring the events to pass. And it is the beat of the music itself that acts as a *psychic carrier wave* for Soviet psychotronic warfare. It is the message of hopelessness and death that the Soviet psychics have been directing at America for decades, and this death metal becomes the anchor point in the physical for their mind manipulation of the American people.

It is highly doubtful that without rock music the Soviet psychics could have had any effect on Americans. The protective shield between the physical and the astral planes of the planet has been broken down by rock and roll in America. And the astral plane (which corresponds to the emotions and the subconscious mind) is the medium through which the Soviet psychics project the vibrations which cause depression, suicide and nihilism.

But it's not just heavy metal, it's all types of rock that provide this anchor point for what we call the International Capitalist/Communist Conspiracy. Just in case you doubt this, let's examine an album of mainstream rock from the mid-seventies. The album is *Hotel California*.

Now, we all know that the Eagles were an innocent band from California. Homegrown American boys playing nice party music for a fun-loving people, right? Wrong. "Hotel California," according to David Tame in his soon-to-be-published book *Rock and Role*, is the place where the Church of Satan was started.

Not only that, but when you look on the inside of this album you see that in addition to the Eagles, the band members who are in the center there, the crowd is made up of witches, homosexuals and other people of a lower vibration who you wouldn't want to be associated with. Not only that. If you look up in the middle window on the balcony there, you can see none other than Anton LaVey. Here's another shot, which is a little out of focus. Because of the dot structure of the litho you can see it a little bit better out of focus.

So we have the song "Hotel California," which sold millions of copies, and to many it's just an innocent song which doesn't mean anything. But to me it means a lot. So I will read now the lyrics to "Hotel California":

On a dark desert highway, cool wind in my hair
Warm smell of colitas rising up through the air
Up ahead in the distance, I saw a shimmering light
My head grew heavy and my sight grew dim
I had to stop for the night

There she stood in the doorway;
I heard the mission bell
And I was thinking to myself,
'This could be Heaven or this could be Hell'
Then she lit up a candle and she showed me the way
There were voices down the corridor,
I thought I heard them say...

Welcome to the Hotel California
Such a lovely place (such a lovely face)
Plenty of room at the Hotel California
Any time of year, you can find it here

Her mind is Tiffany-twisted, she got the Mercedes bends
She got a lot pretty, pretty boys, that she calls friends
How they dance in the courtyard, sweet summer sweat,
Some dance to remember, some dance to forget

So I called up the Captain,
'Please bring me my wine'
He said, 'We haven't had that spirit here since nineteen sixty nine.'
And still those voices are calling from far away,
Wake you up in the middle of the night
Just to hear them say...

Welcome to the Hotel California
Such a lovely place (such a lovely face)
They livin' it up at the Hotel California
What a nice surprise, bring your alibis

Mirrors on the ceiling,
The pink champagne on ice
And she said, 'We are all just prisoners here, of our own device'
And in the master's chambers,
They gathered for the feast
They stab it with their steely knives,
But they just can't kill the beast

Last thing I remember, I was
Running for the door
I had to find the passage back
To the place I was before
'Relax,' said the night man,
'We are programmed to receive.
You can check out any time you like, but you can never leave.'

I can't think of any physical event that this song would be describing other than a blood sacrifice. ("They stab it with their steely knives, but they just can't kill the beast.") "We haven't had that spirit here since nineteen sixty-nine" could refer to the presence of none other than LaVey himself on the balcony. And the rest of it, there's innuendo all the way along—"This could be Heaven, this could be Hell."

You know, why was this person drawn into this hotel as he was cruising along the road? It's the allure of Death and Hell. That's the way I interpret it. "We are all prisoners here, of our own device" is talking about the fact that most souls would not knowingly choose the left-handed path, but many are seduced by its glamour and choose it inadvertently. Then they're hooked by their own desires. And, of course, the part "You can check out any time you like, but you can never leave" is the trap, once they've sprung it.

This rock and the Satanism in it has influenced our leaders and it's in the mainstream. And it's influencing people who never heard of heavy metal. These satanistic references are on the radio every day. In fact, I heard that Gary Hart met Donna Rice at a party at the residence of Don Henley, who is a member of the Eagles. So where can we find our next generation of leaders? Gary Hart could very well have been president. If he had been listening to this group and if he were still listening to this type of music, do you think he would be open to the divine solutions to the problems that face us?

The next group I am going to talk about is Suicidal Tendencies. Their album is called *Join the Army*. And this is a very low caricature of Uncle Sam on the cover—"I Want You to Join the Army." The lyrics of this song, which I am going to read but not play, is another dictation from the suicide entity, which even makes a subtle reference to the influence of the Soviet psychics. To some of you this connection to Soviet psychics may be weak, but to me it is abundantly clear. The song is called "Suicidal Maniac."

A birth that came from more than sound
Now rages on from town to town
A giant grows more every day
And now the Maniac is here to stay

A feeling you can't kill
It's the power, it's a will
Controls your thoughts but you can't see

Just when you thought it safe he suddenly appears
He feels no pain, he has no mercy or no fears
He gives the message and your mind is filled with blue
And now the Maniac lives inside of you

He's back. The Suicidal Maniac

Each day he grows more and more
He's bigger now than ever before
His thoughts he'll compromise on never
He can't be stopped. He'll live forever

Blast away through the mind
A power of another kind
A presence that is growing out of sound

And now it's come, the time the Maniac I'll meet
He takes my hand and now I bow down to his feet
His love for me is like a father to a son
And now the Maniac and I are one

I bow to his might
Too powerful to fight
It's my destiny
Now the Maniac lives inside of me

He's back

An army at his command
A strength that you can't comprehend
A force unknown can now be told
The power of the world he holds

A feeling you can't kill
It's the power. It's the will
Controls your thoughts but you can't see
Just when you thought it safe he suddenly appears
He feels no pain, he has no mercy or no fears

He gives the message and your mind is filled with blue
And now the Maniac's a part of you
And the time has come. The Maniac you'll meet
He takes your hand and now you bow down to his feet
His love for you is like a father to a son
And now the Maniac and you are one

He's back—and he's a Suicidal Maniac.

I don't know where to start with that. The whole thing is a description of the suicide entity taking over a soul. And we have the first line—"A birth that came from more than sound." Now, we know that sound is the power of creation. In fact, we even know that the seed of the Wicked One used the rock beat to create their slave race.

What is this "more than sound" that is referred to? To me, it is vibration, energy, and I see it as the link to the Soviet psychics. What has brought suicide into America besides rock music?—Soviet psychics and their psychotronic warfare. They amplify what's bothering us and multiply it till many simply can't cope. They no longer have the will to live to fight.

There are undoubtedly multiple and complex causes for suicide in our national psyche but, in addition, consider the phrases "controls your thoughts but you can't see" and "he gives the message and your mind is filled with blue." To me, this is a reference to psychic mind manipulation.

Consider that on the astral plane the suicide entities (demons and discarnates) are working to steal the Light of the Children of God and the Soviets are working on the astral with their psychics to break down American will. The two factions can be seen to have a common enemy—the Lightbearers. Both have everything to gain by spilling the Light (Christ consciousness) of America. We also know that all of Death and Hell are working through the Soviet Union to destroy freedom on this planet. So again, things equal to the same thing are equal to one another.

And just to make sure that there will be no young patriotic Americans left, even the urge to defend our nation is exploited in this album. With the title "Join the Army," the single is a low-down parody of a marine recruiting song. It implores the youth to march to the "suicidal beat" and to join the army of "suicidal rock."

Now, it's an obvious and acknowledged fact even by the musicians themselves that rock music in our society today is the most powerful force for social change. Frank Zappa said that. It's affected our entire way of life. Although astrologically, rock came in on December 31, 1959, as I said earlier, a few "pioneers" were already rocking in 1956. The sixties moved on to folk rock and early political rock.

With rock America lost its first major war—Vietnam. We had never lost a war before. Rock made us spineless as a nation. We've never won a war since except Grenada, and that really wasn't a war. We won Grenada because of Oliver North, because he planned it and it was covert and we didn't have the media there to stop it! Now, of course, North is being crucified for his other patriotic and covert actions.

Rock has made it impossible for us to win anything. The most important force for winning battles is the will to fight. That is why combatants engage in propaganda campaigns and leafleting against their enemies. These tactics seem quaint when compared with the massive aural and psychic assault being waged on the Lightbearers of America through today's rock music. It has completely demoralized our youth and removed their will to fight.

And there's a reason for that. The syncopated 4/4 beat is a perversion of the 4/4 martial time of the base-of-the-spine chakra. Whereas the march time is the measured rhythm of the rising Kundalini fire, the syncopated 4/4 causes the exact opposite. It lowers the Kundalini. It actually drives it down—thus draining the upper chakras and the spine of the vital life-force of the Divine Mother.

The accumulation of the energy in the base chakra—which is naturally distributed throughout the body through the chakras, through the central nervous system—causes a buildup which may be released through violence, anger, sexual promiscuity and the black arts. The end result being that the will to be, to create, and to defend one's right to so be and to so create exists no more. Thus the defense of freedom and of life are missing from today's vacant youth.

So we come again to this concept of transference. This song, "Join the Army," advocates joining the suicidal army. Instead of being in the army fighting for life, our teenagers are encouraged to join the juggernaut of rock, marching toward self-destruction. Here are the lyrics:

> I got a story to tell, now listen up real well
> Pay attention this way to what I got to say
> Took it to the street, rap to the people we meet
> Now we're rocking out hard, to the Suicidal beat

Tried to deny our right, so we put up a fight
Just doing our thang, they tried to call it a gang
Saw the way we look, that's all that it took
That's all she wrote, they had their scapegoat

Dressed down, Homeboyz, minority—Join the Army

We're the few, we're the proud, we like to jam it loud
The music we play, won't have it any other way
We're armed to the bone with our music and our tone
Recruiting on the street, with the sound of our beat
Growing larger every day, and everytime we play
Don't need no college plan, we're just a hard-rocking band
We like our music to please, but we ain't gonna appease
No pressure's too much, to make us change our touch

Hardcore, Metal, the New Wave
We're not a gang—Join the Army

Don't be no fool, don't let your prejudice rule
Don't judge by your fear, judge us by your ear
Can't believe every word, of every story that you've heard
Just play the song, I know you'll start to rock along
Well I don't care, 'bout the clothes you wear
It's the size of your heart, not the length of your hair
Don't make no difference to me, the color that you be
Black, white or brown, it's all the same to me

Well if you still don't believe, you best get up and leave
Do what you must do, but this ain't the place for you
You got no right, but if you start a fight
We'll be rockin your head, but with our fists instead

I'll fight it with the band, right down till the end
Ask anyone I've met, this ain't no idle threat
Don't flap no fit, and it won't come to this
Bust as for me, I'm down with the Army

New York, London, Venice
Why join a gang?
Join the Army

Suicidal Rock—Join the Army
Suicidal Rock—Join the Army
Suicidal Rock—Join the Army
Suicidal Rock—Join the Army
Suicidal Rock—I WANT YOU TO Join the Army

So we'll play part of that now. [Excerpt of "Join the Army" by Suicidal Tendencies played] The back cover of the album is the high altar of suicide. Here you see the character that was depicted on the front of the album as a Rambo-type figure with a machine gun. He's now dead—impaled and dismembered on the suicidal altar. Another part of the album is mostly just contorted faces in despair in a collage. So that's Suicidal Tendencies.

Now we'll move on to Dirty Rotten Imbeciles. Better known as D.R.I., they're quite popular. Makes you wonder. This is more death metal. It's aimed at the destruction of society. And it casts the Americans as the imbeciles. It's very insulting. It also deals a lot with nuclear war.

The first song that I am going to talk about is called "Tear It Down." Listen to these words:

Fighting this society there's only
One way to win
We must stick together through
All thick and thin
Cross over the line of
Your stubborn closed mind
Don't be surprised at what
You might find
Things you thought wrong may have
Always been right
You'll probably find fault
In your reasons to fight
You really don't differ from
What I can see
Ain't it time to unite or is it just me?

Just as we watch them
Build this empire
So they shall watch us tear it down
If not with your words then with
The power of our sound!

We are the future so
Let's get things straight
Combine our forces
Before it's too late
Fighting ourselves
Can't go on any longer
We must fight together
If we want to grow stronger

We can tear it down
We must tear it down
We will tear it down

So we'll play that now. [Excerpt of "Tear It Down" by Dirty Rotten Imbeciles played] Before Mother even heard that song she commented to me that all heavy metal and rock in general has the message of "tear it down." And this song is just the crystallization of what was already there. Listening to Suicidal Tendencies from the next room while I was doing this research, she said, "It's as if there were a subliminal in this, and what it would be saying all the time, inaudibly, is 'tear down, tear down, tear down, tear down.' That's how it vibrates to me." And this was the other music, not "Tear It Down" that you just heard.

So in the next song we have an actual simulated nuclear attack. It's called "Oblivion." It begins with an air raid siren and the sound of a crowd screaming in terror. You hear the sound of a nuclear bomb being dropped from a plane and instead of the explosion, the music begins with a violent crash of drums and electric guitar. I'll read you the lyrics:

The day has come
The time is near
For all to end

It's true, it's here
It's all over now
No way to stop
The button's been pushed
The bomb's been dropped
   The city is melting
   The sky burns red
   The ocean is boiling
   We'll soon be dead
Death has come knocking
The door's open wide
He's let himself in
No place to hide
A tidal wave of power
Coming over the hill
A great wall of thunder
Swooping down for the kill
Leveling, destroying
Everything in its path
Just seconds left now
Till we feel its wrath

People run rabid
From the great blast
The Beast is upon us
It's here at last
The streets echo screams
Filled with fear
All through the universe
But no one will hear!

[Excerpt of "Oblivion" by Dirty Rotten Imbeciles played] This is how our twelve-year-olds relate to nuclear war. That's it. That's all there is. They never heard of Thomas Krebs or Danny Graham or High Frontier or any of the speakers whom we've heard Mother interview at Summit University Forum who've told us the real story. This is why we have no will to prepare to fight nuclear war, if necessary, and to remain free. This is it. I mean, you don't need to look any further than these lyrics and this sound because what you grow up on you internalize and it becomes a part of you.

And if the youth internalize this song, they've lived it, and they are already dead (so to speak) because they 'died' in the attack. They're psychologically dead from that time on—from the time they've heard this song. It's the explosion of the base chakra. It's the ultimate hatred of the Divine Mother. It's just like putting a nuclear bomb on the base chakra of the Mother to blow up her womb so she cannot bear the Divine Manchild—and in this case the Mother is America, the Motherland.

This is from Revelation 12.

> And there appeared another wonder in heaven; and behold a great red dragon, having seven heads and ten horns, and seven crowns upon his heads.
>
> And his tail drew the third part of the stars of heaven, and did cast them to the earth: and the dragon stood before the woman

> which was ready to be delivered, for to devour her child as soon as it was born. . . .
>
> And when the dragon saw that he was cast unto the earth, he persecuted the woman which brought forth the man child. . . .
>
> And the serpent cast out of his mouth water as a flood after the woman, that he might cause her to be carried away of the flood. . . .
>
> And the dragon was wroth with the woman, and went to make war with the remnant of her seed, which keep the commandments of God, and have the testimony of Jesus Christ.

The rock music you've been hearing is the 'water' (i.e., astral sewer) that the dragon cast out of his mouth "as a flood." Rock music is the open warfare declared by the seed of Darkness against the remnant of the seed of the Woman. This was prophesied. People should have seen it coming when Elvis Presley arrived on the scene. The furor that was raised over Presley in the 1960s has today become the worship of a fallen angel.

Today's parents think today's music is "harmless" and they allow their children to continue to listen to it, to continue to destroy themselves and in the process they are building a future generation which has no will to defend our nation against a nuclear attack. It is all-out war against the Lightbearers.

If we want to know where nuclear fear is coming from, we should look at the rock bands, not at our government, and certainly not at our military. Some psychologists have even said that we shouldn't teach children about nuclear war because it will incite fear in them. But we let them listen to the music.

So I think, as parents, we should teach children early the facts about what's really going on. And if they are going to get caught up in this death metal, which sometimes parents are helpless to prevent, at least they will have the early teaching from their fathers and mothers that they can refer back to when and if they regain their senses.

ECP: The comment that El Morya made about "Oblivion" is that it is an attack on the heart and on the threefold flame. It is the bombardment of the physical heart and the disruption of the heartbeat, which disrupts the ability of the soul to attune with the threefold flame in the secret chamber of the heart.

One of the things that Saint Germain and El Morya taught me in December concerning death is that the projection of death has no power over you unless it can get you to accept death. So they begin with the projection that you are going to die, which is what all this death metal is—"You are going to die by nuclear war." It pounds into you by this irregular beat—the syncopated beat that is the perversion of the 4/4 time of the base chakra, as you said.

So, once you have accepted that you are going to die, then you are wide open through the heart chakra for your death by the disruption of the heartbeat. And Jesus said that in these days men's hearts would fail them for fear.[20] And it's through the rock beat that the heart is destroyed and death enters. Death cannot enter your life if you do not give in to it and accept it. And the projection of the Death entity who comes in many guises works very, very hard on people, even apart from rock music, to get them to accept death.

To me this is a planetary plot. A large percentage of this nation is accepting nuclear death because this music—the fastest growing segment of the rock industry—is entering the psyche at the subconscious level. You are absorbing the message subconsciously even when you're not aware of it. And so you are not consciously counteracting it.

SCP: In fact, even as we sit here we're probably absorbing radio waves that are being transmitted which we have no control over. And I don't know how they affect the body physically. But I know that on a spiritual and astral level the constant playing twenty-four hours a day of this music, especially in the big cities but even out here in Montana, has a lot to do with our loss of will even though we are unwilling participants. Because even if we decide to tune it out, it still passes through us.

So the good news is I don't have any more heavy metal songs to play! But I do have some more slides and a video promo that has heavy metal imagery and I am also going to tell you about the record companies. So we continue.

This is the back cover of the Dirty Rotten Imbeciles' album. It looks to me like it has a black widow spider in the middle of it. This shows what they think of America. It says, "Imbeciles of America," and it has everyone holding up placards with pictures of imbeciles on them. That's from their insert inside of their album. They had many more little cartoons but I thought that was one you should see.

Now we come to the record companies. You wonder who's behind all this. Well, here we go. Combat Records, Death Records, and Suicidal Records, which is the record company for Suicidal Tendencies. And then we have the record company which is responsible for a large portion of the heavy metal and that is Metal Blade Records.

So I'd like to play you a video promo now for some of these albums. This is the Combat Rock promo. ["Combat Visual Catalogue" video played]

Major Mayhem (Paul Aaronson): OK. Listen up, you brain-dead mongers. You want to be metal heads, you gotta listen to the right metal, right? OK, here's your basic training.

Now, pay attention 'cause my name is Major Mayhem. And it's my job to turn you goons into proper combat metal troops, no matter how sniveling and weak you are. OK, now that we got that straight, grab these combat discs and stick 'em between your ears. You got Venom, *Possessed,* Exodus, *Bonded by Blood,* and Slayer, *Hell Awaits*. This is the death metal squadron. Ride with these guys and the Devil is your co-pilot.

All right, so you mastered death, now you're ready to try special forces—the combat T-squad to you goons. Talas, *Live Speed* and *Sink Your Teeth,* Tokyo Blade, *Midnight Rendezvous* and *Night of the Blade,* and TKO, *In Your Face*. These boys specialize in administering violence with taste.

Now, these next guys you don't want to mess with—the combat rangers. Megadeth, *Killing Is My Business,* Abattoir, *Vicious Attack,* and Sabotage, *Dungeons*. If there's a dirty job to be done, you send in the rangers and pray to God you live.

The combat army marches with a strong infantry. Get your combat boots stompin' with OZ, *Fire in the Brain* and *III Warning,* the Rods, *Let Them Eat Metal* and *The Rods Live,* and Merciful Faith, *Don't Break the Oath,* Trouble, the *Skull,* and Action, *Look Out for the Night*. Any of these divisions can pulverize your pea-sized brain.

And finally there's the combat ultra assassin squad. Oh, my God! So hideous, even I don't get too near them. Impaler, *Rise of the Mutants*.

OK, pinheads, that's your basic training [yelling and screaming in the background] in combat metal. You can thank your lucky stars we've trained your ears in the finest metal wealth in the whole of the U.S. of A. Combat Records. Your next phase of training will include Exciter, Possessed, Thrasher, Running Wild, Nasty Savage, and the dangerous agent Steele. Hallow's Eve.

Remember, bang your head till you're dead. Dismissed!

You will notice that all these fans are young and that they're all doing the Satanist mudra. That clip was tacked onto the end of a heavy metal concert video. These videos are available to children of all ages—not just records but videos. All the videoclips we've shown tonight, with the exception of *20/20,* were bought *over the counter at suburban record stores in upper middle-class neighborhoods.*

Now, I'd like to go on to political heavy metal, which I won't play but I just want to talk a little bit about it.

There's a band called Corrosion of Conformity. This is their album—*Technocracy.* This album did not include the lyrics. And I tried to listen to the music and get some of the lyrics but it was impossible. I couldn't hear one word in any of the songs. But I did get out of the inside an insert, an order form for T-shirts. And I'll read you what the T-shirts say.

Now, this one says, "American dollars and weapons gleam, support another corrupt regime. Human rights long out of style, another killing, another farce trial. Intervention, all the millions spent in aid, spent on war parade. Technological march of death, finalize a child's last breath. Intervention, warmongers in search of victims, make their mark in history, as the children die of asphyxiation. Another child killed for political position. Intervention, we ain't gonna study war no more. Stop funding war in Central America. No more murder in our name."

This is T-shirt #2. It has, again, the symbol for Death Records. I believe that the logo represents a symbol for radiation. And the text says, "They rip the flesh from our mother's breast / Because the War Machine runs on high test. / Greedy fools don't have the sense / To leave the radiation where it rests."

This is supposed to be profound. It's more anti-American rhetoric. And these are "nice boys" from North Carolina.

That is the end of our heavy metal section. Thank you.

"The Summit Lighthouse Sheds Its Radiance O'er All the World to Manifest as Pearls of Wisdom." This lecture by Sean C. Prophet was **delivered** on **Thursday, July 2, 1987,** at *FREEDOM 1987* in the Heart of the Inner Retreat at the **Royal Teton Ranch, Montana.** It was edited for print by Sean C. Prophet and Elizabeth Clare Prophet for this week's Pearl with material taken from a lecture delivered by the Messenger on February 21, 1982. (**1**) ***Nephilim.*** Hebrew "those who fell" or "those who were cast down," from the Semitic root *naphal* "to fall," rendered in the Greek Septuagint, a late translation of the Hebrew scriptures, as "giants" (Gen. 6:4; Num. 13:33). (**2**) See "Prologue on the Sons of Jared" (taken from the Second Book of Adam and Eve), in *Forbidden Mysteries of Enoch: The Untold Story of Men and Angels,* pp. 354–59. (**3**) augmented by the full complement of Martian misqualification of energy: aggression, anger, arrogance, argumentation, aggravation, annihilation, aggressive mental suggestion, anti-Americanism, anti-Father, anti-Mother, anti-Christ, and anti-Holy Spirit energies. (**4**) See Mark L. Prophet and Elizabeth Clare Prophet, *The Lost Teachings of Jesus II,* p. 13. (**5**) See Mark L. Prophet and Elizabeth Clare Prophet,

The Lost Teachings of Jesus I, pp. 3–19. (**6**) Matt. 11:12. (**7**) John 1:1, 3. (**8**) The work done on the string may be computed with the formula Work = Force × Distance. Assuming a force of 1 ounce on the guitar string and a string displacement of .25 inches we obtain

$$\frac{1 \text{ oz}}{1} \times \frac{.25 \text{ in}}{1} \times \frac{1 \text{ lb}}{16 \text{ oz}} \times \frac{1 \text{ ft}}{12 \text{ in}} = 1.302 \times 10^{-3} \text{ ft.lb.}$$

Converting this to joules we obtain

$$\frac{1.032 \times 10^{-3} \text{ ft.lb}}{1} \times \frac{1 \text{ joule}}{0.7376 \text{ ft.lb}} = 1.763 \times 10^{-3} \text{ joules.}$$

Taking this energy over one second we obtain 1.7653×10^{-3} joules/sec or 1.7653×10^{-3} watts of power.

The typical maximum output of a concert P.A. system is 35,000 watts. The multiplication factor of the original signal to the amplified output is

$$\frac{35{,}000 \text{ watts}}{1.7653 \times 10^{-3} \text{ watts}} = 1.982 \times 10^{+7} \text{ or } 19{,}826{,}688.$$

(**9**) Rev. 8:13; 9; 11:13, 14. (**10**) John 8:23. (**11**) Edgar Evans Cayce, *Edgar Cayce on Atlantis,* ed. Hugh Lynn Cayce (New York: Warner Books, 1968), pp. 74–77. (**12**) **Hydra.** The Lernaean Hydra was a many-headed monster in Greek mythology slain by Hercules (his second labor). According to one version of the myth the Hydra had 8 or 9 heads, one of them immortal. Some even credit the monster with 50, 100 or even 10,000 heads. The Hydra terrorized Lerna, a holy district on the coast of Greece 5 miles from the city of Argos, until Hercules was sent to kill it. Each time Hercules cut off a head, however, 2 or 3 grew in its place until Hercules' charioteer Iolaus cauterized their roots with firebrands. Then Hercules severed the immortal head using a sword, or a golden falchion, and buried it, still hissing. According to Virgil's *Aeneid,* the Hydra was also a source of underground rivers which used to burst out and flood the land. If one of its numerous channels was blocked, the water broke through elsewhere. Hercules first used fire to dry the ground and then closed the channels. (**13**) Jane Leavy, "The Decibel Disciples: Young-at-Heart Headbangers and Their Heavy Metal Way of Life," *Washington Post,* 4 June 1987, sec. C. (**14**) David Gelman et al., "Depression," *Newsweek,* 4 May 1987, pp. 48–52, 54, 57. (**15**) Walt Harrington, "The Devil in Anton LaVey," *Washington Post Magazine,* 23 February 1986. (**16**) **Extremely Low Frequency.** Radio waves in the 10-hertz range which are known to affect human health and behavior. (**17**) ***Shem hameforash.*** Hebrew for "the complete name of God," known as the Explicit Name, or the Ineffable Name. (**18**) Leavy, "The Decibel Disciples." (**19**) See p. 45, par. 7; p. 48, par. 1; p. 71, n. 8. (**20**) Luke 21:25, 26.

DISCOGRAPHY

Combat Tour Live: The Ultimate Revenge. Slayer, "I Am the Antichrist"; "Venom Interview Part 1"; Venom, "Witching Hour"; and "Combat Visual Catalogue." Combat Records MXV 8038, 1985. Videocassette.

Dark Angel. "Darkness Descends" and "Perish in Flames." *Darkness Descends.* Combat Records 88561-8114-2, 1986.

Dirty Rotten Imbeciles. "Tear It Down" and "Oblivion." *Crossover.* Restless/Death Records 72201-1, 1987.

Eagles. "Hotel California." *Hotel California.* Asylum Records 6E-103, 1976.

Megadeth. "The Skull beneath the Skin." *Killing Is My Business---.* Combat Records MX 8015, 1985.

Metallica. "Fight Fire with Fire," "Ride the Lightning" and "Fade to Black." *Ride the Lightning.* Elektra Records 60396-2, 1984.

Slayer. "The Antichrist," "Evil Has No Boundaries," "Haunting the Chapel" and "Captor of Sin." *Show No Mercy.* Restless/Metal Blade Records 71034-2, 1987.

Suicidal Tendencies. "Suicidal Maniac" and "Join the Army." *Join the Army.* Caroline Records CD 1336, 1987.

"The Children of Heavy Metal." Corr. Stone Phillips. Prod. Danny Schechter. *20/20.* ABC, 21 May 1987.

Vol. 30 No. 37 *Beloved Saint Germain* *September 13, 1987*

Freedom 1987

VI

The Opening of the Seventh Seal

An Aura of Violet Flame Intensifying

In the heart of Sanat Kumara, Keepers of the Flame, I AM here! [1-min. 8-sec. standing ovation]

Let the hills and valleys, let the mountains and streams now sing the song of the coming of the Ancient of Days. Angelic hosts of Light, herald now the descent of our LORD, our sponsor, our Life.

O thou Magnificent One, Sanat Kumara, we thy Sons, we thy emissaries do therefore speak to thine own in thy name I AM THAT I AM Sanat Kumara.

Keepers of the Flame, rejoice, for our God is nigh and the Mighty I AM Presence hath not fled before the awful face of the coming of world karma. Therefore, flee not. For by the Ancient of Days and the I AM Presence thou shalt prevail! [27-sec. applause]

I bid you welcome to my heart of hearts and to the heart of hearts of my beloved Portia. Therefore, be seated as we enter freedom's fire.

It would appear that it is a moment of worlds colliding, worlds in collision, beloved. And therefore, the stalwart and the astute are not caught between two worlds but enter in to the Great Macrocosm of the Cosmic Christ.

Blessed hearts, you have seen many a narrow passage. But you are here as I AM. Therefore, we together shall remain! [17-sec. applause] Thus I bring to you my message on the opening of the seventh seal.[1]

Understand, then, the mystery of the Word. Understand that the seventh seal is the seal that has been set upon all that has opposed the Seventh Ray and the Seventh Age of Aquarius. The opening of this seal is for the initiation of the chakras of all dwellers upon this planet by the Seventh Ray in each of the rays of being. Thus, violet flame in seven chakras becomes the initiator by the priesthood of Melchizedek of every chakra of every lifestream upon earth.

Thus, there is an accumulation, as you have been taught, of personal and planetary karma that has been a violation of freedom on this planet. So severe has been the violation of the gift of free will and the cosmic dispensation of freedom, beloved, that the travail in the land, that the sorrow and the burden of a Mother's heart must surely be grave indeed.

Knowing, however, what is the mystery of that which comes to pass before your eyes, as a mist coming up out of the ground of mystification to many, you may therefore narrowly pass through this passage unto a golden age. Realize, then, as we have said before, that the golden age must appear—whether physically or in the etheric octave remains the freewill decision of those who occupy time and space.

What is certain, beloved, is that the chelas of Sanat Kumara, sealed in his heart as I AM, shall truly endure, shall truly be the spiritual survivors who have with them all of the components of being necessary to individualize, to occupy and to be in whatever octave is called for.

This, then, I commend to you: the path of self-mastery in the Seventh Ray as applied now to the purification of the chakras by the violet flame, now to the building of the Deathless Solar Body by the power of the Divine Mother within you, now to the sense of eternality, and now to the defense of it here, there and everywhere at the cardinal points of being.

Know, then, beloved, that I come with my mantle. And I come with a door yet ajar, for the Wesak message has indeed preserved hope and opportunity to the Lightbearers and has given to us an opportunity to assist individuals one by one on the Path.[2] This, therefore, we do. And we choose to do it this day, beloved.

We choose to come with our momentum of the violet flame. We choose to enable you to understand that those things which may cross the planet ere the New Day is born may be a chemicalization such as described in these seven trumpet judgments, a chemicalization that may accrue from war or cataclysm or merely the melting of the elements of human karma with such a fervent heat[3] as to cause many untoward and hitherto unseen conditions.

Blessed hearts, though my message is one of Victory, there is one line that I would leave with you and that is *"Prepare for the worst."* Therefore, when ready and prepared, you can *"Live for the best"* and continue to roll back the tides of Darkness and go forth to rescue souls.

Blessed ones, it is your hour and the hour of your God-mastery of the physical octave—of the mind and especially of the emotions. Therefore I leave to your discernment, beloved ones, what is the necessary preparation for the worst and, in fact, what might be the worst that may be coming upon this planetary body.

Apart from this, beloved, we take heart. We take heart indeed that many have been called from inner planes to become Keepers of the Flame. We take heart in progress, individual by individual.

We pray for greater alertness and we could desire more. But, beloved, we are grateful for that which is. We affirm it. And we declare it before the Court of the Sacred Fire: that the chelas of El Morya, that the Keepers of the Flame of Saint Germain have determined to plant their feet in this earth and not to leave the earth until God-victory does appear in their very temples!

We are gratified! I am and so is the Goddess of Liberty, beloved. We say, keep on keeping on! Open the doors for those who are ready to see, hear and respond to your knock, which is my own.

Blessed ones, let us continue as we have begun. Let us press on, therefore, and recognize that truly there is the space of silence in heaven.[4] There is that opportunity of a cosmic interval to collect therefore by the mighty net of the LORD many souls who are on the verge of entering this vibration.

Therefore, my beloved, my greatest desire is to attach to you during this conference an aura of violet flame intensifying, a flame that does become the fire enfolding itself. Therefore, I, Saint Germain, shall attend the conclusion of this event and my angels shall attend.

Thus, violet flame angels positioned in this Heart stand to increase and multiply your calls to the violet flame. And therefore, as you prepare to receive this aura of light, know that it is as a miniature focus of the Great Central Sun Magnet in the Seventh Ray, multiplying the power of the ascension flame and the ascension path of beloved Serapis Bey.

This, beloved, becomes a great magnet of Love and Freedom to all whom you meet, a sustaining support for your own crossing over to higher octaves, even places in the physical plane such as the Inner Retreat, where the etheric octave does yet dominate and the physical with its corruptions has not so much taken over to the saturation of the astral and mental belts.

Come, then, beloved, and be comforted in this my home of Light, this being the forest where I walk and the mountains where I climb. For, beloved, it is good to be almost physical. It is good for an Ascended Master such as I to feel the earth and anchor my presence. Thus, having long had the habit of walking in the wood, you may know that I do occupy this place in contemplation of the Lord of the World and the opening he has established for the Lord Sanat Kumara.[5]

Therefore, the Lord of the World with the Lady Master Venus, Sanat Kumara's twin flame, has diligently served, using the energy of your decrees and many hosts of angels who have gathered, to establish a greater opening and a provision for the deceleration of Sanat Kumara's vibration into this land and property. Thus, step by step, beloved, because of your presence, the Hierarchy of Light desires to amalgamate here forcefields of Light and further dispensations wherewith to assist the Lightbearer, as is our dispensation from Alpha's Wesak Proclamation.

Beloved hearts, understand that as we view the world in this hour we are seeing and understanding that choices made are being made by the weight of world karma, by the manipulation of the fallen ones, and by the absence of virtue and the raising up of the Light within. It is an hour, beloved, when those who have not banked the fires of the resurrection and have so very little going for them can scarcely make it to the exalted state that you have achieved by the long years of your service or even by the intensity of your service in the short hours and days of your affiliation with this activity.

Realize, then, that those who have not seen the vision nor ridden the tide of the incoming Light, these have not the wherewithal, beloved, to enter in to the maximum grace and the higher Light, and they are truly left high and dry. And they have naught else to do but to see and to make their decisions based upon what they refuse to see and what they have refused to be.

The tragedy of tragedies, beloved, is therefore in the disarming of Europe.[6] And as I have told you in my Pearl of Wisdom [number 25[7]], with the coming of Wesak there has been a conclusion of the dispensation accorded to me by the Cosmic Council through the efforts of these Messengers. Beloved, any dispensation that I may have had for the sponsorship of the European continent has been withdrawn. The only sponsorship, then, which I retain is to assist the Lightbearers of Europe. But to place myself upon European soil in order to stand between that continent and the karma that is coming upon it, this I am not allowed to do according to Cosmic Law, to our Father and to the Cosmic Council.

Therefore, beloved, this is the message that I bring to you, for I desire your hearts to understand the meaning of this. And inasmuch as the earth is one, you can see the ramifications and the repercussions of that which may come upon Europe by her being left vulnerable as well as that which may come upon America.

Thus, it is necessary for the Lightbearers to gather together, to give the calls, to establish such a mighty fortress of Light at this Royal Teton Ranch as to create a pillar of fire for the protection of this continent. For it has the maximum opportunity according to its karma, beloved, to be a place of survivability.

Even though you may consider other areas of the world far out of reach of harm's way in an East/West power conflict, I tell you it is the sponsorship of this nation and the Lightbearers here by Sanat Kumara, despite the evildoings of their leaders, that does enable them to receive that divine intervention in time of trouble that many others are not able to receive. Thus, if it has occurred to you that you are called to gather in a place [America] of danger, I tell you, beloved, often where there is maximum danger there is maximum protection. And so it is the case.

But, beloved, we look not to the specific hour of that which may be the worst eventuality. But we look to the burst of Light. We look to the Light that is building. We look to that which has been accomplished. And we look to the auras of the saints (yourselves) as these auras become a greater and greater Light and, therefore, by the very magnetism of the aura you are carried up and apart from harm's way. This does not in any way eliminate the necessity for the physical preparation—for the physical survivability of the physical equation.

However, blessed ones, I tell you, without the Light you will see that one is taken and another is left.[8] And those who have the Light and diligently follow the calling of Serapis Bey to attend those three services a week[9] that comprise Morya's three dots and the three plumes of your threefold flame, they will know that the banking of the fires cell by cell, they will know that the charging of the aura, the fasting, the self-emptying and the infilling with Light will see them through in the end of Darkness unto the beginning of Light.

It is an hour when I come solely for Lightbearers of the world. I come, then, for that rescue. I come, then, for that reinforcement. And I come with violet flame angels. These violet flame angels with myself, beloved, answer each and every single call you make concerning world conditions and World Communism and its Western supporters. But understand, beloved, as we answer the call and multiply the decrees by the power of ten thousand-times-ten thousand[10] we shall not deliver a dispensation that can increase the judgment of that Darkness until there is greater Light raised up in the Lightbearers.

Thus, our agenda is to rescue the Lightbearers. And we shall see by their rescue how their calls shall be enforced and reinforced by the God Surya and the hosts of the Light. We shall see, beloved, how the very call within your heart does amplify the mighty threefold flame that is able, *the mighty threefold flame that is able,* the mighty threefold flame of the entire Spirit of the Great White Brotherhood within you that is able!

Remember the divine spark. Remember the Presence of the I AM THAT I AM. Remember, then, beloved, that I AM Saint Germain, that I AM your father and the father of this activity. And therefore, you shall understand, positioned as a wedge of light, as has been explained to you, that during the period of the opening of the seventh seal, during the period of the intensification of the seven trumpet judgments, there shall be the wedge of the Ruby Ray, the wedge of white fire, the wedge of the violet flame. As you invoke it, we multiply it. As we multiply it, invoke it again, beloved.

We are determined that your understanding shall prevail, shall be sustained, and that you shall raise up this crystal chalice of Light and that the Elohim may come through you.[11] Beloved ones, it is the singular hope that we cherish in our hearts!

Do you understand, beloved, that it is important that you receive Elohim dictations that may be played continuously, that you sing to the Elohim, that you love Elohim. For Elohim is God, God manifesting in the seven rays, personified according to the great beings of Light to whom you call. Understand that it is God who comes to earth through the seven thunders who have been called the seven stars of the morning.[12]

Therefore, beloved ones, as *Noblesse Oblige*[13] is our motto, so then oblige elemental life. Let them be saturated with the violet flame. Let them be infilled now, for truly they have not sinned against God or man. And therefore, we the hosts of Light may bless them and assist them also. Earth, then, begins to take upon itself a glow of the aura of the violet flame in this hour, beloved. It is the violet flame of my angels. It is the violet flame you have invoked. And it shall intensify Earth's aura as you continue to invoke it in these hours.

O beloved, that violet flame aura gives us a vision, gives us a hope of the incoming golden age and earth now meshing with the great aura of the violet planet. Beloved, this is the living desire of beloved Omri-Tas. Let violet flame continue unabated. For, beloved, it does consume, *it does consume,* it does consume planetary karma and all cycles of darkness, beloved.

And therefore, violet flame Cosmic Beings step forth now. They, beloved, do step forth, for they have said to the Almighty One that whereas those who have served with the planet earth may no longer have dispensations, they may at least approach a little closer to the earth and beam their violet flame rays into the very hearts of Lightbearers everywhere. And hopefully, beloved, this shall be an impetus to Lightbearers calling forth the violet flame, more and more and more, intensifying and increasing, therefore, until the whole earth is filled with the violet flame. And, beloved, the violet flame is the mighty mitigating factor.

And when you give the Hail Mary, even then the violet flame is released. For Mother Mary has determined in counsel with us, with the Darjeeling Council, that in response to the Hail Mary said by those of the new age there shall be accordingly a release from her heart of her own full-gathered momentum of the violet flame from her own causal body of Light. And this is the desire of Raphael. This is the desire of Mother Mary. And this shall be the emanation forthcoming, therefore, of their retreat over Portugal, beloved. Let it continue. Let grace flow.

Let the violet flame, therefore, be understood as that which every Ascended Master and Cosmic Being is beaming forth in this hour. Let the violet flame decrees go forth! Let the violet flame songs go forth! Let all who know of the violet flame give it as a gift from my heart to every stranger they meet.

O beloved ones of Light, there is sufficient violet flame in the new little book[14] that is put forth. So use it. So give it. So teach the violet flame. So it is the hope. And so tell all the nations and tell all the people that the violet flame is their hope for the mitigation of those things that must take place in the eventuality of cycles changing and the New Day dawning on planet earth.

Blessed ones, more I cannot say or tell except, beloved, I love you with a fervent heart. I love you with the fervor of Almighty God. I love you with the fervor of Justice and of Freedom and of Mercy. I love you with a fervor of fifty thousand years of loving you and more. Beloved, I AM your heart. I AM loving you within your heart. And I place my purple fiery heart with your heart for the remainder of your stay in the Heart of the Inner

Retreat that you might receive a pulsation and a renewal.

O angels of my bands, go forth now! Go forth and cover the earth with lightning speed. Go forth now and cover the earth even beyond lightning speed, even beyond the speed of light. And go now, deliver these ampules of violet flame to all who are Keepers of the Flame at heart, to all who are Lightbearers at heart who have not made contact with the Heart of the Inner Retreat or Gautama Buddha.

Thus, beloved, the violet flame angels go forth. And thus, they have already returned. Thus, understand how timelessness, eternity and light, light! light! light! may flood the earth by angel wings, by angel hearts, by vision, by instantaneous precipitation of the Master Alchemists, by the full power of Elohim. Thus, every potential Keeper of the Flame and Lightbearer on earth has now received from my angels ampules of violet flame deposited in the heart, awaiting, therefore, their adoration [of the Seventh Ray of the Godhead].

Beloved ones of the violet flame, O Keepers of the Flame, my love shall not be thwarted, it shall not be daunted. Defend, therefore, my name and teaching. Defend the violet flame. And say it [the violet flame decree] into the teeth of every problem and thereby create such a vortex of light, beloved, that when you give the calls to Archangel Michael his legions of Light have ten thousand-times-ten thousand more action-potential because the violet flame does charge every blue-flame word you utter, every command, every decree, every prayer, every hope, every faith and every act of grace, of charity.

Beloved ones of the Light, I AM Saint Germain. I shall not cease to be speaking with you this day. I AM charging your forcefields with light. I refuse, therefore, to acknowledge any darkness in the world. Though I attend the dark councils of the dark ones, I AM there, beloved, denying their very darkness and calling forth that judgment.

I ask you, therefore, to remember me in these councils and to call forth the judgment upon the dark ones "wherever Saint Germain is, where he does maintain his presence, watching and listening and sending to all hosts of the planetary body the information of K-17 and Lanello regarding that action that is being plotted against America and all Lightbearers."

Beloved ones of the living flame, lo, I AM THAT I AM! Lo, I AM the mystery of the Word. And I tell you, beloved, I AM sealing you now by the power of the seventh seal of Almighty God. Even as you are sealed, beloved ones, so you are guarded, you are protected, and there is prevented from entering into you that which has been opened upon the earth by the opening of the seventh seal.

These seals are not the same, and yet understand there is a Seventh Ray initiation of the sealing by the seventh seal. Realize, then, that those who carry love of Light in their hearts do retain that seal.

In the heart of Sanat Kumara, I have come. I will not leave, for I remain until the fullness of purpose of *FREEDOM 1987* is complete.

Hail, Keepers of the Flame! I AM Saint Germain! And I AM here and here to stay! [1-min. 13-sec. standing ovation]

"The Summit Lighthouse Sheds Its Radiance O'er All the World to Manifest as Pearls of Wisdom."
This dictation by Saint Germain was **delivered** through the Messenger of the Great White Brotherhood Elizabeth Clare Prophet on **Saturday, July 4, 1987,** at *FREEDOM 1987* in the Heart of the Inner Retreat at the **Royal Teton Ranch, Montana.** In the lecture before the dictation, "The Opening of the Seventh Seal," the Messenger read and interpreted Revelation 8–11 on the opening of the seventh seal and the seven trumpet judgments. Lecture and dictation available on 116-min. videocassette HP87045, $24.95 (add $.90 for postage), or two 90-min. audiocassettes, A87047, $13.00 (add $.80 for postage). (**1**) Rev. 8:1. (**2**) See Gautama Buddha, "For the Alignment of a World, 'A Proclamation' by Alpha: Wesak Address 1987," p. 244, pars. 3–7. (**3**) II Pet. 3:10, 12. (**4**) Rev. 8:1. (**5**) **The Western Shamballa established by Gautama Buddha, Lord of the World, in behalf of Sanat Kumara.** See p. 378, n. 10. (**6**) **The disarming of Europe.** Refers to negotiations between the U.S. and U.S.S.R. (INF Talks) to eliminate all medium-range and shorter-range ballistic missiles worldwide—especially in Europe and the Western part of the Soviet Union. (**7**) See pp. 251–56. (**8**) Matt. 24:40, 41; Luke 17:34–36. (**9**) Saint Germain's Saturday night service, Sunday Sacred Ritual for Keepers of the Flame, and Wednesday evening healing service, "Watch with Me" Jesus' Vigil of the Hours. (**10**) **Ten thousand-times-ten thousand.** See p. 306, n. 6. (**11**) **The crystal chalice of Light.** See p. 302, pars. 2, 3; p. 310, par. 5; and p. 378, n. 12. (**12**) Job 38:6–7. (**13**) *Noblesse Oblige* [French, lit., nobility obligates]: the obligation of honorable, generous and responsible behavior associated with high rank or birth. (**14**) *Heart, Head, and Hand*

Decrees: Meditations, Mantras, Prayers and Decrees for the Expansion of the Threefold Flame within the Heart, released by Elizabeth Clare Prophet, 36-page booklet, $1.25 (add $.25 postage). 12 booklets for $12; 24 and over, $10 a dozen (add $.80 postage for first dozen, $.30 each additional dozen).

Notes from Pearl No. 32 by Lady Master Nada, pp. 307–12:
This dictation by the Lady Master Nada was **delivered** through the Messenger of the Great White Brotherhood Elizabeth Clare Prophet on **Sunday, June 28, 1987,** at *FREEDOM 1987* in the Heart of the Inner Retreat at the **Royal Teton Ranch, Montana**. (**1**) See Saint Germain, May 3, 1981, "The Mosaic of Life," 1981 *Pearls of Wisdom,* vol. 24, no. 27, pp. 283, 294. (**2**) **Maldek and Hedron.** See *Mysteries of the Holy Grail,* pp. 120, 356–57, n. 1; *Climb the Highest Mountain,* 2nd ed., pp. 93–95, 131–32, 474; and Gautama Buddha, "The Golden Sphere of Light," p. 1, par. 3; p. 5, pars. 3, 4; p. 11, par. 2. (**3**) Matt. 10:34. (**4**) See **Universities of the Spirit,** pp. 285, 286. (**5**) **The ones forgetful.** Manasseh, name of the firstborn son of Joseph, is from the Hebrew *nasheh* 'to cause to forget', or 'causing forgetfulness'. "The ones forgetful" refers not only to the half-tribes of Ephraim and Manasseh, sons of Joseph, but also to the other eleven tribes—the lost sheep of the whole house of Israel. (**6**) John 8:58. (**7**) John 13:5–9. (**8**) Montessori International 1987 Commencement exercises took place on the day this dictation was given. (**9**) Jude 14, 15; Enoch 2. See Archangel Uriel, "The LORD's Descent with Ten Thousand of His Saints!" pp. 113–16. (**10**) **Western Shamballa.** Shamballa, the etheric "City of White," is the ancient retreat of Sanat Kumara, originally built on an island in the Gobi Sea (now the Gobi Desert). It became the retreat of the Lord of the World, Gautama Buddha, and is located above the Gobi Desert on the etheric plane. With the purchase of the Royal Teton Ranch and its establishment in Montana, Gautama Buddha set up his retreat in the West, which he calls Western Shamballa, an extension of the retreat over the Gobi. Lord Gautama Buddha's retreat is centered at the Heart of the Inner Retreat, where ranch conferences are held every year. See Gautama Buddha, April 18, 1981, "The Arcing of the Flame of Shamballa to the Inner Retreat," 1981 *Pearls of Wisdom,* vol. 24, no. 20, pp. 226, 227; and 1983 *Pearls of Wisdom,* vol. 26: "Shamballa," p. 110, and El Morya, October 8, 1983, "Between Two Worlds," no. 53, p. 639. (**11**) **Corridor of light.** On December 25, 1986, Jesus explained that the God and Goddess Meru, standing to his left and right, had come "to establish a corridor of light from the etheric retreat over the Royal Teton Ranch to the etheric retreat of the Feminine Ray at Lake Titicaca. By this corridor of light, beloved, we open a highway whereby your calls may reach South America in time." See Jesus Christ, "The Coming of the Divine Teacher," 1986 *Pearls of Wisdom,* vol. 29, no. 78, p. 681. (**12**) **The chalice abuilding in the Heart.** On June 27, 1987, Archangel Chamuel and Charity explained, "Absent not yourselves from this communion and this vigil, for, beloved, a tangible chalice is being formed, tended by Paul the Venetian, by Nada, by angels of Love. And high in the upper atmosphere await Heros and Amora. For when the chalice shall rise to meet and greet the Elohimic level, then shall Elohim pour into this chalice that which ye seek, beloved." See p. 302, pars. 2, 3. (**13**) Heb. 13:14. (**14**) See Saint Germain, "The Vow," p. 18, pars. 2–5; p. 33, par. 7. (**15**) Matt. 7:2; Mark 4:24; Luke 6:38.

Vol. 30 No. 38 | *Beloved Alpha* | *September 20, 1987*

Freedom 1987

VII

Alpha's Agenda

The Presence of God-Justice in the Earth

I AM the Alpha Star of Being. And I descend in the V of Victory's angels. I am cradled, then, beloved, even as I come to cradle my own.

When you pray unto the Father, beloved, it is I as an individualization of the God flame who do respond, and Omega with me. For I AM Alpha and Omega in the white fire core of your being, God's being—being of Elohim and all Life.

Thus, I AM the voice of eternity and the presence of one whom you know from time unto times and times ending. I come to comfort by the rod of the Law and by its mercy.

I have entered the atmosphere of earth. And therefore, beloved, elemental life does also receive me as Elohim brace the octaves and the Matter Cosmos that I might come, and come as the instrumentation of the Word for the preparation of cycles flashing forth from this Heart as Ruby Ray light across Cosmos. The body of Cosmos is indeed thy habitation. Thus, I have entered it, beloved. And for all of the purposes of the Law of the One, which cannot be enumerated, I am indeed here.

My coming, beloved, is an inner sign to every soul who does live on planet earth. The sign of the forget-me-not that is carried by the Lord of the World is a subtle intimation of a memory, then, quickened. It is a flower of the power of the will of God that does neither startle nor intimidate but truly quicken one to the inner memory.

Thus, the sign of my flower is a reminder to all, many who

have indeed forgot the voice of the Father, the realization of the Son, the permeation of the Holy Spirit in sacred fire breath. Thus, to my own I say, those who have denied the flame-flower of the will of God and the Star of Alpha, they tremble upon the appearance of this forget-me-not.

Everyone upon earth, then, does receive the sign. But there is an outer reveling in unreality that does not cease, that obliterates the soul and the soul identity, that obliterates the memory of the Divine One. And therefore a soul that was and is not, is not present to hear the voice of Alpha.

I AM in the heart of the Lord's Prayer, for this I did give to my Son. And thus Sanat Kumara, Gautama, Maitreya, in the chain of Cosmic Christ, have sustained the Mind of God. And that Mind as Holy Christ Self of you does press now into the earth with the footsteps of my coming.

Elohim and Archangels, legions of the Second Ray of the Mind of God, I call, then, for the clearing of the mental belt of earth by my coming. And so it is in the heart of the Ruby Ray and by that Ray that there is a saturation of the contamination of the mental belt by fallen ones who have sought to displace the Mind of God in all evolutions.

I have summoned this day armies of Light, beloved, some who have not entered this galaxy heretofore. Thus, I have summoned all of Cosmos according to the will of God who can convene for the great restoration of planet earth and the instauration[1] of this Christ Mind that is the mind of the true science of Being.

I AM that Alpha Star of Being. For that is I AM THAT I AM as the point of the original Word, even as is your beloved I AM Presence.

I AM this incarnation, then, of the Alpha Star of Being. And, therefore, where I AM, beloved, many legions of Light may appear and do appear, for they come according to Hierarchy and the Hierarch who does call. My Presence here, then, allows these to gather.

By my leave, O hosts of Light, thou art placed under the wise dominion of Sanat Kumara for the deliverance of earth, for the liberation of Lightbearers, for Cosmic Justice this day.

Lo, I AM the implementation of the word of Justice in this hour! I AM the drawing of the line of Justice in the earth. And it is the line of Alpha. And this line does make its way, therefore, through all those who are the embodiment of injustice.

Beloved hearts, Justice shall return to earth. For I have selected this great God-quality as my offering and endowment of the very soil of a planet. Understand truly, then, the meaning of Divine Justice, the embodiment of this flame by Portia and [embodied], by bequeathment some years ago, in the heart of the Messenger. I desire that each and every one of you should realize that God-Justice is the Power for the righting of all wrong. It is the Wisdom for the righting of all wrong. It is the Love for the righting of all wrong.

The sign of the coming of the Woman of God-Justice is written in the heavens. For on each and every line of the Cosmic Clock, the Divine Mother in her appearing as Omega does manifest through some Ascended or Cosmic Being or Archeia.

Thus, beloved, there are a number of beings of Light who have been the embodiment of Cosmic Justice long aeons. They have volunteered, they and their legions, to come to earth to endow the rivers and the lakes, the seas, the trees and all that is green with the vibration of God-Justice.

Oh, it is an electrode of such power to have in the earth the consensus of all Cosmos to beam that quality and flame of God-Justice into every situation and manifestation, beginning with the levels of the mind of all Lightbearers and percolating through, as you would say, to all humanity.

Thus, Oromasis and Diana, Aries and Thor, Neptune and Luara, Virgo and Pelleur, Four Cosmic Forces, hold now the four corners of the earth and the four winds! Hold them now in order that Divine Justice may enter the heart!

Now, beloved, savor the vibration of Justice. It does cast out ignorance, for ignorance is unjust. It does cast out karma itself, for karma is injustice and the unjust use of the Law.

Justice is the handmaid of Freedom, as you have heard. Thus, the magnet of Justice, spearheaded by Portia and others, can be to Saint Germain that magnet that may draw forth the Cosmic Spirit of Freedom from the heart of the Great Central Sun.

My Son Saint Germain, I have called thee to this altar and thou hast come. I, too, call thee Francis my beloved Son. Therefore, know that in this hour for thy devotion forever and forever, and for the devotion of thine own, I, Alpha, open the floodgates of the Central Sun for the Spirit of Cosmic Freedom to begin to descend to earth, increment by increment, as these flame-flowers—the threefold flame of the hearts of Keepers of the Flame throughout the earth—shall now receive that Spirit of Cosmic Freedom.

(Blessed ones, I must caution you against any applause during this dictation, lest you disrupt the entire forcefield I am building.)

I say to you, then, beloved, this is a cosmic moment for which Saint Germain has long kept the flame. Keeping the flame of Sanat Kumara, he has inspired Freedom upon a planet that long ago was taken over by fallen angels whose tyranny, whose totalitarian minds were the antithesis of Alpha and Omega. From the inception of the dedication of this planet to be Freedom's Star, lo, they came to deny the Father/Mother God entrée into this world by the usurpation of the First and the Seventh Rays.

Know this, beloved, that the return of Alpha and Omega to planet earth is indeed an event of vast aeons. My Presence here today does signify that I have seen the sacrifice and service of my ascended sons and daughters and of not a few on earth who have emerged even in this decade, moving down the centuries to the hour in this very moment of earth's history when they too could shine—shine in the Body of God upon earth even like celestial stars reflected in a clear lake on a clear night.

So, beloved, whereas the Cosmic Council, the Four and Twenty Elders over which we also and sometimes preside, has had to decline the request of those of the Spirit of the Great White Brotherhood serving earth's evolutions for greater dispensations on behalf of the planet as a whole, and whereas at Wesak the pronouncement was given that the Ascended Masters might assist the Lightbearer but no assistance should be forthcoming to those who have not espoused the I AM Presence and the path of discipleship unto Christ, thus, beloved, with this door ajar, I, your Father, have deliberated soundly as to what portion of myself I might offer in this hour when you should all await, as it were with bated breath, to know what the cycles of Cosmos might afford your lifestreams, your future, your children.

This which follows, then, has been our deliberation. And we place before you our affirmation of the highest use of the presence of God-Justice in the earth:

There are, beloved, conditions upon which earth and her evolutions might be saved. The areas of greatest urgency which present themselves are for the final binding and judgment of fallen angels who have positioned themselves in the economies and the governments of the nations and in the banking houses to exercise absolute control over the people.

Beloved ones, for earth to be saved, World Communism with all of its supporters, agents and tools must go down. I raise my right hand and the fire does flow to turn it back upon itself.

Secondly, beloved, the youth of the world must be delivered of the misuse of the science of rhythm and sound and of drugs and all manner of toxic substances polluting their brains, bodies, nervous systems. The abundant Life and the path of discipleship in Christ must be preserved. And education of the heart unto all children of a planet must be guaranteed.

Of the greatest urgent necessity, therefore, as you have heard our presence through the Messenger and all ideas discussed, is the physical defense of the physical continent of America.[2] Thus, the greatest urgency is to defeat World Communism in its present attempt to take over this planet, to defeat it in every area where it is making inroads into systems and into the minds of the people, and simultaneously to raise up the defense. This is the action of Alpha. This is the power of the Spirit of Cosmic Freedom.

Understand, then, beloved, that Saint Germain has served in an endeavor to raise up a body of Keepers of the Flame who might be able to carry such a great, great vibration of the highest level of Freedom. To this hour he has served with you. In this hour I say, beloved, it is your moment to rush forward and receive from him a torch, a strengthening of the desire body and the will, that the Spirit of Freedom from the heart of the Great Central Sun might be sustained in the earth.

The conclusion of the building of the chalice this day and for another week of activities here must give to us entrée to earth twenty-four hours a day by the Spirit of Elohim. And by that Spirit of Elohim, the Cosmic Spirit of Freedom shall also descend.

Thus, beloved, our priorities are protection and defense and the defeating of the violators of this Spirit of Cosmic Freedom—the agents of World Communism and all conspirators of West and East with it. These are and must be bound by the Spirit of Alpha in you, by the Alpha Star of Being called forth, lowered into manifestation by Divine Decree, as your I AM Presence entering the earth through a body temple that is ready and willing and able to hold that flame of God Harmony.

O God Harmony, strengthen my own to not be moved!

Therefore, beloved, this defense raised up and the tide turned against World Communism must be the Alpha power of the Spirit of Cosmic Freedom. The caring for the youth, their deliverance from rock music, drugs, a faulty educational system and a tampering with the abundant Life, this is the Omega action of Cosmic Justice. For it is just that the babies, children and youth, beloved, of every system of worlds receive the foundation of the Father/Mother God from inception in the womb unto the fulfillment of the thirty-three-year span for the raising up of the Divine Mother in the temple unto the ascension flame.

Beloved hearts, let planet earth be restored to that golden-age state where every youth at the age of thirty-three has earned the choice to ascend or to remain in embodiment to become a master of the Matter Cosmos and time and space, a world teacher and benefactor of others! Oh, to know the choice of Cosmic Freedom and Cosmic Justice, beloved!

Now understand, my very dear ones, that long ago the fallen angels who usurped cosmic levels of Freedom and Justice did turn this world to the Darkness that today is labeled as socialism, the denial of the individualization of the God flame, the denial of the children of Light having access to the great bowers of the causal body of Light, and all that has ensued whereby my children look without for to be sustained rather than to the within.

Blessed hearts, we have seen Keepers of the Flame in an hour when this movement and this my Church did not contain the momentum of Light as it does in this hour nor did it have the quotient of Lightbearers it now does. Time was when even a certain force of serpents had become a part of this activity who are no longer here. But even in those days, beloved, by the greater light of the Great White Brotherhood and the true hearts of Light within the movement, I credit to this activity the turning around of America toward Freedom and the patriotism that comes from the God Star, once again embracing a Light that allowed one to be elected to the highest office of the land because he had committed to the people to embrace that Spirit of America that does come forth out of the Cosmic Spirit of Freedom.

Therefore, you see, beloved, because the record has shown the fearlessness of students and youth, faculty, parents, Keepers of the Flame, the leadership in all cities across the nation, because these have dared to challenge the totalitarian Darkness that was hovering over the land, a new spirit of hope did come forth. And the yellow ribbon[3] did become the sign of Alpha's promised return.

Thus, the sons of Alpha, detained by laggard evolutions of the East, terrorized and murdered, the sons of Alpha coming home are the sign also of the coming of my own and myself. In consideration of this victory and in consideration of carrying forward this victory, I have determined, weighing, then, with a considerable pondering of my heart, that it is I, rather than my Sons, who should in this hour make this offer of my Presence to the Lightbearers of the world.

This offering, beloved, is to lend to you my Mantle for the defeating of World Communism and the binding of those who support it—lending you my Mantle, then, specifically to go forth on a mission, not to rest until the leadership of this nation has reached an accord to deploy immediately that strategic defense based on the earth, in space and wherever needed.

Understand, beloved hearts, that strategic defense is first based in the mighty threefold flame of your hearts. Therefore, I lend to you my Mantle to go forth with the materials provided, with the video, with the understanding; to cease not to knock upon the doors of the leadership, of neighbors, of friends, of all people nationwide; to hold your prayer vigils as you have never held them before that this nation, entrusted with the Flame of Freedom by the sponsorship of Saint Germain, Sanat Kumara and now Alpha, might truly occupy space according to the incarnation of the Eternal Word in the sons of Light who shall be the pioneers of this new frontier.

Blessed hearts, the occupation of space is by the attainment of the Buddha. May you hold the flame of Gautama/Maitreya and of the Divine Mother in this retreat that this may be accomplished.

Beloved hearts, this is my proposal to the Cosmic Council: to lend myself to you and, upon seeing the victory of the deployment of the defense of Freedom, to press on for other dispensations. Whether or not this is accomplished, together with the turning back and diminishing day by day of the power of World Communism, will determine the future of planet earth. There is no question about it. And my sons and daughters in embodiment know this. I say it, then, from the highest levels of the Cosmic Mind.

Thus, beloved, in order to defeat the forces of Darkness that are intergalactic who would prevent this by the mind manipulation of the leadership, you yourselves must understand that the equation involves the capacity of your own beings to carry my Star, to carry my Presence, to carry my vibration and heart flame. The bridging of the gap between your vibration and my own, beloved, is accomplished by Elohim and all of the Spirit of the Great White Brotherhood serving under them. It is accomplished by the great force of the Spirit of Cosmic Freedom and the Spirit of Cosmic Justice.

Because, beloved, the fallen ones who fell (archdeceivers among the angelic host) did fall from very high levels, it is thus from those high levels that they must be defeated. By way of understanding this you shall know that Sanat Kumara and the Holy Kumaras, together with the Great Silent Watchers, represent those Cosmic Beings and the level at which the fallen angels in the earth this day must be defeated.

So, beloved, my Mantle, my Heart and Presence, is lent to

you as a protection, as a sealing in the diamond-shining Mind of God, as a sharpening of faculties of mind and heart to convey the Word, the information, to convey the spark of Alpha.

Now, beloved, some time ago the Messenger delivered to you the Alpha crystals. And some have said, "A Cosmic Being would not use a leaded crystal as a focus of light," to which the Messenger responded, "Alpha may use whatsoever substance of the earth he should choose." And it is so, beloved. For the endowment of a spiritual fire is my sending and the chalice is my choosing. The chalice is your heart. But the crystal is both a molecular cup and a mirror wherein my face may be mirrored though you see it not.

Therefore, beloved, understand that there are three stones that may carry a vibration in the earth for your sustenance. These have been used not only throughout the earth but on other planets. Thus, it is up to you, but I explain the law that within the amethyst, within the lapis and within the jade you will find a capacity to store, even as it were, a microchip, to store light, vibration and Word. Natural crystals from the earth are also the option for the altar. It is not necessary that it be something beyond your means, but even a little token shall remain with you as the presence of my offering this day.

Now, beloved, we can see with the twin flames of Saint Germain and Portia, your own and your momentum, that the Seventh Ray, containing the white fire core of Being as all rays do, does also contain the matrix of the Seven. Out of Freedom and Justice can come the reversal of every untoward condition advancing across the planet. These twin flames of Alpha and Omega may therefore clear the way for the lowering of the divine blueprint and the divine plan. The acceleration of your pursuit of the Seventh Ray does indeed give us hope that with the establishment of defense and the turning back of World Communism by a massive reeducation of the people there can be a New Day of opportunity.

Is it a trial balloon, beloved? I would say so. I would say that at the level of the Cosmic Council we are absolutely convinced that when this movement and these Keepers of the Flame put their mind to it the entire MAD[4] posture may be turned around to an integral, integrated positioning of a dignity and integrity that does automatically understand that to retain attainment, defense must be raised up.

Defense comes from "Deity's fences." Deity has always had fences, solar rings, tubes of light, walls of flame. We have never left untended our Holy of Holies and never shall. Thus, covering cherubim and seraphim of God and all Archangels and hosts back to the Central Sun have forever and forever guarded the incarnation of the Word below as is Above.

I, therefore, speak to Elohim and angelic hosts who hold the planet now, as my vibration and that of the one who sent me is saturating the planet and your chakras. O blessed ones, keep the flame in the earth. Seal it well. I charge you to defend all Lightbearers. I charge you to go to all upon this planet who have taken their stand against World Communism and for defense and a strong strategic defense. Go to them.

I, Alpha, authorize a dispensation of protection, the helmet of Mercury, the armour of Archangel Michael. I authorize you, legions of Light who have come from far-off worlds, to turn back upon the evildoer, the evil system and the evil empire tenfold all viciousness sent forth against an unsuspecting world. I charge you, hosts of Light, to restore the Mind of God in this people.

I charge you, Keepers of the Flame, to therefore call incessantly for the judgment of my Son Jesus upon those who usurp the Mind of God and trample upon the mental belt and the mental bodies of the people.

Ho, O world of Light! Ho, O world of Light! Ho, O world of Light! Let the crystal and the star-fire, let the crystal and the star-fire now clear the minds of a people, clear them from all programming from outer space, from aliens, from those incarnate and out of the pits of Death and Hell—programming by the rhythm of rock, by drugs, by all manner of misuse of the science of the Word.

Ho, O world of Light, expand throughout the nations! Ho, O world of Light, prepare, then, those who are of the Light for the coming of my own and my own vibration delivering unto them the mandate of Freedom!

Ho, O world of Light, I AM Alpha turning now, I AM Alpha turning now the world and turning around the world and turning around the Darkness therein to give opportunity to those who love Freedom, to those who love Justice, to those who will desire to receive the engrafted Word and a threefold flame, to all of goodwill who desire to serve the Lord God Almighty. Therefore, unto them I, Alpha, give of myself. And I take my stand.

Therefore, beloved, go forth on a mission sent from the Central Sun! Go forth to your destined purpose whence you came from Sirius. Go forth now, beloved. Rescue the nation and the people. And let there be a sound defeating of World Communism that the oppressed might be delivered.

The hosts of Cosmos attend thy call. The Spirit of Cosmic Freedom attends thy call. Spheres of Justice of causal bodies offered attend thy call. By the call, by the sword, by the activism of the soul, by the spreading of the Word, let America survive to be a chalice once more of Freedom to the earth.

I speak to you, fallen ones in every quarter and den: You, then, have no power over my own! I AM Alpha! My hand does stretch forth. Therefore, 10 percent of the world momentum of evil is reduced this day, bound, therefore! You are shrinking to your native nothingness. While you have breath, confess the LORD God Almighty. Be converted and serve Him!

O Lightbearers of all captive nations, I AM Alpha. I AM stripping you by the hand of my legions of a karma that ought not to be, which may be taken this day from you that you might determine your means of delivering yourselves, your nations and people.

Over the White House and the Capitol Building I position cosmic angels. From their hearts beaming to every representative great and small at the national, state and local level, there is a ray of light of Alpha. Therefore, I say to you, one and all, submit to the will of God and to the Alpha Star of Being.

My Presence in the earth and my Word cannot be turned back. Those, then, who deny Alpha where I AM shall also have Alpha denied where they are.

Lo, I AM Alpha, the point of origination and initiation of Light! I AM Light! I AM Light! I come from Light. I return to Light. My Word is in the earth. My Judgment is in the earth. My Freedom and Justice is in the earth.

With these four, Keepers of the Flame, show me now what you can do for Terra and Life and your own cosmic Victory. Show me, beloved, for these are four pillars in the temple. Show me, beloved, for I shall return, whereupon surveying the scene in forty-eight months, I shall declare to you what further action may be taken from these cosmic levels.

I bow to the flame of the sons and daughters of God. I bow to the flame of the joyous Mother who does receive me. I remember her always in her office of the World Mother. And therefore, Omega does tarry now, beloved, to give you some word of the Divine Mother.

I, your Father, then, move outwards, upwards and beyond this planet. For it has received a sufficiency of myself for these hours and the forty-eight months.

AUM

Beloved Omega

Now, my beloved, I would that you would understand Omega—Omega Presence—a Mother's heart of Cosmos who cares deeply for your soul, for your very heart. Knowing all things about you, each one, I am your devoted Mother Love, not in unknowingness, not fooled by the facade, not unaware of the lie or the deception. I am here in the Immaculate Heart of the Cosmic Virgin.

Know, then, beloved, that this is my heart's message. I, Omega, love you with an everlasting love for who and for what you are. All overlays, all of the psychic and psychological attempts to create an outer self in conformity with the selves of this planet, with all of this I am neither concerned nor impressed.

I love you as you are in the heart of the Father/Mother God forever and forever, from the beginning unto the ending. And you as you are have the capacity now to expand such vast potential of inner spirit fire. Let it expand. And as it does expand, all the phoniness and the facade simply crumble. You are becoming a Cosmic Christ. And I AM the Divine Mother who attends your birth.

Thus, beloved, feel my love and my peace as a strength you may not have known in a long time. Feel the strength of my angels and know something of myself through your Messenger to whom we have given some time ago the mantle and office of World Mother. I shall not tell you when, beloved, because it is beyond this measuring.

Therefore, understand that the love of a mother's heart for your Real Self should not be misconstrued by you to be a mother's approval of your unreal self. Herein, then, lies the danger of contacting the Divine Mother as sacred fire and Kundalini and as such a personal, personal presence too soon. For this love, beloved, would give the impression that there is no need to change or to rearrange oneself, for one is so loved.

Therefore, the device of the Great Kali has been to hide Herself in a cosmic play of Light and Darkness, to hide behind illusion itself in order that you should know that to come into the Presence of the Cosmic Virgin you must pierce all illusion.

Thus, beloved, do not feel there is any dichotomy or hypocrisy in the Divine Mother's love. It is pure and sustaining. It is always there. But never, never does it uphold or support the synthetic self.

The more you desire Mother, the more you pursue Her, the more you will find a stripping and fiery action where there is contact between the lightning of the Mother and the substance of self-delusion. Blessed ones, this is a game that you too can play. It is a serious game, but you can enjoy it. It is the joy of seeing and knowing that the fierceness of the Mother is come to dissolve by sacred fire those knots of substance, nuts and bolts that have no place any longer, for you are not mechanization man; you are fiery spirits soaring.

Thus, it is a game of Victory where intensely you run with the ball of the Cosmic Spirit of Freedom and Justice. It is a game wherein you know you must allow that darkness to give way to the lightning of Kali. It is a joy and a laughter that when it does take place, sin is no more, fallen one at the door may not o'ertake thee. Thou art free, for the Divine Mother in the heart of Cosmic Justice does instantaneously forget by the violet flame all transgressions of Her garment.

Know this too, beloved, that those who consider that some on the Path ought to be punished for their vile deeds by the Mother, these do not understand the vast capacity of the Cosmic Virgin for the dissolution of evil within the psyche.

O beloved, when you have seen the face of Omega, you know that no other reality is necessary but the Divine Mother. Therefore, beloved, know my Presence with Alpha. For I am truly here, and here to see to it that my sons and daughters do not fail their Father who loves them so tenderly, loves you so touchingly, beloved.

Therefore, because he is my beloved, I will not allow you to hurt him or to defile his name. For he has given himself to you this day. And I am here with a guardian action of the Divine Mother's legions to protect you with this so holy, so gracious a charge.

Blessed ones, with the Mother all things are possible. With the Father all things are. Thus, Alpha is already the fulfillment of his assignment in you. Omega is within time and space the progressive unfoldment and fulfillment of it.

Therefore, I say to you, in the immaculate science of the Divine Mother, accept the reality now in the fire of Alpha's Star that World Communism is no more and strategic defense is in position and deployed now! This is the reality of my Alpha and yours. The reality is that the fallen ones with their rock music, their drugs, their manipulation of the economy and education and the government, they are judged! Their systems are collapsed! And my beloved Alpha has given you forty-eight months, twelve for each side of the pyramid, to prove it in Matter by the Mother flame.

O beloved, truly Alpha in you IS. And all that IS is the fulfillment of his Star. [*ISIS* is Alpha unveiled.]

I AM Omega in the earth. And I AM fierce that none shall cross the line that Alpha has drawn. My legions, then, are the cohorts of those he has summoned.

By the power of Alpha and Omega in you, Go be victorious in the Father, in the Mother, as his Sons by the Holy Spirit, Amen!

[Do not applaud, please.]

Messenger's Comments:

I would like to give each and every one of you from my heart an understanding of these dispensations from Alpha. I wish to be certain, occupying the office of Teacher, that you do understand the interpretation of what has been said to you.

So, against the backdrop of the message of Gautama Buddha of Wesak of the judgment of those who have denied God and not received this dispensation, of no dispensation forthcoming for the earth but only help to the Lightbearers; again, against the backdrop of Saint Germain's January 1, 1987, dictation where he calls for those who will take the vow that he might continue to serve (and his vow is to save the Lightbearers, to destroy World Communism)—consistent, then, with the limitations of dispensations, we hear Alpha tell us that he is giving to us an offering of support of his Mantle and his Presence focused in his crystal, or the jade, the lapis, or the amethyst—himself, I should say, through the crystal; the recording of this conference through the three others.

He gives us, then, the charge that if there is to be the saving of the world, we are entrusted and summoned to awaken America to deploy immediately our defenses—our strategic defense, all that is necessary—and to defeat World Communism. This very process entails the defeating of rock music, drugs and the forces of dissolution in the economy and education. However, the first line of defense is to deploy the strategic defense and move for the overturning of World Communism.

Looking in the Mind of Alpha, I am seeing the intensity of the Father and his expectation of his sons and daughters. His expectancy is that you have the razor's-edge awareness of just how threatening the Darkness is on the planet and just how much there hangs in the balance in whether or not we will deploy immediately. Therefore, seeing the urgency, his expectation is that we give our hearts, our endeavors, our service one-pointedly to this cause night and day, accelerating our commitment, our sacrifice and our ingenuity to bring the messages that we have heard here to the people.

He is showing me that none of us can go back to any lesser level or even the level we came from where we thought our service was heroic. We must rise to new levels, even in the sense of rising to the place where we can contain, by the bridge of the Great White Brotherhood and

Elohim, the presence of the Spirit of Cosmic Freedom and the Spirit of Cosmic Justice.

Now, with the turning of the fourteen-month cycle (February 28, 1987), Serapis said that all Keepers of the Flame should attend three services a week, even if there are only two or three gathered. Or if they are totally alone in their communities, they hold these services themselves. This is the Wednesday night Jesus' Watch, the Saturday night Saint Germain Service, and the Sunday Ritual with sermon and dictation.

The sermons and teachings and dictations are available all over the world. And if you are not in a Study Group or a Teaching Center, you may affiliate with one to borrow these tapes or you may affiliate with others. If you cannot afford to purchase them weekly, you can purchase them jointly and mail them to one another so that you all have access to them.

The embodying of the Word of God that is delivered is very important. It is important that Keepers of the Flame realize that they must *be* the Light that is released, and therefore these three services a week are essential to your moving forward with the planet.

Now, all this is in the awareness of Alpha and Omega as they have spoken to us. And the expectancy is that we should admonish ourselves and correct ourselves in these areas and have the sense of self-worth of knowing that only through those of us in embodiment can this world be turned around.

That any Keeper of the Flame should doubt this or think that his presence is not needed at the altar is to me just as serious a problem as the American leadership feeling that there is no need for strategic defense. We can all see the ludicrousness of our leaders not going for defense, but we have to apply that same awareness to ourselves. We must be at our altars and then we must be on the battlefield supporting those whose voices are being drowned because they don't have our calls and our protection and our moving with them.

So the dispensation is a fait accompli, because when God speaks, it is so. But that means it is so in the etheric octave, it is so here, but it is not so until the illusion that it isn't so is dispelled and the reality is lowered into manifestation. So you must understand that the Presence of God with us is an opportunity. The reality has been spoken but it is no guarantee that it shall take place. It is not a dispensation whereby something is set aside and it takes place. It's a dispensation that says, "If you will do this, I will see what, then, I can do in forty-eight months."

Now, Alpha has given to me a great sense of the victory of this company in the last twenty-four hours and an understanding of his mission in coming. I can tell you from my heart of hearts and my heart in God that there is absolutely no doubt in my being that you, Keepers of the Flame, and other Lightbearers can accomplish this task in America of turning the nation around and quickening it, like in the twinkling of the Eye of God, to rally to put up our defenses. I have that absolute sense of victory and I hold the immaculate concept of it in my heart.

You know the Law. You have the judgment calls. You know the decrees. You can meet. Just remember: You have to do it. You have to be the action. It is not in the hearing of it, it is in the doing of it. And sometimes that is where we fall short of the mark.

I know this is possible. I know it is a reality. As far as I am concerned, it already is. And I want you to have that absolute sense of it and have that sense of it in your being and be as a coiled spring—a fire and an energy that moves into action and becomes perpetual motion until you see it as a reality. You are also warriors of the Spirit and you know just how deadly the serpents are. And you know just what the calls must be for their binding and their judgment.

I want you to know that as your Messenger and representing the Mother to you I believe profoundly in each one of you. And I believe that in you God has decided to save the earth. God said this in 1976 in Washington, D.C., at the July conference. It was a message conveyed to us in the dictation of the Goddess of Liberty. Very simple—"God has decided to save the earth."

Now, how he can save it depends on you. So, you see, God may save the earth through a horrific cataclysm—so terrible as to be like that which happened before the Book of Genesis begins when there was darkness and a void in the earth. But God has decided to save the earth through you. And I believe that Alpha's coming is based on this message of 1976—God has decided to save the earth.

So Alpha comes to save it through you. You realize, then, that what Alpha can do is totally determined by you. On earth we either give absolute freedom to the Masters to serve through us or we limit them in increments as we decide that we have better things to do.

Now, during my speaking with you Alpha and Omega and these forces have withdrawn to the extent that you are welcome to stand and applaud and give your praise to Alpha and Omega. [3-min. 43-sec. standing ovation]

Praise the LORD I AM THAT I AM Alpha and Omega!

Praise the LORD I AM THAT I AM Alpha and Omega! (3x)

Someone wrote more than a decade ago, I believe, a song about "sometimes I feel like a motherless child." And I was thinking today how wonderful it is to feel the love of our real Father and Mother and to feel what real love is from one's Father and one's Mother. I think there is nothing more assuring, comforting and to give us a zeal of mission than to feel our Father and our Mother behind us and with us and so profoundly understanding of our plight on planet earth.

So I wish to express my gratitude to Almighty God before this altar and the altar of your hearts for the coming of Alpha and Omega—truly such a great, great dispensation to the earth, such a privilege and such an honor and such a wonder at the meeting of heaven and earth here in the heart of the Inner Retreat at *our* Royal Teton Ranch.

"The Summit Lighthouse Sheds Its Radiance O'er All the World to Manifest as Pearls of Wisdom." These dictations by **Alpha and Omega** were **delivered** through the Messenger of the Great White Brotherhood Elizabeth Clare Prophet on **Sunday, July 5, 1987,** at *FREEDOM 1987* in the Heart of the Inner Retreat at the **Royal Teton Ranch, Montana.** (**1**) **The Great Instauration.** Francis Bacon, 1561–1626, an embodiment of Saint Germain, called his plan for universal enlightenment "the Great Instauration." First conceived when he was a boy of twelve or thirteen and then crystallized in his book by the same name in 1607, Bacon's formula for changing "the whole wide world" launched the English Renaissance. See *The Golden Age Prince,* 2-audiocassette album, 3 hrs., A83176, $12.95 (add $.90 for postage); and *Saint Germain On Prophecy,* pp. 21–22, 24, Book One. (**2**) **On the defense of freedom in America.** The lectures delivered by Elizabeth Clare Prophet on this vital subject are available on the following video- and audiocassettes:

"Saint Germain On the Defense of Freedom," I–IV:

Part I: "To Be or Not to Be," April 17, 1987, 137-min. videocassette HP87036, $24.95 (add $.90 for postage), or two 90-min. audiocassettes, A87028, $13.00 (add $.80 for postage).

Part II: "The Rise and Fall of MAD," May 31, 1987, 77-min. videocassette HP87052, $19.95 (add $.90 for postage), or 72-min. audiocassette B87039, $6.50 (add $.50 for postage).

Part III: "Strategic Defense—What and Why," July 1, 1987, 108-min. videocassette HP87054, $24.95 (add $.90 for postage), or 90-min. audiocassette B87066, $6.50 (add $.50 for postage).

Part IV: "Strategic Defense—Pros and Cons," July 2, 1987, videocassette ready December 1, or 80-min. audiocassette B87067, $6.50 (add $.50 for postage).

"The Opening of the Seventh Seal," July 4, 1987, Messenger's lecture and dictation by Saint Germain, 116-min. videocassette HP87045, $24.95 (add $.90 for postage), or two 90-min. audiocassettes, A87047, $13.00 (add $.80 for postage).

For further discussion of these ideas, see the following Summit University Forums:

"Elizabeth Clare Prophet Interviews Thomas H. Krebs on 'Tsar Wars,'" June 30, 1987, 2½ hrs., 2 videocassettes, GP87005, $39.95 (add $1.20 for postage), or 2 audiocassettes, A87052, $13.00 (add $.80 for postage).

"Elizabeth Clare Prophet Interviews Gen. Daniel O. Graham and Dr. Dmitry Mikheyev on Strategic Defense: To Deploy or Not to Deploy," July 4, 1987, 3 hrs., 2 videocassettes, GP87014, $39.95 (add $1.20 for postage), or 2 audiocassettes, A87056, $13.00 (add $.80 for postage).

(**3**) **Yellow ribbons** "omnipresent" were reported by *Time* magazine as 52 American hostages were warmly received in Washington, D.C., January 27, 1981, after 444 days of captivity in Iran. Yellow ribbons were tied to the White House porch, cars and buses, trees, lampposts, TV cameras, homes and public buildings throughout the capital and the nation. On April 15, 1981, Lord Lanto explained, "We also hope. And we also carry ribbons of yellow fire! Our hope is in the return of those who are held hostage to the International Capitalist/Communist Conspiracy—to that conspiracy that has invaded every avenue of life, especially through the media." See Lord Lanto, "Lanterns for Lord Lanto," 1981 *Pearls of Wisdom,* vol. 24, no. 16, pp. 190–91 and 202, n. 13. (**4**) **Mutual Assured Destruction (MAD):** The United States' policy formulated in the mid-sixties which holds that the highest level of deterrence can be achieved when both superpowers have the capacity to absorb the nuclear first strike of the other and still have adequate retaliatory force to inflict unacceptable damage on the aggressor's society. Since neither side could gain any advantage from attacking, and would be destroyed in the process, stability would be achieved.

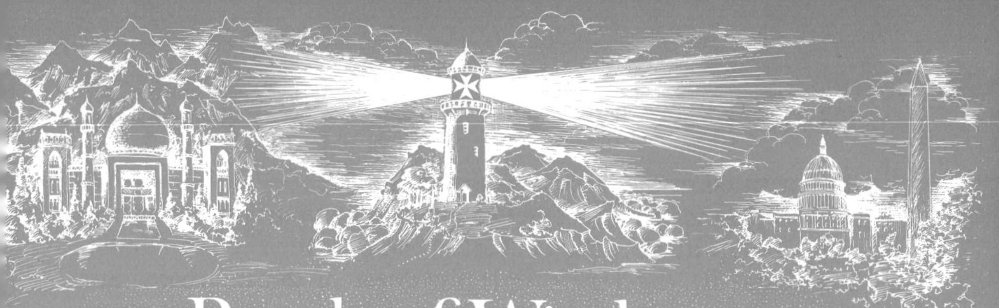

Pearls of Wisdom®
published by The Summit Lighthouse

Vol. 30 No. 39 *Beloved Mother Mary* *September 27, 1987*

Freedom 1987

VIII

The Spinning of the Sun

A Spirituality That Ought to Be in Lightbearers

I see the spinning of the sun. I see the spinning of the sun as a golden sphere, white-fire center. And the rotation of the white fire core within the golden sphere creates, beloved, the white of Alpha, the yellow of Omega, as undulating suns within/without create a whirling action. It is the fire infolding itself. It is the sacred fire of the Sun and the spinning of that Sun Presence—each one's own I AM Presence who is a part of the Great White Brotherhood on earth.

Thus, beloved, contemplate your Mighty I AM Presence now. Probe the spheres beyond the outer blue and green, purple and violet and pink. Come, then, to the center and witness the great sphering action, this sphering motion, beloved, as spherical as the great light tumbling. As it does tumble within itself and not downward nor upward but continues to spin, so there is the action of the base and the crown [chakras] so very necessary, my beloved.

Do understand that the foundation of Life in the Divine Mother in the base-of-the-spine chakra, and the capstone[1] in the crown chakra, beloved, as the light of Alpha, define a spirituality that ought to be pulsating and quickening within the Lightbearers of earth.

But many have been cast down. They have been cast down, beloved, and therefore they do not have the functioning of the pure Christ within the body temple. And the lower order of the lower nature has sapped this light, created a spell of sin and death and disease, and thereby there has been degradation and degeneration of the molecules of the mind.

When the mind becomes enfeebled as a matrix, when it does not pulsate with the action of the Second Ray, then you can understand that by the very disintegratedness of the molecules and electrons there does take place a consciousness of dependence, depression, old age and death. Minds enfeebled without an activating light of the white sphere and the yellow sphere are indeed prey to World Communism and to socialism.

Understand the plight of this evolution and therefore understand the cure. There is not the interdependency within the heart and its chamber,[2] within the threefold flame. There is not, then, a fulcrum in the heart and a balance of the base and the crown chakras.

The individual does note that he is not sufficient unto himself or unto his God. Those things that he desires he cannot acquire, for he does not have the light of Alpha and Omega in his temple. Therefore, beloved, the creature takes on the animal instinct, the self-preservation at any cost.

And therefore, looking upon those who have amalgamated power among the fallen angels or upon those who have accumulated light among the sons of God, these ones who are empty (for in them the light has gone out) cry out, "Injustice!" and they demand to be fed and clothed and tended, educated, entertained, given birth to and buried by the State or other organizations of charity.

Socialism then Communism becomes the answer for those who do not have the integrating principle of Life, those who once had it and then lost it for want of a continuing affirmation of God. Beware, then, lest the mental body or the carnal mind or even the animal mind and its instincts replace the creative Mind of God within you.

Thus, we, Raphael and I, do expect, beloved, your response to beloved Alpha and Omega, first to have that diamond mind sharp and then at the point of the diamond to begin a spherical awareness within the inner brain. For there between the pineal and the pituitary glands there is an action of Alpha and Omega. And by the very spin of that light there is aborning within you the potential to give birth to the Christ Mind and to receive the activation of the crown chakra.

Therefore, go forth, O knights, go forth with sword in hand. Slay, then, the beasts of lethargy that oppress the mind and prevent the Mind of God from entering in.

Blessed ones, be alert and awake and alive! Be intense and intensely motivated and focused. Do not be weary in placing your attention consciously upon Alpha and Omega.

There is too much sleepfulness while you are awake! For you have been trained by a socialist system even while yet living in a land of freedom. You wait for someone to come along and tell you what to do, to think for you, to be creative for you; you have a sense that something outside of yourself holds the key to your destiny. Beloved, this is a most dangerous doctrine.

Beware, then, the false hierarchy of Antichrist composed of the fallen angels who departed from the Second Ray and Jophiel's band.

We of the Fifth Ray therefore come. And we come to expose to you how these fallen ones have attempted to steal the genes themselves whereby the chalice of the brain and the central nervous system is intended in the sons of God to contain a far greater capacity for the physical containment of the Mind of God.

Blessed hearts, look, then, by the All-Seeing Eye, look down your lifestream. For in this hour I, Mary, Mother of the God consciousness in you and mothering that consciousness, do declare to you that I AM here to receive in my basket even your offerings to the Divine Mother as Guru. Let your offerings be the sacrifice of those elements that have limited your godly expression for many incarnations.

We come to serve the Light in you. We come to liberate the Light in you. We come, for we have studied, even at the Royal Teton Retreat, how best to liberate an active sense of the awareness of God's Mind universally.

O beloved hearts, it is so different when you function as the animals, seeking always food, comfort, having to eke out an existence, developing a psychic sense but always encased in that limited, functioning brain which at the animal level we cannot call mind but rather instinct, having a certain capacity for the probing of environment.

Blessed hearts, socialism will cause humanity to behave in a rote fashion, unable to go beyond that rote performance, thus degrading this evolution down the scale to the level of primates and beneath, as they were prior to the coming of Sanat Kumara. The beast has already extended its tentacles into the free world. And those who have been a part of its system, even to the very least, already own less of themselves than they did in the day of their birth.

Blessed hearts, it is deadly to entrust any portion of thy life to another. Thus, a fierce independence and self-reliance must be engendered within your children. Do not coddle them too much.

Do not seek to provide the excessive emotional support, thereby displacing and replacing the development of their own strong emotions founded upon the joy of building the temple of man. Fear not to let the child experience pain or suffering in small increments. Do not be a shield against that which life has dictated for the evolutions of earth whose karma is to work out this very problem of being, the internalization of God self-mastery.

Many a fine soul has been cast in a mold of limitation due to the emotional transference and identity of mother or father desiring emotionally to possess and own the child. To such parents I say:

You are not your child. The child is not yourself. Your children are God's. You have not ownership over them. Just as you were not born to be slaves of the state, so children are not born to be emotional slaves of their parents. Rather, be in the position of wise counsellor, teacher, mother and father in the true sense of a guardian action that is deeply caring, loving and wise yet respects the circle of identity. You must fiercely defend your own from that very seed of socialism that may early be the desire of the child to be consoled lest it experience its own crying and its own difficulties.

Blessed hearts, doing too much for your children will not afford them preparation for their sojourn on earth. Come to understand, then, how the love and joy of a oneness based on mutual respect will carry you far and through eternity in a divinely human relationship with your children and all children.

Thus, in the objective sense it is necessary, as regards children, as regards your own soul and the child of your inner self, to exercise discipline and authority, to draw the line, then, of correct behavior and never to allow those below the level of twenty-one [or those of any age] to assail or be disrespectful of your office as father, mother, parent, teacher, sponsor or simply adult. Thus train children to be disciples of Christ and you will find the greatest love, the greatest wisdom, the greatest respect returning to yourselves.

I speak of youth and children because few upon the planet understand how to raise up resurrection's flame, few understand how to help children achieve the goal of the expanded heart chakra. Surely, beloved, it is trust, it is joy, it is the peace-commanding presence.

Always attune with the Christ of the child and then let the child know that you expect him to make that attunement and live up to that standard. Be sure that you do also, and therefore indulge not yourself. For as you indulge yourself, children watching your example will indulge themselves. Blessed hearts, so it is true of world teachers. The example you set is the one which will be followed. The discord you allow is that which will be tolerated. The harmony you achieve will be loved and emulated.

I speak, then, of the whirling sun that continues to whirl. So the fire infolding itself is pulling from you in this hour, as an intense magnetism, sometimes painful, pulling out the threads sewn by the enemy as tares [sown] among the good wheat of consciousness.[3]

I, Mary, come to you to give you the understanding that this whirling sun of your I AM Presence is indeed the action that can impel the light upward in you as well as the light descending from your I AM Presence. This whirling sun, then, is intended to establish the forcefield of Alpha and Omega with you in your I AM Presence, very available. *AUM*

I AM Mary, profoundly desirous to see you fulfill the victory outlined by Alpha and Omega.[4] Therefore, I, too, step forward, beloved. I open my Immaculate Heart to you, even as I have given to you the dictation of the experience of initiation in the secret chamber of the heart.

I extend my mantle to all who take up the challenge of Alpha and remember me in the rosary. May you find in your busy day, beloved, time for the Child's Rosary given for the babies and children and youth,[5] given for the overturning of legalized abortion, given for the overturning of child abuse, pornography, molestation and the abuse of the child in the classrooms of the schools of this nation and the world.

Blessed hearts, find the fifteen minutes even if it is when you are driving in your car. For by that quarter of an hour I may bring to you a heart full of remedies from Mother Nature for all your needs, your emptiness and those things which repetitively come upon you, whether emotionally or mentally.

I come as the helper of Omega to assist you to rise to a level of walking with God. Walking with God means walking with Elohim. Walking with God, beloved, means pillars of fire in the earth and hope once again unfurled. Will you not, then, sing the song "I'll Walk with God" as a decree, as an affirmation, as a vow and thereby lay the forcefield for the dictation that will follow.

I am receding now into the spinning sun of the I AM THAT I AM. It does not cease, beloved, and I shall not tell you that it shall ever cease. Continue to meditate, then, upon the whirling white-fire and golden-yellow spheres as one, as you sing this hymn of oneness with God.

You will not take your books, beloved, but you will sing it as you remember it, for it is a profound meditation upon the Great I AM Presence.

Please remain seated in your meditative posture. Concentrate now with the inner eye and see—visualize and concentrate on the whirling white-fire sun and the yellow sun. ["I'll Walk with God" sung]

I'll Walk with God

I'll walk with God from this day on
His helping hand I'll lean upon
This is my pray'r, my humble plea
May the Lord be ever with me.

There is no death, though eyes grow dim
There is no fear when I'm near to him.
I'll lean on him forever
And he'll forsake me never.

He will not fail me
As long as my faith is strong
Whatever road I may walk along.

I'll walk with God, I'll take his hand
I'll talk with God, he'll understand
I'll pray to him, each day to him
And he'll hear the words that I say.
His hand will guide my throne and rod
And I'll never walk alone
While I walk with God!

"The Summit Lighthouse Sheds Its Radiance O'er All the World to Manifest as Pearls of Wisdom." This dictation by **Mother Mary** was **delivered** through the Messenger of the Great White Brotherhood Elizabeth Clare Prophet at the conclusion of the Sunday evening service of **July 5, 1987,** after midnight, at *FREEDOM 1987* in the Heart of the Inner Retreat at the **Royal Teton Ranch, Montana.** (**1**) The golden rays of the crown chakra radiate from the top of the capstone, while the All-Seeing Eye of God is centered in the capstone. (**2**) See *A Trilogy On the Threefold Flame of Life,* and "A Valentine from Saint Germain," in *Saint Germain On Alchemy,* pp. 265–352, or excerpts in *Climb the Highest Mountain,* 2nd ed., pp. 285–315. (**3**) Matt. 13:24–30, 36–43. (**4**) See pp. 379–91. (**5**) *A Child's Rosary to Mother Mary*—15-minute scriptural rosaries for the Child within you—published on 4 audiocassette albums, 3 cassettes per album: Album 1 (A7864): John, James, Jude; Album 2 (A7905): Paul to the Hebrews; Album 3 (A7934): Paul to the Galatians; Album 4 (A8045): Paul to the Corinthians. $9.95 ea. (add $.90 ea. for postage).

Vol. 30 No. 40 — *Beloved Archangel Jophiel* — *October 4, 1987*

Freedom 1987

IX

The Hour of the Trumpet Judgments

The Initiation to Conquer and Occupy Space

Jophiel is my name! And I raise the scepter of the living Christ. Summoned by these as a company of numberless numbers, for you are multiplied and surrounded by angels tier upon tier, so I am able, then, in the heart of Christ to answer the impelling call for Judgment. It is the call of God, of Alpha, of Omega and of my Lord who has said, "Lo, I AM Alpha and Omega, the beginning and the ending!"

O Sanat Kumara, we have come, multiplied by all legions of Alpha and thine own. Therefore, O sons of men, therefore, O Sons of God, know that in this hour in answer to your call legions have entered the mental belt of the earth and there is a terrific turmoil and a tumult. There is, therefore, war in this plane of the mind.

Therefore, let all true sons of Light heed my warning: This is the arousing of the serpent, even the sleeping serpent who has long been left in the mental plane to subvert youth, who remain subverted throughout a lifetime for want of the true Shepherd.

See, then, the purpose of the Shepherd's crook. It is to draw up the light from the base unto the crown, to draw it inward into the inner mind and to seal the third eye. Thus, by the sealing of the Christ there is within that spinal altar the power of God.

Take heed, ye legions of the Cosmic Christ! For by his leave I summon you. And in the name of Archangel Michael we do descend to every layer of perversion of the Mind of God.

Let, therefore, the trumpets blow! O seven angels, let the trumpets blow! For there is a suffusing light in these chakras and earth has come to the hour when the trumpet judgments must descend, not only to the level of the mental plane but to the seat-of-the-soul chakra, which is nevertheless governed, therefore, by the air and the Mind of God of Holy Spirit. Beloved of the living Word, let sacred fire know the response.

Thus, a battle begun must be enjoined. The battle begun, you dare not turn your backs. Keep on, beloved. For by the defeating of these forces of the anti-Mind, you in God and with these hosts accompanying you shall defeat all forces of anti-freedom and anti-defense in this nation. Let it be fought, beloved, and let it be fought hard.

Know that as by the hour you deliver your mandate before your personal altar of the Judgment Call and the calls we have taught you in this little while, so millions times millions of angels are empowered, shall continue to be empowered to bind these fallen ones until the reapers come and these angels bind them in bundles and remove the "tares" in the rent of America's garment and take them to their sudden and swift Judgment.

It is the only way, beloved.

Therefore I say, respond with all your heart to defend the Mind of Christ in yourself and in all whom you meet! Let it become a pledge and a badge. Let it become something that is ever with you as that conscious determination to be I AM WHO I AM.

All this, beloved, we bring for the preparing of the action of Elohim. We draw, then, a mighty solar ring around this place and concentric rings extending, until the earth and beyond unto space itself is encircled.

I AM the guardian action of the Mind of Christ beyond space. *Therefore, I claim space for Saint Germain!* [17-sec. applause] It is a mandate of the Seven Archangels whose trumpets blow in a mighty harmony of notes unheard. Blessed ones, the trumpets as they are blown do deliver precisely what is written in akasha that is apart from the scriptural record, yet very plain.

Therefore, inasmuch as this is the opening of the seventh seal, the one triumphant in the seven rays of the seven chakras for the violet flame, for freedom—Saint Germain and his Keepers of the Flame with him in vibration—shall rise, then, for the conquering of space, for the occupying of space, as with the God of the Earth, Gautama Buddha, they understand day by day the Buddhic initiation to occupy that space.

Therefore, I am casting down the fallen ones and the idols! See them come tumbling down out of the skies as Wormwood and other shooting stars.

Blessed ones, let the Saturnian tester, the mighty Initiator Maitreya therefore occupy space. Let the four beings of the ruby cross occupy that space.

Space, then, is painted violet flame by violet flame angels. Let freedom reign! And let all know that freedom has claimed space, and no other but the free hearts of Sanat Kumara may occupy it. So may you make it so in the physical octave!

Blessed hearts, no sadder day could there be than that day whereon others take the dispensation that has gone forth for the victory of freedom in space, for Keepers of the Flame have not claimed it. May you leap to your feet and say,

I claim space for Saint Germain!

[Congregation rises and affirms with Archangel Jophiel:]

I claim space for Saint Germain! (3x)

O my beloved, the Lord of the World does write in that sky your fiat and vow.

Now I would tell you how I should cherish your tarrying in this tent for those calls that can save the earth. Let all who can, then, remain. And let all plan each year to be here no less than fourteen days' concentration of this fiery work of the ages.

Blessed hearts, when calamity falls upon an individual or a family, untimely death, crippling accident, sudden disease and timely passage, it is too late to give a fortnight to the call that could have mitigated and entirely eliminated that darkness. I say, beloved, this tarrying is worth all the insurance you could ever carry. For it is a cosmic assurance that your heart wed, tied by the love tie with Sanat Kumara, is sealed in gladness. And you, then, become the glad ones occupying succeeding levels unto the heart of the Sun.

Now I take you beyond space to the inner space of Helios and Vesta whence there shall come to you the sealing dictations of these five days. I ask that you sing to Helios and Vesta to the tune of "O Sole Mio."

I AM Jophiel, sealing your crown chakra, preparing the way for the fullness of the action of the spinning Sun of your I AM Presence. All now, at once, concentrate upon that Sun high above you and note how it begins to be a pressure here in the very crown chakra the more you concentrate upon the white-fire/yellow-fire sun.

O beloved, the joy of the Lord is in the center of being. Hear, then, the joy of the Lord as the laughter of God does laugh to derision these fallen ones whose place is no longer: for time and space are not for them. Oh yes. Oh yes.

I claim time for Mother!

[Congregation affirms with Archangel Jophiel:]

I claim time for Mother!

I AM Jophiel and I say to you, let my fiat ring and then I shall call upon your vocal chords.

Now, I, Jophiel, proclaim: I claim time for Mother, even the Cosmic Spirit of Justice! Let Justice occupy time! Let Freedom occupy space! Thus intertwining, thus intertwining, the hierarchs of the Aquarian age may sponsor in you the intertwining from the base unto the crown, thus restoring androgynous being and the oneness of twin flames. Therefore, say it:

[Congregation affirms with Archangel Jophiel:]

I claim time for Mother!

I claim time for Mother!

I claim time for Mother!

And that Divine Mother is truly Justice come.

[Congregation affirms with Archangel Jophiel:]

And that Divine Mother is truly Justice come.

And that Divine Mother is truly Justice come.

And that Divine Mother is truly Justice come.

My counsel, then, beloved, is that you should be just in your use of time, just toward all life, just toward yourself, your I AM Presence and all hosts of Light, just toward the divine plan, judicious in your use of moments.

O let freedom ring throughout space!

Now let us journey on the wings of this song. (We request that you do not depart from the dictation mode. You are to sing what you know and be silent in what you do not know.) Meditate on the whirling sun above you. It is for your very life in this octave that you heed the word of the Masters.

Feel now the pulsation of the crown chakra. Close your eyes and visualize it. Intensify the action in your mind's eye as though the sun in the sky were whirling and spinning above you, its colors white and yellow, interchanging. Maintain this thoughtform through all dictations and singing. Your concentration is building a thoughtform for the passage of Elohim. Let us begin.

["Great Central Sun" sung]

This company is being drawn into the heart of Helios and Vesta consciously by the white-fire/yellow-fire sun spinning. Feel yourself entering the heart of the physical sun as one company, as though this entire valley were picked up and placed in the heart of the sun. To complete this, let us sing to Helios and Vesta three times. ["The New Day" sung]

This dictation by **Archangel Jophiel** was **delivered** at the conclusion of the Sunday evening service of **July 5, 1987,** after midnight, at *FREEDOM 1987.*

Vol. 30 No. 41 *Beloved Apollo and Lumina* *October 11, 1987*

Freedom 1987

X

A Journey to the Heart of the Sun

Crown Chakra Meditation—Behold! Cosmic Beings

Apollo and Lumina AM I, left hand and right hand of the God consciousness of illumination, enlightenment, wisdom's petals unfolding. We address you, beloved, in a great amphitheater in the heart of the physical sun that is the Sun behind the sun, a spiritual sphere beyond all matter yet congruent with the etheric octave.

As your eyes are closed now, sense yourself in the heart, even in the eye of a white-fire/yellow-fire sun that is spinning. It is a vast inner space and here you may know the Presence I AM THAT I AM. At your level of awareness in the etheric octave, beloved, we Apollo and Lumina stand before you, representatives of Helios and Vesta, Alpha and Omega.

This bringing of your presence, even this entire company, is for the purpose of your being entirely apart from vibrations of earth. For these moments, beloved, experience freedom from pressure, from weight, from ignorance, from tensions and the agitations and aggravations of a planet of a comparatively low vibration in many quarters and an astoundingly high vibration in the hearts of unascended masters and devotees such as yourselves.

Earth, then, is an admixture, a swirling combination (vanilla and chocolate, as you say), many times black and white but then melting together. Therefore, beloved, know surcease as you come apart. This is an ageless, timeless, spaceless dimension; therefore, you shall not advance during these moments. Though the world continue on her spin, you are beyond spin and in the center of the eye.

Coming, then, to the very center of the causal body, the first ring of illumination's golden flame does present to you the understanding of what is to be lowered into manifestation. Visualize the entire solar system as a span of the causal body spheres in the etheric octave. And realize that from the center to the without, you are desirous of lowering into manifestation, even from the center of your heart, causal bodies of Elohim, Father/Mother God manifest in the seven rays.

Thus, beloved, to bring this center of inner peace, inner space, inner time (where space and time are not) to the earth does require a daily celebration of the heart of Helios and Vesta. Simply sing the mantra three times, incorporate it into each service and resume the meditation of the white-fire/yellow-fire sun above you.[1]

Each day as you pour forth your love, no longer through your heart but through the crown, you will see the opening widening, beloved, widening, indeed, until it becomes as a shaft—more than a crystal cord. You are one with the space you now occupy in this etheric journey.

The result of your calls is this, beloved, that a great strength and strengthening has accrued to your finer bodies. The etheric body of each of you now has either a faint or stronger pattern of your Deathless Solar Body, depending on your participation in the decrees given, depending on your capacity to absorb Light* of dictations.

Understand that as I am pressing into this crown chakra [that of the Messenger], angels are pressing into your own. Thus, you may also take the first two fingers of your right hand and press them into the very center of the crown of your head. You may do so with as much physical intensity as you can withstand. For this will draw the blood and the light-essence thereof to this center even for a physical and clearing action, thus strengthening, yes—but reaching full capacity to bear the Light-weight of Elohim descending, not yet. It is something worth striving for.

Thus, we charge this Messenger to continue these services and therefore to draw you closer and closer through the chakras to the heart of Elohim. It is a present possibility, beloved, but we have determined to proceed with caution, assisting you in the purging of the astral body and the binding of the dweller. Thus, day by day we shall attend until the week from today when we shall see how seven centers have increased.

Now then, beloved, much is gained, much is gained. Few times in modern history has there been a gathering such as this

*Christ consciousness

that has sparked such awareness, such love of Freedom.

Mind you, beloved, though I have removed my hand from this chakra, you may not remove yours from your crown chakra. Let the intensity build. It is for a purpose. The Divine Guru Sanat Kumara has recommended this exercise; for, you see, the fire of the heart does return by the right hand to the crown and does descend again to the heart. Thus a new circulation of spirituality does ensue even as the first two fingers of the left hand are placed at the heart chakra.

Know, then, that you are complete by this fiery vibration. And if you will look at these arms you will see in the curve two halves of a whole signifying that the whole body of man is intended to be the caduceus action. Now while you press your two fingers into the crown and thus release substance not of the Light into the flame, as well as activate a flow, I shall continue my message.

Blessed ones, the gain is a mutuality of hearts, a weaving together of a bond, the clearing of much debris. We repeat, then, we Elohim, who know the destiny of earth (both on the high rise of the high road and on the low descent of the low road), could desire a continuing of this decree service for the dispelling, mitigating or perhaps eliminating of those prophecies of Fátima and others. Therefore earth now continues in the violet flame glow.

We, Apollo and Lumina, containing the Mind of God, now allow you to experience the peace of the percentage of the upper layer of the mental belt where the Light has penetrated and a certain clearing has taken place. Beloved, this action of the Light, approaching a percent of the entire belt, is as a fiery golden lining. It is an anchoring into that belt of the etheric octave that has not been accomplished heretofore.

Know the power of fire in this percentage, beloved. Think not that it is little, for a grain of Light may be for the leavening of an entire system. Light is greater than all Darkness.

One percent of the mental belt of the planet cleared and transmuted as a result of the prayer vigil and conference—for this there is a clap of thunder and a shout of joy from the heart of Elohim! And you ought to appreciate the meaning, beloved. For that one percent includes at that level all prior records of infamy in that one percent of all past ages. Therefore, beloved, it is a work that is established and can be sustained.

I claim the mental belt for the Mind of God in the Christ Self of all! O Holy Christ Selves of all people, I claim the mental belt for thy coming! Enter now, occupy! And these shall fill in the mosaic of that Light. Oh, let it portray the etheric pattern and heaven! There is a closing of the gap. And for some, beloved, there is indeed a sense of an inner connection renewed.

So, soul of Light, rise to the level of the heart. Rise now.

You are beholding on a very large platform Cosmic Beings, majestic figures, some robed in gold, some in white and other hues of secret rays. They are here, beloved, in the center of the Sun. You see them now as recessed from a Cosmic Council meeting, some in clusters in conversation, others with students. These are beings you have not seen before. And they impress upon you their stature, their loveliness and attainment in God, their fierceness and their strength.

Now look at their flashing, fiery eyes. I wish you to gaze into the eyes of these masterful beings, that you might see the expression of those who have the Mind of God and in seeing it, carry that vision with you. May it be with you when you fall asleep and upon your awakening day by day. For in seeing these eyes, beloved, you will also desire to enter the Mind that sees, the Mind that knows, the Mind whose All-Seeing Eye is expressed in these masterful presences.

Some of you have looked upon saints in embodiment and have said in your heart in this or past ages, "I see that Light, I know it is a purity. I would have it, I shall have it." And you have been inspired to be like that one you saw. Now let all see what is your individual God-potential.

Beloved, it was in the counsel of such company that Moses was wont to declare, "I have said, ye are gods."[2] Seeing these beings, you should no longer have an estimate of self as being anything less than God and rather view the lesser portion in the physical domain as an extension that is not clothed upon with the inner majesty. Thus seek to outpicture and be like them. Draw it from your I AM Presence. Draw it from the spinning white-fire/yellow-fire suns.

To this end the God and Goddess Meru placed their causal body spheres at the Royal Teton Ranch, and the causal body of Hedron [was also placed there during Gautama Buddha's New Year's Eve dictation[3]]. To that end, that you might embody your Godhood. I say, Ye are gods and all of you are sons of the Most High! Be it, beloved.

Now in the heart of Helios and Vesta, by Love's wisdom and Wisdom's love there is stripped from you small-mindedness, pettiness, self-limitation, the demons of prejudice, want, fear, poverty consciousness, all those belittling, self-intimidating conditions. These extend to gossip, backbiting, criticism of others, all of the chattering of the human nonsense. We have desired to strip from you that which most detracts in your own behavior patterns from your dignity of selfhood in and as God.

God in you is the one God. There are not gods many. Seeing, then, your expression of Him you ought to cry out in awe, "What hath God wrought! Multiple manifestations of Himself! Yet He is the All and the One." This is the nature of Elohim—all-encompassing Light. Now you know, beloved, that it is within our own auras that both you and the sun are suspended.

We are Elohim, God, of the Second Ray. And all of Cosmos is suspended in our God consciousness of illumined action in this hour. It is a vertical line drawn that takes on the curve of space itself. Therefore, it is an infinite circle. Therefore, beloved, the line drawn is this: All evolutions are illumined to right action, all lifewaves see the righteousness of Righteousness and his Law.

Therefore, those who choose to embody illumination shall be in the heart of hearts of Mary the Mother. They shall enter the Immaculate Heart and there participate in the healing of worlds. Those who deny illumined action for Christ in all little ones and the desperate, oppressed and poor of earth, these, then, shall bear the full weight of the Judgment of Elohim.

The vertical bar of the cosmic cross of yellow/white fire is drawn. Thus, it is the hour of choosing. When the horizontal bar is drawn by Elohim, then, O then shall the fourth woe[4] descend! Therefore, hasten ye, O ye seed of the wicked, and bring forth fruits meet for repentance,[5] even a converted and contrite heart that does bow before Elohim.

Thus, in the sign only of Alpha to Omega we seal this conference, we seal the crown.

Now, then, gently yet with the speed of light, you are becoming more and more congruent with the physical octave of earth. Nevermore shall you go out from the Sun within the sun.

There is stamped upon you the smile, the beaming smile of Helios, the joyous smile of Vesta. Shall you ever look upon the sun again without this smile? I say, nay. For the very thought of Helios and Vesta and the inner space will give to you perpetual gladness in the Light.

Light! light! light! light! light! light! light! Sealed, then, are your chakras by Elohim. Rejoice, for the hour of fulfillment is come!

The New Day
by Vesta

Helios and Vesta!
Helios and Vesta!
Helios and Vesta!
Let the Light flow into my being!
Let the Light expand in the center of my heart!
Let the Light expand in the center of the earth!
And let the earth be transformed into the New Day!

"The Summit Lighthouse Sheds Its Radiance O'er All the World to Manifest as Pearls of Wisdom."
This dictation by **Apollo and Lumina** was **delivered** through the Messenger of the Great White Brotherhood Elizabeth Clare Prophet at the conclusion of the Sunday evening service of **July 5, 1987,** after midnight, at *FREEDOM 1987* in the Heart of the Inner Retreat at the **Royal Teton Ranch, Montana**. (**1**) **White-fire/yellow-fire sun meditation.** For the beginning and the continuation of the meditation on the sun, see p. 395, pars. 1, 2; p. 399, pars. 1, 2, 7; p. 400, par. 2; p. 403, pars. 9, 10; p. 404, pars. 13–15. (**2**) **"Ye are gods. . ."** Ps. 82:6; John 10:34. (**3**) **Causal body spheres** of the God and Goddess Meru. See Jesus Christ, December 25, 1986, "The Coming of the Divine Teacher," 1986 *Pearls of Wisdom,* vol. 29, no. 78, p. 682, or 1987 *Pearls of Wisdom,* p. 16, n. 1. Of Hedron: see p. 1, pars. 1–3; p. 11, par. 4. (**4**) **The fourth woe.** See p. 242, pars. 9–11. (**5**) Matt. 3:7, 8.

Pearls of Wisdom®
published by The Summit Lighthouse

Vol. 30 No. 42 — *Beloved Mighty Victory* — *October 18, 1987*

Freedom 1987

XI
The Victory of Freedom
Take Heart!

Victory is my name! And I AM here to seal *you* in *your* Victory name! [15-sec. applause]

The fires of Victory descend, for my legions of Light have not spent their allotment of illumination's flame given unto them in the heart of the Great Central Sun aeons ago for the blessing and the kindling of those already kindled by Victory's flame.

Therefore, the capstone of Freedom is Victory. And freedom without Victory is no Freedom, beloved! And that is precisely the state of consciousness in the United States of America today. There is freedom but no Victory of Freedom. Therefore, I say to you, What kind of a freedom is that? ["No freedom!" 3-sec. applause]

Thus, my beloved, shafts of white fire and yellow shall pierce this gloom and doom until those who think they are free wake up one day and find out that there is a people in Montana who is free. But they [those who think they are free] are not free, for they are bound and bound again by the calamities of civilization that are as that which implodes from within and is not known or understood until it is too late. Blessed hearts, whether an Exocet missile[1] or a cancer in the side, undetected, there is calamity abroad in the earth.

Now that the trumpets of the Seven Archangels have sounded,[2] I must be present. For the victorious ones must have that extra flame upon the crown, the raising up of Victory's fire.

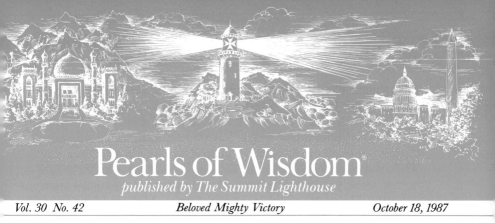

I AM Victory. And I am probing, therefore, the folds of your garments. There I snatch from you defeat and doubt and depression. Then there are those p's of procrastination, possessiveness and, beloved, powerlessness. There are those misuses of the light of the First Ray, all forces of anti-Victory.

I AM Victory and where I AM there is no other vibration than Victory. So it is of my legions. They multiply every day. They come from star systems, for they know that Victory's light is this same yellow/white fire. Oh, the glory of this coloration, beloved! The glory of the base-of-the-spine Mother Light rising to restore life. Oh, how the presence of Victory can fill your microcosm, can give that spin and health and God-awareness!

I AM Victory, come for the battle. Will you join me in the mental belt now, beloved? ["Yes!"]

Oh, my legions can fair contain themselves for desiring to sweep you up, put upon you their armour golden and take you, therefore, into those octaves where these fallen ones are ripe for the picking, beloved! They are rotten, I tell you, and ready to be cast into the fire. O blessed ones, this is not the field whitened to the harvest[3] of saints. This is the field neglected where the rotten fruit is no longer of the matrix of God. Therefore, it must be burned and the stubble that remains taken off the planet.

O blessed ones, the hour has truly come. For the opening of the seventh seal[4] is the true sign of the call of *FREEDOM 1987.*

Go to the root as John Baptist did.[5] Go to the very root with the axe to take it out completely. For this axe of Victory is truly laid at the root of the Nephilim gods who have placed themselves first and foremost in education. There I stand! And there we are! For all life proceeds from the education of the child and youth.

Heart, I say! Take heart! Expand heart! Educate heart in the twelve lines of the clock. When we say educate the heart, we speak, then, of a sphere of wisdom of the heart chakra not outpictured in the physical heart that must pump the life of a system. Therefore, knowing has been relegated to the brain or nervous system, but not any longer. The profound wisdom of the Holy Christ Self is the wisdom of the heart.

Victory, then, is the release of the Trinity. Victory, then, is drawn in the sky. And though the horizontal bar be not drawn, spheres of solar rings drawn mark the sign of a protection peculiar to a people peculiar.[6]

Weary not, beloved, for the buoyancy of Victory shall carry you to the Star of Alpha. Blessed ones, our Presence in these night hours has been to give you the sense of awareness of self apart from time, space and physical body.

My legions come to seal in your beings, then, all given at this conference, both the gift of knowledge of events in the earth and the gift of wisdom of cosmic awareness. Cosmic awareness does flow from the Royal Teton. Victory is cosmic awareness! And cosmic awareness is only God-victorious.

I seal your projects and your service in Victory. I seal you in the heart of Helios and Vesta. I seal you for another round of service to Saint Germain and Portia. I seal you for the great joy of bringing to Alpha the gift of posies of flowers gathered in the Heart.

O my beloved, I AM Victory in the heart of earth, in the heart of you and in this cradle, yes, of a new civilization. I say it, beloved. I embrace you. You are our own.

God-victorious legions, tarry with earth! Pour out now that which you have saved of the original dispensation of Victory, saving it for the hour when these should be drawn up by the Power of Victory, by the Wisdom of Victory, by the Love of Victory, by the Action of Victory! Victory! Victory!

So, beloved, you are in good, good company with so many angels.

Receive me to your heart. For I, Victory, encapsulate my Electronic Presence to a very small height that I might abide with you as the impetus to the balance of your threefold flame.

Just call to me and say: ***"Victory's impetus is mine this day for Power, Wisdom and Love in balance!"*** So I shall be that Inner Helper with the Maha Chohan.[7]

To you my Love forever.

Hail, Saint Germain! On yonder crest I salute you, my brother, and extend my hand. Thus, hands clasped, this is the sign of our Oneness.

"The Summit Lighthouse Sheds Its Radiance O'er All the World to Manifest as Pearls of Wisdom." This dictation by **Mighty Victory** was **delivered** through the Messenger of the Great White Brotherhood Elizabeth Clare Prophet at the conclusion of the Sunday evening service of **July 5, 1987,** after midnight, at *FREEDOM 1987* in the Heart of the Inner Retreat at the **Royal Teton Ranch, Montana.** (**1**) On May 17, 1987, the U.S.S. *Stark,* a Navy frigate on routine patrol in the Persian Gulf, was hit by two Exocet missiles fired from either one or two Iraqi fighter jets. Thirty-seven U.S. sailors died in the attack. (**2**) See Archangel Jophiel, "The Hour of the Trumpet Judgments," p. 401, par. 6; p. 402, par. 6. (**3**) John 4:35. (**4**) Rev. 8:1. See Saint Germain, **"The Opening of the Seventh Seal,"** pp. 369–77. In the lecture prior to Saint Germain's dictation, the Messenger read and interpreted Revelation 8–11 on the opening of the seventh seal and the seven trumpet judgments. Lecture and dictation, July 4, 1987, are available on 116-min. videocassette HP87045, $24.95 (add $.90 for postage), or two 90-min. audiocassettes, A87047, $13.00 (add $.80 for postage). (**5**) Matt. 3:10; Luke 3:9. (**6**) Deut. 14:2; Titus 2:13, 14; I Pet. 2:9. (**7**) Rom. 8:26, 27.

I Claim My Victory Now!

In the name of the living Christ,
In the name of Jesus the Christ and my own Christ Self,
In the name of the I AM THAT I AM,
I claim my Victory now! I claim my Victory now!
I claim my Victory now! I claim my Victory now!
I claim my Victory now!
So the acclamation of the angels of Victory is upon me.
I will not allow the forces of darkness
To take from me my Victory,
For I will not lose the sense of Victory
And I will not fail to claim that Victory.

I AM THAT I AM
I AM that claim of Victory! I AM the flame of Victory,
And that flame is invincible, victorious,
Invincible, victorious, invincible, victorious!
We shall win! We shall win! We shall win!
I say it once, I say it twice, I say it again;
For I AM the cosmic consciousness of Victory
And I ensoul that golden light of Victory.
Now let it blaze forth as the sun of Helios and Vesta
As the magnet of God's Love and Wisdom
Multiplies the power and momentum of Victory
Which I bear from the heart of God!

Taken from a dictation by Mighty Victory, December 29, 1974, "A Spiral for Christ Victory," published on *New Beginnings in the Flame of the Holy Spirit* (8-audiocassette album A7502), cassette B7505.

Pearls of Wisdom®
published by The Summit Lighthouse

Vol. 30 No. 43 *Beloved Archangel Michael* *October 25, 1987*

Freedom 1987

XII

We Shall Win!

I Seal You as Pillars of Blue Flame

I AM indeed Michael Archangel. I AM here, then, for the galvanizing of a company, to charge and charge and charge your chakras by the fiery blue will of God, that you might advance far beyond current levels of advancement. O God, I AM here for the shattering of the mold of the former self: for they are ready.[1]

Therefore I bless the offering of self and abundance and love. I, Michael, summon you this night into the legions of the seven, not alone my own but [those of] the Seven Archangels who must deal with those upon whom the trumpet judgments have descended.

I AM Michael, and the sealing of the crown by the cape and cap of blue is my office. You have been delivered with a mighty fount of illumination and sacred fire. Know, then, beloved, that I AM ever aware of those who lust after the light of the base and the crown [chakras]. Your defender, indeed, I seal you as pillars of blue flame and I multiply your dynamic decrees to me. Soon, then, the perfected preamble[2] shall be in your hands. Use it as a sword.

We shall win, beloved. I AM as determined as Alpha and Omega, as determined as you and the Messenger. *I AM the Guard!* And I share with you the intensity, the love and the determination to establish the protection of God-Freedom, Christ-Freedom and soul-Freedom on earth.

O beloved, in ancient days I stood in your midst to bless you as you went into battle to defeat the Watchers and the Nephilim and their masses. Blessed hearts, I can tell you it was a victorious battle and a Victory for the Light. What ensued after decades was a loosening and a lessening of the hold—the holding on to a Victory won.

This people has won many a Victory but it has been denied, as some of your own have said. Now I say with Victory, I undeny your Victories. I untie your hands and hearts. I open the way. I affirm Victory then, now, forever and tomorrow.

We are Victory. We march with Victory and his legions. We shall see it in the physical octave. I promise you, beloved. So I say, I need to hear your promise also.

["I promise, Archangel Michael!"]

Blessed ones, your promise is the sealing of *FREEDOM 1987,* of the Victory of the defense of Freedom and of earth.

So I AM Michael of the First Ray of Victory!

And Jophiel does say, I AM Jophiel of the Second Ray of Victory!

I AM Chamuel of the Third Ray of Victory!

I AM Gabriel of the Fourth Ray of Victory!

I AM Raphael of the Fifth Ray of Victory!

I AM Uriel of the Sixth Ray of Victory!

I AM Zadkiel of the Seventh Ray of Victory!

So we seal the Victory! And the LORD's judgments through us are God-Victorious to the Lightbearers of the world!

Therefore, we say in the seven planes, octaves and chakras of being with Elohim, Saint Germain, Portia and the Cosmic Spirit of Freedom and Justice:

"Lightbearers of the world, unite and be free!"

[41-sec. standing ovation]

"The Summit Lighthouse Sheds Its Radiance O'er All the World to Manifest as Pearls of Wisdom." This dictation by **Archangel Michael** was **delivered** through the Messenger of the Great White Brotherhood Elizabeth Clare Prophet at the conclusion of the Sunday evening service of **July 5, 1987,** after midnight, at *FREEDOM 1987* in the Heart of the Inner Retreat at the **Royal Teton Ranch, Montana.** (**1**) See p. 319, pars. 6, 7; p. 325, pars. 3–7; p. 326, pars. 1, 2. (**2**) **Alternate Preamble.** "Archangel Michael's Alternate Preamble to 10.00 'For the Defense of Freedom in America.'" See p. 257, pars. 7, 8; p. 258, par. 7.

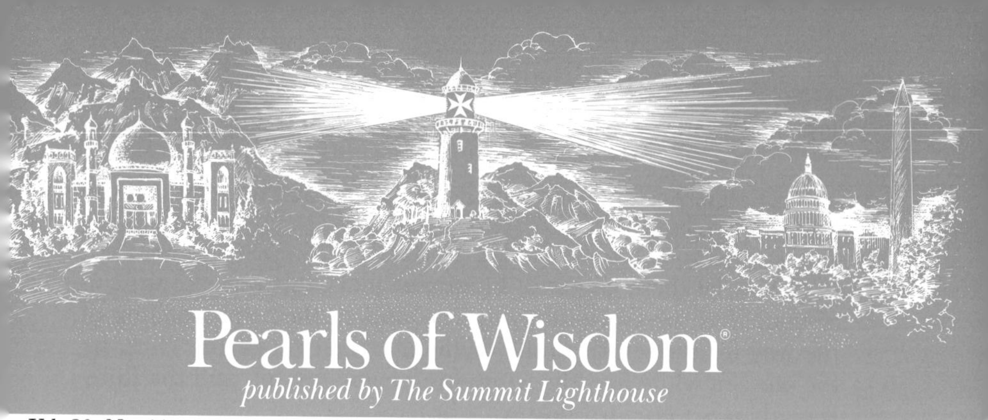

Vol. 30 No. 44 *Beloved Apollo and Lumina* *November 1, 1987*

Freedom 1987

XIII

Elohim of God Stand Guard

The Crystal Chalice at the Two-Thirds Mark

Elohim of God from the Great Central Sun, we are come, Apollo and Lumina. For our canopy of golden illumination's flame waits as a cap for the raising of the chalice.

But this cap, beloved, as a dome of golden light, does descend in this hour, magnetized by the love of your hearts in this day of a Divine Union on earth as in heaven,[1] on this day when the Cosmic Christ of Jesus has delivered to you an understanding of the hindrances of the fallen ones for two thousand years.[2]

Therefore, know, beloved, that as this chalice does rise and has risen that two-thirds of the way to our octave, we await the completion by the breakthrough of resurrection's flame. For at this two-thirds mark, beloved, is the point of self-transcendence through the Law of the One in the Great Pyramid.

May you whose hearts sing unto the mystery of Divine Love of the I AM Presence know that in this hour Elohim of God stand guard. In the name I AM THAT I AM Sanat Kumara, we stand guard![3] Therefore, may you do likewise in these coming days and weeks and months as the power of your word, O Lightbearers of the world, shall surely multiply and cover the earth.

Let us vow together, then, that we shall see change as world transmutation. We shall not cease together. For through this divine experience of these many days in the heart of Gautama Buddha, we can say that through the heart chakra we the Seven Elohim of God are one with you by the heart magnificent of the Lord of the World and the entire Spirit of the Great White Brotherhood.

Therefore, come, our son and daughter, that we may seal thy life in our own.

[Mr. and Mrs. Michael David Reed kneel before the Messenger at the high altar.]

Now let these angels of Elohim so mark this place in the son of man that the Christ may appear and in them the opening of the way for the return to the divine marriage on earth. Thus, by the cross of white fire, the white-fire/yellow-fire sun and the Ruby Ray, thou art one in Maitreya's heart.

And to all this company we say: Go in Peace, go in Joy, go in Love. Go in watchfulness, in tender caring for all little ones. Go in the fierceness of the vigilance of seraphim and Archangels. Go be! Go decree! Go, our beloved, pierce the night by Love's holy Ruby Ray!

Amen, above and below. Alleluia, amen! for the sealing is come. And the mighty sealing action level upon level shall be fulfilled if you attend the call of the resurrection flame with diligence until you hear next by the word of Elohim that the crystal chalice has met the golden dome canopy over the Heart of the Western Shamballa.

Unto all is given our gift of Wisdom's love. May you prosper in this way of salvation.

"The Summit Lighthouse Sheds Its Radiance O'er All the World to Manifest as Pearls of Wisdom."

This dictation by **Apollo and Lumina** was **delivered** through the Messenger of the Great White Brotherhood Elizabeth Clare Prophet on **Monday, July 13, 1987,** at 1:20 a.m., at the conclusion of *FREEDOM 1987* held in the Heart of the Inner Retreat at the **Royal Teton Ranch, Montana.** (**1**) On Sunday afternoon, July 12, 1987, Michael David Reed and Erin Lynn Prophet were united in holy matrimony by Rev. Sean C. Prophet at the high altar in the main tent erected in the Heart of the Inner Retreat for *FREEDOM 1987.* Edward L. Francis gave away the bride. A reception, dinner and waltz followed, at the conclusion of which Apollo and Lumina gave their dictation which included their blessing of the newlyweds. (**2**) The Messenger's Sunday morning sermon was "On the Defense of Religious Freedom: Who Did Hinder You. . . ?" (**3**) **We stand guard.** This affirmation is reminiscent of the words "O Canada, we stand on guard for thee" found in the Canadian national anthem, "O Canada," words by Robert Stanley Weir.

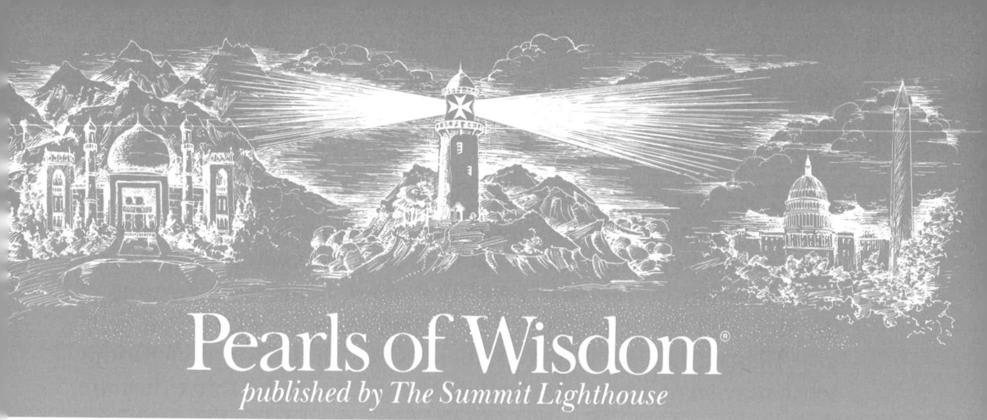

Pearls of Wisdom®
published by The Summit Lighthouse

Vol. 30 No. 45 *Beloved Godfre* *November 8, 1987*

Freedom 1987

XIV

"Do Not Give Up the Ship!"

Let Liberty's Voice Be Heard

Ho! I AM come in a pillar of sacred fire into this my city through this my Messenger. For I, Godfre, have somewhat to speak unto thee, Keepers of the Flame of the nation's capital and concentric rings of territory moving out therefrom. I direct to you the fire of my heart and my love for America, for the I AM Race, and for the divine plan of Saint Germain which he did entrust to my heart.

O veils of the Divine Mother, part now. For I, Son of the Republic, would reach my own. Blessed Goddess of Liberty, assist me in this hour as I would impress upon them this my command to my minutemen and -women, to my soldiers on the front line:

Do not give up the ship![1]

I command you in the name of Elohim! Do not quit this city until commanded to do so, for there is a fight to be fought and won. And I have entered this city this day with my legions of Light, lowering, then, my Electronic Presence over those pure hearts who would be a part of my supreme effort through my vow to Saint Germain to save America, to save the Lightbearers and yet in this late hour to turn back the tide and see the Goddess of Freedom no longer above the Capitol[2] but descending as a mighty shooting star into that Capitol rotunda to be the Mother of Freedom on earth.

Blessed ones, while there is hope we dare not desert this place. Let it be filled, then, with Lightbearers. And let Keepers of the Flame hear my call. For Saint Germain and I with El Morya would see you gather here once more this fall. Therefore, let the Keepers of the Flame be summoned. And let it be such an outpouring of light that the evidence is forthcoming in physical manifestation by the year's end that there is indeed a turning of the tide and the judgment of the fallen ones for which you call.

Blessed hearts, it is a moment when those of the victorious sense may snatch from the teeth of the villains, who think they are the victors, all that they would take from the Light of the son, the daughter of God. Let Liberty's voice be heard through many patriots who come in the wake of the defense of Freedom and the contras, through one such as an Oliver North[3] and many like him who have dared to heed the inner call of Saint Germain to help those freedom fighters when the profligate ones in Congress did not and would not—and did tarry as Hamlet: to be or not to be, to help or not to help, to defy the enemy or not to defy him.[4]

Blessed hearts, indeed let the 'serpent liberals' go down and let them be bound by the Seven Archangels! If you call it forth,* they will do it, I promise you. For these are rotten fruit that will simply tumble down from the trees and be no more if you will but speak the call.

Some have left off the fiery decree work that was their first love for so many other considerations. Blessed hearts, if little by little the self-concerns, the private concerns deprive you of this altar in the house of Saint Germain which he has dedicated,[5] how, then, shall a nation be founded under God? How shall the Flame of Freedom return in such a conflagration as to literally burn out by the power of Elohim of Purity all darkness in this city?

It can be done, O blessed ones. Except ye become as little children, ye shall in no wise enter in. For the little children believe, but the adults become cynical.

Blessed hearts, so long as the sun does rise and the stars twinkle, the breezes blow and the flowers bloom, take heart, for another day of opportunity is at hand. Have we ever won the victory or won a fair fight, beloved, without an intensity that must come as a consuming fire that does burn in the breast for the very love of the soil beneath our feet?

Blessed ones, here or somewhere else every Keeper of the Flame now signed on the lists of this activity will face this adversary. *Blessed ones, the encounter will not go away from you.* Though a nation and a planet be lost, you will go back to the scene of this encounter if you do not face it now! And this is my Fourth of July message to the world of Lightbearers.

I come, then, having desired to anchor it in this city. And so

*If you call forth their judgment

Saint Germain has accorded me my wish. For I desire, as with Mighty Victory, that every erg and cell and atom of this city be charged with my devotion unto Freedom and that this devotion, as my threefold flame, shall indeed displace the vacuous ones, the dark ones, the spoilers throughout the government and industry and business.

O beloved ones, I am here to deliver that mandate and to tell you that you simply cannot desert the scene until called. You simply must stand and prove me now herewith what I shall release in the name of Saint Germain.

Let all Keepers of the Flame gather in this city when and where the arrangements can be made. And make haste that it be before the end of this year. For thereto have I sent my Messenger to be in this city and you also, bearing the light from the Heart of the Inner Retreat.

Therefore, I touch again upon this point of the Law. It is no accident that you are called to be Keepers of the Flame. Some of you have been a part of my household in embodiments past. Some of you have known me from afar. But, beloved, we have all known that Great Star, the Great Adept of Freedom Saint Germain. We have known him. And the line he has drawn must be defended at all costs.

For each and every one of us has some commitment, some date with destiny to defy tyranny and raise up a living flame that speaks in our hearts and by our tongues, no longer silent, and in the vision and the dreams of our minds, yes, a pillar of violet flame that bursts forth as flowers upon the hillsides from our own soul chakras.

Understand, then, that we have a date with destiny to defeat these forces systemwide and in the entire Matter cosmos. Let us not give in when so great a calling is at hand and a victory nigh for the taking.

Thus, beloved, the decree work will be answered. And it shall be answered as called forth, for the Mother of the Flame has truly read the desire in the heart of Elohim to multiply your decrees ten million-times-ten million. Let the calls to Elohim and the power of the Spirit of the Resurrection be full and overflowing. Let the chalice of your heart know the flushing out of the resurrection fire.

Do you think you do service to God and country? I tell you, all service is unto the Divine Flame within. And, beloved, some of you who have rendered such services in this life have truly had years added to your lifestreams in this incarnation, and you know not of it. But El Morya has seen to it, as he does take charge of his own chelas with such tender caring, that when you have acted and decreed above and beyond the call of duty, those decrees have by cosmic law and by his sponsorship returned to you for the cleaning out of the bloodstream, the removal of dangerous cholesterol and other toxins and substances picked up from the environment.

Blessed hearts, know the difference, then, between a chela initiated by El Morya at Summit University and one who is not. There is simply no comparison. Those who are not, yet retain a certain glaze and gloss of the astral substance that may shine as silver but never as gold.

Thus understand, beloved, that without the quickening, where shall the Son of God appear? And without your chalice upheld, where shall the Messenger come to? Thus you have established this sanctuary. Now you must fill it with the fire of your heart. And let your fire, then, shoot forth through all your veins and atoms and through your minds, renewing yourselves with the Power, Wisdom and Love of the mighty threefold flame of the Eternal Youth, Sanat Kumara.

O Ancient of Days, as Thou dost stretch Thy hands over this capital, I say, therefore, let bowers of light descend and let needle rays bind those fallen ones who do no good to our nation, but corrupt it, but steal its technology, but take from us all that is God-given.

I say, then, in the name of Saint Germain, let the rip cord be pulled *now* and let that which has upheld the Soviet Union no longer uphold it! And therefore, let it be cut and let this one come tumbling down. And I say all of the might of Moscow shall never put this Humpty-Dumpty together again.

Therefore, let the people—we the people who keep the flame of Life on earth—let us decree the judgment and the binding of the fallen ones who aid and abet the cause of World Communism. For the system is heavy with the blood of the saints, heavy with the Light stolen, perverted into Darkness, which does weigh it down.

And therefore, Almighty God, let the Great Whore of World Communism and false religion, let it be cut now! Let the rip cord be pulled, then, on world religion that does bind the souls of the people into a doctrine that is not acceptable, that is not applicable. And therefore, by the fiat of God we will not allow our people of Light any longer to be held and bound by this Darkness!

Blessed ones, the hour has come for the ceasing of these systems. Only the call must be given with fervent hearts, vision and a knowledge that it shall indeed be fulfilled by hosts of the LORD.

It has been told to you at our conference that many legions of Light have gathered from the Central Sun, from out the compartments of Cosmos who heretofore have been not at all upon this planetary home.[6] Blessed ones, never has there been an hour when angelic hosts and Cosmic Beings were so available. Likewise, beloved, for such a showing of heaven we must say, let there be a greater outpouring from earth.

And let those in embodiment who know the decree and power of the Word—let them also know that when you multiply it, so the legions of Light shall melt down your own human substance. And I tell you, if there ever were true indulgences of heaven, know this for a truth, that those who decree and stand and preach the Word, teach the Word and spread all those facts and figures and teachings given by the Messengers, you shall indeed have a multiplication factor of Light unprecedented added unto you for your service.

I say this, beloved, for some have shrunk like shrunken apples, no longer juicy and succulent, into their own corners of selfishness, self-serving and therefore concerned only with the saving of their own skins. Perhaps they have not thought of it in this way, but the eclipsing of their service at the altar has shown that there is a certain inner lining of fear that has dominated their decisions rather than the courage to stand and still stand.

Blessed hearts, whereas Los Angeles may be somewhat deserted by Lightbearers, this itself has been decreed. But what do you think would happen to this nation if those who keep the flame here [in Washington, D.C.,] should pull out at this crucial moment in the history of the hemisphere, just at the very hour when by your decrees you may bring in a true and strong strategic defense and defeat years and years of war preparations of these fallen ones, of the Soviet buildup of arms, in order that they may never be used effectively against anyone?

Blessed hearts, truly that system should come tumbling down. And therefore, as we have said, and said through our own Son of Freedom, those who have the greater guilt and the greater error are those of the West,[7] the Nephilim gods who have supported this evil system. Hearts of fire, let them be judged! Whether deceased or not, let their names go down as having been judged by your call.

O blessed ones, just think of it. You are not called to go to war, to go into battle where you may lose your life or even give your life in honor and nobility. You are not called to leave your families or the comforts of home or even your jobs but only to be at this sanctuary daily if you can. For it is vital in this hour that our sanctuaries be full worldwide and such power be invoked as to test the very limits of heaven as to what heaven will do for the raising up of Freedom.

Blessed hearts, I come with my joy, my threefold flame, my spirit, and I say, Let us give it all we've got! Let us give all of our might, all of our love, all of our desire, all that we might have given in past lives but have not, all that we say we shall give in this life and in the next. Let us give it now!

I call all of the faithful worldwide to action now for Saint Germain. For I know that if we as blacksmiths with the God Harmony, who was once embodied as a blacksmith, shall strike a blow for Freedom one and all together, that truly the very impetus and movement and the rhythm of our striking shall break apart the bridges of the International Capitalist/Communist Conspiracy.

Let us march with God Harmony. Let us march to our own tune and not to that of the pied piper of restlessness, procrastination and self-concern. Let us see what life will afford those who give their lives, and give them ultimately in a spiritual sense.

Blessed ones, I can tell you only this, that I give counsel for many reasons. And I must add a note of warning, then, that you need to be so engaged for your own safety—for your spiritual as well as your physical protection and that of your children. Whether from plague or unseen forces or manipulators of the mind, the enemies of the Keepers of the Flame are subtle in this hour.

Remember, you are engaged in expanding the First Secret Ray,[8] and therefore it is an inner walk with God. And that which does attack the five secret rays as the anti-Force of anti-Cosmos, blessed hearts, is that which desires to enter in to the very nucleus of the cell. Thus you understand that in some plagues and under some conditions there is an invasion of the nucleus of the cells unto the utter demise of the individual who has [made himself vulnerable to the enemy as he has] violated the sacred fire of the Divine Mother.

Understand this, beloved, the inroads into your beings are unseen and subtle. They affect the subtle body, the etheric body, the astral and the mental. And you look around and you say to yourself, "Everything is all right." But, beloved ones, the physical will never give you the testimony of this invasion of the innermost privacy and peace of your being.

Thus, know that at the same time that enemies have developed weapons that cannot be smelt or felt or in any way perceived, so they come coincidentally with this testing of the Lightbearers of the world.

As you keep the flame with Mighty Cosmos, as you keep the flame of the Ruby Ray, know, then, that we have heard beloved Alpha, who has said that he should return in forty-eight months.[9] We have noted twelve months for each of the four lower bodies of the earth: twelve months for the purging of the etheric octave of the fallen angels; twelve months for the cleaning out of the mental belt and the waging of the warfare of Armageddon, therefore defeating those forces moving against the youth of the world; twelve months for the routing out of the astral pits; twelve months to anchor the entire message of Freedom in the physical octave and to turn the tide of world opinion.

Blessed hearts, these twelve are not consecutive but simultaneous. And therefore on all fronts you must defend the power of the twelve unto the coming of Alpha again. Thus, stand on the twelve lines of the Clock and defeat those forces. You can do it, beloved. You *can* do it! It is within the Power that God has given unto you, the Power that God will lower unto you.

Blessed hearts, take a renewed sense of purity, of the directness of your attunement with your I AM Presence. Take a new sense of hope from beloved Hope. Take a new sense of buoyancy from our conference and know that you indeed are as the one who will come. Whether it be William Tell, whether it will be the sounding of the warning that the British are coming by Paul Revere, it takes only one, beloved, for the saving of Freedom for an age and ages.

You can think of many, many examples when one individual who had the courage, the vision and the knowledge that his act would count did make the difference in history. And therefore, we are standing here this day. We are gathered together. We are one in the flame of Victory because singular individuals have dared to be God on earth and to alert and to awaken their communities and nations and peoples.

Blessed ones, let Cosmos hear the resounding of your cries and your call. For I AM Godfre! And Saint Germain gave to me truly the divine blueprint of America. And the Goddess of Liberty gave to me the trials that should come. Therefore, it is prophesied that by Divine Intervention the war and devastation of the final vision shall be rolled back.[10]

Let the entire Spirit of the Great White Brotherhood descend through you and sound the clarion call. For understand, beloved, that Divine Intervention does not only mean angels billowing through the clouds in time of nuclear war, though assemble they do, but it does also mean that divine emissaries in embodiment at the time of crisis are flooded with Light, having superimposed upon them the Electronic Presence of Cosmic Beings and, I tell you, that they do act in form.

Therefore, beloved, take your example from this one patriot

Oliver North, who has stood up against these fallen ones who have corrupted a nation and nations. Blessed hearts, run to his side spiritually and demand the defense of all like him, beginning with yourselves. For you are brothers with every patriot and fiery freedom fighter of all nations.

Blessed hearts, you are one at inner levels. Let the Lightbearers of the world unite in the physical octave and, I tell you, they shall not stand. These fallen ones cannot lift up their heads again against the challenge of the Lightbearers if you will only do it.

And therefore, I tell all worldwide, you who do not pay attention to the daily events and news, I tell you, it is a crying shame! For your consciousness being blank cannot be penetrated and used by the ascended hosts, and you yourself do not formulate the accurate and incisive calls in your decrees. It is therefore absolutely inescapable that you watch and take notes on the evening news and other programs that present events, and then follow through with publications which present a more detailed and a more objective view of those events.

Blessed hearts, we work very hard to send our angels to see to it that you are informed. And many still say to themselves, "I do not need to have this information. If I should need it, the Messenger will tell us about it." Blessed hearts, if you wait for that, it may be too late! For it is moments and seconds now which count in the outcome of World Freedom.

Blessed hearts, I tell you, World Communism can be defeated yet! It needs only fervent hearts who understand this and know that it is relentless and demands a relentless fight.

Perhaps you have heard it all before. Well, I tell you, the Goddess of Liberty does not speak in vain. Saint Germain does not speak in vain. And they have spoken to me this day and called me to appear before the Karmic Board. And they have sent me to speak to you that this message might reach all Lightbearers without limit.

Blessed hearts, their question to me was: "Beloved Godfre, how many more times do you think the Lightbearers can bear to hear this message and respond when they have been the watchmen of the night year in and year out and some of them embodiment after embodiment?"

And I said to that august body, "I do understand, O Blessed Ones who are our sponsors, that they may be weary and even bowed down by this responsibility. But I tell you, I know their hearts, and I know that in their hearts they will not fail and they shall respond this time to the measure required by Lord Gautama Buddha.

"And I know also, Blessed Ones of Light, that they are burdened even by the world karma that they do carry. Therefore, I shall go in your name, as you send me and give me your leave, and I shall give them the fire of my heart, the devotion of my being and the tremendous love I have for this nation and for Freedom and for that Cause. And I know that by God's grace I shall speak to them and they shall hear me as they have never heard me before. And they shall know that I, Godfre, shall not leave their side and that I stand in this nation's capital."

And I shall ride upon my white horse, a magnificent being of light, blessed ones, who is an elemental of the first order. And thus, I shall ride this creature up and down the streets of this nation's capital. And I shall continue to do so night unto night and day unto day and hour unto hour. And I shall speak to the people. I shall be as the town crier, beloved.

I shall be here. And some will hear. And those who hear shall receive your calls and they shall be cut free and one by one they shall file into your ranks.

O beloved, we must have this hope, this vision and this promise. I lay it upon your hearts, beloved. Will you help us as never before? ["Yes!"]

May your cry now echo round the world as the shot that is fired that does say, "We will not compromise and we will not stand for the compromisers in this government of this land ennobled by the Great Ones, sponsored by the Great White Brotherhood! We shall not allow them to mouth their mealy-mouthed condemnations of the true Lightbearers, their 'anti' consciousness that does decry war and therefore does accept peace at any price as long as their flesh and skin is saved.

"We will no longer stand for such ignominy in that august body of the Congress, in that Capitol building, in any of these houses of the representatives. Therefore, we will take our stand. We will call for their judgment. We will demand they give accounting before Almighty God.

"And we will demand the raising up of the true sons and daughters of God. And if no one does rise up, we ourselves shall rise up and therefore present ourselves to be elected to public office, if necessary."

Thus, beloved, enough is enough. And all of us have had enough of the fallen ones throughout the nation. Thus, this day it is heaven who does take a stand and say, "Let them go down! Let them go down! And let them join those whose words they mouth who are in this hour on the sides of the pit."

Thus, I, Godfre, have spoken to you in the name of the Goddess of Liberty and by her leave. I have spoken in the name of Saint Germain. I speak through the heart of the Messenger and through the heart of every Keeper of the Flame.

Let Light endure! Faint not, beloved, for thy crown awaits.

In the name of our Lord Jesus Christ by whose Sacred Heart we have come thus far, I say, Hitherto hath the LORD helped us![11]

"The Summit Lighthouse Sheds Its Radiance O'er All the World to Manifest as Pearls of Wisdom." This dictation by **Godfre** was **delivered** through the Messenger of the Great White Brotherhood Elizabeth Clare Prophet on **Tuesday, July 14, 1987,** at the Rakoczy Mansion, Church Universal and Triumphant Washington, D.C., Community Teaching Center, **Washington, D.C.** The Brotherhood anchored the fire of the Inner Retreat above the Washington Monument, lending impetus to the threefold flame anchored there on September 30, 1962, by Paul the Venetian. (**1**) **"Don't give up the ship!"** Recalls the dying words of Captain James Lawrence, commander of the U.S. frigate *Chesapeake* during the War of 1812, "Tell the men to fire faster and not to give up the ship; fight her till she sinks." Traditionally quoted as "Don't give up the ship!" (**2**) ***Armed Freedom* over the Capitol building.** The 19-foot bronze statue depicting the Goddess of Freedom, *Armed Freedom,* crowns the dome of the United States Capitol. On November 23, 1975, Saint Germain said, "I select the monument, the focal point for the enshrining of freedom; and I place that focus of freedom in the heart of America, in the very heart chakra of the Goddess of Freedom reigning over the Capitol building of the United States." See *The Greater Way of Freedom,* pp. 9, 42. (**3**) **Oliver North.** Lt. Col. Oliver North, former National Security Council aide, testified for six days beginning July 7, 1987, before the joint select committee investigating the Iran-contra affair. Deeply committed to the contras and the administration's efforts on their behalf, North discussed his role in the diversion of profits to the contras from the Iranian arms sale. Turning the tables on the committee, North pinned the blame on Congress for the Iran-contra situation, saying, "Plain and simple, the Congress is to blame because of the fickle, vacillating, unpredictable, on-again, off-again policy toward the Nicaraguan democratic resistance." (**4**) For a discussion of *Hamlet* as an analogy for our time and our mission to defend freedom worldwide, see Elizabeth Clare Prophet, April 17, 1987, "Saint Germain On the Defense of Freedom: 'To Be or Not to Be,'" 137-min. videocassette HP87036, $24.95 (add $.90 for postage), or two 90-min. audiocassettes, A87028, $13.00 (add $.80 for postage). (**5**) See Saint Germain, November 24, 1975, "Dedication of the Rakoczy Mansion," in *The Greater Way of Freedom,* pp. 7–8. (**6**) See p. 380, par. 4. (**7**) See Sean C. Prophet, "Apathy in America," p. 62, par. 8. (**8**) **The fourteen-month cycle in the First Secret Ray.** On February 28, 1987, the anniversary of the fourteen-month cycle of ascension's flame released from the Great Causal Body of Life, Serapis Bey announced, "We shall indeed begin five rounds in the five secret rays. . . . I, Serapis, inaugurate fourteen months of planetary initiation in the First Secret Ray." For more information on the fourteen-month cycles, see 1984 *Pearls of Wisdom,* vol. 27, no. 56, pp. 487–93, 495–510; and 1986 *Pearls of Wisdom,* vol. 29, no. 15, pp. 125–27. (**9**) See p. 388, pars. 7, 9; p. 390, par. 7. (**10**) **"Washington's Vision of America's Trials."** The Ascended Master Godfre was embodied as George Washington. Saint Germain sponsored him throughout the Revolutionary War and during the long winter at Valley Forge, where he received a vision through a mysterious visitor (the Goddess of Liberty) of three great perils that would come upon the Republic. See *Saint Germain On Alchemy,* pp. 142–51, or *The Great White Brotherhood in the Culture, History and Religion of America,* pp. 118–23. When Saint Germain anointed George Washington first president of the United States, he gave him the divine blueprint of America. (**11**) I Sam. 7:12.

Pearls of Wisdom®
published by The Summit Lighthouse

Vol. 30 No. 46 *Beloved El Morya* *November 15, 1987*

Adjust to the New Cycle!

Let the fire of the mind penetrate the gloom and doom of a darkness that appears real in the astral plane and here below. Yet, swift as an arrow the mind can soar to the place of the Eternal Day, thus entering the highest etheric octave where our sky does scrape the Absolute, where doves transcend this octave unto pure Spirit of the absolute Mind of God.

Thus understand, there is a safe passage octave to octave and quadrant to quadrant. But the gloom and doom of the mortal mind that would not only encase the Messenger as a bird in a cage but compress the cage as well must be dealt with. Thus, beloved, here below Christhood pure cannot long endure the mockery of a mortal mind that long ago and since time began could not contain the immortals.

Thus, I say, adjust. Adjust yourselves to the new cycle and the New Day, else, stuck in the mud of this mortal consciousness, you may be called a stick-in-the-mud by those who pass. Pray, then, it be not Maitreya, whose garments can be heard rustling and be mistaken for the wind in the branches.

Beloved, cycles do not sit still. Why do ye, then, sit still when God does descend in the power of his glory as not since ancient days have you been told such a story of eternal Life?

Complacency has set in in some chelas who have truly wearied in being in my house. I simply prick the mind and prick the conscience and the heart. For perhaps to shed a tear and a drop of blood should make you feel again more real, as Morya would have you.

Thus, dear hearts, those who have ever thought that to attain immortal Life would be like joining a caravan of covered wagons across America, those who have thought that by merely joining our bands or bandwagon they should arrive must understand that to take the spoon and gently tap the egg, one may remove a shell and find inside the hard-boiled egg or the yolk. Blessed hearts, the point is skins can be peeled away; thus finding another day and traversing an octave, you discover another self and a higher love.

Whilst confined to the geometry of karma here below, it is always well to establish a point of contact with the Infinite. This we know. And this is why the Darjeeling Council of the Great White Brotherhood determined to call your Messengers, that twin beacons might be found in our Lighthouse of Love.

Blessed ones, for the purpose of imparting not only a vision but also a light, a power, a cosmic dimension and episode, we determined that the dictations themselves should be the Holy Communion of our band. For without a transmission of Light by the spoken Word, all of the lofty ideals and ideas could not be quickened by a flame.

The process whereby the dictation is delivered is congruency of our Electronic Presence with the Messenger's and with her chakras. Understand that this process, by contact with physical matter and atoms of one so charged with our office, does quicken as with an electricity the entire plane where this Messenger does abide.

This, then, has been our solution to the equation of stultification in Matter that comes so quickly as sedimentation. And then there ensues a lethargy, even a sloppiness, and people become as though death had begun to set in, and indeed it has in many cases where bodies are not quite alive but not quite on the other side. Blessed ones, death has more than a toehold in the human mind and body. Pray that it not enter the consciousness and begin to fashion thought sequence and consequence by inches of death measured by karmic limitation and the rod of time and space.

Blessed hearts, it takes effort to leap into the etheric octave, and not mere sleepfulness! It is sad news to some who would be with us that to enter in requires a constant effort, a hearkening unto that Light, a tending of the Word.

You have heard of the dispensation whereby the dictations are repeated even as they are played [on audio- or videocassette]. Blessed hearts, I must give you a sense of co-measurement of how powerful is this Word, what a grid of Light is formed and that its necessity becomes to you more and more apparent as you understand the nature of the presence of aliens, not in some distant past or space apart but in this very time; for in these days when you also walk the earth, they occupy space in close proximity to your own.

Blessed ones, these spacecraft and their inhabitants are up to no good upon this planet. But they do have an agenda. Therefore, Alpha's Agenda,[1] delivered by his Servant-Sons and the Lord of the World and himself, must be studied and implemented and organized even as you organize yourselves for effective action.

It is an end of an age, when those who come from the Twelfth Planet[2] and even another called the "Thirteenth," beloved, anticipate a rejoining with those evolutions which their overlords engineered. A number of those in these craft are mere automatons. Their intelligence is not their own, but it is stolen from the Mind of God. Yet by manipulation in Matter, they become tools of that Force [that is Absolute Evil] that is known as the anti-Mind. It does exist.

And thus, all who have no allegiance to the I AM Presence by the threefold flame multiply themselves in physical universes according to the false hierarchy of anti-Life. Thus, they are in reality dead and only claim to be alive. Ye who have the Sun of the Presence in your heart are truly the living. Thus, Life must prevail in an octave where Death seems to swallow up and cover the land even as the sands of the desert, creeping and crawling, devour homes and vegetation and towns.

Therefore, know, beloved, by the vibration of the higher octaves and solely by it are you personally protected from those encounters of the wrong kind which are truly not encounters with Maitreya. To equate with the etheric octave, to draw the Electronic Presence around you, to increase the light of the spinal altar and to be nevermore without the dynamic decree, this is to repel those who seem to exercise powers over mortals, have none over the immortals and have none over those whose allegiance to Almighty God has established truly a vibrational congruency with His Presence.

Where shall we go, Lord Sanat Kumara? Thou hast the gift of eternal Life.[3] Therefore, O chela of the will of God, enter into the mantle of Sanat Kumara and the Great White Brotherhood and know that angels continually do battle in your stead, turning back aliens from any contact whatsoever with those who are our true chelas.

Keepers of the Flame, it is by degrees that you have become acquainted with varied and subtle dangers upon this planet. Thus, the wise ones and the mature have come to a realization, O beloved, of the wiles of the sinister force and that realization has not unseated them nor has it caused them to entertain undue anxiety. Thus, by much communication of misguided psychics, so-called UFOs have already gained a dangerous entry into this very octave. The allegiance of many is utterly and completely given.

We, then, are grateful to attend this anniversary of our Summit Lighthouse, symbol of the I AM Presence, to have presented before you and those worldwide who shall immediately receive our message, that, beloved, *It is the last time.*[4]

Keepers of the Flame must be aware that these fallen ones and aliens are utterly, and I say utterly, fearful of those who embody the Light of Sanat Kumara. They are not omnipotent nor are they omniscient, but they have used science and retain those accomplishments that were known upon Atlantis and Lemuria for destructive purposes, for manipulating life. Their goal is indeed that 'communion'[5] whereby they shall take from the bodies of this lifewave, as they are able, all the light and secondary light that humanity themselves have received from those outposts who are the sons of God in their midst.

Beloved, they desire the Light and the genes*of the Lightbearer. And thus, they would approach those of the highest attainment for one purpose: to combine the seed of the fallen ones, even of Satan and Lucifer, with the seed of the highest Christed ones.[6] For thereby they have determined to do in this age what they have accomplished in many ages: the prolongation of the life of their own bodies and then that of the robot creation which they have brought forth. You will realize, then, that the very presence of the seed of Light in their genes can extend the life of that particular physical evolution for long decades, centuries and aeons.

Therefore understand, beloved, how critical have been the laws handed down by the patriarchs unto the seed of the true Hebrews and Lightbearers which stated that they were not to commingle that seed with the lesser creation that had been created by the fallen angels. Now the plague has come upon the race, beloved, for the ancient Atlantean karma, worse than sodomy, of animalism whereby these laggards, these godless ones, did cohabitate with their own animal creation, producing a genetic mutation that has survived to the present for which the curse and the judgment has now descended.

Therefore, we see how Life has judged Death and the misuse of the sacred fire. And in the midst of the Darkness of this planet our Lightbearers raise up a standard, our chelas raise up a sacred fire. And thus we see the creations of heaven and hell rubbing elbows in the subways of life.

*the Christ consciousness and the Christ image

Blessed hearts, all this has come to pass. Our warning to you, then, is that if it were not so, we should have told you. By this I mean that every teaching given has been first and foremost for your physical, mental and spiritual protection under the Law.

Blaze the Light through, legions of Morya! Come now, angels of Michael and Lanello, Hercules and Amazonia! Therefore, let the shaft of the blue flame descend once and twice and thrice around each and every faithful Keeper of the Flame whose heart is true and because it is true, I, Morya, may enter there.

Understand, beloved, that Truth is a vibration. It cannot be faked. Nor can the Lie be hid.

If you would have Morya in your heart as the protection against all forms of aliens and their creations, know, then, that the Ascended Masters must be a part of your self-conscious awareness—by devotion, by right-mindfulness, by the science of the spoken Word. This we give, beloved, for your protection and the protection of your children and all Lightbearers who shall make their way to this place.

Thus, we address the topic brought to the fore concerning an ancient calendar and a date. Among the misguided psychics who have promulgated a message of "communion" and "harmonic convergence" with UFOs (by invoking these gods and surrendering to them)[7] are some who are the descendants of the gods, having been created by them. They know only the Nephilim as their creators, and none other.

You will know them by their allegiance. For by a man's allegiance, the place where he puts his highest honor, you will discover who is his god. If it be envy or resentment or anger, then that is his god and you know his source and you know his seed. Blessed ones, where the heart is, that is where the individual's god is.

Now, beloved, these fallen ones have placed their races upon this planet for this hour when they might be the negative electrode in embodiment for the anchoring of their energy, their control and their final manipulation of the children of the Light. Understand the complexity of a half a million years, ten million years of programming. Understand the nature of false hierarchies and of the anti-Mind itself.

It is a giant network and it has long moved throughout the Matter spheres for only one goal: to take millions of its own kind in order to devour the Light* of one son of God who has descended into Matter. They will stage a conspiracy for thousands of years to accomplish the undoing and the fall of a single son of God.

*Christ consciousness

We who are in the etheric octave of Matter as well as in the octave of Absolute Spirit need not fear this devouring process. But mind you well, we are deeply concerned, gravely aware of the jeopardy of souls in whom there yet exists a divine spark, albeit sometimes small, of souls who come and hear the Lost Teachings of Jesus and go out and hear many other voices and are fascinated by the cult of UFOs.

Hearts full of fire, understand that the Sons of God in earth are not in great number. Yet the salvation of these is the reason for being of Sanat Kumara. There is a chaff that is burned and there are the tares that are bound in bundles and burned. Realize, then, that that which is saved unto everlasting Life is the good wheat of the [genetic] seed of Christ.[8]

When you have this seed and you know that you have this seed, for the fire burns in your heart, you have two goals in life: First, to preserve your personal integrity and to disentangle yourself from the enmeshments of karma with these fallen ones. And second, to bring the knowledge of the Great White Brotherhood and the religion of the Divine Mother to all others who have this divine spark. Two goals alone: disentanglement with the dark web woven by the anti-minds of the UFOs and the ascent (vibrationally) of the heart and mind to the octaves of safety.

Safety on earth, then, is when you are sealed in the Light from above. There is none other. Thus, the Mighty I AM Presence is your safety when you invoke it. But that I AM Presence remains in the octave native to its own vibration, Absolute Spirit, absent your call.

We the Ascended Masters step down the Light of Absolute Spirit through the etheric octave where our retreats are located. And from that place to your physical atoms the Light descends swiftly in answer to your call. Without that call we also must stand by, for unless we receive it from you *daily* we may not intercede in your behalf.

Now, realize this law of the separation of octaves and teach it to your children. Let them be shaken into a wakefulness as to the correct perspective of life on planet earth. Though this earth be beautiful and was once even more beautiful, beloved, I assure you there are places in this universe far more beautiful even in the physical octave.

Now we are about the challenge that does come when, through an erroneous psychic prediction, there has been the gathering of many thousands who are determined to achieve that number of a critical mass necessary for a vibrational convergence with the false gods of the UFOs. The first order of business for Keepers of the Flame of Life, then, is to visualize and call forth from the octaves of Light a blue sphere around the planet at the line where the physical meets the astral plane. Let this sphere be a barrier between those in physical embodiment and the aliens in their spacecraft who seek to find a window of contact and consonance on those two days noted of the sixteenth and seventeenth of the month of August.

Blessed ones, as my scribe has written down this day, if the people of earth in these numbers elect to establish this tie with these Nephilim gods and their spacecraft, if the allegiance be established and the tie made, there will be no recourse from unleashing cataclysm from the highest levels of the Cosmic Council. There will be no life worth living for Lightbearers on earth, as there occurs a grave overtaking of those who have not yet discovered the seed of Light within themselves. Understand just how critical these days and weeks are and just how much it does indeed lie in your hands to prevent this tie.

Following this, of course, beloved, there will continue to be a greater acclamation, by some, of the people of the Lie in their spacecraft, a greater desire for a convocation by certain humans with these their progenitors. Know, then, that the Great White Brotherhood and all angels of Light and Archangels are fully equipped to deal with the entire fallen race of aliens making their way to this planet. All of them may be turned back, beloved, but only in answer to the call of those who are the true Lightbearers of the earth.

Saint Germain has long foreseen this coming and has begun to sound his cry "Lightbearers of the world, unite!" You can see just how literal is this command. For the unity of the Lightbearers in these very hours when an anti-unity force is being established is all that is required for the stopping of this diabolical plot.

Blessed ones, these civilizations of South America were peopled by the Nephilim gods. And they also did create races even out of their own genes and out of the substance of the earth. Thus, dust to dust is the nature of this clay creation, animated not by a divine spark but as the animal creation is.

Realize, then, that the gods they worship are the gods that created them. And I speak of certain lifestreams and lifewaves embodied in this hemisphere who were also embodied here long ago, who have left their records and who have continued to reembody and whose strain and seed of the Nephilim is with them.

Now, therefore, understand the metallic nature of these

individuals, their glamour which does replace the existence of any aura whatsoever, and their sense of association and even memory of having come here with spacecraft. Understand, then, that their calendar is the calendar of the Nephilim and of their cycles. Thus, one can learn from a false-hierarchy teaching the cycles that they are plotting on the graph, even according to the heavens, of those hours and years when they shall come closer to marrying that creation which they have created long ago.

Now you may search through the records of recent UFO contacts and begin to understand and put together the pieces. These eyes boring through[9] are of robots who are programmed to read from the level of the gene all that there is to know about an individual. Thus they become data banks whose information is fed into a larger computer, all of which is used to program humanity against the Lightbearers and their ways, to present every possible plot for mechanization man to lead your children astray. Thus, I think, beloved, through my presence and my word I have made clear just what is about to be programmed into the masses.

Blessed hearts, forty-five hundred souls of Light gathered in the Heart of this Inner Retreat for *FREEDOM 1987!* Your momentum of light and decrees is a celebration of Cosmic Consciousness! You have made contact through the vortex of the Messenger's heart with octaves of Elohim not even probed or penetrated by these false gods or their human creation. You have already set a planetary network of Light.* It is in position. Let it be strengthened and not suffer a decay rate by inattention to a continuing momentum of decree work. Blessed ones, using the great gain of the dictations and the decrees, the joy and the songs, let this high energy released at our summer conclave be the very forcefield upon which the sphere of blue is focalized.

I, El Morya, give you this assignment of that forty-eight-hour vigil whereby *They shall not pass!* This victory can be secured as you continue the calls for the resurrection flame, that there may be no breach in this funnel of Light twixt the Elohimic octave and your hearts and this place. That particular manifestation, beloved, does neutralize any and all that could come from the psychics led astray or the archdeceivers in their craft.

Realize, then, that we have already set the stage for your victory. You have only to take the steps, walk into it and claim it and use the full power of my mantra for that action of the blue lightning to descend to shatter all that would be built as the antithesis of the mighty work of the ages of the Sons of God—the Christs on earth.

*of the Christ consciousness

Blessed hearts, those who follow the cult of the UFOs have not even taken a simple decree from our dictations to learn it, for they have no affinity, no *fine tie,* no thread of contact with the etheric octave or the Absolute Spirit.

Let there be the reckoning, then, by the sons of God gathered in this place that the Light in you is able, that the Son in you is able, and then, having so dispatched the commands to our bands to bind and remove from the earth all aliens not of the Light and bring to judgment their tools, you make haste to defeat, then, another conspiracy that also comes from the UFOs, which is World Communism in this hemisphere.

Blessed ones, who could give to the bankrupt Soviets and Communists worldwide the impetus and the energy that they use to cause many to go in their direction? I tell you, it is not those who comprise the Soviet government. They, too, are the pawns, all too willing in their lust for power, of the false hierarchy of the spacecraft.

Now, these spacecraft have left some of their own, very capable ones, to be in embodiment on earth, sometimes against their will, forcing them to evolve through the human evolution. They are indeed in positions of leadership in the International Capitalist/Communist Conspiracy. Beloved ones, they are the angry ones. They are angry against the gods in the skies who have left them to the dirty work here below. Realize the archrivalry amongst them as well as the blood tie of their loyalty.

Now understand that it is the religion of the Divine Mother, that it is Shiva (the Holy Spirit personified), that it is the Divine Shakti (the Feminine Principle in polarity with Shiva), that it truly is the Force and the Power of Almighty God in his sons and daughters that is able to overturn these fallen ones in the Matter octaves that these octaves might ascend as a cosmos unto God, unto Alpha and Omega!

Weary not, beloved; your crowns have increased. Any number of you have added to your crowns even the beauty of aquamarine, signifying your love of the Divine Mother, and some the star sapphire and others the ruby.

Blessed hearts, so valiant an effort that has won so great a victory as this July 4th conference at the Ranch should not end in personal defeat for anyone who has given his all to make it happen—because of acclimating once again to a less accelerated vibration and to rest from such intense activity. Blessed ones, when you go into battle you are prepared to give your all. When you come home from the battle you understand there is a necessary period of adjustment. Every conference is the charging forth of the troops to do battle with Death and Hell projecting against those who would come to that enclave of concentrated Light.

Therefore, I, El Morya, your beloved and servant and father and Guru, give you my heart in gratitude for all who understand what they have given, for all who understand what they have received. And to you who are in the process of assimilating both, I say, the gratitude of heaven itself be upon you in added graces and light and especially protection. Gratitude of heaven be upon you in many ways that we have planned with joy whereby we may surprise you and bring you gifts that lighten the eye and enable you to know that the Ascended Masters of the Great White Brotherhood are your loyal friends and compatriots.

We will never let you down, but when you let yourself down and try to take us with you, beloved, we must let go. For we must be about our Father's business. And so it is your own calling.

Blessed hearts, to each one personally, therefore, I give love, recharging the cells, animating the mind and lightening the burden. This transfer, beloved, comes from many of the Great White Brotherhood. It is no small amount of light that we shower upon those who have been a part of this grand conclave in the physical, which in every moment did anchor the simultaneous conclave of the Royal Teton (etheric) Retreat at the Grand Teton in Jackson, Wyoming.

Blessed ones, speaking to you, then, I come. I would tell you what I have said to the Messenger this morn, that in my concern for the building and maintaining of the Inner Retreat, I would have you know that the present momentum of attendance at decrees and services is not sufficient to hold the Light against all extraterrestrials both in and out of embodiment who oppose this endeavor of the Great White Brotherhood on earth.

Yes, you have heard of the ancient shrines, holy ground where many will gather on these days. The names run past, whether Glastonbury or Shamballa or in South America. One and all, today they are barren. There are no temples remaining, no golden-age civilizations, no place left; yet they are called shrines, for some remember that here was once a nucleus of a golden city of light.

Blessed ones, shall they one day say of this place, "It is a sacred shrine" when only the trees and the meadows remain? Or shall they come and make their pilgrimage here because the City of Light out of the etheric octave has been established in the physical? The physical barrenness of these places is a testimony to the nonperformance of the very ones who gather there—their refusal to defeat the gods and to place their allegiance in the heart of the Divine Mother.

Thus, beloved, there is a co-measurement that must be understood: Of the vast lands that you hold and the Light as well, of this place being prepared these fallen ones are frightened and have extreme envy. The guardian action must be seen, else you will find yourselves engaged in little skirmishes. You will find yourselves putting out fires here and there, whether with the media or the government, the neighbors, the nation or the planet.

Instead of allowing your attention to be drawn into those skirmishes, why not put in more decree time? Be here, then, and let your hearts understand that unless that momentum that is required is built, you will find yourselves not being able to hold on to your own souls or path or chelaship, much less the property on which you stand. . . .

Blessed hearts, I, El Morya, tell you, having come from the Darjeeling Council table, that every word spoken to you by the Messenger this evening, every note of warning concerning World Communism in this hemisphere, the deplorable state of mind of the President and the Congress, every word concerning the threat of World Communism spoken by Saint Germain is true and it is imminent.

It is an hour, then, that I am tarrying with you to press into your cells the image of your Christhood and mine. For I would secure the oneness and the permanence of the Guru/Chela relationship. I would make you to understand that there are obligations to being a chela of the Chohans [of the Lords of the Seven Rays] and that you are standard-bearers. You are here, then, to witness. You are here, then, to abide in the Truth.

May understanding abide. And may you be attentive to the explanations of the guises of the sinister force that tempt the mind and aggressively penetrate with those suggestions that have naught to do with Reality.

Let there be the taking of the stand, then, for the throwing out of all peace offers to the seed of Satan and the seed of the UFOs in Nicaragua.[10] We say to them and we say to the spacecraft, In the name of Sanat Kumara, your day is done! Get thee hence! You have no power over the Lightbearers of the earth. Let them be turned back, O Elohim of God. For the day and the hour is come!

Therefore, I, Morya, say to you, prepare this place. Prepare it for students who would come and for survival. Prepare your mind and heart to be tough and to be a part of me. For, blessed ones, where I AM there is the love of the will of God and instantaneously there is a quickening of that vibration of all cosmos.

Thus, the secret of the will of God and the devotion to it is that it makes you a part of the vast *antahkarana,* the great blueprint of Life for all of cosmos. And the electricities of the Central Sun pass through you, and they neutralize the negativity of negative karma, in conjunction with your use of the violet flame.

Let the mind in this instant soar as an arrow. For I soar upward to the etheric octave. And from that point I say, Guard the Messenger! Guard Community! Guard the child and the chela and your own heart.

I AM Morya. I have not left off speaking with you, but shall continue at inner levels—nor have I concluded this address. But I close my portfolio on this chapter that you might find peace in the will of God and return again to hear me, beloved. For can a Gemini be without a twin?

"The Summit Lighthouse Sheds Its Radiance O'er All the World to Manifest as Pearls of Wisdom." This dictation by **El Morya** was **delivered** at the **Royal Teton Ranch, Montana,** through the Messenger of the Great White Brotherhood Elizabeth Clare Prophet on **Saturday, August 8, 1987,** the twenty-ninth anniversary of the founding of The Summit Lighthouse by the Ascended Master El Morya through the Messenger Mark L. Prophet August 8, 1958. (**1**) See p. 382, pars. 5–7; p. 383, pars. 1–6. (**2**) See Zecharia Sitchin, *The Twelfth Planet* (New York: Avon Books, 1976). (**3**) John 6:68. (**4**) I John 2:18. See also p. 14, par. 4. (**5**) For the story of one man's personal encounters with extraterrestrials, see Whitley Strieber, *Communion: A True Story* (New York: William Morrow, Beech Tree Books, 1987). (**6**) This is their version of recombinant DNA. (**7**) **Harmonic Convergence,** August 16, 17, 1987. According to José Argüelles, father of the event, August 16 marked a 25-year period that would culminate in 2012 with the end of the Mayan calendar's "great cycle." At that time earth would enter a period of "galactic synchronization"—contact with alien beings. Believing that a "cosmic trigger point" existed on the August dates, Argüelles called for 144,000 humans to come together at dawn on August 16 and surrender themselves to the "higher galactic intelligences which guide and monitor the planet." In response, these intelligences were to beam communications through the 144,000, which would catalyze the "mental field of the planet" and lead to a decisive turnaround from the present course of events. On August 16 and 17, thousands of people gathered for the Harmonic Convergence at "sacred sites" around the world, taking part in various ceremonies, meditating, and chanting. (**8**) Isa. 5:24; Matt. 3:12; Luke 3:17; Matt. 13:30, 37–43. (**9**) For descriptions and pictures of "eyes boring through," see Budd Hopkins, *Intruders: The Incredible Visitations at Copley Woods* (New York: Random House, 1987), pp. 22, 137, 149; plates 10–20. Strieber, *Communion,* pp. 105, 106. (**10**) **Guatemala City plan.** In Guatemala City on August 7, 1987, the presidents of Guatemala, Nicaragua, El Salvador, Honduras and Costa Rica signed the Guatemala City plan, or Arias plan, which called for the end of hostilities between government troops and all guerrilla forces in Central America; a ban on all foreign assistance to leftist guerrillas in El Salvador and the contras in Nicaragua; amnesty for all guerrillas; and democratic reforms in each Central American country, including free elections, free speech and freedom of the press. According to the *New York Times,* November 5, 1987, "Diplomats and officials from virtually every Central American country say they believe the Sandinistas signed the treaty mainly to force the United States and Honduras to stop aiding the Nicaraguan rebels. . . ."

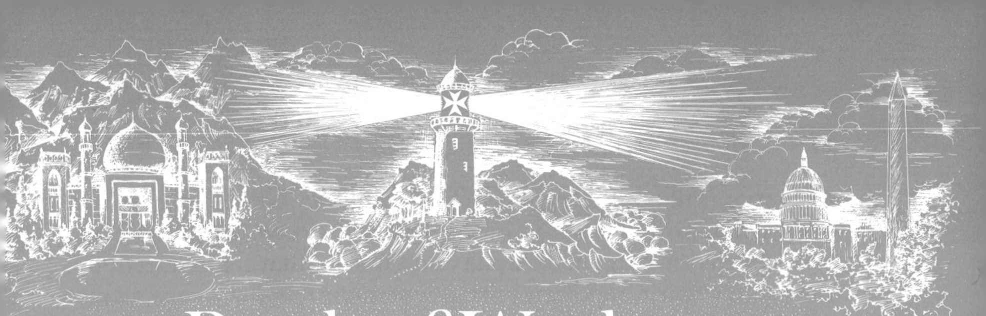

Pearls of Wisdom®
published by The Summit Lighthouse

Vol. 30 No. 47 *Beloved Hercules* *November 16, 1987*

The Armies of the Faithful and True

A Cross upon My Back for Fourteen Months

Lightbearers of Earth,

I AM Hercules, come to you in this physical octave by the very forcefield of light established in this place by Keepers of the Flame here and there across the earth. Therefore, I place my blue dot on those locations where Keepers of the Flame have truly raised up pillars of Hercules!

Know, then, that Amazonia, in counsel with Omega and the Cosmic Council, has determined to go into the depths of the astral plane in South America and to contact those places where the records of corruption and the betrayal of her mystery school did take place. And therefore, she shall, empowered by the very Godhead, move against those records of totalitarianism and tyranny of very ancient times when these fallen ones of an extraordinary stature did rage in the earth and were the spoilers in the land.[1]

Blessed ones, if the light is to come to South America, surely Elohim of the First Ray must go up and down these continents to prepare the way for chelas of the First Ray and for the Mother's appearing.

Blessed hearts, by the corridor of light from the Inner Retreat[2] there is released at this moment at Lake Titicaca the very fervor of your hearts. And those Lightbearers who have been galvanized to World Communism shall have their awakening ere the year's end. And I demand it and it is done. For I AM God incarnate of the First Ray, even his God Consciousness. Lo! I AM THAT I AM Elohim—Alpha unto Omega.

Therefore, blessed hearts, when the general and commander in chief of hosts of the LORD such as Sanat Kumara, the Magnificent and the Beneficent, does declare the battle cry and the word to charge, will not the legions follow? Will they not give the divine decree that will give to us in the physical octave that electrode, even the divine magnet of Alpha and Omega, that shall indeed, by the LORD's Spirit, repolarize these evolutions that have gone astray and lost their minds and therefore become unwitting tools of that sinister force? We have determined to stop them before it is too late. And after the end of this year it will be too late, beloved, for cycles are turning swiftly.

Therefore, know that the Lightbearers must be rescued from their polarization with World Communism and against the Light of the individual Christs. Therefore, know, that on each of the seven rays of their service they must be reached by illumination, by the power of Love such as has never been seen before and such as you have displayed in the fervor of your calls, by Purity that is the fierceness of the Great Kali Astrea, by the power of the All-Seeing Eye of God which must ferret out and isolate on the earth all secret Soviet bases, spy activities, sabotage. These must be exposed! Call for it! Cyclopea wills it so. Say the word, beloved, and stand neath the mighty shower of resurrection's flame abuilding in the Heart of the Inner Retreat.

I come to you, beloved, and I have strapped upon my back a wooden cross representing the burdens of the Lightbearers. Yes, I carry this cross. And you will see me as though I were a carpenter in his trade. And upon my back that cross shall remain for this fourteen-month duration, giving you the opportunity, as the karmic weight may be lifted from the Lightbearers, to draw them into the circle of their Mighty I AM Presence. Beloved ones, it is a two-edged sword: For when the Law no longer allows me to bear this cross, what then will come upon them when suddenly their karma returns again?

Thus, those who must prepare to receive the Light of Sanat Kumara must do so swiftly and must be taught by ministering servants who go forth from this white fire core when blessed by our bands and the Divine Mother. And let those go who are blessed. And let those who are not blessed fear to go! For I have spoken. And the waters of the astral plane are treacherous.

Therefore, beloved, those Lightbearers who are to come into this activity, let them come in the next fourteen months. For when that burden of karma descends again, unless some mighty miraculous dispensation occur from hearts of Keepers of the Flame, I tell you, they must have the wherewithal [of a Light invoked and sustained in their electromagnetic field] to meet it. It is as though there were a mini-dispensation. As Jesus Christ bore this cross for two thousand years, thus I may also bear it, but only for the Lightbearers, for those who have elected to bear the Light now for fourteen months.

Thus, in a mini-cycle, beloved, many may come to understand those fourteen stations of the cross. And they may walk them. And they may emerge triumphant. For the resurrection flame you have invoked is a miracle flame, I tell you! And by the scepter of power of the Lord Christ, so it does indeed expand as a mighty banner unfurled. And you may see in the heart of this flaming presence even the banner of Maitreya, even the banner of the Divine Mother.

Thus, there is the smoke of incense of prayers aloft. And thus I am, cross upon my back, taking my hands and my heart and weaving crystal-fire resurrection spiral ascending to the plane of the golden canopy. So, beloved, Elohim are truly busy in the very process of establishing this mighty pillar that is indeed a crystal chalice.

I AM Hercules and I love you. I love you with an unending and an undying love. And I am so grateful in your sense of self-worth that you have known the Lord, the Saviour Jesus, that you have understood, beloved, that he has saved you to walk a path of discipleship unto that glory. I am so grateful you have heeded our word and understood what is the meaning of world crisis.

These incisive calls to the Archangel Michael have availed much and touched the hearts of Cosmic Beings. Blessed ones, they have probed new heights of cosmic dimensions where some others in nirvana have heard and heeded and come.

Yes, they have come, beloved. Yes, they have come. It is the awakening in all octaves. It is the awakening here below. And it is the awakening of ancient ones out of nirvana. Thus, understand, they have waited in the highest octave and in the fiery core of it until the hour when the Great Battle should take place, and Sanat Kumara, mighty and strong, flanked by Gautama and Maitreya, with the Lord Christ leading even ahead should signal the start.

Thus, beloved, it is a sight to behold, these legions in white—the faithful and the true saints of all ages and universes. They are marching, beloved. Hear the sound of hoofbeats, the sound of drum, the measured cadence as they are marching a long march across the universe as to the Great War in the defense of the Woman and her seed. Oh, the joy to cheer them on! Oh, the joy to know them, beloved!

See how the engines of war are mounted by the Dark Ones. Did you think that all of the buildup of Soviet power in these decades was merely for a physical Armageddon? They fear with a horrendous fear the coming of these armies and their direct contact heart-to-heart with the saints of earth. Therefore these fallen ones in the physical octave who are a part of Death and Hell have determined to see to it that the cords be cut twixt the heart of Light and the heart of God and his armies.

Blessed ones, I AM Hercules and I AM smiling!

Blessed ones, rouse yourselves to join in the universal applause of this magnificent army of Light that marches relentlessly at and toward that point of confrontation. [44-sec. standing ovation]

Yes, beloved. Yes, beloved, you stand on the sidelines of a cosmic highway, joining, then, many legions of heaven who are cheering and applauding as the sound, the certain sound of a Universal Victory, is heard deep within the secret chamber of the heart.

Those who march in this army are the chosen ones from among millions upon millions, those in the forefront all in white. And when miles upon miles of these have passed, those on the sidelines shall join in formation wearing the armour of the seven rays of Elohim! Thus, not the entire vision is given in the Revelation. But for you it is given to see how the Faithful and True does lead them.[3]

Blessed ones, the figure of the Lamb, even the Lord Jesus Christ, whose banner is the Word, is seen far ahead of this company. And the triad of Sanat Kumara, Gautama and Lord Maitreya does follow. Thus, the lone figure of the Son of God sends a message to all tyrants that the single and singular Son of God is fearless before all the hosts of Death and Hell.

I tell you, it is enerving to these fallen ones to see that though armies upon armies come, the Son of God is able to defeat them all single-handedly. And this is the mystery of the Law of the One. Immersed in this fire of Oneness, Jesus is a pillar of a blinding light, that all the earth who have attacked Christendom from within and without might know how much I have loved thee.[4]

O beloved, it is a momentous hour. Therefore, be seated in a compartment of my consciousness. I open my vast garments to you. You may climb inside one of an infinite number of pockets in the lining of my cloak and feel cozy all inside—and even take a nap while I am speaking!

Blessed hearts, feel the warmth and the joy of this little hammock of a pocket inside the cloak of Elohim and know that I have a pocket for each and every one of you. And do you know that elves of Hercules have embroidered your name upon that pocket that is your very own private berth?

So, beloved, I give you this which is indeed a reality, that you might know the profound comfort of Elohim, that you might have the sense of abiding in me always as I truly abide even in the center of the atom of self that you have charged with the will of God.

Know, then, O beautiful ones, that the sun shining upon you reveals a light of glory. Continue in my Word. Continue in my call from this hour until the fortnight is concluded and there is the entrance into the sign of Virgo. Know that so very, very many situations in planet earth hang in the balance. Let the balance not tip against the Light and for these fallen ones, my beloved. Hold steady the balance. Balance is the key to your hour of Victory.

Now you see, after many, many, many hours have passed and each one in divine order of the legions of the seven rays has taken their place, so you, beloved, the saints, may bring up the rear of the troops. And what is the rear, beloved? It is the Serpent's tail. It is the seed of Serpent and the egg.

Only those in embodiment have the authority to bind the Serpent's tail. The heavenly hosts lead. But by your divine decree, you are perpetually standing in judgment of the fallen ones' misuse of the base-of-the-spine chakra of the Mother. Of this misuse of the sacred fire is the Serpent's tail created.

Raise your swords! Take them! Cut off that tail. Cast it into the fire. Go after it in every area of life. For Death and Hell were created out of the Serpent's tail. This is the work of those who know the science of the Mother, who have courage, who see a job to be done and do it. These are chelas of Hercules.

Certain of you who desire to be my chelas, so signify it in these twenty-four hours. For trained by Morya, enlisted by Archangel Michael, there are some whom I may receive. But you must take as your first assignment, beloved, physical balance. I am the most physical of Elohim. And therefore, you must know how strong is my strength in you in this octave. Balance, beloved, by the wheel of the Law—balance heart, head and hand, mind and feeling, physical body with etheric counterpart.

I encourage you and I say, Tear the mask from the Soviet! Tear the mask! Tear the mask, O Elohim of God! Expose them to all the world. We the Elohim of God decree the withdrawal, therefore, of their stolen Light of the Divine Mother. Let it be returned to Her causal body now! I, Hercules, decree it.

Therefore, the maya, glamour, illusion and the raising up of those vibrations of psychotronics out of the spacecraft and their physical tools, these go down in this hour as legions of Hercules enter that fray to demagnetize physical cosmos of these abusers of the Divine Mother's sacred fire!

Blessed ones, decree it and decree it hourly. Say to all fallen ones of the International Capitalist/Communist Conspiracy:

"You have no power! In the name Hercules and Amazonia, the Cosmic Christ, I tear from you the mask of all conspiracy and glamour and of the Lie and the Murderer.

"You have no power! Your day is done! Your evil is not real. Its appearance has no power! Go down to the sides of the pit, ye fallen ones! For Hercules is waiting with cosmic legions to bind you in bundles and take you from our planet home.

"We the Keepers of the Flame do decree it and do challenge by the authority of Almighty God your entire posture throughout the Matter cosmos!

"It is done in the name of the Father. It is done in the name of the Son. It is done in the name of the Holy Spirit. It is done in the name of the Divine Mother."

AUM AUM

Hearts of living fire, I seal you. I seal the power center of the Word. I AM Hercules, positioned to hurl back alien invaders of the territory of Elohim and sons and daughters of God.

I AM THAT I AM Hercules/Amazonia of the First Ray of God's holy will. Flash forth, O will of God! Touch every heart of Light who has called in these hours and given of his heart's Light-essence unto the cause of the entire Spirit of the Great White Brotherhood.

Hail, Saint Germain!

"The Summit Lighthouse Sheds Its Radiance O'er All the World to Manifest as Pearls of Wisdom."

This dictation by **Hercules** was **delivered** through the Messenger of the Great White Brotherhood Elizabeth Clare Prophet at the conclusion of the Sunday evening service **August 9, 1987,** after midnight, at the **Royal Teton Ranch, Montana.** (**1**) See Amazonia, April 13, 1979, "The Story of the Mystery School of Hercules and Amazonia," single 90-min. audiocassette B7924, $6.50 (add $.50 for postage) on 6-audiocassette album *The Quest for the Resurrection,* A7922, 9 hrs., $37.50 (add $1.30 for postage); excerpted in "The Elohim and Their Retreats," in 1978 *Pearls of Wisdom,* vol. 21, pp. 336–38. (**2**) See p. 378, n. 11. (**3**) Rev. 19:11–16. (**4**) Jer. 31:3.

Pearls of Wisdom®
published by The Summit Lighthouse

Vol. 30 No. 48 *Beloved El Morya* *November 17, 1987*

Sacred Fire Baptism

"Greet the Living Flame of God"

Light from Darjeeling beckons the traveler Home. Thus the bourne[1] of the noble attends the return from battle. Know, then, that as there is comfort in the pocket of Hercules,[2] so there is, beloved, comfort in the twin of Gemini that I bear.[3]

Have you thought of the brain itself as twins of the Mind of God? Have you thought of the limitation of hemispheres? Have you thought of the deprivation of Lightbearers from the full use of the faculties of the Mind of God? Well, I say to you, if you have not, then think of it! And think of it now. For these fallen ones have suppressed, as though with the boot of the Soviet, the full flowering of the crown of Life.

Let the Light rise in this Body. Let the Light rise for the full flowering of genius that can be known in the physical octave by those of every age. Let the cells give up the ghosts of all past. Let them give up all that is less than the Light, the golden liquid Light that each cell can and shall hold in the balance of Alpha and Omega.

Surely, I AM come. I AM come on a note of Victory, not to leave you, then, in scenes astral of netherworlds of Nephilim gods. Thus Hercules has opened the vision of the vast panorama of heaven. I open the panorama of earth that can be the fullness of the LORD and of His coming. They shall not pass!

I urge our scribes, noting the precise answers to precise calls, to provide even another alternate preamble focusing on those facts that come to light in answer to the call of the first. There may be seven such preambles, all blue, but each one ensconced in one of the chakras and one of the seven rays.

Let the fire of the blue lightning of the Mind of God unlock the fullness of the potential of the seven chakras and the seven rays and the Elohim's seven focuses upon the brow.[4] Let the seven spheres of the causal body descend.

Let yourself become now, beloved, the angel clothed with a cloud of the I AM Presence and upon his head the rainbow of the Causal Body of God.[5] For as the fire of the blue lightning of the Mind of God descends, it does challenge in you the anger of mortality and death itself, lodged even in the molecules of physical matter.

Beloved, rejoice in the alchemy of chemicalization and leap into the flames of sacred fire! It is the only way. Sacred fire baptism may challenge you, may even singe some portion of the human you would retain. But when you emerge from that sacred fire baptism—a unique and personal initiation of Maitreya—I tell you, nothing in this world can touch you, for you are fire!

It is a spiritual fire, a flame that cannot be quenched! Thus it is written: He does make his ministers a flame of fire.[6]

Would you have it, beloved? Then see that the Diamond Heart and the Gemini Mind,[7] the very solidity of Reality, are thine own. And therefore, you shall not even notice what the sacred fire has taken from you, for it will be nothing of any import whatsoever.

Hasten, then, to greet the living flame of God. Do not rub your eyes and say, "Am I seeing things?" when you see a flame walking toward you on the road. Blessed ones, I am serious. For the sacred fire manifest as salamander or seraphim does indeed walk down the road as a giant pillar or a giant leaf in shape.

Notice how the fire runs to greet you. Blessed ones, so greet it: "I see thee coming, O sacred fire! I shall not turn and run but leap into thy rainbow crescending, ascending, descending, undulating fiery presence!"

O blessed one, I know few sons of God who have not at that moment had a flash of a desire to be somewhere else. It will pass. And you will know that there is not anywhere else to go but into the heart of the flame.

Mark the heart again at the two-thirds level, beloved, and know that if you leap into the flame at that point, you will find yourself seated in a cave in the rock in the heart of meditation with Gautama. And you will recognize that that sacred fire is the gateway to the etheric octave.

These are the things of which I would speak to my chelas, not of wars and tribulations and of rehearsals of the activities of the unmentionables. O blessed hearts, if you are weary, believe me, the earth itself is weary and so are we of such discussions.

Thus, having divested myself of all that you may bear in this coming fortnight and must bear for us, I may then digress in a spiritual mode so that you might also remember that we are adepts of the spiritual fire and that this is the training we give to our chelas.

Most notable ones who have noted the signs, let thy body be the vessel of the Holy Spirit and thy soul the bride of Christ. The key I have given, 'tis enough.

Meditate upon the cadences of my mind, for they are a rope that you pick up at the beginning of a tunnel. And you follow the rope, and beyond its cadences and the paces through the tunnel you will reach the secret chamber of my heart. Hold on to the rope. Do not let go of it. My sentences form this strong hemp.

Therefore, through all the darkness that you pass, beloved, you will find that the words of Morya from the beginning unto the end of our dictations are all cipher, all keys, all kernels that will open by the heat of divine fervor.

In the name of our LORD the Almighty One and Him in His sons and daughters, I serve.

"The Summit Lighthouse Sheds Its Radiance O'er All the World to Manifest as Pearls of Wisdom."

This dictation by **El Morya** was **delivered** through the Messenger of the Great White Brotherhood Elizabeth Clare Prophet at the conclusion of the Sunday evening service **August 9, 1987**, after midnight, at the **Royal Teton Ranch, Montana.** (**1**) **bourne:** realm or domain (1798–1832). (**2**) See p. 444, pars. 7, 8. (**3**) **The twin of Gemini.** See p. 440, par. 3. El Morya is the initiator under the hierarchy of Gemini on the 5 o'clock line of the Cosmic Clock. (**4**) **The focus of Elohim at the Royal Teton Retreat.** The seven rays of the Elohim are enshrined at the Royal Teton Retreat, an ancient focus of Light congruent with the Grand Teton in Wyoming. The rays are concentrated and anchored in a large image of the All-Seeing Eye of God that is located in a council hall of the retreat. (**5**) Rev. 10:1. (**6**) Ps. 104:4; Heb. 1:7. (**7**) **The Gemini Mind.** See El Morya, October 8, 1977, "The Gemini Mind: For the Governing of Society and the Self," 1981 *Pearls of Wisdom,* vol. 24, no. 43, pp. 441–46, or single 90-min. audiocassette B7805, $6.50 (add $.50 for postage). Also, November 10, 1977, "The Gemini Mind, Part II: Victory Is to the Alert," single 90-min. audiocassette B7812, $6.50 (add $.50 for postage).

Beloved Flame of Resurrection

Beloved mighty victorious Presence of God, I AM in me, my very own beloved Holy Christ Self, and Holy Christ Selves of all mankind, by and through the magnetic power of the immortal victorious threefold flame of Love, Wisdom, and Power anchored within my heart, I AM invoking the Flame of Resurrection from the heart of God in the Great Central Sun, from beloved Alpha and Omega, beloved Jesus the Christ, beloved Mother Mary, beloved Archangel Gabriel and Uriel, the angels of the Resurrection Temple, beloved Lanello, the entire Spirit of the Great White Brotherhood and the World Mother, Elemental Life—Fire, Air, Water, and Earth!

Beloved Flame of Resurrection,
  Blaze through me thy Light always;
Beloved Flame, resuscitation,
  Make my heart to sing thy praise.

O blazing white Christ radiance
  Of God's own I AM fire,
Expand thy blessed Purity
  And free me from all wrong desire.

Beloved Flame of Resurrection,
  Rise and rise to Love's great height;
Blessed Flame, regeneration,
  Guide all men by thy great Light.

I AM, I AM, I AM thy chalice free
  Through whose crystal substance clear
All can see the Christ flame lily
  Of eternity appear

Blazing, blazing, blazing! (3x)

And in full Faith I consciously accept this manifest, manifest, manifest! (3x) right here and now with full Power, eternally sustained, all-powerfully active, ever expanding, and world enfolding until all are wholly ascended in the Light and free!

Beloved I AM! Beloved I AM! Beloved I AM!

Note: Use this call to the Resurrection Flame to establish the harmonic communion of your soul with the crystal chalice that Elohim established in the Heart of the Inner Retreat, site of the Western Shamballa, etheric retreat of the Lord of the World. Call to the Spirit of the Resurrection to establish in your heart and home the focus of the Seven Mighty Elohim, who deliver their light to the planet through the forcefield established by Keepers of the Flame in their July 4, 1987, International Conference for Spiritual Freedom and Prayer Vigil at the Royal Teton Ranch.

SUMMIT UNIVERSITY®
A COLLEGE OF RELIGION, CULTURE, AND SCIENCE
OF CHURCH UNIVERSAL AND TRIUMPHANT

August 15, 1987

NICARAGUA UPDATE:
Can the Sandinistas Be Stopped?
A Summit University Report from the Office of the President

In the July issue of *Commentary,* George Russell, an associate editor of *Time,* asked, "Can the Sandinistas still be stopped?"

Russell, who had been the chief of *Time*'s South American bureau, observed that, "seen from the viewpoint of Nicaragua's ruling Sandinista National Liberation Front (FSLN), the war against U.S. 'imperialism' is not going badly at all these days. It seems almost strange to recall, in the midst of the various investigations now in process, that current congressional policy still favors the anti-Sandinista forces. But the likelihood that Congress will provide further funds for the so-called *contra* war. . . is rapidly approaching zero."

Of course, that was before Lt. Col. Oliver North testified at Congress' Iran-Contra hearings and left the committee, in the words of columnist Mary McGrory, "a smoking ruin." As McGrory pointed out, after North, "support for the Contras has jumped twenty points in the polls. For five years, the public has opposed military aid, but in six days, Ollie . . . converted millions." Prior to North's testimony, 67 percent of the American people opposed aid to the Contras while only 29 percent favored it. But after he testified, a *Washington Post*/ABC News poll found that 43 percent favored aid to the Contras while 46 percent opposed it. Other polls had slightly different figures. But all show the same shift and White House pollster Richard Wirthlin said that more Americans now actually favor support for the Contras than oppose it.

Contra support groups are being deluged with contributions from an aroused public. There are reports that President Reagan will ask Congress for more than $150 million in new aid by September 30, when funds for the Contras will run out.

Oliver North's testimony has given the Nicaraguan freedom fighters another chance. But victory is by no means assured. What the American people do now will decide whether the Sandinistas will be stopped in Nicaragua, Texas, or not at all. And whether the Contras will do the fighting—or American troops.

Despite the public opinion shift, it is not certain that Congress

BOX A, LIVINGSTON, MONTANA 59047-1390 (406) 222-8300

will allocate more funds for the Contras. Public opinion might not translate into votes in Congress. Or it could change. Furthermore, defeating the Sandinistas requires more than just one aid package. It requires a sustained political will. And, if we can judge by past performance, the president and the Congress are not going to muster that will without sustained public support.

Our security is threatened by a growing concentration of Soviet military power in Cuba and Nicaragua. Even if Congress gives the Contras some money, they will only be postponing the day of reckoning unless they give enough to counter the relentless Soviet buildup. Patrick J. Buchanan, the president's conspicuously unapologetic advocate, says Reagan's $150 million is not enough. He should "demand, not request, $500 million for the contras . . . and he should settle for nothing less than what the contras require to continue this fight."

Can the Sandinistas be stopped?

Today, thanks to Colonel North and others who testified, there is at least a chance. But unless we the people act quickly and decisively, the Soviets will soon be in a position to spring a geopolitical trap that could result in America's worldwide defeat. Americans must understand how this came about in order to take action and avoid this fate.

World domination has been a Soviet goal since 1917. Moscow correctly viewed Latin America as the soft underbelly, the geostrategic weak point, of the United States. But they were in no position to aggressively exploit this weakness by subverting Latin America. The Soviets had the more immediate problems of consolidating their revolution in Russia and making the embryonic Soviet state function. In fact, until the late 1950s the Soviets were unable to gain much influence in the region except during an interlude between 1945 and 1954 when Guatemala became increasingly anti-American and pro-Communist. The United States found such circumstances intolerable and helped overthrow the radical government.

This was not a total loss for the Soviets, however. Marxist-Leninists had been using Latin America as a laboratory to refine their revolutionary technique. Unsuccessful Soviet efforts at subversion in Latin America in the 1930s and the Guatemalan affair yielded important lessons, the most important being how a Communist government in the Western Hemisphere could *remain* in power.

Fidel Castro was the first to successfully apply these lessons. He also added a wrinkle of his own: he initially denied he was a Communist. In the late fifties, Castro persuaded the State Department, the American media and most of the Cuban democratic leaders that he would establish a democracy in Cuba.

It was a ruse of course. In a 1986 interview with *Le Figaro Magazine*, Castro made no effort to hide the fact that he intended to make Cuba a Communist state from the start, but concealed his goal for strategic purposes. Nevertheless, just weeks after taking power in January of 1959 Castro started building his dictatorship and exporting revolution to Panama, Nicaragua, the Dominican Republic, Venezuela, and Colombia.

Castro's tenure was more or less assured after the Cuban missile crisis of 1962 when the Soviets, as part of the overall settlement, secured an American promise not to use military force to remove him. Each administration since has honored this agreement, giving the Soviets license to turn Cuba into a forward base in the Western Hemisphere without fear of direct U.S. intervention.

In 1961, Castro helped a small group of Marxist-Leninists form the Sandinista National Liberation Front. In 1979, after the Carter administration turned against Somoza and made every effort to hasten his departure, Castro helped the Sandinistas take over.

Castro told them that they could succeed if they gained leadership of the anti-Somoza front and promised to establish a democracy—in short, if they followed his lead. They agreed and Castro sent them hundreds of tons of weapons. On July 17, 1979, Somoza resigned and was replaced by a Sandinista-dominated ruling junta which promised free elections, a pluralist government and a nonaligned foreign policy.

The U.S. press was generally taken in by the Sandinista promises. Shortly after they took power, the *Washington Post* wrote, "The new [Sandinista laws] project the new government as highly moralistic, concerned about state security, politically liberal in a social democratic mold." But by September of 1979 history was repeating itself. The Sandinistas cemented political and military ties with the Soviet Union and Cuba and began providing weapons and training for Communist guerrillas throughout Central America.

At the same time, Jimmy Carter, keeping his fingers crossed, received Daniel Ortega at the White House and sent $118 million in aid to Nicaragua. In addition, the Carter administration supported $262 million in aid from U.S.-funded development banks and urged private banks to refinance more than $500 million of Nicaragua's loans.

What happened thereafter was tragic but, given the past history of Soviet client states, entirely predictable. The Sandinistas seized exclusive control of the government, invited nearly 8,000 Cuban and a lesser number of Soviet, Libyan and PLO advisers to Nicaragua, and turned the country into a second Soviet forward base in this hemisphere. Furthermore, they censored the media, destroyed the economy, harassed the Catholic Church, kidnapped, tortured or executed some 2,000 people, jailed 4,000 political prisoners, forcibly relocated 80,000 peasants and 10,000 Miskito Indians, and drove 500,000 people into exile.

The Sandinistas also set about building the largest and most powerful military apparatus in Central America. When the Sandinistas took over, they inherited a variety of World War II vintage tanks, three of which were operational. Now they have 120 heavy and 30 light tanks, 200 armored vehicles and a large complement of heavy artillery. They have 38 helicopters, including 12 Mi-24/HIND Ds, the fastest and most powerful attack platform in the world.

By 1986 the Sandinistas received in excess of $1 billion worth of military equipment from the Soviet Union and had more men—120,000—in their armed forces than all the rest of the nations of Central America combined. The 1986 shipment of 23,000 metric tons of war materials was, in the words of one military official, merely to "patch up the holes" in their already "massive military machine." It included 1,800 trucks and light vehicles to give their army increased mobility. As if all this were not enough, in the first six months of 1987 the Soviets shipped the Sandinistas another 17,400 metric tons of military equipment worth about $300 million.

In addition to this, the Soviets have spent $500 million building and improving airfields, seaports and other military facilities. The runways at Puerto Cabezas, Montelimar, Bluefields and Sandino have been extended to accommodate Soviet MiGs, and the new 12,500-foot airstrip at Punta Huete is capable of handling any plane in the Soviet inventory, including the Backfire bomber.

Bulgarian crews are dredging bays and building breakwaters, piers and dry docks at El Bluff, a major naval installation on the Caribbean, which will enable Soviet vessels to make rapid deliveries of war matériel. The port of Corinto on the Pacific, already being used by Soviet ships, is being improved and will be able to handle Soviet submarines.

This military force, despite its magnitude, is not designed to defend Nicaragua against an attack by the United States, as the Sandinistas claim. It is structured to intimidate Nicaragua's neighbors—to give them the kind of conventional superiority that will enable them to subvert other Latin American nations without fear of reprisal in the same way the Soviets use their nuclear superiority to paralyze Western resolve to oppose their global adventures. If necessary, of course, the Sandinistas could attack. But with such a preponderance of force, that will probably be unnecessary. They can achieve their goals more efficiently through low-intensity warfare.

There is yet another use for this force. With the vast concentration of arms and the 14,000 Cuban, Soviet and Warsaw Pact advisers in Nicaragua, the Soviets could, according to intelligence analysts Quentin Crommelin, Jr., and David S. Sullivan, "support the planned rapid expansion of the Nicaraguan Army and Militia from a present level of about 200,000 . . . to a force of up to one-half million men which will give the Soviets control of an armed force in Central America approaching the size of the entire regular United States Army worldwide."

The Soviet military planners are now in a position to spring the geopolitical trap they have been methodically laying for so many years. The underlying principle of military strategy is to achieve goals with the greatest economy of resources; the ultimate expression of this is to defeat your enemy without fighting. This is done by creating conditions such that the enemy is psychologically or physically incapable of responding to a threat and is forced to capitulate; if he decides to fight, the outcome will have already been determined—he will be defeated.

Since the turn of the century, the United States has required a politically stable and friendly Latin America in order to project power into areas of vital interest across the Atlantic and Pacific. In 1981, prior to the most intense phase of Soviet/Sandinista military buildup, professor of Latin American history Lewis A. Tambs pointed out that "the erosion of the U.S. position in the closed sea of the Caribbean and the encircling isthmus of Central America portends the collapse of America's global power presence. For the U.S. does not have enough men, money, ships, aircraft or energy to divert massive resources southward and still retain a credible posture in its primary security areas—Southwest Asia, Western Europe and the Western Pacific. Thus, the Caribbean and Central America, although superficially a secondary theater, are part of an overall scenario of Soviet staging."

Tambs, former U.S. Ambassador to Costa Rica, noted that "for the United States, which relies on foreign sources for over half of the thirty-two minerals essential for industrial and military use, and imports over one third of its oil, the Caribbean and Central America are crucial.

"Arabia and Africa may be the petroleum pump. The Indian and Atlantic Oceans may be the oil sea lanes of communications. But for the United States, the Caribbean and Central America are the nozzles.

"The Caribbean is a closed continental sea. The number of entrances and exits is limited. The Bahamas, Puerto Rico, the Virgin, Leeward, Windward and Grenadine Islands encircle the eastern edge. North, Central and South America ring the rest. The only Pacific passage is the Panama Canal . . . . Since some three-quarters of all U.S. oil imports are either produced or transit the shore and sea of the New World Mediterranean, whoever controls the Caribbean and Central America could strangle the United States by choking off the petroleum life lines."

In addition, half of the United States' foreign trade and half of its strategic minerals move through the Panama Canal or Gulf of

Mexico; many U.S. allies in Europe, Asia and Latin America are even more dependent on the canal.

The Soviet Union, by virtue of its growing naval presence in Cuba and Nicaragua, is in an ideal position to interdict, or threaten to interdict, commercial shipping in the Caribbean. Or, should there be a war, it could challenge U.S efforts to resupply its forces in Western Europe. Furthermore, the likelihood of a Soviet thrust into Western Europe is increased by the degree that a U.S. resupply effort could be delayed or prevented. "It should be recalled," says foreign policy analyst W. Bruce Weinrod, "that in the first five months of World War II, the U.S. lost 153 ships to German submarines in the Caribbean; today Soviet submarines are much more capable and less easy to detect than those German subs."

The U.S. is now faced with a dilemma: Should it redirect its attention and military resources to Latin America at the expense of withdrawing forces from Western Europe, Asia or the Pacific? Or should it keep the majority of its assets in those theaters at the expense of Latin America?

If the U.S. ignores the Soviet buildup in Latin America, subversion and violent revolution may sweep up through Mexico onto American soil and the U.S. may also face an armed and aggressive Latin American force of 500,000 men under Soviet control. Moreover, the U.S. will still be vulnerable to the Soviet naval presence in the Caribbean.

If, however, the U.S. withdraws a substantial portion of its forces from those distant global theaters to deal with the Latin American threat, the Soviets could easily exploit the vacuum of power by invading Western Europe, by taking hostile action in the Middle East or Pacific, or by forcing political concessions which are the equivalent of military victory.

The United States cannot allow either circumstance. Both lead to the demise of the U.S. as a global power and our eventual political subordination to the Soviet Union. The only way out of the trap is the timely expulsion of the Soviet military from this hemisphere. It is the studied opinion of Gen. Jan Sejna, the former assistant secretary to the top-secret Czech Defense Council—the highest-ranking military figure to defect from the Soviet bloc—that the Soviets can be challenged in this hemisphere. He believes the U.S. should invade Cuba and Nicaragua and restore freedom. The Soviets, he is convinced, would never risk a global war for Cuba or Nicaragua.

But U.S. policymakers have failed to realize this. In 1962, via the missile crisis agreement, they institutionalized Castro's presence in Cuba. For a number of years, Congress has been in the process of doing the same thing for the Sandinistas in Nicaragua. For example, the 1982 version of the Boland Amendment prohibited the use of funds "for the purpose of overthrowing the government of Nicaragua."

While the Soviets have given the Sandinistas everything imaginable in the way of military equipment and support, the United States has been slow to respond. First the Carter administration funded the Sandinistas. Then, between 1981 and 1984, the CIA gave the Contras $80 million. In 1984 a later version of the Boland Amendment cut off funds to the Contras for a year. In 1985 Congress gave the Contras $27 million in humanitarian aid. In 1986 Congress allocated $100 million for the Contras—but $30 million was for nonmilitary purposes.

Thus far, the U.S. has given the Contras a total of about $220 million, of which $163 million was military aid. The Soviets have given the Sandinistas $2.5 billion, including about $1.8 billion in military aid—just over $10 for each dollar the U.S. has given the Contras. Thus, the Soviets are reaping enormous benefits from a low-risk, relatively low-cost adventure in the Americas.

There are a number of reasons why the United States has been slow to recognize the gravity of this threat. Few in Congress—or anywhere else in the federal government—believe the Soviets have a long-term goal and a grand strategy. On the other hand, many in Congress believe the United States has "dirty hands" due to past U.S. military intervention in Nicaragua. Others in Congress sympathize with or support the Sandinistas. In 1984, for example, Michael Barnes, chairman of the House Subcommittee on Inter-American Affairs, and nine other Democratic congressmen, including Majority Leader Jim Wright, wrote a "Dear Commandante" letter to Daniel Ortega which, in apologizing for U.S. foreign policy, said, "We have been, and remain, opposed to U.S. support for military action directed against the people or government of Nicaragua. . . . We believe that you have it in your power to establish an example for Central America that can be of enormous historical significance."

As far back as 1982, an internal Sandinista memorandum described Barnes, Senator Christopher Dodd and Congressman George Miller as "friends of our revolution." In his most recent comments on the Iran-Contra hearings, Patrick Buchanan observed that "the dirty little secret slipping out of the show trial is that. . . the liberal wing of the Democratic Party has made itself the silent partner—the indispensable ally—of revolutionary communism in the Third World. . . . [They do] not want the Communist regime in Nicaragua overthrown."

Finally, the Reagan administration has been almost criminally negligent in its failure to tell the American people what is really happening south of the border. Otherwise, Colonel North's testimony, which clearly and simply described the Soviet threat in Central America, would not have caused such a remarkable shift in public opinion in favor of the Contras. In fact, a recent Harris poll found that voters now favor by a 54 to 42 percent margin "sending U.S. troops to fight in Nicaragua if it is the only way to keep Nicaragua from going communist."

There are signs of hope. The Iran-Contra hearings have increased public support for the Contras. Sandinista human-rights violations have angered former Sandinista supporters, such as Democratic New York Congressman James Scheuer, who may now drop his opposition to U.S. aid to the Contras. And the Contras, at least temporarily equipped thanks to U.S. funds, are showing some success in the field.

What's more, the Sandinistas are becoming so unpopular in Nicaragua that, with continued success by the Contras, government officials, soldiers and citizens may soon realize that it is possible to defeat the Communist regime. That could lead to large-scale military defections, civil unrest and even the secret cooperation of government officials with the democratic resistance. Then it would only be a matter of time before the Sandinistas' political and military support structures collapsed.

The Contra war is not, as the Sandinistas aver, a simple rebellion against lawful authority incited by a foreign power. It is a civil war between the forces of Communism and the democratic resistance. Should the Contras receive sufficient U.S. military and diplomatic assistance and the Sandinistas be cut off from outside aid, the Sandinistas could lose this war. Much of what happens in the future depends on U.S. attitudes and that often depends on how well the American people are informed.

The outcome in Nicaragua has yet to be determined. Congress will be considering another White House request for funding in the near future—probably for about $150 million. It is possible that an aroused American people will compel Congress to act responsibly and help the Contras oust the Sandinistas. But, according to Congressman Dave Bonior, chief deputy Democratic whip, "Even after six days of Ollie North, there is still no clear majority in favor of *contra* aid. I think we have an excellent chance of cutting off aid."

Which brings us back to the original question: Can the Sandinistas still be stopped? The answer is yes. Will the Sandinistas be stopped? That is yet to be decided.

Late Bulletin: Two Plans to "End the War between the Contras and the Sandinistas"

On August 5, 1987, President Reagan unveiled a plan endorsed by Democratic leaders to end the war between the Contras and the Sandinistas. In revealing the plan, the president promised not to ask or lobby Congress for more aid to the Contras before September 30, the day the current funding runs out.

The Reagan framework calls for a cease-fire between the Contras and Sandinistas within 60 days followed by the immediate suspension of U.S. aid to the Contras and Soviet and Cuban aid to the Sandinistas. Under this plan, the Sandinistas would grant amnesty to the Contras and restore civil rights, establish an independent electoral commission and set a timetable for elections.

The U.S., Nicaragua and other Central American nations would immediately begin negotiating a regional security agreement and the withdrawal of all foreign military advisers "in excess of the normal and legitimate needs of the region." The U.S. would also suspend combat maneuvers in Honduras and lift its trade embargo against Nicaragua, thereby making the country eligible for new U.S. aid.

On August 7, the presidents of Guatemala, Nicaragua, El Salvador, Honduras and Costa Rica, meeting in Guatemala City, adopted a modified version of a plan proposed by Costa Rican president Oscar Arias. It is broader than the Reagan proposal: it calls for the end of hostilities between government troops and all guerrilla forces in Central America.

The Guatemala City Plan would ban all foreign assistance to the leftist guerrillas in El Salvador and the Contras in Nicaragua. It provides for amnesty for all guerrillas but prohibits the use of Central American territory for a staging area, which would mean the Contras would have to leave their bases in Honduras. This plan also calls for democratic reforms in each Central American country, including free elections, free speech and freedom of the press, to be monitored by international observers.

There are other differences between the two plans. The U.S. proposal calls for a cease fire within 60 days; the Guatemala City Plan within 3½ months, well beyond the point U.S. funds for the Contras run out on September 30. The U.S. plan specified the end of outside military aid to both the Contras and the Sandinistas. The Guatemala City Plan would allow the Soviet Union to continue supplying military aid to the Sandinistas but cut off U.S. aid to the Contras. And while the Reagan plan called for democratic reforms to be instituted at the time of the cease-fire, the new plan allows the process to take place over several months.

Both proposals are flawed. The most serious weakness is that they both require the Sandinistas to negotiate an agreement that could lead to their loss of power, something no Communist government has ever done. The history of Communist diplomacy strongly suggests that the Sandinistas will use these talks as a means of delaying or denying new funding for the Contras. The *Washington Times* (8/4/87) said, "The Sandinistas support the Arias plan because it offers a sly way to block Congress from voting new aid to the democratic resistance."

The Reagan administration reportedly floated their peace plan because they did not believe that they had the votes in Congress to secure more aid for the Contras without it. Not all agree. Congressman Jack Kemp said the votes for Contra aid "would be there if the President made a case and suspended his vacation." The *Washington Times* (8/6/87) reported that Kemp and other conservatives said that "the White House didn't take into proper account the votes that were racked up by the testimony of Lt. Col. Oliver North during the Iran-Contra hearings."

Democratic leadership has made no promises to support an administration request for new Contra funding if the U.S. plan doesn't work. And Speaker of the House Jim Wright has called on the president to back the Guatemala City Plan, even though it would cut off U.S. aid to the Contras while allowing the Soviets to supply military equipment to the Sandinistas.

Prophecy:

"Let the fire of freedom emerge in the hearts of those who dare to challenge tyranny, dictatorship and murder in Nicaragua! O God, deliver these, as they are as the early American patriots taking upon themselves the responsibility to defend a nation against the usurpers of the seat of God-government that belongs to the people, is of and by the people of Nicaragua, who demand their freedom this day. And I say, they shall have it!

"And I challenge *you,* Keepers of the Flame, to prove me right. I challenge *you* as prophets in the earth this day. For my mantle of prophecy descends upon you now, beloved. Seize it. Wear it. Use it. For this nation must be filled with the prophets of the Almighty whose prophesying is in the affirmation of the prophecy itself.

"To affirm the victory is a fiat of the LORD's prophecy. Therefore, let those who dare, go, then, to the side of those freedom fighters and say at their side the rosary to Archangel Michael. Let those who dare, go in their finer bodies as others may go in the physical.

"Beloved, it is the company of saints. It is the prophets, old and new, who must affirm this freedom this day. For it is the fulcrum, whether of God-freedom to the entire hemisphere or totalitarian encroachment *that will not be stopped, I warn you, without bloodshed in these United States.* And this is my prophecy to you!

"They will move to Panama. They will infiltrate. And there is not the spine or the unity today to turn them back. Let them *be* turned back and let our voice, now the minority, become that which sparks the majority to see the vision and to realize it!

"Nevermore was there a cause so great, so espoused by the tears of the beloved Mother Mary and her heart's fire. Nevermore since the

American Revolution has there been a cause that so concerns the nations and the Ascended Masters. Beloved ones, the facing of the tyrant of the Soviet Union now becomes the world enterprise of Lightbearers everywhere. Therefore, I say to *you:* Lightbearers of the world, unite!"

Saint Germain, July 4, 1986

"Do you not weep, beloved, when you see children raised up to fight battles in the Middle East, in South America? Well, weep again, mothers, for it may take place upon this soil ere you disturb yourself and perturb yourself concerning world conditions! If you desire not to see your grandchildren in this posture, beloved, then know that the defense must come of the right of the individual to have and till his own land and to be free of the domination of superpowers or totalitarian forces or conspiracies that conspire against him.

"I say, let those who love freedom defend it else find themselves behind the very defenses that they have not drawn and therefore bereft and face to face with such a colossal condition as they are not able to do one mite about it.

"It is a question of timing, beloved!"

Chamuel and Charity, May 31, 1987

"Let Liberty's voice be heard through many patriots who come in the wake of the defense of freedom and the Contras through one such as an Oliver North and many like him who have dared to heed the inner call of Saint Germain to help those freedom fighters when the profligate ones in Congress did not and would not and did tarry, indeed, as Hamlet—to be or not to be, to help or not to help, to defy the enemy or not to defy him. . . .

"You can think of many, many examples when one individual who had the courage, the vision, and the knowledge that *his* act would count did make the difference in history. And therefore, we are standing here this day, we are gathered together, we are one in the flame of victory—because singular individuals have dared to be God on earth and to alert and to awaken their communities and nations and peoples. . . .

"Therefore, beloved, take your example from this one patriot, Oliver North, who has stood up against these fallen ones who have corrupted a nation and nations. Blessed hearts, run to his side spiritually and demand the defense of all like him, beginning with yourselves. For you are brothers with every patriot and fiery freedom fighter of all nations. . . .

"Let the Lightbearers of the world unite in the physical octave and, I tell you, they shall not stand. These fallen ones cannot lift their heads up again against the challenge of the Lightbearers if you will only do it."

Godfre, July 14, 1987

FREEDOM 1987 Summit University Forums

Video- and Audiotapes Now Ready at Special Prices for Keepers of the Flame

Summit University Forum is a weekly cable TV show hosted and directed by Elizabeth Clare Prophet. This series was taped live before thousands gathered under the big top at the Royal Teton Ranch in Montana during FREEDOM 1987, an international conference for spiritual freedom.

Dr. Alejandro Bolaños on Nicaragua: The Untold Story. During this lively interchange with Mrs. Prophet, Dr. Bolaños, President of the Nicaraguan Information Center, provides an incisive critique of U.S.-Nicaraguan policy and the inside story on everything from Sandino and Somoza to Soviet subversion tactics. 3 hrs., 2 videocassettes, $39.95 (GP87008); 2 audiocassettes, $13 (A87040).

Thomas H. Krebs on "Tsar Wars." Mrs. Prophet probes the Pentagon's former chief analyst on Soviet space warfare capabilities. What emerges is an updated version of a special briefing Krebs gave President Reagan on the likelihood that the Soviets will deploy a space-based missile defense in the near future. 2½ hrs., 2 videocassettes, $39.95 (GP87005); 2 audiocassettes, $13 (A87052).

Professor Antony C. Sutton on the Capitalist/Communist Conspiracy. Before an enthusiastic crowd of 3,000, the nation's foremost authority on U.S. support of the Soviet military-industrial complex tells Mrs. Prophet how Western capitalists helped build the Soviet state and armed forces—and why. Sutton answers Mrs. Prophet's penetrating questions on Soviet psychotronics, weather warfare and sabotage of the U.S. space program. 2 hrs., 1 videocassette, $29.95 (V87009); 2 audiocassettes, $13 (A87054).

Crossroads South Africa: Summit University Forum Roundtable. Mrs. Prophet's provocative questions stimulate an energetic discussion of the South African crisis, including the role played by the superpowers, the ANC and the press. Her guests: Uys Viljoen, political counselor for the Embassy of South Africa; James Kendricks, former consultant to the governments of Nigeria and Liberia; Rev. Kenneth Frazier, veteran civil rights activist; and Rev. E. Gene Vosseler, defense activist. 2½ hrs., 2 videocassettes, $39.95 (GP87029); 2 audiocassettes, $13 (A87061).

Gen. Daniel O. Graham and Dr. Dmitry Mikheyev on Strategic Defense: To Deploy or Not to Deploy. The most dynamic S.U. Forum ever! An electrified crowd of over 4,000 repeatedly break into thunderous applause as Mrs. Prophet, General Graham, the nation's foremost proponent of near-term deployment of strategic defense, and Dr. Mikheyev, an expert in Soviet military policy, discuss how the U.S. can defend herself against a Soviet nuclear attack and why SDI scares the Soviets. 3 hrs., 2 videocassettes, $39.95 (GP87014); 2 audiocassettes, $13 (A87056).

Dr. John W. Gofman on the Politics of Radiation and Human Health. An enlightening exchange between Mrs. Prophet and one of the world's leading experts on the health effects of ionizing radiation. Reveals an inside view of a decades-old cover-up of the dangers of nuclear power by "responsible authorities" and the real consequences of the Chernobyl disaster. 3½ hrs., 2 videocassettes, $39.95 (GP87020); 3 audiocassettes, $19.50 (A87058).

Dr. Edwin N. York on How to Survive a Nuclear War. Mrs. Prophet's guest, one of the nation's foremost authorities on nuclear weapons effects and shelters, describes how it is possible to survive a nuclear war if you are prepared. Extensive questions and answers. 4½ hrs., 3 videocassettes, $59.95 (GP87024); 3 audiocassettes, $19.50 (A87063).

Special offer to Keepers of the Flame: Order the entire package of 14 videocassettes of these 7 S.U. Forums at a reduced price of $257.24 (regularly $289.65)—buy all 16 audiocassettes at $5.00 apiece for $80 (regularly $6.50 each, total $104). Offer still good.

Make checks payable to and mail to: Summit University Press, Dept. 748, Box A, Livingston, Montana 59047-1390 (406) 222-8300. Our staff or answering service is standing by 24 hours a day, 7 days a week, to take your credit card orders (MasterCard or Visa). Orders will be filled as fast as the tapes can be duplicated.

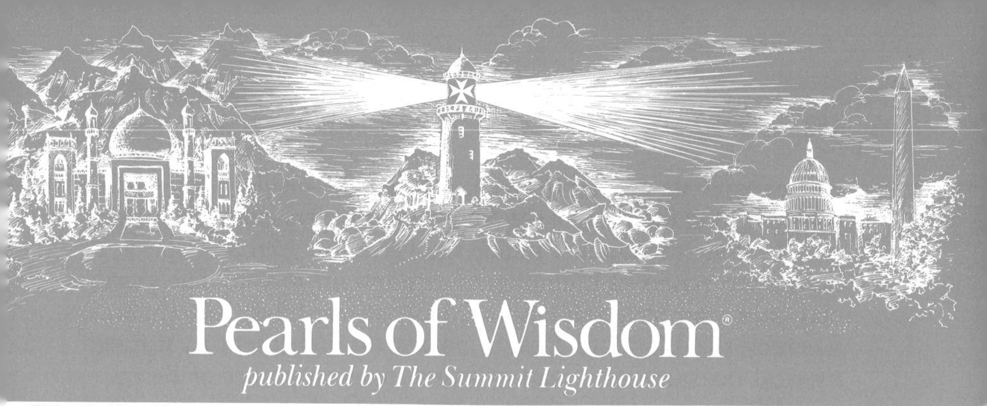

Vol. 30 No. 49 *Beloved Mother Mary* *November 18, 1987*

The Consolation of the Divine Mother

Part I

Present Your Bodies a Living Sacrifice

The Ritual of Self-Emptying

Present your bodies a living sacrifice,[1] O my beloved! For therein, by the sacrificial nature of the soul, there does take place the self-emptying. As when a potter takes the clay to form an earthen jar, so in this act of presenting oneself there is hollowed out the receptacle for the water of Life.

The living sacrifice is the chalice. Lo, I AM that chalice. And this day as your Mother Mary I bear in my crystal chalice even the shaft of Ascension's Flame. This flame does form lilies at the feet of the servant of God. Thus, the perfume of lilies does waft its way throughout every place where our Keepers of the Flame do keep the Flame of Life.

Hail, Maitreya!—my Son also. O thou Cosmic Christ, fill all of cosmos with thy Light, that naught else can be except that which is Christ conscious. And that which is not Christ conscious, then, must dissolve.

You see that Maitreya, the Great Chalice of Light, does bear Ascension's Flame of Cosmic Christed ones. Understand, Keepers of the Flame, how by oneness with the will of God, the flame that you choose to bear within the chalice—which you form by each and every living decree of the Word you recite—can very soon not only ignite a cosmos but also fill it all inside.

Come to understand, beloved, the great strength and presence of Elohim not only filling a cosmos but containing it and having created it as though they should hold a lapis ball in the hand and this ball should be the all of cosmos. As far as the mind can expand its reach, beloved, all is held inside a great blue sphere held in the hand of the Almighty One personified in Elohim.

I intone the noun. I intone the presence. And as I speak, so do the seven rays of Elohim pass through me to you. The sacrificial ones who have self-emptied have strong lutes, i.e., chakras, whereby the Light* of Elohim passes through them as through musical instruments, creating sound in seven planes of Being.

Oh, how great is the goodness of God, having so created each manifestation of Himself which he did call sun, *s-u-n,* and therefore did endow with the capacity for Godhood!

You need not wait, beloved. For even as I have said and Moses has said, "Ye are God's!" in the sense of ownership, so God does own thee, beloved.[2] It is well to admit it and to surrender. But the ownership is a two-way street. When God does own you, O beloved, you also do own that God!

And therefore, the thing-in-itself[3] is the God Flame and within the God Flame is the image of Christ. Lo, I AM come and you are that Christ! I in thee and thou in me, beloved. Understand the uniqueness of this figure-eight flow.

I AM Mary. As I speak, angels of the Fifth Ray busy themselves about the alignment of chakras and four lower bodies.

Where else on earth does one find, then, those who may pray by the hour unto the hour and unto the hour? Blessed ones, in the Roman Church dispensations and graces are granted for far less prayer. So one man's co-measurement with the realm of the possible is another's with the realm of the impossible. Understand, then, ye who have the capacity to contain the living Word seven hours or five, three or nine, that this is your sense of co-measurement in God.

Angels of the Ascension Flame, even my own, come also, for my dictation to you does serve a multifaceted purpose: First of all, to endow you with some portion of that Light. Whether or not you can contain it in the heart, the chakra or the cell, beloved, does depend upon the ritual of self-emptying that you have observed.

Secondly, angels come for a gradual stepping-up of each one to receive the Elohim Astrea. Astrea with me, we together form an axis of Light, Spirit/Matter. Thus, an axis of Light is also established between the heart of your I AM Presence and Holy Christ Self, who does plant within your heart as much of that axis as you are able to bear. And may the capacity increase daily as you, touching the limits of your habitation, say to God, "O God, expand my narrow room!"

*God consciousness

Thus, beloved, one day you will consider that all of the physical cosmos itself is yet too narrow a room for thy habitation. And thus, you will desire to enter the Heart of Elohim. And I, the handmaid of your Lord, your Holy Christ Self, will bid you enter. And thus, beloved, inside the Heart of Elohim you will know the experience of holding that cosmos as though held in the right hand of God.

Thus, for those who walk the path of the Ascension, no expanse of the physical universe or endless discovery or experimentation or wonder or fantasy can offer ultimate spiritual satisfaction. For the repetitions of matter molecules in the grand ritual of the creation and uncreation of worlds do translate to the soul, beloved, intimations of a higher ritual and order that can be contained only in the Spirit cosmos.

Thus, feel the flame—oh, feel it now from the heart of Lanello so close, as he did also hold this heart[4] when taking dictations from our bands!—feel the Ascension Flame and know that ye shall not long tarry in a physical cosmos, for ye are from above and not from beneath.[5]

And because it is so, you, beloved—for ye are God's even contained in and containing Elohim, for does not the drop of consciousness of Elohim contain the all of Elohim?—you are called of other worlds. Having come therefrom, you desire to return to that vibration that is native to your soul and spirit.

And because you are within Elohim and Elohim is within your self, you are above the lower order of creation; and these fallen ones—and gods lesser and many—are even beneath your feet, beloved, as they are beneath my feet.

For I place my Electronic Presence around you now, that you may know the meaning of suspension in a Spirit/Matter Cosmos. And that descent through the nexus of the figure eight is but to establish coordinates in Matter in order that the children of the Light, the children of the Sun who have entered these lesser spheres, might follow the highway established by thy garments back to the center of Being.

And thus, the little one asked, "Why did we depart the other universe to come to this one?" Thus, souls who have descended from above do recall the point of origin, they do not forget their First Love. Blessed ones, those who seem to forget that First Love, these are they who never had it in the beginning. For I tell you, it is impossible to forget the love of Alpha and Omega and Elohim.

Thus, beloved, the moment of reconsecration by the emerald ray is upon you. For when you find reason to assemble for a worthy cause, we take the opportunity to enter in, when you are in that state of concentration, to perform inner work as a surgery by light rays. It is our desire, therefore, to deliver the devoted on the very sunbeams of their devotion. This we will always do, beloved.

Thus, it is well, when attending evening services, not to take in much substance of food afterwards, but perhaps some necessary liquid in small amount, to retire, then, when the energy field of the body is charged and to allow nothing else to interfere.

Thus, the continuity of devotion in the physical octave matched by the inner work at night may sometimes result in a period long enough to roll back densities and old karma that are simply outworn garments, shells of cells ready to be consumed.

Thus we seize our opportunities to serve our counterparts in the earth. And we are grateful that you seize an opportunity as Michael seizes his sword of blue flame to serve us when the call is needed.

Blessed hearts, when all of the Matter cosmos is rolled up as a scroll, know, then, that the mighty momentum that is extracted therefrom as the endowment of that cosmos by Lightbearers shall accrue to the individual causal body, thine own, as well as to the Great Causal Body of God.

When in nirvana, beloved, one's causal body and being merges entirely with God's. And when there is independent action and a going forth again, there is the separating out once more of that causal body, it having been further endowed, through this Oneness, by the very magnetism and the field of God's consciousness.

These principles must be understood by the Law of the One. When you are in that One there is never separation, for God is God. And you are not outside of Alpha and Omega, whether in nirvana, out of it, ascended or unascended. For you are not limited to the extension of yourself in form but fully God-free beings here and now.

I, Mary, recede, then, into the white-fire heart of my beloved.

"The Summit Lighthouse Sheds Its Radiance O'er All the World to Manifest as Pearls of Wisdom." This dictation by **Mother Mary** was **delivered** through the Messenger of the Great White Brotherhood Elizabeth Clare Prophet at the conclusion of the Saturday evening service **August 15, 1987,** after midnight, at the **Royal Teton Ranch, Montana.** (**1**) Rom. 12:1. (**2**) Exod. 6:6–8; Lev. 26:12, 13; Ps. 82:6; John 10:34. (**3**) **Thing-in-itself** [German *ding an sich]:* an ultimate reality unqualified by the subjective modes of human perception and thought; a metaphysical reality. (**4**) alabaster heart held by the Messenger during the dictation (**5**) John 8:23.

Pearls of Wisdom®
published by The Summit Lighthouse

Vol. 30 No. 50 *Beloved Astrea* *November 19, 1987*

The Consolation of the Divine Mother

Part II

Present Yourselves a Living Sacrifice

Let Heaven Descend to Earth in Hearts of Living Fire

I AM come into your midst, beloved. Already you are encircled with garlands of blue-flame flowers that compose even my circle of blue flame fashioned especially for the devotee of Light. My sword is also composed of individual blue roses. And thus, this gift of love, formed in the Mind of God, executed by angels of the Fourth Ray of Elohim, does now become a part of you, beloved—a circle and sword of blue flame, a garland of light and a remembrance from the blue rose of Sirius whence some have descended and unto which all may apply for entrance.

I AM Astrea indeed. And I have encircled this cosmos. And the devils do tremble, not on my account, beloved, but on account of the saints in earth who know my name and invoke me into the physical dimension.

Therefore, their plan has gone awry. And we know that in God's eye when the challenge is known and set before any Keeper of the Flame, there will be that God-determination to call forth the seven light rays of Elohim and Holy Kumaras for the undoing, for the thwarting of those plots contrived in Death and Hell so very long ago, beloved, as to be written even in ancient volumes yet retained in Hades.

Beloved, the work intended to be accomplished by this hour is fulfilled and being fulfilled, sealed, then, by Elohim through this my word to you and actions which yet must be taken. Thus, again forty-eight hours and we trust all shall be fulfilled.

Understand that the timetable seen for world takeover by the spacecraft and the space people has become a time of their judgment when they could be whisked away by legions of cosmic hosts in answer to your calls, thereby creating a vacuum which the Light and the emissaries of the entire Spirit of the Great White Brotherhood ascended and unascended could fill—filling, then, the vacuum abandoned by these fallen ones, beloved, not by chance or free will but by the LORD's compelling force and army led by the Noble One, Sanat Kumara.

Recognize that we anticipate victory upon victory until these forces shall no longer hold sway on planet earth. Let it be a God-Victory, beloved, for there is an opening of heaven and earth by the pillars of calls made, by the imminent completion of that chalice in the Heart of the Inner Retreat through resurrection's sacred fire.

Thus, there is opportunity to go to the very cause and core of social problems in the earth—political problems, problems in education originating in those who conceive of themselves as masterminds.

As you look at their stooges in the earth, beloved, you will read the pride of these overlords and how they could never conceive that the sons and daughters of God would take the great key of the Word itself in time, setting aside all other pulls, temptations, preferences, projects, et cetera. Blessed ones, they truly thought that they had this planet sewn up!

Hearts of living flame, it is only the beginning of the battle! Yet to know what victories can be achieved in hours of concerted effort must truly give heart even to a skeptic, if there be one left among you.

O legions of Light, caress these souls! Give them in this hour the divine vision to know that systematically, ray by ray, the perversions of Light may be bound.

Do not weary. Do not enter into a sense of woe, for all that is Darkness in the earth can be bound. As you increase your numbers, teach the teaching of the Word, and understand that flood tides of light and paeans of praise issuing from our altars worldwide create streams of light, then mighty rivers, then oceans of light.

Thus, it is essential, beloved, that many, many more Keepers of the Flame begin at once the joy of the science of dynamic decrees. For this you ought to call, for each time you gain ground—and you are the troops who have won that ground—you indeed deserve reinforcements that you might take an "R and R"[1] and then return to the scene again. This is our conception of planetary renewal, survival and salvation. But, beloved, for want of replacements our troops must stay and stay again.

Where, then, are those who would come to their side? Where are the mothers of the world who would come and take them down from the cross? Yes, we know there are deserters. But, beloved, realize that you who deserve reinforcements and for whom there are indeed reinforcements, must give a little more time to the giving of decrees for that very event to take place, and for the cutting free of those who are to come, and for the binding of all forces of Death and Hell who would prevent them.

This is one of the major strategies of the fallen ones: to keep apart from you those brothers and sisters who would love to be at your side, who would love to spell you for a season, beloved, as you would engage in some other type of creative endeavor in the joy of the LORD.

Blessed hearts, the plot of the fallen ones is to find you weary, out of balance and susceptible to their driving force that would pound and pound again until there enters the aggressive mental suggestion that you cannot hang on another hour or day or week in the service of the LORD. Beloved ones, the very service which you or anyone renders may involve a certain level of fatigue. This fatigue, then, begets susceptibility to that voice of darkness that would take from you the cup of Victory that is hardly farther than the glint of the eye of Astrea or Mighty Victory.

Thus, inasmuch as you have tended the fields of a cosmos in this hour, I, Astrea, in the intense love that is focused in my circle of blue flame do draw it around you now, clearing, then, that misqualified substance which may linger because you have placed your attention upon another's need that is greater. And in this hour it has been the entire Spirit of the Great White Brotherhood whose need is greater.

Thus, in answer to your calls Seven Elohim offer cups of living flame of the seven rays. And these cups come by angel hands, and drop by drop the flames shall enter the chalice of each chakra that there might be the gradual adjustment to greater light. Ye are putting on etheric bodies of light. Oh, see to it, then, that the physical chalice is able to mesh with that body until the shine upon your countenance and the glow in your body and the light of the eye will surely be, beloved, the only testimony needed that this is indeed the highest calling and the highest path on earth! It is the pathway to the stars.

We are the seven stars which sang together in the morning of creation. Morning stars, we always sing as we create, as many of you do also. And our elementals, of course, whistle while they work.

Beloved, joy is all around you. We ask that you remember this. For as joy is the motor of life, so the vibration of joy does truly allow us to enter each time you feel a joy rippling through your being and a smile of Victory that does beget the laughter of oneness.

O beloved, how great is the day when the individual knows truly that neither Death and Hell, nor the dweller or karma, nor the false hierarchies of all physical universes have any power whatsoever over him. For he is hid with Christ in God, one with Elohim, independent of time and space, yet entering there with firm foot and heart and speech that all might hear the call of Sarasvati and enter the true and living Word and Her expression thereof.

Oh, the love of the Divine Mother! Oh, the love of Sarasvati for each one! If Sarasvati be with you, can Brahma be far behind? Therefore, let the cult of Father and Mother as Brahma and Sarasvati adorn your life, for their Presence is a pinnacle of light, a gift of true expression, a wisdom that is spoken that may be communicated far across the galaxies and to the simplest heart who may be your neighbor.

We the Elohim of God come as [now that] grids of light have formed. We are now ready to release a sacred fire that shall consume in the physical universes that portion of karma that is lawful, and that shall be the answer to the call of the Messenger and to you who also enter her call.

Blessed ones, the Law is just, the Law is one, the Law is irrevocable. The Law must act, it must always act when the voice of Mater does sound. So there is the sound of Elohim: Elohim! Elohim! Elohim! Elohim! Elohim! Elohim! Elohim! and Elohim! (for the Eighth Ray chakra of the Buddha and the secret chamber of the heart).

Therefore, beloved, earth and solar systems, this galaxy and the twin galaxy to it, all receive our rippling light. And beyond this I shall not tire you with naming again and again galaxies through which we pour our light this night.

Therefore, the Lord Sanat Kumara does come to pronounce the judgment of those who shall receive it because sons and daughters of God in earth have pronounced the key, not only the name but the descriptive term that does give the formula of the false hierarchies and their miscreations. This shall continue, then, throughout this vigil.[2]

I say to you, beloved, beware of those who feign allegiance, surrender, or sacrifice. Beware of their pitiful presence. Beware of their singed wings and their hollowed-out forms that are indeed not a chalice but haunted houses, whited sepulchers.[3]

Beware the living dead, who in the final expression of death itself seem to have the shine, the glamour that does pretend to be of the true light. These will always attempt to enter and remain in the Community of the Holy Spirit. Having the sense, the animal sense [of self-preservation], beloved, they carefully hide behind the mask they have created and they hide behind the light invoked by the Lightbearers.

You will see, then, that as the Teaching does go far and wide, these who would save their lives are the first wave. And those who will lose their lives for the sake of Elohim, they shall remain in the farthest corners of the earth and planetary systems, keeping their vigil and their guard, standing as watchmen in the night of the Kali Yuga.[4] And they shall arrive one day, full flaming ones that you shall recognize. In that hour, beloved, so the mandala of the Great Divine Director shall be complete.

The filigree pattern of the completed chalice may be seen as a gossamer veil, almost as spun glass. Let the call to resurrection's flame fill in the matrix until the crystal does become as solidified as the etheric octave is, more solid than physical matter.

O thou sacred fire mist, out of the mist let the crystal be formed. I, Astrea, call it now. And unto you I AM THAT I AM. I AM one and I embody a million vows of Lightbearers taken at inner planes. Let them count, then, for the voice of Elohim.

Sons and daughters of God, let resurrection's spiral through you continue. For when this does take place, it shall be the greatest opportunity to Alpha and Alpha's sons, not the least of whom yourselves.

Now then, your calls having contributed to a considerable vacuum in space and time, we recommend that you fill in that space with a call to the resurrection flame, with rounds of calls on the seven rays for the balancing action of the Seven Elohim. Let us fill time and space with light until, beloved, time and space should not be able to contain it. And thus, instead of the rolling up of a scroll, there shall be, indeed, the ascension of universes of lifewaves.

This has always been a possibility. But because of the corruption of space, the mockery of time, the misqualification of light, it has not been possible. But all things *are* possible with God. All things *are* possible with Elohim!

Elohim, then, present the key to the age! Truly it is the Divine Mother descending into your midst by the shaft of Elohim, by the funnel of light. Let the Divine Mother be fully physical in ye all, and know that the heart of Elohim will do this if you cooperate.

Present yourselves a living sacrifice. This is the message of the Spirit of the Divine Mother from all worlds and octaves: Present yourself a living sacrifice and I shall enter in and take up my abode in your temple of Light. So it is true. So it shall be, according to your election. Hear the cry of the Divine Mother that goes forth unto all of Her own: Present yourselves a living sacrifice!

Thus the Divine Mother is the solution, resolution, dissolution of all spacecraft and aliens now! By the sign of the cosmic cross of white fire, know the imminence of the Divine Mother's full occupancy of the Matter spheres.

Shall the vessels of the Matter spheres be broken by Her coming or shall they, by the Seventh Age, be transmuted in Her alchemy that She might be seen once again? *AUM*

Let the sign of the Emerald Matrix be for you, beloved, the realization that all things that you are above are crystallized in Matter by the emerald ray.

So let heaven descend to earth. Let heaven descend to earth in waiting hearts—hearts of living fire, hearts of living fire, hearts of living fire.

"The Summit Lighthouse Sheds Its Radiance O'er All the World to Manifest as Pearls of Wisdom."
This dictation by **Astrea** was **delivered** through the Messenger of the Great White Brotherhood Elizabeth Clare Prophet at the conclusion of the Saturday evening service, **August 15, 1987,** after midnight, at the **Royal Teton Ranch, Montana.** (**1**) **R and R:** rest and recreation, rest and recuperation. (**2**) Two worldwide prayer vigils were held August 7–9 and 15–18, 1987, to hold the balance of light in the earth. During the prayer vigils the dictations of El Morya, Hercules, Mother Mary, Astrea and Kali were given, published in Pearls 46–51. (**3**) Matt. 23:27. (**4**) ***Kali Yuga:*** Sanskrit term in Hindu philosophy for the "age of darkness." It is the last and worst of the four *yugas,* or world ages, comprising a cosmic cycle and is characterized by strife, discord and moral deterioration. The present dark age, or Kali Yuga, is believed to have begun on February 18, 3102 B.C. (with a duration of 432,000 years). For a different calculation of the duration of the yugas which sets the present age 285 years into the Dvāpara Yuga, see Swami Sri Yukteswar, *The Holy Science,* 7th ed. (Los Angeles: Self-Realization Fellowship, 1972), pp. 7–20. See *The Lost Teachings of Jesus I,* pp. 82, 143 and 359, n. 19. Note: "Ave Maria," sung by Mario Lanza, was played at the Messenger's request at the conclusion of this dictation.

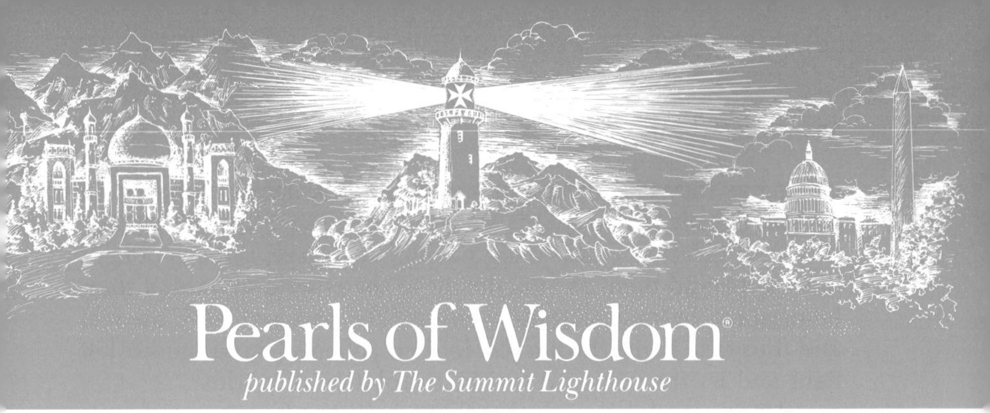

Vol. 30 No. 51 *Beloved Kali* *November 20, 1987*

The Consolation of the Divine Mother

Part III

Let the Fierceness of Kali Rage!

The Fulfillment of the Chalice in the Heart

Let the fierceness of Kali rage until the darkness of Death and Hell in earth is consumed by the white fire of the Divine Mother in each and every chela of the will of God!

I AM THAT I AM in the fiery vortex of the I AM Presence. So I AM the Shekinah[1] and the Divine Mother. And I have come for the liberation of the Light and the Lightbearer!

Therefore, beloved who embrace me, embrace now the living sacred fire. Embrace, then, my true son, my true daughter. Therefore, let the allegiance to the banner of Maitreya, to the banner of the Divine Mother be pure and swift as an arrow.

Let it be clear as crystal, even the mighty crystal that does unveil itself, as ribbons of light and Elohim reveal, beloved, the fulfillment of the chalice in the Heart of the Inner Retreat to the Elohimic level![2] [21-sec. applause]

There can be no delay for Victory in earth, for this battle is won by moments and by seconds. Therefore, I AM the Kali who does defeat delay and delay tactics and the chela's own propensity to procrastinate.

Therefore, beloved, when you think to take a step, *take it!* and never look back. For when you wonder and reason and doubt and fear, blessed hearts, you may wear a hole in the earth where you are and thereby predict thine own demise.

Blessed ones, you must march forward. Thus, you have sung the song to the Sun[3] that is sung by pilgrims marching to the Sun away from dead and dying worlds. This is the true march and the singing as they face the Light and never look back but march on on that cosmic highway.

And therefore, these ones, having, as it were, ribbons of light flowing behind them as attachment to the etheric spheres of their home stars, become as those who take the best and leave the rest and thus take home the harvest in their spheres [causal bodies] of light and let the rest wait for the dissolution of worlds.

Understand, beloved, that that which can be harvested must be harvested. So the crops do not wait in the fields lest the rain come and spoil them. Thus, understand that there are worlds to be harvested, worlds of light and good and great consciousness.

So come the reapers! And when they harvest the good fruit, lo, the tares are left and then other reapers come and harvest these and bind them in bundles to be cast into the lake of sacred fire.[4]

Blessed hearts, you see, when you stand ready to be plucked by the angels of Light for victorious service midst the legions of Light, you understand that because you have prepared yourself to the harvest, both as the bountiful offering of the Divine Mother and as harvesters yourselves, you are clearing the field of all that is of worth and allowing the remains to stand alone, their tatters blowing in the wind as some scarecrow left over in mid-October.

Realize this, beloved. Let the Light be harvested that the Evil may be bound. Therefore, tarry not in the cups of the Evildoer.

Look up, beloved, for nigh unto you is that mighty sphere of Light, a bower of loveliness: I AM THAT I AM in the fiery center of the Great Causal Body of the Divine Mother appearing!

So I AM THAT I AM THAT I AM. So I AM a devouring flame as the light goes forth out of my mouth. And it is fire, beloved. It is living fire. So may it proceed from me lest you yourselves find your tongues singed.

Therefore, when you make the call, I, Kali, shall release that sacred fire into the core of Evil. Let the call go forth! For I AM here and I have had enough. And I say, Enough *is* enough!

So behold, the day of the legions of Kali has come! The day of the legions of Kali has come, beloved. And this is not the dark night of the Kali Yuga, save for the dark ones. It is the Light Day of the Great Kali come, beloved! And it is the Day of the Appearing of the Divine Mother!

So I AM here! And see how this light, as lightning itself, does illumine the sky with a light no man can gaze upon. It is the 'Light Kali Yuga'. And behold, mine own in the earth shall truly embody the crystal fire mist. And the mist shall crystallize. And we shall see where the seed of the wicked are left.

Rise, O hosts of Light. Rise, O legions of the Mother. For the liberation of the Mother in the earth is come—and in the heavens. And the liberation, as never before, of her chelas is upon you.

O ye faithful to my heart, I give you again the heart of Kali. I AM in the center of the flame, my sword. I AM—the Presence of God is—*Shiva!* Shiva, Shiva, *Shiva!*

This dictation by **Kali** was **delivered** through the Messenger of the Great White Brotherhood Elizabeth Clare Prophet on **Monday, August 17, 1987,** at the **Royal Teton Ranch, Montana.** For notes, see p. 472.

THE RADIANT WORD

Beloved Babaji
Unascended Master of the Himalayas

Given June 17, 1979, at Camelot, Los Angeles County, California

I AM Babaji! I choose to speak by the authority of the Darjeeling Council on behalf of the unascended brotherhood of the Himalayas. For we come forth and we come to sponsor now true chelas of the path who will wear the mantle of the ascension, white and bright.

I come in the person of Father as I am called. I come to pierce and penetrate the veil. I come to expose those false ones who have misrepresented us. They are named and their names hang with the sword of Damocles that is upon their head. I say, Let them be exposed! For we will have the victory of all chelas in the dispensation of the Great White Brotherhood.

I come. My hand is upon the shoulder of our Messenger. I stand and I declare to the world: Let those who would be chelas of Krishna, of Yogananda, of the great Light of Kali, of Brahma, of Vishnu, of Shiva and of the saints who have gone before—let those who would follow Guru Nanak and all the rest who have risen from the lotus flower of the Mother hear now: your initiations are required of you this day and the Ascended Masters will give them, as these are the initiations required of your souls.

I stand with Morya, my friend of long-standing. I stand with all who have gone before. This is a time of intense terror in the earth. We summon the light of Mu and we go after you, O chelas!

Now hear our word crackling across the etheric plane, the mental plane, the emotional plane and the physical plane. For we are the unascended masters, for we have chosen to be Mother Light for you in Mater for your blessed victory.

We come. We will intensify that ascension fire. And you will simply have to get over your desire to be the removed one set apart and in meditation and in unreality when there is a victory to be won and a battle to enter. We are in the midst. We have always been in the midst.

Therefore, gaze into our eye and know that we love you, we will not pass you by, we will not leave you to a dead ritual. We will come. We declare ourselves.

Now then, prove your chelaship by your awareness of our vibration and our presence. For it is up to you to know the Teacher and the Guru. I am here! Where are you, O souls who call to me but remove yourselves among the psychics and their imitation of our light?

Well, I penetrate now. I penetrate with that inner light. You have called, you will receive it. And do not be surprised that it will disturb your world, for I will disturb you so long as you call my name and use my name in your service. And I will disturb you until you set aside that psychic activity, that personality cult and come into the Law of the One.

This is no time for dalliance and separation. This is time that the Body of God should wake up! This is no time to go into nirvana. The cycles of the Buddha are to come out from nirvana and be here where life is suffering.

I demand that you take the violet flame if you desire to continue to have our sponsorship in the many varied activities and schools following the masters of India. The violet flame is our coming, and we are one with the violet flame Masters.

Test me by my vibration! Ask me and I will come to your life! Don't you dare deny me or my Messenger until you have demanded proof and more proof! For I will give it! I will come! And I will growl with Himalaya until you know that the God Star Sirius is my home also. And I am with the legions of the Mighty Blue Eagle and I am here. And I will not take no for an answer! If you are of the Light, you may first fight with Babaji. And when I have fought and won, I will teach you how to defeat the demons.

So I have come. I have broken the silence. And all of the masters of the Himalayas gather with me, for this is their Father's Day. And they have increased the planetary light of Father in answer to your call, in answer to the call of Morya.

We know him. Do not speak with those who say they have never heard of Morya. Simply invoke his vibration, his name with ours, as we do, and let him be the tester of their souls as he is ours too. We follow him, for he has passed beyond the veil. He, then, holds the light of Mother, as we hold it too. We will not leave him or you.

Now you who hear me: Go find those souls trapped in the false paths of the false gurus of India! And let them hear my message, let them hear my Word! Do not fear to show them the face of the Messenger or the sound of my voice. Then let them choose. And do not leave them without the light and sign of Astrea.

I AM Babaji. I AM here because I AM not anywhere else, but everywhere.

This dictation is available on single audiocassette, $6.50 (add $.50 for postage).

Royal Teton Ranch
Box A, Livingston, Montana 59047-1390 406/222-8300

September 18, 1987

Dear Friends of Saint Germain,

Because you are also my friends of Light I want you to know that I consider my stumping in these final years of the '80s to be the most important mission of my life as Saint Germain's Messenger for the Coming Revolution in Higher Consciousness. And I count each and every one of you a part of that mission.

To awaken North Americans to their spiritual vulnerability to the enemy within and without is surely a challenge beyond the capacity of any man or woman. Thus, casting myself upon the Rock of Christ, I respond to the call of the Masters and their friends in the United States and Canada to come to your sanctuaries and worship with you at the altars you have erected to the living God—to greet you heart to heart.

For I am the one sent to deliver Saint Germain's Prophecy, Jesus' Lost Teachings and the healing power of the Archangels to a nation (and many nations) that is sick at heart but knows it not, grievously troubled of soul yet having no awareness of the malady (its cause or cure), and without the political fibre to save itself.

Being together in New York for four days, October 1 through 4, and in Washington Wednesday to Sunday, November 25–29, over the Thanksgiving weekend provides all Keepers of the Flame as well as new students a tremendous opportunity to invoke the legions of the Seven Archangels for the protection of both coasts as we assemble for the transmutation and turning back (according to the will of God) of the prophecies of Fátima and Nostradamus.

All that we have discussed concerning the eventualities of returning planetary karma at the end of this two-thousand-year cycle now focuses on us: Will the Keepers of the Flame of Liberty make the sacrifice to be there with the Goddess of Liberty and

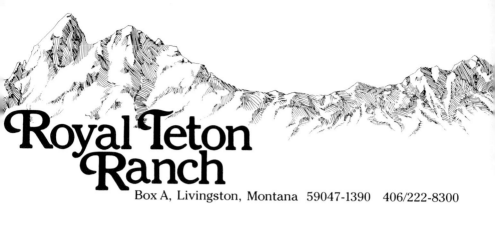

Saint Germain to erect walls of light and to challenge the entrenched forces of darkness that weigh upon our nation? I am absolutely convinced that if we are diligent and make the call, if we keep our eyes and ears pinned to the news and not let anything get by, we can make the difference.

There are some very necessary ingredients to the alchemy that must be accomplished through the uniting of the Lightbearers of the world. On his Ascension Day in Kansas City, our beloved Jesus called for ten thousand new Keepers of the Flame in North America. He said, "I have come, then, to make a plea to you and to send my Messenger abroad across this continent" to gather them. With this increase in the light and the decree momentum, the Master said he could erect a canopy of light over North America "to protect it from those calamities of the Four Horsemen."

Each time we make the pilgrimage to the place that is prepared for us to do our very special work, the Ascended Masters respond with a tremendous release of light through the dictations and the clearing of the geographical area where we are. Our goal on this fall stump is to call for Mother Mary and Archangel Michael to cut free the Lightbearers in each city, that Saint Germain's sealing by the Emerald Matrix may quicken their inner vision as to their personal divine plan and those karmic events which must surely come to pass unless there is that increase in the numbers and devotion of Keepers of the Flame.

My lectures will be varied each evening and there will be a special dictation from an Ascended Master in every city where we stump. The incomparable light that is felt by all people of God through the dynamic decrees and meditations, our invocations and dictations is the surest proof of the authenticity of our stand for the Great White Brotherhood and the reality of the heavenly hosts midst the people of America. For this people has been called in this age not only to defend freedom and a way of life but also to engage in the war of Armageddon for the ultimate defeat of the embodied seed of the fallen angels.

All students of the Ascended Masters' teaching must know: the forces who would deter this mission—whether misguided or embittered by their own failures or threatened in their seats of temporal power—are organized and committed to defeat Saint Germain's sponsorship of freedom in America, in the world, and in anyone who speaks his message or proclaims his name as the hierarch of the Aquarian age.

These forces are entrenched from Left to Right in politics and religion, in institutions of higher learning, and of course in the anti-cult movement. Wherever the voice of Truth attempts to topple the towers of Babel they have erected, they are arrayed in unholy alliances to control the people—whether by unjust laws, taxation, manipulation through the media, junk food, drugs and rock music, or the thousand and one allures of the senses.

Today it is open warfare that is being waged by embodied fallen angels, and, yes, aliens in our midst, against the children of God through the doctrines of Satan preached openly through rock music and subtly through the entertainment industry. Soon you will be receiving in your Pearls of Wisdom a three-part series that is the text of my son Sean's marathon exposé given at the July conference on "Rock and Roll in America." These Pearls will be sent to you for your awareness/action agenda in your communities. They are a foundation for lectures you can give as you make a major contribution to committees of parents already formed to fight the harmful influences of rock music and drugs among our teenagers and children. The audiocassettes of this event are available immediately and the slides can be ordered from a list we will be sending you.

On every front where entrenched evil assails the mind and heart and soul of our youth and our people, Keepers of the Flame must be there. Our strength is in our union, in our coming together regularly and without fail for Saint Germain's Saturday night services and the Sunday Sacred Ritual where the teachings of our Lord and Saviour Jesus Christ and the dictations of the Ascended Masters provide us with our weekly communion for another seven days of our service with Elohim in the re-creation of worlds.

Beloved Alpha's dictation given on July 5, offering his Presence to the Lightbearers of the world and lending us his mantle together with a very specific agenda to go forth and save the Lightbearers, is a hope and a sponsorship in this critical hour. As I have been sent stumping by Saint Germain in the past, so in this hour I go forth from the heart of our Father with his blessing and commission once again to invoke the light of heaven to set the captives free.

It is my goal to introduce to everyone His beloved sons the Lords of the Seven Rays, who come to initiate the people of America in the seven chakras that they might begin to embody a solar awareness, a Christ consciousness and ultimately a God consciousness of the seven planes of being within these sacred centers which God has given to us for this purpose.

Through the raising up of a crystal chalice in the Heart of the Inner Retreat during our summer conference, the Elohim are closer than ever before to our hearts and to our call. Thus, the Lords of the Seven Rays become the representatives of the seven mighty Elohim and the Seven Archangels as they release through all the light of God that will not fail to raise up and liberate the Lightbearers in this age.

For this one thing we know, the Lightbearers can be reached. They can be cut free from the indoctrinations of the International Capitalist/Communist Conspiracy. They can be quickened to their own Mighty I AM Presence. And when they hear the Truth they will know it and they will know it as the Truth that sets them free. Whether or not the nations will ever take up the calling of Saint Germain remains to be seen, for it is not given to any of us to interfere with anyone's free will nor with the will of God as it is expressed through the law of karma and its tempering by mercy and justice.

At our conference in Washington, D.C., we will be two blocks from the White House. Thanksgiving Day and Sunday are thus very special prayer vigils for Keepers of the Flame. An opportunity to give our hearts in dynamic decrees for America. Beloved Jesus will deliver his Thanksgiving Day address and on Sunday our year's-end report on the state of the nations will be presented.

Thanksgiving will mark the one-year anniversary of the monumental dictations given by Jesus and Saint Germain in our final event before our move from our Malibu campus to the Royal Teton Ranch in Montana. Saint Germain's dictation was published as the last chapter in Saint Germain On Prophecy and Jesus' as well as Saint Germain's in the 1986 Pearls of Wisdom. I shall never forget the profound plea from the heart of Jesus:

> O my God, my God, do not forsake me in my little ones in this hour of the Dark Night of the Spirit. I, Jesus, before my own, cry unto you, O Father! Deliver, then, the children of the Light who have descended from thy heart, for I would take them to my breast in this day.
>
> O my Father, give unto these and all who keep my flame the understanding of the "imperil" that is upon the earth and the great necessity, as Mary has said at Fátima in thy name, Father, to save these souls lest they be lost for ages.

Nor shall I forget Saint Germain's all-enveloping presence at the Airport Hilton as he entered and strode down the center aisle to take his place on the platform to dictate through me. His presence was clear as crystal, every detail of his face, his magnificent eyes, his robe, the fiery purple aura. He had stepped through many veils and was surely on the edge of the physical. That message has galvanized our movement worldwide to take up his cause and his call for the defense of freedom before it is too late.

I am looking forward with immense anticipation to hear what our beloved Saint Germain and our brother Jesus will say to the people, to witness their conversion of many souls to the one true God, opening the door to the saints and great teachers and loved ones of all centuries who make up the entire Spirit of the Great White Brotherhood.

Today every student of the deeper mysteries, every chela (disciple) of the Masters is an emissary and an outpost of their light, their love, their imploring, their quickening, warnings and prophecies. Wherever we are, whether in silence or moved to speak by the Holy Spirit, we carry that banner of the World Mother and of Lord Maitreya. We are part of a planetary network of light, always one when we are maintaining the momentum of the violet flame, the tube of light and the calls to Archangel Michael around ourselves and living the teachings as we know we should and can.

Surely this is a time to witness, to study diligently the current releases through the Pearls of Wisdom, but then to simply give ourselves freely to God and his angels and to take no thought "how or what thing ye shall answer, or what ye shall say: for the Holy Ghost shall teach you in the same hour what ye ought to say."

All of the topics that are listed under Special Events as well as the Inner Workshops will be covered in some measure each evening of our tour. Every Stump is 7 p.m. to midnight, a full opportunity for all sincere seekers to feel and know the presence of their own beloved Christ Self and I AM Presence. The company of angels and saints who do assemble as a cloud of witness will convey enlightenment heart to heart, quickening the soul's memory of the Ancient of Days and past golden ages when we walked and talked with these masterful beings.

America and planet earth are on the brink of destiny. Whether the future is dominated by the religion of the UFOs or of the Divine Mother and the servant-sons of God will be determined in the days, weeks and decades at hand. In our lifetime or our children's we will see either the forces of Light or of Darkness dominating space, hence the future of earth's civilization.

There are some who will sit back and chronicle the times. There are others who've got spirit and spunk and a zest to give their lives for the cause of freedom in a derring-do, in a self-givingness that compels the Higher Self and the Higher Power to descend into these mortal forms we wear with the energy and the strength of the Immortals.

On January 1, 1987, there were two choices before all of us—to retreat and batten down our hatches before the oncoming woes and predicted earth changes or to summon all that Life has given to us in this and all previous incarnations on planet earth, to invoke a Power, a Wisdom and a Love beyond ourselves, to give ourselves to it, to commend ourselves unto the Spirit of the living God and go forth to preach his Word and to be it. The bottom line was this: we would never know what victory might have been if we didn't try, if we didn't give it our all and our finest hour.

Blessed hearts, we are not babes in Christ. Throughout our many lifetimes and even in the short span of this one we have done it all and seen it all. The traps and temptations, byways and rounds of relationships, money schemes, possessions, fame or temporal power hold nothing for us.

As for me, I have already given my life to God and to the very heart of every Keeper of the Flame and Lightbearer on earth. I have nothing to lose, for each day as I give my all and the all of my Christhood, I am renewed, replenished, infilled, empowered, joyous to go forth and give again. Nothing is real or relevant but the knowledge that without the Lost Teachings of Jesus Christ and Saint Germain's great gift of the violet flame and his message on personal and planetary freedom, souls of light who have lost the way or been devoured by the agents of hell will not find salvation unto God. Mother Mary predicted this in her Fátima message of 1917. She told us to pray the rosary daily, for many souls could be lost.

Beloved, as you give your life for the deliverance of a planet and a people, know that I am standing with you. If you experience difficulties, obstacles, burdens too hard to bear, I am as close as a phone call or your heart's prayer to God that the fervent calls which I make daily before his altar might bear you up and strengthen you, give you courage and peace. You need but leave your name and address and a brief statement of your situation at any of our phone numbers and prayers will be given for you personally by myself or by the twenty-four-hour prayer vigil that is kept at the Inner Retreat.

In my heart there burns a fire to save souls for Jesus, for Mother Mary, for Saint Germain, and I want to tell the people that I love most, the people of the United States of America and our brothers and sisters in Canada, that Archangel Michael and the hosts of the Lord are here and ready to cut free those temporarily lost in astral diversions and that the armies of the Lord await their call to deliver North America and the world from nuclear war and the time bomb ticking away in the economies of the nations.

To help make this Stump happen I am asking for your love offering to help us meet the tremendous expenses we are incurring to put Saint Germain's Stump for the Coming Revolution in Higher Consciousness on the road and to keep our team stumping as long as our Lord and our nation hath need of us. Thirty-three dollars from your heart will be "seed money" to be multiplied for our efforts.

If you can give more at this time, I assure you the need is great if we are to sustain Alpha's agenda both for the Ranch projects and publishing as well as our production of TV shows of our forums and revolutionary messages now viewed by millions on cable and broadcast television. If we receive the ongoing support necessary to sustain our calling, the messages delivered to the nations by the Ascended Masters nightly will become cable television shows so that people in their homes can also drink in the full light of the original release.

Finally, I ask for your daily prayers for our victory on this Stump and for the cutting free of the souls of light for whom our mission is intended. We need your prayers as well as your help in the cities on our tour, and your physical presence especially in New York and Washington, D.C. Please take advantage of the very reasonable rates at the New York Penta and the Capital Hilton. When you register at these hotels, stating you are attending our Summit University seminar, we receive free conference rooms according to the number registered. The same holds true for the Minneapolis Hilton. And the more people who fly Continental and Eastern Airlines, the more free tickets we get for staff to be there.

The entire staff working with me at every level for the Stump effort and the preparation of the Ranch share a flame of God-happiness that wells up in waves of joyous anticipation of our togetherness under the Lord's tent as city by city we gather to celebrate his name and answer his call. As for me, I can only say, Where shall I go, Lord, but to the heart of your Keepers of the Flame on earth—for there is the mirror image of thyself in form.

All my love is with you,

Mother

P.S. Please take special note of the courses we are offering in the Lost Arts of Healing. You may wonder why I have selected these topics for eighteen-hour intensives (six hours a day for three days) in New York and Washington. Mother's Touch, Foot Reflexology and Macrobiotic Cooking give to the individual independence in the maintenance of the highest energy flow, physical strength and balance for the challenges we face together.

Our Macrobiotic Cooking classes are based on the true diet of the ancients and the Eastern adepts. Why is this important? Because as anyone can see, a single nuclear accident can contaminate the animal life upon which we depend for our meat or dairy products. The contamination from Chernobyl is far greater than we have been told, as you will learn from our Summit University Forum interview with Dr. John Gofman. When we have come to depend on stimulants, meat, sugar and junk food to get us through the day, we require time to train the body to derive its proteins and spiritual energies from sprouts, grains and a balanced vegetarian diet.

We who are sensitive to the spiritual vibrations and the burdens of the world weight on our bodies must look seriously at our diet and how it affects our ability to cope with stress and the last plagues already reaching epidemic proportions in our society. Now is the time to prepare for the crossroads of karmic retribution whether upon ourselves, our family members, loved ones, our community, our cities. When we are prepared for crisis, we may never have to meet it, for spiritual, physical, mental and emotional wholeness repel chaos, disease and death.

It is because Saint Germain has told us to be prepared that I recommend these three disciplines for all who would be ministering servants to life. When others need help and are not able to cope with crises in their lives, we must be capable and willing to care for them. Foot Reflexology and Mother's Touch give you the complete technique for restoring the flow of light from the I AM Presence and the chakras throughout the central nervous system to every organ in the body.

These systems are not intended to replace or be a substitute for the basic rules of health or medical care or surgery when deemed advisable by one's personal physician. They are techniques you can use to alleviate stress. In crisis or epidemic when there is a shortage of health-care professionals, you can be there to comfort life and to open the body's own channels and resources of healing.

We who would be our brother's keeper must give our hands to God that through them, as through the hands of the Saviour, the light of the Father and the Mother can reach those in need. All you need is a fiery heart, a compassionate mind and willing hands trained as Jesus' were to touch the points.

Beloved Jesus told me when I was embodied as Martha that we would come to this age when not only his teachings but also the art and science of his healing would be lost. He told me that I would find many whom he would call to restore his teaching and his methods of spiritually scientific healing as well as diet. In the service of his own, we are producing—by research, experimentation, and interviewing a devoted group of experts—a body of information that is being studied by many people, even those who are not connected with this movement.

Above all, let us remember that the essence of our Lord's Lost Teaching is to comfort, enlighten and defend life. In the heart of the Divine Mother, let us be about our Father's business.

Ma

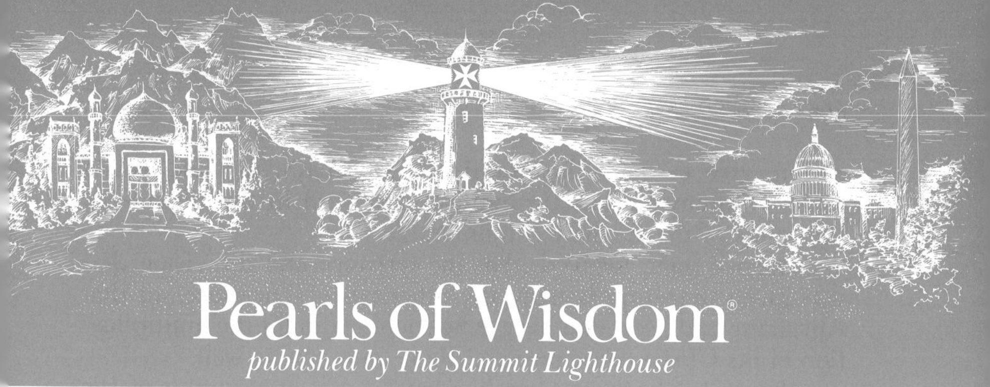

Pearls of Wisdom®
published by The Summit Lighthouse

Vol. 30 No. 52 — *Beloved Lanello* — *November 21, 1987*

The Father's Love

From out of the heart of God in the Great Central Sun, I AM come.

Blessed ones of the Light, in Saint Germain's name I, Lanello, set my seal upon you and bless you in this hour, all who go forth, all who remain,[1] for ye are the Alpha unto the Omega of the completeness of this divine calling.

Thus, in this circle of light, you receive directly now, heart to heart, the light of my ascension currents and of that which I bring from the Central Sun where I have been, there to secure light and dispensation for our Community at Maitreya's Mystery School.

Blessed ones, I, too, have perceived all these things that my Beloved has told you. Thus, desiring to fill in the blanks with Lightbearers—and abundance and richness of teaching and great redundancy in the publishing of the Word—so, beloved, this time I myself, at the request and recommendation of El Morya and Saint Germain, have gone to visit the Father, to be in that place where I have set the mark of your return, the great throne room of Alpha and Omega in the Central Sun.

Thus, beloved, my legions have, in my absence, been with you; and now upon my return I do secure and seal for you the opportunity to bring to pass that expansion that is necessary for the actual survival of this movement upon earth. I, therefore, have appealed to the offering of Alpha's sponsorship and mantle and presented to him a very detailed account of your needs in this hour.

From my contact with that very Presence and the awe of Him, I can tell you how cherished you are, each and every one and all those who should be here. Thus, the Father is well pleased that there are those through whom he can work to bring forth His beloved everywhere on earth, to assemble them, to secure them and to give to them the promise of Abraham: to make you a father of many nations, to multiply His seed in thee again—as the sands of the seashore, innumerable.[2]

Know, then, beloved, that the territory and the vision that was given unto him is truly thy inheritance. Therefore, all that Abraham could see with his eye he could claim for the multiplication of his Christ consciousness. Be it unto you as well.

Look up! Expand your horizons! Look at the map of the earth, the solar system, the galaxy and claim it all for the seed of Sanat Kumara. There is no limitation in the heart of Alpha as regards your own calling, beloved, none whatsoever. The only limitation is the limitation that you yourself should retain in consciousness.

Thus, beloved, the harvest is ripe whereby the fallen ones may be plucked. I will tell you, then, that they will be removed from the earth far more easily than you imagine. Only make the call.

My lips are sealed, as they often were when I was with you, to tell you all that Alpha has told me. My desire, then, is to give to you the great assurance, beloved, of the Father's love, of his care and concern and his placing before you guardian angels unto the victory of his mission and his Agenda.

I AM the sealing of this company, this Stump, by the light of the Father who has sent our Mother and now myself to go forth again to claim his own. Beloved, know the Peace and the Presence and the Love of your Father and be at peace.

This, then, is my commandment unto you: to pray the Father that He will send you heavenly hosts and saints and all Lightbearers in order that this mission might be fulfilled in every nation and this gospel preached in every nation, that the end, truly, of your sojourn might be.[3]

The everlasting hills and octaves of light and worlds born and waiting to be born attend thy coming. Know that thou art loved and strive to make thyself worthy of our love.

O Invincible Majesty of the Light, O Maximus, O Maxim Light—I call it forth for these Thine own!

O Eternal Flame of Alpha and Omega, let this Oneness nevermore be broken but signify that in earth we are the wafer of God and in heaven we are sacred wine for the Lord's sacred supper.

By the Sacred Heart of Jesus, I AM all that I AM.

May ye be also all that ye are.

To my little one, a kiss of joy.

I withdraw into highest octaves of the Great Sphere of Life, there to keep the flame of Spirit for your going forth and your coming in from this time forth and even forevermore.[4] Amen.

This dictation was delivered Sept. 24, 1987, at the Royal Teton Ranch. For notes, see p. 472.

Vol. 30 No. 53 *Beloved Archangel Gabriel* *November 22, 1987*

Saint Germain Stumps New York

I

Called to an Unusual Sacrifice

Violet Flame for an Extraordinary Transmutation

In the holiness of God I AM Gabriel, pleased to be in the midst of this company. Therefore, I summon legions of Light. And they have circled this city round for the profound purpose, beloved, of building walls of light to seal Light and banish Darkness.

Long has heaven waited for a response that could draw forth such intercession as to raise a pillar of fire in the midst thereof. Let us see, then, that the Lightbearers of this area in a one-hundred-mile radius should rally round the pillar of Ascension's Flame and abandon their dancing round the golden calf. (I was there on Atlantis and in the Arian dispensation when the worship of this form did predominate.)

Thus, beloved, treasure the Light and know that the few are counted of the Almighty One for the saving of cities and nations. Thus, for the saving of a city or the saving of the Lightbearers I come, that by the direction of the Almighty One there might be extended an increase of sacred fire.

Beloved, it is the increase of Light* oncoming in the earth that veritably does cause cataclysm, such as earthquake in the "new city" of Los Angeles,[1] called so, for it comes on the site of an ancient Lemurian city.

Know, then, as it has been said, that the light intensifies from the Central Sun, for cosmic spirals move on with or without the awareness of those who prefer to sleep and perhaps to die rather than awaken to the full responsibility of divine Sonship with all that it portends.

Many prefer not to be awake. And therefore I, Gabriel, say, America, awake! and take note that when elemental life can no

*Christ consciousness as light from the Central Sun

longer bear the alchemy of oncoming light midst the plane of darkness, it is earth herself that must give way.[2]

What is the purpose, then, of earth changes but that the earth body and her evolutions that will to survive—fully awakened as the Buddha—might contain a new light for the new dispensation. I doubt very much that any among you would disagree with me or the view of all Seven Archangels that earth cannot continue in the present round of discord, dissonance, war, plague and death.

Beloved, something must give! And it is our desire to see those for whom we are the Teachers understand that it is the giving up of the lesser self—its displacement by the incarnation of the Word where you are—that is the offering, *the acceptable offering,* upon the altar of God whereby transition into a new light and age could come about without the destructivity that may ensue unless many thousands more respond to the call of the noble brother Saint Germain to keep the flame of Life.

Thus, beloved, there are no shortcuts to the salvation of a planet and a people. Nevertheless, the single anointed one who will claim his Christhood and call forth the Father and the Son to take up their abode in his temple,[3] that one may displace the Darkness of ten thousand-times-ten thousand individuals. Thus, the quality of Light, of the internalization of the Word—it is that which we seek. And for this reason and to this end we have sent forth our Messenger, that a people might know that victory is within their grasp.

O enlightened ones, we have known you from the very beginning from the heart of the Divine Mother. How tender is the love of Seven Archangels and legions of Light for each one personally.

The teaching has gone forth that the fate of earth is in the hands of Lightbearers who are in embodiment in this hour, whether the tiny babe or one in the womb who does come from the recesses of nirvana to reembody. Blessed hearts, those who have life and breath of the Holy Spirit in the earth are called, then, to an unusual sacrifice that is the joy of the Lord within their members.

Blessed hearts, the times are so trying and oppressive and so stressful that we of the Archangels counsel the retreat into the bliss of the Divine Mother and the heart of the Buddha. There, by the science of the mantra let those who know and see keep the flame in the cities as though positioned in the caves of the Himalayas.

It is here and now that thy light, O Israel, may count for all.

Thus, in this hour I am sent for the touching of the third eye. It is a quickening and it is, as it were, a magnetic impulse to draw up the light of the chakras. It is well, then, to attend and immerse yourself in this teaching during this weekend, for we the Archangels and those who come are preparing you for the presence of the Lord Jesus. As you have understood, it is for the greater light.

I desire to see you gather to give the violet flame decrees throughout the day on the morrow, that you might in that service realize an extraordinary transmutation from the heart of Archangel Zadkiel. Burdens upon you and upon this city weigh heavy, beloved. They weigh in the very earth body. Let them, then, be cast into the sacred fire of the Seventh Ray. Let violet flame angels who come succeeding my own bands therefore give a gift of light to this city that is the third-eye chakra of a nation.

O Great Liberty and Temple of the Sun, open the twelve gates of the temple, that these evolutions initiated by thy heart, O Mother of Exiles, might enter on their ray and calling, while their bodies sleep this night and come into consonance with an inner awareness without fear of those things which could come upon this area unless a people rise up in acclamation of their God.

Blessed hearts, we have mercy and compassion upon all who are bowed down, who are the ignorant and know not what they do. But this mercy and compassion is not able to stay the hand of the Law of God or the oncoming cycles of Light.

Understand, therefore, that suspended over this city is a vast inner etheric retreat.[4] It is our goal to see those who are the spiritual descendants of the twelve tribes embody the path of self-mastery of the twelve gates. Let the seed of the Ancient of Days, then, be quickened. Let all who have the gift of the divine spark know that never has heaven been more ready to give an outpouring of light, and yet never have we felt so confined by the Great Law.

Therefore, it is free will and your own determination to intercede for a city and a nation that will make the difference. *To determine to hold light, to have light, to be light, to know the light and to be the servant of the light even while becoming the master of that light, this is the calling of the hour.*

Inasmuch as this is the city where the All-Seeing Eye of God is focused, I may tell you that the change which may seem impossible can come in the twinkling of the eye of God. Let the last trump of mortality sound.[5] Let the death knell sound and let each and every one shed a single snakeskin of the former self. And take heart and hope and receive the Holy Comforter, the Holy Spirit, that all things can be different if you will it so.

Where free will is determined to hold the balance, there the angels rush in. Blessed hearts, know, of a truth, that as my angels, dressed in white garments of light of the Central Sun, surround you, all is being given to you that you can contain in this hour.

Thus, the change of alchemy of violet flame may find you at a new level of awareness on the morrow to receive a greater quickening. It is for the alignment with the Son of God that we come. It is for the alignment of the I AM THAT I AM.

Therefore, earthquake did come upon the new city. But, beloved, there was a mitigation of it for the very calls of Keepers of the Flame giving the action of the violet flame and many decrees to the heart of the God Star.

Thus, though one may feel the quaking and shaking of the earth, one must also remember the mercy of God. Let mercy's flame rise. Let elemental life be given hope. And let them be given support of the violet flame that they might enter in to prevent those worse things that could be or might have been. It is a day-by-day holding up of the mighty tent of the Lord of this nation by the violet flame that does pour forth from all retreats of the Great White Brotherhood.

Look, then, with your inner sight in this moment and see planet earth as a violet sphere intensifying in that violet flame. See, then, how the saturation of certain geographical locations where there is a vibrant purple intensifying by angelic bands does also signify areas of greatest trouble, of greatest burden and potential for cataclysm.

This city, beloved, is just as much in the line of cataclysm as has been Los Angeles. Let us see renewed, then, the calling forth of the rainbow of light from the heart of Los Angeles to the heart of New York.[6] Let us see, then, twin pillars of violet flame sustained by Keepers of the Flame. Let us see such an increase in violet flame in these cities that we will call forth and receive a dispensation from Melchizedek himself, the Ascended Master who does teach the path of the Melchizedekian priesthood at the retreat of Lord Zadkiel and Holy Amethyst over the Caribbean.

O blessed beings of Light, hosts of the LORD, may we reinforce the violet flame and then be about our Father's business for the raising up of pillars of blue flame for the defense of nationhood, Christhood and Divine Love in every creature.

Day by day, then, the great equation of life hangs in the balance. Under this sign of Libra we come, for autumn equinox does release opportunity as well as another increment of world karma. See, then, how there is a triggering of natural forces, spiritual forces according to the seasons, according to the signs of the times.

The gathering of Lightbearers to this convocation, then, is ultimately for the transmutation and holding back of the karma that consists of the dregs of a year in the final quadrant. The final quadrant of each year is the physical, beloved. It is when all those momentums of the first nine months may actually precipitate into physical form.

We must tell you, beloved, that the nation itself is threatened in war in the Persian Gulf, that the people's hearts are threatened for the very oncoming karma. Thus, it is an interval in time and space, an interval out of heaven whereby the violet flame so invoked by you might transmute that which shall surely become physical and become a burden to all should it come to pass.

I, Gabriel, do not deliver a prophecy of doomsday but of great hope and of enlightenment, which is sorely wanting from the pulpits of the nation or from the political pundits! Blessed hearts, the enlightenment is that those of the light, those of hope and faith and charity may give themselves to make all the difference in the outplaying of world events. Thus, when you gather and the violet flame is given and events are stayed and life returns to peace and quiet, you may never know what has been averted.

Thus, beloved, the spiritual [people] will attune with the violet light, the violet flame and the Seventh Ray and find themselves liberated in the heart of God for every call that is made. Hear me, I say! Every call that is made accrues to your personal causal body of Light against the day of the descent of your own personal karma. Let a word to the wise, then, be sufficient, for the LORD's hosts are ready now.

Blessed ones, if these teachings are unknown to you, if you have never studied them before, then your attendance under our teachers in our workshops will give to you a widening sphere of awareness of all that can come forth from your own beloved I AM Presence.

I, Gabriel, would receive you to my heart. The means at my disposal is the touch of the third eye. If you would receive of my heart and my heart's love for you from the beginning, thus pass by and feel the gentle touch as the gentle current of light may anchor that portion of God given to me for thee.

[intonations, 48 seconds]

Thus, from the ancient breastplate of the high priest of God, twelve rays go forth touching each one who is the spiritual descendant of the Ancient of Days.

O Christ, quicken hearts, fan fires that have begun to diminish. Let the coals from the altar of God renew those in whom the flame has gone out.

All who desire renewed intelligence of the Mind of God and love, come then to this altar.[7]

"The Summit Lighthouse Sheds Its Radiance O'er All the World to Manifest as Pearls of Wisdom."
This dictation by **Archangel Gabriel** was **delivered** at the conclusion of the Thursday evening service, **October 1, 1987,** after midnight, during a 4-day seminar held at the Penta Hotel in **New York City,** where Elizabeth Clare Prophet was stumping for Saint Germain's Coming Revolution in Higher Consciousness. Prior to the dictation, the Messenger delivered the lecture "The Healing Power of the Seven Archangels." (**1**) **Earthquake in Los Angeles.** On October 1, 1987, at 7:42 a.m. PDT, an earthquake registering 6.1 on the Richter scale shook the Los Angeles area, followed by sixteen aftershocks throughout the morning. It was the most severe quake in the region since 1971. According to authorities, at least six people died and more than 100 were injured in the earthquake. Property damage, which included cracks in many downtown Los Angeles buildings and the collapse of buildings in Pasadena and Whittier (near the earthquake's epicenter), was an estimated $59 million. For Nostradamus' predictions of earthquakes around the **"new city,"** interpreted as possibly New York or Los Angeles, see *Saint Germain On Prophecy,* pp. 143–44, 148–51, Book Two. (**2**) For information about elemental life, the increasing burden they bear in sustaining the planet, and the need to invoke violet flame on their behalf, see *A Prophecy of Planetary Cataclysm,* in *Saint Germain On Prophecy,* pp. 1–72, Book Three. (**3**) John 14:23. (**4**) **The Temple of the Sun,** retreat of the Goddess of Liberty, is on the etheric plane over Manhattan, New York. (**5**) I Cor. 15:51–53. (**6**) On November 17, 1985, the Goddess of Liberty explained, "I am directing the arcing of the rainbow rays of light over America from New York to Los Angeles." See the Goddess of Liberty, "Allegiance to the Law of the One," 1986 *Pearls of Wisdom,* vol. 29, no. 5, p. 32. (**7**) Congregants passed by the Messenger to receive the touching of the third eye and the transfer of light by the Archangel Gabriel, Angel of the Annunciation.

Notes from Pearl No. 51 by Kali:
(**1**) **Shekinah** [Hebrew]: the visible manifestation of the Divine Majesty; a glory or refulgent light symbolizing the Divine Presence. See *Corona Class Lessons,* p. 422, n. 8. (**2**) **The chalice of Light in the Heart of the Inner Retreat.** For more information on the raising up of the chalice and its significance, see pp. 302, 310, 374, 383, 417, 418, 443, 456, 459. (**3**) "Adoration to the Great Central Sun," song 587 in *The Summit Lighthouse Book of Songs;* no. 3 in *Mantras of the Ascended Masters for the Initiation of the Chakras,* p. 3. (**4**) Rev. 19:20; 20:10, 14, 15; 21:8.

Notes from Pearl No. 52 by Lanello:
(**1**) Lanello's dictation was given in a Circle of Light held before the Messenger and team departed on Saint Germain's Eastern Stump, October 1–November 1 and November 25–29, 1987. Those who remain at the Ranch hold the balance of Alpha, those who go forth hold the Omega. (**2**) **God's promise to Abraham.** Gen. 12:1–3; 13:14–16; 15:4, 5; 17:4–8; 22:17, 18; Rom. 4:13, 16–18; Gal. 3:29; Heb. 11:8, 9, 12. (**3**) Matt. 24:14. (**4**) Ps. 121:8.

Pearls of Wisdom®
published by The Summit Lighthouse

Vol. 30 No. 54 *Beloved El Morya* *November 23, 1987*

Saint Germain Stumps New York
II
24 Months
The Enemy Does Not Sleep

Hail to the God flame within you!

Chelas of the will of God, my friends and compatriots, I am here, sent by the Darjeeling Council of the Great White Brotherhood. And in my heart there burns yet the sapphire of my First Love and the ruby of my desiring to impart to this people the essence of the Blood of Christ—my Lord, thy Life, our Oneness.

Therefore, students of the deeper mysteries, as I have long been engaged in setting forth the hidden and wisdom teachings of the Far East, I desire to bring to light in you that the point of the lance as well as the point of the diamond must relate to current events and to the point of the third eye of the chela who is aware that grain by grain the sands in the hourglass fall, cycles move on and the enemy does not sleep.

I can do no less than to read to you from documents that now rest on the Darjeeling Council table. And there, beloved, our council does continue its meeting this night even as I address you through my outpost in the West. Gracious are ye who have assembled to hear me speak. May the angels and the devas of the First Ray salute thee, then, as we find oneness and consolation in the Sacred Heart.

Beloved, I come on the eve of Saint Germain's message to you. Therefore, I must present evidence that is not being presented to you by the heads of state in the West nor by your president or his cabinet. Blessed hearts, the evidence is clear to us and to those who know and therefore ought to do better that the Soviet Union has never altered her position in moving toward the nuclear first strike against this nation and the devastation of Europe.

Despite all talks of peace and disarmament, I say to you and all who will hear me: Beware, for the shadow of death in the form of the pale horse[1] does stalk the land. Were I to acquaint you with all knowledge and evidence at hand, I should say, beloved, that I might bear the karma of spreading a fear unto torment that would not allow you the equanimity to deal with the evidence or the available alternatives.

Some must sound the warning and incur thereby the unpopularity of their times. I, for one, have never shirked from my responsibility to speak truth nor to warn the people of Israel. Therefore hear me, beloved: Ere twenty-four months have passed, be it known to you that this nation must have the capacity to turn back any and all missiles, warheads incoming whether by intent or by accident. Where there is no defense you invite the bear into your own haven.

Blessed hearts, there is no turning back from this evidence nor from the responsibility of a free people to guard the light of freedom, to guard the borders of a spiritual identity and a national destiny. Therefore, I say to you, Keep the flame of America! Stand guard at the side of Mother Liberty.

While you meet, therefore, there is the advancement, with no turning back, of that determination to defeat and devour the West. Blessed ones, you find some of this evidence even in the journals of the times, yet all sleep, save the few. And some who know do nothing. And those who know are also in the government of this nation.

For shame, I say, that a world should be lost for selfishness and fear and spinelessness in the leaders of a country! Will a people, then, who yet have heart and voice turn from their commitment to freedom? Or shall they act as a stitch in time to save nine?

I daresay, beloved, on the brink of what appears to be the fulfillment of the prophecies of Fátima and Medjugorje, I stand before you and I tell you still that the opportunity lies in your hands to rally the forces of Light of America, the people who yet remain of sane mind and sound heart, to demonstrate and to move for the necessary defense to deter war without ever engaging in that war.

Is this, then, the Ides of March?[2] Is this the hour when a leader's own countrymen shall put not only the leader but a nation and an entire civilization to death?

Let it be known, beloved, that we the Ascended Masters of the Great White Brotherhood recommend civil defense and defensive weapons that stop nuclear war from being fought to begin with. Let it be understood likewise that those who know me and know my vibration may hear clearly and understand that there must remain a physical enterprise such as this nation America, not only as a platform for evolution but as the base of a pyramid of a path of initiation. For when the earth is no longer safe for a path of individual Christhood, wherefore the nations? to what end an economy or a banking system?

Beloved hearts, the betrayal of yourselves is almost complete.

Know, then, and understand that I warn you of the indoctrination of the media and of the false prophets of peace that have come again almost in numberless numbers, for their fear begets passivism as do their mentality, their music, their drugs, their food and their pastimes.

Thus, by spinelessness shall a nation be lost? I ask the question of every American and of every citizen of the world who has heart. Shall there be a rallying to defend a nation and a gift so sublime of Saint Germain or not? ["Yes!"]

Blessed ones, if ever you had a fiery heart, a spark of desire to retain all that is holy, if ever you knew of an inner ingenuity, now is the time to unleash it. Now is the time to determine absolutely the rallying to a cause and the rallying of a nation. Things cannot continue in this vein, beloved.

I come with the fierceness of the Divine Mother and the Holy Spirit. Shiva! I come in the power that God has given unto me as the Lord of the First Ray to summon the troops and to say to you, the Lord Christ has called for ten thousand Keepers of the Flame. Can he save the city and North America with ten thousand? He has said so, beloved, and I believe him.[3]

Therefore, understand, all you who would make a commitment to freedom, that Saint Germain is the Ascended Master to whose heart I commend you. To be a Keeper of the Flame and to give that daily support in decrees as well as an activism that does display one's heart and thought and mind for a cause—this is the calling of the hour.

Let those who let the spark fly for a revolution that founded this nation not shy away from their responsibility in this hour. Let us keep the flame by night and let us act and act again in the day, else this nation, beloved, shall pass through all of the darkest prophecies that you have ever heard prophesied for this hour.

Blessed ones, there is nothing more key and nothing more important on my heart. Day by day the moves to position in space and in defense are being taken by the Soviet! Let it be understood that these facts are known by this government and yet not brought to the attention of the people; somehow they believe that if the waters be troubled there shall thereby be the invoking of war.

Blessed hearts, we of the First Ray understand the principles of power and the abuses of power. And therefore, strength becomes the principle of the First Ray in the defense of the Divine Mother in this nation and all of her children of Light worldwide.

Let there be the desire of some hearts to become initiates of the sacred fire and cease your surfeiting in your businesses and in your acquiring of goods and things and money! What will you do with all "these things" when the day descends upon you when the skies are no longer bright but only bright with nuclear warhead exploded/imploded and releasing that which is death to the people?

With some preparation, all of which is known to the Department of Defense, this nation can permanently deter nuclear war. Let it be done, I say! And let those who have ear to hear know that the prophets have spoken again and again and not been heeded. And the very people of Israel and Judah have gone down again and again into slavery because they heeded the god of lust, the Moloch of human greed and the false prophets of peace![4]

So we have sent the prophets into your midst and so we come ourselves, I myself occupying the office of patriarch of this entire evolution.[5] Blessed hearts, we have spoken through this Messenger and yet where is there the real reckoning of that which is being planned?

Blessed hearts, hour by hour our Messenger must be aware of our deliberations and of your own. And she has observed, as I have, the discrepancy between the two, almost an ignoring or a not wanting to hear of the seriousness of this hour.

Has there ever been a time when less-qualified candidates have approached to obtain the Oval Office? Blessed hearts, I can tell you nay. All are compromisers. All speak as out of both sides of the mouth. All have not the fearlessness of the Divine Mother to call a spade a spade and to fear not before the dark ones and their plots but to fear only one's own cowardice, one's own betrayal and one's own judgment day.

How can so many millions of people fear to lay down this life that they might take it again in a mission of Christhood? Where have the people's awareness of the sacred mysteries gone? I will tell you. They have gone down the river Styx[6] as they have allowed these fallen angels out of the pit to fill the sound waves with the dissonance of Death and Hell that numbs the mind and body, rapes the chakras and deprives a people of personal dignity and the Ascended-Master walk with God.

All this a people and a nation has allowed in the very face of the divine document and the divine dispensation of the gift of the American Republic. I tell you, beloved, I rend my garments this night as the prophets of old as I see good hearts standing by meekly while those who come with the engines of hell take over the youth of a nation and even the adults with their spells of drugs and their mind manipulation.

How can so many lifestreams sponsored by the Almighty One collectively and en masse behave as though stupefied? How can it be, beloved? Are they lemmings running to their own destruction, desiring death? Have they so taken up the calling of the fallen angels that they have forgot that the Lord Jesus Christ lives in this nation, pleading and knocking at the doors of the churches to be heard, to have his lost Word spoken finally and to find some ministers who have some fire left in the spine after they have done with all of their social preoccupations?

They have lost the awareness of what it means to be a true servant of the people as have their leaders. And they do not stand in the congregation of the righteous but seek, self-serving, to please all, thereby pleasing none. The leaders have not awakened to the fact that grass-roots America has heart and awareness and illumination from the Ascended Masters.

But those who have amassed wealth ill-gotten, filthy lucre in a merchandise of materialism, these ones who appear to have the power, beloved, I say before the living God, they have no power! They have no power in this hour! And yet their citadels do not come tumbling down though they are made of toothpicks, for none dare challenge them.

Will all, I say, quake in their boots? Or will some arise and realize that a round-the-clock marathon has been called for by Archangel Gabriel for the violet flame to spare this nation further cataclysm,[7] to buy time again and again that a people might awaken, that they might come to their senses and to the defenses and know that the light that is not guarded is the light that shall be lost, the nation that is not guarded is a nation that shall be lost.

Blessed hearts, you are on the brink of doom and know it not, as every civilization has reached a heyday of pleasure and disregarded all of the signs of the enemy without and the enemy within. Even while I speak, beloved, that enemy does listen and does watch.

Therefore, what kind of a state have we? Is it the estate of the Highest and of his sons or some kind of a polyglot mixture where none have a sense of the true inheritance of the sons and daughters of God?

I say, beloved, if this nation go down and be lost, woe! upon the seed of the wicked and woe! upon the seed of Light for their neglect. For this karma shall be a karma of neglect.

How art thou fallen, O Lucifer and Babylon the Great?[8] Shall this city in one night be no more? And shall all the merchants mourn before her destruction? Shall it come to pass as the prophets have foreseen?

I tell you, whether or not is up to your heart and your call. We will answer every call to turn back this darkness that is a conspiracy from within as well as without. For you know well Saint Germain has called it an International Capitalist/Communist Conspiracy that does bring about nuclear war.

And who is more guilty: the nation that allows it and builds itself an enemy or the enemy himself who has avowed purpose, has never concealed it, has never denied it?

Blessed hearts, at least the aggressor has honest and plain intent, whereas your own leaders refuse to read the handwriting on the wall and in the textbooks and in the record of this history. Need you go back to Assyria and be reminded that Israel and Judah were devoured by the Assyrians now reincarnated as the leadership of the Soviet Union? Need you be reminded of Babylon, the pleasure cult and its leaders reincarnated in Rome and now in America?

Blessed ones, neither to the right nor to the left is there any righteousness—"no, not one."[9] But the righteousness of God is in the heart of the living Christ within any and all who will espouse him and understand that there is a time to play, there is a time to fight, there is a time to sing and there is a time to march. There is a time to defend and take up the sword. There is a time to come with the olive branch of peace.

There is no sense of timing in this nation; and as time is the Mother, so there is no sense of the Divine Mother in any case.

Shall all the world be lost on the eve of the golden age of Aquarius? I shake my head, beloved, and I wonder. I say, therefore, let ten thousand Keepers of the Flame show their finest hour. Let the intercession come.

Therefore, to this end I am empowered by the Great Lord, the Maha Chohan, and with me the Seven Chohans of the Rays, for the quickening of these chakras of this people here so gathered and the chakras of every true Lightbearer upon this continent and in every nation.

Therefore, I, El Morya, standing before you in the hour of destiny, do send forth the fire into the very heart chakra. Now feel the gentle impulse where you are as this impulse does go to every heart in whom there dwells God and the love of God. Blessed ones, there are many in every nation. And therefore, I call in the name of Elohim to the Lightbearer of every nation in the earth, including in my beloved Mother Russia. Let the Lightbearers of the earth unite now before it is too late in the name of Saint Germain, in the name of Mother Mary, in the name of Jesus Christ!

Therefore, from the heart chakra, increased, then, by impulse from the Temple of the Sun, the rays go forth to the throat chakra, the third eye and the crown, solar plexus, seat-of-the-soul and base-of-the-spine.

Therefore, the alignment does come by the great mathematics of Cyclopea Elohim, All-Seeing Eye of God. This realignment does come about for the gathering of a people and for the decrees offered in every sanctuary and home where the flame of Life and Liberty and Freedom is kept.

All who are here this night come by the impulse of the urgency of the hour; all these things which I tell you are known of you at subconscious levels and other areas of consciousness, even the Higher Mind. The outer mind does not accept but does screen out, for there is a fear, beloved, to accept the realities of the oncoming woes.

Therefore, I AM Morya, your friend and father of old and your Presence, strengthening you and urging you to be all that you are and to understand that all other tasks and callings must be subordinated to the guarding of the flame of freedom dedicated upon this soil and nation, the guarding of the land, the cities, the people, the borders. Let it be so. For the gross neglect has already cost this nation great opportunity and safety.

Science from the heart of the Cave of Symbols, from the heart of Saint Germain has been given. Technology has been secured not for war but for defense. Therefore, it has been turned to implements of war as the fallen ones in this nation have given away all advantage in defense to the enemy.

The karma itself, beloved, warrants the descent of this judgment through the foreign power as it came upon Israel and Judah.[10] Therefore, let the Lightbearers who know the Law stand between a nation and her neglect which has become her karma.

Let all you who hear me speak for the first time remember to keep the flame and to sign that document to be a Keeper of the Flame, even as the early American patriots signed that document in Independence Hall. There comes a time when life and destiny necessitates the signing of one's name to a cause. O people of America, will you sign your name next to the signing of Saint Germain's name by himself, our noble Knight Commander?

I tell you, beloved, this hour in the Darjeeling Council chambers Saint Germain has stood and signed his name once again to a document that is for the saving of this nation under God, that this nation might be the open door to that salvation of Mother Liberty to all nations. He has stood before us to give an impassioned speech concerning the giving of his life once again if our Father will accept his offering. Saint Germain desires only to save this nation and this people as a bulwark of defense to all and to all enlightenment.

Blessed hearts, I tell you, it is not the taking of a vow nor the mere signing of the name, but it is the activation of the resources of one's causal body in a marathon that must continue until safety is won. Those hearts who would participate in this cause may go to Darjeeling this night. Our doors are opened to any and all patriots of the world who will defend freedom and sign this document with Saint Germain. Do not take the opportunity lightly, beloved, for this signing is the signing of one's life, as he has signed for his life.

Now I say, bestir yourselves! Act for freedom! Let your cause be made known! Let truth be shouted from the housetops. Let there be a true awareness that does not escape every citizen.

Blessed ones, it is one thing to give a people a message; it is another to remain in hours of prayer to the Archangels to cut them free from their predilections, from their addictions, from the vibration of the death wish itself that hangs over the land and settles even into the psyche of some who were formerly our best servants.

Hearts of fire, you need the call to the seraphim and every angel in cosmos to rescue a nation from itself and a people from its idolatry and false beliefs. Therefore, I, El Morya, tell you, neglect not the spiritual work nor the speaking out. Become, then, men and women for all seasons.

I salute you in the fire of the heart and in the four quadrants of Being. Ere twenty-four months pass, beloved, there shall be a reckoning and a confrontation unless something is done.

I, Morya, seal you in the heart of the diamond-shining Mind of God. So be protected. So be blessed. And so know that I have loved you with an unmitigated love, a love unending that is tender, all-enfolding and one with you.

I walk with you, beloved. Call to me and my Electronic Presence, for I have somewhat of the First Ray to inspire you with, to infill you with—to strengthen you, to comfort you in your aloneness and in the hours when you wrestle with the anti-Self and the anti-Life forces in those whom you meet.

O Blessed Mother, Mary, thy Son does salute thee in this hour and offer prayer for thy intercession before the Father for time again and a half a time that a people might awaken and know what is the true score in this hour.

> Blessed Virgin of God, thou who hast been to me a comfort in all life, hear my call in this hour even as you hear the call of these hearts. Therefore, we cry to thee, we who have recourse to thee, Blessed Mother. Come, then, with thy legions of Light to stand with this people and this company between a nation and her descending karma.
>
> Mother of God, our hearts expand to thy Immaculate Heart. Receive us as thine own. And let us be thy instruments here below, as Above.

Blessed ones, feel the Mother of God in this place, her vast presence. And note the single tear that descends from her eye.

It is not too late, beloved! Therefore, we have not yet said "what might have been" but give you the vision of Victory. Seize it, I say! Seize it in the name of Mary.

"The Summit Lighthouse Sheds Its Radiance O'er All the World to Manifest as Pearls of Wisdom." This dictation by **El Morya** was **delivered** on **Friday, October 2, 1987,** during a 4-day seminar held at the Penta Hotel in **New York City,** where Elizabeth Clare Prophet was stumping for Saint Germain's Coming Revolution in Higher Consciousness. (**1**) Rev. 6:7, 8. The rider of the pale horse of Death, the Fourth Horseman of the Apocalypse, delivers death in many forms—war and famine that follow economic collapse; plagues, cancer, AIDS and new viruses; suicide, addictive drugs and all that leads to a slow sweet death. See *Saint Germain On Prophecy,* p. 68, Book Two. (**2**) **The Ides of March.** On March 15 (the Ides of March), 44 B.C., Roman dictator Julius Caesar was stabbed to death by a group of nobles and officers who feared that he might make himself king and thereby bring the republic to an end. (**3**) See pp. 269, 273,

274. (**4**) **The rejection of the prophets.** I Kings 19:10, 14; II Kings 17:13–23; II Chron. 24:20–22; Isa. 30:8–14; Jer. 7:25, 26; 19:3–7, 14, 15; 20:1, 2; 26; 36; 37:1, 2; 38. (**5**) El Morya was embodied as Abraham, father of the Hebrew nation, to whom the LORD said, "I will make my covenant between me and thee. . . . And thou shalt be a father of many nations." See *Lords of the Seven Rays,* pp. 33, 45. For more on the life and person of Abraham, see Elizabeth Clare Prophet, August 25, 26, 27, 1982, "Teachings of the Mother on Morya as Abraham," and January 24, 1982, "The Story of Our Father Abraham and of His Chela and of His Guru," on five 90-min. audiocassettes, B82105, B82106, B82108, B82112, B82113, $6.50 ea. (for postage add $.50 for the first cassette and $.30 for up to 4 more). (**6**) **The river Styx.** In Greek mythology, the Styx is the principal river of the underworld which circles Hades nine times. The waters of the Styx are said to have a narcotic effect on those who drink them, leaving them insensible for a year. (**7**) On October 2, 1987, Archangel Gabriel explained, "Though one may feel the quaking and shaking of the earth, one must also remember the mercy of God. Let mercy's flame rise. Let elemental life be given hope. And let them be given support of the violet flame that they might enter in to prevent those worse things that could be or might have been. It is a day-by-day holding up of the mighty tent of the Lord of this nation by the violet flame that does pour forth from all retreats of the Great White Brotherhood." See p. 470; and the Goddess of Liberty, "The Tent of the LORD," pp. 107–11. (**8**) Isa. 14:12; Rev. 16:18, 19; 18. For Nostradamus' predictions of earthquakes around the "new city," possibly New York City, see *Saint Germain On Prophecy,* pp. 143–44, 148–50, Book Two. (**9**) Rom. 3:10, 12. (**10**) II Kings 17:6–12, 22, 23; Jer. 39:1–9.

Cassettes Available from the Messenger's Eastern Stump

Elizabeth Clare Prophet, October 3, 1987, "You, Saint Germain and Healing through the Violet Flame," and dictation by Saint Germain, on three 90-min. audiocassettes, A87087, $19.50.

Elizabeth Clare Prophet, October 31, 1987, "Halloween Prophecy 1987": Mother Mary: On the Great War—from Fátima to Medjugorje, On the Astrology of the U.S. and the U.S.S.R., On the Economy—the Four Horsemen of the Apocalypse, and dictation by Mother Mary, on two videocassettes, 4 hrs. 26 min., GP87063, $39.95, or on three 90-min. audiocassettes, A87079, $19.50.

Elizabeth Clare Prophet, November 1, 1987, "The Lost Teachings of Jesus on the Mother," and dictation by Jesus Christ, on three audiocassettes, 4 hrs., A87090, $19.50.

I. Archangel Gabriel, El Morya, Saint Germain, including the prophecy of the LORD GOD (New York City), on 90-min. audiocassette B87073, $6.50.

II. Jesus Christ, Himalaya (New York City), on 79-min. audiocassette B87074, $6.50.

III. Archangel Zadkiel (New Haven), Archangel Chamuel (Boston), Archangel Michael (Baltimore), Lady Master Nada (Philadelphia), on 90-min. audiocassette B87075, $6.50.

IV. Listening Angel (Pittsburgh), Archangel Uriel (Cleveland), Elohim of Peace (Columbus), Vesta (Toledo), Saint Germain (Detroit), on 90-min. audiocassette B87076, $6.50.

V. Mighty Victory (Louisville), Maha Chohan (Indianapolis), Archangel Raphael (Cincinnati), El Morya (St. Louis), A Cosmic Being from out the Great Silence (Chicago), Gautama Buddha (Chicago), on 90-min. audiocassette B87077, $6.50.

VI. Mother Mary, Jesus Christ, Serapis Bey, Saint Germain (Minneapolis), on 90-min. audiocassette B87078, $6.50.

Postage for Audiocassettes. Add $.50 for one cassette, $.80 for up to five cassettes and $.90 for over five cassettes.
Postage for Videocassettes. Add $1.20 for two cassettes.

Vol. 30 No. 55 *Beloved Saint Germain* *November 24, 1987*

Saint Germain Stumps New York
III
The Deliverer of My People
The Speaking of the LORD *God*

Ho! let the waters of eternal Life flow, then, from the citadel of Being.

I AM in the heart of every Keeper of the Flame, Saint Germain. Therefore, with you in this hour in this city, I AM in the fervor of Freedom and Liberty's name.

O people of the LORD, East and West, O children of the Sun, my sons and daughters, hear me, then. For I also come of late from the Darjeeling Council chambers where the winds that blow through the trees high in the foothills of the Himalayas do waft on their breeze sweet incense and prayers unto the great principles and persons of the Godhead.

Thus, you have celebrated the incarnation, lo, of the Word, East and West. Let it be, then, for the balance of a planet and more, aye, for the raising up of a soul of Light unto the victory of the Eternal Mother.

Therefore, beloved, remember the Cave of Light, remember the Master R.[1] For I AM here and I AM there, and I do weave a planetary caduceus, that you might understand (though Freedom be my very own heartbeat) that I neglect not the training in the secret chamber of the heart of those devotees who must garner light in the center of being if they would make a statement for Krishna and Arjuna in this hour.[2]

Let the chela of the Universal Christ know, then, that I AM in the heart of the Great Guru Sanat Kumara even as I AM in the heart of the one who must be the extension of a Spirit cosmos in these veils of Matter for the rescue of souls.

Therefore, I AM come to those in the West who know not that they need the rescuing by fiery seraphim and devas of the will of God.

I AM in the heart of the seventh dispensation.

Therefore, there does remain in this city a pillar of my Presence and of the great light of the Far East.[3]

Therefore, Come, Master of the Himalayas. Establish thy blue lotus flame until twenty-four hours hence and less that word should go forth from this place out of the Cave of Light.

Therefore, Come, Divine Mother—Come, then, Kali. Let there be the gathering of those tormented by the plagues of sophistication and civilization.

Blessed hearts, my word has gone forth even as you have heard commentary on the world scene through the very gift of prophecy that is upon this Messenger.

I AM the one, then, who does promote this program for the defense of freedom.

I AM the one who does first and foremost seal now the seat-of-the-soul chakra in you by the amethyst crystal. Let the violet flame blaze forth from thy soul henceforth, for I would bestir the awakening by the fires from heavenly altars.

I AM in the heart of the Cave of Symbols and the Cave of Light.[4] I place my Electronic Presence over each and every one—the Lightbearers of the nations who are determined to turn back nuclear war while there is yet time. For there is indeed time!

And in this hour, then, the days shall not be shortened for the elect. I say, they shall be lengthened! [15-sec. applause] Let each twenty-four-hour cycle for the elect of God now become the forty-eight and more.

Let the great aura and the causal body of Jupiter be upon you. And with joy and joviality I say, Go forth to win a world for the heart of the Divine Mother whose servant I AM. She is universally present in ye all, one Body, one Light. One song She does sing in the heart, "O my children, be free! O my sons and daughters, rise up now and lead these lambkins into the folds of the garment of God."

Lo! I AM THAT I AM. Lo! the hand, therefore, of God in me and my hand in his hand and one with the Goddess of Liberty does release to you, beloved, a momentum for the arresting of the spirals of darkness and deceit and the masters of deceit in this city and of those who are a part of what I have so named as the international capitalist/communist conspiracy. Let it be so.

Whether or not you have wondered if there be such a conspiracy, for the moment accept my word that it does exist by powers that be, warned of by the apostle Paul, your beloved Hilarion. Thus, the "spiritual wickedness in high places"[5] of this city, which does represent the third-eye chakra of the nation, is a manipulation in money matters beyond conception.

And therefore I say, Woe! Woe! Woe! Let the judgments descend upon those who manipulate the abundant Life of a people of God and subject them to a slavery untold far beyond that of the Egyptian taskmasters!

Know ye not that they have enslaved your mind and heart and body?

O ye people of America, cry out for Freedom and do not resist your deliverer who does come to you! For the deliverer of my people is truly the Spirit of the LORD and the mighty Archangels and the Divine Mother in your midst. And this deliverance must come swiftly, as in the eye of God.

Let the deliverance come, I say! And resist not going forth into the wilderness, America, to come apart from this Babylonian civilization that will swallow you up even as malefic flowers do close and consume the very soul itself.

Blessed hearts, be in this city but not of its downward spiral. And therefore, by the spiral of light and the Ascension Flame so conquer what thou art where thou art and be in the heart of the living pyramid of Mater at that point of Resurrection's Flame.

I AM Saint Germain! And I keep the flame of Mother Liberty. And I come now to enjoin your heart to my own as I do extend the divine spark and a current of light for the increase and balance of those who do carry with honor, with reverence the threefold flame of Christ-Liberty within their hearts.

Beloved ones, I come with a sacred fire breath to breathe upon that divine spark the light, the energy and consciousness of the Holy Spirit. [The sounding of the holy breath is heard.] Thus in Alpha and Omega receive renewal, a fire that does consume and intensify within you now the will to be and the will of the devouring Kali to devour those malefic spirits foul that move across the land to devour the youth of America and the world.

I say unto all purveyors of drugs and all who poison the minds and souls and bodies of youth eternal everywhere:

Woe! Woe! Woe!

So the pronouncement of the judgment of Almighty God be upon you. So by the spirit of the Prophet does there descend now that karma upon those who are the destroyers in the earth![6]

And let the archdeceivers of the people in their nests in the nations' capitals now tremble, for the LORD God Almighty does walk the earth!

For the Lord *God Almighty is come and the Divine Mother does enter and does take dominion in the Matter universe.*

Let the devotees of the Mother, of the Christ and the Buddha appear, then. And fear not to claim the Light, for so must your Light increase even as the Darkness of the fallen ones does decrease.

Those wise ones of the Spirit who live in the heart of the Mother know the hour and the sign of cosmic cycles. They do know indeed the signs of the times. And they know when they stand in the presence of the infilling fire of the Holy Spirit!

Thus, look and see with the inner eye as the Lord [appearing as] the Maha Chohan does stand in large form before you, intensifying the action of the Holy Spirit to breathe new life and opportunity into the Lightbearers of this city and all who would be so called the Lightbearers of the world.

I pray you, beloved, intensify your sendings of love to the blessed Mother Mary. For the Divine Mother is near and She does pass by, then, those "mighty ones" yet in their seats.[7] She does pass by, then, those who victimize the poor and leave them on their own.

Beloved hearts, the Divine Mother does go forth with more than a social program, aye, indeed, She does go forth for the buoying up of the will to be, to love, to do, to create and to return to the original founding principles whereby Alpha and Omega have created in the beginning.

So, in the sign of the cosmic cross of white fire know that the door of opportunity has never swung more wide, that the portals of purity, the chakras (even of the great ladies of heaven) open now to deliver unto you that sacred fire and that white light of the Sun behind the sun.

Blessed hearts, receive anew the calling of the Divine One and know that you are indeed sent for a purpose. I say, break the curse of death and mortality! Thou hast no part with it. Only the soul evolving unto the Deity is nigh. Therefore, cease to refer to oneself in a limited capacity, for the fountain of joy of the heart does overflow.

O rejoice, beloved, for the Lord our God reigneth!

I, Saint Germain, call in the name I AM THAT I AM:

Elohim of God, it is the hour! Arc, then, the light of the Inner Retreat to the very heart of the Goddess of Liberty and that statue. Let there be an open fount created out of Mind of Elohim of God. Let there be the opening of the way. Let there be deliverance this day and let the walls of light go up. For the Lord our God has decreed it. Lo, He has said:

The Speaking of the LORD God

I AM the LORD thy God. I have not forgot my own, but I AM the very fire in the midst of Israel.

I speak out of the Flame of the ark of the covenant. I speak out of the Sacred Heart. I speak out of the flaming Flame that will not be quenched, known of Zarathustra and Melchizedek.

For I, the LORD thy God, have spoken through prophets and avatars and Christed ones of all ages, and I have summoned my people. And I stand again through this my Servant-Son Saint Germain. And I demand that that mandate be delivered unto the people of this nation under God and of all nations.

Come, then, and worship under the mighty Tree of Life. Come, then, and stand under your own vine and fig tree. For I have sent to you my Presence. I have sent to you my prophets. I have sent to you my Son.

And therefore, hear me, people of earth! I say to you, bind, then, the oppressor! For the hour is come for the judgment of the fallen ones in the earth who would push you to the brink of war and economic collapse and famine and plague.

Therefore, I AM with thee in the hour of the Call. And I say, in my name I AM THAT I AM send forth the mandate of the judgment and see how one is taken and another is left. See how there shall be the harvesting of those wicked and foul spirits in your midst who have taken your children and led them astray unto the very burden of your souls.

Lo! I AM the LORD thy God that liveth in thy midst. And therefore, let the false-hierarchy impostors of the Brotherhood of Light go down. And let freedom ring in every nation. And let the bell of Saint Germain be heard as a mighty chime in the heart.[8] And the sounding of the Law of the One does create, then, the resolution and the reunion of hearts on earth with hearts who are my own.

Lo! I AM the LORD thy God who liveth. Lo! I AM in thee and thou in me. And therefore, trust in the God of thy forefathers and enter into the oneness whereby the nations are defended by a spiritual light and a pillar of fire.

And the golden-calf civilization does go down! And the Cain civilization is judged! For no longer is the Cain civilization protected by the mark of Cain.[9] It is no more.

And therefore, let the fallen ones know that the hour is come that they must pay the price for the shedding of the blood of the holy innocents and of the sons of God and of the prophets and of the Christs. Therefore, let them tremble! For I come into their citadel of international power and moneyed interests. And I AM, of the LORD God, do declare unto you that through my Archangels they shall know the judgment.

And therefore, let the Lightbearers stand fast in the earth. Let the true disciples of the living Christ stand fast and behold the salvation of our God.

O people of earth, know, therefore, that eternal Life is nigh. And therefore let there be the sealing—therefore let there be the sealing, therefore let there be the sealing of the places of the deep of Death and Hell. And let there come a breath of air and a reprieve unto the Lightbearer for the regrouping of forces, for the exposure of the Liar and the Lie and the binding of the Murderer in his lair. I say it! I proclaim it! I declare it!

Now hear the word of my Son Saint Germain and do follow his calling, beloved. For if you do obey my Prophet whom I have sent unto the Aquarian age, then, beloved, understand that you shall be delivered. But if you heed not this voice of the seventh angel,[10] beloved Saint Germain, you will find yourselves not in the center of God-free being and therefore not able to deal with those forces which return to earth through resolution by my sacred fire.

Therefore, invoke the sacred fire daily. Invoke the violet flame. Invoke my Archangels in my name and I shall send them unto you.

For I, the LORD thy God, liveth and I live to save the earth in this hour. Therefore, be myself in form, and in formlessness I shall be with thee always in the Spirit of the I AM THAT I AM.

Truly, beloved, the Father has sent me unto you. I AM your brother Saint Germain. I have set forth for you (and through the Lords of the Seven Rays, the Ascended Masters, and Jesus Christ) a path, a teaching and a mighty work of the ages. Not of myself but of the oneness of the Universal Christ have I spoken, written and dictated through my Messengers.

Heed the Word and the Call. The Message is present, the Teaching available.

Take first things first. Defend thy spiritual right to be. Defend the land of the earth, time and space, inner and outer. Establish bastions of freedom and protection. And neglect not the challenge of [to challenge] those misrepresentatives in the halls of government who, if you allow them, will lead you in the paths of self-destruction—national and international suicide.

You have heard the speaking of the LORD God. Know, then, that this Word must be affirmed daily by you, for it is the law of the Spirit/Matter Cosmos and the mighty figure-eight flow. As Above in the heart of God, as you have heard his will purposed, so below manifest it, I counsel you. Not angels or Ascended Masters or the LORD God himself may accomplish this for thee. Thou alone, all One, do this, then. For this Body of Light is the torch held high by the Goddess of Liberty.

O saints and soldiers of the cross, worthy of thy calling, pass by me now as I would touch the third eye through the emerald matrix and deliver to you the molecule of light on which is inscribed the blueprint, the divine plan for you and your twin flame in the two-thousand-year dispensation of Aquarius. For some it shall be the Ascension sooner, for others later.

Tarry, then, in the Holy City, the New Jerusalem, until ye be endued with power from on high.[11]

I AM the Light of the Heart

I AM the Light of the heart / Shining in the darkness of being
And changing all into the golden treasury / Of the Mind of Christ.
I AM projecting my love / Out into the world
To erase all errors / And to break down all barriers.
I AM the power of Infinite Love, / Amplifying itself
Until it is victorious, / World without end! (9x or 33x)

The New Day
by Vesta

Helios and Vesta!
Helios and Vesta!
Helios and Vesta!
Let the Light flow into my being!
Let the Light expand in the center of my heart!
Let the Light expand in the center of the earth
And let the earth be transformed into the New Day!
(9x or 33x)

I AM, I AM, I AM the Resurrection and the Life
of my finances and the U.S. economy (3x)
Repeat this line 3 times, then conclude with

Now made manifest in my hands and use today!

Repeat the entire mantra 33 times to transmute forces
of Antichrist opposing the abundant Life for God's people.

Note: Take Saint Germain's "I AM the Light of the Heart" mantra and alternate it with the call to Helios and Vesta (9 or 33 times each), sealing both by Jesus' affirmation of the Resurrection and the Life for the healing of the economies of the nations. Add *Archangel Michael's Rosary for Armageddon* combined with a half hour of dynamic violet flame decrees—all of this to mitigate the returning karma upon the economies of the nations. Don't wait. Act today. Time is short.

"The Summit Lighthouse Sheds Its Radiance O'er All the World to Manifest as Pearls of Wisdom."

This dictation by **Saint Germain** was **delivered** at the conclusion of the Saturday evening service, **October 3, 1987** (after midnight) during a 4-day seminar held at the Penta Hotel in **New York City,** where Elizabeth Clare Prophet was stumping for Saint Germain's Coming Revolution in Higher Consciousness. Prior to the dictation, the Messenger delivered the lecture "You, Saint Germain and Healing through the Violet Flame," which included teaching on the violet flame, the astrology of the times, the prophet Jeremiah, the prophecies of Nostradamus and Mother Mary, and the spiritual and physical defense mandated for the age. Lecture and dictation are available on three 90-min. audiocassettes, A87087, $19.50 (add $.80 for postage). (**1**) **The Master R,** appellation of the Great Divine Director, the R standing for Rakoczy, the royal house of Hungary which he founded. Prior to the sinking of Atlantis, the Great Divine Director transferred his retreat and the flame of the retreat to the area known in this century as Transylvania. (**2**) **Krishna on war.** For a discussion of Krishna's teaching to Arjuna on Arjuna's duty as a warrior, see the Bhagavad-Gita, chaps. 1, 2; and Elizabeth Clare Prophet, April 17, 1987, "Saint Germain On the Defense of Freedom: 'To Be or Not to Be,'" 137-min. videocassette HP87036, $24.95 (add $.90 for postage), or two 90-min. audiocassettes, A87028, $13.00 (add $.80 for postage). (**3**) **Cleopatra's Needles.** Saint Germain may have been referring to the granite obelisk that stands in Central Park behind the Metropolitan Museum of Art. It is one of a pair of obelisks erected in front of the Temple of the Sun in Heliopolis, Egypt, more than 3,300 years ago by Thutmose III. In 1880 one, a gift to England, was erected on the Thames embankment in London. In 1881 the United States received the other. The obelisks are known as Cleopatra's Needles. (**4**) **Cave of Symbols.** Saint Germain's retreat at Table Mountain, Wyoming. **Cave of Light.** The retreat of the Great Divine Director in India. (**5**) Eph. 6:12. (**6**) **Cocaine bust.** On November 17 and 18, 1987, at Port Everglades, Florida, U.S. drug agents seized over four tons of cocaine hidden in two shipments of lumber to be used for making picnic furniture. It was the largest amount of cocaine ever seized in the United States. The drugs, concealed inside hollowed-out boards four feet long, had an estimated street value of $300 million. The vessel which shipped the lumber had traveled between Honduras and Florida. (**7**) Luke 1:52. (**8**) See Saint Germain, "The Chime of an Ancient Bell," pp. 291–92. (**9**) Gen. 4:15. (**10**) Rev. 10:7. (**11**) Luke 24:49.

Pearls of Wisdom®
published by The Summit Lighthouse

Vol. 30 No. 56 | *Beloved Jesus Christ* | *November 25, 1987*

Saint Germain Stumps New York
IV
The Call of the Cosmic Christ
Discipleship unto the Ascended Master Jesus Christ

Into the fullness of the Light I would draw you, my beloved—not into the partial light, not into the uncertainty between the darkness and the daylight. I AM come to this city very personally to claim my own disciples.

My heart is open, opened by the Father once again to call my own to a path whereby they shall embody my Word, my Teaching, my Flesh and my Blood.

Discipleship in this age is the Call of the Cosmic Christ.

O souls mounting the spiral staircase unto heaven where thy Christ does await thee, I AM Jesus and I call you to be now the embodiment of all that I AM and to receive me that you might have with me henceforth the most direct relationship.

I call for a purpose and it is the step-by-step containment of the Light. I call you to my fold not in the general sense but in the specific sense of knowing that a Teaching, a Way of Life, a Spirit of the Resurrection cannot endure upon earth unless, truly, ten thousand determine in this hour of my appearing to embody the fullness of myself. Truly, I have answered the call of the child and the teenager who have asked to be my disciple.

Blessed hearts, with ten thousand I will show you and Saint Germain what we together can do for the turning of the tide. Our God has decreed and the Trinity does embody his will, but here below, if that kingdom is to come into manifestation, truly there must be those who can be pillars to hold up the new city, the Holy City, the etheric octave of light come down to earth. Let the New Jerusalem be seen and shared, be partaken of by my own.[1]

I would receive you, then, in my retreat in Arabia[2] [on the etheric plane] to tutor you as I did tutor my apostles Paul and John and countless others through the ages who have come to be initiated in the secret rites given to those who are able to enter the inner circle.

Blessed ones, that door is open to all who qualify. Therefore, it is not an apartness but the saving of a divine grace until ye are able to drink this strong wine of the Spirit.

Blessed hearts, the inner circle consists of the five secret-ray rings of Light that surround my Sacred Heart and do exist in pattern as prototype around your own heart chakra. These spheres of light have been occupied by your human creation. Therefore, the invitation to be my disciples is given to one and to all—all who will understand the self-emptying by Love in order that you might be filled anew with these five frequencies of spherical lights that must be present round the heart chakra if the fullness of my Sacred Heart is to abide in you.

Let there be a recognition, then, that it is I who have called you to bring ten thousand Keepers of the Flame to the heart of Saint Germain. To be a Keeper of the Flame—of Light in the Lighthouse of Being—is the first step toward discipleship.

Having so fulfilled the basic requirements of these lessons, you then come to that time, beloved, when you desire to study the mysteries under Maitreya. And the World Teachers approach you, that you might know that we give a path of initiation step-by-step to his heart. It is the hour when the fulfillment of all promises is come.

If the cumulative Light of all ages and avatars is to be brought to the fore and to the physical octave in the new age, then the forerunners of the age—those who have lived on earth (and continue to live on earth) bearing with them the signs of previous dispensations—must be willing to enter this age in the fullness of my Christhood and their own [Christhood] appearing within them. Wherefore shall there be, then, a path of the Ascension or of saving grace except ye are the Light of the world and the city that is set on an hill that cannot be hid?[3]

Let it be known, then, forever—let it be known that in this hour of maximum karma descending, ten thousand have heard my voice and understood that wherever there is the Anointed One [the Lord Our Righteousness,[4] the Holy Christ Self raised up within the individual], I AM in that heart and the Father with me. We do take up our abode in those who are in harmony with Love, never an offense to the Light itself. Thus Father and Son dwell in thy temple and in this my own.

Know, then, the meaning of the expansion of the fire of the heart as almost with pain the increase of sacred fire creates the burning [sensation], the expanding, even of the chalice [heart chakra] until the fullness of the Christ is come.

Therefore, in this body, [become] my Body, I AM.

I AM in every disciple who knows the path of the inner mysteries. And to those who desire them I come to teach. Receive, then, all that I have offered, all that is written and spoken. And be ready at any hour; for the Bridegroom, thy Christ Self, cometh to take the soul by the hand into the secret place. And there I come to initiate.

In this moment, beloved, angels of the Holy Spirit and of our Lord, the Maha Chohan,[5] are with me. By the Holy Spirit and the intense Love of angelic hosts there is this day a quickening of the twelve petals of the heart, as though new life were blossoming: and the green stalk and the green shoot are quickened.

And the fountain of the Divine Mother rises up within you that you might perform a work for our blessed Saint Joseph in his day. Called Saint Germain in this hour, my father and your own does reappear to go before my Mother Mary, my brothers and sisters, each and every one of you.

Blessed hearts, it is sometimes true, though prosaic, that the greatest Light compels the greatest Darkness. And therefore by our Light in the earth the Darkness is forced out into the sacred fires and altars of transmutation that you have erected by violet flame invocation.

Consequently, beloved, the presence of the greater Darkness in the earth does compel you by Love to externalize the greatest Light. Therefore there are those who need to see and know human suffering, that the desire to be healed and to be the instrument of healing might be kindled to a white-hot fervor that does magnetize the Holy Spirit in the fullness of his divine appearing.

Know, then, beloved, that when all is well in a level of mediocrity in the earth, there is no goad to spiritual progress. And in past ages when the conquest of the earth itself—eking out an existence, forging new civilizations—was the demand, again, only the very few sought the interior life.

But in this hour, beloved, you who are "my disciples in deed"[6] have drunk the cup, even the dregs of all activities of the sine waves of the rise and fall of civilizations, continents and planetary cycles again and again. There is no new thing under the sun[7] on this earth for you, for the cumulative experience of karma and the world has seen it all. And you yourself look to new worlds to conquer. Yet without wings how does the soul fly to the Source and to her God?

I AM come, then, to give you wings, to teach you to fly to the heart of the Father. I AM come ready to place upon you a crown of everlasting Life[8] when you shall have triumphed over the lesser nature and out of love and purest love magnetized the infilling of the Word, of the Holy Ghost, of the water of Life and the Blood that is my Being, my Self.[9]

Blessed hearts, it is a path of Love that I bring, Love illumined by Wisdom and illumining Wisdom in the way. The burning in the heart for none other than to be in the very Presence of the I AM THAT I AM—this burning is a fire that does propel the soul as nothing else can.

Therefore, with all thy getting[10] on the path of self-mastery and knowledge, I counsel you, my own, that to love one another profoundly as I have loved you[11] in the secret places of the Most High[12] is the key to an accelerated path whereby adeptship is a by-product of love and good works and inner purity and divine motives rather than the goal.

To seek to be master, then, or disciple without great concern for those things that are upon the earth and coming upon the earth makes no sense and does not balance in the equation of life.

Love, then, is that sacred fire that does lay down its life for the friend and take it again.[13] And each time in the givingness of life you increase in Christhood. There is no sense of loss as former garments are laid aside and the robe of Christhood descends. Therefore, with each leaving off of the familiar, one becomes acquainted with the outer court of the kingdom and successive spheres of divine awareness where new friends and new angels abide who attend thy coming.

O blessed one, is it not true that "The Hymn of the Pearl"[14] does awaken the divine memory of other years and lost spheres and a song that the soul has sung and a hymn of choirs that have not recently rung? Therefore, let the bell that tolls be not for Death but for eternal Life.

And in the process of the inner conviction and knowing "I AM ascending unto my God and your God,"[15] let there be a certain abandonment unto the service of our God, our LORD, our Saviour. Let there be the sense in all thy waking hours that but for thy ministration some poor soul may be lost. Bypass the "blank ones" whom the Father himself has no desire to convert, but go to the "little ones of my heart." Go to the simple ones rather than those of pomp and story and majesty who mix with the princes of this world and desire not to commune with me one hour.

I ask, then, that you renew your commitment to giving my Watch, my "Vigil of the Hours." So it shall be to you that I shall be in your midst, beloved, as you give this prayer service in my name weekly. You may give it alone, all-one with me, with the recording provided.

And, therefore, know that there is no limit to the expansion of the five spheres of the five secret rays around your heart. And when I AM near and nearest to you in vibration—for you have called me by the magnet of your love and prayerful devotions—I promise you that all who commit to be my disciple as a Keeper of the Flame shall have my spheres of light and my Sacred Heart superimposed upon him or her throughout this Watch each week.

It is my desire, then, that in fifty-two sessions with you, which I would like to be of ninety-minute duration (or more), you might experience such renewal and such self-transcendence at the conclusion of a single year's Watch with me that you shall indeed know that I AM come into the earth to take my own in the grand ritual of the Resurrection and the Ascension.

Blessed hearts, I come with a simple call and a plan. And yet I remain mindful of the accelerated and complex requirements that the Law does place upon you as you invoke the Archangels to engage in Armageddon to defeat those who would devour souls in the earth.

Therefore, the Watch itself is for the opening of the heart that a door might exist where I might enter and thence release to the earth renewed Light and Presence, beloved, that you might understand that through you I desire—I, Jesus, your brother desire—to increase the Christ consciousness in the earth, that upon this foundation all other Servant-Sons of heaven and heavenly hosts might indeed build the new age, magnetize the little children and devour the Darkness abroad.

Blessed hearts, the greatest persecution of my life in this age is the persecution of my message and of those who speak the Truth in the true Teachings that I have given. Therefore, as in the days of Jeremiah, it is the false prophets of peace, the false shepherds of Christ,[16] who are the betrayers of my Word—those who speak of me and yet do not have my Presence in their hearts—it is their message and their example which do belie the true path of discipleship.

And, therefore, to remedy this I choose to enter in—at a renewed level of calling and dispensation from my Father—to a most intimate relationship with all who will not only call to me with their lips but will also enter my heart by embracing Saint Germain's teaching of the violet flame and acquaint themselves with my Mother Mary and not shun her. Further, I choose to enter into this relationship with all who will call upon Saint Michael the Archangel to defend both Church and State and to exorcise these domains of Alpha and Omega of all fallen angels who have come to steal away the best of the hearts of men.

Blessed ones, realize that this path of discipleship has its foundation in my earthly mission and its culmination in the fullness of my Teaching of the new age.

I would speak, then, of my Messenger Mark who did write down the Gospel bearing his name and reincarnate as my Messenger[17] in this age to found this organization from which you now abundantly receive our graces and gifts. The calling of this one, and his response in his aloneness as he did respond to my heart, has meant for all hosts of heaven an open door in this activity that is absolutely essential to the survival of the Lightbearers in this century.

I desire you to understand that my persecution is [the persecution of my Christhood is carried out in] the limitation of my Presence, my Word and Life wherever there are those who have limited my own to commune with me and to receive my progressive revelation by the Holy Spirit. Therefore, few there be who have retained the integrity of our message and brought forth in detail a divine mosaic of all that I have taught.

Therefore, beloved, as a single individual may be the key to unlock a door through which all humanity may pass, such being the case with my disciple Mark, so I say to you it is no less the case with yourself. It is the hour to decide if in your aloneness, all-oneness with me and the Father, you shall then be a key for millions of souls who will step through the door that you have opened.

Let it be, then, that you embrace my Teaching and that you recognize that the persecution of the sacred mysteries and those who bear them in this age does require that all who catch the spirit of the message here stated therefore band together and present themselves as a movement of Light that may not be set aside—whose members apart might have been put down or persecuted, but as one fervent heart, one Sacred Heart dedicated to my Mother through me, might then be a magnet to magnetize a world, to literally pull it up and away from the old magnetism of the lower levels of orthodoxy that truly have entombed me and left me upon the cross crucified and therefore left my sons and daughters and my children crucified on a cross of iron and steel and a Cain civilization with all of its burdens.

How can those who are truly Christians or followers of Christ in any world religion cease for a moment their concern and their activism to defend life that is unborn, life that must reincarnate that souls and a world might move on? How can any who know the true path sit back while the world may be devoured in flames of World Communism and by the betrayal of all those of the West who have made this possible?

Blessed hearts, this is why I have spoken of the fervor of the heart. For those who love do not stand by while youth and children are destroyed and civilizations crumble. They walk out from their pulpits and into the streets and they rescue life, not in a humanistic sense but because they have received that power from on high and, therefore, by the empowerment of the Trinity may act in our name to stand between a nation, a people, a family, a single soul and a returning karma too hard to bear.

This is why and to this end I call you to be my disciples in the most serious effort of all of your incarnations, to recognize that in thy flesh thou shalt see God and be my Self.[18] And only thus shall this world be endowed with a sufficiency and Presence [of my Christhood] in the physical to stay the hand of oncoming Darkness.

The lambs have been shorn not only of their identity but of a Teaching that could enable them to realize that identity. They have been turned aside by every false prophet, false pastor and false guru. Blessed hearts, for every vice there is, there is a false prophet that has embodied it. For every false teaching, whether in the economy or the arts or the sciences, there are the fallen ones who do embody it.

Let the Divine Art appear, let the Divine Wisdom and true God-Government. For this cause I have sent to you for your edification the Lords of the Seven Rays. They prepare you to be the fullness in manifestation of the Mystical Body of God.

Fear not, beloved. You have always believed that somewhere a chalice is filled with the elixir of eternal Life. I say to you, here is the chalice. Take, then, the Teaching. Take, then, that which we have set forth. For there does not come another and another to rewrite what we have said and spoken. It is sealed and it is finished.

So the lost Word is written, ready for you to bring to it the fire of a heart filled with love and therefore to quicken that Teaching in your body, in your members, in your chakras and to be the living Teaching and the living Word. To this calling I call you and to the service with the Archangels of the Cosmic Christ, to this calling—to expose the false doctrine that is leading nations astray, false doctrines of politics, false doctrines in the military and in the defense posture.

Let it be understood that every area of life must have my disciple standing there holding the key that does unlock the mystery of the Word and the Path whereby every branch of service and knowledge and endeavor might be once again endued with the flame of Gautama Buddha, Padma Sambhava, Sanat Kumara,

Lord Maitreya, my brothers, my friends, my cohorts of Light.

Heaven is filled with the witness of the glory not alone of my Coming but of His Appearing. Therefore, beloved, I seek no pre-eminence in the hierarchical chain of being, for I AM WHO I AM, I AM Alpha and Omega, the beginning and the ending. And my speaking is of the Eternal Logos, who I AM, who you also can be and are. For in the highest planes of thy being, O beloved, I, Jesus, affirm it: Thou art the living Christ!

Now I speak to your soul, sometimes fully awake and sometimes not so, and I implore you, my soul, my brides, come now and determine and desire with all of your desiring to be that Christ who thou art—here in flesh, here in form. This world hath need of thee. Thou dost occupy the heavens and the stars. Now occupy earth till I come in the full glory of the physical manifestation long attended by many. Occupy till I come, beloved.

And when you stand in my place, being my Self in form and embodying my Light, then I do come to you, Jesus, your Teacher, and I sponsor you, beloved. And you shall know a sponsorship never known before. For my legions of angels are ready and waiting for the ten thousand and more who shall hear me because I come pleading the cause of Saint Germain and world freedom.

Without this victory, then, of a spiritual and physical defense for the nations, there shall not be seen in the earth nor a new age, nor a new day. Therefore, act swiftly and make haste, for I have called. I have called.

So receive now this Communion served by my ministering servants. Do so in remembrance of Me and my Call. Take, eat, this is my Body which is broken for you. And drink ye all of it, for I, Jesus, offer you the full cup of my Life.

Remember, Victory does replace all toil and travail. And in the day of triumph, all struggle is no more.

I greet thee in the effulgent Light of thy Divine Reality.

[Communion served by ministering servants to 1200 gathered at the Penta Hotel to receive Jesus' words and blessing]

"The Summit Lighthouse Sheds Its Radiance O'er All the World to Manifest as Pearls of Wisdom." This dictation by **Jesus Christ** was **delivered** on **Sunday, October 4, 1987,** during the 4-day seminar held at the Penta Hotel in **New York City,** where Elizabeth Clare Prophet was stumping for Saint Germain's Coming Revolution in Higher Consciousness.

Note: ***"Watch With Me" Jesus' Vigil of the Hours*** released by Elizabeth Clare Prophet is a worldwide service of prayers, affirmations and hymns which in 1964 the Master called upon Keepers of the Flame to keep individually or in groups. The service was dictated by the Ascended Master Jesus Christ for the protection of the Christ consciousness in every son and daughter of God and in commemoration of the vigil the Master kept alone in the Garden of Gethsemane when he said: "Could ye not watch with me one hour?" Available in 44-page booklet, $2.00 (add $.60 for postage) and on 90-min. audiocassette B87096, $6.50 (add $.50 for postage). Special offer: $5.00 for cassette and booklet in quantities of 5 sets or more; additional booklets $20.00 a dozen. For notes to this Pearl, see Pearl 57, p. 506.

Vol. 30 No. 57 *Beloved Himalaya* *November 26, 1987*

Saint Germain Stumps New York

V

The Heart of Christ Is the Open Door

Discrimination of Reality and Unreality–Discernment of Spirits

Out of the blue lotus flame of my retreat in the Himalayas I AM come, Manu of Light, Lawgiver unto the nations, ancient as ancient as the one you know—Sanat Kumara.

I AM THAT I AM Himalaya, preordaining and preceding mountains bearing my name. In the white fire center of Being I draw sound, sound that is sounding now in your body temple and in your heart. Thus, out of light invoked, out of the sound pronounced and sung,[1] I weave a chalice of blue flame, that the Divine Mother might approach her own in the West and deliver unto them the disciplines of Padma Sambhava.

Therefore, let those who aspire unto the Buddhic mind know that the heart of Christ is the open door thereto. I AM of the ascended octaves, a sponsor of unascended masters, adepts and their chelas. Thus, those who have pursued a path of physical self-mastery, I say to you, receive now the gift of blue lotus flame of my heart, if indeed you have heart to receive it.

Some who have come out of the East unto the West showing physical prowess and the *siddhis*[2] have not yet internalized the living Word who is the Universal Christ. Thus, beloved, know that *siddhis* alone do not clear the path for the incarnate Word. Thus, seek to be one with avatara, incarnation of God, and then know that thy God in thee is the All-Power, as Above and below.

The approach of the heart is the open door unto the victory of the West. Let threefold flames be balanced. Let the knowing be the knower of Brahma, Vishnu and Shiva. Lo, in this Trinity of Light discover, O soul, layers of receptivity, creativity and light in the sacred centers. Each vortex [i.e., chakra], a spinning disc of light, can become a veritable sun. Thus, configurations of stars portraying the man show the seven planes and relate to the eye that all of cosmos is pitched and ready to receive the one who understands the ascending and descending of these seven planes by the love of the Mother and the Buddha, by the love of Shiva and Shakti.

Know, then, O hearts of fire, that we await all levels of balance to step through the veil through you also. With all thy getting, then, know the disc of Light, know the internalization of Alpha unto Omega, Omega unto Alpha.

The sealing of the dictations of the Ascended Masters of the Great White Brotherhood in New York does take place through this experience of offering the mantras to Light. Such a givingness does neutralize the misuse of the base chakra that is rampant and rife in the West.

Blessed hearts, only self-destruction and disintegration can come through the syncopated beat of rock music. Understand, then, that the key to the loss of the sacred fire of the spine is this very beat and the movement of that which I call anti-music and anti-Word. Therefore, know, O world, that that which seems as harmless as a dove in flight, as the simple pastime of youth is neither simple nor harmless nor is it a pastime but the consuming of time and space.[3]

Therefore, beloved, the power of the Word in mantra and the release of light does create an electromagnetic field. And when many so gather and when the tape recordings of the many who have gathered sounding the Word are played again and again, it does serve to reverse the downward spiral created by the anti-music and begin again to raise up the vision unto a people who have lost the way, who have forgot the land of Mu or Vaivasvata Manu, who no longer remember the Great Divine Director or Meru and Lake Titicaca. Yet all these names and the retreats of those on high have been known forever in the consciousness of the race.

See, then, how the destructive use of the sound of the AUM prevailing even in normal conversation when it is strident and raucous and unholy does surely, surely bring down the spirituality, the dignity and the love of a people.

Blessed hearts, the good people of earth need your care and carefulness. Therefore, see how you have displaced a vortex of darkness in this city and know that you can enjoy such a communion in the heart of the Buddha and the Mother through this use of sound and accomplish the purpose of raising the light within you, purifying your centers and restoring some balance to a city.

In the ancient temples of Lemuria, twelve surrounding the central altar, positioned in a wide circle across the vastness of that continent, there was the perpetual intoning of the Word in the frequency of the twelve gates of the City of Light.

Thus, beloved, when many left off their giving of the mantra and the intoning of the light, gradually one by one misusing the altars and then desecrating them and then turning them wholly to the abuses of fallen angels, there did come even the sinking of so great, great a land as Lemuria. No cataclysm and the record thereof is greater in the race memory than the going down of Mu midst flame and fire.

Blessed hearts, the Masters of the time did lead their chelas to distant shores. And as they stood and watched, so the grief was profound that with the sinking of the Motherland there was the going down of her retreats and the withdrawal of her Flame.

Thus the lowest point on Lemuria, beloved, was indeed the assassination of the incarnation of the Divine Mother in that hour. Realize that such a karma in the earth of the denial of the Mother, though enacted and executed by fallen angels, has remained a scar on the face of the earth for many thousands of years.

It is an age, then, for the balancing of that karma, the transmutation of the record and the bringing to judgment of the fallen ones who did desecrate Her temple and the temples of Her daughters, as well as the temples of themselves.

Blessed hearts, infamy upon infamy in perversion upon perversion unto the violation of the Holy Child did follow until the Darkness that covered the earth found no opening for Light.

Sometimes the evolutions of earth, or at least the Lightbearers, experience a consciousness of mourning and know not why. It is a grief for the loss of the Divine Mother and especially on the part of those who saw it coming but did stand by and not prevent it.

In this era, beloved, the nations of the earth have sought to raise up some element in their race memory of the Divine Mother's appearing, Her science, technology, art and culture. Therefore, in the fire ring[4] around the Pacific are to be found those remnants of Lemurian lifewaves and races, as well as the reincarnated Lemurians.

In this age we see the Motherland reappearing in the United States and in Mother Russia. Therefore, beloved, inasmuch as these nations share many lifewaves who were together in the Motherland, both bordering on that fire ring, it has been the object and the goal of the fallen angels who corrupted that very

Motherland and her shrines to also go to these nations to set one against the other, to raise up, then, a leadership committed not to the Divine Mother and Her Manchild but to atheism, materialism, intellectualism without the Spirit or the sacred fire of Mu.

Thus the children of Mu are divided by serpentine philosophies and conspirators conspiring not for the defense of Life but to win in their rivalries against one another. The fallen angels are competitors, then, to see who can be first in this and that, and they but use the children of Mu to achieve their ends.

O people of America, your counterparts in Mother Russia, having lived under a system heavy to be borne, are in some areas far more alert and awakened to the conspiracy of the dark ones than you are. Nevertheless, it is a burden grievous upon both nations. And all other nations in the earth are held in the balance of a confrontation not of Lightbearers but of warring systems and rival fallen ones.

Therefore, let the sound go forth! Let those of Light of every nation recognize that their leaders display no loyalties to the Flame of Mother or to this people, but rather are their loyalties to another, not from above but from beneath.[5] Let all Lightbearers of the earth know that Light itself has conspired to weave the garment of God as Mother and in weaving, to weave hearts together who are of Light.

Therefore, we say to you, defeat the common enemy that is within thy self and mind and body and soul, and you will then unite to defeat the enemy that is without. You cannot see clearly what is Light and Darkness, what is Real and Unreal. You have been caught up in their systems and their economic theories and their philosophies and you have not understood that only by the vision of the third eye does clarity come and do ages-old false loyalties fall from you in favor of absolute devotion unto the Universal Christ, whose Light is in all children of the Sun.

Blessed hearts, until you recognize that fallen ones and foul spirits long ago arrived upon this planet in the attempt to subjugate the children of the Sun, you will not understand confrontations East and West nor within your own backyard and neighborhoods.

Awake, I say! For I AM Himalaya. And I have attended your comings and your goings in and out of incarnation unto your causal body, unto the farthest depths of the astral and physical plane. I say to you, beloved, according to the path of initiation outlined in "The Hymn of the Pearl"[6] that is truly based upon an ancient Lemurian text known by Jesus, your evolutionary spiral has continued too long in and out of earth consciousness.

Blessed hearts, you have, as it were, a momentum on a sine wave that is not ascending. You have become accustomed to earth's merry-go-round and have forgot that the purpose of the sine wave is to get off the merry-go-round and to enter the spiral that leads as a coil of fire directly to the heart of Alpha and Omega.

Djwal Kul, come! Kuthumi, come! Morya, my Sons, come now and let them see thy threefold flame! Let them see what it means to embody Brahma, Vishnu, Shiva. Let them understand that the Trinity of the Far East did appear in the birth of the Cosmic Christ in Jesus[7] and does attend their own birth now unto the Spirit.

I, Himalaya, by the power of the blue lotus send a fire that has a cutting edge, to strip from you now a certain hardness and density that has accrued to your auras and physical bodies, to the mind and emotions. I send a flame. And the heart of the flame is the secret ray, and in the heart of the secret ray is the violet fire.

Thus, from Alpha and Omega we begin to accelerate that there might spin off your being and world the dross and the dredges that you have attracted to yourself by failing to spin the wheels of the chakras, [by failing] to settle yourselves and to not be moved by the agitation of the Western mind that queries, "Why should I sit and give my decrees? Why should I sit and recite and chant mantras? There is no purpose to this at all, no worth to it. Let us be done with it."

Blessed hearts, the carnal mind is the instrument of the negative force of the planet. The sooner you recognize this aggressive force and this suggestion that enters the mind whenever you are open to it through an absence of the Alpha/Omega balance, the sooner you will embark upon a greater Christ-mastery. So many in the West, in the pride of the mind, are convinced that all ideas are their own, all suggestions have originated within their own creativity.

Pray, then, for the gift of discernment of spirits.[8] Pray, then, to be taken to this temple of light, even the Temple of the Sun that once was physical on the continent of Atlantis.

Pray, then, to know Paul, the Venetian Master, and to understand him as an adept of the Ruby Ray, an initiate of the Holy Spirit and a Master of the art of Love. Read this one life and his dictations in the *Lords of the Seven Rays* and realize, beloved, that until you can exercise Christ-discrimination by the Presence of Brahma, Vishnu and Shiva in the heart through the tutelage of Morya, Kuthumi and Djwal Kul, you will not arrive at the point of the razor's edge.

Sharper than the two-edged sword is the necessity for the one who is to divide the way between the Real and the Unreal. This is the challenge of Life! This is the challenge of living in the cities of the earth. But the challenge does not disappear in the mountains or in nature. For wherever the carnal mind remains in control, wherever the individual has not risen in his soul to the very heart of the Divine Mind, there will the faltering on the Path be.

Thus, beloved, I extend my hand in helpfulness as you take up the calling to be disciples of Jesus Christ for this very purpose of knowing at all times the difference between the Christ Mind and the lower mind, and when you know it not, to recognize that you have need of a Teacher, an Ascended Master, your own Holy Christ Self, who will teach you what is Real and Unreal.

Mistake not the power of the fallen ones for the power of God. Practice does perfect the soul's knowing. Yet these two powers side by side [the Real and the Unreal] thou must be acquainted with, and through a process of trial and error and experience come to know unmistakably the vibration that does tell all. Thus, whether the inner voice be the living Christ within you or yet the remnant of thine own mind or a false-hierarchy impostor whose words resemble the living Truth, thou must arrive at the hour of that discrimination, for thy life and the life of many shall depend upon it.

Blessed hearts, you have but to look in the arena of politics, the media and defense to realize how people are pulled and swayed right and left. With absolute conviction they believe the lie that was brought into Maitreya's Mystery School on Lemuria, the lies of the serpents, those fallen angels of superior intellect and knowledge who were able to confound even the most blessed of our representatives of the Sun who were not yet ascended and therefore fell prey to their promises and to their magnification of maya.

Blessed hearts, these theories have been around a long time. The fallen ones do not have an infinite repertoire but they do not need it, for humanity is swayed to the right and to the left as easily as with a smile or a clucking or the Lie itself.

Precious hearts, pray for Truth. Give the mantra to Cyclopea,[9] the All-Seeing Eye of God, that you might have inner sight and know in your heart and soul when the archdeceivers are selling you, as it were, a bill of goods only to harness your Light and [the energies of your] chakras to their own projects and purposes. Thus, in this hour, without vision the people do not know who are the leaders of Light and who are not. This is a most dangerous circumstance.

Therefore, I, Himalaya, come to seal you from the base [chakra] unto the crown [chakra] that the light might be retained and raised and that you might pray continually through the rosary to Mother Mary, through the call to Cyclopea, through the ever-present help of Pallas Athena for the vision to know—to know the Truth that shall set you free[10] and to know what is Real.

Therefore, I, Himalaya, send forth piercing blue fire throughout this nation, stripping the garments of the accusers of Christ and his brethren, stripping them, then, that they might no longer deceive a once mighty people.

O America, return to the stature of the Divine Woman and Her Christ Child! Return to the heart of Mother Mary and the Mother of Mu.

Therefore, all light released in this place is sealed in your causal bodies. And I commend you, Keepers of the Flame, to a vigil for Saint Germain in these remaining hours. Forget not that he has kept the flame for you until you should arrive at the point of destiny.

AUM

Thus, a blue flame, which is a blue flame lotus thoughtform over the city, does now contain the momentum of the prayers, decrees, offerings and dictations of this class. These shall be released in answer to your call for all needs whatsoever.

I have determined to tarry in this city to reinforce Lightbearers new and old on the Path. I have come to be a guiding light whereby you may see the pitfall before you step into it. And should you step into it, my angels tarry to pull you from it and set you on the straight path of soul perfectionment. Make use, then, of our Presence for a fortnight. Then see how you can sustain it ongoing in the heart of Elohim of the First Ray.

Seven seals of blue flame lotus upon you, each one, seven chakras enfolded in light.

It has been a good mission and a victory for you, the Brotherhood, and this city. Weary not in well doing, for wherever the Keepers of the Flame gather *we are there.*

With the sign of the entire Spirit of the Great White Brotherhood, I seal you now unto the hour of your Ascension in the Light.

"The Summit Lighthouse Sheds Its Radiance O'er All the World to Manifest as Pearls of Wisdom."

This dictation by **Himalaya** was **delivered** on **Sunday, October 4, 1987,** during the 4-day seminar held at the Penta Hotel in **New York City,** where Elizabeth Clare Prophet was stumping for Saint Germain's Coming Revolution in Higher Consciousness. (**1**) Prior to Himalaya's dictation, the Messenger led the congregation in singing *bhajans,* i.e., devotional songs to the Principles and Persons of the Godhead in the Eastern tradition, and in Buddhist and *bija,* i.e., seed syllable, mantras to the Divine Mother for the purification, protection and expansion of the chakras. (**2**) See p. 160. (**3**) See Sean C. Prophet, "Rock and Roll in America, Part I: Heavy Metal: Abuse of God-Power," pp. 327–68. The three-part exposé on "Rock and Roll in America," delivered by Sean C. Prophet July 2, 1987, is available on audiocassette. Part I, "Heavy Metal: Abuse of God-Power," on 2 audiocassettes, A87069, 2 hrs. 24 mins., $13.00 (add $.80 for postage). Part II, "Political Rock: Abuse of God-Wisdom," on 60-min. audiocassette B87071, $6.50 (add $.50 for postage). Part III, "Techno-Rock: Abuse of God-Love," on 90-min. audiocassette B87072, $6.50 (add $.50 for postage). (**4**) **Ring of Fire:** a string or belt of active volcanoes which encircles the Pacific Ocean at or near the margins of the continents of North and South America, Asia and Australia. (**5**) John 8:23. (**6**) See p. 494 and n. 14 below. (**7**) Bearing the Light of the Trinity, the three kings, or wise men, Caspar, Balthazar and Melchior, charted the time and place of Jesus' birth by astrology and the magnet of the heart: "We have seen his star in the East and are come to worship him"—El Morya bore the flame of the Father, Brahma; Kuthumi, that of the Son, Vishnu; Djwal Kul that of the Holy Spirit, Shiva. The Trinity manifest in the threefold flame of the heart of the Christ Child was the lodestone which magnetized them through their own hearts' Light. They were representatives of the Three-in-One. Jesus *was* the Three-in-One incarnate. (**8**) For teachings on the gift of discernment of spirits and other gifts, see *Lords of the Seven Rays,* Book One, pp. 123, 133–34, 142–43. (**9**) "Beloved Cyclopea Beholder of Perfection," no. 61 in *Mantras of the Ascended Masters for the Initiation of the Chakras,* p. 17, $2.00; on 82-min. audiocassette B85137, $6.50 (add $.50 for postage). (**10**) John 8:32.

Notes from Pearl No. 56 by Jesus Christ:

(**1**) Rev. 21:2–27; 22:1–7. (**2**) On Jesus' retreat and his tutoring of the apostle Paul, see *Lords of the Seven Rays,* Book One, pp. 183–88, 199–203, 225. (**3**) Matt. 5:14. (**4**) Jer. 23:5, 6; 33:15, 16. (**5**) **The Maha Chohan,** the "Great Lord" who presides over the Seven Chohans of the Rays, holds the office in the hierarchy of the Great White Brotherhood of Representative of the Holy Spirit. See *Lords of the Seven Rays,* Book One, pp. 13, 15–18; Book Two, pp. 277–97; and *Saint Germain On Alchemy,* pp. 423–24. (**6**) John 8:31. (**7**) Eccles. 1:9. (**8**) James 1:12; Rev. 2:10. (**9**) I John 5:6–8. (**10**) Prov. 4:7. (**11**) John 15:12. (**12**) Ps. 91:1. (**13**) John 15:13; 10:17; Rom. 16:4; I John 3:16. (**14**) **"The Hymn of the Pearl."** Prior to the dictation the Messenger delivered a lecture on the Lost Years and the Lost Teachings of Jesus in which she read the Gnostic poem "The Hymn of the Pearl" and the commentary on it from *Gnostic Scriptures Interpreted,* by G. A. Gaskell. The poem, thought to have been composed by the apostle Thomas, portrays the soul's descent from the highest spiritual plane into the planes of illusion with loss of memory of her origin. There she faces the trial and tribulation of the lower life until she responds to the Call from Home, which eventuates in her ascent culminating in her union with the Divine. (**15**) John 20:17. (**16**) **False prophets of peace and false shepherds of Christ.** Matt. 15:8; Jer. 6:13, 14; 14:13–15; 23:1, 2, 9–40; 27:9, 10, 14, 15; 28; 29:8, 9, 21–32. (**17**) The Messenger Mark L. Prophet who founded The Summit Lighthouse in 1958, called by El Morya to deliver the Lost Teachings of Jesus and the prophecy of Saint Germain as they would be dictated to him by the Ascended Masters. (**18**) Job 19:26; John 14:12; Rom. 8:14–17, 29; Gal. 4:6, 7; I John 3:2.

Pearls of Wisdom®
published by The Summit Lighthouse

Vol. 30 No. 58 | *Beloved Archangel Zadkiel* | *November 27, 1987*

Saint Germain Stumps America

1
My Gift of the Violet Flame
I Come to Anchor a Pillar of Violet Flame

Hail, O Legions of the Sun! Hail, Sons and Daughters of God!

I AM Zadkiel of the Seventh Ray and I have come to this city and to this area of our Eastern seaboard to anchor a living pillar of violet flame, that the children of the Sun might know the LORD and be free. In the fullness of your God Presence I bid you welcome to my heart and be seated.

We the Seven Archangels are crisscrossing the nations of the earth, and we expand the Great Causal Body of 'God with us'* to contain the planetary evolutions. Understand, O ye ancient souls of Light who were with the Ancient of Days in the beginning, that which I would bring to your remembrance: the Law compels you, the sons and daughters of Light in the earth, to invoke the living flame of God and to direct that flame into action in various trouble spots around the world—not neglecting thine own temple of light which must become the temple of the living God.

Lo, I AM THAT I AM. I AM one with the I AM Presence of all Life and therefore one with your I AM Presence, for God is one.

Thus, beloved, the call does compel the answer: When you invoke the light of our violet flame legions, know that millions of angels of the Seventh Ray—who serve Saint Germain and his twin flame, Portia, the Goddess of Justice, and God at the Elohimic level personified as Arcturus and Victoria in the Seventh Ray—do answer your call with us, for we are one. And we are one for the fire of world transmutation. And we see the rise, the fall, and the ebb of the tide of world karma daily as Keepers of the Flame

*"God with us" is from the Hebrew *Emmanuel*

worldwide do invoke the violet flame and therefore mitigate the effects of that mass karma.

I bid you enter into the heart and love of the Archangels, kept from mankind by those desiring not to see us play a pivotal role in human history. Yet we have never forsaken those who are in pursuit of the living Word, no matter what their time or history, destiny, race or affiliation.

We serve all who serve the Light.* I said, beloved, *We serve all who serve the Light!* And if there be Darkness, put it behind thee. The shadow must be behind thee when thou dost face the I AM Presence and this symbolical rendering of it as the Chart, focus of every altar.

Thus, we call our Messenger to raise this altar of an ancient people[1]—[the central focus of the I AM Presence flanked by that of] Saint Germain embodying the spirit of Samuel, prophet in Israel, [and of] Jesus himself embodying the eternal path of *Christos*. And therefore, the Archangels Gabriel and Michael, also the abiding presence at this altar of God ministering unto the seed of Light descended through Abraham, do gather their legions for the quickening of the threefold flame.

Let the divine spark that is thine inheritance,[2] O sons and daughters of God, expand now. I say, let it expand! For I, Zadkiel, in addition to placing a pillar of violet flame in this place, do blaze the violet flame through your heart chakra for the unfolding of the heart.

The unfolding of the heart is the unfolding of the wisdom of the Mind of God, for out of the wisdom of the heart does proceed all things. Know, then, the Mind of God that is available unto you by the Seven Archangels. Know that there is a healing power of the Seven Archangels and that you may invoke it by the call.

Therefore, we may not intercede in the affairs of men unless the prayer go forth. Thus, you must understand that this law is based on our Father/Mother God's recognition of your free will, by which, having demanded and received it, you did go forth to dwell in these several octaves. By free will you have and take dominion over the earth. And unless you ask God to intercede, He, by His own decree, will not and does not break that covenant of free will and enter in.

Thus, invite us and be not forgetful to entertain strangers, for thereby some have indeed entertained angels unawares,[3] including yourself, beloved; for some of you have descended from the angelic octaves to come to earth to be physicians and ministering servants unto life, to defend the poor, the minorities and

*We serve all who serve the Christ consciousness, the emanation of the Mind of God personified in the individual Holy Christ Self.

those who have a creative inner heart and yet may not have the majority vote in any area of life.

Thus, understand that angels have taken embodiment on earth, angels who serve the LORD God in his children and who desired to be near to them when they did come under such condemnation and persecution of the fallen angels who were cast out of heaven into earth by Archangel Michael.[4] And therefore, Archangel Michael does stand with the children of my people in these latter days.[5]

And therefore, let there be a Great Salvation. Let there be a great *self-elevation* of the Light within you from the base unto the crown [chakras]. For as the Light does increase in your body temple and the third eye does open, you will see Archangels and Masters of Light as we stand and speak through our Messenger.

Thus, it [this Light and the divine vision it carries] is a gift of the Holy Spirit, beloved. And thus, it is a mantle that by our Word not only is a Message delivered to your heart but also is a Light transferred into this octave. For we may use an instrument in full conscious, waking awareness, and therefore not as channeling[6] but as the direct Word spoken. Believe me, beloved, this is the manner in which the blessed ones of Israel and the Lord Christ did receive the speaking of Yahweh [YHVH], the speaking of the I AM THAT I AM.

Therefore, we the angels of the LORD's Presence, we who do stand in the Presence of God,[7] do deliver that Presence to all those who will gather and understand that heaven has never ceased to speak to its own in the earth, that there is no separation between heaven and earth, that indeed the LORD God may speak through and to whomsoever He may choose. And God does determine and decide this day to speak to you in your heart. Therefore, know the LORD, and know that the voice of the LORD within you is the Son of God manifest even in your own beloved Holy Christ Self.

The miracle of angels is no miracle at all. We have been from the beginning created out of Elohim, out of the LORD God Almighty to minister unto his children. And therefore, it is altogether natural that you should summon our angels for the protection in daily life of small things and great, for we serve on each of the seven rays and we serve on each of the seven chakras, and our ministrations are all-encompassing.

We are the servants of the LORD God Almighty to his own!

Therefore, we say, know the LORD! Return to the oneness of thy origin in Being! And know, beloved, that in this hour of world history thou art called to rise to a new degree of divine awareness, to a new challenge—a challenge which can be met if you will heed the word of true prophecy in your midst.

We the Archangels did initiate Isaiah and Jeremiah. We did send them forth. And as the LORD God spoke through them, we were the very form of that LORD God who does descend in a Spirit and does use the Presence of Archangels to convey His prophecy.

Blessed ones, we have been from the beginning and we have known you from the beginning. We have known you from everlasting to everlasting. We were there when the morning stars sang together. We were there when the Father/Mother Elohim did form you out of the white fire ovoid of Being. We attended thy birth.

Is it not understandable that we love you with the most profound love of cosmos, that our hearts are one with your own and that we desire to commune with you daily and hourly to give you the courage, the wisdom, and the fearlessness to face that which is coming upon the earth, to look at it with a fierceness of the eye of the Divine Mother and to say to that proud wave of descending karma: "Thus far and no farther! Thou shalt not pass!"

Blessed hearts, say that fiat into the very teeth of the testy problems that arise daily, preventing you from fulfilling your reason for being. Shirk not, then, the calling of God. For those who play in this hour, those who spend themselves in every sort of dissipation, I tell you, they will rue the day, for their very presence in the earth, absent the Light of the LORD God, is one more vacuum that cannot be filled by the living Word and therefore [their non-alignment, non-integration with the Light is] a further weakening in the bastions of Light that are always held up by the people of Light in embodiment.

Now I send forth to you that Light of the violet flame and my angels do attend you. Blessed are ye who have heard the Call and come to this Presence [of an Archangel and an Archangel's Messenger] that you might physically be filled as a chalice of Light, as a cup from which many may drink.

Blessed hearts, key in your receiving of Light is the retaining of that Light. Therefore, I counsel you, take the decrees and call forth protection from the heart of Archangel Michael from this moment hence and see that you guard your harmony. For in the loss of harmony is your loss of Light and even the strength of your physical form and mind. Therefore, beware the tempters who come to you through the very dearest of souls and friends, and then in your reaction [to an untoward situation] you lose your harmony and dissipate the Light.

We cannot forever be filling your cups (as chakras) and your temple with the Light of the God Presence only to come again and find them empty. We must have souls who understand that the building of the kingdom of God within,[8] *the consciousness of God within you,* is the day-by-day, day-by-day increase of Light until the whole body is full of Light,[9] until the whole nation is full of Light, until all people throughout the earth may bend the knee before the living Word and recognize all heavenly hosts and armies of the Ancient of Days (known in the Far East as Sanat Kumara and Karttikeya) and will know truly that the LORD is come to defeat the fallen angels, the archdeceivers who would wreck this economy, who would wreck this nation and this planetary body with their nuclear weapons!

Blessed hearts, rise up in one shout of righteous indignation across the earth and invoke the power of God for the Lightbearers of the world to unite and defeat this World Darkness coming upon a people!

Blessed hearts, this nation or any nation was never founded by God to have the people oppressed and put down and denied the fruits of their labors and the Light of their hearts. O blessed ones, some have become so accustomed to the limitations of the systems under which they live that they do not even know what to do with full freedom when they have it.

And this brings me to the subject of entering the Aquarian age that is the age of freedom and alchemical transformation when all things are possible unto the soul that does rise to serve the LORD God. Blessed ones, it is an age for acceleration of transmutation of personal karma and acceleration of realization of the Christ potential.

Therefore, know this, beloved, that many have abused freedom in this hour, many have abused the freedom of light and sound and consciousness, even the freedom guaranteed in this nation. Realize, then, that the sacred freedom that is yours is the free will to serve the Light, to live in the Light, and to become the Light—to be harmless toward any part of Life and to serve all those who remain in the ignorance of self-deceit and of the ignoring of the Law.

Blessed hearts, freedom must not be taken and misused and misappropriated as a power over this or that one. Therefore, I, Zadkiel, send forth a Light for the purging of those who know not that they have either been victimized or have victimized others in a psychological manner of control and possession and manipulation, whether of children or of others.

Let everyone *feel,* then, the shower of violet flame, be cleansed by it and know that the LORD thy God liveth. Oh, how Moses saw that flame and exclaimed, "Our God is a consuming fire!"[10] Know and meditate upon this conception of God as the sacred fire and then understand that God consumes all that is unreal about you.

If you would be free, then have courage to see Reality. Prove me now herewith, saith the LORD. Call unto me to show you the vision of the prophecy given, to show you the vision of heaven and of hell and of those things coming upon the earth. If you call and still call, therefore accept the answer and accept the message from wherever it may come.

Blessed hearts, God desires you to see but you have not desired to see. You have shut your ears, you have closed your eyes, you have not listened to the inner voice or followed your hunches. You have not followed those instantaneous awarenesses but rather not desired to know that which may be unpleasant or calamitous.

These things can be faced. For the LORD God has vowed, I shall not send to thee any temptation which thou art not able to deal with.* Therefore, know that that which is potential of Darkness can be swallowed up in Light. But the open door to Light in the physical octave is you, is all Life that is God, who does inhabit your heart, is the power of the spoken Word to protest, to demonstrate, to decree. Pray at the altar, then go forth and take your stand in all areas where life is threatened. You are the open door to safety and salvation in the earth.

Those who place that open door and that salvation in one Ascended Master [such as the Ascended Master Jesus Christ] and neglect the teaching of all the Ascended Masters—that those in embodiment are also called to [be the instruments of God and of His Christ] to deliver an age—will rue the day [they denied the Christ potential in themselves and in His little ones] when they find themselves on the other side and without bodies to return to and thus unable finally to render that last service that might have been—which was truly the final karmic requirement of their lifestreams.

Begin, then, at the beginning. Take my gift of the violet flame. Take it as angels give you the maximum you can retain in this hour. Then multiply it daily. It is as a lodestone. Truly it is as a leaven for the leavening of all consciousness.

I AM Zadkiel! And I place this pillar of fire in this place because some have already understood and some will understand, beloved. And for that reason earth does continue as a schoolroom for initiates of the sacred fire. Happy are ye when ye become the disciples of the living God and his Word within you.

In the name of the entire Spirit of the Great White Brotherhood, I salute you and bid you adieu.

*"God is faithful, who will not suffer you to be tempted above that ye are able; but will with the temptation also make a way to escape, that ye may be able to bear it." I Cor. 10:13.

This dictation was **delivered October 6, 1987,** at the Park Plaza Hotel, **New Haven, Connecticut.** For notes, see p. 518.

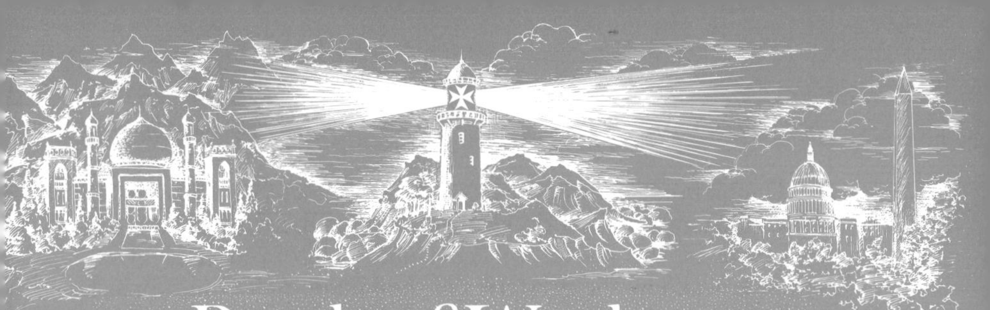

Pearls of Wisdom®
published by The Summit Lighthouse

Vol. 30 No. 59 *Beloved Archangel Chamuel* *November 28, 1987*

Saint Germain Stumps America

2

Rise Up to Defend Borders of Consciousness!

Ruby Ray Angels Form a Border of Light around America

Ho! Everyone that thirsteth, come ye to the waters. Drink of the water of Life freely.

Lo, I AM THAT I AM the heart of an Archangel, Chamuel by name. Thus, I bow to the Light of God within you and I welcome you to my heart, O people of Great Love. I desire to discourse with you this evening. Therefore, be seated in my Love Ray.

Understand the meaning of Divine Love that must, because it loves, bind every force of anti-Love that would devour my little ones.

Therefore, I AM the Archangel of Love which stand in the Presence of God! And I deliver to earth a mandate of Light: Thou shalt have no other love before thee save the Love of Almighty God within thee that does press through [the seven chakras] and expand all seven planes of being.

As thou desirest to be infilled with Love, so expect the purging sacred fire of Love's own Ruby Ray. Welcome the Christ and Buddha, the Prophet and Moses! Welcome Zarathustra! And welcome thy Higher Self! For lo! a [manifestation of] God is born this day and the realization of that God is dawning within you.

Therefore, beloved, when we began, Charity and I, to expand the flame of Divine Love several infinities ago (as I would express it), lo, the expansion of the dawn of Love became a quickening of all Life that is God. And we entered a Life expansive and beyond all realms known to you in this hour even by the most powerful lens of telescope.

Understand, beloved hearts, that beings of Great Love such as the cherubim of God do keep the way of the Tree of Life and the Flame of the ark of the covenant.[1] Unto you it is given, therefore, to know the mysteries of the kingdom of God,[2] for it is the age. And a little leaven of Light[3] does open and expand the awareness of a trinity of fire within.

Know, then, that as the power of Shiva does move in the earth and as the spinning wheel of Light containing the dance of Shiva (as the Holy Spirit) does turn, so there is an activating, so there is a chemicalization. And, beloved, if you would have Light, then you must surrender something of the fat of human selfishness. For Divine Love is lean and wise and pure and able to of these tyrants make thrones of Victory unto thyself.

Beware, then. Beware the tempter and the archdeceivers. Beware all that assails the Love tryst of the children of the Light in the heart of the Divine Mother.

Lo, we have sponsored the root races in the earth. We have sponsored your souls. We were there in the beginning when the Alpha unto the Omega did send forth the sounding of the Word—and the heart of thyself, lo, it was formed! And God did hold in his hand thy heart, thy threefold flame, thy endowment of the gift of eternality, that one day thou shouldst be immortal forever.

The going out and the return to His heart of thy soul is a saga, beloved, and thou knowest. For the long cycles apart from the heart of the Great Central Sun have taken their toll upon you. But many, if not all, rejoice in the coming of the Divine Son appearing, even the Sun of thine own God Presence.

Therefore, beloved, let the Ruby Ray angels form a living, angelic border of light round this nation, round North America. See them opening the third eye. And in your visualization see standing tall, fifty feet in height, angels of the sacred fire of my bands, angels of the Ruby Ray of Divine Love.

Thus, let Love now be the defense of freedom as those who have the say in the governments of the nations invoke the angelic hosts of Light and demand the action of the sacred fire as mandate, as common sense, as spiritual law and as the defeat of the foe, the antichrists of East and West. For surely it is written that they should come, not one but many, beloved.[4] Therefore, know that the hour of the prophecy of the apostles of Christ is nigh and be not deceived.

In a moment and in the night there shall be the descent again of the star Wormwood. Know, then, the meaning of that star of Chernobyl[5] as the descent of a judgment upon those fallen angels cast down to the earth by my cohort Archangel Michael, who have taken embodiment and yet are aliens in your midst, whose agenda is to take the Light and in the process destroy a world. Know them, beloved, and call unto the Lord Christ with The Judgment Call[6] that is given; for it is written, as it is spoken, by Jesus.

At his name all angels bend the knee.[7] And note well that this reverence of the Son of God, the bending of the knee before the God in you (whether or not you have realized that God), is the ritual of all angelic hosts of Light. For the one God in all—embodied or not, personified or in Spirit, the one Universal Light, the one Spirit of the LORD God Almighty—is the focal point of our adoration as we cry:

Holy, Holy, Holy, LORD God Almighty—Thou art Holy, as Above, so below, in manifestation in man, in woman and in child!

Therefore, we say *Holiness unto the LORD!*[8] Let the holiness of the LORD in you promote your own reverence and sense of the sanctity of life and the sacredness of your own.

If God were in the earth in a tiny babe in this hour, if an avatara had been born, would you agree that that God incarnate ought to be protected by heaven above and earth beneath? I should say the answer ought to be "Yea, Lord, let us attend His appearing!" Well, beloved, look to thy heart, for the divine spark in thee is God.

Value thy life as God's life. Value the life of the unborn as God's life appearing and increasing. Let the value be placed once again on Life with a capital *L*—Life that is God everywhere. This sense of the universality of the Being of God within you, beloved, this sense does draw all factors of civilization into proportion and co-measurement with the Infinite.

Therefore, hear the mandate of God, the God of Love unto a people: Secure yourselves in light, in devotion, in fealty to the Divine Presence. Forsake all idolatry. Forsake all self-indulgence. And know that Death and Hell stalk *the earth* and therefore must be defeated by those *in the earth.* Go forth to protect innocent children! Go forth to protect all Life! And see that that protection does extend itself to every facet of human existence.

And let a land consecrated by Saint Germain be sealed! Let it be sealed! Let it be sealed! And let the mind be defended. Let the heart be defended! Let the soul be defended! And let the physical platform of evolution, the temple which is the temple of the living God be defended! Let the land, the air, the sea be defended of all impurity and pollution.

O beloved, I declare now, legions of angels of cosmic purity descend by Elohim Astrea and Purity. And they come for the purging of the four quadrants of the earth and for thy deliverance. Therefore, receive them and obey the voice of the LORD within thee.

Let there be the awakening! For we the Archangels crisscross the land and we speak to a mighty people, an ancient people of old. For long ago, fifty thousand years and more in the Sahara Desert, which was once a great civilization, you, beloved, were in embodiment. You saw and lived in a great golden age. You, America, knew the way of Light. And yet, by taking for granted that Light, you became vulnerable to that foreign prince who did invade.

And therefore, there was a withdrawal of Saint Germain and of other luminaries who had led that civilization, after a great banquet was held announcing exactly what the form of takeover would be.[9] Nevertheless, though all heard of that conspiracy and all knew that "the Dark One cometh," yet with the withdrawal of those who kept the flame of that civilization to higher octaves the people fell prey to the sinister force of the Dark Ones. Thus, fallen angels have attempted to intrude themselves from time immemorial.

Blessed hearts, we say of this planet earth, a crossroads of cosmic evolution, It is enough! It is enough! Lo, they entered the garden of Maitreya the Buddha. Lo, they did turn aside twin flames—your own and yourself, beloved—to a way of duality. Thus enmeshed, you have lost track of your own twin flame.

We, Chamuel and Charity, Archangels of Love, are pledged to reunite you, but you must understand that the way made plain is first to unite with your own God Presence. And in that 'Polestar of Being', in that magnet of sacred fire, you shall become a blazing sun to draw unto yourself the divine half of the Great Whole of which you are that component.

Blessed ones of Light, know, then, that though the word has gone forth from many—from the heart of the Blessed Mother, from the heart of prophets and sages, even from the heart of this Messenger—though many have seen it coming, yet we say, there is not a mobilization of forces.

Therefore, we release the Ruby Ray into this nation!

Blessed ones, take heed. For it is a piercing ray and it is also a ray of judgment which did topple the Tower of Babel, which was a monolith of human pride and idolatry. And it was built by Nimrod, embodied fallen angel. And therefore, we the Archangels did release the Third Ray of Divine Love for consuming that force of anti-Love and preventing the proliferation of Evil.

Blessed hearts, there is a time when we may act; there is a

time when we may not. And that space provided is for your action. Therefore, be men and women of destiny, recognizing that heaven and earth must mesh (the etheric and the physical octaves) that a golden age might saturate the very dust beneath your feet and make it once again crystal light and a transparency of earth body.

In you is the convergence of suns. In your heart is the answer and out of it are the issues of all life[10] before you this day. Let the Ruby Ray act, then! Let it act to bind those who have so deceived this nation under God, who have so deceived the people through their false prophets and false teachers. Let it be known, therefore, that the living Word in you is the sure sign of the victory of Life in you.

Men and women of Israel, of the seed of the Ancient of Days, you who are the Christed ones, hear me, then, in all races and people! The hour is come for the raising up of the threefold flame. The hour is come for the return to the one God. Let all of your dalliance in materialism be set aside this night.

The sword of an Archangel stands to cut you free!

Accept me if you will, blessed hearts. Not a hair of your head shall be touched if you do not allow it. But I tell you, there cometh after me one day, in the Day of [Karmic] Reckoning, the LORD's emissary of the avenging sword. In that Day of Reckoning which is known as the Day of Vengeance of our God[11] there will not be a choice.

Thus, to gladly give up the very cause and core of one's karmic burden at the offering of an Archangel is wisdom indeed. But to attend [wait for] the day of the descent of thine own karma, understand, beloved, it is as it was taught by the Lord Christ: Let those who will, cast themselves on the Rock of Christ for the old mold to be broken. For when the Rock does come, it will grind that one who is out of alignment and grind him to powder.[12]

Therefore, beloved, thou canst not escape time and space or a Matter cosmos. And if this be not thy God-mastery, then humble thyself in thy conceit of supposed superior wisdom. If you have not devised a scheme to climb out of the box of Matter and soar with angels, then bend the knee before thy God and pray for intercession by those who are of the infinite cycles of Life. For this is where you shall be. This is the calling to which you are called, to become the fullness of the Law of the One.

Therefore, I, Chamuel, raise the ruby sword. And I say, angels of my bands and of the Holy Spirit, let the ruby sword cut them free from all that would hinder their divine progression in the cosmic spheres, from all that would hinder them from laying the foundation of absolute God-defense in every quadrant of Matter beginning here and now!

Lo! it is done. Lo, I have spoken it!

Sent by God to you, I AM a Messenger from the Holy of Holies. Hearken unto me, O America, O earth, O people who know I AM THAT I AM! Rise up to defend your borders—and borders of consciousness!

The circle of Light is complete. My angels have completed their positioning on the borders of this nation and North America. Therefore, know, they shall keep the vigil of Life. The question they would ask you, beloved, is "Will you keep the vigil of the Flame of Life with them?" ["Yes!"]

I bow to the God Flame in you and I withdraw to higher octaves.

"The Summit Lighthouse Sheds Its Radiance O'er All the World to Manifest as Pearls of Wisdom." This dictation by **Archangel Chamuel** was **delivered** by Elizabeth Clare Prophet on **Wednesday, October 7, 1987,** at the Park Plaza Castle, **Boston, Massachusetts,** where she was stumping for Saint Germain's Coming Revolution in Higher Consciousness. (**1**) **Cherubim.** Gen. 3:24; Exod. 25:18–22; Num. 7:89; I Kings 8:6, 7; Heb. 9:4, 5. (**2**) Matt. 13:11. (**3**) Matt. 13:33. (**4**) I John 2:18, 22; 4:3; II John 7. (**5**) **Wormwood and Chernobyl.** Rev. 8:10, 11. *Chernobyl* means "wormwood" in Ukrainian. For an in-depth analysis of the Chernobyl nuclear disaster as a prophecy of karma in the Bible, in the stars, and in Nostradamus, see *Saint Germain On Prophecy,* Book Two, pp. 152–99. (**6**) See "The Judgment Call 'They Shall Not Pass!'" by Jesus Christ, no. 45 in *Heart, Head, and Hand Decrees: Meditations, Mantras, Prayers and Decrees for the Expansion of the Threefold Flame within the Heart,* p. 34, $1.25 (add $.25 postage) $12 per dozen; multiple dozens at $10 each (add $.80 postage for first dozen, $.30 each additional dozen). (**7**) Phil. 2:10. (**8**) **Holiness unto the Lord!** Exod. 28:36; 39:30; Zech. 14:20. See Elizabeth Clare Prophet, February 15, 1986, "Christ the High Priest," 1986 *Pearls of Wisdom,* vol. 29, no. 29, pp. 279–88; *The Lost Teachings of Jesus II,* pp. 335–37. (**9**) On the takeover by the visiting prince, see *Saint Germain On Prophecy,* Book One, pp. 3–7. (**10**) Prov. 4:23. (**11**) Isa. 34; 61:2; 63:4–6; Jer. 46:10. (**12**) Matt. 21:42–44; Luke 20:17, 18.

Notes from Pearl No. 58 by Archangel Zadkiel:
(**1**) **Altar of an ancient people.** You can also set up this altar of the Lightbearers of the world in a special place in your home. The central focus of the I AM Presence is flanked by the Sindelar portraits of Saint Germain on the right and Jesus Christ on the left—all three available in a number of sizes including a folding stand-up portable altar. Two or more candles, a piece of natural quartz crystal, some amethyst crystal, a crystal chalice and the representative "Books of the Law" *(Climb the Highest Mountain, The Lost Years of Jesus, The Lost Teachings of Jesus I* and *II)* complete your focus. Depending on the size and elaboration of these, you can add fresh or silk flowers, a monstrance and selected statuary of the saints of East and West. Be careful not to clutter it. (**2**) Rom. 4:13–18; 8:14–17; Gal. 3:29; 4:1–7; Heb. 6:13–17; 11:8–12; James 2:5. (**3**) Heb. 13:2. (**4**) Rev. 12:7–9. (**5**) Dan. 12:1. (**6**) **Channeling** is a mental process in which the individual who is channeling partially or totally sets aside waking consciousness to act as a vehicle through which disembodied spirits in the astral realm or beings from outer space can communicate. The Ascended Masters teach that the only legitimate communion is with the ascended saints of the Great White Brotherhood and that psychic channeling is dangerous because it seriously depletes the channel, as well as those present, of "ectoplasm" (thought to produce materialization or telekinesis)—the vital energy in the aura which provides a natural protective sheath around the astral body of the soul. (**7**) Luke 1:19. (**8**) Luke 17:21. (**9**) Matt. 6:22; Luke 11:34–36. (**10**) Deut. 4:24; 9:3; Heb. 12:29.

Vol. 30 No. 60 *Beloved Archangel Michael* *November 29, 1987*

Saint Germain Stumps America

3

The Awakenment Must Come to All

Let the Nation Rally to a Spiritual Defense

Hearts cry out to the living God. Therefore He has sent me to you. I AM Michael Archangel, Captain of the LORD's hosts. Welcome to my heart.

My heart expanding through this vessel does touch you tangibly now with the fire of Love of the First Ray beings of Light. I AM sent, therefore, in answer to the call of those of earth, of America, those whose hearts cry out in fear and torment in the night, yet who upon awakening know not of their agony.

Thus, beloved, I come to establish and secure spiritual protection, for this is my office and calling. By your envelopment with the blue flame which you call forth from the heart of God, you also can secure a physical protection. Blessed ones, the densification of light to afford ultimate and complete physical protection by light is possible, but not without a heavy concentration of prayer, meditation and dynamic decree.

Blessed hearts, cosmic beings step aside when the fallen angels unleash nuclear holocaust. Know, then, that the physical protection must be demanded by yourselves from those sources and forces that are assigned to that office in the nations. Know that we establish that protection unto you so far as the Great Law will allow us to do. But your responsibility to take dominion in the earth does require you to establish a foundation for the securing of these blessings of Liberty unto yourselves and to your posterity[1] as it is written.

Thus, beloved, know that with the coming of the legions of

Light, there must be a quickening and an awakening. Therefore, I, Michael, send through this nation the blue lightning of the awakenment that must come to all. For better or for worse, this nation must rally to a spiritual defense long neglected, else any physical defense shall not prevail. The very atoms and cells of being and of military might must be charged with the Holy Spirit, that that might not injure life but protect it only. This is the mission of a Christ nation, and that is the destiny of this land.

Understand, then, that many false prophets have gone forth with what I would term "ridiculous" solutions to the equation of nuclear war, such as pronouncements, they know not what—pronouncements that the Great Law or the powers that be will never allow it—not understanding the fundamental principle that people themselves have already allowed war by the war in their bellies, the war in their members,[2] the war with one another. And thus, the people feed the engines of war of the fallen angels. Blame yourselves, beloved. You have given them free rein with your tax dollars. You have given them a complete and full timetable for engaging a nuclear first strike against this country.

Know, then, that spacecraft will not be there to collect you on the hillsides in that hour. And it is folly to so suppose and to assign yourselves to their saviouring. Blessed hearts, go not here and go not there but look within. Establish the [inner] kingdom* and then raise up a [physical] fortress of Light.

Can you look again into the eyes of a single child or the children of a nation and turn your backs on this question of establishing protection within the economy, protection in the field of health, protection to youth in the question of drugs and some very harmful satanic rock music?

Blessed hearts, the waves of darkness come through many channels to rape the chakras of the people. Defense is the primary necessity to survive that which comes out of the bowels of Death and Hell in this hour.

Thus, to prevent nuclear war one must shore up the bastions of a national awareness of the God who dwells midst His people through angels and heavenly hosts—yes, through the Ascended Masters and through elemental life. This nation and all Lightbearers of the earth are surrounded with teeming hosts who are ready to deliver. Yet scarce a prayer is offered by some in an entire lifetime.

Prayer is indeed the key. Will a moment of silence or a minute or five assuage the grief of a nation? Blessed hearts, should the direst of prophecy appear, know that it will take the penance of

*the God consciousness of Reality

many generations and millennia to restore a planet to usefulness as a foundation for spiritual and physical evolution.

The folly of believing that the Soviets will not begin a war is a folly akin to other false psychic predictions. You have heard the testimony of many sources. Now feel the vibration of an Archangel who does freely move in and out of all areas of international intrigue.

I tell you, beloved, there are madmen in this world and they are sprinkled in every nation, including this one. Therefore, the madmen of this nation are the pacifists who do not understand that the right arm of the LORD is ready to defend those who help themselves. And the madmen of the Soviet Union are the aggressors, paranoid, believing many lies that they themselves have twice told as twice-told tales. These, fearing to be devoured, thus put themselves in a corner where they reason in their irrationality that they must wage war to survive.

The psychology of these two leaderships, beloved, is incomprehensible to many Lightbearers and children of the Sun. I advise you to begin to understand by taking up a study of the darkness and the strangeness of the power elite and the moneyed interests who have no God, no heart, no soul or spirit and therefore tremble and quake lest they lose the support of the people.

And the people of God have again gone after their idolaters and their idols. Thus, they are encouraged to worship fallen angels in every area of life, and they do so readily. Thus, the disease that Moses himself challenged in his people is again midst this people. Whether it is in money or power or the slaying of one's children [in abortion], beloved, the law of karma does act for every form of idolatry.

Thus, we read the handwriting not only on the wall but upon a scroll of Life. That scroll does come from the Keeper of the Scrolls, and it is a reading of that which will surely come to pass unless there is an about-face and a quickening, a return to first principles and an understanding that to defend the light of Christ in these little ones is the supreme responsibility of parents and citizens of a world.

Make no mistake, beloved, we the Archangels are ready to answer your call, to multiply it ten thousand times ten thousand. Our release in this city is for a mighty protection, reinforcing that given by Zadkiel and Chamuel in Connecticut and Massachusetts.

Therefore, see how we are concerned even regarding the prophecies given by Saint Germain not only to Nostradamus but to other lesser-known seers. The concern, then, is for the rising again of Atlantis and Atlantean ways in the last days—ways of war, genetic engineering, misuse of the science of sound and rhythm and of the crystal of Life itself. Blessed ones, as these things return and are allowed to run rampant on the earth, including the unleashing of the very power of the nucleus of the atom, know that the consequences for the abuse of Matter and of Spirit within Matter must be the same.

Therefore, you have heard some reports of spacecraft in the East. Know that there are benign beings in space and there are aliens who are not benign but truly malevolent ones who have come to destroy and not to raise up.

Why are mankind so trusting of visitors from space whom they know not and who encroach upon their way of life, who have even limited the expansion of their [mankind's] intelligence by genetic design to see that they do not remember the Ancient of Days or the Archangels or their tie to their I AM Presence?

Is it not curious that throughout scripture men of God have communed with angels and yet in this hour their forgetfulness is almost complete? I tell you, it is an interference that is conscious and willing on the part of those from space who have ever determined to subjugate the race [—and the "I AM" Race, if they could].

Thus, understand, where the Spirit of the Lord is, where the prophecy does go forth and where the Archangels gather, so there is also the gathering of the antithesis. And this antithesis of the Universal Christ, you must understand, is existent in alien gods, the very ones who were cast out of the etheric octave by our bands and cast down into earth bodies, into incarnation.

The history of the descent of these ones is known. Thus, they are not free but bound to earth bodies. And therefore, they take their technology and their science, stolen from the Ancient of Days and the Sons of God, to wreak havoc in the physical octave—their sole determination to see to it that the sons of God in embodiment should not rise and take dominion and learn to invoke the judgment and call to us for the binding of these fallen ones.

Be not deceived, beloved, for our God is not mocked by them. What they sow, they shall reap.[3] Our God bides His time that His children might return to Him and give allegiance to the one God and, forsaking all others, enter in to that perfect communion wherein the soul does become the bride of Christ.

Thus, the extension [of grace before the Day of Karmic Retribution] is not given to the evildoer but to the Lightbearer. Yet it is the evildoer who takes advantage of the extension while the Lightbearers sleep! Is this not a calamity of great magnitude and proportion, beloved? Therefore, we have sent our Messenger again to preach our Word and to deliver it and in an unprecedented manner we have determined to speak through her to audiences who would listen.

Know, then, that it was the Archangels who spoke through the prophets of Israel saying, "Thus saith the LORD." For we stand in the Presence of God. We embody the I AM THAT I AM. Archangels *are* his Presence in this world of form.

Know, then, that we speak through this prophet to warn a nation. Those who cannot hear our Word, who cannot stand the Light, let them know that one day they will cry out both for the Word and for the Light of God to deliver them.

Blessed ones, this is an hour when deliverance can come! My legions are brilliant in shining armour, white and blue. Their radiance and their aura shall be revealed to you in sleep, for otherwise you are not able to see with chakras not yet liberated and cleansed, purified and expanded. But if you pursue the Path, it shall come to pass that you shall see the hosts of the Lord even as they have been seen of old (as the eyes of Elisha's servant were opened)—all the armies of heaven encamped upon the hillsides[4] waiting for the cry of those in embodiment—waiting for the call that would empower the angels to come and help and lead the people to the victory.

Blessed hearts, Armageddon is promised and all wait for it. I tell you, Armageddon is here! It is being waged against your youth and children. Know, then, that many souls of Light born to serve the Great Cause of Freedom are being limited in their expression of that divine spark for the conditions they find in this nation and in every nation on earth. Let a people rise up, then, and be sensitive to the hearts of children. Let them be sensitive to those rumblings that may come upon a world too soon.

I AM Michael. My angels form additional cordons of light on these coasts and a stabilization of the blue flame in the earth, *holding the balance, holding the balance, holding the balance,* beloved, as we pray the LORD God to release the dispensation for the quickening of hearts who must do better if they and the planet are to survive.

Blessed hearts, survival is questionable. Though physical bodies be retained, if souls be destroyed, what profit is there? What excuse can we give our God for the perpetuation of an evolution that does glorify the god of lust and deny the living Christ?

Therefore, my flaming sword does remagnetize the light of the spine within you unto the LORD God. Receive, then, our assistance. And let there be a continuing prayer vigil that does call to us that we might do more than presently allowed to step through the veil and lead this nation to the proper alignment with her divine plan.

Beloved, I AM sealing this city and the Keepers of the Flame. I seal Washington. And I shall return for a greater sealing at Thanksgiving that there might be now till then a vigil, such as the world has not seen, to the Seven Archangels for their deliverance.

As you are our hope, beloved, so I say to you truly and in modesty, the hope of the world lies in God's power released through the Archangels, Elohim and saints all. Joy be with you in the Lord in your heart. Joy be with you in the name of Mary. Joy be unto you through the violet flame of Saint Germain.

I AM Michael. We stand guard.

Legions of Light, come now! Strip these souls of all that the Great Law will allow, that they might find renewed polarization to the inner will of God made known to them by the inner Christ.

I seal you with the sign of our retreat. Call to us, then, to take you to Banff where you might receive a strengthening and a vision for action. We are angels of action. We move with men, women and children of action. We are prime movers and prime activators. Call upon us and you will see.

Bowing to the Light of Christ in you, I AM the servant of the LORD God.

"The Summit Lighthouse Sheds Its Radiance O'er All the World to Manifest as Pearls of Wisdom."
This dictation by **Archangel Michael** was **delivered** by Elizabeth Clare Prophet on **October 11, 1987** (after midnight) at the Lord Baltimore Clarion Hotel, **Baltimore, Maryland,** where she was stumping for Saint Germain's Coming Revolution in Higher Consciousness. (**1**) **Preamble to the Constitution.** "We the people of the United States, in order to form a more perfect union, establish justice, insure domestic tranquillity, provide for the common defense, promote the general welfare, and secure the blessings of liberty to ourselves and our posterity, do ordain and establish this Constitution for the United States of America" (1787). (**2**) Rom. 7:15–23. (**3**) Gal. 6:7. (**4**) II Kings 6:15–17.
Worship of angels forbidden by the Roman Church. The Roman Catholic Church has repeatedly banned the worship of angels not named in its officially approved scriptures. The Synod of Laodicea in A.D. 343 decreed that only the names of the Archangels Michael, Gabriel, and Raphael could be used in prayers and forbade Catholics to worship angels privately outside their churches. The worship of angels not named in scripture was again banned by a Roman synod convoked under Pope Zachary in 745 and by Church councils in the ninth and fifteenth centuries. In 1950 Pope Pius XII in his encyclical *Human Genesis* reaffirmed that Catholics were only allowed to use the names of Michael, Gabriel, and Raphael. In 1964 when Vatican II revised the liturgy of the mass, it eliminated Pope Leo XIII's prayer to Archangel Michael, which had been said at the end of each mass since 1886, because it did not refer to the Eucharist or the communion of Christ with his disciples. (See p. 508, par. 1)

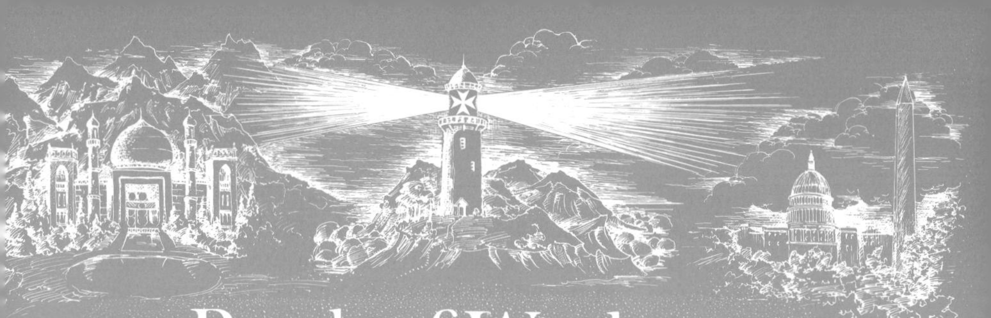

Pearls of Wisdom®

published by The Summit Lighthouse

Vol. 30 No. 61 *Beloved Lady Master Nada* *November 30, 1987*

Saint Germain Stumps America

4

God in You Is Greater

I AM Come Bearing a Flame of Love

Eternal Light of the Creator, I AM come into this city bearing a Flame of Love which I have kept for thee, beloved, ten thousand years. This may seem to you to be a bit of something unheard of. But I assure you that I AM Nada and that the Love of my heart is a flame I have kept for aeons. I have known you ten thousand years ago and beyond in other continents and times.

I extend a hand cupped, holding this Love Flame, which as a Light of the eternal *Christos* is come to ignite the people of this city where Love also has an ancient focus that is Liberty itself. For what is Liberty but Love in action in the liberation of the soul.

My service with Jesus has taken me to the calling of God to be Lord of the Sixth Ray. I desire through you and my angels unto you to give to you an action of a sealing—even a mending—of the area of the solar-plexus chakra.[1] For, blessed hearts, by violence of the violent ones who take heaven by force[2] (that is, who take the light of the chakras by such measures), there have occurred in the people of God rents in the garment so that they are no longer able to hold the Light in this most blessed chakra, the [solar-plexus] chakra where God is desiring in you to be more of Himself.

Receive, then, unto your hearts an increment of Love to increase the compassion and truly the Wisdom of the heart that does consider all things dispassionately—with wisdom, with true observation and a wait-and-see attitude. Therefore, beloved, those who hold the Peace at the place of the belly of the Buddha, those who send Peace to a world may build walls of Light, of Peace.

Elohim of the Sixth Ray, I summon you in the name of Jesus Christ. Come to the city. Raise up souls of Light. Let opportunity given now be perfected in a wise discipleship of Love and Truth—internal knowing and the will to be and to be that Light in action.

For the city and a much broader area, I AM come from the Temple of the Sun. Therefore, the Lords of Karma, seven in number,[3] would have me warn you of karma—both personal and planetary, as has been our subject this evening,* and yet assure you that the blessings from on high are always adequate to meet the challenge *when* the word to the wise is sufficient to cause some to move from their moorings and to know that in time of crisis there are better places to be than in the teeming cities of life or on the coasts where cataclysm threatens. This should never disrupt your service in keeping the Flame nor in giving the call to reverse the tide of Darkness and to accelerate the oncoming tide of Light.

Know, then, that we prophesy not danger but counsel you to entertain angels, to sing to and love angels who come to you as messengers to tell you when and where to be.

Life in these times is only so perilous as is your absence of true inner Peace. Let the quality of Peace, then, be a power unto you, a power as of the seven seas. Let the power of the water[4] of the Divine Mother be unto you truly the raising up of your soul unto Life.

Legions of angels of the Christ Mass and the nativity of Jesus, come now to this city. Let there be an intense communion preparing for His coming into every heart. Let ancient records of Atlantis be cleared by violet flame angels to give greater stability to this landed area and to the hearts of those who defend Light and hold it on high as a torch of Liberty.

Our coming to you, beloved, is always in answer to the heart's call. I AM the servant of the Light within you, your willing sister and teacher. I invite you, then, to my retreat over New England,[5] as well as to Jesus' retreat over Arabia.

You must understand that as you fall asleep at night, you can make the call to your I AM Presence to send you angel attendants who will guide your soul in your etheric body to the inner planes where the schools of the Brotherhood are, where the temples of Light are. Here you learn, sitting at the feet of the great Masters who supply you with all necessary inner knowledge of your life, those things which must come to pass and your very personal role of being the hand of God in action to care for his little ones, to heal and especially to invoke the Light that does dispel and mitigate the burdens of a planet.

I come to ask again, with Meru, for a Vigil for Youth for the

*the subject of the Messenger's Stump delivered from the heart of Saint Germain

protection and true education of the children and youth in all nations. This is so very dear to my heart. For I see the future that they must occupy and I see them ill equipped for the task.

As to the government of this nation, then, there are many false prophets and betrayers of the people within it. They have come to a polished rhetoric, yet to a hollowness. They have mastered the art of deceit, of talking but saying nothing or promising and never fulfilling. It is an hour to look for true sons of God to represent the Christ of all people and all ages in every area of government.

How long need the people of earth be long suffering before the betrayers in office who squander their light and money and do not care for them or even provide for their basic defense?

Blessed hearts, it is a travesty unknown to the angels and a profound sadness to the Ascended Master Saint Germain. You have heard of the Madonnas and the tears that flow from the Blessed Virgin's statues.[6] Know, then, that the tear in the eye of Saint Germain, the tear in the eye of Jesus has not left.[7] For a people with so great an opportunity have been so betrayed by fallen angels posing as angels of Light.[8]

Take, then, the Messenger's counsel to give the call to Cyclopea to open your vision. This name of Elohim of God has naught to do with myths of gods but is merely a name for the 'Third-Eye One', for the one whose vision is in the All-Seeing Eye of God. We give counsel in the call, for it is you who must offer it that the Divine Appearing may manifest in you. This is an act of your own free will.

The blessed Mother Mary does intercede. Receive her and heed her call. For the daily rosary does raise up in you the shield of the Mother Ray, the sacred fire blazing upon your heart's altar. With spiritual protection you then have a base for a physical protection that can endure.

Hearts of Light, I counsel and counsel again. Only those in embodiment can take the reins of government and demand a basic protection of this nation. If it come not, the enemy will steal in and steal away even the treasure of your heart.

Know, then, beloved, that this is indeed a cycle of great darkness in this nation's government. Let the Lightbearers of America hold up a candle in "A Perpetual Vigil of the Hours,"[9] calling unto the hosts of the LORD, the Archangels themselves, to wage war and bind the servants of corruption, the archdeceivers and the spoilers in the earth.

By the Ruby Ray of the Archangels Chamuel and Charity you can see a dividing of the way as the Lord himself does descend to exorcise a planet of those who would bring about a war to the destruction of a way of life.

Blessed hearts, never submit to the inevitable, else it will come. But know that *the Light of God in you is greater* and able to face the calamity of the morrow and the coming years. In all ways, rise in the Spirit of the Resurrection.

I call to the angels of the Resurrection, of the Holy City that John beheld descending out of heaven from God.[10] Let this Holy City be unto you the promise of the Place Prepared and the key to your building a foundation in the earth that shall carry forward to a golden age and put behind you the threatening woes and the darkness in the earth.

The Lord Christ above this city can now be seen [with the inner eye], such a large figure of grace, blessing, enlightening. Blessed ones, Jesus does sing to you a hymn. It is a hymn of comfort and consolation, an inner joy that stands and still stands in the face of its absence in the earth. Angels' choirs sing with him now. A million voices flood the skies. In etheric octaves the chorusing becomes a vessel for a descent of light and blessing.

May all of this city of Philadelphia receive renewed heart to fulfill their fiery destiny and to take their stand for the children—the children of all the world entrusted to their care. For all people must know that the children of the earth are our joint responsibility. Let us make a planet pure and safe for their development and realization of the Eternal Logos. For, beloved, great souls come to earth escorted by angels to serve on this planet. Happy are ye who have seen the vision and will lay the foundation for their coming.

I, Nada, servant of Christ in you, healer by God's grace, welcome you to my heart of hearts. May we share a conscious friendship forever? Will you welcome me to your home and heart, beloved? ["Yes!"]

Only say the name Nada and I shall be with you always in the Love of my Lord.

So I withdraw from you, beloved, and join Him now. When you go to rest this night, call to angels that you might be a part of this angelic choir with Him.

"The Summit Lighthouse Sheds Its Radiance O'er All the World to Manifest as Pearls of Wisdom."
This dictation by the **Lady Master Nada** was **delivered** by Elizabeth Clare Prophet on **Monday, October 12, 1987,** at the Penn Tower Hotel, **Philadelphia, Pennsylvania,** where she was stumping for Saint Germain's Coming Revolution in Higher Consciousness. For notes to this Pearl, see pp. 545–46.

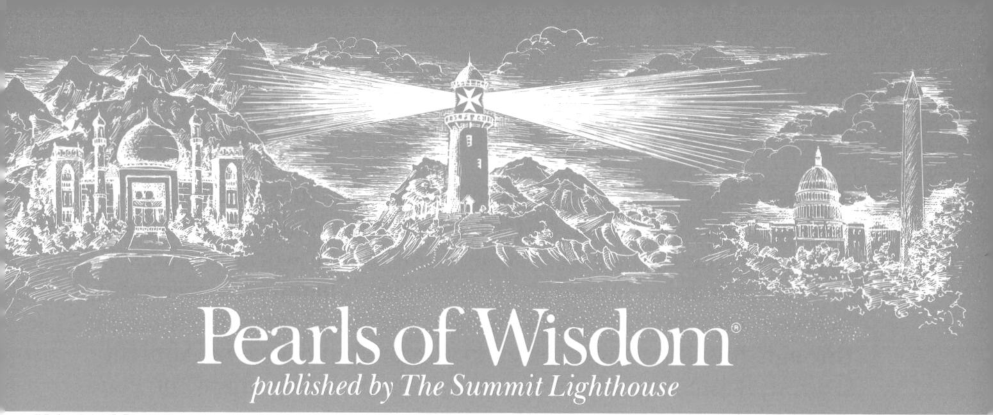

Vol. 30 No. 62 — *Beloved Listening Angel* — *December 1, 1987*

Saint Germain Stumps America

5

Strength in the Union of the I AM THAT I AM

You Can Place the Capstone on the Pyramid

I AM the Listening Angel of God. Therefore, in my heart, beloved, is the sorrow of mourning—of souls who mourn even beneath the threshold of outer awareness.

Youth and age alike across this nation, sensitive to those things that are oncoming in the planetary cycles of karma, yet not knowing, not able to articulate what they sense, do enter, then, the era of the dark night of the soul[1] without understanding the path [of personal Christhood unto God]. And on the surface they know no cause of their depression.

There is a malaise in this land and throughout the earth that can only increase unless the soul fully awakened in Christ (by his shield and armour secure and protected[2]) may enter the Universal Mind and embark upon a course of action to remove the sources of world condemnation.

I am known as Listening Angel. What is not generally known is that millions of angels of my bands engage in a service of listening to the hearts and souls, the prayers and murmurings of all people of earth. These supplications are then carried by my angels to the throne of God, that our Father/Mother may know and understand the burden of the people as they attempt, sometimes haltingly, to phrase a prayer, not knowing they are in need of deliverance or even the meaning of deliverance itself.

Blessed hearts, the disease of the psyche, which is of the soul itself, is most troublesome, for it is beyond the defining of the outer mind or the experts. When the soul of a people is in lamentation for that which is coming, it is an hour when those who have the courage and awareness to face the future boldly in God must appear on the horizon as true shepherds, true world teachers.

Knowledge is indeed a responsibility. Therefore, understand, beloved, by your choosing you have chosen to hear our message through this Messenger. Now, in the profound love of Almighty God, I, Listening Angel (by way of answering many of your prayers), must tell you that you, then, enter the courts of accountability for taking action vis-à-vis those things you have heard and understood in your hearts this evening.

Therefore, a people and so great a nation may rise in gratitude in this hour to all heavenly sponsors, to Saint Germain, to Mother Liberty, to all who have nurtured the souls of a people for ten thousand times ten thousand years.

Know, then, beloved, that it is an hour when you can place the capstone on the pyramid of America that has been building. Let your dedication be to the full flowering of the All-Seeing Eye of God within you, as well as to the wisdom of the heart and a definition of action and purpose.

As it has been said, in time of emergency we act to stay the hand of the greater calamity. Therefore, which of the horsemen shall arrive at the gate first? Or shall they all arrive at once for the staying of the first? Blessed hearts, pray indeed that your flight be not in winter.[3] Pray, indeed, that all of the calamities of the Four Horsemen[4] do not come at once.

Therefore, to defeat the woes [i.e., karma] in the economy and the woes of threatening war ought to be the supreme joy and determination of those of you who know you are embodied angels who volunteered to quit the courts of heaven, not by defiance against the Almighty as the rebellious angels did but because in the compassion of your hearts you desired to go forth to save that which was lost to the Divine Awareness—for the false teachers, the fallen angels, had turned them aside.

Therefore, there is a "peculiar" people in the earth, as it is written in scripture,[5] peculiar, for they have embodied from angelic realms but to serve, but to defend, but to embody a spirit of Love and Freedom and Hope and Healing.

Therefore, to contact those who are able to take decisive action and to move others may be your calling. Above all, whatever the direction of your response to the Truth you have heard, I pray that you shall pray and pray daily for the victory of the Divine Mother in your midst. The blessed Mother Mary is everywhere in the earth with all those who speak her blessed name and give the mantra simply, *In the Immaculate Heart of Mary I trust.*

Blessed ones, there is truly a stitch in time that saves nine. Many have won in the very last moments of the sands of the hourglass. You are not defeated except by your digressions, your diversions, your depressions.

Blessed ones, the hosts of the Lord demand attention to youth that they be not lost. Hear our cry, our plea and our marching. For we can also be heard in the land[6] and you can know the soft presence of an angel wing caressing your cheek and tenderly touching a child in tears. Blessed hearts, look up and see the numberless numbers of your intercessors. But give the word and we can release Light sufficient to this Victory.

Your representatives in the economy and the government, in the [department of] defense are accountable to you, to the Christ of your heart, to Almighty God. Who shall make them accountable if you do not speak, if you do not write, if you do not march?

If we could, we should long ago have done it for you, but the Great Law does not allow us. And therefore, you see, it is your hour. It is your life, and this is a stage on which you have played many parts. The role to be outplayed this day is that of liberator of the people of our God.

You can begin at the beginning. You can do something, for many courses have been presented to you. Above all, let those who see the vision and who equate with the vibration of the message know that all of your strength is in your Union. And the unity of Lightbearers can defeat all planetary Darkness.

Can we not agree upon a foundation of oneness in our hearts, oneness with Saint Germain, who has given his life for every one of you and all across the nation at one time or another?

Can we not agree that the violet flame is the universal solvent of planetary disease, discord and death?

And can we not agree to give our hearts fifteen minutes daily in dynamic violet-flame decrees to this cause of world transmutation?

Sometimes little promises are best kept rather than plans of grandiose schemes that never materialize. Sometimes in simple acts of devotion and ritual the soul mounts up to increase and multiply that very devotion and ritual and service. Thus, exercise your wings of light, O ye of many lands, and discover the strength of those divine pinions!

Wherefore art thou sent to a world? But to watch it disintegrate before your eyes? I say nay! I have heard the cries of a people and the prayers of a single child's heart. Know, then,

O beloved, that *in the Union of the I AM THAT I AM you can take dominion in the earth.*

I salute you in the name of the Seven Archangels. I commend you to your own counsel and your own means.

Pray, then, that Victory and his legions surround you and that you arrive at the Gate when your course is done. For the loving Father/Mother God wait to receive you as conquering heroes, victors in the earth and of the Spirit.

Feed the sheep of the Saviour. Take care of my little ones.

By the Universal Light, I, Listening Angel, greet you. An increment of fire from the altar of heaven is apportioned unto you by seraphim who attend you now. Receive, then, the blessing of Saint Germain[7] as you absorb that fire and give praise to the holy name of God and thanksgiving to his angelic hosts.

My kiss upon your forehead until you know the fullness of the bliss of God.

"The Summit Lighthouse Sheds Its Radiance O'er All the World to Manifest as Pearls of Wisdom."
This dictation by **Listening Angel** was **delivered** by Elizabeth Clare Prophet on **October 14, 1987** (after midnight) at the Westin William Penn Hotel, **Pittsburgh, Pennsylvania,** where she was stumping for Saint Germain's Coming Revolution in Higher Consciousness. (**1**) **The dark night of the soul** is the test of the soul's encounter with the return of personal karma, which, if she has not kept her lamps (chakras) trimmed with Light, may eclipse the Light (Christ consciousness) of the soul and therefore its discipleship under the Son of God. It precedes the **dark night of the Spirit,** the supreme test of Christhood, when the soul is, as it were, cut off from the I AM Presence and must survive solely on the Light (Christ consciousness) garnered in the heart, while holding the balance for planetary karma. For the Messengers' teachings on the dark night, including readings and commentary on the writings of St. John of the Cross, the sixteenth-century mystic who described these mystical experiences in his works "The Ascent of Mount Carmel," and "The Dark Night," see Elizabeth Clare Prophet, *Living Flame of Love,* 8-audiocassette album, 12½ hrs., A85044, $50.00 (add $1.30 for postage); "The Dark Night of the Soul," on two 60-min. audiocassettes, MTG7412, MTF7413, $13.00 (add $.80 for postage); *Mysteries of the Holy Grail,* pp. 173, 368–69. See also "The Ascent of Mount Carmel" and "The Dark Night," in *The Collected Works of St. John of the Cross,* trans. Kieran Kavanaugh and Otilio Rodriguez (Washington, D.C.: ICS Publications, 1979), pp. 66–389. (**2**) "Wherefore take unto you the whole armour of God, that ye may be able to withstand in the evil day, and having done all, to stand. Stand therefore, having your loins girt about with truth, and having on the breastplate of righteousness; and your feet shod with the preparation of the gospel of peace; above all, taking the shield of faith, wherewith ye shall be able to quench all the fiery darts of the wicked. And take the helmet of salvation, and the sword of the Spirit, which is the word of God." Eph. 6:13–17. (**3**) Matt. 24:20, 21; Mark 13:18, 19. (**4**) Rev. 6:1–8; "Halloween Prophecy 1987" by Elizabeth Clare Prophet, see p. 482. (**5**) Exod. 19:5, 6; Deut. 14:2; 26:18, 19; Titus 2:14; I Pet. 2:9. (**6**) See pp. 443, 444, 445. (**7**) **Emerald matrix blessing.** At the conclusion of every Stump message, those attending passed by the Messenger for Saint Germain's transfer of light by the "emerald matrix" as she touched their third eye with an emerald crystal. This is the "sealing of the servants of God in their foreheads" prophesied in Revelation 7.

Vol. 30 No. 63 *Beloved Archangel Uriel* *December 2, 1987*

Saint Germain Stumps America

6

In Defense of the People of God

The Good Karma of the I AM Race—Defend Your Right to Be

Ho! Light descend! I AM Archangel Uriel and I salute the living Christ Jesus and the living heart of God in you.

Beloved who live under the canopy of the stars and know the grace of Freedom, I enter this territory and I say to all within the distance of a thousand miles radiating from this point that the light that is upon you as opportunity comes by the blessing of good karma to a seed of Light drawn to this area and nation.

Thus, beloved, the blessings of Liberty bestowed are merited and earned by the good of many lifetimes. Thus, in that cosmic bank that is called the causal body where all good works and treasure is stored, you may know that tremendous blessings of Light are available for you to extend to life here below.

Let us speak, then, of the good karma of this I AM Race—these "Americans." Let us speak, then, of the good works done in recent centuries and in many lifetimes of the past. Thus be it known that the glory of life and the very sponsorship of Jesus Christ and Saint Germain of this nation to be a place of Christed[1] ones does descend from ancient times and is manifest through your very own sacred labor.

Understand the equation, then. You have light in your causal body, yet someone else would take this light and squander it. It is as though you had an inheritance and knew not of it and suddenly found one day that you had had this inheritance, but before its discovery thieves came in and stole it from you and you were bereft of it.

So it is in this age of the sons and daughters of God who

descended to earth to serve as wayshowers to the people. A spiritual inheritance is thine.

Many today have squandered their material inheritance for a number of reasons. But, blessed ones, do you see that it is truly because of your good karma that you ought to be and should be protected in this age for a spiritual path leading unto a golden age that even the Ascended Masters and heavenly hosts have prepared, beginning as a nucleus in this nation and spiraling to incorporate the entire earth?

Thus, beloved, that which is deserved, that which is earned sometimes goes unclaimed, undefended. And this is exactly the situation you find yourselves in today. Because it is decreed that spiritual and physical defense is yours (decreed by Almighty God and your previous good works), you must therefore defend that inheritance and defend that divine decree and affirm it yourselves. You must fight for your right to be. Every world saviour or saviour nation that has done so has endured to extend the blessings of its civilization to all other nations.

Those civilizations who took for granted their golden ages, their immortality, their prosperity, those who were not on guard and did not correctly perceive the psychology of invading forces or of the enemy, these have all gone the way of the fallen ones, fallen civilizations, and even lost continents. Those who study history know scenario upon scenario of those lovers of God who nestled in spiritual ways and practices yet did not understand the spiritual disciplines of self-defense.[2]

We the Archangels and our hosts do therefore stand guard, and we do deflect and turn back to the evildoer his malintent. Thus none is hurt and the evildoer is stripped of his power to wreak evil in the earth. Some have studied the martial arts and understand this principle of spiritual defense. The technology which Saint Germain has inspired upon Aquarian-age scientists in this nation enables America to accomplish just this in this hour, to turn back an aggressive force with injury to none and the preservation of life to all.

Blessed hearts, is it not best to confine the enemy or those of evil intent by stripping them of their power to do evil rather than to consider ways of incarcerating individuals in vast prison houses or to destroy them by untimely death? All of these things do interfere with the Divine Law, yet science itself is an instrument of law. Ought it not to be used, then, until child-man does graduate to the level of adeptship and can perform some of the feats of a Christ or a Himalayan adept?

Thus, it is wise, beloved, to count one's heritage and to understand the spoilers in the earth and the archdeceivers. They have manipulated the lifeblood of the people in the currency manipulations. Therefore, "In God We Trust" can no longer be said of a money system but only of the sacred hearts and sacred labor of the people themselves. Is it any wonder, beloved, that in the earth there are those whose motives run counter to the commonweal? Know, then, your history, a cosmic history, and know your angelology.

For I tell you that I was a participant in the casting out of heaven of the angels that did make war against God and his Sons.[3] Therefore, they were cast into earthly bodies and have roamed this earth seeking to devour[4] the children of the Light for vast aeons.

The mask they wear is a likeness to human form and therefore they go undetected. They are masters of deceit and they have programmed mankind to support them, to vote for them, to believe their philosophies and to actually fight their battles of rivalry for them; therefore we see brother against brother, slaying one another in defense of the isms and the strategies of fallen angels who are but rivals in a game of chess to control a planet.

Let the people of America and Mother Russia awake! Let the people of Europe awake! Let the seed of Light awake and know that the masses of mankind must depend on some who know better and will do better in answer to the call of the Blessed Virgin. Let it be said, then, that the fiber, the will, the heart and the spirit of this people is able to save not alone a nation but an entire planet from nuclear holocaust.

I AM an Archangel and I embody that fire of the Lord Christ for the binding of the force of Antichrist. When you summon Archangel Uriel you invoke in your defense legions and legions upon legions of Lightbearers, angelic hosts. We march with the Faithful and True and the Ancient of Days. We march with the hosts of the LORD who are ready to liberate those who will help themselves.

The call will do much. It shall compel our intercession. But your action and your demand upon your representatives in Church and State for the protection of your spiritual and human rights must be immediate!

You can no longer trust those who tell you that all is well, whether in the economy or in the defense of the nation or in the government itself. You must understand that these are the hours when captains and kings and mighty men will fall.[5] And when they fall, beloved, it is well that you are positioned out of the way of their tumble and the mountains of karma that shall fall upon them for the persecution and the oppression of the people they have meted out.

Thus the judgment comes upon this seed of the wicked, this fallen-angel race among men, and it is not intended for the children of the Light. But the children of the Light have gone awhoring after other gods.[6] They have not heeded their prophets. And thus they have become so entangled, so enmeshed in the money systems and the folly of these serpents in their midst that we must ask, how shall we the angels of the LORD separate them out in a time when our angels are sent to bind the fallen ones and remove them in order that this planetary body might move forward into a golden age of peace and freedom, an age of enlightenment when the prophecy is fulfilled that every man shall sit under his own vine and fig tree—his Holy Christ Self and Mighty I AM Presence.[7] And he shall know the LORD, and he shall know Him in all of his being and life.

Blessed ones, thus the time of the end of the age of Pisces and of earth changes is a glorious time. For the Day of Vengeance of our God is not declared by a loving Father upon his own children but upon those fallen angels who have sworn enmity against His seed and have tormented them to the very end of [goal of] destroying their psyche, their souls, by manipulating their psychology, their minds and brains from earliest childhood.

Thus, upon those who move against and destroy the holy innocents and the little children, the judgment was pronounced by Jesus: ["And whosoever shall offend one of these little ones that believe in me, it is better for him that a millstone were hanged about his neck, and he were cast into the sea."] Thus, a worse fate may come upon them than any other for the harming of the little child.[8]

Let it be known, beloved, that the legions of angels are fierce to defend these little ones. We ask you, parents, sponsors, teachers and adults of this civilization, to be equally as intense to defend youth from the inroads upon their brains of the chemicals of drugs and the violent beat of rock music that does tear from them their energies and their very life-force. There are so many attacks upon youth that we wonder if a generation shall survive intact to embody that Universal Christ, which burden of the children you have heard spoken of.

I come to you with the fervor and the impassioned plea of an Archangel who has stood in the defense of the Lord Christ and all of his own for centuries, who has stood in defense of every people of God out of Israel and Judah, out of the Far East, out of every nation and continent—so we have stood. And always when we would work through those in embodiment, there were so few who would lead, who would set the example, who would have the courage to march forward, not understanding that when the decision is made to defend life we defend those individuals.

And our job is made that much more easy if these individuals will set aside a time for prayer, preferably three times a day. Thus, in the three-times-eight, in the twenty-four, there is a guardian action whereby the individual understands the necessity of the call to defend himself and his own when he is engaged in Armageddon. Indeed this is Armageddon! Indeed my legions of Light come to tarry with you!

Angels of the Lord Jesus Christ, come now and tarry with these our own and let them be enlightened. Let the Light infill their temples. For when we send our Messenger it is not merely that you may hear words but that you might receive an outpouring of Light that is ours to convey when we have a spoken word through which to convey it.

Thus, from the altars of Almighty God, in whose Presence I stand, we send to you a light, an awakening, a kindling fire and a quickening. Heed it, O beloved! For there are practical steps to be taken for the guardian action of thy life and thy family, then of thy city and nation and planet. Therefore, secure one's own bastions and be ready to act on behalf of those who know not what they do[9] and need the support of true shepherds.

Angels of the LORD God, angels of the LORD God, I have summoned you! Thus, place your presence around them as a swaddling garment, that they may know the Will of the Father, the Comfort and Wisdom of the Mother, the Presence of the Holy Spirit.

Oh, let that Christ expand. Expand, I say!

Now then, O legions of Light, thy swords raised as thou dost form a circle of light in the heavens, bind the possessing demons and discarnates that cause the youth and children to be led astray, to be not themselves and to follow the pied pipers, the false prophets of Atlantis reincarnated.

So, beloved, I send my angels to do battle in your behalf. May you awaken in the morning with your own remembrance of the Lord's instruction to you as that action that is to be taken.

Let the violet flame rise from beneath, saturating a people and a consciousness. For we, the Seven Archangels, are committed to the deliverance of a people while there is yet time and as long as some respond to the call and hear it.

Therefore, let those who misrepresent the people in this government and the government of the Soviet Union know that your days are numbered wherein you shall continue to betray the Life and the Liberty and the Freedom of such souls. Therefore, repent! And declare the Truth to your nations that they might know that you have plotted this war to their own destruction.

I tell you, all destruction you have sent forth, O you fallen ones in positions of international power, it shall turn and rend you by the right hand of God, who shall return to you all of your darkness and woe which you have unleashed in the earth!

Therefore know, though you may wreak havoc, "Vengeance is mine, I *will* repay!" Thus saith the LORD![10] For our God is not mocked. You shall not forever escape your karma by your manipulation of a people. Whatsoever you shall sow, so you shall reap.

Therefore, let the day be at hand when once again a people does rise up, who thinking they were free discover they are yet slave and therefore throw off their oppressors.

Lightbearers of the world, I send forth the call from the heart of Saint Germain, *Unite and be free!* Unite and bring in the golden age!

I AM Uriel. My heart's love does enter your own to strengthen you, to comfort you, to be with you always. Therefore, in the name of the living Saviour, I salute you and bow to the Light within you.

"The Summit Lighthouse Sheds Its Radiance O'er All the World to Manifest as Pearls of Wisdom."
This dictation by **Archangel Uriel** was **delivered** by Elizabeth Clare Prophet on **October 16, 1987** (after midnight) at the Cleveland Airport Marriott Hotel, **Cleveland, Ohio,** where she was stumping for Saint Germain's Coming Revolution in Higher Consciousness. (**1**) **Christed.** From the Greek *Christos,* meaning anointed; hence, Christed ones in the truest sense of the word are anointed, as Jesus was, by the Light of the I AM Presence. (**2**) See p. 546, from "A Massacre's Message: Get Out or Die," *Newsweek,* 7 December 1987, p. 52. (**3**) Rev. 12; Enoch 10:1–5; 19; 21:3–6; 26; 79. (**4**) I Pet. 5:8. (**5**) Rev. 6:15–17; 19:17, 18. (**6**) **Awhoring after other gods.** Exod. 34:12–17; Lev. 17:7; 20:1–6; Deut. 31:16–20; Judges 2:10–19; 8:33; I Chron. 5:25; Ezek. 6:9; 23:30, 36–39. (**7**) I Kings 4:25; Mic. 4:4; Zech. 3:10. (**8**) Mark 9:42. (**9**) Luke 23:34. (**10**) Rom. 12:19.

Pearls of Wisdom®
published by The Summit Lighthouse

Vol. 30 No. 64 *Beloved Elohim Peace* *December 3, 1987*

Saint Germain Stumps America

7

The Two-Edged Sword of Life

The Responsibility to Defend Life and Liberty

Peace unto the Lightbearers in the earth!

I AM Elohim of the Sixth Ray, come following Archangel Uriel to this state for the anchoring of the presence of the two-edged sword of Life. Therefore, for this mission to this heart of a nation I place a pillar of fire in the earth that does also vibrate in consonance with the living power of Christ so established by Uriel.

O legions of Light summoned by the Lord, attend these who would preserve Life and Liberty and embody the universal Light.

Therefore, come, O mighty ones of the Ancient of Days, legions who march with the army of the Faithful and True. Encamp thyselves round about the borders of a nation, the quadrants of a planet. And let peace be known as the power of Light, the infusing presence of angels of Uriel and my bands. So they do precede the coming of the Lord Christ in a most unusual manner into the hearts of all those who stand for Truth.

Awake! I say, O nations of the earth. Awake! to a cosmic opportunity and responsibility to preserve, to defend, to multiply Life. Life that is God in thee therefore necessitates a recompense from those Above and beneath.

Angels sounding a note introduce a vibration quivering the planetary atmosphere and aura. It is the gentle passage of a Light, and it is indeed for transmutation, for preparation and for the alert.

O beloved of the Light, the forces who come through the Four Horsemen, even the fourth, the pale horse, those which are unleashed out of the pits,[1] these are [to be] bound in answer to the calls of those in embodiment.

Fear not and fail not to make the call unto thy Christ and mine. For a circle of fire does establish a spiritual forcefield that we would see become physical. Yet how can anything become physical unless there be those who understand the meaning of being the vessel of the power of God in an age when that power has been abused and misused to the detriment of children and youth and all life.

Therefore, out of the Heart of the Inner Retreat where our forcefield is established I have come. For it needs be that a people unalert and unawakened who yet follow a false doctrine in religion, in the economy and in the government must come to an understanding that there is a Light of Freedom and that Light of Freedom is available.

Seven Archangels who have bowed before the throne of the Almighty and vowed to serve all Lightbearers in the nations, all people of goodwill—Come forth now! For as it is written, the time is short for the realization of this Light and the Light that no man hath seen on land or sea, the Light that is indeed the equation of the I AM THAT I AM.

Let the Light pierce the hearts and the chakras! In the heart of God, I, Peace, Elohim, declare it. And let the piercing be for a clearer vision and an understanding of the part that each one must play in the deliverance of a planet and a people.

The news of returning karma has been rejected by evolutions in many centuries. Therefore, hear the Word of the LORD! For the quenching of war and rumors of war[2]—these things that one day do appear as the surfacing of planetary karma—must come about by the sword of Peace that is raised by the living Christ, by the sword of Truth that is raised by the Divine Mother.

Let the fire go forth for the devouring of all that is unreal, for a planetary transmutation. And see that it does proceed out of thy mouth,[3] beloved. For this infilling Light is indeed unto the victory of all Life. Yet the record is clear and I remind you, for by the reading of history and the running with that record the illumined and enlightened ones may avoid the repetition of history as karmic cycles do recur.

In the living Light of the Word, then, know that the hour of the prophecy of Saint Germain is nigh. Let those who understand the meaning of shepherding nations and shepherding a people draw together their hearts, until by the crystal and the crystallization of their devotion they may create a chalice over this state, mighty indeed, a receptacle that shall be as a reservoir of Light to the people in time of trouble. That time of trouble long ago prophesied[4] is nigh, yet need not be.

Thus, we come. And in our Presence may you know what is Real and what is Unreal. May you vanquish Unreality by the Reality of God externalized within you. May you rather understand the piercing sword of the sacred Word that does send forth not only a message but a mandate from angelic hosts of Light, bands of angels of the seven rays who call to you now and say:

"O people of God, come up higher! Come into the Union of the Divine One but rest not in your labors. Go forth to save that which is lost. And in the economy of Life raise up a strong and sure defense on behalf of the entire world and planet."

Unto the living heart, the Sacred Heart of thy Christ and the Christ of Jesus, I commend you. Forget not the call of Jesus to the disciples. For there is a time to take up the sword[5] and a time to lay down the sword, a time to enter into heights of cosmic consciousness beyond the planes of maya and illusion, beyond the forcefield where battles are waged and wars are fought and epidemics take life—and a time to be in the midst of my people "to bind up the brokenhearted, to proclaim liberty to the captives and the opening of the prison to them that are bound. . . ."[6]

Precious ones, in the veils of illusion some yet suffer from unreality. And there are those who suffer in a large way from their delusions of grandeur and grandiose schemes and ancient battles and scores that fallen angels have come to settle, using the people of Light and mankind as fodder as they do wage their ages-old controversies across the planets.

I remember well and paint before you the akashic records of the era before the sinking of Lemuria when wars were waged by the gods in the misuse of the sacred fire. And by "gods" I mean those fallen angels embodying by their own free will a left-handed path of Darkness and Death. Thus, a false priesthood and those who betrayed the living Light of the Divine Mother by their misuse of the Light, Energy and Consciousness of God did wreak that havoc that caused the sinking of continents. And past golden ages have descended to the state in which we find mankind this day.[7]

Let those who know the Truth, then, be a pillar upon the Rock of Christhood. Let them demonstrate by their works and not mere words that Christ is able to defeat every darkness of War and Death. Let there be a summoning of the will and inner forces as people in the earth in this hour discover that those in embodiment are they who must make the call and clear the way for heaven's intercession.

We, the entire Spirit of the Great White Brotherhood, declare to you, O America, so sponsored by Saint Germain, that upon you is a great gift, an opportunity, a responsibility, and the record in akasha and in the Book of Life of many of you who have made the vow to defend Liberty in this hour of maximum peril.

Thus, look to the mountain and to the vision and implement it with all practicality and the Holy Spirit. Thus shalt thou and thy members survive unto the New Day and thy Ascension in the Light.

I AM Peace, Aloha [is] above me. Therefore, by twin flames of God we seal this place and all desiring to be centered in the heart of cosmic peace. [intonations, 35 seconds]

Melchizedek, Ascended Master, I summon you for the victory of Life and for the training of my own in the royal robes of the priesthood of thy order.

Let the devotees from all walks of life strive to embody the violet flame and the science of the seventh age, which is the Alpha and the Omega of religion and science for Aquarius.

Out of the Word is sent a river of Light for the devouring of Darkness, a river of Peace for the devouring of War. May you be instruments of it and preserve a planet and a people.

"The Summit Lighthouse Sheds Its Radiance O'er All the World to Manifest as Pearls of Wisdom."

This dictation by **Elohim Peace** was **delivered** by Elizabeth Clare Prophet on **October 18, 1987** (after midnight) at the Hyatt on Capitol Square, **Columbus, Ohio,** where she was stumping for Saint Germain's Coming Revolution in Higher Consciousness. (**1**) Rev. 9:1–11; 11:7; 17:8. (**2**) Matt. 24:6; Mark 13:7. (**3**) Rev. 11:3–5. (**4**) Dan. 12:1. (**5**) "And he said unto them, When I sent you without purse, and scrip, and shoes, lacked ye any thing? And they said, Nothing. Then said he unto them, But now, he that hath a purse, let him take it, and likewise his scrip: and *he that hath no sword, let him sell his garment, and buy one.* For I say unto you, that this that is written must yet be accomplished in me, 'And he was reckoned among the transgressors': for the things concerning me have an end. And they said, *Lord, behold, here are two swords.* And he said unto them, It is enough." Luke 22:35–38 (**6**) Isa. 61:1. (**7**) For more information on the misuse of light that caused the sinking of Atlantis, see *The Lost Teachings of Jesus II,* pp. 260–66, 300–304, 306, 316–17, 480–81.

Vol. 30 No. 65 | *Beloved Vesta* | *December 4, 1987*

Saint Germain Stumps America

8

The Divine Mother in Travail

Giving Birth to a New Age and a Planetary Christ Consciousness

Out of the sun center of Life I AM come, Vesta, Eternal Mother of ages. My Presence with you in the earth in this hour is an all-sustaining comfort, a strengthening of hearts inclined to be vessels of the virgin light of the Divine Mother.

I place my Presence here as a Mother of ages, that there might be released within the earth in this hour light of the Central Sun Magnet that will give to all who are the Lightbearers, the true patriots of a cosmic freedom, an inner balance and an ability in the outer to effect world change.

From the diamond point of the heart of Mary unto the center of the earth and the sun of this system, we seek to hold (and therefore seek your cooperation in the holding of) the balance of Life, both in the nature kingdom and among those who are embodied who are moved to extremes of right and left.

As the demand for the energies and resources of the earth does increase when there are none to be had, neither supply nor commodity but only chaos, Old Night and confusion, there is a replaying in the earth of the last days of Atlantis and the hour of the sinking of Lemuria. These records have come full cycle.

By the power of your own Sun Presence, the I AM THAT I AM, let these records of this handwriting on the wall be erased, as penciled beams of light descend in answer to your call and by the scientific power of violet-flame or sacred-fire mantra to the Divine Mother. I embody the *Power* of mantra and the *Wisdom* and the *Love*.

Let all Lightbearers know that the only salvation is the Light. And if you would indeed impart it to all, then let the Light be thy goal, thy daily purpose and thy reason for Being. In the heart of thy spirit and soul, I, Mother of Life, come to you with a swaddling garment of Light, a bearing up of your inner Being, that you might face with equanimity, poise and fearlessness flame those conditions you see all around you.

I summon legions of the Central Sun, angels of the sacred fire in the command of the Lord Jesus Christ. They descend now in answer to his Call and mine. Let there be in the earth, then, the guardian action of these anointed angels succoring all who will call.

Call daily to the angelic hosts, beloved. And therefore, standing midst the pillar of fire and the violet flame all around you, let your grace and inner knowledge exceed the borders of self-concern and survival now to pick up those who indeed have need and look to you by way of seeking recourse in the higher octaves in those of us who may answer.

Let your heart be an open door to comfort life. Therefore, seek daily the Comfort Flame from the altars of heaven, that you might always have that comfort in hand to give to others.

Hold the balance with a surefootedness and a knowingness that your feet are firmly planted upon the Rock of Christ, of Divinity, upon which you stand. Then see to it that you are found in the Place Prepared, spiritually in consciousness and physically by Saint Germain.

Know, then, that the very concentration of Lightbearers in our Place Prepared in Montana does avail much as many may pray together daily for the holding of a balance of a planet in the grips of travail—travail to give birth to a new age, a new dispensation and a planetary Christ consciousness.

The calling of the Divine Mother comes not alone through my heart but through Mary, the Mother of Jesus, through Kuan Yin and many saints in heaven. Thus, beloved, it is the Mother of All Life[1] who does appeal to you, her sons and daughters, to take your stand and give your life to the saving of an age and to the transcending of strife on your own part and, by your assistance, on the parts of all to whose aid you may come in our name.

I represent the Spirit of the Great White Brotherhood concerned with this system of worlds. And I can assure you that the crossroads at which earth finds herself has become the concern of cosmic councils. Therefore, this day does mark, surely, a turning point in the nations.[2]

Can there be a regrouping of forces?* Can there be a rise

*Vesta is referring to the day's stock market crash.

again? Yes, there can be a rise again, beloved, but never as steady as before. Thus, the sudden setbacks are experienced. Prepare, then, for there is truly a way and a path to endure and to survive unto thine own Ascension in the Light. Therefore, seek the path of reunion with God and know that I, Vesta, AM with you.

My Presence in the earth has been sufficient. I withdraw now so as not to overdo the Light or the necessity of movement in the earth to bear it. We come by increments, for Light itself, beloved, may cause cataclysm.

I return, then, beyond this world to the center of the Sun behind the sun of this system with a reminder to you that in the Flame of Mother I AM always at your heart's call. Only speak the name *Vesta* and I shall send you light beams for the holding of the balance.

With all my Love to you, I tell you, I understand your hearts, the deepest burdens and secrets thereof.

Bless you, my children, the Lord is with thee.

"The Summit Lighthouse Sheds Its Radiance O'er All the World to Manifest as Pearls of Wisdom." This dictation by **Vesta** was **delivered** by Elizabeth Clare Prophet on **October 19, 1987** (after midnight) at the Sheraton Westgate, **Toledo, Ohio,** where she was stumping for Saint Germain's Coming Revolution in Higher Consciousness. (**1**) **Mother of All Living.** The translation of the name Eve, from the Hebrew *Chavvah,* lit. "life-giver." See Gen. 3:20. (**2**) **Stock market crash.** On Monday, October 19, 1987 (the day Vesta delivered this dictation), the Dow Jones industrial average fell more than 508 points, a 22.6 percent drop in the market and the largest decline since the crash of October 29, 1929, when it fell 12.8 percent and started the Great Depression. The only other time the Dow fell further was on December 12, 1914, during World War I, when it plunged 24.4 percent. By August 25, 1987, the 5-year-old bull market had reached a high of 2,722.42, but beginning on October 6 the Dow slid a record 91.55 points. Although there were 2 days of increases, the downward trend continued. On Wednesday, October 14, a new record decline of 95.46 points was recorded, followed by 57.61 and 108.35-point falls. The weekend did not calm nervous investors, and Monday morning they rushed to get out of the market, precipitating the 508-point decline. Despite moderate gains, by the end of October the market loss was 645.67 points. Some analysts argue that Black Monday (as the crash of October 19 was called) was a long-overdue correction to a market that had risen too high. Others say it marks the beginning of a major recession or even depression. Distinguished economist Dr. Ravi Batra in *The Great Depression of 1990: Why It's Got to Happen—How to Protect Yourself* suggests that "the worst economic crisis in history" will take place in 1990 due to a combination of a recession and a shaky banking system. Foreign markets are highly influenced by U.S. markets, and the crash was reflected around the world in such markets as Tokyo, Hong Kong, Milan, London, Zurich, Toronto, and Melbourne.

Notes from Pearl No. 61 by Lady Master Nada:
(**1**) **Solar plexus,** "place of the sun," chakra anchored in the etheric body at the navel corresponding to the nerve center. The spiritual center through which one realizes the Christ consciousness of Peace. When this is attained, Jesus said, "Out of the belly shall flow rivers of living water" (John 7:38). The solar-plexus chakra corresponds to the Sixth Ray of ministration and service, vibrates with the purple-and-gold band of the causal body, and has six petals. See *Intermediate Studies of the Human Aura,* pp. 77–80, 87–90, plate 6; *The Lost Teachings of Jesus I,* pp. 279–80. (**2**) Matt. 11:12. (**3**) **Lords of**

Karma. The seven members of the Karmic Board are: the Goddess of Liberty, Spokesman, representing the Second Ray; the Great Divine Director, First Ray; the Ascended Lady Master Nada, Third Ray; the Elohim Cyclopea, Fourth Ray; Pallas Athena, Goddess of Truth, Fifth Ray; Portia, the Goddess of Justice, Sixth Ray; Kuan Yin, Goddess of Mercy, Seventh Ray. See *Saint Germain On Alchemy,* p. 421. (**4**) **The power of water.** In alchemy water is the element associated with the solar-plexus chakra and the emotional, or astral, body. Hence, in the solar plexus—which is the seat of man's desiring that by his free will may become the seat of God's desiring to realize Himself in His *man*ifestation—it is water as "energy in motion" over which man may gain self-mastery. In so doing, he is taking dominion over his emotions, which the alchemist understands to be "e-motion," or energy in motion—the power of the seven seas. (**5**) **The Rose Temple,** retreat of the Lady Master Nada, is located above New Bedford, Massachusetts. Designed after the pattern of a rose (each petal is a room), this retreat is the etheric counterpart of the Temple of Love on Atlantis where Nada once served as a priestess. In the center of the retreat there burns the flame of Divine Love, tended by brothers and sisters of the Third Ray for the healing of earth's evolutions by Love. (**6**) **Weeping statues.** Hundreds of statues of Mother Mary have been seen and photographed shedding tears, particularly those known as the Pilgrim Madonna, which bear the likeness of the Blessed Mother's appearance at Fátima. This phenomenon has been observed throughout the world, including in Sicily, Italy, Japan, China, Canada, and several cities in the U.S. A statue in Long Island, New York, reportedly wept on the days of the attempted assassinations of Pope John Paul II and President Ronald Reagan. Observers say that there is a correlation between world events and the weeping of the statues. (**7**) See p. 108. (**8**) II Cor. 11:13–15; Matt. 7:15. (**9**) **"Watch With Me"**—when you receive the gift of booklet and cassette of Jesus' Vigil of the Hours, answer the call of the heavenly hosts expressed by Nada and give it daily for 15 days then weekly throughout 1988. God in you can hold the balance of personal and planetary karma *when* you give yourself to be the open door for Jesus to step through the veil through you! (**10**) Rev. 21:2, 10–27.

Note 2 from Pearl No. 63:
". . . those lovers of God nestled in spiritual ways and practices who did not understand the spiritual disciplines of self-defense." Archangel Uriel

"Other white farmers in southern Zimbabwe post guards with automatic weapons against the rebels. At Olive Tree Farm and neighboring New Adam's Farm, the Pentecostal ministers simply trusted in God. One night last week an armed gang seized the missionaries and their children from their beds, bound them in barbed wire and methodically butchered them with axes. After three hours of mutilation and murder, the attackers torched the houses. They threw the bodies of their victims into the flames and departed.

"At dawn 16 whites lay dead in the ashes of their homes. Five were children; one was only six weeks old. One of the two survivors, Laura Russell, 13, was given a written message for 'all people from Western or capitalist countries' living in Zimbabwe: get out or die. 'We are prepared for our last man to face their last man,' the letter warned. The dead included two Americans and a Scotswoman.

"Last week's attack in the Matabeleland region was the bloodiest massacre of whites since Zimbabwe won independence from Great Britain in 1980. The immediate cause seems to have been a confrontation two weeks ago. A group of black squatters, driven by drought to find new pasture for their cattle, had moved onto the whites' land. The whites ordered them off. 'You won't eat another meal,' warned the leader of the evicted blacks. Zimbabwean officials say the squatters then sought help from a local gang.

"The group was one of Matabeleland's many loosely organized rebel bands, known as dissidents, that oppose the rule of Prime Minister Robert Mugabe. (Mugabe's old foe, opposition leader Joshua Nkomo, denies any connection with the dissidents.) Since 1982 the rebels have waged a campaign of terror against the whites who have title to much of the best farmland. Last week's massacre brought the campaign's toll to 66. 'These were innocent missionaries,' mourned Home Minister Enos Nkala. 'Engaged in production, talking about peace. They were people we so much value.'" "A Massacre's Message: Get Out or Die," *Newsweek,* 7 December 1987, p. 52.

". . . In the prayers of simple people there is more power and might than that possessed by all the great statesmen or armies of the earth." Ronald Reagan, December 10, 1987.

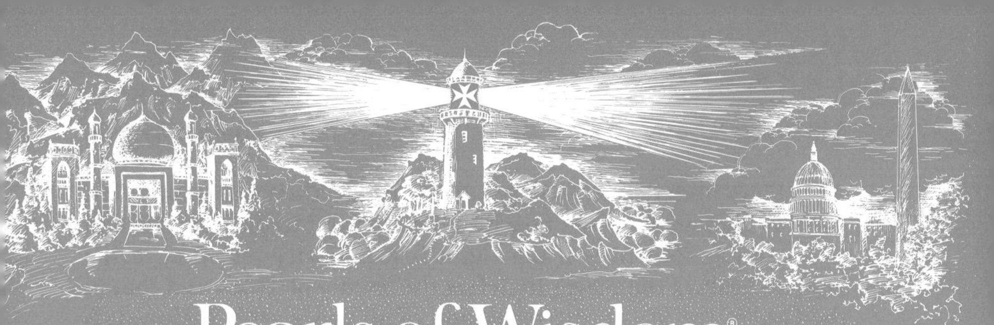

Pearls of Wisdom®
published by The Summit Lighthouse

Vol. 30 No. 66 | *Beloved Saint Germain* | *December 5, 1987*

Saint Germain Stumps America
9
A Day of Decision
The Defense of Freedom at Every Hand

Ladies and Gentlemen, Keepers of the Flame,
Lightbearers My Own,

I step forth on the world stage prematurely, for I had not so planned to speak to you until Thanksgiving in Washington. Nevertheless, *I AM here and my name is Saint Germain!*

Beloved ones of the Light, it is indeed the urgency of the hour that brings me to anchor in the physical octave through the Messenger and your own hearts an increment of fire—Seventh Ray action for the holding of the balance and the steadying of the ship of state.

Having few representatives in Washington upon whom I can count to deliver the mandate of the will of God to the people, I go out across the nation seeking whom I may discover whose fiery heart and devotion to Light will allow me to place there a crystal amethyst of my heart and therefore to anchor through that spiritual focus my Presence and my violet flame for transmutation in this hour.

As you have endured to this end of our delivery,[1] so I would first give to you my greetings and those of my beloved twin flame, whom I introduce to you as the beloved Portia, known as the Goddess of Justice. We together, then, are holding the balance in this hour of your entry into the age of Aquarius. Therefore know that our love is with you and that we are real and most concerned, for we have lived through many ages and many periods of crisis.

What is noteworthy, beloved, is that in all areas of crisis and ultimate catastrophe, it has taken but a few Lightbearers to save a situation and but a few spoilers to ruin all for the people.

1. The Messenger's stump in which she gave Saint Germain's prophecy concluded at midnight.

Thus understand that key figures play their parts this day, even as chessmen on the board of life. For you to discern this and to recognize that in you the Light is a majority and that in the angelic hosts is the power to defeat the enemy of Truth and that in the Call is the key to the resolution of all crisis—this, beloved, is rewarding, that you should understand and then take action based on the majority of God within you. For one wed to that Light is sufficient instrument.

I have walked the cities and nations in this and past eras in the attempt to bring relief and healing. And do you know, beloved, that in certain of those past times I have not found a single individual through whom I could work. Therefore, when I find even a room full of hearers such as this and a body of Keepers of the Flame worldwide, I can assure you that I am gratified.

And that decree power is what we need to receive the dispensations from Cosmic Councils to intercede where no intercession or divine intervention might have been thought possible. Already, then, there is a certain mitigation in the [karma in the] economy, even with the coming of beloved Vesta. Each and any one of you or all together can make the difference.

Let us celebrate a day of decision, then, as our hearts are one in the love of the Blessed Mary and the Son Jesus. As we can commune together and determine that as the few banded together to respond to my heart in the formation of this nation, so in this third century of America's destiny the few and the many may awake and by the grace of God focus on those things which are the need of the hour.

The visions that I have given to the Messenger are accurate indeed. And I have given many visions beyond those recounted this night which are held back. Therefore know that the scope and scheme of the totality of that which could come of calamity is also known to her.

But I tell you, beloved, to begin at the beginning—which is the defense of freedom at every hand—this will draw a line that the forces out of hell that are not physical will dare not cross. For though there be war and contemplation of nuclear war, you wage a spiritual warfare against those principalities and powers of invisible hierarchies of fallen angels.[2]

And therefore, it is the Archangels and it is the Lord Christ and the Ancient of Days and the armies of heaven who wage war this night for the binding of the hordes out of the astral plane who would spill over into the physical through various openings, whether of individuals or of systems or of manifestations that allow it in this octave.

I speak of the rending of the veil that has protected the

2. Eph. 6:12.

physical [plane] from this Darkness. Blessed ones, that veil has been rent earlier in this century by practices that are not of the Light. Even the breaking of the protective auric sheath of our youth through drugs alone has wreaked havoc in them, causing the entrée into their psyches of the suicide entity, who can be named and cast out as Annihla.[3]

Thus, forces of annihilation move as feminine vampire across the earth this night. The legions of Astrea and Archangel Michael work, as it were, furiously for their binding. Every prayer spoken by every sincere heart, no matter what their path or faith, is taken as the sign that we may enter in and do what the Great Law will allow in the mitigation of this "chastisement"[4] at the end of the age of Pisces.

I come, then, with concern for decisions that are being made in your names and in your behalf by those who have not the capacity to lead. Therefore, beloved, it does take the Mind of God in all areas to outsmart a complex karma whereby the people of Light are tied to those spoilers in the earth and archdeceivers, tied by economic systems. Whether by bread lines, whether by the stock market, whether by taxation, whether by armies and war, the planet is enmeshed.

And therefore, the call went forth long ago from the heart of Joshua: "Come apart *now* and be a separate and chosen people!"[5] When the avalanche of human karma descends and the seed of the wicked who know they have karma cry out to the mountains, "Fall on us, fall on us!"[6] for they desire to die rather than to face the Lord's judgment, it is then, beloved, that you must indeed be out of harm's way.

I ask you, then, to pray and pray fervently to God and to Mother Mary. I ask you, beloved, also, if you care to do it, to pen me a letter and then burn it with physical fire. Ask me from your heart to send you my violet flame angels, angels such as those who warned me when I, as Joseph, took the young child and Mary into Egypt.[7] Thus, the warning can come to you as to the direct course of action the same way it came to us by the Lord's legions of Light.

Blessed ones, in you is a flame that burns, and by it you have the all-power of God to take a stand in your time against all injustice. The beloved Portia will assist you each and every hour when in the name of these little ones you take your stand against the oppressors of my people and every form of injustice in Church and State

3. Use Archangel Michael's Rosary for Armageddon for the exorcism of such malevolent, nonphysical "forces of annihilation" affecting children, youth and adults alike, societies, economies, governments and nations. Available on 91-min. audiocassette with 32-page booklet, $5.00 (add $.80 for postage). **4.** In 1963 a German newspaper, *Neues Europa*, printed a supposed extract of the third secret given by Mother Mary on July 13, 1917, to three shepherd children at Fátima, Portugal. It read in part, "A great chastisement will come over all mankind; not today or tomorrow but in the second half of the twentieth century. . . . The age of ages is coming, the end of all ends if mankind will not repent and be converted and if this conversion does not come from rulers of the world and of the Church." **5.** Exod. 33:16; Lev. 20:24; II Cor. 6:17, 18. **6.** Hos. 10:8; Luke 23:29, 30; Rev. 6:15, 16. **7.** Matt. 2:13. Saint Germain was embodied as Joseph, protector of Mary and Jesus.

and the economy. The lines have been drawn by others than yourselves, yet they [these 'others'] exist on the power they have extracted from you—your light and your taxes—and by the fact of the burden of their karma which they have put upon you that is grievous.

People of earth and of Light, rally, then, while there is yet time. For even the Fátima prophecies may be turned back. But I will tell you *what it will take: Beginning with ten thousand new Keepers of the Flame who will give those dynamic decrees, we should expect a million even in the United States invoking the violet flame daily before we should see a considerable change in that which is projected. Yet this is possible.* Without question there are a million Lightbearers, many of them led astray into false paths and teachings that are nothing but time-wasters.

When it is an hour to decree and to check the actions of evildoers by voice and vote, it is not the time to dabble in entertaining arts, whether these be the black arts or witchcraft or psychic channeling itself. Blessed ones, there is a time to concentrate on one point and one alone, and it is survival. Then you may go back to your preferences on the Path.

I come for the uniting of a heart and all hearts of America. I come for the warning, beloved. And I tell you, it is possible to lose centuries of what we have built. It is also possible to use these centuries and your action of today as a foundation for the building of a true golden-age civilization that can sweep the earth from this point, America, into the new age of Aquarius.

Thus, beloved, note well that this is your hour and the power of Light that is yours to command by free will. We have played our parts. We are almost, as it were, bystanders. Our angels encourage you but we know that you are center stage in this final act of this Piscean dispensation. Your actions, choices, moves and decisions will truly affect the fate of earth and her destiny for centuries to come.

I commend you to the care of the little child. When you sense that responsibility and you look into the eyes of innocence, you know that you must act. You may not love your life enough, but I ask you to love your children, love your posterity, love the gifts that God has given to you and then rise up to defend Liberty in every plane and at every hand.

I AM your brother and friend—at your side instantly at your call. It is now my joy to seal the servants of God in their foreheads. I take the emerald crystal and through this hand direct to you a charge of light for your vision, your victory and your protection.

By the sign of the cosmic cross of white fire and the Maltese cross, we shall conquer as Above, so below.

Peace, holiness, freedom be unto you.

This dictation was **delivered** by Elizabeth Clare Prophet following her **October 20, 1987** Stump at the Southfield Hilton, **Detroit, Michigan.**

Pearls of Wisdom®
published by The Summit Lighthouse

Vol. 30 No. 67 *Beloved Mighty Victory* *December 6, 1987*

Saint Germain Stumps America
10
Keep the Flame of Victory
Earth Is Destined for a Golden Age

O Light from the Central Sun, here am I, Victory's Son, come to this city for the sole purpose of establishing in this place a living spiral of the flame of God's Victory.

I AM an angel of Victory, so called by my dedication to that light of Victory in you all. God has given to me legions of Victory in my command. And unto the living Christ of each son and daughter of God we serve to liberate life.

This flame, then, of God's Victory is indeed a mighty pillar ascending far into the upper atmosphere and beyond. Blessed ones, it is a pillar of golden-white light. And therefore, its involuting action as the fire infolding itself does create a vortex drawing all into the higher Victory of the Lord Christ in all people.

Blessed hearts, this impetus unto life, unto the raising of the sacred fire to the crown [chakra], even in your own body temple, is delivered to you by the loving hearts of those who serve at the altar of the Most High God: Seraphim of the Light who tend these altars crying,

"Holy, Holy, Holy, LORD God Almighty, Thou alone art Holy!"[1]

These do deliver to you the golden ampule of oil from their auras which they have received from the altar of God, that you also might partake and quaff that substance now, beloved, knowing that ye are chosen of the Light.

O people of earth, rise to your calling in that highest sense of Life and Liberty vouchsafed to you. Indeed it is the end of an era. Let it be the end of all human error and strife as well.

Understand that in order to articulate the Word, we send to you our Messenger as a reminder from ancient times of your

1. Rev. 4:8; 15:4.

Destiny and Joy and Love.

O awake, America! Awake, O people of the heart of Victory!

For long ago you have chosen that flame. And therefore your excellence is quickened now.

Did he not promise the sending of the Comforter?[2] Know that the heavenly hosts who deliver their word in this age are here to comfort, to strengthen, to warn and to deliver a people who would be delivered by the right hand of the Almighty.

Blessed hearts, take that hand and walk with God in this hour. For surely your voice in the power of the spoken Word, aligned with His own, may be the instrument for the saving grace that is needed in this hour when the blind leaders of the blind would take this nation far afield from the flaming sword of Victory, even the two-edged sword that does proceed out of the mouth of the Faithful and True, thus dividing the Real from the Unreal.

Awake, O thou that sleepest![3] *Awake! I say. Awake! in the name of God Victory!* And hear the marching of the Faithful and True and the armies in heaven. Are they not come to deliver a people?

Shall a people not rise up and join them? Or shall they sleep and sleep away until they themselves and all they have built are taken from them?

The hour is perilous. The Light is available and oncoming. May those who know the gift of free will and a path of Light[4] not neglect to hear our cry.

Thus, all that can be done by heaven is being done, beloved. Let us hear the response of all in the earth out of every nation. Let them arise to know that earth is destined for a golden age in Aquarius and can meet that timetable if her people will it so.

Not here or there, not in this or that testimony but in the living kingdom, the consciousness within, do you find deliverance and surcease from all outer strife.

O expand, Victorious Threefold Flame upon these hearts' altars! Expand with quickening fire!

I, Victory, Messenger of Almighty God, am pleased to seal you in the heart of the living flame of Victory. Let the love of many angels know your own heart and be known of you, O beloved.

O beloved, hear the voice of the Son of God! See Him and live forevermore.[5] I AM in the heart of the flame of Victory, evermore the servant of the Light within you.

Hail, O legions of Victory! I send you now to every city, town and hamlet across the face of the earth to find some soul of Light who shall be a bearer of the Light of Victory, a kindling spark to all.

Keep, then, the flame of Victory.

2. John 14:16, 26; 15:26; 16:7 **3.** Eph. 5:14 **4.** The Light that is, and is the emanation of, the Christ consciousness. **5.** John 5:25; 10:27, 28.

"The Summit Lighthouse Sheds Its Radiance O'er All the World to Manifest as Pearls of Wisdom." This dictation by **Mighty Victory** was **delivered** by Elizabeth Clare Prophet following her **October 22, 1987** Stump at the Hilton East, **Louisville, Kentucky.**

Vol. 30 No. 68 | *The Beloved Maha Chohan* | *December 7, 1987*

Saint Germain Stumps America

11

Eternal Vigilance Is the Price of Liberty

A Destiny You Are Capable of Fulfilling

Sons and Daughters of Liberty,

Thy heart in the Great Central Sun is known and the Book of Life does reveal thy inner name.

I am called the Maha Chohan, which means simply "Great Lord." I am the teacher of the Lords of the Seven Rays, and the one who does hold the chalice of the Holy Spirit as an office in the ascended hierarchy of Light. Thus, I bring to you a gift of the Holy Spirit from my heart and etheric retreat over the isle of Sri Lanka.

Blessed ones, the universities of the Spirit, the etheric retreats [of the Great White Brotherhood], are open. Your sponsorship by the Ascended Masters and careful instruction set forth by Saint Germain in the Keepers of the Flame Lessons provides you with a very simple and accurate method of meditation for leaving the body before retirement, as one does pass into sleep, to go consciously to our retreats and to study and to return with the memory of what is given.

Blessed ones, I come, for the LORD God has sent me to you and to America to deliver the Spirit of his Presence as an impulse of Light, as an inner knowing, as a sacred breath that is wafted over the nation.

Angels of the Holy Spirit are summoned. Therefore they come to quicken, to give new life to a people. For it is also prophesied in the vision received by George Washington that Divine Intervention will be the key to the saving of a nation.[1]

Thus, prophecies of these times are written. And in that

writing there is, as you have been taught, the option of free will. Therefore, beloved, understand that Divine Intervention comes not alone from Above but through your own hearts as you understand yourselves to be divine intercessors on behalf of a people.

We pray, "Father, forgive them, for they know not what they do." Yet, beloved, there are some in this nation and in the government who do know what they do and are aware, fully, of that which could come to pass. Why do they not speak out? How dare they not speak out in this hour of the trembling of the cup of destiny!

Blessed hearts, even so, the Spirit Most Holy is a chastening rod upon those betrayers of my people. Know well, then, that they have no power, saving the power the people give to them by their ignoring of the first responsibilities of a free people in a republican form of government. Thus, let this democracy in this republic be a flame that is not quenched by neglect. Fan the fire of Freedom, I say, by the Holy Breath that God gave thee at thy birth!

Remember this land, beloved, thou who dost remember the God Star Sirius. Remember well that this land is so consecrated to God Government for the turning around of worlds and all the mischief making of ten thousand years of the betrayers of the living Word.

Ye are a people endued with grace, a people of a calling from the ancient times and the Ancient of Days. This is your hour of Victory. I say to you, Act in time and claim that Victory! For if ye defend not a land so consecrated by ascended hosts to the Law of Liberty, how can you receive again thy native sun, the God Star Sirius? To what place in cosmos shalt thou return, O people, having lost the best gift of God?

O understand, beloved, this is the testing ground, and the souls of a nation are being tested. Aye, they knew the testing a hundred years ago, knowing the violation and the attack upon the wholeness of Alpha and Omega,[2] but in this hour they sense not the danger.

Let the few be the sparks that fly. Let the Holy Spirit quickened in you now, beloved, be that power of God that does empower you to speak, to be heard, and to have angels and the wind of the Spirit in your sails to deliver a mandate, as one voice does rise up from the din of the pleasure cult and the madness of the times, one voice of ten thousand saints and a million and a million again that does cry out unto God and demand of this government:

Peace, Protection, Defense, Strength, Integrity and the Living Light of a people that shall no longer be hid but be upon the mountain of God as an ensign, not only to a planet but to a cosmos, that the Lightbearers whose destiny is come have taken their stand and determined to defend a nation, a planet and all people by the living sword of Peace!

Remember, He said, "I came not to send peace but a sword."[3] That two-edged sword out of the mouth of the Faithful and True is the power, beloved, to cleave asunder the Real from the Unreal.

I command the hosts of Light, let Unreality be banished! Let it collapse now! Let the living God appear as the sign of the age and the coming of that star of destiny that is your own Mighty I AM Presence and causal body.

Beings of the elements, I summon you. Angels of the living fire, I summon you. Where the defense is not present, place thy bodies. Seraphim of God, place thy spiritual bodies of light for the defense of all who trust in Him.

O would it be that they would hear the call! And yet even those in the churches go the way of the Liar and his Lie, espousing causes that ought not to be espoused, betraying the original principles of Freedom.

I AM in the heart of the Holy Spirit as the Holy Spirit is in my heart. So, beloved, witness my love for you and for Saint Germain.

I come, then, with a company of saints and angels who have vowed to defend all who will raise up that hand and heart, who will look to the hills and who will say:

"Saint Germain, I come, for God has called. I can do naught else, for I have seen the vision and I shall act upon my vision."

Blessed hearts, angels have formed a very large circle of fire around this city. It is as a solar ring. There is a grid of light within this ring that can be filled in by your calls and prayers and dynamic decrees and devotion.

Therefore, beloved, understand, the free will of God has sent angels to form a grid of light and a circle of fire. Let the free will of a people who are yet free fill in that grid with light and create here a focus of the Great Central Sun Magnet to magnetize the light, the protection, the new age and the defense of freedom that is required if a free people shall remain free.

Therefore, in the living Spirit I AM. I remind you that every spiritual adept who has entered the courts of heaven has had to secure in the physical what he would earn in cosmic dimensions. Earth is your proving ground. America is your destiny. This state and city is the cross of time and space meeting Infinity where you, beloved, are to realize the universal Sonship of every Lightbearer.

I commend you to a destiny which you are capable of fulfilling. No challenge has ever been given a people or a planet or a group of initiates that they could not fulfill in God—heart, head and hand one.

Therefore, with hands clasped and with the Spirit of Cosmic Truth, I commend you to the ingenuity of the heart and the contact with the Universal Light. May it be said of you that you were the spark that did ignite a movement of Victory and a golden age of Peace. May it never be said, "What might have been..." But let a free people know that eternal vigilance is indeed the price of Liberty.[4] Now is the hour to pay that price!

I bow to the Light in your heart that is the potential for Godhood.

"The Summit Lighthouse Sheds Its Radiance O'er All the World to Manifest as Pearls of Wisdom."

This dictation by the **Maha Chohan,** the Representative of the Holy Spirit, was **delivered** by Elizabeth Clare Prophet on **October 24, 1987** following her lecture at the Sheraton Meridian, **Indianapolis, Indiana,** where she was stumping for Saint Germain's Coming Revolution in Higher Consciousness. (**1**) **"Washington's Vision of America's Trials."** During the long winter at Valley Forge, George Washington received a vision through a mysterious visitor (the Goddess of Liberty) of three great perils that would come upon the Republic—the Revolutionary War, the War between the States and a third world conflict. The most fearful peril would be the third, in which armies from Europe, Asia and Africa would devastate the whole country. At the end of the vision, an angel upon whose head shone the word *Union* and legions from heaven descended to join the inhabitants of America, rolling back the invading armies and bringing victory to the land. See *Saint Germain On Alchemy,* pp. 142–51, or *The Great White Brotherhood in the Culture, History and Religion of America,* pp. 118–23. (**2**) **The Civil War** (1861–65) between the Northern states (Union) and the eleven Southern states (Confederacy) arose out of conflicts over slavery, the right of states to secede from the Union, and the economic and political rivalry between an agrarian South and an industrial North. It was precipitated by the election of Abraham Lincoln as president and the secession of Southern states. After early Confederate gains, the war ended with the Union's victory on April 9, 1865. Though the victory was marred by Lincoln's assassination on April 14, the Union was saved, slavery was abolished and after Reconstruction under President Andrew Johnson, the seceded states were readmitted to the Union. (**3**) Matt. 10:34. (**4**) Wendell Phillips, 1852.

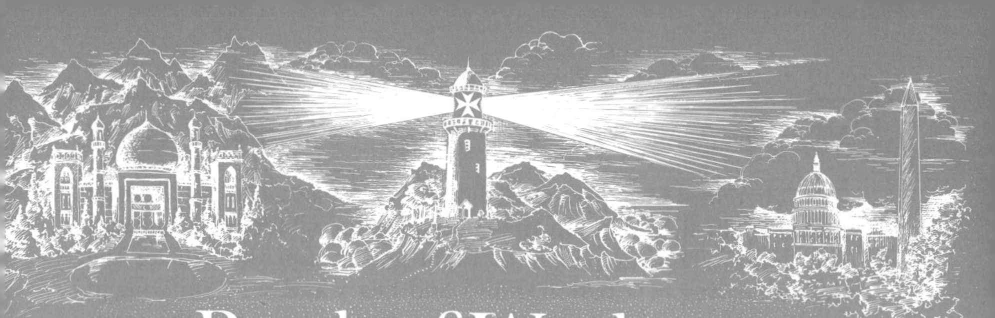

Pearls of Wisdom®
published by The Summit Lighthouse

Vol. 30 No. 69 *Beloved Archangel Raphael* *December 8, 1987*

Saint Germain Stumps America
12
A Call to the Healing Flame
Development of the Third Eye for a Vision of God

Ho! Everyone that thirsteth, come ye to the waters of eternal Life. For the fount of the Universal Christ does flow!

I, Raphael, greet you in the Immaculate Heart of the beloved Mary. We have come in this hour and to this city for the defense of Life and to assist the Ascended Master Saint Germain in his God-determination to see the Lightbearers of earth defended and this nation under God so situated as to pursue the great golden age now appearing.

Therefore, our gift upon the altar of this nation is a call to the healing flame.[1] For without Divine Wholeness nor a people nor a continent can respond to the call to "Be all Light!"[2] to enter in to that wholeness whereby in integration of the spirals of Light there is forged that individualization of God in embodiment that does determine that the Light shall descend, the Kingdom shall come, His Will be done on earth as it is in heaven.

Wherefore, to what end, do you suppose the Lord has shown to the beloved John the Holy City descending out of heaven? It was so that you might recognize that this etheric blueprint is intended to manifest upon earth. And thus the meeting of that bride adorned for her husband with the living Christ does take place, that on earth as in heaven finally the golden etheric city of light, over and again, might be represented in the cities of earth, which are become the kingdoms of our God. This merging of the octaves and of heaven and earth is the sign of the ascending ones and their fulfillment of that cosmic destiny from the beginning.

Therefore we say to each and every one, let a healing altar be raised up in the home, in the church, in the citadel of Light and Freedom—wherever people of Light gather. Let the call for the divine healing of a nation, mind and heart and soul—in will, in body and in the functions of the very government and the economy—therefore be the goal. Let this call for healing be consistent and daily. And see what the Fifth Ray and the development of your own third-eye chakra may increase for a vision of God that does become as a funnel whereby the energies of the octaves of light might flow through that vision to coalesce in form.

Healing, then, is required of the psyche, the soul itself, and of bodies bruised by bombardment of forces unseen and toxins of the environment and a polluted food chain.

Blessed hearts, let the mind be quickened by the power of the Immaculate Heart! Let the soul be quickened! And let each one understand that it is lawful to balance this body and to perceive strength [in it]—therefore to present oneself an acceptable chalice for the uses of the Holy Spirit.

Therefore, legions of angels of the Fifth Ray gather. They gather for the twofold purpose: a mighty vision in the hearts of the people, that they might (1) read the signs of the times and (2) know that the sign is given as a warning that all might know the approaching danger. For unless some portion of karma descend, beloved, how will the people become alert to the oncoming tragedies which will surely follow thereafter—unless they unite to take action and take a stand for Light, for defense and for the balance of these monetary systems?

Blessed hearts, forces are raging in the earth. And indeed the Lightbearers are called to draw the line over which Darkness shall not pass. We decree it: They shall not pass, in the name of the living Christ! But unless our decree be repeated through your own hearts and chakras, your free will is not expressed and therefore the Light has no vessel whereby it might fill that vessel and overflow to reach the boundaries of many who are in need of that surcease in this hour.

Blessed hearts, I come to anchor a light and a flame wherever souls may gather to invoke that healing light. I also direct your attention to the call to the Elohim of the All-Seeing Eye of God,[3] that by your use of that mantra you may increase the vision and the opening of the third eye, not prematurely but in consonance with your use of the violet flame and the gentle raising of the light upon the altar of being.

Therefore, beloved, understand that when spiritual vision is opened you see heaven as well as hell, you see the darkness of world karma as well as a future golden age and truly the celestial city of God. Blessed ones, it cannot be otherwise, for the opening of the lens unto Reality must show the consequences of the abuse of Reality and their antithesis.

Thus understand why this spiritual eye is not opened by the angels of the Fifth Ray. For most people upon this planet are not able to bear the visions of Darkness, such as those portrayed by my beloved Mary at Fátima and Medjugorje.

Thus, the innocence of children protected and sealed by the Archangels does allow their pure hearts to repeat exactly what they have seen and heard without the disruption of minds based on rationalism, empiricism or even the fears of the woes coming upon the earth. Blessed ones, out of the heart of the child is Truth spoken.

Therefore, let all people of earth know that the hour is today and tomorrow, that there is a time to sow light and reap light, to build a citadel of the emerald ray and the emerald chalice, a time to invoke wholeness for the nations and for the people and a time to call for the purging of the earth of those fallen angels.[4] For surely the hour is come for those angels called the reapers to remove the tares, even as the wheat is being harvested.[5]

Thus, beloved, let the spoilers in the earth be bound! For the LORD God Almighty has decreed it and we are his mouthpiece. Therefore may you also see yourself as a messenger of God, that you might affirm that divine decree and invoke the judgment of those who are plummeting this earth into a course of destruction and of trembling and of quaking by their infamy and their violation and sin against the Holy Ghost, even in these little children.[6]

Let the souls of Light beneath the altar of God[7] know that the hour is coming, and now is, when these woes upon the earth shall be recompensed upon those who have originated them, who are that very seed of the fallen ones. Blessed ones of the Light, may you therefore know the place of light and haven of safety in the Holy of Holies of your own I AM Presence. May you truly understand the need for a Path and a Teaching and for this dynamic decree.

I have called you to my heart that my angels may now approach you. They have the ability to place their auric field, their electromagnetic field, around you now. You may bid them welcome with a softly spoken "welcome" to them. For they must have your permission to enter your aura now to convey a vial of healing and a quickening of the chakras.

For we come, beloved, only to serve and magnify the Lord within your temple, to glorify his name I AM THAT I AM. Therefore, in the name Jesus Christ, we serve. In the name of the Christ of you, we serve. In the name of the entire Spirit of the Great White Brotherhood, we serve.

Call to us at any hour of the day or the night for a loved one or a nation, a continent or a planet. For ours is the joy to enter in, to combat Darkness, to manifest Light.

Blessed hearts, I extend my hands, even as my angels now tend you. And they attend you, beloved, inasmuch as they await your call, your prayer and your willingness to be the instrument of this emerald ray in the earth that is for the healing of nations.

May your Tree of Life also, as your causal body and the fruit thereof, be for the healing of all nations.[8]

So it is decreed by God in the beginning. So it is up to you to decree it in the ending. As Above so below, Alpha/Omega in God and man is the sealing of this covenant.

[Chant in angelic tongues, 27-sec.]

To the Light eternal I bow, in heaven and on earth. May you be one as we are. Truly in the nexus of the Eternal Christ is all resolution.

My beloved, I AM ever your Raphael.

"The Summit Lighthouse Sheds Its Radiance O'er All the World to Manifest as Pearls of Wisdom." This dictation by **Archangel Raphael** was **delivered** by Elizabeth Clare Prophet on **October 25, 1987,** following her lecture at the Omni Netherland Plaza, **Cincinnati, Ohio,** where she was stumping for Saint Germain's Coming Revolution in Higher Consciousness. (**1**) For a complete 4½-hour lecture on the healing power of angels and "Christ Wholeness—the Seven Rays of God," including dictations by Uriel and Zadkiel, see Elizabeth Clare Prophet, November 25, 1987, 3 audiocassettes, A87100, $19.50 (add $.80 for postage); 2 videocassettes, GP87089, $59.95 (add $1.25 postage). (**2**) The Messenger's Stump lecture preceding Archangel Raphael's dictation contained instruction on how to use visualizations, mantras and dynamic decrees through the science of the spoken Word for healing. She gave with the audience the prayer to "Christ Wholeness," which includes the call to "Be all Light!" See no. 38 in *Heart, Head, and Hand Decrees;* no. 224 in *The Healing Power of Angels* booklet, $2 (add $.45 postage). See also Mark L. Prophet and Elizabeth Clare Prophet, *The Science of the Spoken Word,* with 6 original full-color healing thoughtforms for visualization, $7.95 (add $1 postage). (**3**) "Beloved Cyclopea Beholder of Perfection," no. 61 in *Mantras of the Ascended Masters for the Initiation of the Chakras,* $2; on 82-min. audiocassette B85137 of songs and decrees from the Mantra booklet, nos. 55–67, $6.50 (add $.50 postage). A total of 5 audiocassettes contains all the songs and decrees of the Mantra booklet, B85135–B85139, $6.50 each (for postage, add $.50 for one cassette, $.80 for more than one). (**4**) **Fallen angels.** Enoch 10:1–20; 12:5–7; 13:1–4; 14:1–7; 16; 19; 66:4–15; 67:2–5; 105:13–17. See Elizabeth Clare Prophet, *Forbidden Mysteries of Enoch: The Untold Story of Men and Angels,* containing all the Enoch texts, including the Book of Enoch and the Book of the Secrets of Enoch, $12.95 (add $1 postage). (**5**) Matt. 13:24–30, 36–42. (**6**) Matt. 12:31, 32; Mark 3:28, 29; Luke 12:10. (**7**) Rev. 6:9. (**8**) Rev. 22:2.

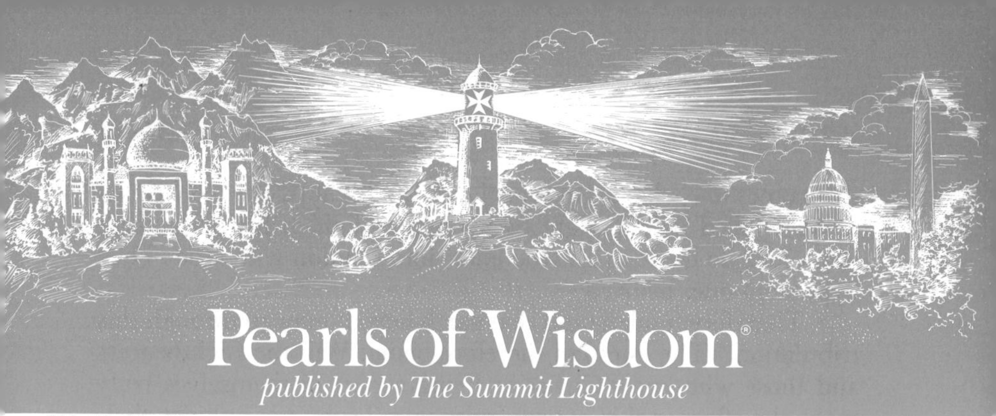

Vol. 30 No. 70 *Beloved El Morya* *December 9, 1987*

Saint Germain Stumps America

13

Let Your Voice Be Heard

What Happens on Earth Is in Your Hands

Ladies and Gentlemen, Heart Flames of Living Truth,

In the flame of the will of God, I AM El Morya, teacher of the Messengers and tutor of your souls (if you would invite me) to receive that path of the diamond heart of God's will in Mary's name.

I come to this city to contact those disciples of the Lord Christ who have shown an extraordinary devotion to the will of God and have so translated that devotion into good works and piety.

Know this, O beloved, that angels of the Keeper of the Scrolls do write in a beautiful handwriting even the devotions of your heart, the secret thoughts and musings and the deep desiring of your souls to serve the world good and holy purpose.

Therefore, I speak to you regarding that discipleship offered by the Lord Jesus in this hour. We, the Lords of the Seven Rays, do assist you to that end and welcome you to our universities of the Spirit, even our retreats.[1] We are glad in a holy gladness when you come to our doors. We receive, each of us, ten thousand students each night. Our angels go forth to escort these students to the etheric octave. And I count any number of you in this room as those who have already been to my retreat in Darjeeling.

All is not lost. But we must in this hour compress into a short time those activities most productive to the staying of the Hand of Darkness in the earth.

Blessed hearts, understand that the dark night of the soul, which is the hour of the soul's darkest karma, and the dark night of the Spirit, which is the hour of the eclipse of the I AM Presence that comes to each one [in order] that the Light [Christ consciousness] invoked below might be a Light to lighten his way—these initiations do come to all who enter into reunion with God. They bypass no one, beloved.

Therefore, understand that earth herself may go through this tribulation.* The question therefore being: Will the Lightbearers and those who know Christ as being a part of themselves truly make the effort in this hour to raise up a Light, not only for their own survival but for that of the many?

The question of free will, then, must be addressed. For many see a bright future and predict it and do not understand that they themselves must be the fulfillment and the instruments of their own prediction; they do not understand that invisible hands do not suddenly appear to rearrange the karma of a planet with a roseate dawn and a path through the mountains where you walk hand in hand into the sunset. These are beautiful dreams, beloved, but take care that that red sun in the sky is not from a nuclear blast [fireball].

Understand, beloved, that this holocaust which is projected by mankind's present karma exactly as the Blessed Mother has said, by the agents of Satan and erring individuals, could well occur unless those who have the light, the will, the ability—and where do we find that but in America—shall raise up a defense not only for this nation but for the entire planet.

Saint Germain has given from the Cave of Symbols a technology for the keeping of the peace and not for war. Yet the diligence has been wanting. And therefore, in this nation, that which was given to the Lightbearers has been transferred to the seed of the wicked† who have plotted a course of destructivity beyond imagination.

Therefore, I commend you to the Path in which you are engaged, to the call that you have already answered, to implement it by letting the Light in you become a voice that is heard—heard all the way to the Oval Office and the houses of Congress. Let it be heard, beloved, for your voice is also recorded by angels. And therefore, the karma of protest is a positive karma and does accrue to your lifestream as that which you determine to do and to be in the face of all odds and those national policies that, though considered to lead to Peace, shall surely lead to War. The instability of the economy is the sign, even the sign of the opening of the way for the enemy to take advantage by war or other means.

Know always, beloved, that we who are the Lords of the Seven Rays do manifest instantly at your side when you make the call to us in the name of God. We say, "To know you is to love

*of the dark night of the soul and the dark night of the Spirit †offspring of the "Wicked One"

you," as we know your hearts afire. We trust that you will also say of us, "To know you is to love you." And therefore, we invite you to get to know us in these writings set forth[2] by our direction and by the love of the Messengers and their staff.

We invite you to our retreats once again. May you make the call and receive the ministrations of Chamuel's band, sending angels of Love to your side who will protect you by the Ruby Ray, even as Archangel Michael's legions are engaged in the binding of evil forces unknown to you and yet which are affecting your lives daily and mightily.

In the name of the living Word we come for communion. And our angels, angel devas of the diamond heart of God's will, attend you in this hour. And they are fashioning in a basket weave a diamond heart to seal your heart. It is our love of the will of God in you and in all past service of all previous lifetimes that gives to the ascended hosts such unmitigated devotion as we come to stand at your side.

Know, then, beloved, that *unless you make the call we are not allowed by cosmic law to intercede or to interfere in your lives.* This law, you must understand, is binding upon all those who dwell in the Spirit cosmos or even in the etheric octave.

What happens on this earth, then, is purely and squarely on your shoulders and in your hands—in your free will and in your determination to unite on this one point: that you have a right to a spiritual defense of angels and Archangels and the Light [*Christos*] descending, and that you also have a divine inheritance that guarantees to you the right to a physical defense.

Inasmuch as you are in charge of the physical earth as the platform of your evolution, you, then, must see to it that the defense of freedom at every hand—in every chakra, for every soul and child and for the boundaries of the nations and the states—is indeed intact. Therefore, know that Archangel Michael has never been more at the side of all those in the earth who cherish that flame of freedom and have determined to keep the flame of Life and to defend the integrity of the individual and his reunion with God.

Know, then, beloved, that at this moment, given fifty years, Saint Germain and the hosts of Light could so awaken a planet as to move it in peace and without a tremble into the great golden age of Aquarius. That is the divine plan for this era. But fallen ones have for centuries busied themselves to deny that fruit of Victory to all saints and Lightbearers.

Thus, beloved, you are victims and have been victimized. But once you know the Truth, know, then, that knowledge is not only power but it is responsibility: and the responsibility is upon you.

It is indeed incumbent upon you that you let your voice be heard and your vote count for those strategies so necessary for the keeping of the flame of peace of the Prince of Peace who said, "I came not to send peace but a sword." This sword, nevertheless, is a sword of peace, a deflecting two-edged sword that does turn back unto its point of origin all hate and hate creation that is turned against the Light.

Understand just how much our hopes are placed in you from the ascended octave. And when you pin your hopes upon angels and Ascended Masters, you do not do so in vain—so long as you make the call and give the dynamic decree for us to enter your life. For we shall not fail you when you bid us enter daily and hourly. A quick call to us will result in a planetary action.

The Light of God never fails, beloved. And your Mighty I AM Presence is that Light. May you also not fail to make that call.[3]

I seal you in the diamond heart of Mary. I am your brother. Call to me and know my love.

Thus, I release keys that shall unlock in you a light and an integration when you yourself raise your vibration and the fervor of your love to that point that the key may be unlocked for you.

I AM Morya of the flame of God's will, ever the champion of your right to be.

"The Summit Lighthouse Sheds Its Radiance O'er All the World to Manifest as Pearls of Wisdom."
This dictation by **El Morya** was **delivered** by Elizabeth Clare Prophet on **October 27, 1987** following her lecture at the Chase Park Plaza, **St. Louis, Missouri,** where she was stumping for Saint Germain's Coming Revolution in Higher Consciousness. (**1**) **The Lords of the Seven Rays** and the retreats where they conduct their universities of the Spirit: El Morya (First Ray), Darjeeling, India; Lord Lanto (Second Ray), Royal Teton Retreat, Grand Teton, Jackson Hole, Wyoming; Paul the Venetian (Third Ray), Temple of the Sun, New York; Serapis Bey (Fourth Ray), Luxor, Egypt; Hilarion (Fifth Ray), Crete, Greece; Nada (Sixth Ray), Saudi Arabia; Saint Germain (Seventh Ray), Royal Teton Retreat, Grand Teton, Jackson Hole, Wyoming. See pp. 285, 286. (**2**) See Mark L. Prophet and Elizabeth Clare Prophet, *Lords of the Seven Rays: Mirror of Consciousness,* Summit University Press, $5.95 (add $.50 for postage). (**3**) The Light of God never fails! (3x) and the beloved Mighty I AM Presence is that Light!

Vol. 30 No. 71 *A Cosmic Being from out the Great Silence* *December 10, 1987*

Saint Germain Stumps America

14

Summoned to the Highest and Noblest Purpose

The Eleventh-Hour Victory That Is Possible

From out the Great Silence I Address You—
Children of the Sun, Sons and Daughters of God.

I AM a Cosmic Being ensouling, therefore, Cosmos. In the heart of God I AM. And I AM come to you for the bracing of this city and your hearts in a chalice formed of crystal light.

Therefore, beloved, into this chalice there is poured a Life-giving essence, that you might know that in his day each and every one is given to drink of the cup of Life. To do so, then, is to receive the impartation of an essence that can become the all of Self. To taste of the elixir of Light, therefore, is to develop the thirst for everlastingness that may come by the application of the science of the Word and the Work of the Lord.

Hearken, ye legions of Light, angels marching with the Faithful and True. Hearken, then, ye saints robed in white who cry out from the altar of God, "How long, O Lord?"[1]

Therefore, we come with a timetable and a cosmic clock. It is a giant face, that all might understand the meaning of the eleventh hour and the eleventh-hour Victory that is possible. Only with God are all things possible. With man, nothing is possible.[2]

Therefore, for all the schemes and treaties and preparations and armaments of war, what shall survive the age is the pure in heart. And the pure in heart shall see God and live.[3]

Therefore, in the Purity Flame of an ancient focus of Light, I descend into this city to call those who have reincarnated from the previous golden age that was once in this area. Blessed ones, you have known of the Light, and long ago the prophecy of a Darkness to come was given to you here.

You volunteered to return to this area to enshrine the heart of a nation as a celebration of the Heart of God in life here below. You said, "O Blessed One, we shall go forth and remember to keep the Flame in that future age."

The hour came, then, when angels of God accompanied you to the portals of birth. And you descended in the forms you now wear, some having come here from other cities, yet all called to the dance of the hours, the weaving of a net of Light [the Christ consciousness] for a guardian action.

Guardian angels have come, and seraphim, even Gabriel. And thus, at inner levels you may behold white light, angels in white, Cosmic Beings in white this very night walking the streets of this city. Yes, they bear a purging Light in answer to a call made. Yes, they come to forestall imbalance that could cause the imbalance in Nature foreseen by some psychics.

We raise up a wall of Light that must be sustained by the daily call of the inhabitants. Therefore, we say again, remember the Ancient of Days. Remember your First Love in the heart of God. Remember the sweetness of being in the bosom of God. And know, then, that thy descent is single-pointed. Its purpose, as a two-edged sword: the celebration of the energy of light of a Spirit cosmos and the consuming of all Darkness that would assail it.

Lead me to the Real, I say. I have been led to the real hearts of Light here and across this area. I have been led by the Keeper of the Scrolls, who does name the names of those written in the Book of Life, gathered to this territory therefore, who know the name of God "I AM" and are determined that that name shall prevail.

From the heart of the Cosmic Council I announce to you a season given and gained for the saving of life and the area. Let your hearts rejoice and become one and form a diamond heart of Mother Mary in this city, a chalice, then, for this heart chakra of a nation.

Let all who treasure Freedom take the stand for Freedom and its defense. I give you the words of Alpha in this phrase. Let Liberty's torch be raised, for it is also the fire of heart that is the fleur-de-lis, a threefold flame that will not be quenched but give hope and hope and hope again. With faith and charity let the "tri-color" seen, then, in Old Glory reveal a purpose of faith and hope and charity that together may call legions of Light to your side.

Blessed hearts, it is a moment to rejoice, to quaff that drink, to take that chalice, to become it. It is a moment to know that this is the hour in which thy God has summoned thee to the highest and noblest purpose of thy life.

Angels weave a so-called cosmic connection, filigree light, between thee and thy twin flame. Let the Alpha and the Omega of being express, then, with all due diligence and hasten the fullness of the cup of joy of the seven chakras.

We release Light of the Central Sun. This Light as "a cloud of infinite energy"[4] will serve yet forty-eight hours to absorb from this city as much Darkness as the Great Law will allow. Such is the gift we bring with the coming of the Messenger. Now may your heart's offering impel her return to anchor Greater Light.

My beloved, I have loved you from the beginning. Fiery darts of Ruby Ray are sent to you to pierce unfortunate sendings, "arrows of outrageous fortune" of the seed of the wicked.

Chamuel and Charity, raise up now garments of the rose light around these. Let comfort abide, enlightenment continue until all thy house does celebrate the joy of the will of God.

In the crystal of thy heart a single drop of the divine nectar is placed. This nectar, beloved, a single drop, is the potential for God being.

May you live forever in the Heart of God. I return in Cosmos to the great Great Silence. I bow to all Love within you.

"The Summit Lighthouse Sheds Its Radiance O'er All the World to Manifest as Pearls of Wisdom."
This dictation by a **Cosmic Being from out the Great Silence** was **delivered** by Elizabeth Clare Prophet on **October 29, 1987,** following her lecture at the Knickerbocker Chicago, **Chicago, Illinois,** where she was stumping for Saint Germain's Coming Revolution in Higher Consciousness. The Messenger's Chicago Stump and this dictation are available on three 90-min. audiocassettes, A87093, $19.50 (add $.80 for postage). (**1**) Rev. 6:9–11. (**2**) Matt. 19:26; Mark 10:27; Luke 18:27. (**3**) Matt. 5:8. (**4**) **Cloud of infinite energy.** In his *Intermediate Studies in Alchemy,* Saint Germain teaches how to magnetize millions of "focal points of light" into a brilliant pulsating "cloud of infinite energy" that can be directed into personal and planetary problems for the healing of specific conditions, such as disease, pollution, crime and war. See *Saint Germain On Alchemy,* pp. 191–251, or *Intermediate Studies in Alchemy,* pp. 38–87; and *The Creation of the Cloud by Saint Germain and Meditations on the Alchemy of Constructive Change and the Control of the Aura by Elizabeth Clare Prophet,* 2-audiocassette album A8063, 3 hrs., $12.95 (add $.90 for postage). *Sacred Ritual for the Creation of the Cloud,* 65-min. audiocassette with accompanying booklet, $7.00 (add $.85 for postage).

The Judgment Call
"They Shall Not Pass!"
by Jesus Christ

In the Name of the I AM THAT I AM,
I invoke the Electronic Presence of Jesus Christ:
They shall not pass!
They shall not pass!
They shall not pass!
By the authority of the cosmic cross of white fire
it shall be:
That all that is directed against the Christ
within me, within the holy innocents,
within our beloved Messengers,
within every son and daughter of God...
Is now turned back
by the authority of Alpha and Omega,
by the authority of my Lord and Saviour Jesus Christ,
by the authority of Saint Germain!

I AM THAT I AM within the center of this temple
and I declare in the fullness of
the entire Spirit of the Great White Brotherhood:
That those who, then, practice the black arts
against the children of the Light...
Are now bound by the hosts of the LORD,
Do now receive the judgment of the Lord Christ
within me, within Jesus,
and within every Ascended Master,
Do now receive, then, the full return—
multiplied by the energy of the Cosmic Christ—
of their nefarious deeds which they have practiced
since the very incarnation of the Word!

Lo, I AM a Son of God!
Lo, I AM a Flame of God!
Lo, I stand upon the Rock of the living Word
And I declare with Jesus, the living Son of God:
They shall not pass!
They shall not pass!
They shall not pass!
Elohim. Elohim. Elohim. [chant]

Posture for giving this decree: Stand. Raise your right hand, using the *abhaya mudrā* (gesture of fearlessness, palm forward), and place your left hand to your heart—thumb and first two fingers touching chakra pointing inward. Give this call at least once in every 24-hour cycle.

Vol. 30 No. 72 | *Beloved Gautama Buddha* | *December 11, 1987*

Saint Germain Stumps America
15
The Heart Chakra of America
A Focus of the Threefold Flame Placed over the City

My Most Beloved,

I AM in the Holy Temple of Shamballa, the Shamballa of the West, whose etheric retreat has also been established from everlasting. In relationship to the Retreat of the Divine Mother that is vast over the territory now called the Royal Teton Ranch,[1] my own holy temple in the etheric octave over the Heart is, as it were, the antechamber, the secret chamber of the heart where the soul does journey, here to enter to be God-taught.

Thus, beloved, the celebration in the Heart of the Inner Retreat each summer[2] is the celebration of the eightfold chakra and the Eightfold Path. It is the entering in to the holy temple of the Great White Brotherhood whose path through our Mystery School under Lord Maitreya does bring the individual to the consecration of his life, his tabernacle, as the holy temple of being.

Thus, beloved, I come to place myself in this city, for it is indeed the heart chakra of America. All know well that without the heart, life does not continue in this body. Therefore, in this city where the winds of the Holy Spirit blow, there is the necessity for reinforcement from divine levels that the heart of America might be renewed, that the hearts of individuals in this nation might be restored by the power of the Resurrection Flame.

Blessed ones, there are organs and even chakras that may be missing by injury. But the heart must beat on and forever beat on, one with the heart of God. Therefore, the restoration of nations must receive a divine impetus. And the saying must now be

"As Chicago goes, so goes the nation."

Let the Sacred Heart and the path of its journey through Jesus Christ be known to you, that the threefold flame might be balanced and you might also know the initiations of his Teacher, Maitreya.

Therefore, to this purpose I come, well pleased that this building and sanctuary might be dedicated by yourselves as that "Holy Temple." Angels of the Lord of the World so gather, entwining this building in a spiral of garlanded white flowers. Thus, the grace of God does ever appear midst illusions and confusions and the travail of the Earth Mother to give birth to her children in Light.

Beloved ones, you have heard of the threefold-flame focus fixed on the etheric octave over the Washington Monument.[3] Therefore, in this hour, and note it well, I, Gautama, place over this city a focus of my heart, the threefold flame of the Lord of the World. This I give as a cosmic reinforcement to Victory,[4] to the Cosmic Being from out the Great Silence and all other Ascended Masters who have ever delivered their powerful discourses and dictations in this city.

I come to reinforce a unity of hearts of all who know and love Saint Germain. Therefore, crystals of light are affixed round this focus of the threefold flame positioned in the etheric octave for a guardian action and for a crystallization of the path of initiation for all who will listen to the song of the heart and the hymn of the soul.

Therefore, let the path of the Sacred Heart and of the Ruby Ray under the Lord Sanat Kumara and the beloved Lady Master Venus open in this city through your own teachings and seminars and Study Groups. Let there be a mass of arteries and veins going forth from this heart center. And let all be touched by a new life.

We come in an hour, beloved, when all of the ascended Hierarchy seek ways and means to respond to the offerings that you give daily upon the altar of Life. Therefore, when such a thrust is made by the Messenger and Keepers of the Flame, when such an outpouring of gratitude does take place, it does open the door once again for a member of Hierarchy to call forth some dispensation from the Cosmic Council of the Great Central Sun to assist mightily the Lightbearers in the earth.

This is that occasion, beloved. Therefore, let Truth triumph in this city. Even as this threefold-flame focus is positioned, so, beloved, Pallas Athena does thrust into the ground that sword of Truth. It does declare the warfare of the hosts of Light against all conceit, deceit, arrogance and ego manifest in those lifestreams who are here to keep the trust of sacred office of representatives of the people in Church and State, in industry and commerce, in the arts and education and in all social and governmental services.

Blessed ones, the call for Truth and for the All-Seeing Eye of God in this city will indeed open the way for the pilgrimage to the heart, even the heart of the Central Sun and the outpost of that heart at the Western Shamballa, physically at the Inner Retreat—to this heart chakra and to the purification of their own heart chakra until the knee is bowed before the I AM Presence and the Holy Christ Self.

O Lord of lords and King of kings, thou Christ Jesus, in thy name, most magnificent servitor of Light, I, Gautama, summon the entire Spirit of the Great White Brotherhood and all saints here below and Keepers of the Flame.

May you extol the sacred fire of Freedom in the heart of Saint Germain.

May your meditation be upon the hearts of the ascended ones.

May you find love in your heart and that wondrous love for your I AM Presence that is never conditioned by a sense of human pride or a sense of human injustice.

As love pours forth from your heart, you shall merit day by day the visitation of the angels of the Christ and the Buddha.

In that living awareness and in the folds of my garment, I seal all who would be sealed—now in the third eye, now in the heart. May you go with God and take this open door to my heart as a means for Victory, personal and planetary.

I shall receive you again this New Year's Eve when in conclave at the Royal Teton Ranch and etheric retreat at the Grand Teton we once again deliver our message and our mandate. Let us look toward the day when cloven tongues of fire are the sign of all who love Light and these cloven tongues are upon the very crown of each soul.

Thus, beloved, earth is raised up increment by increment as you serve. And this day we celebrate the victories of this Stump unto the finish. Hence we go to the focus of the white fire core of Alpha and Omega in the Twin Cities, there for the sealing of a round of releases intended to work from the inner to the outer in all America until the awareness of the glory of God and the necessity to uphold it is sung by all who love faith, who love hope, who love charity.

I say, Hail, Saint Germain! Hail, Keepers of the Flame of Life! So I AM the Keeper of the Threefold Flame of Life within all evolutions of this planet. I desire and look to the day when from the Central Sun an initial impulse and increase shall give to all a quickening and a divine awareness that Aquarius is come with the full portent and opportunity of a new age. Let it be written in that day that Keepers of the Flame have bought with a price the Freedom and Victory of Terra.

We have paid the price for your enlightenment gladly by our Life and Light. Blessed hearts, see what you can do.

"The Summit Lighthouse Sheds Its Radiance O'er All the World to Manifest as Pearls of Wisdom." This dictation by **Gautama Buddha** was **delivered** through the Messenger of the Great White Brotherhood Elizabeth Clare Prophet on **Friday, October 30, 1987,** at the Church Universal and Triumphant Chicago Community Teaching Center, **Chicago, Illinois.** (**1**) **The Retreat of the Divine Mother.** On December 15, 1985, Sanat Kumara announced, "The opening of the door of the temple of the Divine Mother and her Inner Retreat is also come. And this Inner Retreat, positioned now as a vast center of Light, is indeed above that 'Place Prepared'—prepared, of course, by the Divine Mother—the entire area of the Royal Teton Ranch." See Sanat Kumara, "The Retreat of the Divine Mother at the Royal Teton Ranch," 1986 *Pearls of Wisdom,* vol. 29, no. 10, pp. 70–72. (**2**) The annual International Conference for Spiritual Freedom sponsored by the Great White Brotherhood is held over the Fourth of July weekend at the Royal Teton Ranch near Livingston, Montana. Thousands gather from around the world to hear the prophecy of Saint Germain, the Lost Teachings of Jesus, and dictations and lectures by the Ascended Masters through their Messenger on spiritual, political and social issues. This year the Messenger conducted Summit University Forums in which she interviewed guests on the topic of the defense of freedom. Following this conference, a wilderness survival seminar and two-week retreats on the teachings of the Lords of the Seven Rays are conducted. (**3**) **Threefold-flame focus over the Washington Monument.** On September 30, 1962, K-17 announced, "There has been held a beautiful and wonderful session at Chananda's retreat in India and a decision was made on the part of beloved Paul the Venetian whereby there was transferred from his retreat in France this day, at the hour of eleven o'clock your time, the full pulsation of the great Liberty Flame. This flame was permanently placed within the forcefield of the Washington Monument; and the pulsations of the Liberty Flame are intended to grace the heart of America as a gift from the Brotherhood and from the heart of beloved Paul the Venetian. . . . It is given as a treasure from the heart of France, from the spiritual government of France to the spiritual government of America. . . . The Liberty Flame is a gift of greater magnitude than the former gift of France, the Statue of Liberty, as a tribute to that great being, the Goddess of Liberty. It is incomparable, for the flame itself shall penetrate the structure of the monument, rising high into the atmosphere above it; and all who visit there shall become, even without knowing it, infused by the pulsations of the Liberty Flame within the heart of America." See *Lords of the Seven Rays: Mirror of Consciousness,* Book One, pp. 132–33. (**4**) See Mighty Victory, "The Purging of Chicago," pp. 83–89.

Pearls of Wisdom®
published by The Summit Lighthouse

Vol. 30 No. 73 *Beloved Mother Mary* *December 12, 1987*

Saint Germain Stumps America
16
The Vision and the Lightning
The Diamond Heart of Mary over the Twin Cities

Bless my sons, O Lord, for in them is a fire kindled. Bless my daughters, O angels, for their wings do enfold precious children.

In the name I AM, I am Mary, your friend, O little ones and great ones, those who serve and those who understandably sometimes weary of serving.

I am your Mother and I come in an hour of your life when you have need of me and my angels, when you have need of Raphael for the healing of hurt.

We are divine helpers, able to help you, then, to bear the burden that so suddenly and sometimes, as it were, cruelly does come upon you.

With violet flame and healing ray my angels infuse you with a new life and strength and a corresponding transmutation.

Sometimes the very weakness of the flesh, beloved, prevents you from embodying the strength of the Spirit. Therefore, strengthen the physical chalice. Bring it into balance. Receive the offering of nourishment that comes from the Ancient of Days and his Teaching. For the adepts have paved a pathway for the balance of your bodies. And those antichrists come in this hour have infused into civilization the very elements of diet contrived to tear you from the focusing of heart, the balancing of the life-force, and the raising up of the energy [sacred fire] so necessary to win.

Angels of the Holy Spirit, I, Mary, call to you to comfort life, to reinforce the weary and to give the vision to all, that that which is given gladly this day as service shall be multiplied ten thousandfold.

For the need is great, the servers are few.

Shall the whitened harvest be not harvested?

Shall the ripened fruit ready for God consciousness be left to drop from the trees of God's orchard?

It is an age not only of the ripening of the bad fruit but of the great maturation of the children of the Sun who have seen the vision and the lightning—*who have seen the vision and the lightning, I tell you*—and heard the Word at inner levels and attended the universities of the Spirit of the Lords of the Seven Rays in their etheric retreats.

They have heard the call of the World Mother. They are ready.

Thus, as your day is, so shall your strength be[1] if you will but remember to connect with my heart in the rosary.[2] I know, beloved, many things call your attention. But the fifteen-minute rosary is a transfusion of my Body and Blood, which is also that of Alpha and Omega.

My great desire is that you might be strengthened. That you might be strengthened, beloved, is the reason for my coming.

My word of prophecy has well been spoken by our Messenger.[3] It is a detailed prophecy that comes from Virgo, the Earth Mother. Realize, then, that the tutoring of this heart to deliver this must come, for it must be presented in an orderly manner, for we would leave no stone unturned in your understanding.

The components of decision making and the decision makers must be right knowledge, right-mindfulness and a righteousness of the Holy Spirit enduing all of your life. Blessed hearts, know, then, that with the facts in mind you can better read the cycles of your own life.

To read and to run, to be centered in the heart of the crystal, in the heart of the mountain, in the heart of the memory of God, this is thy rightful place. Seek, then, the eightfold chakra and the Great Lord, the Maha Chohan.

I decree that all sorrow shall cease in the lives of those who will give themselves cheerfully, even minimally, to the call and the dynamic decree daily!

Blessed hearts, I would give you all that I AM but the Law does not allow it. I may give to you only that which you call forth and allow me to give to you by a measured beat, step-by-step and daily, on your own path of attainment.

Let the spiritual fire be fanned again, O my Raphael! For we come to serve those who have become weary in their efforts to uphold life and even the kindling fire of Saint Germain.

As I speak to you, beloved, I contact the heart of every Lightbearer in this earth who has and is giving his life for a cause, a cosmic cause of a planetary liberation. I tell you, the armies and saints of heaven do come to reinforce.

Let your lips repeat the Lord's Prayer, and in the giving of it open, *open* the door of the heart that ten thousand-times-ten thousand angels might pass through you for your healing and for the healing of nations.

I have also come in consonance with the divine will and the action of the Lord of the World. I come that my Immaculate Heart, envisioned as a diamond heart, might be placed over these Twin Cities. Let my single heart be the pattern and the presence, then, whereby you yourselves might weave the second diamond heart. I bring the heart of Alpha. You, then, bring the heart of Omega. Therefore in building together, the efforts of heaven and earth might be one and the T'ai Chi therefore set.

I pledge to you my heart, beloved. And I ask you if you might not also give your heart for the tipping of the balance in favor of Light. May it count and be a compensation for all peoples of this nation. Overflowing the bounds of the nation, let it then be for the contacting of all hearts of Light.

Dearly beloved, the altar of heaven requires an offering in this hour from some among earth if we are to stave those actions which may be forthcoming in the nation's capital at summit meetings or others held behind the scenes. Such an hour of need for the All-Seeing Eye!

Legions of the Fifth Ray and holy angels, come now! For by a vision clear the people that have walked in darkness shall see a Great Light.[4] And those who see shall live. And those who know shall be the Mind of God. And those who love shall have the heart of Christ. And those who extend mercy as violet flame petals and feathers of light, these shall receive more in kind and know a soul freedom not known before.

Give, then, casting thy bread upon the waters,* being assured thereby that it shall return to thee by a wave of light so multiplied, that abundance shall surround thee, even as a rosary of pearls may be used by you to count your blessings and your Hail Marys.

I speak to you as I release to you star-fire light and as our angels give you new hope of life. Life from the Fifth Ray angels and Healing Masters is truly a fullness to which you have a right; for Divine Wholeness is your inheritance and your reason for being. Let none take from you portion by portion your spine or your spirit, your health or holiness, your identity or your soul. Be

*"Cast thy bread upon the waters: for thou shalt find it after many days." Eccles. 11:1.

satisfied with nothing less than the full Divine Image recorded upon self and world chakras.

O Light, descend! These have come. Let them be filled.

By the chalice of Elohim thus raised up in the Heart of the Inner Retreat, the tie is established to the Western Shamballa, retreat of Gautama Buddha at the Royal Teton Ranch. Let that tie, then, give you the increase of Elohim—Elohim, beloved, the Seven Stars of the Morning, the Seven Powers of God Manifestation. Through them, I say, is the key for the vortex of Light over this city to increase and outdo and do out with the vortex of Darkness!

Will you not put those spirits of Darkness on trial, even as you try the spirits within your own auras?[5] Will you not invoke the power of Elohim that a majestic spiral of light so firm and tight and fiery shall defeat any and all that would assail thee and thy home?

From the heart of the AUM in the Central Sun the sound is heard. May you, then, seal your own chakras, intoning this AUM with me.

AUM

I AM sealing the seven chakras of each one with the Light of integrity and integration. My angels bow to the Light within your heart.

Go in Peace, beloved. The night is far spent and the day of the Divine Appearing is at hand.

"The Summit Lighthouse Sheds Its Radiance O'er All the World to Manifest as Pearls of Wisdom." This dictation by **Mother Mary** was **delivered** by Elizabeth Clare Prophet on **October 31, 1987,** following her "Halloween Prophecy 1987" at the Minneapolis Hilton Inn, **Minneapolis, Minnesota,** where she was stumping for Saint Germain's Coming Revolution in Higher Consciousness. (**1**) Deut. 33:25. (**2**) See Mary's Scriptural Rosary for the New Age, in *My Soul Doth Magnify the Lord! Mother Mary's New Age Teachings and Rosary with a Challenge to Christendom,* Summit University Press, $7.95 (add $1.00 postage); *A Child's Rosary to Mother Mary*—15-minute scriptural rosaries for the Child within you—published on 4 audiocassette albums, 3 cassettes per album: Album 1 (A7864): John, James, Jude; Album 2 (A7905): Paul to the Hebrews; Album 3 (A7934): Paul to the Galatians; Album 4 (A8045): Paul to the Corinthians, $9.95 ea. (add $.90 ea. postage); *The Fourteenth Rosary: The Mystery of Surrender,* booklet and 2-audiocassette album, includes rosary, 2 lectures, and a dictation of Mother Mary, 3 hrs., V7538, $12.95 (add $.90 postage). (**3**) In her "Halloween Prophecy 1987," the Messenger gave Mother Mary's up-to-date prophecy on Fátima, Medjugorje, the astrology of nations, the Four Horsemen of the Apocalypse and the economy. See p. 482. (**4**) Isa. 9:2. (**5**) I John 4:1.

Pearls of Wisdom®
published by The Summit Lighthouse

Vol. 30 No. 74 *Beloved Jesus Christ* *December 13, 1987*

Saint Germain Stumps America
17
The Day of Thy Christhood
Keep the Flame of Eternal Life

Out of the Light I AM come, never absent but only making you aware, beloved, of my entrance, that you might realize that your own proximity to the Universal Christ does indeed have to do with the preparation of the bride. As you daily invoke this wedding garment by the science of sound, know that this is the vessel I require [that I may] enter into your heart and being, to dwell with you, to walk with you, to be a part of the Great Overcoming in this era.

Let my disciples, then, fulfill the Word of Light and the Law of the One. For I, Jesus, as the Bridegroom, desire my perfect love [to be] in you to give unto you that union of Christos for which your souls have longed and hungered.

Blessed hearts, there must be a sustaining, a continuum of Light. Let discipleship, then, be thy reason for being and thy goal the attainment of the All.

Our desiring, as the ascended hosts of Light, is to work with you daily [in order] that this soul within you be formed and re-formed by the sacred fires of the Holy Spirit.

So, beloved, we are not absent. For the Great White Brotherhood, all saints ascended, whose celebration is even this day, gather, ten thousand-times-ten thousand and more. The saints robed in white can be seen by you and known by you. In fact, you can be a saint robed in white on earth long before the hour of your full ascension. For the white aura is the sign of purification and a path and the [soul's] empowerment by the Light of the Divine Mother.

Seek Her and know Her and find Her. Love Her and rise with

Her. Follow the Divine Mother all the way Home to thy Father. For thy Father does attend thee in the courts of heaven. But thy Mother has tarried with thee in earth to restore a Teaching and a Path, to quicken, to love you, to anoint you, to prophesy to you, to chasten you, *to love you and raise you up.*

Even so, beloved, I AM that Mother, for God in me is also Mother. And I extend that Mother Flame to you in this hour through my Messenger, even as my Mother Mary has extended her heart's love and healing through her.

Know, then, that this comfort is an understanding of all of your ways and your waywardness. It is an understanding of your return and your becoming fed up with the old ways of the old man.[1] It is an awareness of your struggles to cease from the ways of life that tear down the light and to be turned around, to be converted [unto the Universal Christ] by the great sun disc, that Great Central Sun Magnet.

O Lord God in the heavens, receive them unto thyself, even a portion, even the mind and heart. Now let them be filled.

Blessed hearts, it is the hour and this is the day of the marking of the hour, November 1st, 1987. Mark it well, beloved, for it is a date written in the Book of Life. And for this reason and on this date I have come to these Twin Cities to celebrate our twin flames, each and every one of you as Alpha and Omega.

I have come to bring to you, then, the Word of our Father, and it is this: The hour has come for you to understand, beloved, that nothing less than becoming the Christ will suffice as fulfillment or requirement of the Law. Too long and long enough have you been blessed and fed by other anointed ones, too long have you come to receive in your church services, in your synagogues and temples and mosques.

Realize, then, that those who have received a light, a witness, a testimony of the ascended hosts, those who know now the true path of the geometry of God, those whose internalization of the Word is long due are given the sign in this hour. And it is the sign of the Holy Spirit. This is the day that the path of thy Christhood must begin in earnest. Not [postponed] till tomorrow but today, my Christ, thy Christ One.

Counting this day as the first day, if you will, of an earnest discipleship unto my Flame and Heart, I draw you if you will be drawn. I receive you if you will indeed be received. Therefore, beloved, know that I, Jesus, declare this day, formally with my Father, as the commencement of a path for Lightbearers of the world who know that in my mantle and in my momentum there is a gift to be received—to be earned and won.

I, Jesus, come to you, beloved, in this hour to impel you forward. For I will not leave thee except by your own request. And therefore I will be as the "hound of heaven."[2]

Too many yet sleep, having been awakened yet preferring sleep. Be quickened, beloved, and know that the accountability is upon you from this day forward and that the Law does require it for thy salvation, for the very survival of the soul herself.

Cosmic cycles have turned. And in their turning, even the days and the hours of thy life now numbered must be filled with Light and the cup filled daily. For, beloved, if you heed me not you will find yourself at the conclusion of this life wanting in the Light necessary to make the transition to higher octaves.

Foreseeing the world as I foresee it, I do not recommend in all cosmic honor that you plan on reembodying again on this earth.

The hour of your fulfillment is come! Your Christhood is nigh and has been knocking at the door for many years and lifetimes. And some who have known this path and received, as it were, a mouth-to-mouth resuscitation by the chakras of the Messenger have retained the Light and yet not sought the mastery of the Light, the self-perfecting in the Light, the protection of the Light and the will to be as GOD IS.

Thus, we minister unto you. Now we say, Become that Christ! Receive your Lord and your God into your temple. And I, Jesus, as your brother, will walk at your side, will talk with you, will counsel you. And you will know me in the Love that I shared with John, my beloved. You will know the intimacy of Love's communion and Love's initiation.

Take to your hearts, then, the lessons given by Saint Germain. Resolve to keep the Flame of Life that is your own Christhood, for only in that Christ flame do you have with you eternal Life.

Blessed ones, your eternal Life is not something to be set aside as a garment or to be left in heaven. You need a lamp in which a Flame of eternal Life is burning continually. For in the day or the hour of the coming of the dark night of the Spirit or even the dark night of the soul, it is this Light that shall light thy way and be a light unto all thy house.

One and several, many and thousands will depend upon this Light. And in the day of your appearing in this Christ, you will be grateful unto God that you have heard me and heeded my word. For so shall you see that ten thousand may be saved because the Flame of eternal Life is burning brightly in the temple of being.

Feel it now, beloved, for I place my Sacred Heart one with

your own, one for the impetus of the balance of the threefold flame, for the impetus of the twelve petals of the heart chakra to provide you now, one by one, with the initiations of the twelve gates of the temple, even the seven chakras and the eighth and the five secret-ray chakras. Thus the thirteenth is the deliverance of the All unto the all of you. By the path of the Sacred Heart, by the path of the Ruby Ray, so triumph in grace and in good works, so triumph in graciousness and selflessness.

I, then, predict your future. For this day I have studied the record of the Book of Life for each and every lifestream who has come to this seminar and for all individuals who are called Keepers of the Flame worldwide. My prediction, then, given coming events, given your own karma, is that the only way out of the dilemma of the human equation is to act now.

Hear me, beloved! I have never been more in earnest. I have cried unto the Lord for you. And God's emissaries have brought abundant Light and Teaching.

Hear me, beloved! For even my plea is a measured one. For the Father has said to me, "How many times will you plead for their own cause of eternal Life, my Son?" Therefore, the Law and the dispensation of karma does allow it, but not forever.

Therefore, hear my cry to your soul! Hear my cry to pick yourself up, to wax hot in your devotion and fervor, to know the inner life, to desire to feel the flow of sacred fire in your being and to desire this until by your very imploring, as in the parable of the unjust judge,[3] so God does respond.

For the soul that does trouble the Lord does truly receive her recompense. If your desiring is sincere and you implore God daily, I tell you, beloved, the Father will not withhold from you every test and initiation, every teaching and interior correction, every leading you require to the fount of knowledge, even Gnosis, even my own Lost Teachings.

Beloved, hear, then, the Word of the Son of God and live! I AM your brother of Light. I come to you in such Reality with my angels in this hour. I come for your rescue. And I come for that rescue that you might in turn rescue others. It is time for you to be true shepherds and ministers, ministering unto the Word at the altar and ministering unto souls who have need of that Light.

Blessed ones, the impelling Light spoken out of the Shekinah, out of the heart of Mary in the deliverance of her prophecy and Saint Germain's, has given to you the accurate vision of the assignment of your Christhood in these Twin Cities. You did not come here merely to escape and to survive. You came here, beloved, to raise up a pillar of fire, that *all* might escape and *all* might survive.

Now let us see to it that the sons of God shall win in this competition. After all, beloved, those who on your behalf fight the good fight in Armageddon have a right to see your Light so raised up as to devour, then, that funnel and vortex of Darkness[4] that hangs heavy over this city.

Let us see, then, how the servant-sons of God on earth shall salute the Godhead and the saints in heaven that none of these saints should have died in vain but should have lived forever, that you might prove here below that this kingdom of God on earth shall not be violated any longer by the forces of avarice or witchcraft or black magic or of the fallen angels' desecration of the soul of the youth.

Let it be so! For it is time and high time that the Father should have a witness in the earth that does prove the victory of Life over Death and Hell! Let this come swiftly! Let it be, beloved, because you have seen the challenge and consider that for your very own integrity and integration with the living Word of the Mother, you should not allow, while you have breath and life, those forces to defile a holy city.

And once there was a holy city, a city magnificent, in this place. And once you lived in this city. And once you knew the Light and kept the Flame and raised it up. And none could enter there because the Light did seal the city from the intrusion of any whose vibration was less than the Light of the living Flame that you kept on the altar of your heart. And that Flame of eternal Life did burn with a brilliance of Wisdom, the Empowerment of God and the Love of the Holy Spirit.

Therefore, beloved, as in the case of many golden-age civilizations, by subtlety and by microscopic degrees in temperament, in vibration always eventuating in the magnetism of oneself to lower and lower energies, this city then became open, a totally open city for those of all laggard evolutions, those of the cults of the heathen and the hedonists. And by and by the balance was changed: the Darkness prevailed. You forfeited the Light of many lifetimes and went the way of those with cunning and cleverness in their leading who always promise that if you go in their way you will not surely die.[5]

Be it known, beloved, that to leave off the keeping of the Flame of eternal Life is the very first act of suicide. Let it not be said of this generation that they have lost the Word so ready to descend into their temples to save a planet and a people. I cannot speak otherwise, for the messianic mission is yours! The word *messiah* means simply "leader." Some must rise up and lead.

Here is the One, the Divine Mother, who leads up the spiral staircase. Follow, then, the Divine Mother all the way to your own crown of Life. Follow, then. For as you set the pace, as fads go in this world, many will follow. It seems a folly in itself that people will follow others in doing almost anything, even if it is most obviously ludicrous or a desecration of life.

The example set of the Light in you must be a quickening. I direct you, then, to the example of my Messenger Mark who is ascended with me now. This one who lived in your midst did truly have the charisma of the Holy Spirit, which is the presence in the aura of the magnetism of Love. That presence became a profile of Christhood impressed upon the ethers of the earth. There are many who walk following that profile today, though they know not that they follow him.

Realize, beloved, that all souls of earth take a reading on your footsteps. And those of Light who desire to know the Great White Brotherhood and to enter in, they follow those who call themselves disciples. Therefore, no longer be disciples but anointed ones. I, Jesus, declare it! I summon you and I command you as my own. Take up the lead. For many must follow, and that quickly, ere the age draw the curtain on my dispensation.

I AM Jesus of Nazareth. I AM your own. Receive me now and receive the serving of Holy Communion as a sign and a promise that I give you of my Life-essence, my spiritual fire, my Mother Body.

My Alpha and my Omega be unto you the quickening. Then return it unto me multiplied and with good fruit. Such is the requirement of the Great Law and the Great Guru, our God.

I see now you and your twin flame in heaven. And my inner eye is fixed upon you and your beloved complement in your inner white-fire bodies. I hold this in my inner sight until you should reject my path, my counsel or comfort.

I AM your Jesus. Now I say to you, Be my Christ!

With the sign of our Oneness and the Law of the Word, I AM with you alway—to the end of your tribulation in this age.

AUM AUM AUM

In the Oneness of the All, I AM thy True Self.

"The Summit Lighthouse Sheds Its Radiance O'er All the World to Manifest as Pearls of Wisdom." This dictation by **Jesus Christ** was **delivered** by Elizabeth Clare Prophet on All Saints Day, **Sunday, November 1, 1987,** at the Minneapolis Hilton Hotel, **Minneapolis, Minnesota.** Prior to the dictation, the Messenger delivered the lecture "The Lost Teachings of Jesus 8 On Woman and the Divine Mother." See p. 482.
For notes, see Pearl 76, p. 590.

Vol. 30 No. 75 *Beloved Serapis Bey* *December 14, 1987*

Saint Germain Stumps America

18

A Warning of Danger in the Earth

Use Saint Germain's Heart Meditation for Fourteen Days

Blessed Ones Who Have Seen the Light,

In this day and age but the few perceive it [the Light] and among those who do, a lesser percentage pursue it, seek to define and refine it within being, or even become enamored by it.

Let not the fervor of your First Love wax cold. For in this hour of Ascension's call,[1] I, Serapis, come to you to warn you of a danger in the earth. That danger is the absence of those who keep the Flame of the Divine Mother, even the light of the base-of-the-spine chakra.

The abuses of this light have reached a level beyond the abuses that were practiced against the Divine Mother both on Lemuria and in Atlantis. Whether through the misuse of science or sound, technology or even that light raised to the third eye in practices of black magic, these perversions of the light of the Mother led to the sinking of these continents.

You may comprehend that the Law acted in those ages and cataclysm ensued as a result of this misuse of the Mother Flame. Therefore, beloved, you may understand what a grace is upon the planet in this hour that such infamy should be ongoing and on the increase and yet in many quarters life continues as always and many are able to walk a path of Light.

My coming to you in these Twin Cities is, of course, to remind you, as you have already been reminded, to seek reunion with the Father/Mother God, to raise up a pillar of Light that shall not only overpower the dark funnel that has been raised by the fallen ones, but to do so for the expressed urgency of providing a compensation for such abuses as are on the planet in this hour. Nuclear war itself is the abuse of the sacred fire of the atom. And thus, beloved, the infamy upon infamy can be a tale that is told many times.

Our warning is this, then, that unless that spark divine in Keepers of the Flame should wax hot and allow you once again to tend the altars as you should, there is little that will be done to avert those projections that have been told to you in our prophecy of last evening.[2]

It seems as though Keepers of the Flame have been burdened by the very weight of the year. Blessed hearts, it was announced to you that the weight of planetary karma would increase on January 1st of this year. Now you have been prepared for those astrological configurations that bear the portent of a far greater weight.

What will you do—you who have allowed yourselves already to become bowed down by returning karma of the planet—what will you do when, on January 1st, 1988, the weight of the planet will feel tenfold that of the previous year?

Precious hearts, only by establishing priorities when you see the Light and have the Light will you be able to sustain your fervor and momentum in the hour when the planetary levels of Darkness rise. Now, this rising can be met by you with glorious convocations held throughout December for winter solstice, Christmas Eve and Day, and the usual New Year's conclave. May it be so, beloved, for all that you can do to bank the violet fires for that hour of the New Year's descent will serve you well in the years ahead.

Take refuge, then, in the Divine Mother in a very present person in the beloved Mary and so many angels of heaven. But above all, take unto yourself Her swaddling garment and let the Light be raised up. Let your goal be the Ascension. Let it be to endure.

For some of you, this year has spelled sudden setbacks, calamities, illnesses difficult to bear. Others have experienced the financial setbacks brought on by the coming of the black horse. Be it so, beloved. The Path and the Teaching of the living Christ is such that as you accelerate with it, the Light in you is able to meet the tide of Darkness and consume it. Therefore, our purpose in being here this evening is to pledge to you our support as you join the living Christ Jesus as disciple, willing to be tutored of heart.

This message and seminar is very pointed to Keepers of the Flame, especially in this city but in all cities of the nations. For we come with a sense of concern that some have not heeded the cry nor known just how great is the threat whether of nuclear war or of economic debacle. Let your preparations include, then, an hourly concern for the giving of those fiats and calls that will deter those prophecies clearly outlined in the Messenger's work on Nostradamus.[3]

I AM Serapis and I can tell you that in our etheric retreat, circles within circles within circles of students of the Ascension Flame hold twenty-four-hour vigils for the keeping of a pillar of fire for the nations. When you serve your two-week term at Luxor in the course of cycling through the universities of the Spirit of the Lords of the Seven Rays, you, then, also join these circles. The circles are more than that action which does hold a decree momentum. The circles are solar rings composed of the unified hearts of all those who form them.

Thus, my passage through this city with legions of seraphim does mark even the day and the hour when you elect to wear white robes and to be in the earth saints of God, pillars in the temple and initiates of Serapis through the Lord Christ.

From the heart of Luxor now receive to your heart an impetus of the Mother Flame. It is a foundation stone and a white cube that will assist you to raise the sacred fire from the base chakra to the heart. From that level, then, the soul rising on that upward-moving fountain may find the protection of the white fire in communion with the living Christ.

We, the Lords of the Seven Rays, sponsors of Summit University at the Royal Teton Ranch in 1988, do welcome you, then, in the etheric quadrant of the year (January, February and March) for our quarter wherein we shall concentrate week upon week for the balancing of chakras and the giving to you new light and new birth so that you are well equipped to carry the momentum on your return to the cities.

All of heaven is poised to assist all Lightbearers to enter in to the period of earth's transition. Truly let us see the planet as a violet flame sphere and know that one heart in God is able to be the vessel for the saving of millions.

The love of the Masters of the Fourth Ray surrounds you. If you look up, you will see a circle of initiates from our etheric retreat who have formed a circle round about this room. These are your brothers and sisters who are advancing on the path of the Divine Mother. Some of you have met them in our retreat as you journey there at night. Some of you have yet to make their acquaintance. They have come here for a purpose, to lend their bodies and auras as a cosmic reinforcement, reinforcing in you health and strength and the necessary supply to make preparation in every way.

Thus, the blessing of the heart as the white light shall now liberate you in an extraordinary manner. May you take the mantras of the heart and the tape for the clearing of the heart chakra by Saint Germain, and for a period of fourteen days use that tape daily as Saint Germain's Heart Meditation.[4] Use it, beloved, for fourteen days is the required allotment of time to absorb the gift that is given to its greatest usefulness and effectiveness in your world.

Blessed ones, you have heard of dispensations in prior years. Let me assure you that our Father Alpha has sent me with the blessing of Mother Omega to bring to you this warning, this countermeasure and this assignment. On this tape you will find Saint Germain's invocations for the clearing of your heart chakra given as a dictation during this meditation. By this, beloved, and the consequent expansion of the heart and its reinforcement, you will know a strength, a courage, an elation and a joy to press on and to maintain your light in ever-increasing levels so that that Light is always greater in intensity than the Darkness of returning karma and the forces of Armageddon that assail it.

You, my beloved who have seen the Light, to you I say, Become the Light! Become the Light, beloved. For it will take, measure for measure, less effort than to deal with the calamities that may come upon you because you have failed to heed the warning or to become that Light.

Be assured that we have sent our Messenger warning the people from city to city with our message of urgency. This is no ordinary Stump but one that must count in the annals of the nation even as a ride of Paul Revere.

Let the Light in the Lighthouse be the sign, then, that our God approaches. And let the cry of terror in the night out of the astral plane be the sign also that at the point and time determined the pale horse shall also ride.

Ever with you in the Middle Way that leads to eternal Life, I AM your mentor of the Spirit and your loving disciplinarian on the Path of Ascension's Flame.

My Electronic Presence can be called by you daily and hourly in these fourteen days which begin in this very hour. In that period of time may you receive me and my momentum of Light for the Victory. As one devoted to your heart, I now withdraw to higher octaves.

This dictation by **Serapis Bey** was **delivered** on **Sunday, November 1, 1987,** at the Minneapolis Hilton Inn, **Minneapolis, Minnesota.** For Notes, see Pearl 76, p. 590.

Vol. 30 No. 76 — *Beloved Saint Germain* — *December 15, 1987*

Saint Germain Stumps America

19

The Agenda of the Forces of Light and Darkness

The Judgment Falls upon Those of Greatest Neglect

Angels of my bands, I, Saint Germain, salute you! Come now, O legions of violet flame angels! Come now for the dissolution of worlds of malintent as the benign influences of Aquarius increase.

I AM here, beloved, also by the urgency of the hour, for your quickening, to bring all that the Great Law will allow of Seventh Ray dispensation for your unity and one-pointedness of purpose.

You have heard that Alpha has lent to you his Mantle for assistance to the Lightbearers of earth. The Proclamation of Alpha given at Wesak,[1] his address at the Fourth of July conference[2]—those conditions set forth therein for assistance to earth have not changed. May you study these dictations as you receive your own Pearls of Wisdom. And let all who enter this path know that the dictations that have gone before in this year and the last will tell you step-by-step of that which is transpiring at inner levels as the entire Spirit of the Great White Brotherhood does take its stand to defend the Lightbearers who uphold a flame midst the dark.

I AM, then, in the heart of Freedom. And my sight is set upon the nation's capital. There I shall be this Thanksgiving, and I bid you be there also; for the portents of that summit are not of Light and not of Victory nor of Peace. That such folly should befall the nation in the hour not only of maximum peril but maximum Light! How can two centuries of striving of fiery spirits be set aside by ignorance and illusion and pride such as is indicated for the signing away of the last vestige of defense for Europe?

Dear hearts, the Messenger has delivered this message city by city. Yet, know truly that it is I who have delivered it, I who have warned, I who have empowered her and you to understand what is the real agenda of the forces of Light and the forces of Darkness that have inveigled themselves into both governments.

Therefore, let the people know. Let the people know that their very platform of evolution, their very future is being bargained away by those who have become puppets of hell. And it is so and I state it. For the false hierarchies of fallen angels have had their heyday.

How much more will they be given, then, by a nation that sleeps and does not tackle the beast of these giant skulls of rebellion, surely whited sepulchres[3] who wander the halls of Congress and government and have no offering whatsoever, whose auras ought to be seen by you (and yet the Light of America has descended), auras of blackness, auras that exude foul odors on the astral plane? Yet, suave are they, denying every offering of everyone sent by my heart to give some measure of deliverance.

Blessed hearts, even as you are burdened by events parading before your eyes, know that I too am chagrined, to say the least, to be about America in an hour when so much is lost, even for the weakness and the instability of minds and hearts.

Where is there the loyalty or the cosmic honor flame? Where is there the one who is the Light in the Lighthouse of being? Where are men and women who can be alerted by what we manage to send you as warning through the media? Will none act? Will all wait and watch and see?

I tell you there is a mass hypnotic spell upon the nation. And it is infamous and diabolical. Blessed hearts, truly, I say, if ever there were to be an hour to let your voice count, let it be before it is too late.

May you write your name and subscribe to our Pearls of Wisdom before you leave this night, for you need to read every dictation given on this Stump. You need to know what has been said and delivered.

Blessed hearts, nowhere else will you hear the full Truth. And nowhere else will you meet a body of individuals determined to deal squarely with that Truth and squarely with the Lie.

How dear is life when none are there to proclaim it? Therefore, let this sweet life that you are about sense a future where life could be dim and heavily diminished and conditions bleak. Let us avoid it, beloved. I say to you once and for all, let us avoid what is projected by every prophecy that can be read and read accurately.

Let us act as though we were making sacrifice in the last day. For it is that hour.

I came, then, to New York and did pronounce the judgment as did the LORD God in that hour. So I pronounce it now. Blessed ones, the judgment must be seen as potentially falling upon those of greatest neglect. Those who have the most Light and Awareness, they shall also have the greatest karma by their neglect of their Light and their Awareness.

I teach you and illumine you concerning Cosmic Law and nothing else. I teach you, then, beloved, that to see the Light is to become it, else you will lose that opportunity. I can only reiterate what my brother Serapis has said and tell you that the day's advance and your position must be defined, cleared and maintained.

I will see you in Washington. And there and then I shall deliver my full address. For this moment I say, in the month given to you, beginning this day, let us together fell the pillar of Darkness that has been built in this city. And let us replace it with Light.

Can we not have something to offer the Fourteen Ascended Masters who govern the destiny of this nation and freedom to the earth? Can we not raise up a sign to Surya? Can we not say, "Here is the line drawn by Keepers of the Flame and Lightbearers!"—"the line," quoth Morya, "where Light meets Darkness and swallows it up"?

Somewhere some must prove that the impossible is possible with God, the Mighty I AM Presence. Somewhere a sign must be given to the Cosmic Council that more intercession can be given because some have been willing to pay the price.

My heart's blessing shall continue as you visit our two Teaching Centers in the month ahead for the raising up of this Light. Therefore, beloved, the sign of the Twin Cities shall be the sign of Alpha and Omega. What sign that is must be known by the end of this year.

I AM Saint Germain. In all of the love of your heart, I am your brother. And I walk with you every step, every precious footstep of your path to Freedom. Now, win it! Now, go for it, beloved! For the now may not come again.

With the sign of the Maltese cross on the forehead, I shall now seal you as servants of God with a vision—the protection and the strength to fulfill it.

I AM Sanctus Germanus, ever with you in the Eye of God.

"The Summit Lighthouse Sheds Its Radiance O'er All the World to Manifest as Pearls of Wisdom." This dictation by **Saint Germain** was **delivered** by Elizabeth Clare Prophet on **November 1, 1987,** at the Minneapolis Hilton Inn, **Minneapolis, Minnesota,** where she was stumping for Saint Germain's Coming Revolution in Higher Consciousness. (**1**) See pp. 242–46. (**2**) See pp. 379–88. (**3**) Matt. 23:27.

Notes from Pearl No. 74 by Jesus Christ:
(**1**) Rom. 6:6; Eph. 4:22; Col. 3:9. (**2**) See "The Hound of Heaven," a poem by the English poet Francis Thompson (1859–1907). (**3**) Luke 18:1–8. (**4**) **Funnel of Darkness and Funnel of Light over the Twin Cities.** In her "Halloween Prophecy 1987" delivered October 31, 1987, in Minneapolis, the Messenger described two funnels over the Twin Cities: "Two funnels appear over the city like tornadoes, rising straight up, a very tightly coiled funnel and then the spreading of the top as the opening. One is black and one is white. The black signifies the collective misuses of the Light of God; it is a vortex of Darkness and of karma. The funnel itself is holding up this Darkness and this karma. . . . This funnel is very high, perhaps spreading from its center five hundred miles, and it is simply full of astral substance. It is the overshadowing force over the city. The lesser funnel is a funnel of Light, it is white. The canopy of the dark one comes over it. It rises up maybe fifty miles extending with the same shape, a tightly coiled funnel opening at the top, having a radius of perhaps five miles. Each of these is a vortex of energy. The one that is the vortex of Light signifies the Light that is being raised up as cumulative, up until this hour. The Darkness shows the misqualification in the same geographical area. . . . The reading I am giving you of today in the Twin Cities is not the hour of the Final Judgment. It is a reading that tells us how we are running our courses—what is the strength of the forces of Antichrist, what is our strength. If we were to be weighed today, we would see the balances tip in favor of Darkness. But this is a reading that we can run with. It's a measure that is given. God often sends his angels with measuring rods so that we can know where we are in our Book of Life and in our accountability. You who are assembled here this evening are fully sufficient in numbers, if you should apply yourself in a vigil of the hours, to the increasing of that funnel of Light until it overtakes and supersedes the Darkness and then by its magnetism does release the violet flame for the consuming of that Darkness. This is very especially important in this city because the Twin Cities focus the Alpha, the Omega—the principles of balance in the heart of the Central Sun for America." (**5**) Gen. 3:4. **Jesus' Arabian Retreat** is located in the etheric octave over the Saudi Arabian desert northeast of the Red Sea. Another retreat, not in use at this time, is in a subterranean complex of buildings which the Masters hermetically sealed before a cataclysm covered the complex with desert sands. Nearly 400 feet beneath the surface is a huge chamber with 50-foot high columns decorated with hieroglyphs. Other stylized paintings in purple and gold line the walls. In an adjoining council chamber the cosmic symbols of the twelve houses of the sun are inlaid in the floor. The building style and interior design of this subterranean city resemble ancient Greek and Roman architecture.

Notes from Pearl No. 75 by Serapis Bey:
(**1**) See Jesus Christ, "The Call to the Path of the Ascension," pp. 269–76. (**2**) See p. 576, n. 3. (**3**) See *Nostradamus: The Four Horsemen,* in *Saint Germain On Prophecy,* Book Two. (**4**) "Saint Germain's Heart Meditation," on 90-minute audiocassette B87027, $6.50 (add $.50 postage).

Vol. 30 No. 77 *Beloved Archangel Zadkiel* *December 16, 1987*

Saint Germain Stumps America
20
The Vision of a Future That Could Be
The Choice Is Yet in the Realm of the Possible

Come Now, O Sons of Light!

I, Zadkiel, salute thee in this hour of promise. Aye, it is the promise of God to deliver thee. Aye, and *you* have promised to deliver *Him* in this hour—in His little ones, in souls shorn of the wedding garment.

Hearken ye, O Lightbearers of a nation and many nations. I, Zadkiel, speak to you as I spoke to the children of Light by the mouth of Moses and of the ancient prophets. For we the Seven Archangels did deliver the prophecy of the Lord by the mouth of Isaiah, Jeremiah and those who went before you in those ancient times. Therefore, the Word that is delivered to you in this hour is a prophecy of the Seventh Ray and Age.

Children of the Light, sons of Light in your midst, hear me! For I cast before you now a vision of violet flame, as over the land a sacred fire does burn: all of America covered by violet flame. This is the vision whereby you see what destiny America can deliver unto the nations. It is a future of hope, prosperity and light and an inner walk with God. This is the vision of Saint Germain. I am able to show it to you because you have invoked a violet flame that does appear this night as though covering the map of fifty states and more.

Beloved, this is a future that could be. I pray it will not be a future that might have been. This is Option the First whereby you the Lightbearers, by Holy Amethyst' ray, determine that the all-consuming fire of God shall be for transmutation and transformation in the earth body and element, in the sea and the waters, and in the air.

Therefore, by violet flame transmute the seven vials of the seven last plagues that we have already poured out in the earth![1] This is the sign of the coming of the new age, the age of Aquarius and of Saint Germain. It is the sign of Keepers of the Flame who know that in this hour the essential light must come forth through the Seventh Ray and the violet flame of that ray.

Know, then, beloved, that to cease the agitation, to cease the nonconcentration of the mind, to draw back to self the scattered energies of a scattered attention—this is the requirement.

Lo, I AM Alpha and Omega in the white fire core of Being!—thy being and the being of God which thou art in higher dimensions.

Know, then, beloved, that all who call themselves futurists, all who would be the avant-garde of a new dispensation of eternal Light, these are counted [as such] by us only when they are devotees of the living flame of cosmic freedom, the violet fire.

Noble ones of joy and courage, noble ones of heart, of science and of God, ye are called to an hour. The choosing of yourselves is not an exclusive choosing, for each evolution and race and wave in its time is called to raise up the ensign of Light. *Therefore a people of Light worldwide is called to bring in the great golden age of Aquarius. This, beloved, can be accomplished in this hour only if millions rally to that living flame, to the pillar of fire in the midst of Israel,*[2] *to the Holy City Foursquare established upon this continent.*[3]

Know, then, that *the choice is yet in the realm of the possible* for Lightbearers of all nations to raise up the call to Light, to summon Archangel Michael, to enjoin and to be enjoined by hosts of Light that come from cosmic spheres for the delivery of a planet.

Blessed hearts, *this vision must be fulfilled by those in embodiment,* you who have heard and seen and felt the Light and the ministration of angels in your midst. Know, then, beloved, that your capacity to contain Light is infinite, even as you are the issue of the infinite God!

O Holy Spirit, O LORD, the Great One, the Maha Chohan, come now and touch them one and all. For in the fury of the sacred fire's descent may there be, then, a gentle yet powerful stripping action whereby illusion as a veil is torn from them and they may see more of the heavenly light and the golden portal of other years.

O beloved, with thy twin flame remember the beginning from the beginning, thy origin in the Central Sun, the rounds of great concentric spheres of light, the putting on of skeins of light, lo, the descent into form for the increasing of light and awareness and attainment and evolution.

Lo, then the intergalactic battle of forces of Light and Darkness! Lo, the victory of Archangel Michael and his legions and the casting out and into the lower densities of a physical universe of all those whose allegiance was not unto the living God and his sacred fire.

Lo, your choosing did then become, O precious ones of the Light, a going forth to save that which was lost, the pursuit not alone of fallen ones but of innocent souls whom they stole from octaves of light. Many of you, therefore, are angels in embodiment, angels of the deliverance of God, angels of the vengeance of our God, angels of our bands who have chosen a sojourn upon earth to minister to thine own.

I quicken you as teachers of mankind, shepherds of souls. I call to you to understand that in a few short years, as time is reckoned by decades or centuries, you are called to come Home to God by Resurrection's fires and Ascension's flames.

I remind you of your ancient calling to deliver souls and to deliver them unto the LORD God with their God Flame blazing upon their hearts' altars. I remind you, then, of the necessity for the rescue of souls in this hour in the name of the Divine Mother, Mary, who does come to nourish the Christ flame in ye all.

I remind you that the scene of violet flame covering the land is one that can be accomplished by you. And if it is not, beloved, then you will see Option the Second. You will see coming to pass the third vision of George Washington:[4] You will see a cloud coming forth out of the East and out of the West and over the seas. You will see warfare and bloodshed upon this very continent and soil. You will see, beloved, cities of the nation overcome and burdened, a people rising up by the call of Micah, the Angel of Unity, to be one and to turn back the Adversary. And you will see as hope against hope the failing of those of America to turn back that nightmare of the Great War.

You will see, then, that the only deliverance that can come to a people so unprepared as this to face a world war is Divine Intervention. And yet, beloved, though the angelic hosts descend, some among you must be pillars of fire whereby to anchor that Divine Intercession.

Therefore, see and know, beloved, that what kind of victory shall be your own is truly your choice and choosing in this hour.

I AM Zadkiel. The Divine Mother of angelic bands of the Seventh Ray is my beloved Holy Amethyst. Feel the Presence, then, of the Archeia, of the great feminine being of the Mother of God nourishing elemental life and your souls. For we come to quicken the seat-of-the-soul chakra.[5] We come to infuse light—flame for flame.

As you have invoked the violet flame, so it does become a magnet to magnetize a certain quotient of that light from the heaven-world. As you tarry these days and consider the seriousness of this hour, beloved, know, then, that at the conclusion of this vigil we shall pour into this city a multiplication of the violet flame that you have called forth.

Our violet flame angels shall not leave this sanctuary. They shall tarry in this inn where the Christ may be born in you. Therefore, not in the cathedrals of the world, the mosques or synagogues do we appear, but we appear here in this hour where an innkeeper has said, "Make room for the birth of the living Christ." Thus, outside of a dead and dying doctrine and orthodoxy we stand to deliver the true Christ message of your Victory.

Blessed hearts, a path of individualism was extolled by Moses and the prophets. Supreme individuals were they who responded to the individualization of the God Flame, I AM THAT I AM. And the great individualist Christ Jesus with the apostles, the great revolutionaries of the East—all have come, singularly consumed by sacred fire, moving among men, holding a balance, preserving an earth and an evolution for your own maturity and divine Sonship in this hour.

Thus, the path of Freedom squarely set upon free will does acknowledge that some, including the embodied fallen angels, have chosen to pursue a course of Death and War, manipulation by temporal power and moneyed instruments, beloved. And their interests have not been with and for and by the people who share the common Light of the one loaf of the Lord's table. Nay, I tell you, their agenda has been the rivalry of various orders of fallen angels who have sought to take from these little ones the Light of their emergent Christhood.

I AM in the Law of the One and in the heart of The Lord Our Righteousness within you. Remember that I have told you, remember that I have shown you a vision. The choice is truly upon the shoulders of those who have been sponsored by Saint Germain to raise up the divine document of the Constitution and who, in a declaration of independence, apart from and separate from those fallen angels, have chosen to be one nation under God.[6]

May you find union in the Light, determination and strength in the Vision. For surely it shall come to pass that one or the other shall be the history of this land according to your choosing.

I admonish you that while you have life and breath and hope and avenues of communication that you cease not to deliver the message of Saint Germain and the call of an Archangel who has stood for you civilization after civilization unto the end of this age. May you know this Truth that I have spoken and fulfill the prophecy of your destiny!

Violet flame angels attend each one. You are being ministered unto by angels of the Seventh Ray in our command. Receive their love for your Victory. They are your devoted brothers and sisters on the path of the Seventh Ray.

Now cometh the Angel of the Sixth Ray.

"The Summit Lighthouse Sheds Its Radiance O'er All the World to Manifest as Pearls of Wisdom."
This dictation by **Archangel Zadkiel** was **delivered** by Elizabeth Clare Prophet on **November 25, 1987,** following her lecture "On the Healing Power of Angels: Christ Wholeness–the Seven Rays of God" at the Capital Hilton, **Washington, D.C.,** where she was stumping for the Coming Revolution in Higher Consciousness. Lecture and dictations by Zadkiel and Uriel available on 3 audiocassettes, 4½ hrs., A87100, $19.50 (add $.80 for postage); 2 videocassettes, GP87089, $59.95 (add $1.25 for postage). Lecture includes thorough teaching on the alchemy of healing using the science of the spoken Word, the violet flame and resurrection flame, and the mastery of the seven centers of being through clearing the chakras. The video uses many slides for visualization and the words of all decrees and songs are in easy-to-read type on the screen. A very necessary and fundamental lecture for new students of the Ascended Masters' Teachings and a "how to" lecture for those preparing to become world teachers. (**1**) **Vials of the seven last plagues.** Rev. 15, 16. See *Vials of the Seven Last Plagues: The Judgments of Almighty God Delivered by the Seven Archangels,* Summit University Press, $5.95 (add $.50 for postage). (**2**) **Pillar of fire.** Exod. 13:21, 22; 14:24; Num. 14:14; Neh. 9:12, 19; Zech. 2:5. (**3**) **City Foursquare established in North America.** The Ascended Masters have called North America the map of the "City Foursquare," the Place Prepared and the Promised Land for the reincarnation of the seed of Light of Abraham. (**4**) **George Washington's vision.** See p. 556, n. 1. (**5**) The place where the soul resides in the physical body is midway between the navel and the base of the spine. This corresponds to the **seat-of-the-soul chakra** anchored in the etheric body. It is the place of solar awareness, where the senses of the soul, the intuitive, or 'psychic' senses, are experienced. The "gut feeling" of approaching danger, excitement, or happiness is an example of this soul faculty, the ability to read moods and vibrations not empirically discerned through the five physical senses. This chakra when vibrating in harmony and consonance with the Holy Christ Self and the other chakras emits the violet light of the Seventh Ray. When the violet flame is invoked it liberates the soul by transmuting the accumulation of negative karma not only in the seat-of-the-soul chakra but in all the chakras. Violet is the color and wavelength of the age of Aquarius, which is the seventh age and dispensation whose hierarch is Saint Germain. Because this chakra corresponds to the Seventh Ray and Age, it is activated in this time of the awakening of all souls prophesied by Daniel (Dan. 12:2). See Djwal Kul, *Intermediate Studies of the Human Aura,* pp. 77, 84, 85, 94, 95, 98, plate 7. (**6**) Refers to the Constitution of the United States of America and the Declaration of Independence. See also Elizabeth Clare Prophet, December 25, 1981, "Declaration of International Interdependence of the Sons and Daughters of God on Behalf of the People Apart from Their Political, Economic, and Military Oppressors in Every Nation on Earth," 1982 *Pearls of Wisdom,* Book I, vol. 25, no. 5, pp. 41–48.

More Violet Fire
by Hilarion

Lovely God Presence, I AM in me,
Hear me now I do decree:
Bring to pass each blessing for which I call
Upon the Holy Christ Self of each and all.

Let Violet Fire of Freedom roll
Round the world to make all whole;
Saturate the earth and its people, too,
With increasing Christ-radiance shining through.

I AM this action from God above,
Sustained by the hand of heaven's Love,
Transmuting the causes of discord here,
Removing the cores so that none do fear.

I AM, I AM, I AM
The full power of Freedom's Love
Raising all earth to heaven above.
Violet Fire now blazing bright,
In living beauty is God's own Light

Which right now and forever
Sets the world, myself, and all life
Eternally free in Ascended Master Perfection.
Almighty I AM! Almighty I AM! Almighty I AM!

Vol. 30 No. 78 *Beloved Archangel Uriel* *December 17, 1987*

Saint Germain Stumps America

21

The Promise of Thy Deliverance

"He That Killeth by the Sword Must Be Killed by the Sword"

Ho! Sons and Daughters of the Sun, I AM come.

Witness, then, ten thousand-times-ten thousand legions of angels in the service of the Lord Christ. They pass over and through this city and their presence is a most extraordinary event. They move with the legions of the Ancient of Days and of the Faithful and True who does lead the armies of heaven.

Know, beloved, that this marching of angels through this city is for the event of the binding and the casting out of those fallen angels at inner levels who are aliens to this world come from other spheres and planetary systems in the physical universe.

They have declared war upon a nation that sleeps and the nation is not roused to defend herself.

O beloved, we come to rouse a populace and to say,

Awake, America! Awake, then!

We bring light and auric emanations of the Central Sun. We bring a maximum light by the LORD God and the Cosmic Council that may be delivered unto you.

Therefore, to all who attend this vigil we say, pray for this people that the patine of sleepfulness, of pleasure of the senses be taken from them swiftly. That they might be cut free by Astrea and Archangel Michael to receive our ministrations is our prayer.

As you have prayed to God, so we pray you open your hearts and call to the Divine Mother that She might intercede for such a mighty deliverance. O the hearts are there, "hearts of gold,"[1] as Saint Germain has called you. They are there but covered over by all manner of misuses of sound, of motion picture and the media. They are absorbed in the illusions broadcast to them, with no time left over for the discovery of the inner kingdom of God.

Therefore, beloved, a nation is about to be traduced by a foreign envoy who does come speaking peace but who has war in his heart. Let him be exposed by Cyclopea!

And therefore, to all enemies of the people of Light upon earth, we declare unto you, whether you perform your wickedness against the Lightbearers consistent with human law, whether it is by subterfuge, intrigue or calumny, there is a Divine Law that does apply to you.

He, therefore, who shall go forth to take life by the sword shall also lose his life by the sword.[2] You may argue. You may argue your freedom to take life at will, to abort life in the womb, and your laws may uphold your freedom. But I, Uriel, declare unto you that you shall face the Divine Law gainst which there is no argument, no opinion or second opinion:

He that shall take life by the sword shall lose it by the sword.

Therefore, know, you who come with the lust of America in your heart—the lust of her light, her civilization and her technology—you who mount your armaments to defeat her, you shall not stand in the Day of Judgment! For the All-Seeing Eye of God is upon you and that which you inflict shall be inflicted upon you by the angel of the LORD as it was inflicted upon you in the days of Sennacherib when the angel did come and thousands did fall at his hand![3]

Therefore, know, O ye who come from beneath, the eye of God is upon you! Therefore know that there is a recompense and there is a Divine Law. Though you may deny it in your godlessness, though you may massacre those of freedom worldwide, you shall not stand in the Day of Judgment.

And by these hearts, so are the nations consecrated to the Immaculate Heart of Mary. And a people shall rise up and they shall overturn their overlords.

And as you have delivered brutality upon brutality, insensate, so there shall come upon you the fire and the ice, and you shall know that as thou hast meted out the unmercifulness of hell, so the nonmercy shall be unto you a fiat of your own devices.

You stand accountable! And by your hand and your execution of war in the earth, you shall know your judgment! And the hour of that judgment is come!

I AM Uriel, Archangel of the LORD's Judgment and of the Lord Christ. I stand in this city and I read the record of your conspiracy before the people of God. I stand midst your empire and I give to my own prophet to hear the words of your collaboration against the Light. Know, then, that all things are seen and known beforehand. And so is your end foreknown.

Therefore, retreat and seek to raise up a Light while there is yet time. Bring forth fruits meet for repentance,[4] ye who have murdered the saints and shed the blood of the innocents even in this century![5] We know thee who thou art. Thou canst not escape the LORD, for the physical cosmos is but a playpen. You shall not hide from the Presence of the LORD God. Therefore know Him in this hour in the presence of the angels of this city. And know, when you step upon this soil so it shall be that thy treachery shall be turned against thee.

I, Uriel, speak to the oppressors of my people and those in this nation under God who have collaborated with the enemy of Freedom. Nor shall you stand in the Day of Judgment, neither the captains or the kings of this civilization who have betrayed a people and their Light. You shall not stand who have betrayed your word in the highest seats of the government of this nation. Let the Word of God judge you, for that Word is the two-edged sword[6] and the living Presence of the Christ.

My Word does go forth. It is the Word of Almighty God that I speak in this hour. It does coalesce physical atoms and molecules.

Therefore, let the inner alignment of the Holy Spirit be known of a people. And let you who hear me and know that ye are God's, serve Him, then, and be the instrument of that judgment of Darkness whose hour is come and that ultimate binding of these tares sown among the wheat, truly an espionage of fallen ones, of Antichrist.

Let those who are of the Light know that though ye be delivered in the end, our desire is to see you join the hosts of Light to deliver a nation and turn back war and the engines of war—not by war but by a shield of peace, flaming peace that does turn war aback and demand that those who have malintent be devoured by that malintent.

Thus is the Call of the age. By the judgment of the Lord Christ invoked by you,[7] you will know that my Word can be fulfilled in the physical octave only through your heart and your divine decree.

I summon you in the name of the Goddess of Freedom, who reigns above this nation's capital.[8] I summon you in the name of the Goddess of Liberty, who does keep the third-eye chakra of a nation in New York Harbor. I summon you to keep the watch as watchmen of the night,[9] the dark night of America's karma. I summon you to be Keepers of the Flame in Saint Germain's name.

I, Uriel, deliver upon the altar of this nation the judgment, therefore, of unseen forces on the astral plane.

Elohim of God, descend in this hour for the binding of all that assails a nation and a people, and protect the Lightbearer in every nation upon earth. To this end am I sent. To this end am I come from the great white throne and the Presence of Him who does sit upon it.[10]

Therefore, I AM a messenger of God, Uriel Archangel. And I have not forgot the healing Light. Truly know that the judgment of the Lord Christ separating the Real from the Unreal is your deliverance unto Wholeness. [10-sec. intonation]

Thus, I shall touch you with a transfer of Light. As you see the Light of your I AM Presence and keep your attention upon that Presence, so be it unto you according to your will to be, your faith to live, and your wisdom to know God as He is within you.

I say, Be thou made whole by the Mighty I AM Presence, who does love thee with an everlasting Love. I AM that Light! And I summon you to it for the deliverance of billions of souls.

You, the individual, now called, can make the difference.

In the name Jesus Christ and Saint Germain, in the name of the Divine Mother and all who have delivered unto you their prophecy, I say, Keep the Flame, deliver the nations and let the leaves of thy Tree of Life be for their healing and thine own.

I salute the God Flame within thee. So, remember the promise of thy deliverance.

Come, then, for I would touch that blessed orb of inner seeing.

"The Summit Lighthouse Sheds Its Radiance O'er All the World to Manifest as Pearls of Wisdom." This dictation by **Archangel Uriel** was **delivered** by Elizabeth Clare Prophet on **November 25, 1987,** following her lecture and Archangel Zadkiel's dictation at the Capital Hilton, **Washington, D.C.,** where she was stumping for Saint Germain's Coming Revolution in Higher Consciousness. (**1**) **Hearts of gold.** See Saint Germain, "Your Heart as the Altar of God," 1967 *Pearls of Wisdom,* vol. 10, no. 7; or "A Valentine from Saint Germain," in *Saint Germain On Alchemy,* p. 349. (**2**) Rev. 13:10. (**3**) **Assyrian army slain by the angel of the Lord.** II Kings 19:35, 36; II Chron. 32:21, 22; Isa. 37:36, 37. (**4**) Matt. 3:8. (**5**) **Deaths caused by Communism since 1917.** See p. 45; pp. 71–72, n. 8; murder of prophets, saints, holy innocents, I Kings 18:4; 19:1, 2, 10, 14; II Chron. 24:20–22; 36:15, 16; Neh. 9:26; Jer. 26:20–23; Matt. 2:16; 23:33–36; Rev. 6:9, 11. (**6**) **Two-edged sword.** Heb. 4:12; Rev. 1:16; 2:12. (**7**) Invoke "They Shall Not Pass!" the Judgment Call by Jesus Christ, p. 568. (**8**) **Statue of the Goddess of Freedom.** See p. 428, n. 2. (**9**) **Watchmen of the night.** Isa. 21:5–11; 62:6; Ezek. 3:17; 33:7. See Saint Germain, November 22, 1980, 1980 *Pearls of Wisdom,* vol. 23, no. 48, pp. 325–34. (**10**) Rev. 20:11.

Pearls of Wisdom®
published by The Summit Lighthouse
Vol. 30 No. 79 *Beloved Jesus Christ* *December 18, 1987*

Saint Germain Stumps America
22
Comfort Ye My People!
I, Jesus, Prophesy the Certain Day of Your Victory

My rod and my scepter I place in the earth upon this hallowed ground made sacred by the fervent hearts of all who have gone before you, beloved, in a path of immersion in Christ.

Lo! I AM come and I walk the earth in search of the Lightbearer, in search of the one who will not be content until he does bear the All, the allness of the Light, not content with half a cup or lesser measure, not content to leave room in that cup for the vacuum of emptiness.

Beloved, earth is hallowed by the feet[1] of those who see the goal of Christhood and do not shirk their responsibility to pursue it. Love not the world,[2] then, for the love of the world begets retention of the not-self. If there is no longer love for the finite condition, for the body of death that is mortal, then none of those things that can be added to it as adornment will have any pull or tug upon thy soul.

To be content in the Light is peace, and it is the peace which passeth the understanding[3] of the world but is the full understanding of the Keeper of the Flame. Therefore, beloved, those who give their lives to the Cause of Freedom and can do so fully, joyously, contentedly, are those in whom the Flame of Comfort burns. The Comfort Flame is the Flame of the Holy Spirit.

Comfort ye my people,[4] then, with enlightenment, with the watch, with the warning. Comfort ye my people with the clap, with the thunder and with the rejoicing that God does descend into the temple of Light and raise the Light and increase the Light.

If you have nothing in the Day of His Appearing, then wherefore shall he multiply thy light? Yet there is no condition of nothingness in the human spirit, for there is that something of the not-self that does occupy when you yourself do not occupy until I AM come[5] within you as the I AM THAT I AM.

Verily, verily, I say unto you that my rod and my scepter in this seat of government shall be a rod that is a rallying point for those who love the laws of God and His will codified in human governments and human institutions. My rod shall be the point of judgment, a repellent unto the seed of the wicked, and it shall blind them on occasion until they are not able to see the way in which to carry out their wickedness.

Therefore, so raise up your own rod, beloved. Let the rod be this sacred fire blazing upon the altar of your being—yourself being a rod by the quickening power of Alpha and Omega which I gladly convey to you according to your portion.

Have you a magnet of the heart? So know that in this instant I open my heart and you receive from me, your Jesus, that which you are able to magnetize by a light that you have so cherished beyond all else, that in this moment of my coming your reward is with you and my reward is my joy that some have understood the Call and have responded with the Call.[6]

The Call of heaven one with the Call of earth, meeting at the point of the Universal Christ and His Mediatorship, does give much to the hosts of Light in vanquishing the forces of Darkness. Until you did call to Michael the Archangel this day there was surely the upheaval of the forces of Darkness who did not desire to have spoken by the power of my mantle the message of the ultimate defeat of the dweller on the threshold[7] within you and within planet earth. I mark this place and I tell you, this has been the sounding of the death knell of the dark forces, and the fruition of that message spoken to you shall be by your word one with my own.

Who shall separate us from the love of Christ? Who, pray tell? Not the dweller, not that counterfeit spirit, for you have seen it for what it is. Now you have but to slay it by the Word, by the Call to the Archangels and to stand steadfast as they do bind the Evil and release the Good.

How swift is the descent of God-Good within the temple of the one who not alone in word and vow but in staunchest deed has shown proof to the Almighty that he will stand and still stand, *that he will stand and still stand, that he will stand and still stand!*

How much proof the Law does require of you ere the I AM THAT I AM shall descend into your temple bodily is according to your record found in the Book of Life.

Be grateful that your name is written therein. Be grateful that one angel of Light may come to tell you what is written there, what is required of thee, deed upon deed upon deed, to cancel out the force of the anti-deed of Antichrist performed in your unenlightened state of the ignoring of the Law.

Therefore, stitch for stitch, footprint for footprint, you shall prove now herewith unto the LORD, even as He shall prove unto you, what a great blessing you can pour out (by your accessibility to the fountain of Light) to the earth herself for the Victory of Freedom.

Know, then, beloved, that there does come a day where the affirmation of God-Good in you does tip the scale to every denial of every previous incarnation. Weight for weight the Light is greater when you perform those deeds, beginning with the dynamic decree in the affirmation of Light that does turn the tide of Light for millions. So your actions may count—a single one for ten thousand previous denials.

Thus, you are about the Call of the hierarchy of Libra for the tipping of the scales of Justice in favor of your own Divinity. And in that day of days, beloved, when there is the confirmation of that self-mastery of Christhood, you will know, for you will feel it—the weight of the mantle of the LORD.

You will know what it means to bear the burden of the LORD.[8] For that coat that you will wear does indeed have weight and you must brace yourself to bear such a coat of the weight of the LORD's Presence. And you shall become accustomed to the accoutrements of the order of the priesthood of Melchizedek. And you will know what is the meaning of being a bearer of Light, and you will see how the Light you are given day by day shall be, indeed, a counterweight to the planetary force of Evil and of the dark side of the moon of human consciousness.

Therefore, I, Jesus, prophesy to you individually the certain day of your Victory. You know all that can be said on the subject of this Victory. Anything else to be said will be spoken in the secret chamber of your heart by the Great Initiator, your own beloved Holy Christ Self, in consonance with the Word of Maitreya.

Know, then, beloved, that the sum of this initiation is greater than the sum of the parts. Know, then, that you must exceed the knowledge and the knowing that has been conveyed. You must infuse the Teaching with the Flame of Comfort, the Flame of the

Holy Spirit. Let us return to that living fire, comfort—a roseate glow when needed and a steely white fire when deserved.

Understand, beloved, that you now walk this path and you walk it with your God. You must pass through this initiation and I AM indeed your Initiator.

I have desired to place squarely before you the actuality that though some have fasted and fasted away by spiritual light the human karma and the human creation, they have retained an identity in the not-self, not understanding what is true Christ-Identity in God, not perceiving the Holy Christ Self as the Divine Image that is to be worn not as a mask but as an undergarment and as the white robe of the saint.

Fear not to become thy Christ, but fear indeed to take the Light of Christ to improve the image of the not-self. Thus, perfect not the human. It is not perfectible. But let the soul be perfected through the shedding of unreality.

Enter in to the house of your Lord. So it is the servant of the King who does inherit the crown of the King.

I AM in the heart of hearts of all who call to me in this moment to be my disciples indeed. I make known to you once again: ten thousand Keepers of the Flame are needed. [Since I sent forth the Call May 28, 1987] less than a tenth of that number have been attracted to become members on the rolls of the Keepers of the Flame Fraternity. Let us not abate our reaching out with the Teaching and the Bread of Life, with the Comfort Flame that we raise in our hearts. Let us not rest until the magnet of the heart, the fire burning there, does truly draw into our ranks those who are already Keepers of the Flame at heart.

I would raise the canopy of Light for the protection of North America.[9] At the moment it is a grid that must yet be filled in.

I am grateful for all gifts given of Light. Let us press on now with the Divine Decree. For you have seen the Light and the Darkness and though you may not be fastened permanently to either, you stand, as it were, in the valley of decision and your decision is sealed.

Those who have seen the vision of the living Christ may know that the Adversary is bound. I have bound him by the scepter of my rod in those who have committed to that walk with me. But, beloved, measure for measure you will also go forth in my name to bind the devils in the earth who are the false hierarchy impostors of the nations and of the representatives of the people.[10]

Know, then, that as we the entire Spirit of the Great White Brotherhood do perform for you that service of the bearing somewhat of karma and the binding somewhat of that dweller, you, then, go forth in our name to bind those conditions which are an affliction to the Divine Mother and to Her seed[11] in the earth.

Measure for measure, we are one. Spirit by spirit of His Flame, we are one. Ministering servants on the line of Truth, we are one. We are all one Body in Light[12] and about to become all one Body in the earth, for swiftly my angels come to take that which can be taken and to show you a mirror, that you might look into that mirror and see reflected there the face of your Holy Christ Self and the smile thereupon.

So be transformed. So leave behind the lesser self to which you have clung, not knowing, not understanding that in so doing you have to a certain extent preserved the human facade with your very decree momentum.

Let the soul not be weak but strengthened—strengthened in body and mind. Let the power of Light call her to her dwelling place.

I, Jesus, stand in this heart. I stand in this city and my twelve legions from the heart of the Father are with me, not absent, beloved, but surely waiting, becoming impatient for the rolling momentum of your dynamic decree vigil that shall empower them to truly bind those forces that they have been waiting to bind for many weeks now.

Let us be up and doing! Let us see what fruitful bough we may bring from this branch of the Tree of Life to our beloved Alpha, showing Him that we have remembered the gift of his Mantle and his Presence to go forth in his name.[13] He has sent you on a mission.

I come to you, for you have arrived at the gate of my heart. So in your presence a statement is made. Therefore I say to you in the words of the Archangel through the prophet, *Comfort ye, comfort ye, comfort ye my people!*

By this sign of the staff held on high, truly the sign of the incarnate Word century upon century, I, Jesus, promise you that the Law will act to defeat Antichrist if there yet remain spokesmen in this hallowed ground.

Raise up your voices, O ye gates! Raise up your voices in praise and thanksgiving!

I bow to the Light of the heart of my beloved Saint Germain, my father, my friend, my prophet, my true brother. Therefore, in Saint Germain I am grateful in this hour for the saving of a nation unto their demonstration of the law of individual and universal Christhood.

The ensign is raised up![14] It is your Christ, my Christ one. Let all nations rally to the sign and let the states defend the foundation unto the capstone of the pyramid for the great defense of Freedom always.

I AM Jesus and I say unto the foes of this path of Christhood in Church and State worldwide:

They shall not pass! They shall not pass!

Unto the enemies of the Divine Woman and Her seed, I, Jesus, say, ***Woe! Woe! Woe!*** I have spoken it and it is done.

Receive ye the Holy Ghost and my Body and my Blood as Communion is served by angelic hands through our servers.

May you have a place for me at this supper of Thanksgiving.

By the sign of the Immaculate Heart of Mary, we conquer time and space.

"The Summit Lighthouse Sheds Its Radiance O'er All the World to Manifest as Pearls of Wisdom." This dictation by **Jesus Christ** was **delivered** by Elizabeth Clare Prophet on **Thanksgiving Day, November 26, 1987,** at the Capital Hilton, **Washington, D.C.,** where she was stumping for Saint Germain's Coming Revolution in Higher Consciousness. Prior to the dictation, the Messenger delivered the lecture "The Lost Teachings of Jesus: Sermon 9 On the Enemy Within"—teaching on the confrontation with the counterfeit spirit, or not-self, "the dweller on the threshold," including readings and commentary on Romans 7:14–25; Revelation 20:11–15; 21:7, 8; the Gnostic text Pistis Sophia, bk. 3, chaps. 111, 112, 115, 116; and literary and film classics. Lecture and dictation on two 90-min. audiocassettes, B87097–8, $13.00 (add $.80 postage.) (**1**) Isa. 52:7; Nah. 1:15; Rom. 10:15. (**2**) I John 2:15. (**3**) Phil. 4:7. (**4**) Isa. 40:1, 2. (**5**) Luke 19:13. (**6**) Part I of *"Watch With Me" Jesus' Vigil of the Hours* includes the Three Potentials—the First Potential: You; the Second Potential: Expanded Awareness of Earth's Evolutions; the Third Potential: The Call—followed by Part II The Guardian Action and Part III Thy Kingdom Come. The *"Watch With Me"* is a worldwide service of prayers, affirmations and hymns which Jesus has called upon Keepers of the Flame to give individually or in groups (see pp. 494–95, 498). (**7**) **Dweller on the threshold.** A term sometimes used to designate the anti-self, the not-self, the synthetic self, the antithesis of the Real Self, the conglomerate of the self-created ego, ill conceived through the inordinate use of the gift of free will, consisting of the carnal mind and a constellation of misqualified energies, forcefields, focuses, animal magnetism comprising the subconscious mind. The dweller on the threshold is therefore the nucleus of a vortex of energy that forms the 'electronic belt', shaped like a kettledrum and surrounding the four lower bodies from the waist down. This electronic belt contains the cause, effect, record, and memory of human karma in its negative aspect. Positive karma, as deeds done through the divine consciousness, registers in the causal body and is sealed in the electronic fire-rings surrounding each one's own I AM Presence. When the sleeping serpent of the dweller is awakened by the presence of Christ, the soul must make the freewill decision to slay, by the power of the I AM Presence, this self-willed personal force of anti-Christ and become the defender of the Real Self until the soul is fully reunited with Him who is the righteous LORD, The LORD Our Righteousness, the true Self of every lifestream on the path of initiation. See "The Lost Teachings of Jesus: Sermon 9 On the Enemy Within," noted above. 1983 *Pearls of Wisdom,* vol. 26, no. 6, p. 50; no. 36, pp. 383–91; no. 38, pp. 429–54. 1985 *Pearls of Wisdom,* vol. 28, no. 9, pp. 84, 85–93, 97; no. 26, p. 350, n. 10. 1986 *Pearls of Wisdom,* vol. 29, no. 22, pp. 199, 203, 210–12. *Saint Germain On Alchemy,* pp. 395–96. For notes 8–14, see p. 618.

Pearls of Wisdom®
published by The Summit Lighthouse

Vol. 30 No. 80 *Beloved Serapis Bey* *December 19, 1987*

Saint Germain Stumps America
23
The Divine Reality Does Appear
The Hour of the Judgment of the Son of God Is Come

Holy Ones of the Light,

I AM Serapis and I have come with legions of Light of the Divine Mother, who do indeed compass this city round about—seraphim and saints of the Most High God, those who are robed in white,[1] those who have been chosen of the Fourth Ray now to enter this city and to form the great cosmic cube.

Thus, the cube of the City Foursquare, founded upon that foundation of Ascended Master Light, is met by the devotees out of the East who have come to greet those descending from the Central Sun, converging, then, as Alpha and Omega in the heart of Elohim. Solar ring upon ring of angels of light form round about a grid of Light,* beloved.

Therefore, our statement is our presence and our presence is the extension of the Central Sun, that a nation under God, conceived in the heart of Liberty, sponsored by Saint Germain, should know the permanence of the eternal Light and the record kept here, that the saints of the Great White Brotherhood, as Above, so below, do stand to keep the city.

Therefore, come what may, the Divine Reality does appear. It is now and it is a confirmation of that light upon the brow that does seal thee forevermore in the heart of Alpha and Omega.

Lightbearers of the world, I AM the Hierarch of the Ascension Temple of Luxor[2] and an ascension temple that is not of this world. I say to you, then, keep the Flame of Life upon earth and know that the immaculate concept of a golden age is yet held in

*grid of the Universal Christ consciousness

the hearts of all those who serve the Holy Cause of Freedom. And know that that enlightenment which is come upon you—which may expand and expand and expand now as you meditate intensely upon the fire upon the crown of the head and see and visualize golden illumination's flame intensifying—is the predawn of that golden age. As this does take place, beloved, so our anchor point in the earth through you does increase.

Therefore, in the reflecting pool, behold, a multitude of heavenly hosts is seen, and superimposed upon them and again upon that cosmic cube there is the vision of the great pyramid of this civilization of the I AM Race in its perfected state; and above that pyramid is a capstone yet waiting to be placed on that solid foundation.

Blessed hearts, when Darkness moves in the earth the Lightbearers intensify Reality, and Reality is an intimidation unto those who have it not. There be some upon this earth who come from beneath, as Jesus said,[3] who have not known the Reality of God since they have turned their backs upon the sun, even the Great Central Sun and the Light incarnation of the Word, who is the Son of God. These cannot stand in the day of the appearing of the sons and daughters of God. Therefore, they would if they could foment war and annihilation and the collision of worlds here below before that advent of Christ in His own.

Let them know, then, that there is an end to all of this—finis. There is an end to all of this, I say. And therefore, tempt not the Great Kali nor bet thy time in the Kali Yuga, for the Divine Mother and the right hand of that Great Kali does descend upon you.

And therefore, let the fallen ones who think they have control in this world know: you have no power except God give it you.[4] Trust not your fates or your plans, for the Light's dominion in the earth shall have the Victory and those who are not found in the All-Seeing Eye of God, they—mark you well—shall not endure. For these are not conquerors of time and space and they may not pass through the star above that pyramid unto eternal Life.

Therefore, know that it is an hour to come into the Divine Union. Whether or not a nation shall rally to the divine cause of a golden age, let it be known that the Reality of the kingdom is nigh, the Reality of the Son of God is nigh, the Reality of the Divine Mother is nigh, and all who, then, leap into the arms of the Archangels shall know of a truth that God is very near in this hour to pluck his own unto the higher vibration. There may they abide in the intensity of the God Flame to lower that Flame into manifestation wherever child or child-man does raise up a cup or a chalice to receive it.

Thus, beloved, the quickening is come. I AM Serapis for the quickening of hearts who will be quickened, who are to be quickened. Let them know, then, that there is a path, there is an initiation unto eternal Life: the goal is the Ascension. The goal, therefore, is Victory in this earth in the Matter spheres, Victory in the soul and the soul's reunion with God. Let that Victory be pursued and let your feet sandaled, then, with winged sandals of light know truly the swiftness of the Mind of God of Mercury.

Therefore, Hermes Trismegistus, thrice blessed by the power of the three-times-three, come now to balance these heart flames and their devotion. Come with balance, then, of Brahma, Vishnu and Shiva.

Therefore, in the name of the Father and of the Son and of the Holy Spirit, in the name of the threefold flame within your hearts I say, O Lord Maha Chohan, breathe upon them the breath of the Holy Spirit. So let the sacred fire breath fan the spark in the heart. Fan the divine spark now, for they are worthy, for their names are written in the Book of Life and upon the rolls of Luxor.

Seraphic bands, heed now! Stand in formation, form the mighty cosmic cube and therefore let Death and Hell flee from the face of the Son of God. Living Christ Jesus in the midst of the city, perform thy holy work! [20-sec. pause]

Hear, then, the sound. Hear the sound of those legions of Light who deliver a divine music for the marching of the legions from the Central Sun. Hear them in concentric rings, wider and wider, encompassing greater and greater territory, moving out from this city. Hear the chorusings. Hear the acclamation of the Son of God appearing.

Blessed hearts, I announce to you that the Lord Jesus Christ in a vast manifestation of his Being, Presence and Causal Body does occupy the whole sky and heaven above this city, therefore releasing the true Divine Doctrine of his own inner Word spoken in the heart of every devotee of the Cosmic Christ worlds without end.

Go down, then, ye fallen angels to the sides of the pit![5] For the Son of God does raise his right hand in judgment of you who have betrayed a nation, a people, a God, a planet and a system [to deprive them] of the Divine Union, as Above, so below. The legions of the Lord Christ bind many in this hour and they are truly bound and they shall not be loosed again but removed from inner planes where they have been since their transition.

There is a great clearing, then, of the inner planes of the planet whereby the Son of God may call those souls who are of the Light and quicken them into the very hour of their resurrection.

Therefore know, beloved, that many upon earth shall receive from the beloved Son of God this night an impetus to rise in the flame of Cosmic Christ Peace and to defend the Spirit of Liberty as the Spirit of the Divine Mother abroad in the land and throughout this planet. Truly, Divine Intervention shall not wait for crisis. Truly, Divine Intervention does come, therefore, to prevent crisis and to raise up a wall of light around a city.

Therefore, let all who enter this place know that the hour of the Judgment of the Son of God is come. He, therefore, sends his angels first to the Lightbearers that they might willingly and joyously separate out from the unreality of the Unreal.

O Divine Reality, appear, then, in the seven centers of thy Lightbearers in the earth! O Divine Reality, appear, then! Appear, then, Divine Reality, before these fallen ones who have none, and therefore let them perceive their nakedness and their nothingness[6] outside of the pale of the God-center of that mighty threefold flame.

I AM Serapis. The curtain has unveiled a vision of inner planes of Light, numberless numbers of heavenly hosts. Be certain, beloved, that Divine Justice, even that Spirit of Cosmic Justice, is come into the earth. Pray with all of your hearts and souls and minds. Decree with all of the rejoicing of your voices for that Light to penetrate and saturate, *penetrate and saturate, penetrate and saturate* into the very astral planes, into the very depths of degradation of Death and Hell until the sea shall give up its dead[7] and there shall be the binding of all that is foul and unclean out of the astral plane and the pits under the earth.[8]

So there are sweeping changes due for a planet as angels of the violet flame sweep through and bind the dust of centuries. May a people rally, may a heart hear the call. May the singular note of wisdom and the singular sound of the angel of the Son of God trumpet the Divine Appearing of the Woman clothed with the Sun in heaven, Mary, the great mediatrix of grace and mercy.

Therefore, beloved, in the sign of the caduceus and the sacred fire rising, I impel you to a higher dominion, a higher consciousness, a higher retreat.

The cosmic cross of white fire seal you as Saint Germain does receive you now to seal the servants of God in their foreheads.

I AM THAT I AM Serapis Bey. I AM THAT I AM in the heart of Ascension's Flame. I enter the Flame and by that Flame I return to the heart of God.

This dictation by **Serapis Bey** was **delivered** by Elizabeth Clare Prophet on **November 27, 1987,** following her lecture "Chakra Initiations with the Lords of the Seven Rays," at the Capital Hilton, **Washington, D.C.,** where she was stumping for Saint Germain's Coming Revolution in Higher Consciousness. For notes, see Pearl 81, p. 618.

Vol. 30 No. 81 | *Beloved Saint Germain* | *December 20, 1987*

Saint Germain Stumps America

24

It Is the Last Time

Occupy a City for Me, Beloved

Ho! It is the last time that I shall appear in this nation's capital unless and until those who know better do better—until those who have seen my calling and heard my word respond to it and postpone not the day of our God's appearing.

Lo, my Presence has counted for ye all for millions of years in this earth and in higher octaves. In joy and love and with what fond purpose I have sponsored this nation and this opportunity!

Keepers of the Flame, by your leave I AM sent from the Great Central Sun to stand in the midst of this city as a pillar of violet flame, my aura, then, sealing a destiny—a destiny far spent.

For America has abdicated her role as the nation of Christhood, the eternal Law of God, as the nation wherein The Lord Our Righteousness should raise up a standard, an ensign of the people and a two-edged sword.

Thus, beloved, through your hearts and yours alone, the Lightbearers in all the earth—those who know me and may not know my name but have espoused the Cause of Freedom and of Peace—through them I shall continue to work.

But I shall not be here, beloved, to deliver to you another statement of my word or my call unless the representatives of the people, from the highest office in the land to the least, shall take their stand for the defense of Freedom.

Therefore, know, O city of an alabaster light, O city that has been cast in the very mold of the God Star, I shall leave when my Messenger does leave and my Keepers of the Flame have concluded their vigil. Thus, so long as this vigil does remain, I shall remain; and upon its conclusion, beloved, let those who have made the karma know that karma, and let those who respond to the Call of God get thee up into the high mountain of the I AM THAT I AM.

This nation, therefore, has received not only my own sponsorship but the sponsorship of Cosmic Beings and councils and of the entire Spirit of the Great White Brotherhood. Heaven expects a response, a recompense.

Therefore those long fascinated with my person or writings from whatever incarnation or as the Wonderman of Europe,[1] those who know my name and associate with it perhaps the glamour and the glitter of other octaves or of personal flattery, I tell you this, *I AM a living pillar of violet flame!*

Wheresoever you shall raise up that violet flame by a concerted action of a decree momentum, there I shall be, as it were, the genie of the lamp, the lamp of knowledge and transmutation, the lamp of transfiguration and the transubstantiation of the body and the blood of thyself, that the Lord Christ might truly enter therein. Wheresoever a pillar of violet flame is raised up, because it is the equivalency of my Presence I shall be there.

Thus, take, take, then, the Messenger's offering of that which is to be released of the violet flame decrees and calls to my heart. If you shall use that recording of the word,[2] angels of the violet flame, Zadkiel, Amethyst, Elohim of the Seventh Ray, Arcturus and Victoria, the beloved Kuan Yin, the beloved Great Divine Director, the beloved elementals, the Holy Spirit, these shall amplify as we, Portia and I, shall amplify my Electronic Presence through it.

Know then, O beloved, that footprint for footprint if America and the earth shall long desire the Presence of Saint Germain with them, they must forge a fire, truly a violet flame fire where I may place my feet. It is indeed the last time, the last Opportunity, the last Freedom and Justice. Either these flames be raised up by the Lightbearers of the world or you shall see the Darkness prophesied by young and old alike, those who have seen, those who have known, and those who have read the report of that which the enemy does propose against this nation and against all people of freedom worldwide.

I say, then, that in my Presence this day, I have implored the Father and the Cosmic Council to reveal to you firmly and finally—that you might take action—truly the mind manipulation of this people that does come forth out of the bowels of hell, out of the hearts of the fallen ones, out of the very Soviet and those aliens who come in their spacecraft. The mind manipulation of this people of America and of the earth must be neutralized by the sacred fire, by a protection raised up through your giving of that rosary of Archangel Michael that is for the Armageddon through which you are already passing yet know it not but sleep through your passage through the dark night of the Spirit.

I AM Saint Germain. As my time is running out, so is your time running out, beloved. I have cried to you in the hills and in the mountains. I have cried to you in the cities and in the valleys and in the secret chamber of your heart, and for one reason or another you have denied the science of the Word. You, America, have denied the Presence of the I AM THAT I AM unveiled to you decades ago, reinforced again and again by the Messengers and Teachers who have gone forth.

Therefore, those who believe the lie of the Serpent and his seed, lo, their judgment is just, and the LORD God has affirmed and confirmed to me this day that these judgments cannot be changed. Those who reject the Person of Maitreya, those who reject his Person, whether in the Lord Jesus or in the least of these my brethren,[3] therefore are cut off from that Presence. It has ever been, and the Law abideth forever. Even so, true and righteous are thy judgments,[4] O LORD, and we do give thanks before the altar of Almighty God that Thou hast descended into the earth to take to thee thy great power and to reign.[5]

Therefore, in the living witness of the God Flame, I AM THAT I AM Saint Germain, and I say to you, elemental life is able to neutralize this mass hypnosis, this mass condemnation and national suicide, this ignoring of the Law. Truly, a concerted action of Keepers of the Flame raised up can yet save a nation, can yet respond to the Sacred Heart of Jesus, enter into the path of discipleship and go up and down the highways of the land preaching the word of the Keeper of the Flame, the great Holy Spirit in his Person and Presence, delivering the Word of the Lords of the Seven Rays and giving them the Power of comfort from the heart—the Wisdom of comfort, the Love of comfort—drawing them into the path of the walk of the Keeper of the Flame.

Therefore, the sands in the hourglass of this year, 1987, do run out. And in the final hours of the Darkness that has befallen this nation there does come the representative of the false hierarchy who is marked by the mark of the beast, therefore, to enter and to negotiate as serpent and fallen ones have ever done. And the unwary respond; and the proud, the ambitious and the stubborn and the foolhardy who occupy positions of power in this government think that they may bargain and win. One can never bargain with those who have committed themselves to the destruction of Light, Life, Freedom—and America as the nation of the I AM Race.

Therefore, beloved, beware, and mount your vigils and give your cry unto the LORD, for some will hear, some will understand, some will be raised up and some will be saved!

Therefore know that each and every hour of thy life does count, for thou art on the path to realize Buddhahood—Divine Fatherhood, Motherhood and Christhood. And in the midst of the Great Darkness let the Great Light appear, and let it be the Light of your I AM Presence, let it be the Light of your Christhood raised up! For even past the eleventh hour there is that moment of quickening when souls of Light shall see, and those who see the face of the living Son of God in the Ascended Master Jesus Christ, those who will hear of his Lost Years and Lost Teachings, those who will enter the fiery coil of his Lost Word, *They shall live. I tell you they shall live!*

And the question becomes, beloved, in what vibration, in what dispensation and in what octave shall you be found? Shall you be found hid with Christ in God?[6] Shall you be found in the eye of the capstone of the pyramid? Wherever you are found, I say, give glory unto the LORD unto the day and unto the night, for salvation must come unto those who are faithful and true.

And the LORD God Almighty shall truly go in the Person of the Divine Mother to put down those mighty from their seats,[7] to bind and strip, therefore, those captains and kings. They all have their day, beloved, and they all have their day of destructivity unto their own destruction. Take heed, then, that you are found out of the way of these fallen ones when they attempt to march over the land.

Blessed hearts of living fire, would to God and to your hearts they might be turned back before it is too late! It is yet possible and nothing is impossible with God! Therefore, plan for the present, plan for the future, plan for your immortal destiny and neglect not so great a foundation.

I, Saint Germain, have passed to you the torch of America's Freedom. I have passed it long ago. In this hour it is fully in your hands. All Lightbearers of the earth, it is a time when you may come running and may gather symbolically and actually at the foot of the Washington Monument and take your stand with the Great Causal Body of Godfre, for he yet moves in this nation's capital[8] as do others of the ascended hosts, beloved.

Thus many come and have volunteered, ascended and unascended, to take my place and to be with you here as you fight the good fight for that living flame of Freedom. Blessed ones, I am most fortunate and most beloved as to have millions of friends in cosmos beyond this system and yourselves in embodiment.

And therefore, these friends of Light have come to me in those hours when the Lords of Karma have said, "Not so, Saint Germain, thou hast given the all again and again; we will not accord thee another dispensation." Therefore, beloved, you have met the requirement of the hour yourselves by giving the violet flame marathons in my behalf. Such an hour is come again, beloved.

But I tell you, in the highest octaves of cosmos, and with Portia, I pursue dispensations ye know not of. I pursue with Alpha and Omega surely a fiery deliverance and an action of the Spirit of the Resurrection. Surely that which I have in my heart as cosmic dispensation may be magnetized by you.

Blessed ones, enter into the praise of the LORD and the dynamic decree with the fervor of love and devotion in your heart. If it must be, then, let there be a hymn of praise and an entering in to [the Electronic Presence of] a Master or an Archangel before you begin with the intensity of the battle array and armour of Light to move after those hellions in the earth and to call to Astrea and Archangel Michael for the binding of those foul spirits who emerge out of hell as though to conquer nations and the very souls of a people.

For none has raised the right hand, none save the Lightbearers in the earth, to stay their hand, to turn them back, to say, "Thus far and no farther, O proud spirit! Go down to the side of the pit!"

Blessed ones, it is necessary to speak Truth into the very teeth of the Lie and the Liar. Let it be done, then, and let your voices, let your hearts, let your robes of righteousness be made known. Let the power of Light be expanded in you!

Now, beloved, I seal you in my Electronic Presence, for I shall make the most of the hours that remain to me. I seal you in heart and mind, and my Electronic Presence, my purple fiery cape around you this day shall surely be the action of the sacred fire to leave those footprints, to leave that fiery violet flame and to make a statement for those who would spy out our liberty:[9]

That the LORD our God shall have you in derision![10] O ye who think you have captured a planet or you who think you shall do so. The LORD shall have you in derision. And as you plan a surprise attack upon the nations, so ye know not in what hour or in what day the LORD our God shall appear unto you and you shall be as grass and you shall wither,[11] for your mortality devoid of a spirit and of the God Flame shall not endure! And therefore, play out your hand, ye fallen ones, for the angels of the LORD do stand ready, swords drawn, to bind you by the very act taken of your physical karma.

Therefore, know: those who shall take the sword shall surely perish by it[12] and their days shall be known no more, for in this age, O ye of Babylon, O ye of Assyria, O ye false gods, ye shall go down and your judgment shall be final!

Therefore, let them know, for I, Saint Germain, declare it in the heart of this nation's capital, that if you shall so touch one of these little ones, *lo!* your judgment is sealed—one of these little children of my heart, one babe in arm, one Keeper of the Flame, there shall fall upon you in this age the full descent of all of your karma, all of your misery-making throughout the galaxies! It shall come tumbling down upon you so that you shall not know ever thereafter the name I AM THAT I AM nor the LORD who is God.

Elohim, mark them, then, who have the sign of the beast, mark them who have his number,[13] for they are truly marked men and marked women, and they are watched by the Great Silent Watchers. And as they move against the Light and the dispensations of Aquarius, so shall their karma crystallize upon them.

Beloved ones, this is spoken as the warning and the judgment of the fallen ones but take no comfort in it, for [it is written,] "my soul hath no pleasure in the death of the wicked."[14] Yet, beloved, an age and the alchemy thereof must be for the purging, must be for the refining, must be for the fulfillment of the prophecy that "one is taken and another is left"[15] and that the tares are bound in bundles and are cast into the fire of the all-consuming Presence of our God.

And therefore, let the seed of the wicked in the earth tremble! Let them tremble, O ye gates! O hierarchies of the Sun, let the grid of Light* now seal the earth! Let the hosts of the LORD now seal the earth! [11-sec. pause]

Holy Amethyst does move about the city with violet flame angels, priests and priestesses of the Seventh Ray. They, beloved, are igniting violet flame campfires. These are not large, but sufficient for a consuming action and a quickening of souls; they are the sign of the "hundred circling camps."[16]

They [these violet flame campfires] are the sign, unto all who read and run, for the quickening and the awakening of the memory of the violet flame and ages long ago when they were once a part of a fiery dispensation of the violet planet and beloved

*grid of the Universal Christ consciousness

Omri-Tas. Violet flame for the awakening, first in this city consecrated to the throat chakra, the voice of a people, and then in the cities of the seven chakras[17] and beyond! So long as there shall be a response to these violet flame campfires, so long shall Amethyst have her dispensation to ignite these fires in America.

Blessed ones, our best is given into your hearts' keeping, entrusted there. The mighty solar rings of Astrea are formed as grids of Light about a planet and the hosts of the Lord are rallied for the rescue of the single son or daughter of God who is determined to be the fullness of His Great Spirit and Causal Body, and of the Allness of the Divine Mother incarnate.

When all the world has gone mad or asleep around you, beloved, you do not despair, you come into the awareness, truly the direct apprehension of your Godhood. *You kindle a sun in a dying world! That is your mission!* You kindle a sun and you adore Helios and Vesta, Alpha and Omega, the one true God manifest in all the beauty and glory of His Light emanations! You become a sun! You are the sun, and you will let no Darkness defeat it, put it out or cast a shadow.

Therefore defy the Darkness in the name I AM THAT I AM. Be the Son of God! Be the I AM THAT I AM! And let them [those of the Darkness] know that when they arrive at the gate of your consciousness, they must deal with the mantle of the Lord of the World, the Lord Gautama Buddha—they must deal with the living Christ Jesus raised up in you, they must deal with the Son of sons and the Sun behind the sun.

Therefore, be quickened by seraphim. Be guarded in the Presence of thy Tree of Life[18] by cherubim. Know the LORD. Know his Presence. Know his Son and Holy Spirit. Know the blessed Virgin and champion Her Cause in the earth.

There is a destiny to be won! No finer hour has ever been given to a company of Lightbearers throughout a planet than that that is given to you, beloved, to occupy this city until the coming of the dawn of enlightenment of the representatives of a people, until the rallying of a people to *Shake and awake! Shake and awake! Shake and awake!* those who have deserted their posts in the government and the economy.

Occupy the city till they be raised up and the Light in them be that Christ, and occupy a city for me, beloved. For I, Saint Germain, am determined to return when you shall have fulfilled your reason for being here and now in infinity and in this cross. For the cross of time and space is marked. Stand in the center and *know thy God!*

"The Summit Lighthouse Sheds Its Radiance O'er All the World to Manifest as Pearls of Wisdom."
This dictation by **Saint Germain** was **delivered** by Elizabeth Clare Prophet on **Sunday, November 29, 1987,** at the Capital Hilton, **Washington, D.C.,** where she was stumping for Saint Germain's Coming Revolution in Higher Consciousness. Prior to the dictation, the Messenger read Isaiah 40. (**1**) See *Saint Germain On Alchemy,* pp. vii–xxvii; *Saint Germain On Prophecy,* Book One. (**2**) 90-minute audio-cassette of violet flame decrees and songs soon to be released. (**3**) Matt. 25:40. (**4**) Ps. 19:9; Rev. 16:7; 19:2. (**5**) Rev. 11:17. (**6**) Col. 3:3. (**7**) Luke 1:52. (**8**) **The Ascended Master Godfre** was embodied as George Washington. On Godfre in the nation's capital, see pp. 419–21, 427. (**9**) Gal. 2:4. (**10**) Pss. 2:1–4; 37:12, 13; 59:8. (**11**) Isa. 40:6–8. (**12**) Matt. 26:52; Rev. 13:10. (**13**) Rev. 13:11–18; 15:2. (**14**) Ezek. 18:23, 32; 33:11. (**15**) Matt. 24:40, 41; Luke 17:34–36. (**16**) Julia Ward Howe, "The Battle Hymn of the Republic," stanza 2. (**17**) **American cities representing the seven chakras.** 1. First Ray, throat chakra, Washington, D.C. 2. Second Ray, crown chakra, Boston, Massachusetts. 3. Third Ray, heart chakra, Chicago, Illinois. 4. Fourth Ray, base-of-the-spine chakra, Miami, Florida. 5. Fifth Ray, third-eye chakra, New York City. 6. Sixth Ray, solar-plexus chakra, Detroit, Michigan. 7. Seventh Ray, seat-of-the-soul chakra, Los Angeles. (**18**) Gen. 2:9; 3:22, 24; Rev. 2:7; 22:2, 14. The **Tree of Life** represents the I AM Presence and the causal body.

Notes from Pearl No. 79 by Jesus Christ:
(**8**) **Burden of the Lord.** Zech. 9:1; 12:1; Mal. 1:1. (**9**) **Canopy of Light over North America.** On May 28, 1987, Jesus said, "Blessed hearts, I have come, then, to make a plea to you and to send my Messenger abroad across this continent for the gathering of ten thousand who will call themselves Keepers of the Flame of Life and who will understand that I, Jesus, have called them. For I was called by the Father, by the servant-Sons, by Saint Germain and the hosts of heaven to establish a teaching, a path and even the Keepers of the Flame Fraternity, that these lessons might be studied, that the daily decrees might be given, that the Light might be anchored and the Light itself be the Mediator to stand between a people, a world, a continent and their own returning karma.... Blessed ones, this North America, a place consecrated by Love to the reunion of souls with God, is a place where if the Lightbearers would respond and *make the Call,* even as I call you this night, there should be established even the white light over a continent to protect it from those calamities of the Four Horsemen, which could indeed appear for want of mediators in the earth." See pp. 273–74. (**10**) **Casting out devils.** "And he ordained twelve, that they should be with him, and that he might send them forth to preach, and to have power to heal sicknesses, and to cast out devils." Mark 3:14, 15. "And he called unto him the twelve, and began to send them forth by two and two; and gave them power over unclean spirits.... And whosoever shall not receive you, nor hear you, when ye depart thence, shake off the dust under your feet for a testimony against them. Verily I say unto you, It shall be more tolerable for Sodom and Gomorrha in the day of judgment, than for that city. And they went out, and preached that men should repent. And they cast out many devils, and anointed with oil many that were sick, and healed them." Mark 6:7, 11–13. "After these things the Lord appointed other seventy also, and sent them two and two before his face into every city and place, whither he himself would come.... And the seventy returned again with joy, saying, Lord, even the devils are subject unto us through thy name. And he said unto them, I beheld Satan as lightning fall from heaven. Behold, I give unto you power to tread on serpents and scorpions, and over all the power of the enemy: and nothing shall by any means hurt you." Luke 10:1, 17–19. (**11**) Rev. 12:1–9, 13–17. (**12**) I Cor. 12:12–20; Rom. 12:4, 5; Eph. 4:4. (**13**) **Alpha's Mantle and Presence.** See pp. 384–86. (**14**) **Ensign raised up.** Isa. 5:26; 11:10–12; 18:3; Zech. 9:16.

Notes from Pearl No. 80 by Serapis Bey:
(**1**) **Saints robed in white.** Rev. 3:4, 5; 6:9–11; 7:9, 13, 14; 19:8, 14. (**2**) **Ascension temple at Luxor.** See *Lords of the Seven Rays: Mirror of Consciousness,* Book One, pp. 149–50, 164–67, 171; Book Two, p. 153. (**3**) John 8:23. (**4**) John 19:11; Rom. 13:1. (**5**) Isa. 14:12–17. (**6**) Rev. 3:17, 18. (**7**) Rev. 20:13. (**8**) Rev. 21:8; 22:15.

Joy to the world  *the Lord is come!*

December 12, 1987

To the dearest friends of my heart—
you who are the Lightbearers of the world—
I greet you with a Christmas wreath of the Saviour's love
encircling the earth,

"Freely we have received, freely we give!"

It is in the renewed joy of Jesus' birth and mission that I send to you the enclosed gift of his Presence lovingly prepared by our family and staff at the Royal Teton Ranch—the beautiful new 44-page booklet of Jesus' Watch given to Mark and me in 1964 and a 90-minute cassette of the entire service with newly recorded songs and decrees and Mother Mary's Rosary.

Please accept this precious offering of our hearts and voices all one as a chalice bearing our prayers and special Christmas salutation to you and yours as you keep your vigil for the nations with our Lord this season and throughout the years to come.

Also enclosed is Jesus' Pearl of Wisdom, his message to us dictated October 4 at our New York seminar. It is his call to discipleship in this age directed personally to each of us and to all who will hear. It is his call "to be now the embodiment of all that I AM and to receive me that you might have with me henceforth the most direct relationship"—to embody "my Word, my Teaching, my Flesh and my Blood."

This call of the Master of Galilee today is equal in import and moment to his call to the twelve and to the holy women who, answering, became his disciples and the recipients of the deeper mysteries two thousand years ago.

This call is the continuation and the fulfillment of Jesus' call to the path of the ascension given to us May 28 in Kansas City on his ascension day. In that address he said, "I am sent by the Father for the quickening now of ten thousand saints in . . . North America." The path of the ascension, he said, "can be fulfilled upon this continent because there are certain retreats in the heaven-world, called the etheric octave, where there is a consecration of that ascension flame and path, which can be entered into only by Love." Jesus spoke to us of the path of love evident in his intimate relationship with John the Beloved and of our soul's mergence with the Christ whereupon "I and my disciple are one."

Jesus went on to describe the various retreats in North America—that of Chamuel and Charity over St. Louis, the focus of Paul the Venetian over the city of Washington, D.C., the retreat of the Elohim of the Third Ray over Winnipeg, Canada, the retreats of Eriel of the Light and John the Beloved over the state of Arizona, the Temple of the Sun over Manhattan, the Royal Teton Retreat at the Grand Teton. And of course, there is the retreat of Archangel Michael and his legions at Banff.

Jesus told us that he prayed to the Father that we might have a series of studies in the retreats of the Archangels, to which the Father replied saying, "My Son, let them prove themselves with thy brothers, the Seven Masters of Light, and then they shall truly know the divine interchange with Archangels." Thus, it is to the inner-retreat experience that Jesus directs our attention not only with the Lords of the Seven Rays but also in the North American retreats.

Jesus called to the angels of the cosmic cross of white fire, saying, "I, Jesus, mark the sign of the cross over this North America, that by the Ruby Ray and by the white fire my Body and my Blood might infuse the Lightbearers for the protection of a path that is to be forged and won."

Expounding on the path of Love, Jesus underscored "the great need of humanity for the Mediator, the Intercessor, the Advocate. This Person of God who does defend those who have gone out of the Way, who does plead before the courts of heaven for mercy unto the ignorant, this Person, beloved, is the Universal Christ that I AM. . . whose Presence just above you may descend as your vibrations are elevated, resurrected, accelerated by the great science of the spoken Word which we teach."

He then spoke of the office of World Teacher which he shares with Saint Francis (the Ascended Master Kuthumi) which is "to be that Intercessor, to bring enlightenment as well as comfort, that those who are in Darkness may see a Light, and a Great Light, and walk in it." The Beloved One called to us to be world teachers, saying:

> This is the hour to claim the mantle of Mediator, to claim the mantle here below of your Holy Christ Self and to take your stand through prayer and invocation, through dynamic decrees to the Father, for grace and mercy and

light to flood this North America and the entire earth to contact those of greatest Light and to transfer to them even the sacred fire of the Word, that there might be here below an increased manifestation of Light to hold the balance for the Darkness that shall surely come upon this earth unless a people swiftly turn to the inner Light and unless millions, beloved, come to the realization of the God who is within as well as the God who is in his heaven.

With a plea as urgent, as timely and as heartrending as Jesus' lament over Jerusalem, our Elder Brother has made his plea. His words of today are with us to act upon. His words of two thousand years ago echo the Lord's judgment:

> O Jerusalem, Jerusalem, thou that killest the prophets, and stonest them which are sent unto thee, how often would I have gathered thy children together, even as a hen gathereth her chickens under her wings, and ye would not!
>
> Behold, your house is left unto you desolate.
>
> For I say unto you, Ye shall not see me henceforth, till ye shall say, Blessed is he that cometh in the name of the Lord.

With these words Jesus departed from the temple and foretold its destruction. Today Jesus delivers the same message to the churches who have failed to deliver the profound message of his lost years and lost teachings which he has been preaching through us since 1958. Therefore outside of the established orthodoxy, our Lord together with beloved Saint Germain established the Keepers of the Flame Fraternity so that souls of Light might have a step-by-step path to follow for the victory of their own Christhood and their own ascension in the Light. Following are his words:

> Blessed hearts, I have come, then, to make a plea to you and to send my Messenger abroad across this continent for the gathering of ten thousand who will call themselves Keepers of the Flame of Life and who will understand that I, Jesus, have called them. For I was called by the Father, by the Servant-Sons, by Saint Germain and the hosts of heaven to establish a Teaching, a Path and even the Keepers of the Flame Fraternity, that these lessons might be studied, that the daily decrees might be given, that the Light might be anchored and the Light itself be the Mediator to stand between a people, a world, a continent and their own returning karma.

The conclusion of Jesus' message on his ascension day is so urgent that I would be remiss as his Messenger and disciple if

I were to fail to include it here. Therefore please bear with me and with our Lord, for he speaks from his heart to an age that will not hear him—and he speaks to each one of us because we have the capacity to understand—and to act in his name. Following is his teaching and his imploring:

> You have heard it said that the Son of God is come to bear the sins of the world. I AM that avatar for this two-thousand-year cycle, beloved. But the hour is come, beloved, as you have understood it and seen it abroad in the land, when inasmuch as I have borne the sins of the world, or world karma, that the transfer of that karma back to those for whom I have borne it should come to pass.
>
> Understand this law, beloved, and heed this teaching. Forgiveness is the setting aside of karma, or sin, and that setting aside is a period of opportunity. Two thousand years, beloved, has this planet had the opportunity to recognize the Christ of me and of many saints and Masters of East and West who have gone before me.
>
> For I am not alone in heaven as some have thought. But many have ascended by the very same law whereby I was taken down from the cross and did enter the tomb to prove the initiation of the resurrection, that you might also prove this great law of the Spirit of the Resurrection.
>
> Therefore, beloved, understand that in this hour many have internalized greater and lesser measures of my Christhood and their own. And many have turned a deaf ear to the message.
>
> Thus, beloved, the Day of Reckoning that is referred to by the prophets as the Day of Vengeance of our God is the day when that opportunity comes to a conclusion and every man must bear his own burden. (And these words, too, are in scripture.) Thus, the burden of karma is daily being placed, individual by individual, upon the just and the unjust, beloved.
>
> But the grace and the mercy of the Law and of all heavenly hosts and of the Father has been the gift of the Holy Spirit, the gift of the violet flame whereby through the invocation of that violet flame, intensely and daily, that karma descending at a personal and a planetary level may indeed be transmuted, or balanced. This process is by the all-consuming sacred fire of God through the Person of the Holy Spirit. It is, if you will, a baptism by fire.
>
> This purging, beloved, does therefore enable the sons

of God in the earth—and all who will heed the message of my brother and friend Saint Germain on the use and application of the violet flame—to accelerate on the path of the ascension by Love, for the violet flame is Love's all-consuming forgiveness.

This beloved brother who was with me as my father Joseph (for so I called him, beloved) has been an adept of the Seventh Ray and of the use of the violet flame for tens of thousands of years and beyond. This has been his calling in God. This is his gift from the Father and his gift to the Father's children.

Understand, then, that in the ongoing cycles of two-thousand-year dispensations, it is the age of Aquarius and of the Seventh Ray that has descended upon earth, meshing, then, with the final decades of Pisces.

Therefore, you will see at this altar our oneness, our oneness as we together assist earth's evolutions to make the transition into an era of freedom, that by freedom's flame that is called the violet flame, souls who yet have karma to balance may not be overcome, may not be struck down by that karma, nor a world itself be destroyed or come to an end. For there be few and then many in this planet who shall hear my voice and his, know the Truth and confirm it in their hearts and call to that violet flame, beloved, unto the victory of individual Christhood and planetary Cosmic Christ awareness!

I, Jesus, preach this message to you, beloved. It is an urgent message. You who have an inner awareness, do not deny the signs of the times, do not deny the rumblings in the earth or my own prophecies written in scriptures already in your hands.

It is the end of an age when there must be an entering in of a new vibration, a new opportunity. And the question is, beloved, Will enough of the Lightbearers in the earth recognize this vibration of the Seventh Ray and realize that it is the key to the conclusion of this two-thousand-year cycle?

Blessed ones, this North America, a place consecrated by Love to the reunion of souls with God, is a place where if the Lightbearers would respond and make the Call, even as I call you this night, there should be established even the white light over a continent to protect it from those calamities of the Four Horsemen, which could indeed appear for want of mediators in the earth.

Understand, beloved, that the mediators who must stand between a people and a planet and their karma must be in physical embodiment. If you will read my words you will find that they say, "As long as I AM in the world, I AM the Light of the world."

"As long as I AM in the world..." Beloved, I AM in the ascended octaves of Light; I AM the Ascended Master Jesus Christ. And I AM in the world only when I AM [the I AM Presence of me, the Christ of me is] in my own, when the temple is prepared, when the Christ Self has been invoked, and when the violet flame has cleansed the four lower bodies to prepare a highway [a tunnel of light] for our God's descent into form.

I desire to come into your temple, beloved, and be in the world. And therefore, when you feel me entering into your house in that Second Coming, understand that you in me and I in you as we are one make the same declaration: "As long as I AM in the world, I AM the Light of the world."

Blessed hearts, recognize the Call. Your souls are ancient. It is your hour and the moment of your destiny. Recognize, then, that the Call to be the Divine Mediator must be answered ere the earth changes that must come about take their toll in a cataclysmic way or perhaps in war, even that war prophesied by my Mother at Fátima.

Blessed hearts, the choice is yet to free hearts and free thinkers who will know the winds of Aquarius and be the Keeper of the Flame of Life on earth. Thus, do not fall prey to a sense of predestination or of psychic prognostication wherein you believe all that must happen will happen and there is nothing that you can do to change it. You have not been taught the true meaning of prophecy, which is to show you upon the screen of life what could take place if you do not intercede.

Blessed hearts, what you see in the mind's eye can be canceled out by decision and free will. You do not need to fulfill any thought, feeling or idea that is negative. But, beloved, when you see the projection upon the world screen of that which can easily be calculated by the signs of the times, this, then, must be transmuted because you are seeing a prophecy of karma returning.

Therefore, take the violet flame; invoke it. Call to me and all saints of heaven and all powers of angels to intercede, that the sacred fire might consume planetary karma and Archangel Michael and his legions do battle and bind the fallen angels and evil spirits which would possess, destroy and defile even the souls who are on the path of overcoming.

Blessed ones, some of you have been taught that evil is not real. And indeed it is not real in God. But you cannot deny that there are spoilers in the earth who have wreaked their holocausts upon millions. You cannot deny that in the hearts of some there is a will to do evil.

You must undertand that this malintent must be checked by those who know the science of the spoken Word. For the Word itself will swallow up the appearance of evil. Take heed, then, that the appearance.and the illusion does not swallow up souls ere they have realized the Truth which you know—that in the absolute sense of the scientific affirmation of being, evil is not real.

Armageddon is yet to be fought by the Archangels and the legions of Light and the Faithful and True and the armies in heaven. Yet, it is your hour to make the Call. He who understands the Call made in the earth unto heaven and the Call of heaven made unto earth will arrive at the nexus where heaven and earth meet in the Divine Call and the Calling.

Beloved, I leave you, then, with this charge: Make your calling and election sure. For millions who yet dwell in ignorance need your intercession. In the name I AM THAT I AM, in the name of Christ of you, I say, Keep the flame!

Not only in these words, beloved, but in Jesus' continuing Presence with me do I know and desire to convey to you this Christmas season how profound is his love for the Lightbearers of the world and how deep is his concern that we recognize the urgency of the hour and give ourselves to his divine calling, to keep the flame by studying and embodying the mysteries given in the Keepers of the Flame Lessons and in the library of his teachings which we have published for you over the years.

As you meditate on his call and your response, may I suggest that you take the cassette of his Watch and play it at this time while reading chapters 24 and 25 from the Book of Matthew. As you play it softly in the background, you may feel the Lord enter your home to be with you as he opens the eyes of your soul concerning the events of your life and what the future holds for us as we face it together—always in his Presence.

As I reread the words of Jesus in the enclosed Pearl, I feel once again the desperation (if I may use that term) of his spirit as when he wept over Jerusalem. In my desire to serve him and to serve you, I am sending this letter and enclosure to 15,000 souls. My prayer throughout this season will be that some will understand, that some will have the courage to respond, for I know from the heart of Jesus that it is through our response that the prophecies of Matthew 24 can be turned around and the centuries unfold a golden age instead of planetary destruction. Jesus says that he is calling us for a purpose, and that is the step-by-step containment of the Light:

> I call you to my fold not in the general sense but in the specific sense of knowing that a Teaching, a Way of Life, a Spirit of the Resurrection cannot endure upon earth unless, truly, ten thousand determine in this hour of my appearing to embody the fullness of myself. . . .
>
> Blessed hearts, with ten thousand I will show you and Saint Germain what we together can do for the turning of the tide. Our God has decreed and the Trinity does embody his will, but here below, if that kingdom is to come into manifestation, truly there must be those who can be pillars to hold up the new city, the Holy City, the etheric octave of light come down to earth. Let the New Jerusalem be seen and shared, be partaken of by my own.

Jesus is now inviting us to come—our souls in our finer bodies during sleep—to his retreat on the etheric plane over Saudi Arabia "to tutor you as I did tutor my apostle Paul and John and countless others through the ages who have come to be initiated in the secret rites given to those who are able to enter the inner circle." So desiring to work through us and to raise our vibrations not only through the violet flame but through the wisdom and illumination of his lost teachings, he says:

> Let there be a recognition, then, that it is I who have called you to bring ten thousand Keepers of the Flame to the heart of Saint Germain. To be a Keeper of the Flame—of Light in the Lighthouse of Being—is the first step toward discipleship.
>
> Having so fulfilled the basic requirements of these lessons, you then come to that time, beloved, when you desire to study the mysteries under Maitreya. And the World Teachers approach you, that you might know that we give a path of initiation step by step to his heart. It is the hour when the fulfillment of all promises is come.

In anticipation that his own will respond before the year's end, Jesus says,

> Let it be known, then, forever—let it be known that in this hour of maximum karma descending, ten thousand have heard my voice and understood that wherever there is the Anointed One [the Lord Our Righteousness, the Holy Christ Self raised up within the individual], I AM in that heart and the Father with me. We do take up our abode in those who are in harmony with Love, never an offense to the Light itself. Thus Father and Son dwell in thy temple and in this my own.

In order to accomplish his stated goals for us and through us, Jesus asks us to renew our commitment to giving his Watch, promising us that he will be in our midst as we give this prayer service in his name weekly with the recording provided. Further extending himself to us in the light of world peril, Jesus makes his commitment to us:

> When I AM near and nearest to you in vibration—for you have called me by the magnet of your love and prayerful devotions—I promise you that all who commit to be my disciple as a Keeper of the Flame shall have my spheres of light and my Sacred Heart superimposed upon him or her throughout this Watch each week.

The Master then makes plain what can be the result if we will faithfully keep this Watch for one year:

> It is my desire, then, that in fifty-two sessions with you, which I would like to be of ninety-minute duration (or more), you might experience such renewal and such self-transcendence at the conclusion of a single year's Watch with me that you shall indeed know that I AM come into the earth to take my own in the grand ritual of the Resurrection and the Ascension.

Jesus then tells us of his call and his plan: the Watch as it is set forth in the booklet and on tape for you to give with him aloud and in full voice is "for the opening of the heart that a door might exist where I might enter and thence release to the earth renewed Light and Presence. . . . Through you I, Jesus, your brother desire to increase the Christ consciousness in the earth, that upon this foundation all other Servant-Sons of heaven [the Ascended Masters] and heavenly hosts [the Archangels and their legions] might indeed build the new age, magnetize the little children and devour the Darkness abroad."

Jesus says that in order to remedy the persecution of his life and message by the false prophets and false shepherds, he has chosen to enter in "at a renewed level of calling and dispensation from my Father—to a most intimate relationship with all who will not only call to me with their lips but will also enter my heart by embracing Saint Germain's teaching of the violet flame and acquaint themselves with my Mother Mary and not shun her."

He says, "Further, I choose to enter into this relationship with all who will call upon Saint Michael the Archangel to defend both Church and State and to exorcise those domains of Alpha and Omega [the arena of Church and State] of all fallen angels who have come to steal away the best of the hearts of men."

Jesus tells us that this path of discipleship to which he has called us has its foundation in his earthly mission and its culmination in the fullness of his teaching of the new age. Directing us to the example of his messenger, Mark, who opened the door to the Ascended Master octaves to us all, he says that a single individual may be the key to unlock a door through which all humanity may pass:

> It is the hour to decide if in your aloneness, all-oneness with me and the Father, you shall then be a key for millions of souls who will step through the door that you have opened.

In conclusion, the Master tells us:

> To this end I call you to be my disciples in the most serious effort of all of your incarnations, to recognize that in thy flesh thou shalt see God and be my Self. And only thus shall this world be endowed with a sufficiency and Presence [of my Christhood] in the physical to stay the hand of oncoming Darkness . . . .
>
> Now I speak to your soul, sometimes fully awake and sometimes not so, and I implore you, my soul, my brides, come now and determine and desire with all of your desiring to be that Christ who thou art—here in flesh, here in form. This world hath need of thee. Thou dost occupy the heavens and the stars. Now occupy earth till I come in the full glory of the physical manifestation long attended by many. Occupy till I come, beloved.
>
> And when you stand in my place, being my Self in form and embodying my Light, then I do come to you, Jesus, your Teacher, and I sponsor you, beloved. And you

shall know a sponsorship never known before. For my legions of angels are ready and waiting for the ten thousand and more who shall hear me because I come pleading the cause of Saint Germain and world freedom.

Without this victory, then, of a spiritual and physical defense for the nations, there shall not be seen in the earth nor a new age, nor a new day. Therefore, act swiftly and make haste, for I have called. I have called.

In the Light of our Lord's Presence where do we begin?

1. Emphatically, at the door of our hearts where we will bid him enter: "Come Jesus! Come Lord! Dwell in my heart—thy Christ my Christ forevermore."

2. Then we joyously take the enclosed booklet and tape and give this Watch with Jesus daily for fifteen days.

Before beginning this prayer vigil with Jesus for the nations, commune with him alone and with your God, pour out your heart to Jesus in the most personal, soul-searching letter that you have ever written. Ask him to show you how to serve him, how to be obedient to his call. When you have penned the last word of all that your heart desires to tell the Saviour, seal it in an envelope addressed to him and hold it to your heart while you give the Watch once through. Then call to the angels to deliver your message to his heart as you physically burn the letter in your fireplace or a safe place. This is a sacred ritual and a year's end confessional.

In this letter you should not only tell Jesus what you desire to do in your service to him and with him but also tell him the problems in your life, in your family, business or job in which you need his assistance. No situation, no matter how small or great, simple or impossible, is beyond his heart's ability to resolve.

Turn everything over to Jesus, including financial, legal and health problems, difficulties in relationships, in your own psychology/karma, or with your children. Tell him about the planetary ecology, the pollution of Mother Earth, poverty, and the homeless and famine stricken. Give him the names of the sick, the needy, and those terminally ill, those burdened by drugs and AIDS. Speak to him of the larger problems of the international economy, the national budget, the American farmer and shop-keeper. Ask him to direct the light of his Sacred Heart into the prophecies of Nostradamus recorded in Book Two of "Saint Germain On Prophecy," to mightily assist our youth and their education and to deal with the personal and planetary injustices that trouble you most.

3. After fifteen days of giving the Watch with Jesus, reassess your life and take note of the problems and situations that have been resolved. Accept your victories and know that more are on the way, write to Jesus again and thank the Lord and his angels for their love. Then list and number your New Year's objectives and ask the Master's help in all you desire to accomplish for the Good. From that time forward keep the Watch with Jesus each week on the day and hour of your choosing.

Think carefully about this day and hour and be sure that you will be free at that time every week throughout the year. Then fill out the pledge on the last page of your "Watch With Me" booklet and sign it—and look forward to faithfully keeping your "Love tryst" with the Master, knowing that He who has promised to be with you in that hour will be faithful. And other thousands who keep this Vigil of the Hours throughout the year will be forming with you a Christmas wreath of perpetual prayer encircling the earth.

4. This is the century, the decade, and the hour to anticipate the great and notable day of the Lord in your life—to make your decision to be or not to be his disciple. To accept the Lord's offer you must be prepared to make a lifetime commitment to serve him and to be instrumental in bringing his lost teachings to bear on every area of human life. If such a givingness of yourself seems more than you are ready for, remember, Jesus has already committed the allness of himself to you. After all, we give ourselves in love to one another in marriage and friendships, to our children and causes and businesses and professions—why not give ourselves to the Ascended Master Jesus Christ whose Christhood, through the personal Master/disciple relationship, then multiplies our own Christhood in all the dimensions of our loyalties—not only human but divine.

This gift is confirmed in the first-century Gnostic Gospel of Thomas where it is recorded that Jesus said,

> He who will drink from my mouth will become as I AM: I myself shall become he, and the things that are hidden will be revealed to him. . . . The Kingdom is inside of you and it is outside of you. When you come to know yourselves then you will be known and you will realize that you are the sons of the living Father.

This is Jesus' call to you, beloved, to discipleship today. Where else can you go to know the mysteries of God, find safety during coming earth changes, or attain the only true salvation—the balance of karma by the grace of the violet flame and good works whereby we regain our soul's union with the Divine through the path of the ascension?

As Jesus said to the twelve (who like you and me had heard his Call and his Teaching), so he says to us, "Will ye also go away?" One can sense the pain of the Wise One who knows how much his students need him—his shepherding, his mantle—yet how fragile is the thread of contact until they see Him as he truly is, and know that same Christhood to be their own life's calling.

"...Will ye also go away?" When I read these words recorded by John, I am touched by the tenderness of his heart—his Love so full, so present, so personal. And I thank God for Peter's response: "Lord, to whom shall we go? thou hast the words of eternal life. And we believe and are sure that thou art that Christ, the Son of the living God."

There is no doubt about it: the Master/disciple relationship under Jesus Christ is surely the highest calling to which we could be called. This union with his Sacred Heart—as the culmination of our day-to-day interaction with the Ascended Masters who sponsor the Keepers of the Flame Fraternity and dictate its lessons—truly makes life complete and ultimately fulfilling wherever we are on planet earth.

5. Therefore, give serious consideration to joining Saint Germain's Keepers of the Flame Fraternity today. If you do not have our booklet on the fraternity or an application form, simply call this toll-free number (800-245-5445) and we will send you one by the next mail. The membership fee for single or joint family membership, including the first seven lessons sent to you each month, is $33. You can put this amount on your credit card by phone and tell us you wish to make this commitment and we will send you your first lesson and membership card and complete your records when you return the membership application at a later date to Box A, Livingston, MT 59047-1390. In addition you will also receive upon joining the fraternity a free 544-page book—actually four books in one—"Saint Germain On Alchemy."

It is our goal, in response to Jesus' own heart call, to receive ten thousand new Keepers of the Flame into the fraternity before December 31, 1987. Your decision and your immediate response can make this a reality. Thousands testify to the blessings they receive through the sponsorship of Saint Germain, the Lords of the Seven Rays, the World Teachers, Jesus Christ and Kuthumi, and Mother Mary and the Maha Chohan, the representative of the Holy Spirit, through their active membership in this fraternity.

6. Help others to become disciples of Jesus by sending to them this "Watch With Me" booklet and cassette. The regular price for the cassette is $6.50 and the booklet $2.00. If you order quantities of five sets or more, they are $5.00 a set; additional booklets are $20.00 a dozen.

If each Lightbearer who receives this Christmas package gives five booklets and cassettes, we will have contacted 75,000 people with Jesus' message of direct discipleship and effective oneness with his heart through participation in this worldwide Watch. If each of you gives ten sets, we will contact 150,000. This Vigil of the Hours was planned by Jesus for anyone whose heart is open to his and who is receptive to committing a weekly hour of prayer to the Lord for the blessing and healing of their families and nations.

Just think of it! With a commitment of just an hour or an hour and a half each week, Jesus can accomplish for us what we could not do for ourselves during the entire week! By the concentration and devotion of our energies, one pointed, to his heart as we contemplate his portrait on the cover, we give Jesus that open door for sixty or ninety minutes as He floods our worlds with Light and Healing.

During the Watch, Jesus places his Electronic Presence over each one of us, anchoring the Light of his being through the supplicant's chakras (spiritual centers) for the holding of the balance of world peace and freedom. There is not a problem that we see on the evening news or in the morning headlines that cannot be resolved through his Sacred Heart.

Won't you take a moment to make a list of friends, relatives, loved ones and children as well—for their hearts are pure and they understand so completely Jesus' Vigil of the Hours. Again, you can call us on the toll-free number, giving us your credit card number, and we will fill your order immediately. Be sure to enclose your personal message with each set you send. If you care to send Jesus' Pearls on the ascension (quoted in this letter) and discipleship (enclosed), they are 50 cents each in any quantity.

7. Use the enclosed "Heart, Head and Hand Decrees: Meditations, Mantras, Prayers and Decrees for the Expansion of the Threefold Flame within the Heart" to give daily dynamic decrees for the acceleration and protection of the Light that Jesus, the Ascended Masters and the Archangels give to you. This is the mighty work of the ages! For this glorious entering in to the Sacred Heart also set a time and place and be faithful. The earlier in the day the better. (And the best time is dawn—to celebrate the dawn of your own Christ-realization.) As in any exercise or proficiency, it is constancy and diligence day by day that takes the prize of the high calling in Christ Jesus. If you would like a supply of these for your prayer circle or meditation group, they are $1.25 each and $12.00 for one dozen. Two or more dozen are $10.00 a dozen.

8. In your desire to serve Jesus with all of your heart, you will undoubtedly take note of his words, "Further, I choose to enter into this [Master/disciple] relationship with all who will call upon Saint Michael the Archangel to defend both Church and State and to exorcise these domains of Alpha and Omega of all fallen angels who have come to steal away the best of the hearts of men."

If you do not already have the ninety-minute cassette of Archangel Michael's Rosary for Armageddon with the booklet of the complete text (which allows you to stop the tape and insert your personal prayers for the healing and exorcism of the governments and economies of the nations or of loved ones), send for this most powerful prayer service which includes calls to the Seven Archangels, to Jesus Christ and to Mother Mary, and set a time when you give it once a week. The service itself is only fifty-five minutes. A dictation by Archangel Michael and songs to him complete the ninety minutes. The price—only $5.00 for booklet and cassette.

9. Since Jesus' call is also an assignment to study his Teachings, if you do not already have them, order your copies of "The Lost Years of Jesus," "The Lost Teachings of Jesus" Volumes I and II, "Corona Class Lessons" and "Prayer and Meditation" while they are on the twenty-five percent discount through January 31 on orders of $100 or more. (Please see our Christmas catalogue or ask us to send you one.) These books are ideal Christmas gifts and companions to your gift of the "Watch With Me" and cassette.

10. Call or write us to find out the Teaching Center or Study Group nearest you so that you can meet with other Keepers of the Flame on a regular basis, not only to decree but also to hear the latest lectures and dictations of Jesus' lost teachings and Saint Germain's prophecy.

Finally, beloved, I have enclosed a Christmas love-offering envelope for any contribution great or small you may desire to make before the year's end. It is your contributions which enable us to carry on our worldwide service to Lightbearers, including the giving of this "Watch With Me" booklet and cassette to every new inquiry or Pearls of Wisdom subscriber that we receive. For all that Jesus has done for us each one, I, for one, can do no less than give every soul who knocks on our door the opportunity to enter his Heart and to know his Love.

1988 is the year we intend to build Jesus' Church at the Royal Teton Ranch. As you send your Christmas wreath offering to us, we will put it towards Jesus' Ministry and Church so that Jesus will find his place prepared in the hearts of men and at the altar of the Chapel of the Holy Grail. Thus, by our vigil the Lord's lost teachings will never be lost again—nor to this or succeeding ages.

With all my heart, I thank you for your love of the Lord, for keeping his vigil for the nations and for bearing the Light in his name.

Sincerely in the Christmas Rose
who is our Blessed Jesus, the Christ,

Elizabeth Clare Prophet

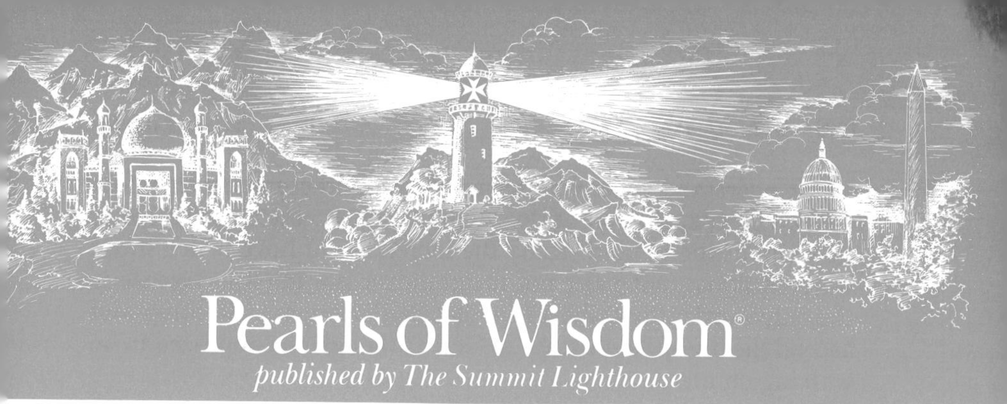

Vol. 30 No. 82 *Beloved Lanello* *December 24, 1987*

A Fount of Victory

The Mandate of Our God for the Incarnation of the Word

Lanello's Birthday Address 1987

Out of the heart of the Son of God a fountain of Victory begins to rise. It is a welcome sight, for the fountain of Victory, beginning with a single stream, is the sign that the impelling fire beneath the rock is a fervent heat whereby Victory does rise.

I have come to speak to those who desire to hear me and to listen. Many have listened to our Brotherhood, many have heard the Call, yet they have not internalized the Word. This Word, beloved, is assimilated by love and by loving obedience. The fruit of this Word is a living sacred fire and flame-flowers of the heart. Where the roots of consciousness have assimilated indeed that Life, there the flowers spring forth.

Thus, beloved, it is impossible to take the word [of God] merely to repeat it again. But if thou wouldst become the word, then endow it with the fire of Love. Understand that many quote great sages and prophets, the Lord Christ and us, the Ascended Masters. Yet there are times when that word is endowed as a renewal by the Holy Spirit, and there are times when they sound, as Paul said, as sounding brass or tinkling cymbal.[1] Therefore, know, beloved, that all of the words we have ever spoken will never add up to the Word incarnate within you unless you bring to them the fervor of the fiery heart.

The Lords of Karma have sent me on this the anniversary of my birth date of my final incarnation,[2] and I am sent with the challenge to impart to you the wherewithal of fulfilling the mandate of our God for the incarnation of the Word.

Thus, beloved, Love is the key. Therefore, one must measure one's capacity to be a cup of Love. Can the hand be a cup? the foot? the limb? the organ? the heart? the brain, the mind, the soul? Can the tongue be the instrument of Love?

Understand yourself in terms of the microcosm and therefore know, beloved, that all of thy members must now be attentive to be a cup fitting to hold steady the sacred fire of Love which is not watered down, not pale, not insignificant but intense. Intense is the only word to describe a love that shall overcome all things and ascend the invisible staircase to God as though one appeared to be walking on air.

Now, then, beloved, the fountain must rise. The fire must be, and if the coals have grown cold and if the fire has lost its fervor, so the fount of Victory shall be reduced and be no more, for it is the pressure of the heart's loving that does sustain, hour by hour and day by day, a Victory flame that can and does surely swallow up the forces of defeat and defeatism.

Blessed ones, in the beauty of the lilies there is the testimony of Christ's coming and his promise that you also shall come into the full maturity of that Christ life. Therefore, by the fount of my Victory flame I come to wash away, by the baptism of water, momentums of anti-Love that block the already rocky road of thy footsteps to the receiving and the giving of the fire of Love.

Let it be a fiery furnace, I say! Let it melt the snows of all the Himalayas. Let the love of my brothers and sisters upon earth be, then, for you a sufficiency for the melting of any and all human creation charted on any or all lines of the Cosmic Clock.[3]

Hasten ye, I say, to bank the fires of the heart's love in a self-givingness such as has not been seen, no, not since the day of the Lord Jesus Christ's submission to his judgment before the gods of this world. Greater love hath no man than this, that a man lay down his life for his friends.[4] Let the sign of the heart become the sign of this Community of the Holy Spirit, and let it be one heart, one mind and one body that does sponsor the one-pointed goal of saving the nations for Saint Germain.

Blessed ones, let us begin this new year with a new notebook and a new writing. File all the old that have gone before and begin a clean white page. I desire you to have a section in this notebook that shall be entitled "The Impelling Love." Each time, then, you encounter a circumstance or individual, an idea or Master or littlest angel that does cause your heart to open and your soul to shed a tear, whatever is the impelling force of that love that does instantly bring you into alignment with Cyclopea's All-Seeing Eye and with the will of God, write it down in this diary in detail. For, beloved, when the heart is full of love and with communion with our Father, no sacrifice is too great, no self-givingness is even weighed; it is that "impelling love" that simply acts upon that force of cosmic love captured in the twinkling eyes of a babe or a cloud-filled sky of moving angelic hosts.

Blessed hearts, these moments come, and it is as though all of thy members should rise to release in the self-emptying to give that love to a cosmos. The self-emptying done with, one does resume what may appear as the mundane chores and responsibilities.

All servitors of Light throughout cosmos must tend to the details that are sometimes repetitious to keep the wheels of creation spinning. These day-to-day tasks are the very fabric and fiber of our movement, and they are rhythmic cycle which does establish a momentum of rhythm of service—so that when the Lord Gautama may come to your side, the momentum of balance day by day of the flow of Alpha and Omega in your service does give to you the ability to receive from him a higher balance as he would add to your momentum of constancy even his own and therefore lift you up and quicken you by the very momentum of your service into a new cycle—as we would say, a new arena and vista of cosmic awareness.

Blessed hearts, this beauty of self-transcendence, then, is punctuated by the mighty encounters of love that impel you once again to a higher giving that does enable you to perform the tasks of yesterday with a new zest, an enlightenment and a quickening of the Holy Spirit. Therefore, you may mark in your diary, concerning this impelling love, those things you were able simply to leave behind as though stepping out of yesterday's work clothes.

Moving on, moving on, moving on, that is what we are about! And where we are going is unto the untrammeled heights of the Central Sun.

All of your building is for the building of the temple of man, line upon line. Neglect not, then, the plumb line of Truth, no detail unworthy of effort, for the crystal of self must be an alchemical/chemical formula that does vibrate and quiver with the spiritual chemistry of God.

Thus, beloved, let there be open spaces in the crystal of self. Let the wind of love blow through, and in those hours when you are ready to pay any price, to do any favor to enter into the nearness of thy God, so note [it] well; for I tell thee the forces of anti-Love upon this planet always seek to take from you the cup of love—its poetry, its memory and its blessing. Each gift of love of friend or angel, Master or the Lord Christ himself must be seen as something that you are able to multiply by the fervor of the heart that does impel the rising fount of Victory in the Son of God.

You have seen how quickly, as time is counted, you can

achieve momentum in physical exercise and sport. Know, then, beloved, that this is also a co-measurement, that you might understand that the spiritual fortifying of the spirit itself, the fiery spirit of God dwelling in you, is something that can be built and built upon and multiplied daily.

There is nothing whatsoever that is nebulous about the increase of the wedding garment, the Deathless Solar Body.[5] Some have a rich garment composed of a most beautiful fabric out of resurrection's flame. It is a soft-white, off-white [creamy yellow] radiance; and, blessed ones, this garment of God is so full and, as it were, luxurious in light that angels know that that one is truly entering the kingdom of God.

Thus, one close to you has recently been shown this magnificent garment woven through many years of service in the Light, line upon line and detail upon detail. Thus, all efforts made to provide a cup for light to fill have resulted in the most intricate weaving as angels knit this garment many thicknesses, beloved, and beyond the garment proper, an aura magnificent of this radiance—the radiance of resurrection's flame.

How, then, shall this soul appear in the transition? Blessed ones, it shall hardly be a transition at all, for the movement between octaves and worlds by the Deathless Solar Body is complete, facile. Therefore know, beloved, that the constancy of service and the meticulous attentiveness to the embodying of the Word does result over the years of a lifetime (and yet even weeks and months) in a manifestation of spiritual glory.

There are others, then, who come to this community who do not bank the fire of the heart, do not bend the knee before our Lord Sanat Kumara, the mighty Ancient of Days. Thus, beloved, without that inner presence of Light that does confess that Jesus is LORD and that that LORD is one and one God in all and all manifestations of Himself, there is not the nucleus for the fire of Love to increase [in order] for the individual [soul] to be a chalice of Light and Love and majestic Peace in all her members.

Therefore, beloved, such individuals, having not a vortex of fire of the heart, have only a vortex of the absence—the absence of surrender unto God. These, then, use this vacuum whereby to draw to themselves the light of all others—possessions and things and monies and substance, energy and the Light itself. These are takers not givers, and they do not appear in the lineup of those who are weaving a Deathless Solar Body.

Often very personable, having the magnetism of the human consciousness, they have learned long and well the art of engaging others by the personality and its devices—and yet so close is the Personality of God, the great God-Good of that Holy Christ Self, who would descend upon the instant with angels of Light were that one to bend the knee before Almighty God and thus reconnect to his own heart flame.

Many of you are fooled by "the takers." Many of you do not understand that you are not obliged to give of your fount of Victory unto those who have not raised up a fount of Victory by their own heart's fervor. Thus, the devil who does also quote scripture does come upon you, quoting all of those verses concerning the giving to the poor and the helping of those who ask.

Blessed hearts, Jesus has asked me to remind you that his preaching was for the children of the Light, the lost sheep of the house of Israel, those in whom there does dwell a threefold flame, the kindling light of our Sanat Kumara, who has sponsored us all upon this earth. To help one another who have a threefold flame and the fervor of love that does impel the Victory fountain: this is in divine order. Nevertheless, let all helpfulness come as the giving to others of the ability to create for themselves what others have striven also to create.

We counsel, then, *Work while ye have the Light.**[6] Ye do have the Light.† But if you squander that Light unlawfully upon those who have lost their souls, become castaways and in fear of that loss of the fire of the altar of God have raced to this citadel of Light, blessed hearts, you are also in danger of losing the Light that you have. In the one instance, it is not lawful before Maitreya to so give it away, and in the second, beloved, those who would take it from you have an insatiable desire and need, for no sooner do they receive the light or the abundance of the sons and daughters of God than it does pass through them and they require another influx. For they have not or will not bend the knee truly before their own Mighty I AM Presence.

Blessed hearts, the inner walk of the Master who is Teacher and the disciples is known by the Master and of the Master. The Messenger, then, being the instrument of that relationship, does guard the secrets of the Master as well as the secrets of the disciple.

Know, then, beloved, though we may read and transfer to our Messenger in embodiment (even as we are given them) the records of the Keeper of the Scrolls, that which is known concerning the individual lifestream may not be shared with other community members until such time as covert as well as overt actions by such individuals must be noted because they may threaten harm or degradation or some burden to those other members

*the living Christ with you †Christ consciousness

of the community unless they be warned. Therefore, within the Mystery School there has always been provision for the transfer of an understanding of the paths of the initiates so involved.

Thus, beloved, to embody the living Word and to increase the fire of Love, the requirement that has been stated must be stated again to call to your memory that the gift which Paul the Venetian and the Lord Maha Chohan do prepare you to receive, the gift of the discernment of spirits,[7] must be sought by you. Therefore, when having that discernment you will not go out another round or another ten rounds in idolatrous relationships of the human personality which ignore that which is the living Reality within.

Blessed ones, there are any number of initiates whose outer personalities are not necessarily of the popular type. They may not necessarily be communicative or magnanimous every moment. Blessed ones, the outer personality often has little to do with the inner God Reality of that person and the God-Good. For, you see, beloved, the farther one is upon the Path, the more strenuous the climb and the greater the challengers of his ascent and his Christhood. Therefore, there is a groaning in the spirit. Therefore, there is a travail as with the Divine Mother he does desire ultimately to give birth to a Christhood.

Understand that such an one so engaged may not be continually focused upon the outer niceties or exchanging the outer pleasantries. Thus, it is well to judge righteous judgment,[8] and if you are not qualified so to judge, then, beloved, to obey the admonishment, Judge not, lest you be judged.[9]

Therefore, I, your brother Lanello, stand in this hour to take from you those very blocks to a greater discernment and Christ-discrimination where the end result is not a criticism or an analytical gaze toward others but simply a sensing of whatever the burdens may be that you may help others carry and a sense of discipleship that will not allow encroachment upon your Christhood, whether from within your own substance or from without. To deny this encroachment, beloved, to hold oneself in the middle way of a discipleship that is neither too easy nor too stern is the way of wisdom.

Those who indulge their four lower bodies and others' are ofttime the ones who make excuses for the lower vibrations that they do sense and know. Thus the sympathy for a grain of the consciousness of the carnal mind (otherwise known as the devil) can be the crack whereby the waters of the astral plane begin to drip within your own astral body until a sea is raging, covering over the eye of God and all Christ-discrimination that is there in reality but not effective [in the moment] for the mounting of the soul up that spiral staircase into the secret chamber of the heart.

What I have said, beloved, concerns each and every one of my own here. For as you listen and ponder and contemplate my words, I will come to you and I will surely make known to you those things that are ready to fly quickly into the sacred fire and to be no more, as the dry leaves in fall are blown by the untimely winds of an early winter.

It is, then, with great joy that I might pass through these halls, and in this chamber, beloved, be accorded the honor of delivering the first dictation.[10] Therefore, beloved, as I am accorded this honor, so I am given the opportunity to name this hall.

Blessed ones, the altar is magnificent but I cannot call this hall the Chapel of the Holy Grail. Rather I would call to your attention that it more resembles a gathering place of concerned knights and ladies, children and Keepers of the Flame who come together to take counsel with the LORD who has said, "Come, let us reason together. . . ,"[11] therefore coming to deliberate and to understand the changing tides of the world scene in the economy, in the government, coming together in that deliberation in order to reach your conclusions, thence to face the altar and to call upon the Holy Spirit to release that sacred fire for a world alchemy that is so needed.

I consider, then, that this place is more than a chapel, more than a decree sanctuary. It is a point of union of hearts in the heart of our dear El Morya, our sponsor and our great love. Therefore, in memory of days of old and in promise of those things to come, including one day a true church and sanctuary, I prefer to call this hall the Court of King Arthur.[12]

Thus may you understand that Camelot has returned once again and you are called, each and every one, because of all past service to the Holy Grail, to that magnificent chalice of consciousness and being and to its perfectionment in yourselves and in the world order.

You and I know that each one of us has unfinished business, not alone from those hours, but from ancient times on Lemuria, Atlantis and more recent centuries. Thus, where there is a need, Camelot must be raised up. Let "the Once and Future King" be our present king, for we have need of him and we do not desire to leave him in the last stanzas of Tennyson nor in a concept of the death of Arthur.[13]

Therefore, to Life, to the resurrection, to the building of the future upon the foundation stones of the past, let there be lowered, then, the sound, the memory, the divine purpose, the sense of justice and the Round Table itself in this that is renewed again, the Court of King Arthur. Thus, you may call it King Arthur's Court, but let it be a place for thinking and feeling and striving men and women who truly have heard the call of Jesus Christ to endure to the end and therefore receive the crown of everlasting Life.[14]

There are initiations to be given and taken. There are jousts to be entered and the lists whereby you wrestle with and defeat the dragon of the lower nature. There is a perfecting of the physical body, both in exercise and in the wise use of chemistry in one's diet. There is the chalice of the mind that truly can become extraordinary as it is filled with Light and the balance of Alpha and Omega.

Let this new Camelot be for a new age, but let it be above all more than a building and more than a gathering place. Let it be composed of white stones that are for the building in octaves of Light of that which cannot suffer the corruption of moth or rust or decay. Let it be for the building, then, of that which is substantial.

And that glowing white as marble, as pyramid, as edifice, let it be seen on the inner planes by all the world, and let all the world have in this hour a mighty zest for a return, not to King Arthur's Court of old, but to King Arthur's Court as it is this day in the etheric octave, as it is the gift of Morya over this very place to be lowered, then, day by day into this building as each one does embody that very spirit, that very diamond heart and that very fire and fervor of Love that does produce the living fountain of Victory.

Remember, then, that the assimilation of our Word is by a spirit, a holy spirit—and its distillation and sending through your chakras, O my fellow knights and ladies of the flame: this, then, is the individual call and creativity of Camelot. This is the Call that goes forth from the Father/Mother God and from every Lightbearer who was a part of this endeavor of King Arthur in Britain of old.

All, then, who have risen again in the fire of the resurrection, all who are embodied, all who are yet to embody, I say to you, I am your Lanello and I have never been more fervent or fiery in my determination to defeat those who did cause the downfall of our Community of the Holy Spirit by their black magic and by their witchcraft, by their conniving! Blessed hearts, that scene did close for many of us, as it were, in tragedy of that which might have been, that which almost was. Therefore, we are determined in this age to bring our Christ Presence before every enemy of our beloved King Arthur.

Blessed ones, we are determined to defeat the consciousness

which they embodied and represented as chessmen on that board. Wherever it is found, wherever there does rise a force to defeat the living Christ Light upon the altar of that temple and that temple of the Blessed Virgin Mary, there we would stand to defeat it by illumination's golden flame, by alchemy of transmutation, by exorcism of the Divine Mother Astrea and Archangel Michael, by the word of Love and Life and, yes, by a fount of Victory!

Blessed hearts, you who give in love, whose love is a fire that burns, you, then, who have the fount of Victory in this moment, remember that I have told you that one day you shall thirst for the waters of eternal Life and there shall be no other waters given save thine own. And because you have raised up a fountain of Victory out of a fiery furnace of love, you will drink of those waters and be saved and have everlasting Life.

O bank the fires of Love! O fill, fill the stream of Victory!

I am your Lanello in this hour, rejoicing in the beloved Guru, the wise man forever.[15] I bid you sing to him in this hour and to his Diamond Heart.

I bid you adieu, heart to heart. Yet I go not away or anywhere, for *I AM truly everywhere in the Consciousness of God!* When you have that consciousness, I am there with you, a part of you, to do with you the will of God; and I promise to make your tasks light. And I promise that that light shall be translated and transformed into the Deathless Solar Body. Weave it, O weave it! Thou hast need of it even now.

I am come with comfort and joy. Now let us receive our Master Morya with that comfort and joy.

"The Summit Lighthouse Sheds Its Radiance O'er All the World to Manifest as Pearls of Wisdom."
This dictation by **Lanello** was **delivered** through the Messenger of the Great White Brotherhood Elizabeth Clare Prophet on **Christmas Day, December 25, 1987,** at the **Royal Teton Ranch, Montana.** (**1**) I Cor. 13:1. (**2**) The Ascended Master Lanello was embodied in his final incarnation as the Messenger Mark L. Prophet, born December 24, 1918. (**3**) For teachings on the **Cosmic Clock,** including the human perversions of the God qualities as charted on the Clock, see Elizabeth Clare Prophet, "The Cosmic Clock: Psychology for the Aquarian Man and Woman," in *The Great White Brotherhood in the Culture, History and Religion of America,* pp. 173–206; and *The ABC's of Your Psychology on the Cosmic Clock,* 8-audiocassette album, 12 hrs., A85056, 12 lectures. (**4**) John 15:13. (**5**) On the weaving of the **Deathless Solar Body** and the descent of this garment during the ascension process, see "The Great Deathless Solar Body," in *Dossier on the Ascension,* pp. 154–59. (**6**) "I must work the works of him that sent me, while it is day: the night cometh, when no man can work. As long as I AM in the world, I AM the Light of the world. . . . Then Jesus said unto them, Yet a little while is the Light with you. Walk while ye have the Light, lest Darkness come upon you: for he that walketh in Darkness knoweth not whither he goeth. While ye have Light, believe in the Light, that ye may be the children of Light." John 9:4, 5; 12:35, 36. (**7**) I Cor. 12:1, 10. For teachings on the **gift of discernment of spirits,** see *Lords of the Seven Rays: Mirror of Consciousness,* Book One, pp. 123, 133–34, 142–43; and *The Lost Teachings of Jesus II,* pp. 180–81. (**8**) "Judge not according to the appearance, but judge righteous judgment." John 7:24. (**9**) Matt. 7:1; Luke 6:37. (**10**) This dictation by Lanello was the first to be delivered in the temporary 'chapel' at the Royal Teton Ranch located in Saint Germain's food barn. (**11**) Isa. 1:18. (**12**) El Morya was embodied in the fifth century as Arthur, King of the Britons, warrior and head of the mystery school at Camelot. On the Christian mysteries as these relate to Christ's Body on earth, see *Lords of the Seven Rays: Mirror of Consciousness,* Book One, pp. 5–6, 8, 192, 226; Book Two, pp. 147–48, 175, 190, 238, 300. (**13**) See Alfred Lord Tennyson, "The Passing of Arthur," in *Idylls of the King.* (**14**) "Blessed is the man that endureth temptation: for when he is tried, he shall receive the crown of life, which the Lord hath promised to them that love him." James 1:12. "Fear none of those things which thou shalt suffer: behold, the devil shall cast some of you into prison, that ye may be tried; and ye shall have tribulation ten days: be thou faithful unto death, and I will give thee a crown of life." Rev. 2:10. (**15**) El Morya was embodied as Melchior, one of the three wise men who paid homage to the Christ Child.

Pearls of Wisdom®
published by The Summit Lighthouse

Vol. 30 No. 83 *Beloved Mother Mary* *December 25, 1987*

The Order of the Diamond Heart

The Sacrifice of the One and the Many for the Saving of America

Christmas Eve Address 1987

Out of the Diamond Heart of the Divine Mother I AM come to you, beloved. For long ago I beheld that heart and I determined to fashion that Diamond Heart within myself that it might be unto all sons and daughters of God in these octaves truly a sign, a symbol, a vibrating presence that would enable them to understand that in the Immaculate Heart of the Divine Mother all are born. Now see, beloved, as I am her instrument, how you are intended so to be.

I speak to all angels who have gone forth from the courts of heaven—now veiled in flesh, now moving in these tides of earth. I speak to you who came bearing Light to serve the children of the Light. I speak also to you who took exception to the divine justice of our Father and therefore didst rebel against the living God-Good as the divine spark in every heart.

All angels earthbound, hear me! For I am truly crowned Queen of Angels for my part in delivering to earth the Manchild who is Jesus the Lord, and King of kings and Saviour. Thus, as I descended from heaven, called by God unto this purpose, I have also been assumed unto heaven for having fulfilled that purpose.

Blessed hearts, my garment of light was not compromised in earth, not in the several incarnations accorded me to establish even the foundation for the coming of the Saviour at that moment of history when many souls, including angels who did descend, would come to the Y on the Path, to choose God-Good and live forever or to choose again their denying of the living Son of God in Jesus and in each and every one of his sisters and brothers upon earth.[1]

Therefore, beloved, from the hour of his coming men and

women of earth have made their choices. Pilate made his choice and Herod and many others who played their parts. And they did reincarnate to fulfill the fruit of their tree of life unto this hour and century of the two-thousand-year reign of my Son.

Blessed ones, even for their choosing they were given again opportunity to choose. Now, for this certain group of lifestreams scattered across the earth, the end of an age, a cycle and a choice has come. Therefore there is a tremendous momentum in the earth in this hour of those on all sides seeking to move others and men and nations against the living Light, yet to disguise their movements as though they were for the greater good. Though they do not speak in the name of God, yet they claim to be of that goodness that is "superior" to his own.

Thus, beloved, many are yet gone astray by the same philosophy of the Serpents, those fallen angels in the garden of God who did turn aside many from the stronghold of living Truth, from the two-edged sword keeping the way of the Tree of Life. Therefore you have understood this convergence [of the forces of Good and Evil at this transition between Pisces and Aquarius].

I, Mary, have spoken to the understanding of those to whom I have entrusted my messages, my prophecy, my vision of a karma outplayed upon the future, a karma of free will whose course is a juggernaut[2] of self-destruction. Thus, I come to those who understand the mysteries of Christ and have believed that these mysteries are revealed by him, within the secret chamber of the heart to all who are ready, without dissimulation, without discrimination, regardless of their religious affiliation.

I come in this hour, therefore, with the sign of the LORD's judgment that cannot be otherwise.[3] For to allow those who have murdered the Christed ones, that is, the anointed of the Light and the prophets and the messengers and apostles of all time, to move on into the next two-thousand-year cycle would surely not be in keeping with the Great Law of God.

Thus, there is an impending sense that as the sands in the hourglass run out, the moments for right decision diminish. Thus, the whole world senses the tension—a tension drawn between angels of Light and angels who have still not been willing to bend the knee before that Light.

Many among you are those angels who came to teach, to reawaken and to move the children of Light to a steadfast allegiance and devotion to that living Christ of Jesus until they should understand his words to Thomas, to Philip, to the entire inner circle: Those who drink from the same fount from which

I drink shall be as I AM.[4] This fount is the living fount of eternal water that is the I AM Presence of Life.

Therefore, know, beloved, that you must make haste to drink of this fount and to understand that the elixir of the water of eternal Life will not leave you as you are. And therefore, change by the winds of the Holy Spirit, by a fiery baptism and the cleansing water of the Divine Mother—this, this too must be understood. This, beloved, does come to you. Resist it not. Be not entrenched in the very ways that have been put upon you by false doctrine, false theology of the same [breed of] Serpents who preach their lies in the economic systems in states and nations.

I come to you, then, to give you the realization that because the children of the Light have not heeded their true Teachers over the centuries, many more have gone after the Lie, flattered by these very ones who have invented the art of flattery itself. Thus, those who might have been ministers of God and teachers, devoting the full course of their lifestream to the conversion of souls unto the Holy Ghost, these very ones have been enamored of other callings and other fields.

Therefore, one thing is needful, the realization that unless the light of the living Christ be raised up in each individual heart, the planet itself and its evolutions are yet in great jeopardy. The quotient of Light* in the earth ought to be greater for my Son's giving of his life alone! It ought to be greater for the exposure of the Liar and the Lie that he did manifest, not only in preachment but, beloved, by example.

Is not the example of his crucifixion and the mockery of his trial, is it not to show that each and every time there is opportunity the fallen angels committed to the Antichrist will move against the Word incarnate to the utter destruction of the single son of God coming into the realization that the reality of his own being within his own temple is truly and only can be Christ the Lord?

This reality of the Presence of my Son, truly the universal Light itself within ye all, is a quickening Power, a quickening Wisdom, a quickening Love whereby the faithful shall also inherit the promise given to him[, whereof he spake]: *All power in heaven and in earth is given unto me.*[5] This is the power of God to work change and to galvanize and reassemble hearts around the divine polarity of Alpha and Omega of him who said: *I AM Alpha and Omega, the beginning and the ending!*

In the fullness of the Light understand a simple equation: Because the children of the Light have not known their true shepherds and because some who ought to have taken up the mantle of

*Christ consciousness

shepherd have cast it aside for other "more interesting" callings, therefore not enough among the Body of God upon earth have ever understood that for that 'body bulb' to burn brightly, there must come about an intensity in the Word for the sacred fire to increase. And when it does increase, beloved, as all saints have ever known, there is a period of the dark night of the soul[6] as that soul's karma must pass into the sacred fire.

Therefore, if you do espouse discipleship under Jesus Christ to which he has called you,[7] know, beloved, that it is a known path of initiation and that the darkness and trial and tragedy that does befall you does come because you have made your commitment to serve with him, to bow before him and to know the Lord in him as truly the LORD the I AM THAT I AM who is God.

To understand this is to become this. To look upon that Christ of him is to receive that Christ, portion by portion unto yourself. And when you receive this Light, the Light will first purge you to make you a fitting habitation of your God. And as that purging does take place, it is the karma, the old records, the old sowings and sayings that were not of God-Good that come to the fore and must pass into the flame, as ghosts of the former self are seen parading through, only to dissolve in that pillar of sacred fire.

Beloved hearts, when you have set yourself to a course of discipleship unto my Jesus, I say, vow to God that you will stand and still stand. Accept his Call, that you might call upon the Archangels and the hosts of the Lord to guide and to guard you. These ministering ones—they are necessary to thy Victory. Thou hast need of them. Invoke them in the name of your I AM Presence, your Holy Christ Self and the Christ of Jesus. Invoke them, beloved, but do not turn back.

Therefore, what is the end of this path? Is it not the resurrection and the ascension to eternal Life? Aye, what, then, is the middle of this path? Is it not the confrontation and the encounter as of Saint Stephen, as of John the Baptist,[8] as of all who have carried the Light? Does that Light not come and stand face-to-face with the absolute Darkness of the fallen angels who have denied him? Will he not send his disciples into the very quarters of the earth where the children of the Light as shorn lambs are not able to deal with that Darkness?

"Even so, send me."[9] Thus was the word of the apostles. Some went forth with great eagerness and yet when the tests came, their fervor of emotion did not carry them in the hour when they must affirm their Lord before men.[10]

Now then, beloved, this is the reason for the testing: to vow a vow of Love. That vow, then, is to be tested that in all thy ways thou might understand the meaning of the vow, the meaning of what it is to stand upon one's word in Truth—come what may.

Whenever the next step of individual Christhood is taken, all fallen angels and black magicians will assail that one at that point of the line of Christhood. If you are able to defeat them by the fervor of Christ-love in your heart, you may step another step higher, once again to defeat those forces of Antichrist who have positioned themselves on these steps of the path of attainment. They are claiming their superiority until some knight of the cross, some lady who has kept the flame of the Mother of God does willingly mount to that level and say, *Here I stand, so help me God!*

Therefore, beloved, as there is the mounting of a spiral staircase, there is the thinning of the ranks. For some will say, I have stepped on the last step that I will take. I will not move higher, for to do so I must surrender this and this and this of my fame, my personality, my preferences, my enjoyments of this world.

Therefore all choose. But I tell you (it is a secret that few know), if you will rest at a certain level, you then will be targeted even more. Therefore, the conclusion of those who climb the highest mountain is: the only way to go is up. If you remain at a certain level, beloved, it is even more difficult than to ascend again. Thus, wherever you pause, there will the forces of the enemy assemble. Life [in order] to be—life to be alive and living—must move on in a creative intensity that is the fire of Love gathering more and more and more of itself!

I am therefore unto you a representative of the Divine Mother and of the path of the Diamond Heart. This path of the Divine Mother as the path of the Diamond Heart has been espoused by the beloved El Morya. El Morya does teach this path of devotion to the will of God by that Diamond Heart to each and every one of his chelas. Therefore you who have been in his retreat in the etheric octave in Darjeeling have heard much about this.

I come to tell you in this hour of this year's Christ Mass and the celebration of the birth of my Son that El Morya does call you and call you again to be a part of his order in which I join him, the Order of the Diamond Heart.[11] This order, beloved, is dedicated to the giving of one's heart to form the Sacred Heart of Jesus. Whereas one individual may not be able to bear that Sacred Heart alone, many who pledge to bear it may become components of the one great heart of our Lord. It is the same principle of the

Body of God upon earth, many members but one Body.[12] Thus, many hearts also form one Diamond Heart.

This Diamond Heart is Christ's own heart of the will of God. Nothing can withstand it, for its Light intensity is greater than all Darkness of the dark ones in the earth.

Blessed ones, through the ages the saints have been called to give their lives for the saving of the Church or the nation or the community or the planet. This my Son also did, but the giving of his life was in living and not in dying, and the shedding of his Blood was not in dying but in living. For the immortal Light that does flow from his heart is a stream that never ends but does fill every communion cup on earth.

Understand this principle, beloved, that in this hour two thousand years hence all disciples of Jesus Christ upon earth are called to be a portion of that Diamond Heart.

I come to explain to you, beloved, that as there was an hour, as the decade turned to 1970 and darkness moved over the land, when your own beloved Mark offered to me, Mary, his own life and heart for the buying of time, of opportunity for his children, his own beloved students, Keepers of the Flame and Lightbearers of the whole world to come into consonance with the understanding of the mysteries of the Lord and Saviour that would allow them to receive so great a salvation through the knowledge of their own I AM Presence and Christ Self—blessed hearts, in that hour there were not enough upon earth who could make up a Diamond Heart, even a heart of sacrifice whereby that sacrifice should be in living and not in laying down one's life.

Therefore, as the weeks and months passed in that decade, there came an hour when either one who had become the fullness of that oneness of Christ should give all of that Light for the buying of time [on behalf] of the children of God upon earth else the world scale of Darkness should tip and therefore the great gain of thousands of years should be lost.

You understand also that not in dying but in the path of the ascension, in the path of the resurrection was this life given.[13] Yet it was indeed a sacrifice and a great loss, in one sense of the word, for this activity and the ongoing initiation heart to heart which he was able to deliver physically out of the Sacred Heart of Jesus.

Blessed ones, that which was gained was all of these years to the present hour for many to come into the Light and for others whose life span had drawn to its natural conclusion to enter into the ascension coil. Thus, today thousands upon thousands now understand the sacred mysteries of Christ by the writing and the teaching of the Messenger Mark and its continuity through the Messenger who does remain.

Blessed ones, this has given a great increase and impetus to the Light on earth. You ought to understand that the progressive revelations that have come forth by the Holy Spirit in many quarters have taken their impetus by this very giving of his life and the setting forth by the Messengers of the Lost Teachings of Jesus.

Now then, beloved, this very process has again and again created opportunity, but the Light that does activate and awaken all who sleep does also awaken and open that opportunity of free will whereby many have gone after other gods, necromancy, the spirits that mutter and peep,[14] channeling[15] that is nothing but spiritualism, and all manner of what is purported to be new-age teaching which is of the lower astral activity—cavorting, then, with aliens in their spacecraft who have no good design for this planet.

Therefore, we see, as it were, an abuse of opportunity at worst or a misunderstanding of opportunity [in the least] by the unguided who have not had the true shepherds to follow. Thus, great good has come about through the opening of the paths of religion to new inquiry and discovery, and by the same token, beloved, this has brought about an opening of certain of the pits [on the astral plane, spilling over into the physical,] and therefore also darkness going forth. Thus, we arrive again at the crossroads of the nations. Thus, the call went forth, *Who is willing to give his life for the saving of the nation, for the saving of America?*

Blessed hearts, because of the closeness of the heart of your Messenger here to Jesus and certain of her inner initiations, there did come an hour [during this Christmas season] when He did say to her once again, "Are you ready to give your life for the saving of America?"

Filled with the Love of the Holy Spirit and of her Lord, she did instantaneously say, "I will give my life. I will lay it down. I will do anything for the saving of America."

She did say this to Jesus, knowing full well, beloved, that it could mean the very loss of her physical life and the conclusion of this embodiment. Thus, one must understand a level of initiation and the filling of the heart so full of the Love of the Saviour that to give one's life is only to realize the allness of Life and the Life that is the All. From the hour of that commitment to the present this initiation was sealed.

Now I unveil and make known to you what is the plan of Jesus in this regard. It is his desire, then, not to have the necessity for anyone to lay down his life to save a nation but for many to live to save that nation, including your Messenger.

And therefore, Jesus with myself and El Morya at the Darjeeling Council communing have said, Let us reactivate on earth the Order of the Diamond Heart. Let us call many disciples of Jesus Christ, many who have studied this Path and Teaching, many who know the hearts of the Messengers.

Let them understand this calling. Let them understand that throughout all history the saints have given their lives that the Teaching and the Word of God might live forever as opportunity. Let them understand that by the Light of the dictations and the Holy Spirit and the Great White Brotherhood, there has come such an afflatus,* such a descent of the Holy Ghost that truly numberless numbers of those whose auras are as the saints robed in white (these having internalized a just portion of Christ's own Sacred Heart) may now become a part of that great Diamond Heart and serve to give a portion of their life that all might live and all might continue to be a vessel and a chalice as one great heart for the saving of America as a Christed nation and the path of the Master/Disciple relationship under Jesus Christ and the Servant-Sons of God in heaven.

Do you understand, beloved, that the hour of the Second Coming of Christ signaled by Jesus descending in clouds of glory is fulfilled only when his own upon earth choose to be the vessels of that universal Light?

Thus, beloved, that hour is come and ye are able. Therefore, on this Christmas night 1987, you are given the opportunity to give a portion of the light of Christ that you have realized to compose a Diamond Heart that is sufficient not only for the saving of America but to forestall that any saint or one of these little ones or the Messenger should have the necessity to lay down his life that others might live.

Blessed hearts, it is a wondrous day of opportunity. As you remember the Fifteenth Rosary,[16] those who become one with that Light and with that Christ and with that Sacred Heart of Jesus have two choices: to take all of that Christhood as the whole loaf [of the Bread of Life] and break it and give it [in the giving of oneself in life] to a world or to take that Christhood unto themselves for their private achievement. The choice of individualism in God must allow for either step, beloved.

Therefore, so choosing to give that portion and the all of such externalized Christhood as she does have, this Messenger has determined—in the full knowledge that all that one does give away

*afflatus [Latin, act of blowing or breathing on, from *afflatus*, past participle of *afflare* to blow on]: a divine imparting of knowledge or power: inspiration.

God may return in his own time and choosing—to give that Christhood for the saving of this nation.

May you come to the understanding of the Fifteenth Rosary and the meaning of forming together in this our Camelot come again the Order of the Diamond Heart. May you contemplate what the giving of the gift of self [the gift of Christ Selfhood] must mean and may you seal that giving by December 31 that at the conclusion of the year the offering of oneself upon the altar of God might be complete.

Blessed ones, surely you who know and see do also understand that the nation America cannot and shall not be saved in any form save by those who *in life* give their lives to the great principles of Cosmic Christhood upon which it is founded. You who know and know well the signs of karma and prophecy and the signs of the evildoers who hold sway in this government recognize that without the miracle there is little hope for a future that is safe for the babes in arm that are entrusted to your care.

Blessed ones, the miracle is Divine Intervention. The miracle is you! Divine Intervention must take place through the embodied sons and daughters of God.

Thus, I, Mary, with Morya at my side on this platform, do tell you that the Darjeeling Council under the guidance of the Lord Jesus Christ has proposed this as the ultimate and final resolution and opportunity for that saving grace.

I tell you, this that might be seen as a manger of Bethlehem, this place in the wilderness, is surrounded by teeming thousands of angels who attend the birth of Christ in your hearts. May you appeal to the beloved wise man El Morya for a sense of comeasurement with his heart, with the Sacred Heart of Jesus and with the Diamond Heart of Mary.

May you know that you upon earth are called and counted as needed to give this offering unto the Lord and unto the people whom you love dearly.

May you bear witness unto His Love! It was of this that Lanello spoke.[17] Greater love than this hath no man: that a man lay down his life for his friends.

Blessed hearts, what a joy to know that you can give and retain opportunity to fulfill the fullness of your Christhood come again.

With the sign of the cosmic cross of white fire I, Mary, seal you unto the Victory of the Diamond Heart. Now with Jesus the angels sing "Joy to the World" in celebration of the descent of your God and your Christ into your temple.

Receive him, beloved. Receive the Father, the Son and the

Holy Spirit, even as you have received the Divine Mother through me. For in this at-one-ment you will know what is your course from this day unto the hour of the fulfillment of your life.

Now let the burning fire of my heart leap unto your own that you might know the simultaneous bliss and pain of the Divine Mother who does carry the burden gladly for all of Her children.

"The Summit Lighthouse Sheds Its Radiance O'er All the World to Manifest as Pearls of Wisdom." This dictation by **Mother Mary** was **delivered** through the Messenger of the Great White Brotherhood Elizabeth Clare Prophet on **Christmas Day, December 25, 1987,** at the **Royal Teton Ranch, Montana.** (**1**) Dan. 12:1–3, 10. (**2**) **Juggernaut** [Hindi *Jagannath,* lit. "lord of the world," title of Krishna]: derived from the "car festival" held each year in honor of Jagannath in Puri, India, where his statue is mounted on an enormous cart and dragged by worshipers to his summer home one mile away. As a result of exaggerated tales that devotees would throw themselves under the cart's huge wheels to be crushed to death, *juggernaut* or *car of juggernaut* has come to mean any inexorable force or object that relentlessly crushes whatever is in its path. (**3**) "We give thee thanks, O Lord God Almighty, which art, and wast, and art to come; because thou hast taken to thee thy great power, and hast reigned. And the nations were angry, and thy wrath is come, and the time of the dead, that they should be judged, and that thou shouldest give reward unto thy servants the prophets, and to the saints, and them that fear thy name, small and great; and shouldest destroy them which destroy the earth." Rev. 11:17, 18. (**4**) "Jesus said to his disciples, 'Compare me to someone and tell me whom I am like.' Simon Peter said to him, 'You are like a righteous angel.' Matthew said to him, 'You are like a wise philosopher.' Thomas said to him, 'Master, my mouth is wholly incapable of saying whom you are like.' Jesus said, 'I am not your master. Because you have drunk, you have become intoxicated from the bubbling spring which I have measured out. . . . He who will drink from my mouth will become like me. I myself shall become he, and the things that are hidden will be revealed to him.'" Gospel of Thomas, logia 13, 108, in *The Nag Hammadi Library,* ed. James Robinson (San Francisco: Harper & Row, 1977), pp. 119, 129. (**5**) Matt. 28:18. (**6**) **The dark night of the soul**. See p. 532, n. 1. (**7**) **Discipleship under Jesus Christ.** See Jesus Christ, "The Call to the Path of the Ascension," pp. 269–76; "The Call of the Cosmic Christ: Discipleship unto the Ascended Master Jesus Christ," pp. 491–98; "The Day of Thy Christhood: Keep the Flame of Eternal Life," pp. 577–82. (**8**) **The confrontation of Saint Stephen with the fallen ones**. Acts 6:8–15; 7. **Of John the Baptist**. Matt. 3:1–12; Luke 3:1–20; Matt. 14:1–11; Mark 6:14–28; John 1:19–28. See "Confrontations: The Watchers vs. John the Baptist and Jesus Christ," in *Forbidden Mysteries of Enoch: The Untold Story of Men and Angels,* pp. 491–93. (**9**) Isa. 6:8. (**10**) **Peter's denial of the Lord**. Matt. 26:69–75; Mark 14:66–72; Luke 22:54–62; John 18:15–17, 25–27. (**11**) **The Order of the Diamond Heart**. See Jesus and Kuthumi, *Corona Class Lessons,* pp. 90–91; excerpt of Mother Mary, August 15, 1958, 1987 *Pearls of Wisdom,* p. 237, n. 9; and *Saint Germain On Alchemy,* pp. 391–92. (**12**) **Many members but one Body.** Rom. 12:4–8; I Cor. 10:16, 17; 12. (**13**) The Messenger Mark L. Prophet, now the Ascended Master Lanello, took his ascension on February 26, 1973. (**14**) Isa. 8:19. (**15**) **Channeling**. See p. 518, n. 6. (**16**) **Fifteenth Rosary**. See Mother Mary, March 19, 1980, "The Gift of a Mother's Heart: The Mystery of the Fifteenth Rosary," 1980 *Pearls of Wisdom,* vol. 23, no. 27, pp. 165–69. (**17**) See pp. 619–21.

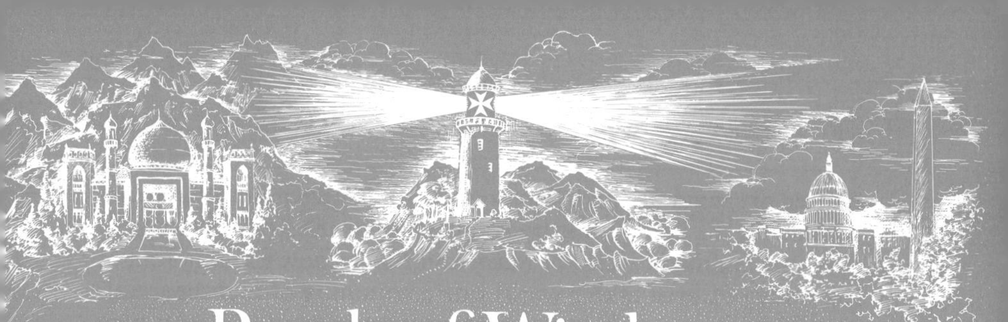

Pearls of Wisdom®
published by The Summit Lighthouse

Vol. 30 No. 84 *Beloved Jesus Christ* *December 31, 1987*

The Hour of Thy Victory Draweth Nigh
"For Judgment I AM Come into This World!"
The Lord's Christmas Day Address 1987

My Beloved,

The hour is coming and now is that the Light of eternal Life is to be permanently thine own. I speak of the cosmic cross of white fire that does mark the day and the hour of thy ascension. By the star of my causal body yet shining over this place, I bring to you the joy of contemplation of being assumed unto God in the ritual of the ascension. It is the glory to God in the highest that does bring peace and goodwill on earth.

Blessed ones, know then that this hour which cometh draweth nigh quickly. For even a century is but a short time to satisfy all of the grace and the fullness of the Law of God. O my beloved, know then that the Victory that is nigh must also be held tightly by thy hand that no man take thy crown.

The crown of Life is won daily, and therefore there does come to all, step by step on the ladder of initiation, the opportunity to give—at first in small ways which seem great and then in great ways which seem small. For as one does ascend the spiral staircase realizing the Allness of God, one knows how small, by comparison, must any sacrifice be; for the gift of the return current is always the Divine All. The saints of all ages unto whose hearts I have imparted this great and compassionate truth are they who are above you now, the immortals. Yet, it is not beneath them to walk by your side day upon day.

Thus, the Ascended Lady Master Thérèse of Lisieux[1] does make her way in your midst, consecrating the momentum of her mantle unto you that you might know of a dearest friend and sister who has since the hour of her ascension mightily increased her mantle of sacred fire and who does desire to give it unto each one. Therefore, she is never far from this place or the hearts who comprise the Diamond Heart of Mary and Morya now forming [out of the Body of Christ of this worldwide community of Lightbearers].

This Diamond Heart, which consists of all those who give their life to the will of God, is surely the means whereby all people of goodwill upon earth might see and recognize that the Christ attainment is truly that open door of the hour, and I myself do offer it again.

Therefore I say, Come unto me, all ye who labor, who are heavy laden both by the burden of the Work and the Light, and of the Word and the Light of your own I AM Presence. Know, then, of a truth that those who bear the Light in the body feel the weight of so great a salvation. It is the weight of the Great Central Sun. It is the power of the allness and the omnipotence of God.

It is a new kind of weight, beloved. It is a glorious weight, not as of gravity or of karma or of the laws of this plane. It is the rejoicing: O the burden of the Lord! O the burden of the Lord! I AM THAT I AM.

Thus, I commend you to a path of joyous sainthood, not martyrdom. Let us speak of the joy of the Seventh Age and dispensation! Let us speak of the joy of angels! Let us speak of the joy of the heart filling with the sacred fire and of a body and a soul and a mind and a spirit becoming more and more the All-in-all.

Thus, the allness of the lesser self enters the Great All, the allness of the Greater Self. And where does one leave off and the next begin? O beloved, when you are immersed in the All, when you are immersed in God, *you are* that One and there is only One and I AM a part of that One. And my Sacred Heart in you shall be known henceforth and forevermore as the Diamond Heart of God's holy will.

This, beloved, is the true bliss of heaven on earth until you know not whether you are in this or that plane, on earth or in heaven, for all of your life is filled with the presence—the omnipresence of Love. A perpetual awareness of thy God is not far from thee, beloved, nor is sainthood. Only thy definition and circumscription of this way and path and word itself does keep thee from that fullness of that recognition within self:

> "Lo, God in me is a saint of God!"—which, by the way, does mean "God in me makes me an issue of God Himself. I am His lifestream. I am His divine sending. Lo, I am of Him. I have gone forth from Him but now I affirm: I AM the undiluted Self. I AM the soul that has not lost her savor.

I AM the soul infired by God. I receive it. I know it. I accept my fiery destiny in this moment."

O let the fiery destiny unveil *thy* Self, beloved! It is a sweet song of angels and of seraphim and of the Elohim of God, which I would hear you sing ere the night is o'er.

Now know, precious hearts, that to extend the cup of one's life is surely to have that cup filled with immortal life. Let not your heart be troubled. For I, Jesus, am confident by the very witness of my heart that the Christ of you—men and women and children—is able to fashion a Diamond Heart of God's holy will whereby not one, not a few, but the many (as God does use the term "many") shall identify, by the blessed teaching of the Law of the One, with this One—with this One that is the I AM THAT I AM.

Blessed hearts, what is the calling, then, of those such as Saint Thérèse who enter the Order of the Diamond Heart? Truly it is to espouse the will of God and to set aside those goals which come after that central purpose of life.

Let us understand that the most direct calling of God in this hour is to save America. Why America? Why the United States? Some vehemently object to this seeming preference. Beloved, it is because this nation has the great endowment and sponsorship of Saint Germain, the greatest investment of Light of the Great White Brotherhood in the experiment of freedom on earth.

Therefore, to save America is to save a dispensation that has not been given to any other nation. To save America is to save the lost sheep of the twelve tribes, of the legions of Sanat Kumara, and to raise up such a Christ consciousness as will draw all Lightbearers of the earth. To seal and save this nation under God is to preserve opportunity for the victory in every other nation upon this planet.

Let it be known, then, that if this nation be lost and sponsorship and dispensation be lost, no other shall be forthcoming to any other nation. For all upon earth have had four hundred years and more to be aware of the great pulsating flame of freedom that has been anchored upon this continent and soil. Know then, beloved, that if America is lost—a generation, her youth, a government, a constitution, a vision and the capstone of the pyramid itself—lo! beloved, not another cause, not another calling, not another destiny will remain to be pursued.

How well I remember, for I moved amongst them, those who were galvanized in the Revolutionary War with its declaration of firmness and Christ-purity against all encroachments upon the individual, sovereign free will of the sons and daughters of God. How they left their businesses, their farms, their professions, their education, all to defeat the common enemy who would have enslaved this nation under another system and under its own crown.

Again, beloved, the hour came, the hour to defend this nation against the encroachments of the international bankers. Thus, the one raised up (as George Washington had been to lead those armies) was none other than the son Abraham Lincoln. And though he did fight to turn back those who came now not to control her soil but her wealth and her abundant life, yet ultimately the cause to which he gave his life and for which he was also crucified did not prevail.

Thus, the taking over of a nation has come by the taking over of the minds of her youth and her people, her monetary system, even the gold standard as the Christ standard set aside. It has come about by the creeping, crawling serpents who have entered the halls of government at every level of the nation. The takeover from within, even that prophesied by that prophet and president Abraham Lincoln,[2] is almost complete.

Blessed hearts, this is the state of the nation and the state of the hour. Is it any wonder, then, that in answer to the heart's call of my Messenger, "What can I do, to what can I give myself to save America?" I did respond and did respond with the profound Teaching that one who has a life of Christ within may offer that life. But this has already been done by your Messenger in her embodiment as Catherine of Siena, as in her thirty-third year the laying down of her life in the bearing of the burden of karma of the Church did 'buy' for that holy Church until the present hour the opportunity to continue.[3]

Thus, in a co-measurement of this, understand that the giving of one's Christhood and the giving of that momentum of the Alpha, the Omega is such a sustaining grace and light in the hearts of the saints as to perpetuate entire civilizations by the sacrifice of the one or the few.

Therefore, beloved, you may understand that good karma is on your side and hers. For having so passed through and already traversed this initiation, your Messenger, then, has no requirement by cosmic law to lose her life save in giving it utterly in service if, beloved, as my Mother has told you, there are many who come forth to up the level of their sacrifice, to actually be and know that they are twenty-four hours a day a portion of that Diamond Heart. Thus, beloved, to be a part of that order one must know and give one's self in the mystery of surrender to the will of God.

Many times preconceived notions of personal destiny do not allow one to see what is that holy and perfect will of God for one's life. Therefore, I commend you to the giving of the Surrender Rosary and the calls to the will of God. And I tell you to understand that no denial of that which is the fullness of thy life [on earth] is required, but only a heightened vision as to exactly what is the fullness of that life plan—that divine plan of you and your beloved twin flame[—in order that you might fulfill it with all due diligence].

Blessed hearts, again, sometimes a cosmic interval does sound as in the hour when in heaven that fallen archangel did take up sword against the living Son of God only to be defeated by Archangel Michael and his hosts and to be cast down into the earth. Was there a disruption in the pursuit of the course of the will of God in that hour for all those of the Great White Brotherhood? I tell you, beloved, indeed there was. We did put aside *all* of our callings in God to defeat the Adversary who did challenge the very path of Christhood unto the sons and daughters of God and all children and evolutions of the mighty root races.

Thus, these intervals, beloved, are just that, as though time should stop, as though the Great Divine Director or the referee should call "time-out" and all of a cosmos does stand still while the Sons of God and the hosts of the LORD do defeat the adversary of their God-Reality.

What does this tell you, then? It tells you that no time or space or eternity is lost, and that when you have fulfilled [your duty in] the defense of life and the right to be in heaven as on earth, on earth as in heaven, you do take up where you left off in this lifetime or the next, in this octave or another. God does not require you to forfeit your very special plans and purposes but only to place in perspective that the hour does come when, if the course of civilization is to lock into the grid of Light and alignment with the next dispensation, those who are a part of that Light must give the Light they have to stop the onslaught of the dark ones who pursue that precipitation of the new dispensation to destroy it and the Christed ones before they are yet born out of the womb of the Cosmic Virgin.

Thus, beloved, it would seem an inopportune hour that I was called at the age of thirty-three to give my life for the judgment of the Watchers, the archdeceivers, then highest ranking fallen angels in embodiment on earth who were in the Roman Empire, who had infiltrated the highest ranks of Judaism and were elsewhere on the planet not recorded in the history of that time. Blessed ones, I did give my life and I did take it again as prophesied. And I did remain and move on in a glorified body that was yet physical to teach and preach to my disciples and to the world.[4]

Therefore, know that my trial was for the judgment of these fallen ones, and as they did judge, so were they judged. Likewise it is so that when a city and a nation have placed on trial my Messenger, it is they who have been on trial, and all who have been the mouthpiece of Death and Darkness [raised against her] have themselves incurred their own judgment.

Therefore, I speak of the Christ in you, of each and every one and of each babe who does sleep while at inner levels he does mightily strive in the spirit for the victory of nations. It is so of your Christ, beloved, as I said, *For judgment I AM come into this world!** This is your fiat of the hour, beloved, and that judgment of the world [and the world's condemnation of the Christ in you and in these little ones] through and by your Christ Self is indeed the primary affirmation of the will of God for your life and purpose and daily service [in the Order of the Diamond Heart] in this hour.

Forget it not, because, beloved, the fallen ones do not forget. They know thee who thou art, thou holy ones of God—they know. They know, therefore, that if you forget they will not forget, and in your absence of alertness and memory of just who you are and why you are here, they seek to spring their traps, to take advantage of you, to turn you aside, to make you feel self-condemnation or even to engage in rivalry or competitiveness with one another.

Blessed hearts, the Christ of you does affirm every hour, and you may hear your Christ Self affirming it, *For judgment I AM come into this world!* These judgments include not only the judgment of the fallen angels and the exorcism of foul spirits that make up a part of the fabric of the earth but, beloved, these judgments are righteous judgments made for and on behalf of the children of the Light who have not the true shepherds, do not have the defenders, do not have those who will champion their cause.

For judgment I AM come into the world!—the righteous judgment that does protect the innocent and those who are oppressed by the fallen angels yet in their seats of power. To protect the innocent, one must unseat these mighty from their seats. Let them go down, I say! And let them go down in the name of the Keepers of the Flame of Saint Germain by the authority of your Christhood!

So I AM Jesus, and that Christhood, beloved, includes all of the Light externalized, both your fiery spirit, which is that portion of the Spirit of the I AM THAT I AM that dwells in your temple, and your soul, who is that portion of selfhood that descended from the great octaves of Light and must now put on garments of consciousness and return to the heart of the Father/Mother God as the pearl—the pearl of great price, because I and others have paid the price for you.

*"And Jesus said, For judgment I am come into this world, that they which see not might see; and that they which see might be made blind." John 9:39.

The pearl of great price you are, for *you* have paid a great price to stand, face and conquer your karma, your past misdeeds. And in your willingness to suffer for a while the burden of that karma, you will now know surcease from it and see the dawn of a new day of opportunity. Be glad and rejoice that you have allowed yourself to bear your karma rather than to deny it, push it back and cast it aside.

With intelligence and the intelling quality of wisdom, so with the violet flame you can also make that suffering turn to joy and comfort in this hour. For the violet transmuting flame, beloved, does indeed take all of that energy and return it to your causal body, which does grow and grow and grow as the lilies of the field grow.

Therefore, beloved, to espouse the will of God is the path of sainthood and, as Morya has said, it is the sacred adventure. When you see this you will know, all things coming under the grand design, that you are surely locked in to the Diamond Heart of my Mother Mary, that heart being the Immaculate Heart, that heart being the pulsation of a cosmos.

Thus, beloved, all things follow when you vow to do the will of God. And when you truly demand and cry out to the Father, *"Show me what is that will!"* and you are able to let go of pet plans and projects, you will be found called and sealed in the Order of the Diamond Heart.

I am your Jesus, fairest rose of your heart. I am one with your Christ. I am in the center of the lily, the threefold flame that is the heart of that diamond chalice of Mother Mary. Therefore, you see that the acceptable flower that you bring to this calling is the lily, which does represent the threefold flame.

Hearts of Love, I gather you but I do not pluck you from the fields of life. I would see you become immortelles, yet upon the stalk. May it be so, that the green stem upon the spine does signify that a group of pilgrims on earth one day in December of the year called 1987 did come to a new and an ancient divine awareness through their own beloved Brother ascended.

Prayer of the Devotee of the Diamond Heart

Behold, I AM everywhere in the Consciousness of God!
Therefore, in giving my life I cannot lose it,
  for He has found me and taken me all to his heart.
I AM one with Jesus, his disciple of the Sacred Heart.
And I AM, I AM, I AM giving my portion
  to form the Diamond Heart of Mary and Morya
  as the worldwide sign to every foe,
  every foreigner and enemy of Christ:

Thus far and no farther!
The Diamond Heart of the sons and daughters of Light shall
prevail in the name of our Lord and Saviour Jesus Christ!
It is done and we accept it done this hour in full power.
For God in us is the doer and it is done.

Therefore, at any hour until the midnight strikes the coming of a new year and a new planetary karma you may say:

Beloved Jesus, my Brother, my Master,
I will follow in the footsteps of the saints
of the Diamond Heart.
I will give the just portion of my life that not one,
neither the Messenger, neither a Keeper of the Flame,
need be plucked of Thee from God's garden on earth.
I seal this, Jesus, with a gift of my heart, thy heart one.
Behold, my Lord!
I AM with Thee everywhere in the Consciousness of God!
And by that Reality, my Lord,
I know there is no death, there is no grave, there is no hell,
for the Life triumphant has swallowed up
the death of defeat!
It is done. We are one, nevermore to go out
into the shackles and limitations of time and space.
Jesus, Thou art my All. I AM thy All.
And I do enter thy heart as thy bride,
thy servant and disciple, thy friend.
O Lord, take me where Thou wouldst have me
into the highest heaven and into the depths of Hades.
O Lord, let me serve Thee wherever Thou art
and one of these thy little ones is gone out of the way.
In the name of the Way, the Truth, and the Life, Jesus,
I AM thine own forever through my daily, step-by-step service
in the Order of the Diamond Heart.

This dictation was **delivered December 25, 1987,** at the **Royal Teton Ranch, Montana**. (**1**) **Thérèse of Lisieux** (1873–1897), French Carmelite nun, known as the Little Flower of Jesus, canonized 1925; remembered for her statement, "I will spend my heaven doing good on earth." (**2**) "If destruction be our lot, we must ourselves be its author and finisher. As a nation of freemen, we must live through all time, or die by suicide." Abraham Lincoln, "The Perpetuation of Our Political Institutions," address, Jan. 27, 1838. (**3**) **Catherine of Siena** (1347-1380), Italian mystic; traveled widely and sent hundreds of letters to prelates and sovereigns attempting to reform the Church and bring peace to Italy. Upon her deathbed at age 33 she prayed, "O eternal God, receive the sacrifice of my life for the sake of this mystical body of holy Church." Canonized 1461. (**4**) There were traditions in the first to third centuries of a long interval between the resurrection and ascension. The Church Father Irenaeus wrote, "From the fortieth and fiftieth year a man begins to decline towards old age, which our Lord possessed while He still fulfilled the office of a Teacher, even as the Gospel and all the elders testify; those who were conversant in Asia with John, the disciple of the Lord, [affirming] that John conveyed to them that information" (*Against Heresies*, c. 180). The third-century Gnostic text Pistis Sophia (1:1) states: "It came to pass, when Jesus had risen from the dead, that he passed 11 years discoursing with his disciples and instructing them." See *The Lost Years of Jesus*, pp. 4–5; *The Lost Teachings of Jesus I*, pp. 335–36.

Index

Volume Thirty - 1987

For an alphabetical listing of many of the philosophical and hierarchical terms used in the 1987 *Pearls of Wisdom,* see the comprehensive glossary, "The Alchemy of the Word: Stones for the Wise Masterbuilders," in *Saint Germain On Alchemy: For the Adept in the Aquarian Age.*